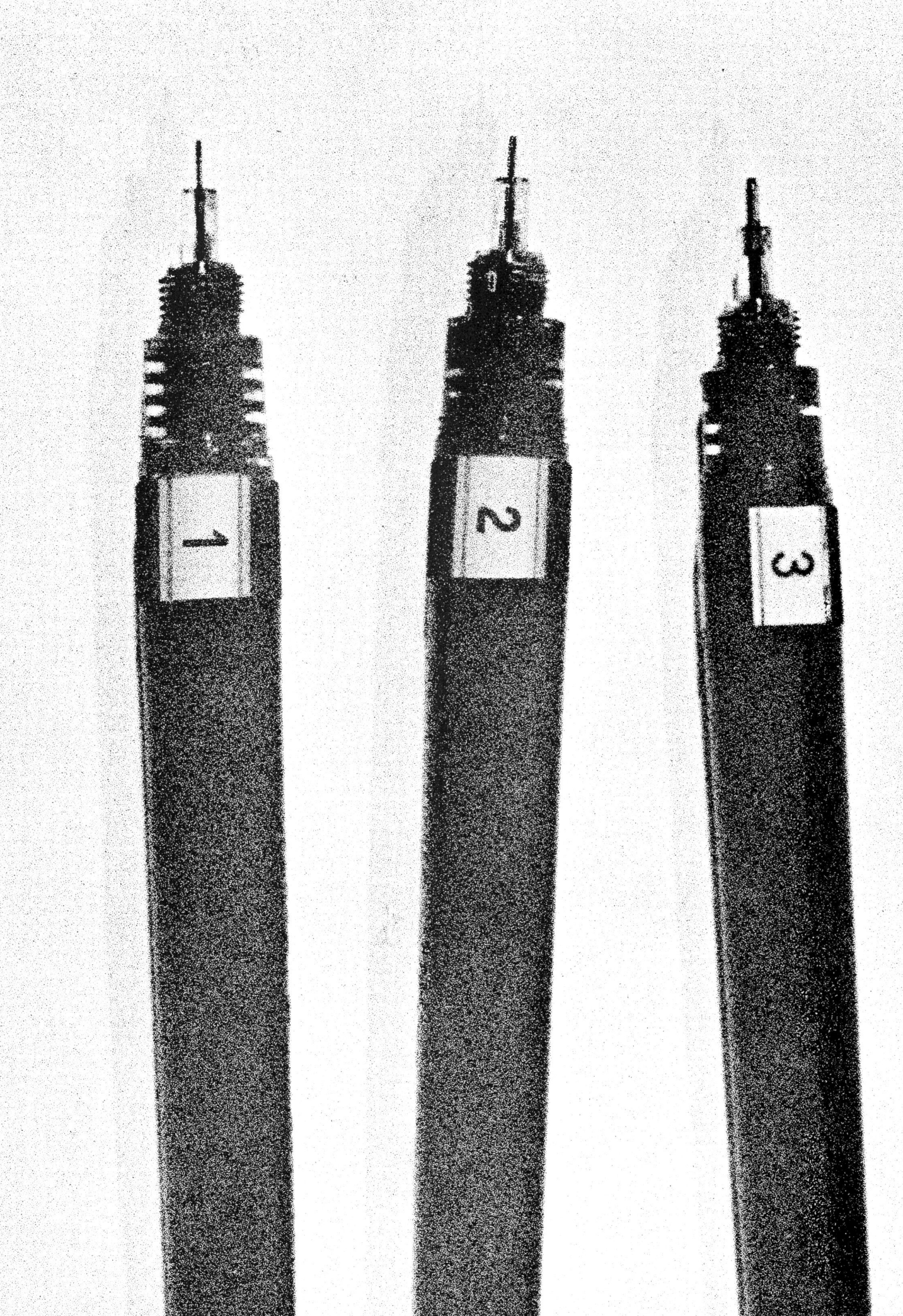

A photographic review of Creativity'73, displayed at The Conrad Hilton Hotel, Chicago, September 11-13, 1973, Th

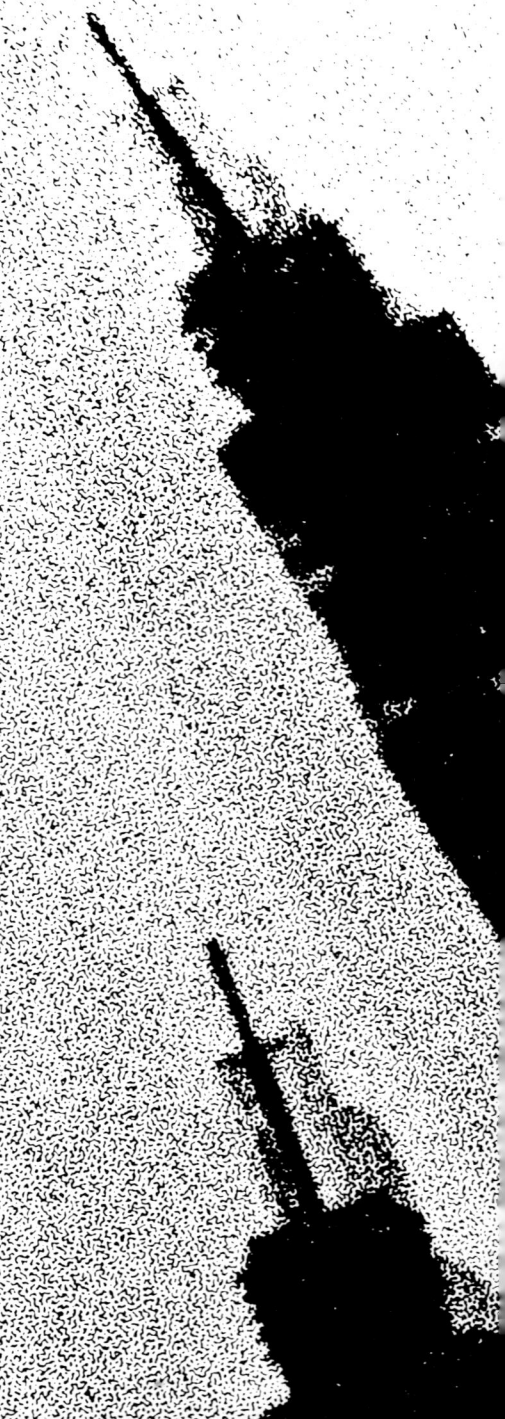

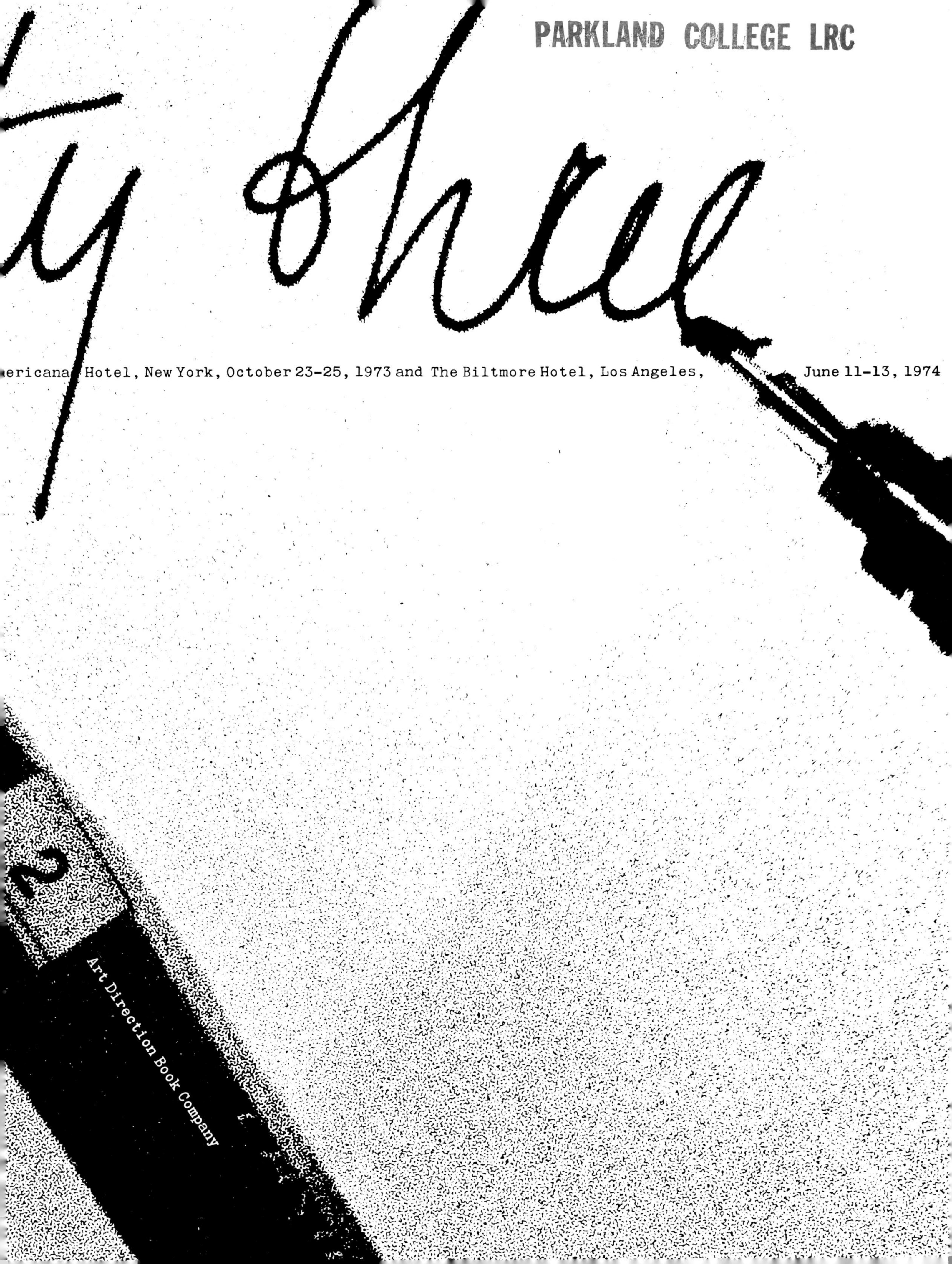
ericana Hotel, New York, October 23-25, 1973 and The Biltmore Hotel, Los Angeles, June 11-13, 1974
2
Art Direction Book Company

This Annual displays a vast amount of work expertly prepared and designed. Technical skill is evident everywhere. The handling of type for the long headline, heavy copy ads could serve as classroom models for years to come. The Annual Reports are superb for their over-all design, selection of photographs, and, again, type selection and treatment. Packaging design is on the quiet side, but precisely on target.

Nostalgia was a major design element of this period. Note the old-timey props, art deco typefaces, sepia tones and tints for everything from business cards to TV.

The defiant, belligerant anti-Establishment layouts so common

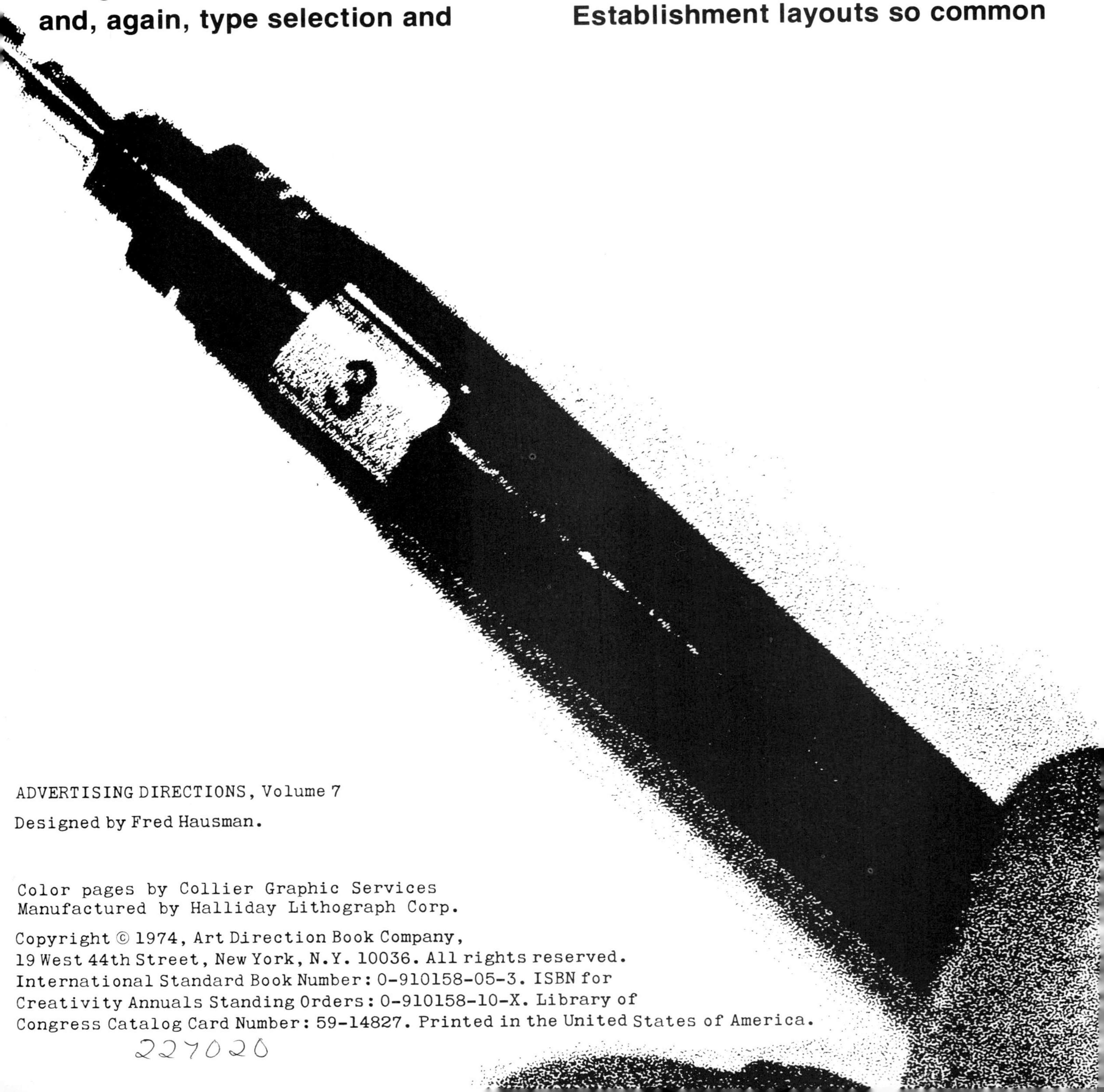
3

ADVERTISING DIRECTIONS, Volume 7

Designed by Fred Hausman.

Color pages by Collier Graphic Services
Manufactured by Halliday Lithograph Corp.

International Standard Book Number: 0-910158-05-3. ISBN for
Creativity Annuals Standing Orders: 0-910158-10-X. Library of
Congress Catalog Card Number: 59-14827. Printed in the United States of America.

a year or two ago practically disappeared except for record albums, and an occasional poster. Humor, except in the TV commercial or a flash here and there in packaging or on a letterhead, is notable by its absence. It was a somber, sober year in advertising.
Creativity 3 records these changes in visual advertising:

- Photography began to move towards the dramatic, and away from the reportorial. Perhaps it felt it had to, for illustration, already tight and realistic, continued its attempts to outperform the camera for detail, texture, highlighting, vérité.
- Letterheads have split into two separate design approaches. The

classic continues the trend towards simplicity, and the anything-but-classic allows anything, even up to billboard effects.
- Copy gets longer and longer, and better. Liquor copy developed a style all its own—long, tongue in cheek, preposterous but charming "fables."
- Tight typography seemed to be coming to the end of the road. An increase in serifs in turn increased the use of larger than expected type sizes, and pried type just a bit apart; at least by recent standards.

In overview, it's obvious that this wasn't a year for much innovation or experimentation. Creativity was confined within unyielding budgets. As a result, visual professionals exposed their skills, talents, and disciplines in the fundamentals of advertising art; not in its spectaculars. This Annual marks, in effect, the final resting place — at least for now—of gimmick, or, as it is more nicely known, conceptual advertising

CONTENTS

1–55	Color Folio
56–67	Photography
68–95, 273–298	Editorial Design
96–179	Consumer Advertising
180–272	Trade, Political, and Public Service Advertising
299–360, 400–438	Brochures, Catalogs, and Magazine Covers
361–399, 706	Posters
439–499	Annual Reports
500–563	Promotional Pieces
564–605	Packaging
606–620, 640–649	Books & Book Jackets
621–639	Record Albums
650–688	Illustration
689–705, 707	Typography
708–748	Trademarks & Logotypes
749–793	Letterheads
794–843	Television Commercials and Film
	Index

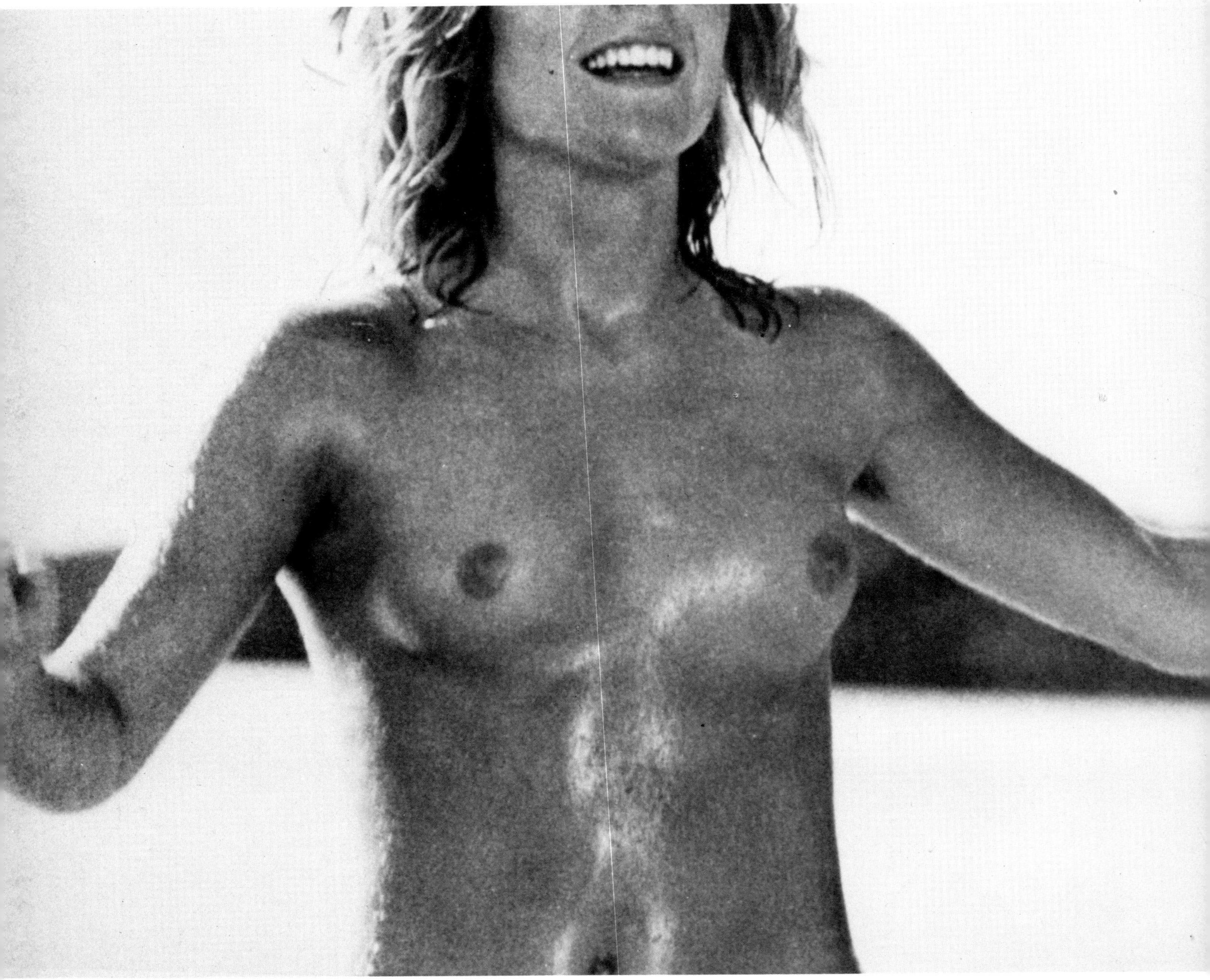

1
Marknads Kommunikation AB Entrant
Jorma Kosunen Art Director
Christer & Arne Production AB Photographers
Barnängen AB Client

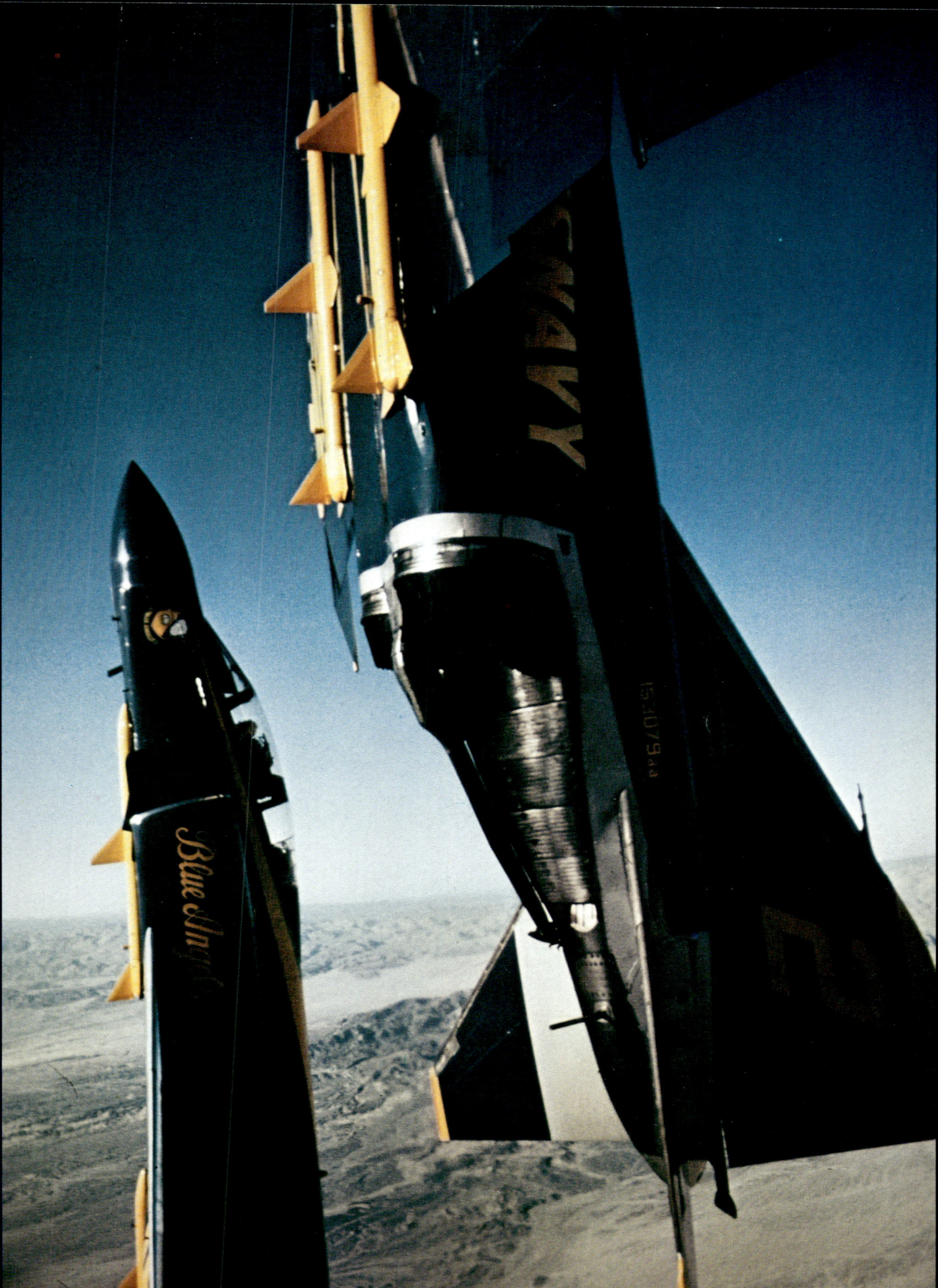

2
Wesley B. McKeown Entrant

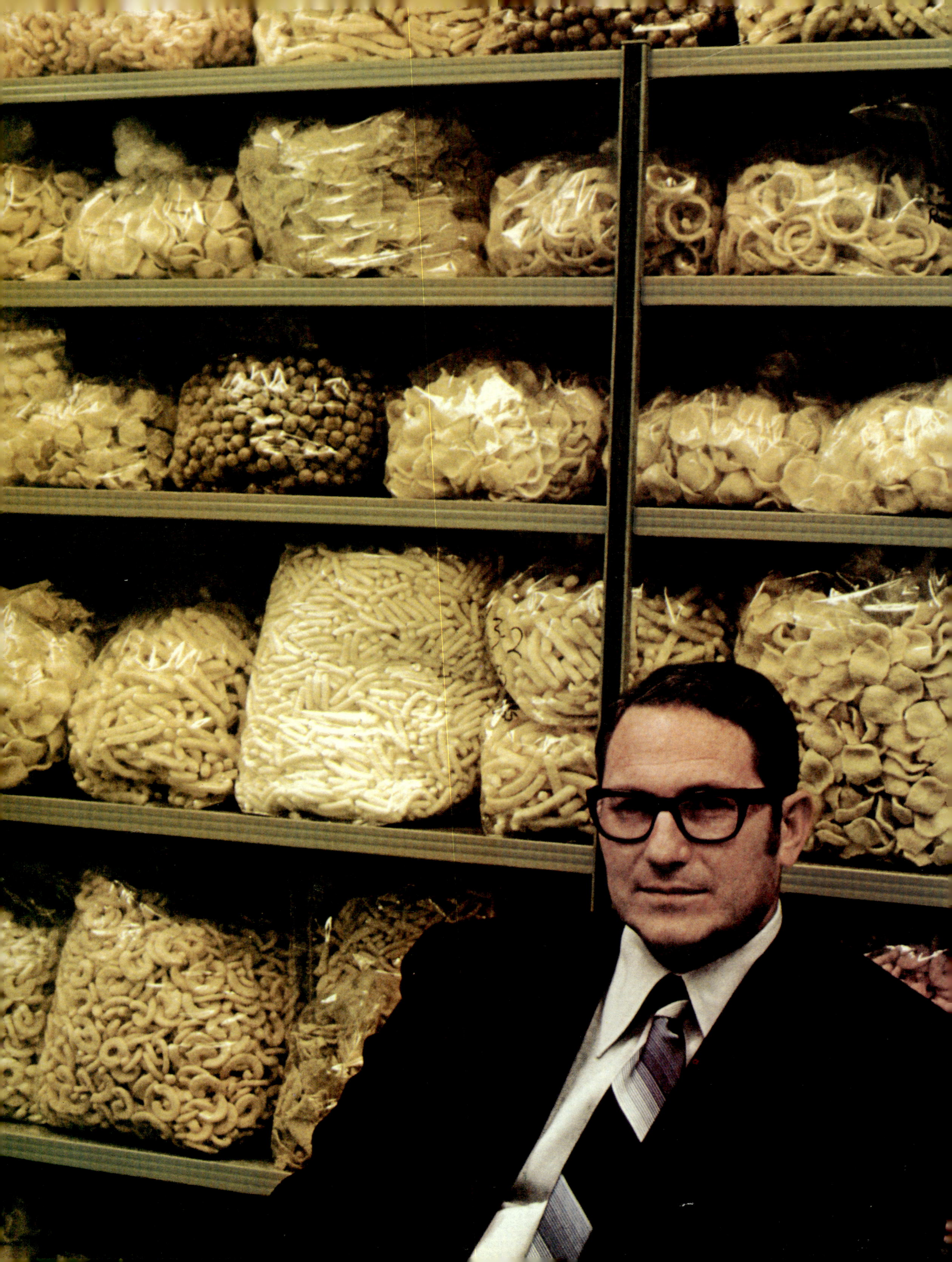

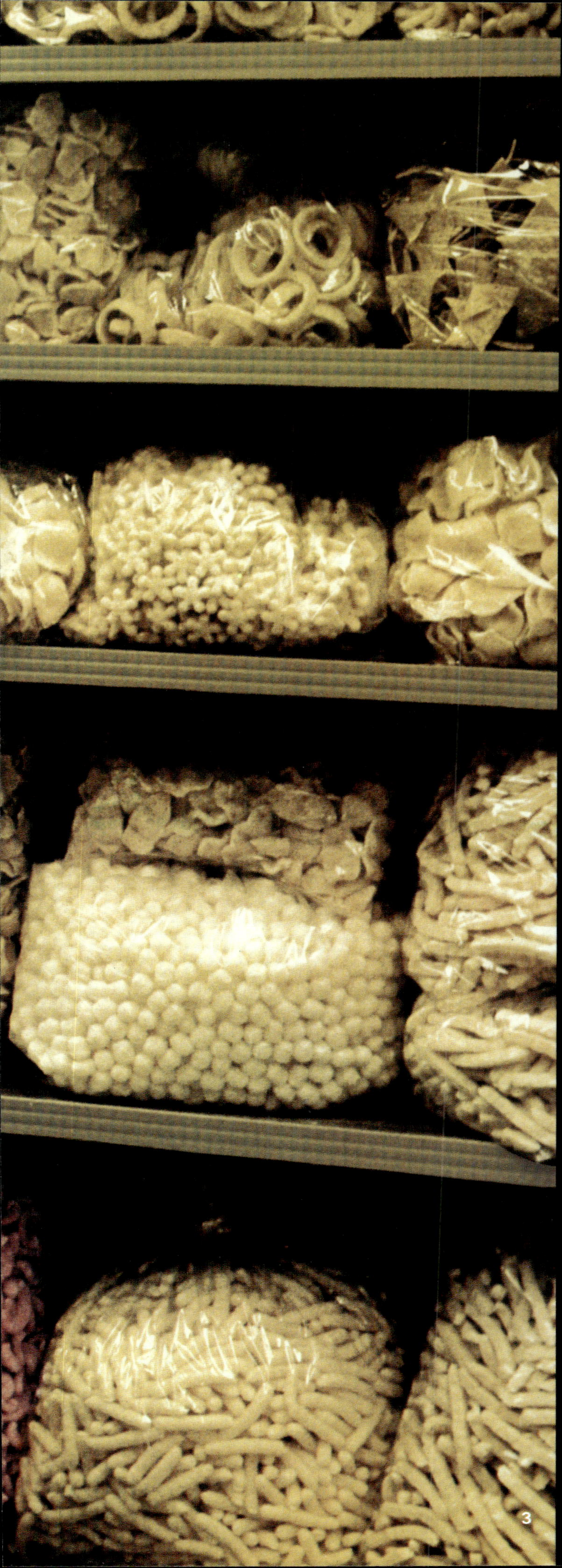

3

4

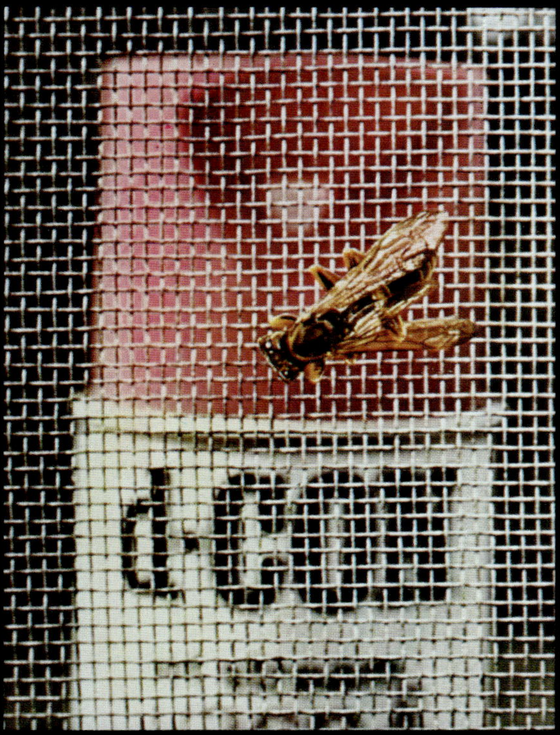

4
Corporate Annual Reports Entrant
Len Fury Art Director
Marvin Koner Illustrator
Sterling Drug Inc. Client

3
Eisenman and Enock Inc. Entrant
Stan Eisenman, David Enock Art Directors
Burt Glinn Photographer
PepsiCo, Inc. Client

5
Sport Magazine Entrant
Al Braverman Art Director
Bob Peterson Photographer
Rebecca Baxter Designer
Lubalin, Smith, Carnase Studio

6
Playboy Enterprises, Inc. Entrant
Arthur Paul Art Director
Kerig Pope Designer
Frank Lafitte Photographer
Playboy Magazine Client

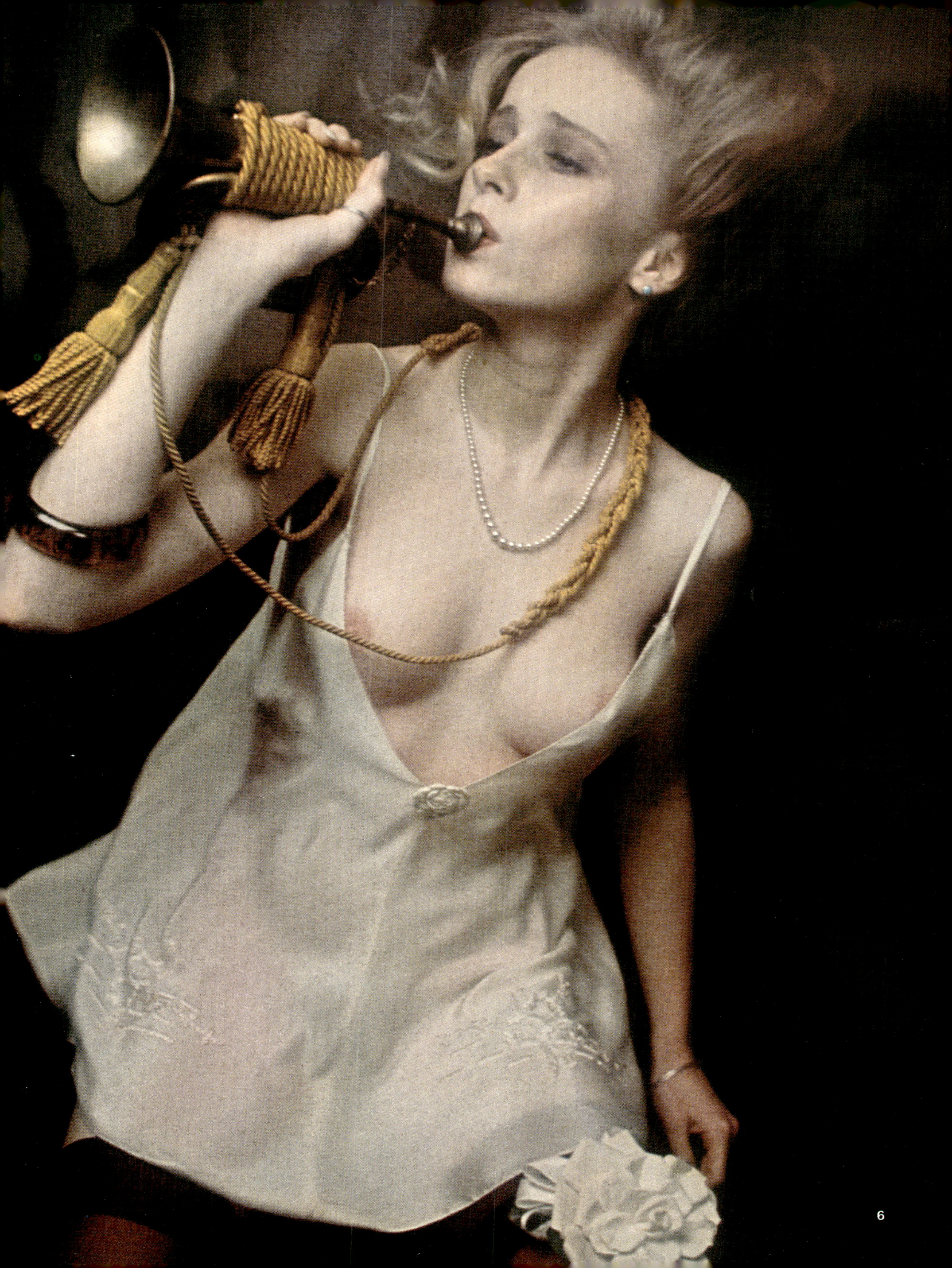

7

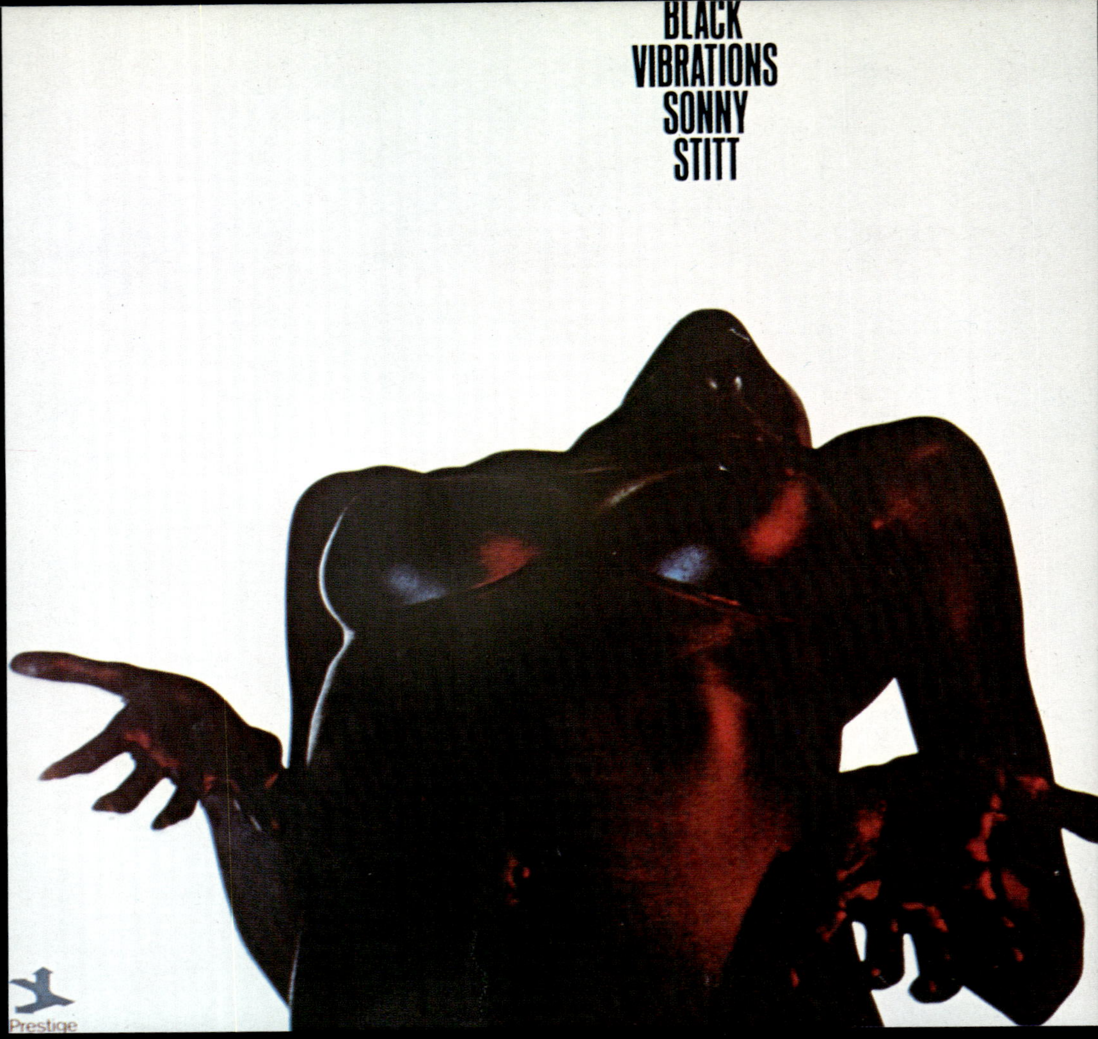
BLACK
VIBRATIONS
SONNY
STITT
Prestige

7
Tony Lane Entrant
Fantasy/Prestige/Milestone Records Client

8
Designers Ross Stewart & Winner Entrant
Frank Ross, Dan Stewart, Harriet Winner Art Directors
Warren Lynch, Photography Inc. Photographer
Hart Products Company Client

9
Ian Gunn Entrant
Raymond Fedynak Art Director
Ken Ambrose Photographer
Muller Jordan Herrick Inc. Agency
Foster Wheeler Corp. Client

8

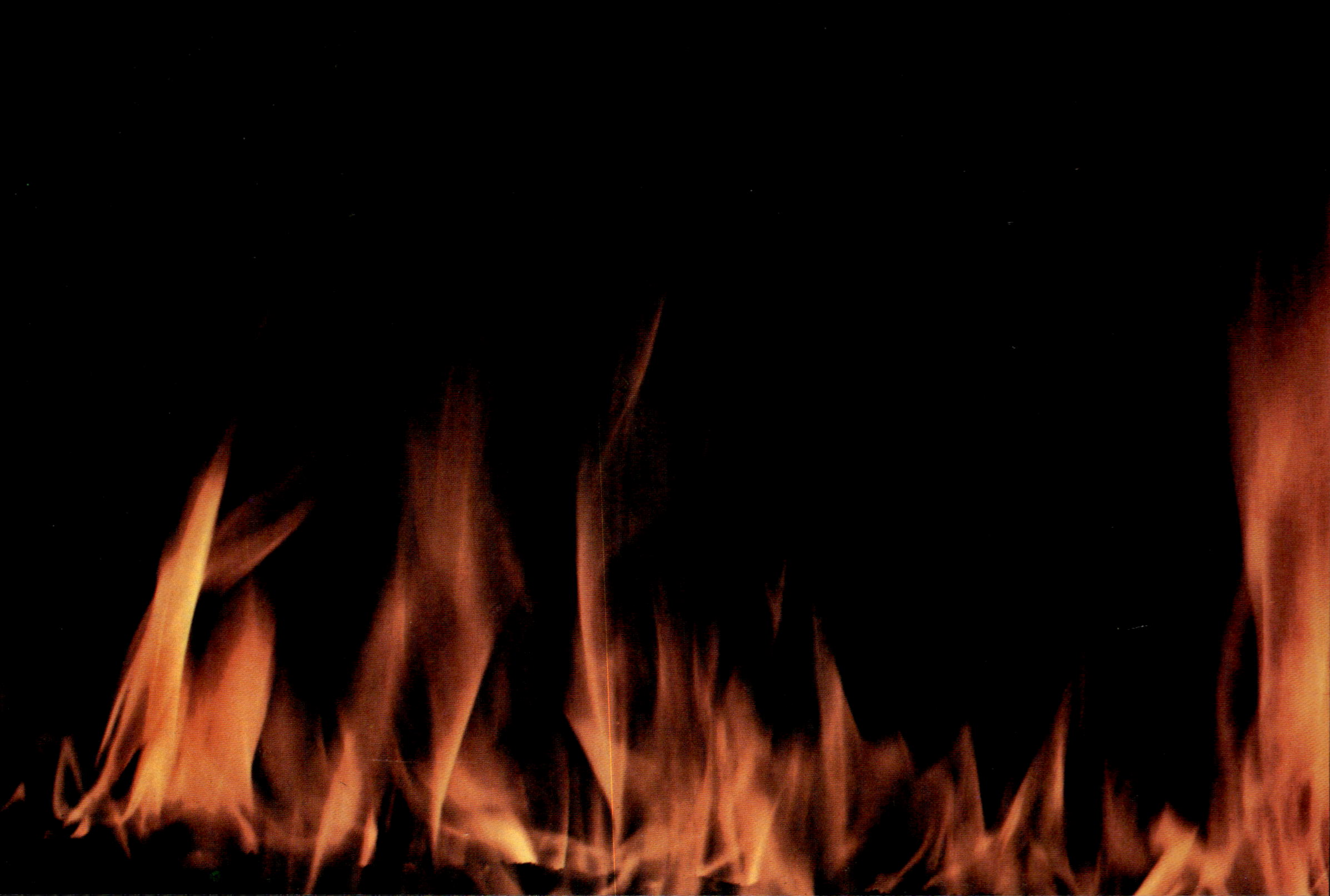

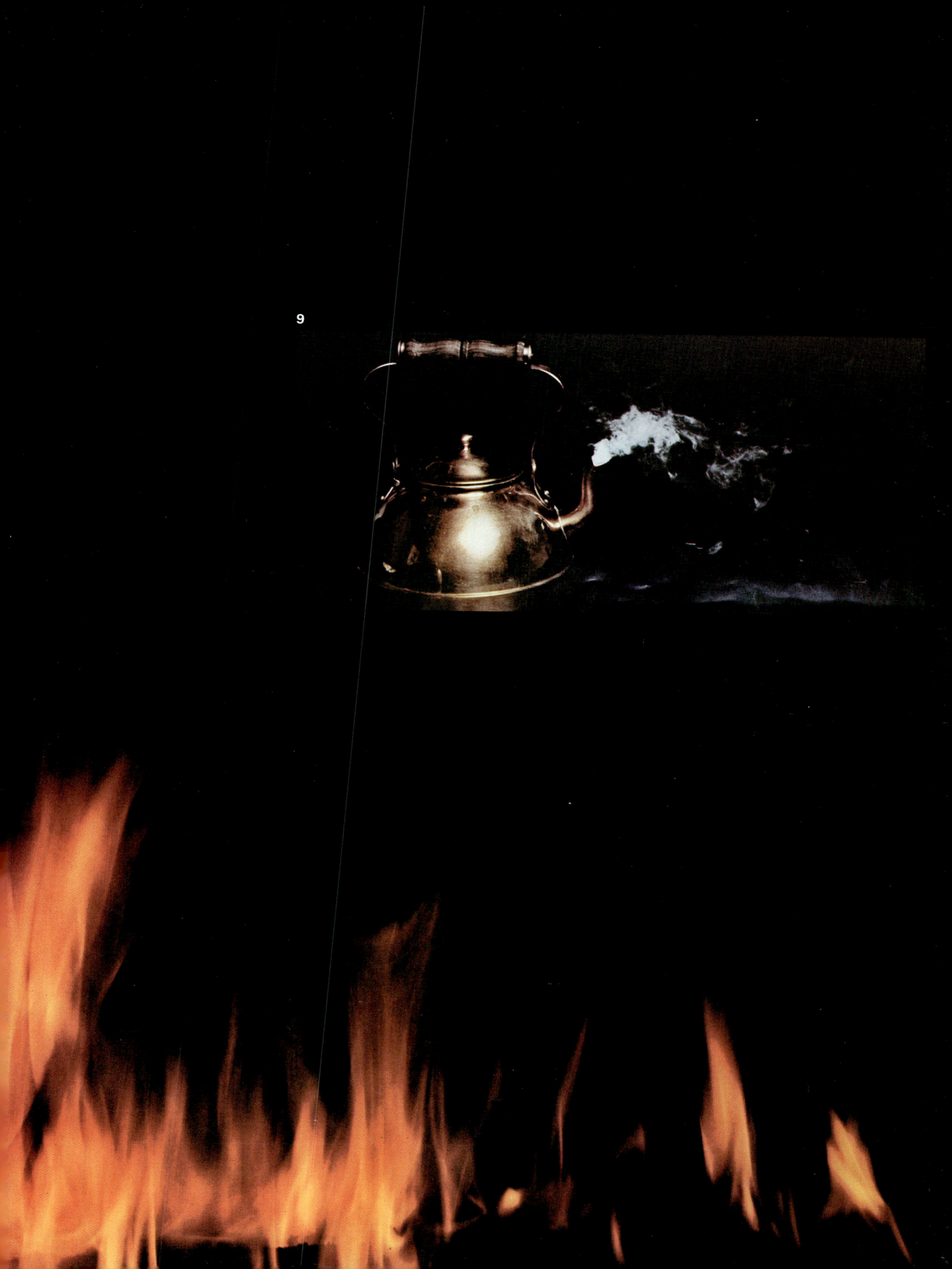
9

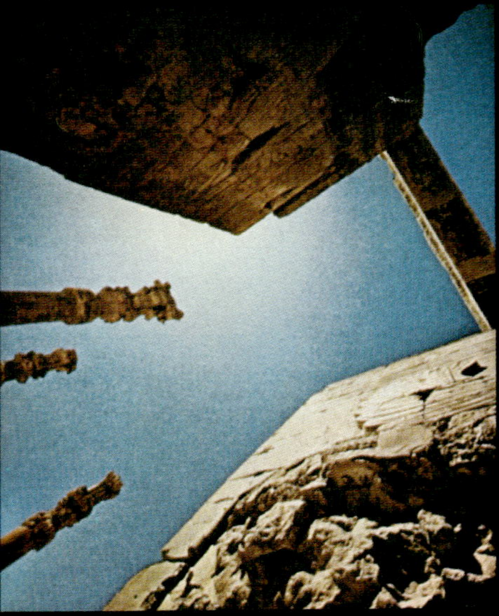
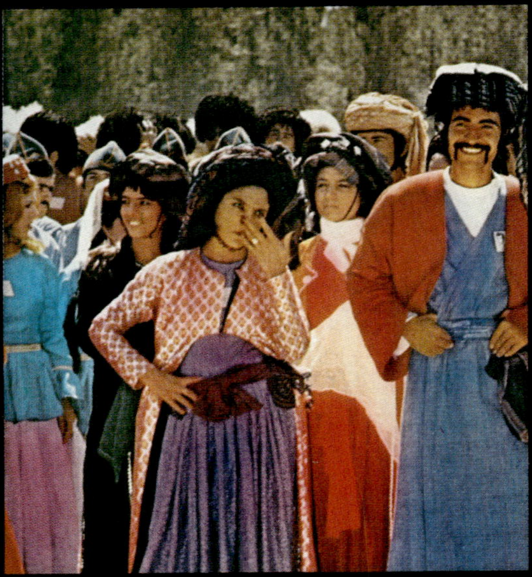
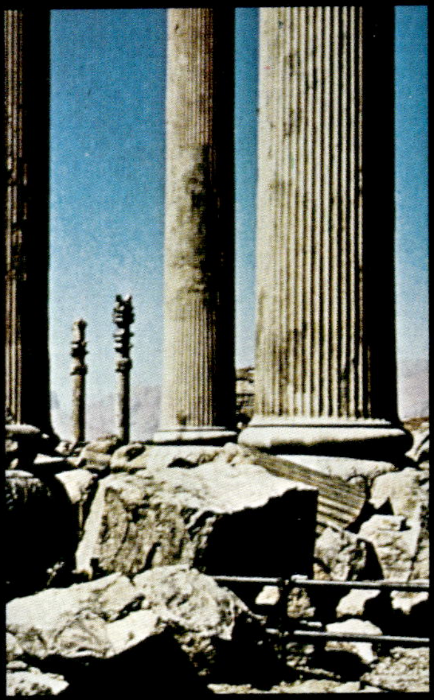
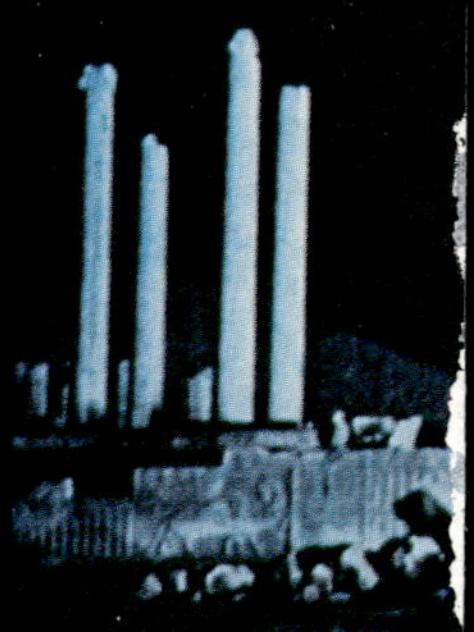
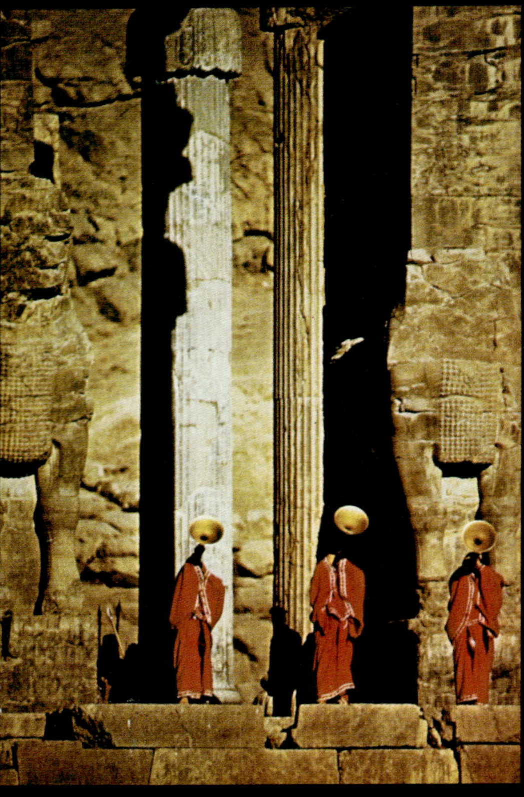
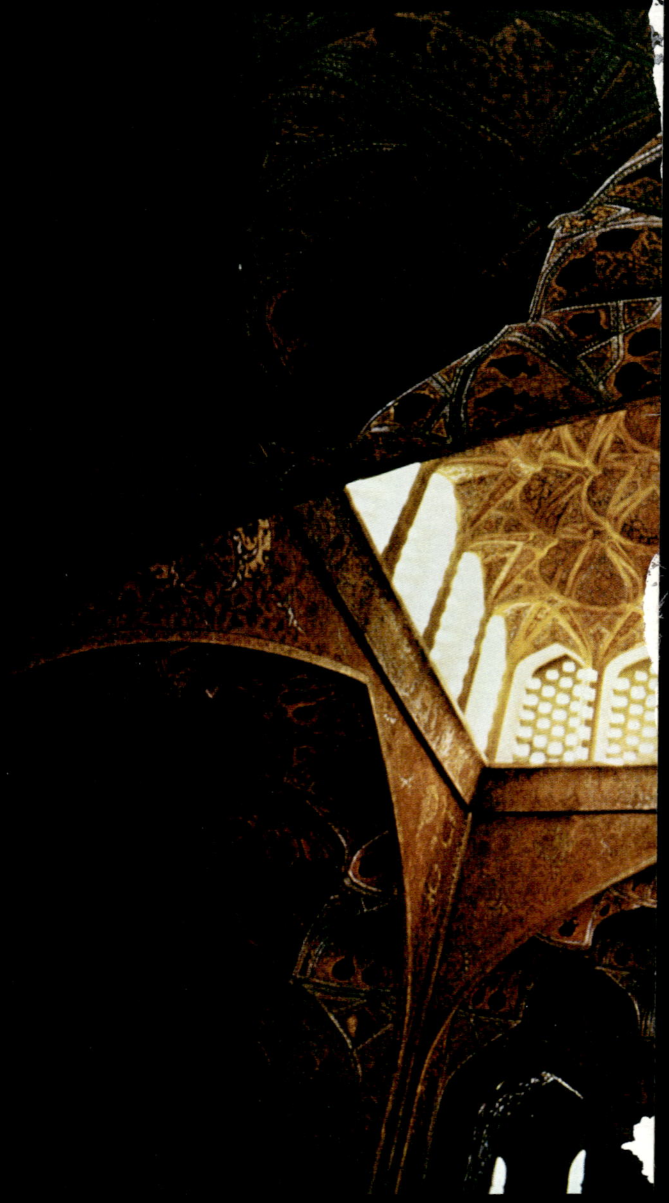

10-17
Jay Maisel Entrant
Jacques Lowe, Heinz Heimann, Nimal Jayserka
Art Directors
Creative Communications S.A.,
Franklin Book Programs, Inc.
Clients

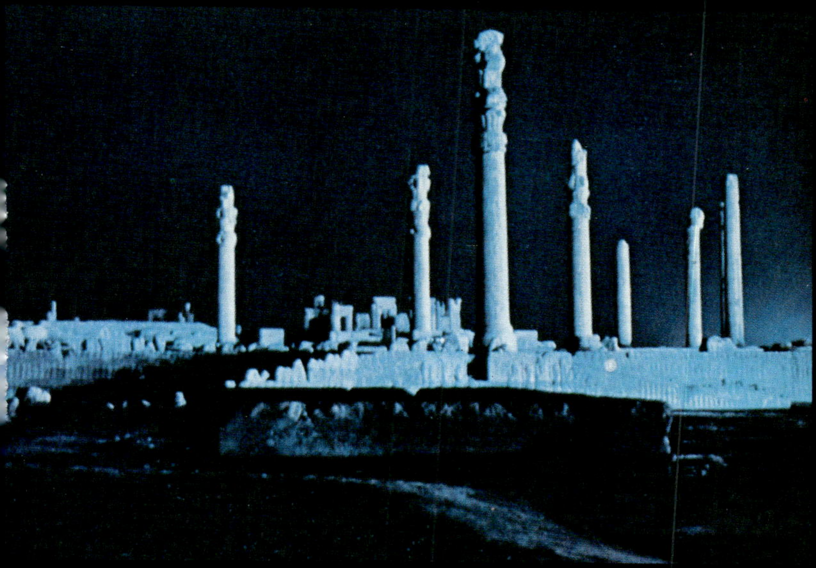
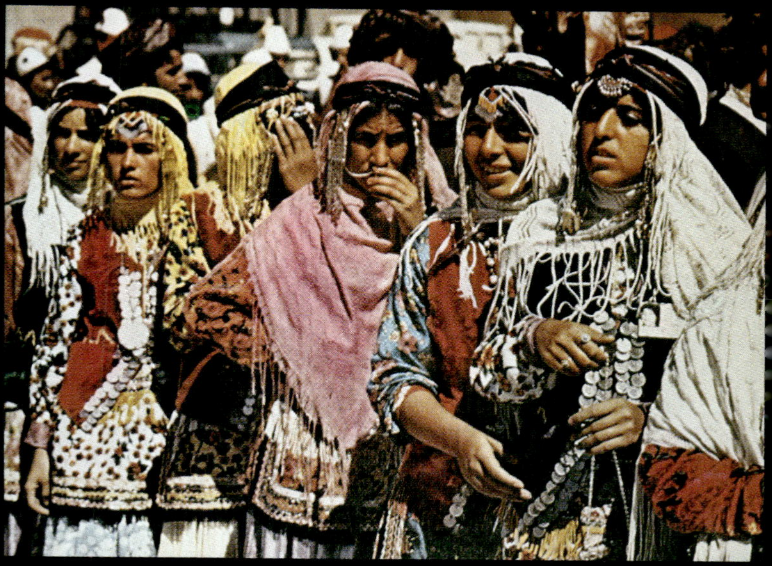
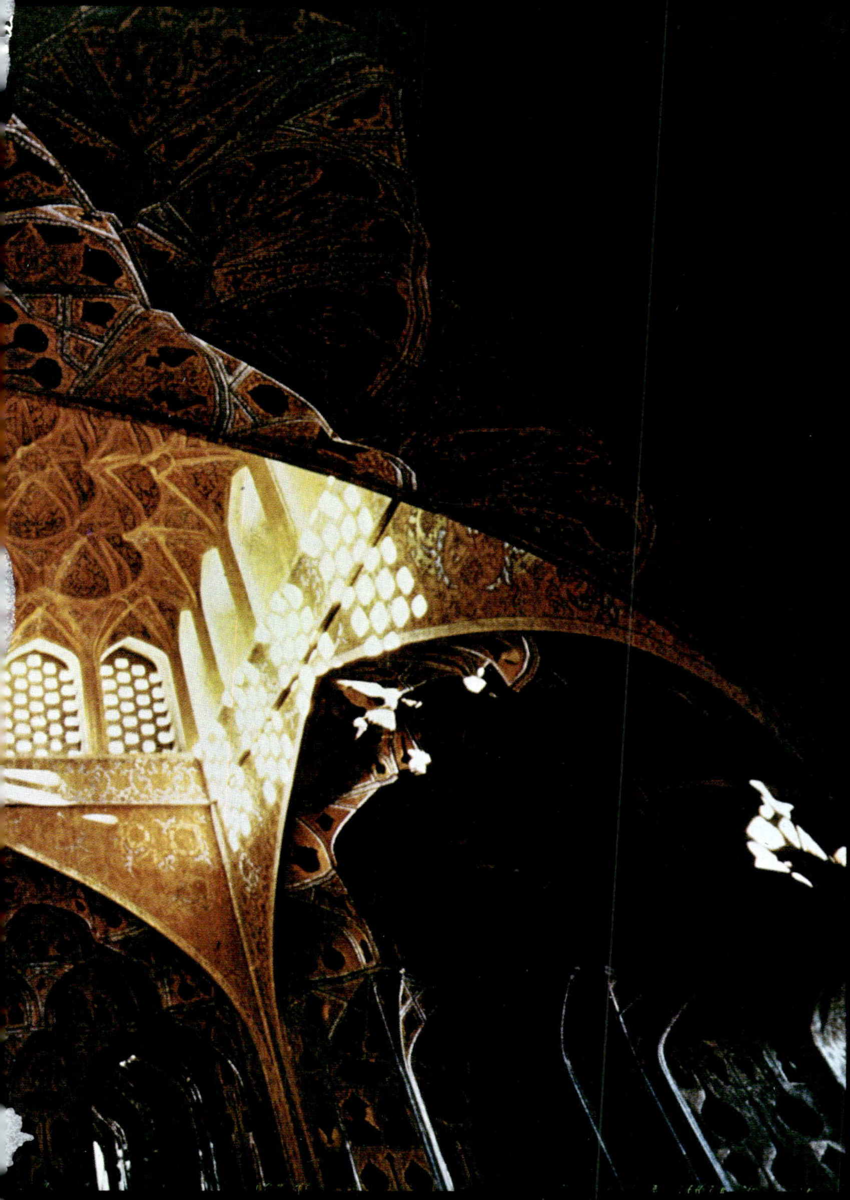
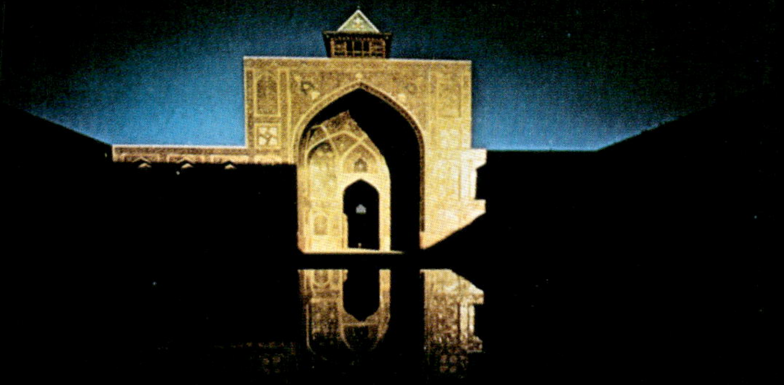

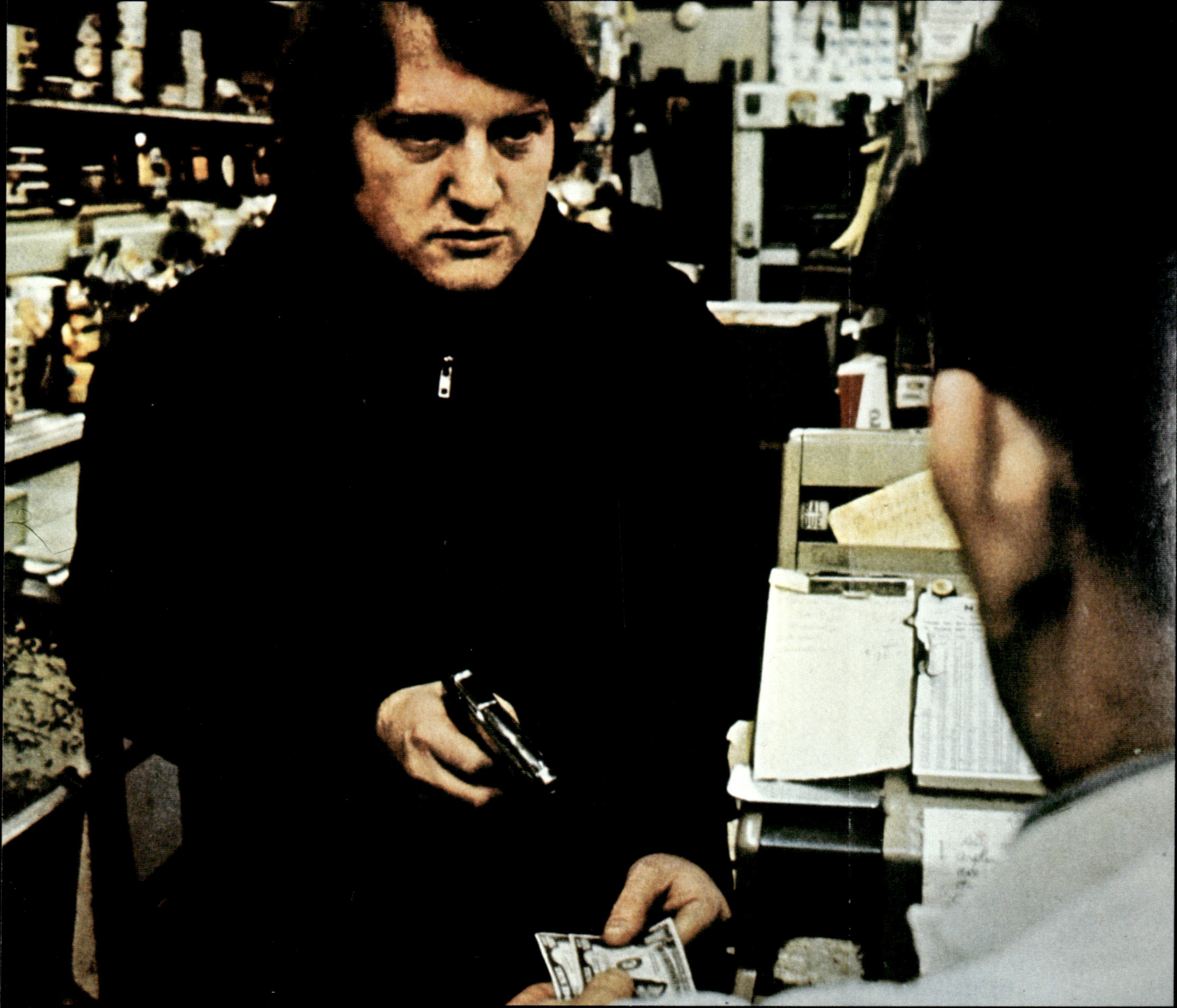

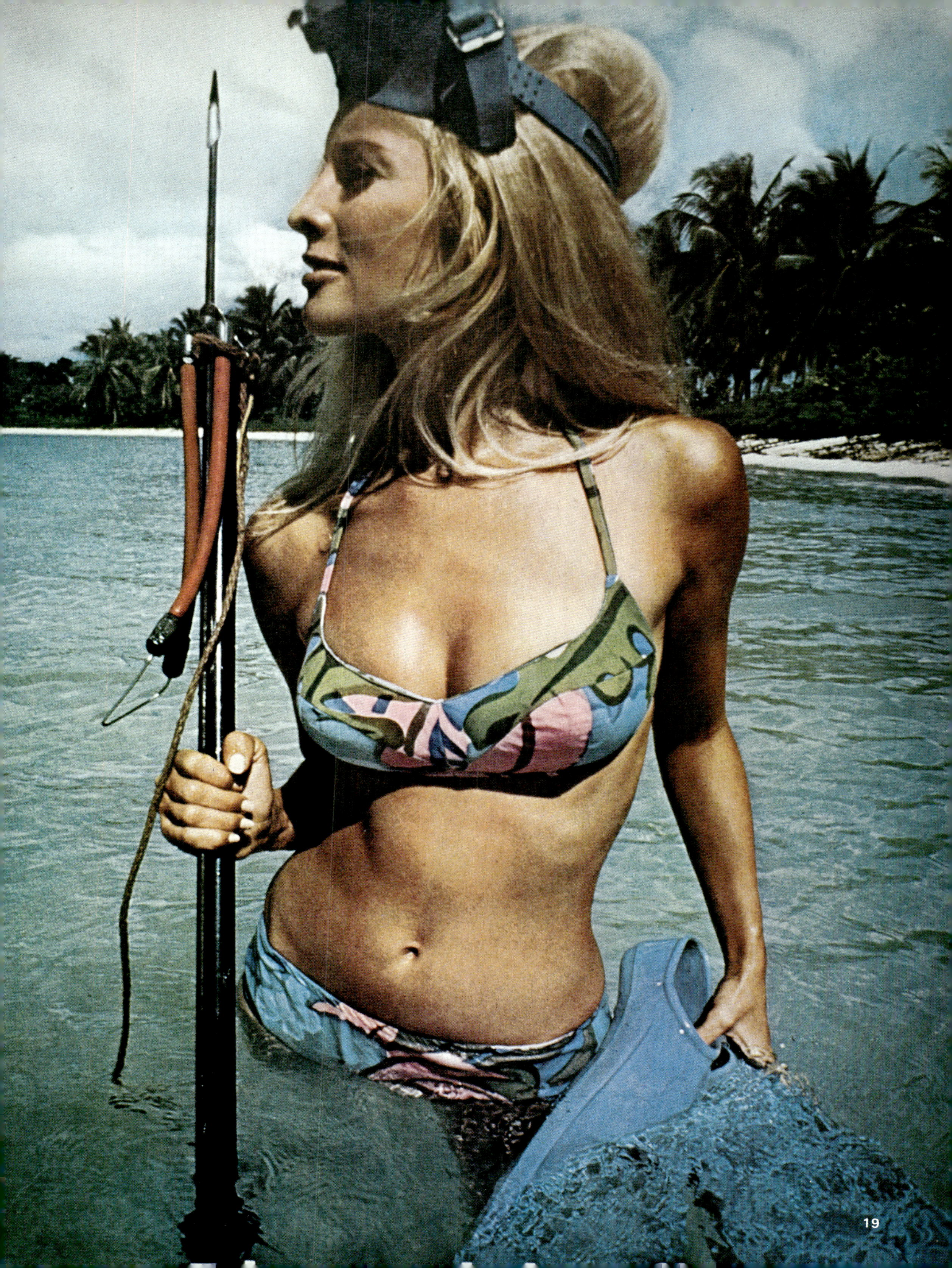

20

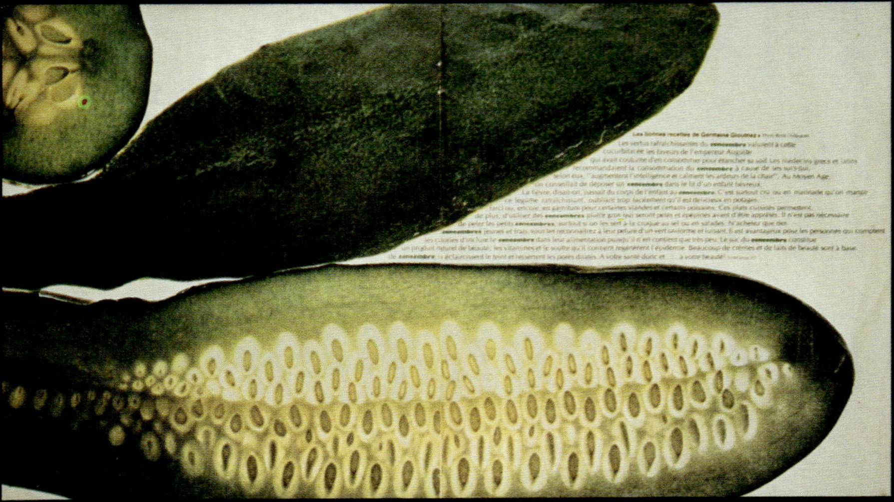

20
Perspectives Inc.
Entrant
Gilles Daigneault
Art Director
Concombres
Agency

21
Michael Love
Entrant
Jim Galati
Photographer
Katz, Jacobs, & Douglas, Inc.
Agency
Tempees
Client

22
Katz, Jacobs & Douglas Inc.
Entrant
Rick Katz, Robert Jacobs
Art Directors
Ed Silano
Photographer
Herb Zucker
Studio
House of Ronnie
Client

23
McRay Magleby
Entrant
Graphic Communications
Studio
Brigham Young University
Client

21

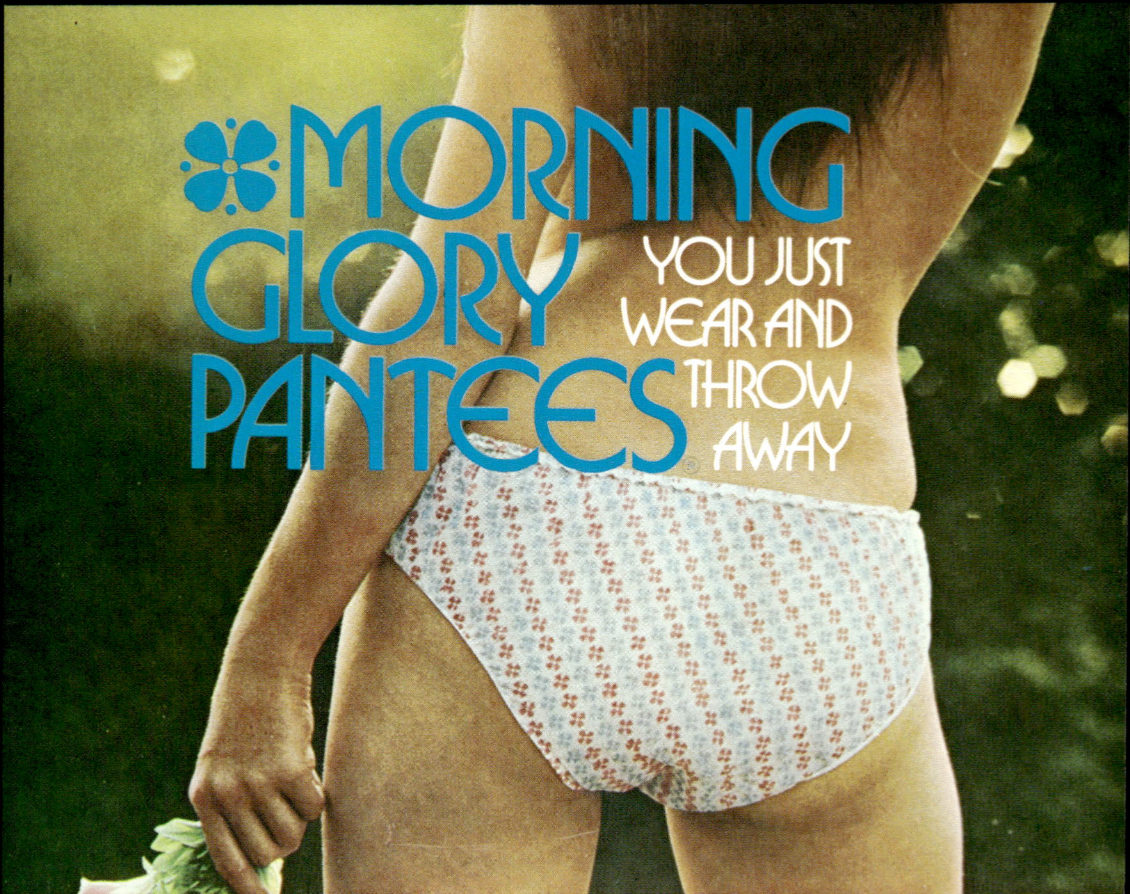
MORNING GLORY PANTEES
YOU JUST WEAR AND THROW AWAY

23

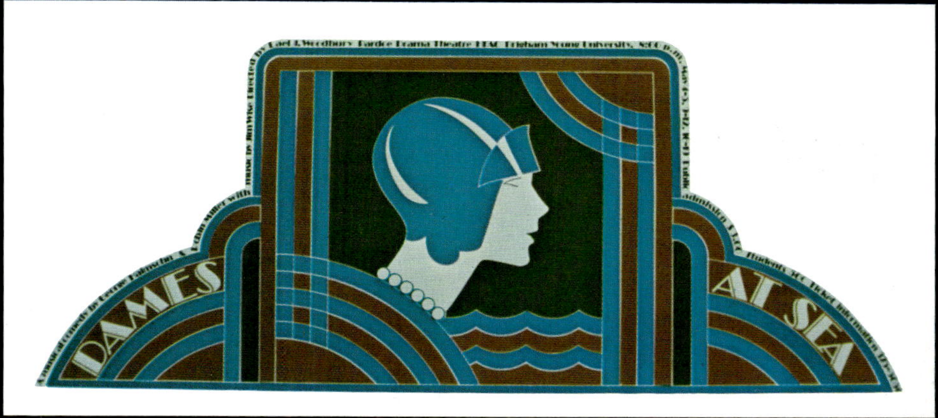
DAMES
AT SEA

22

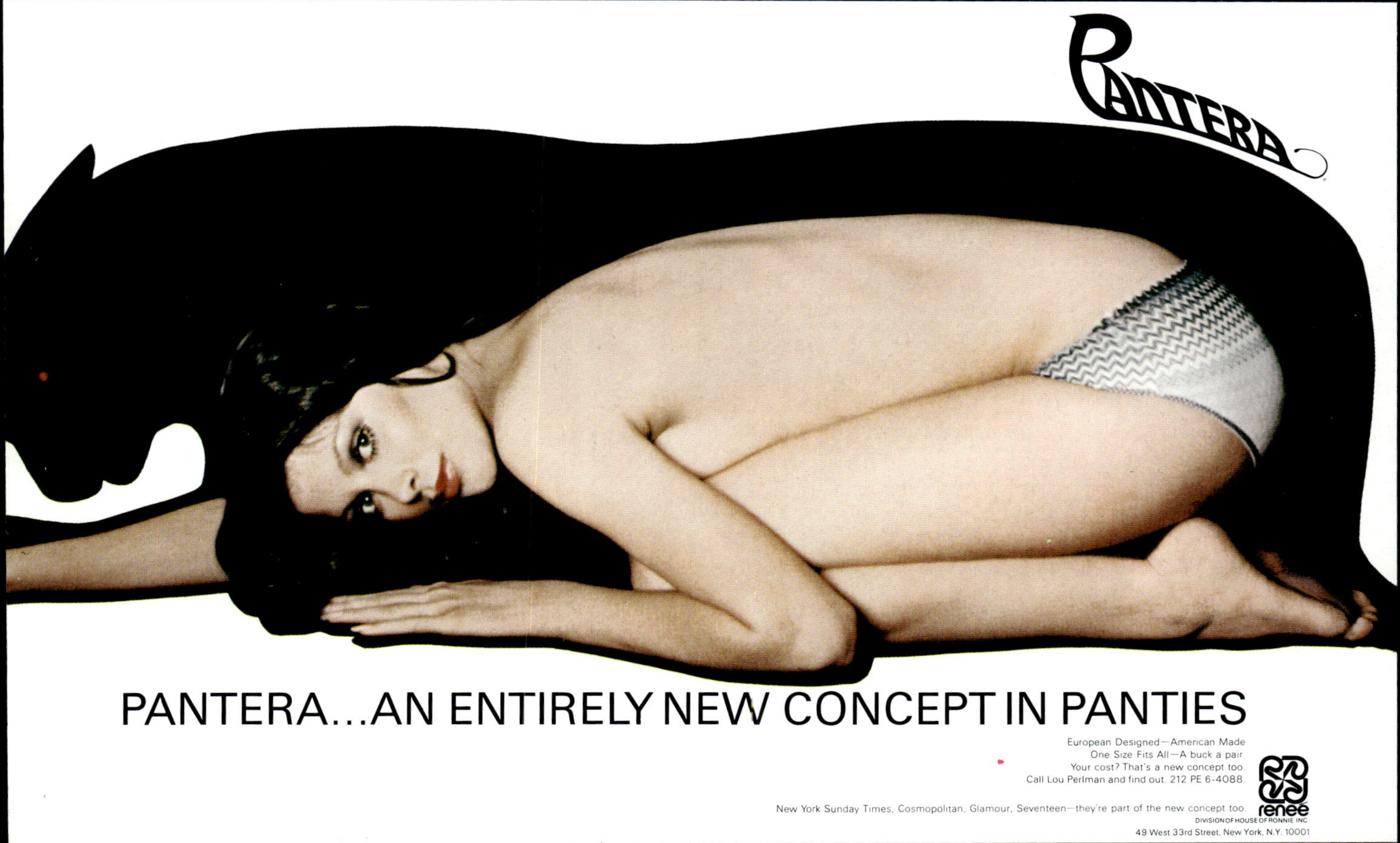
PANTERA
PANTERA...AN ENTIRELY NEW CONCEPT IN PANTIES
European Designed—American Made
One Size Fits All—A buck a pair.
Your cost? That's a new concept too.
Call Lou Perlman and find out. 212 PE 6-4088.
New York Sunday Times, Cosmopolitan, Glamour, Seventeen—they're part of the new concept too.
renée
DIVISION OF HOUSE OF RONNIE INC
49 West 33rd Street, New York, N.Y. 10001

24

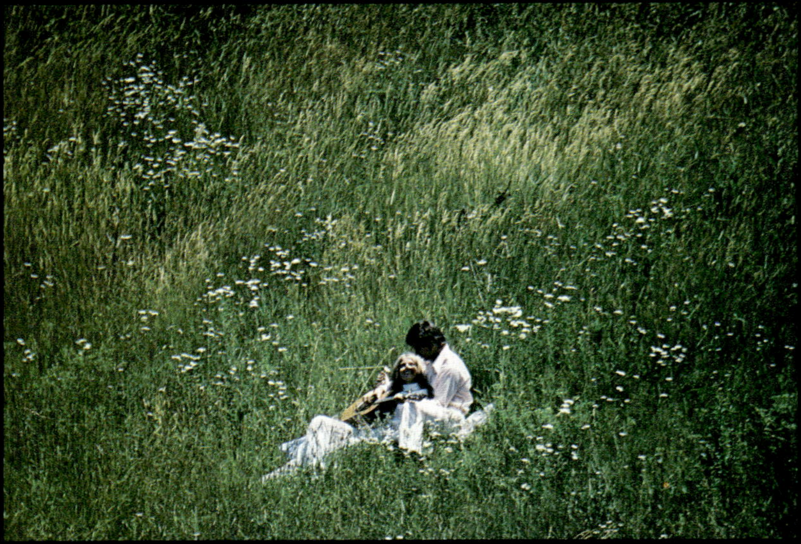

25

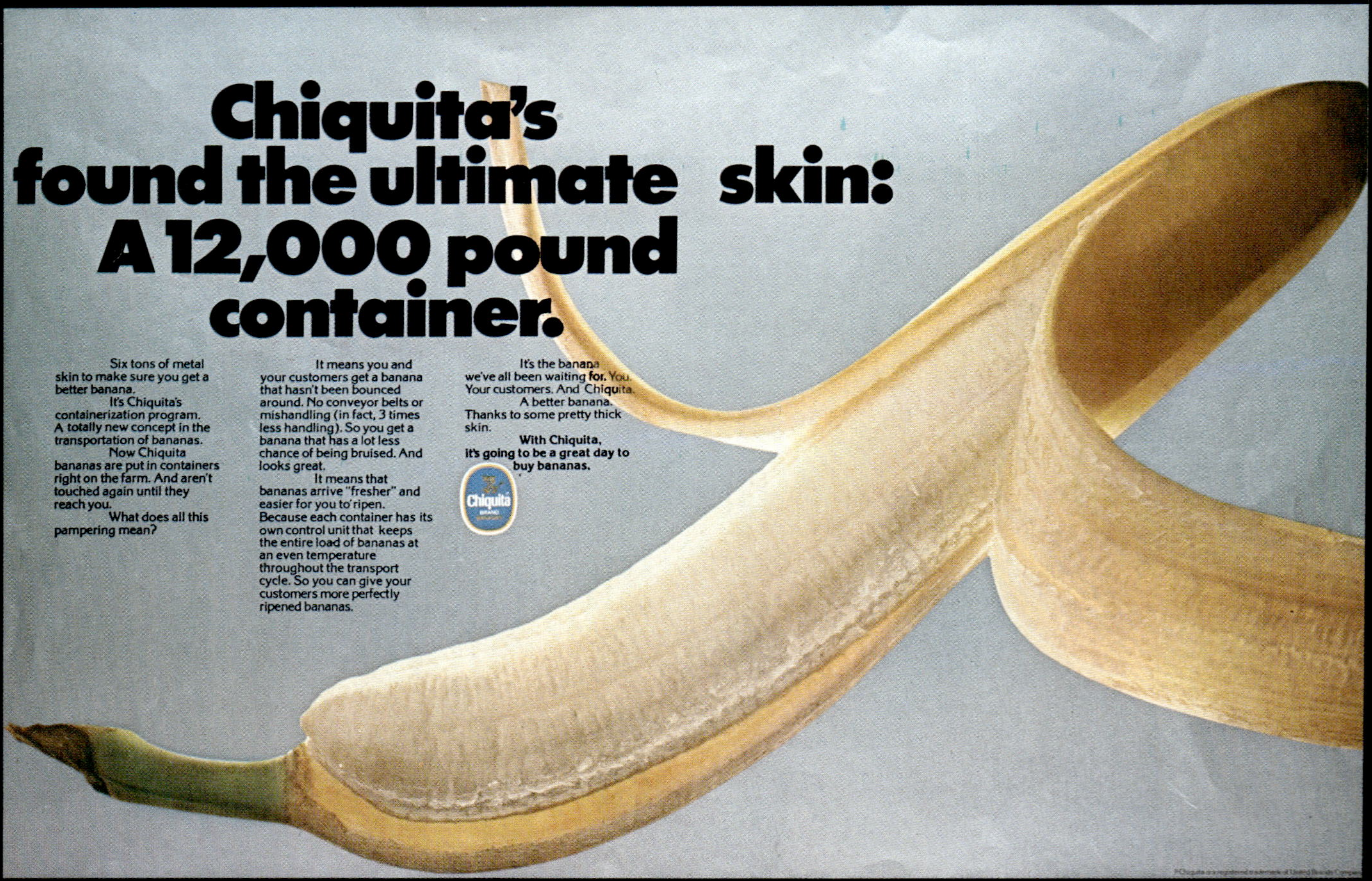
Chiquita's found the ultimate skin: A 12,000 pound container.
Six tons of metal skin to make sure you get a better banana.
It's Chiquita's containerization program. A totally new concept in the transportation of bananas.
Now Chiquita bananas are put in containers right on the farm. And aren't touched again until they reach you.
What does all this pampering mean?
It means you and your customers get a banana that hasn't been bounced around. No conveyor belts or mishandling (in fact, 3 times less handling). So you get a banana that has a lot less chance of being bruised. And looks great.
It means that bananas arrive "fresher" and easier for you to ripen. Because each container has its own control unit that keeps the entire load of bananas at an even temperature throughout the transport cycle. So you can give your customers more perfectly ripened bananas.
It's the banana we've all been waiting for. You. Your customers. And Chiquita.
A better banana. Thanks to some pretty thick skin.
With Chiquita, it's going to be a great day to buy bananas.
Chiquita

24
Nicholas Zarkades Entrant
Stock Photos Unlimited of New York Photographer
The Gillette Company Client

25
Ken Etheridge Entrant
Anthony Barboza Photographer
Woody Connor Copywriter
Young & Rubicam Inc. Agency
United Brands Co. Client

26
Playboy Enterprises, Inc. Entrant
Arthur Paul Art Director
Kerig Pope Designer
Frank Lafitte Photographer
Playboy Magazine Client

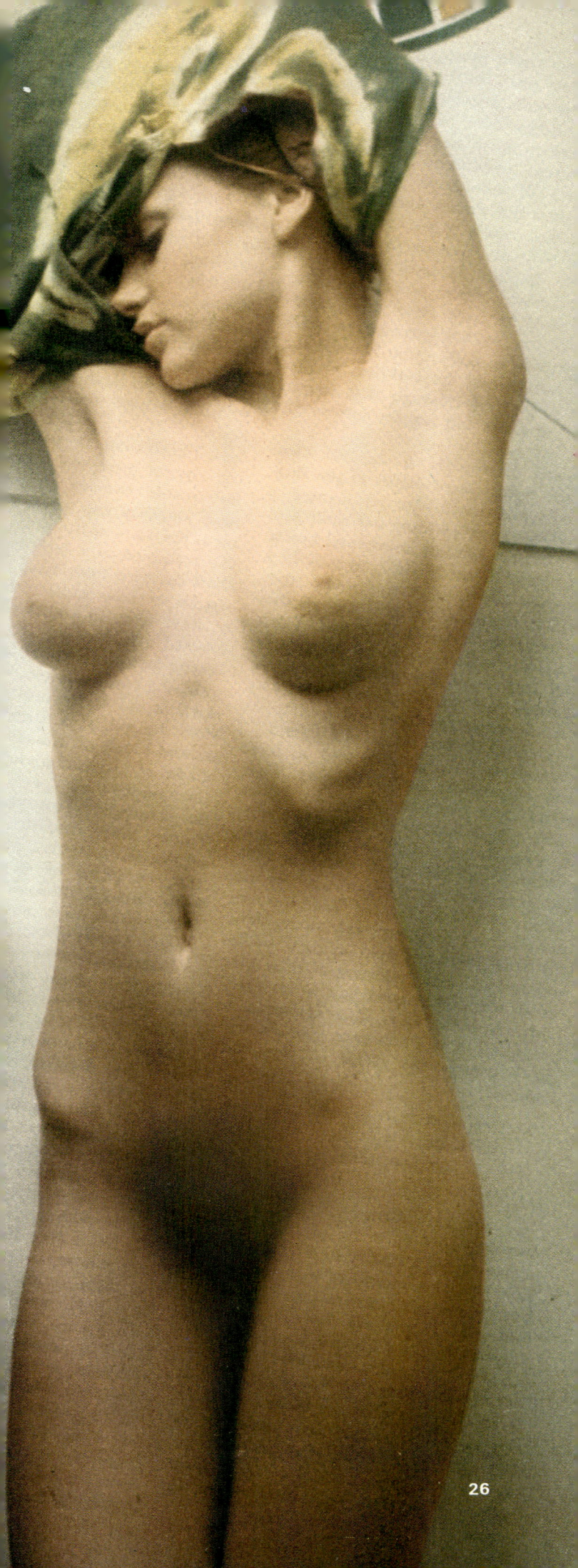

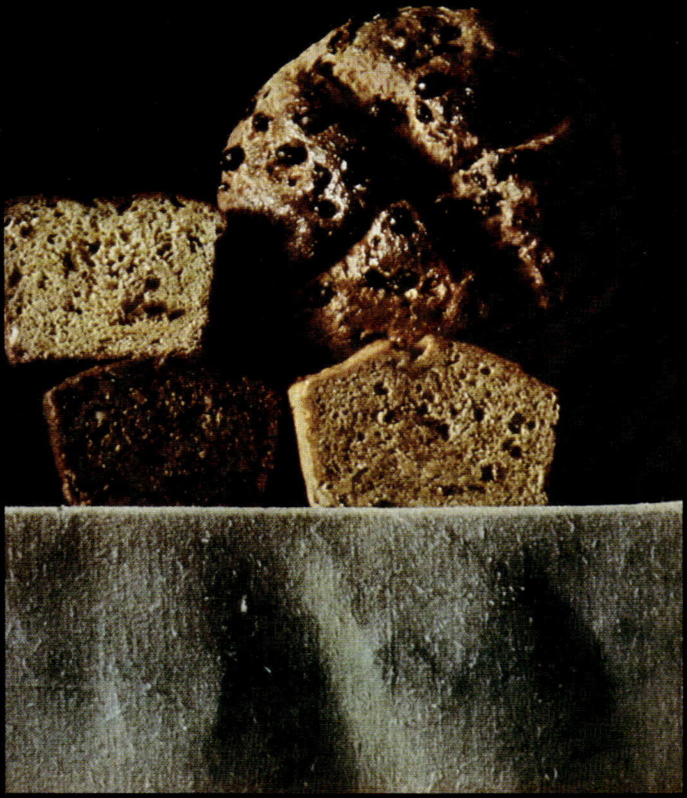

28

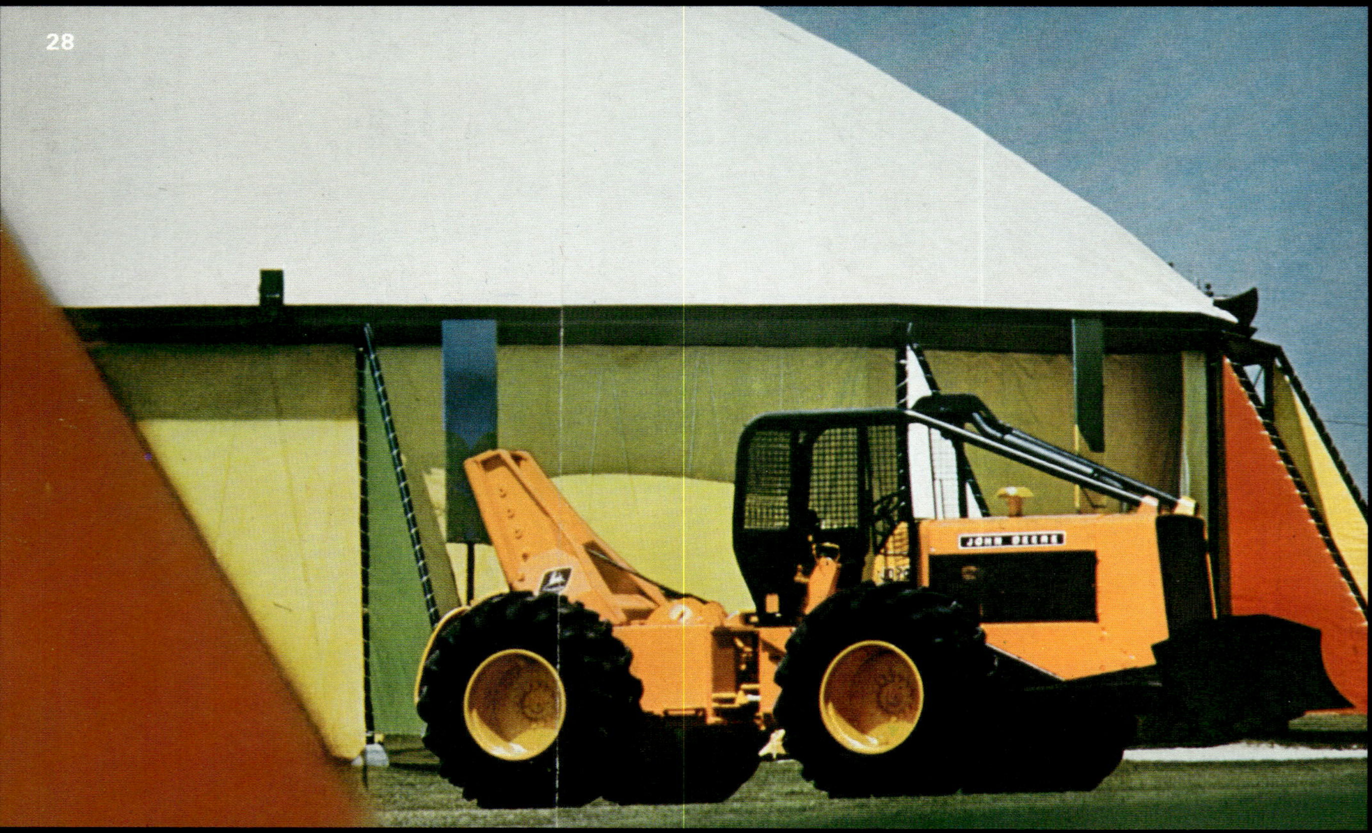

27
Redbook Magazine Entrant
Valerie Kleckner Art Director
Jerry Sarapochiello Photographer

28
Murrie White & Assoc. Entrant
Gary Springer Art Director
Jim Lienhart Designer
Archie Lieberman Photographer
Deere & Company Client

29
Redbook Magazine
Entrant
Valerie Kleckner
Art Director
Morecraft/Oliwa
Photographers

30
Eisenman and Enock Inc. Entrant
Stan Eisenman, David Enock Art Directors
Burt Glinn Photographer
PepsiCo, Inc. Client

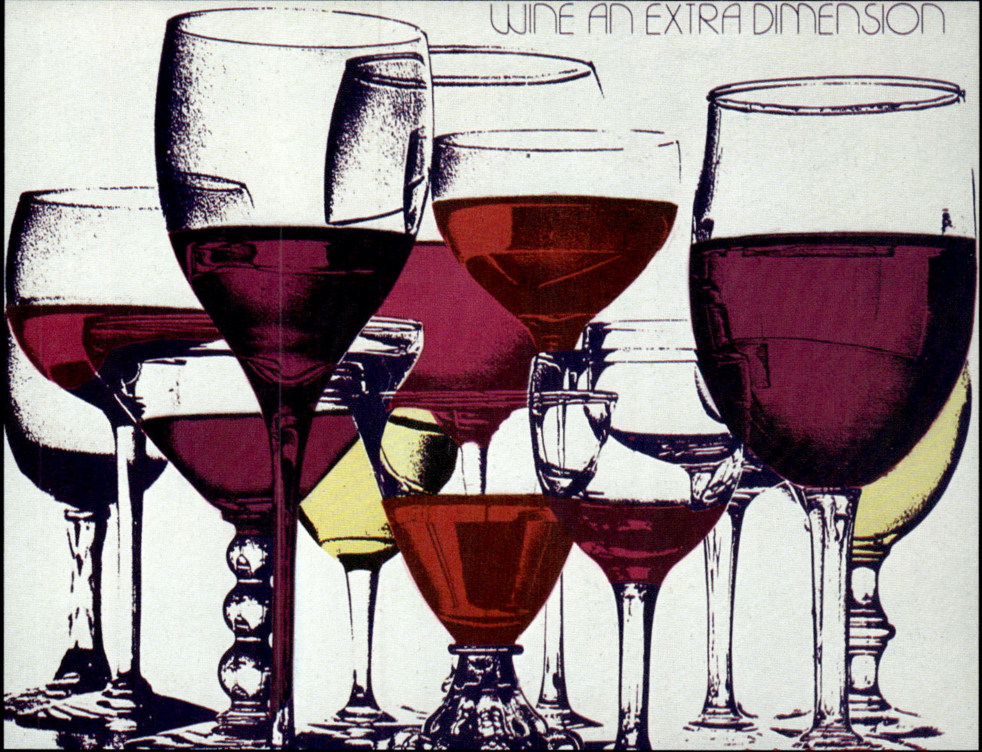
WINE AN EXTRA DIMENSION
29

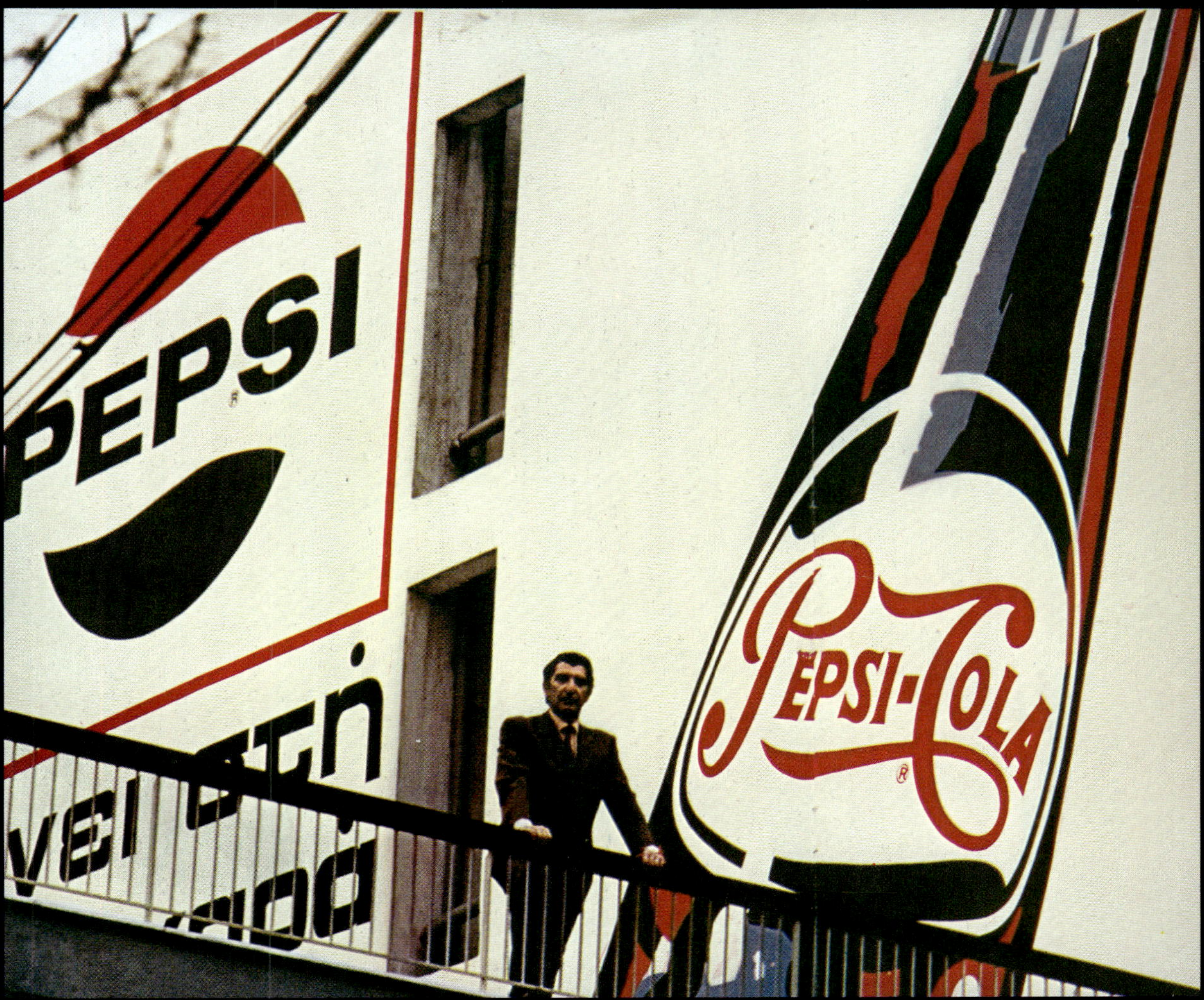
PEPSI
PEPSI-COLA
30

31

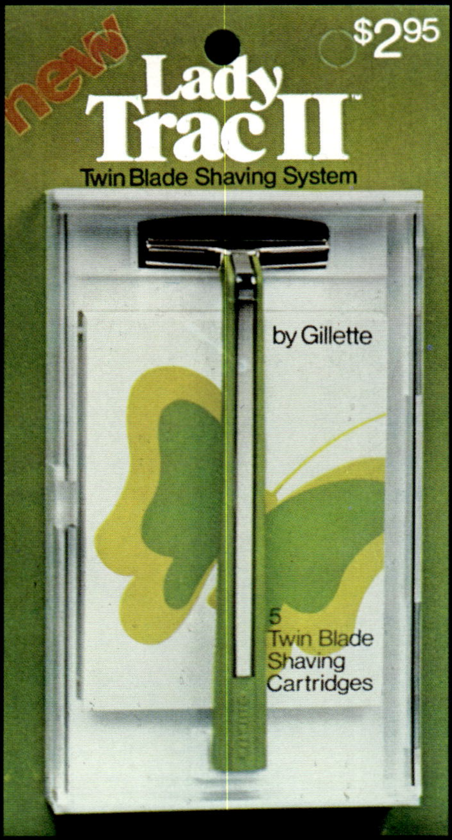
new
$2.95
Lady Trac II
Twin Blade Shaving System
by Gillette
5 Twin Blade Shaving Cartridges

34

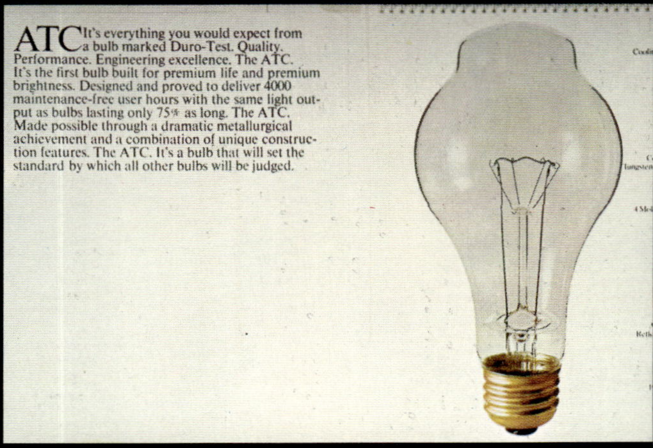
ATC It's everything you would expect from a bulb marked Duro-Test. Quality. Performance. Engineering excellence. The ATC. It's the first bulb built for premium life and premium brightness. Designed and proved to deliver 4000 maintenance-free user hours with the same light output as bulbs lasting only 75% as long. The ATC. Made possible through a dramatic metallurgical achievement and a combination of unique construction features. The ATC. It's a bulb that will set the standard by which all other bulbs will be judged.

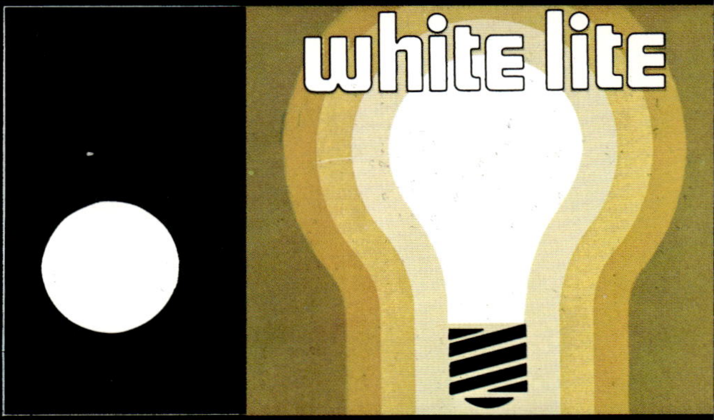
white lite

35

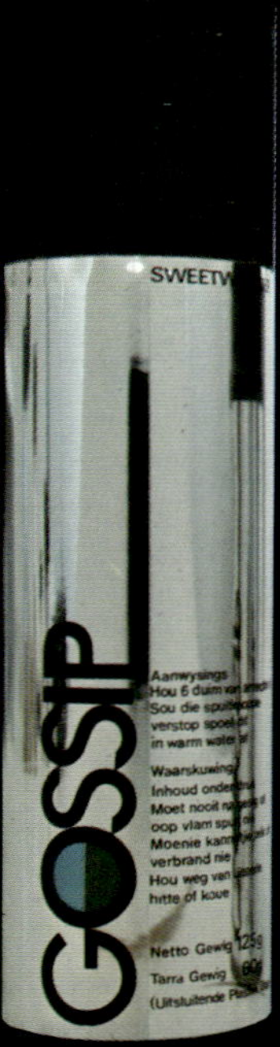
GOSSIP

32

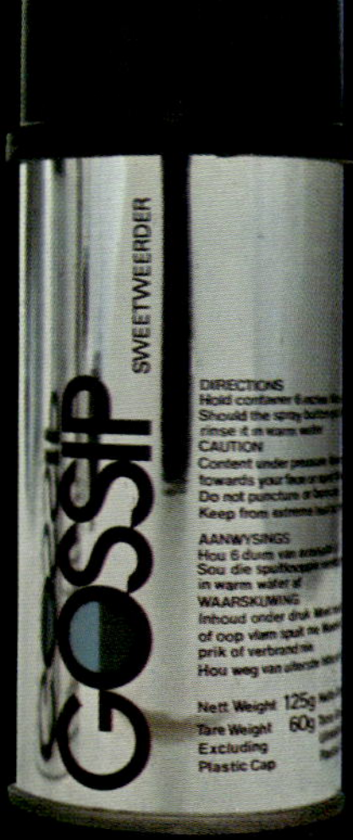
GOSSIP
SWEETWEERDER

33

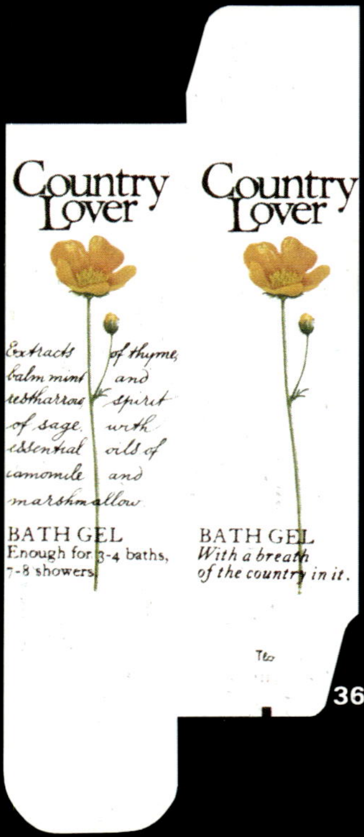
Country Lover
Extracts of thyme, balm mint and restharrow spirit of sage, with essential oils of camomile and marshmallow
BATH GEL
Enough for 3-4 baths, 7-8 showers
Country Lover
BATH GEL
With a breath of the country in it.

36

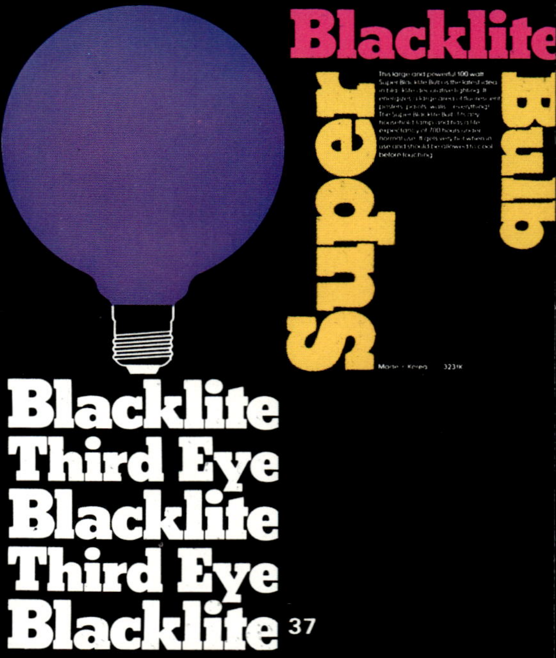
Blacklite
Super Bulb
Blacklite
Third Eye
Blacklite
Third Eye
Blacklite

37

31	32-33	34	35	36	37	38
Ray Shaw Entrant **Bruce Ray, Nick Fader** Designers **Gillette Safety Razor Division** Client	**Arie J. Geurts** Entrant **Unimark International, Johannesburg** Agency **Bristol-Myers** Client	**Hinrichs Design Associates** Entrant **Kit Hinrichs, J. Wright** Art Directors **Durotest Corporation** Client	**Irwin Hanopole** Entrant **Torch Bulbs** Client	**Lloyd, Clark, Rowe Ltd.** Entrant **Linda Butler, Kim Clark** Art Directors **Country Lover** Client	**The Third Eye, Inc.** Entrant **Linda Brewer** Art Director **John Brewer** Illustrator	**Ursula Flurer** Entrant **Margret Malast** Letterer **Southland Corporati[on]** Client

38

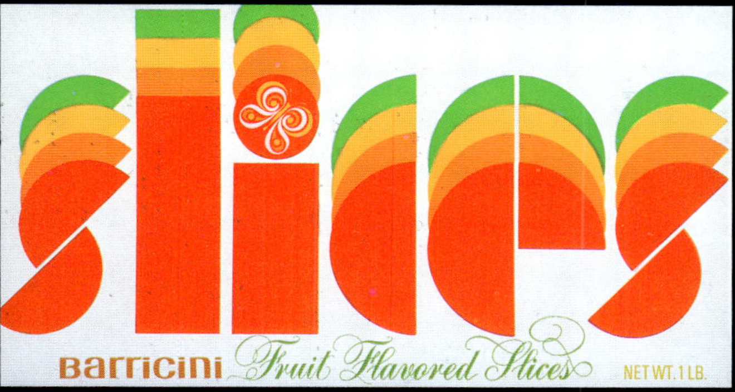
slices
barricini Fruit Flavored Slices
NET WT. 1 LB.

39
Murrie White & Assoc. Entrant
Gary Springer Art Director
Jim Lienhart Designer
Deere & Company Client

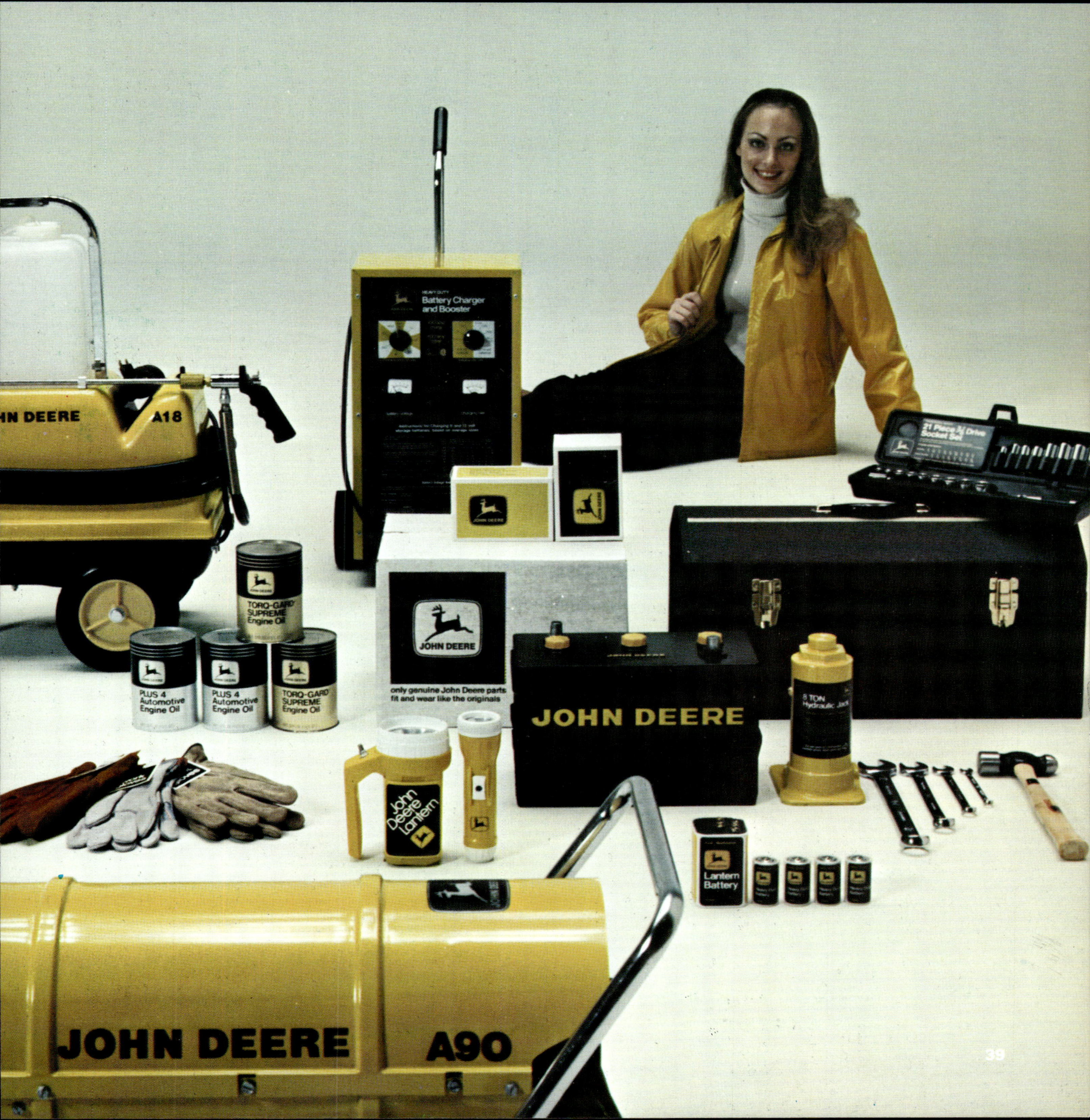
JOHN DEERE
A18
Battery Charger and Booster
TORQ-GARD SUPREME Engine Oil
PLUS 4 Automotive Engine Oil
PLUS 4 Automotive Engine Oil
TORQ-GARD SUPREME Engine Oil
JOHN DEERE
only genuine John Deere parts fit and wear like the originals
JOHN DEERE
8 TON Hydraulic Jack
John Deere Lantern
Lantern Battery
JOHN DEERE
A90

40

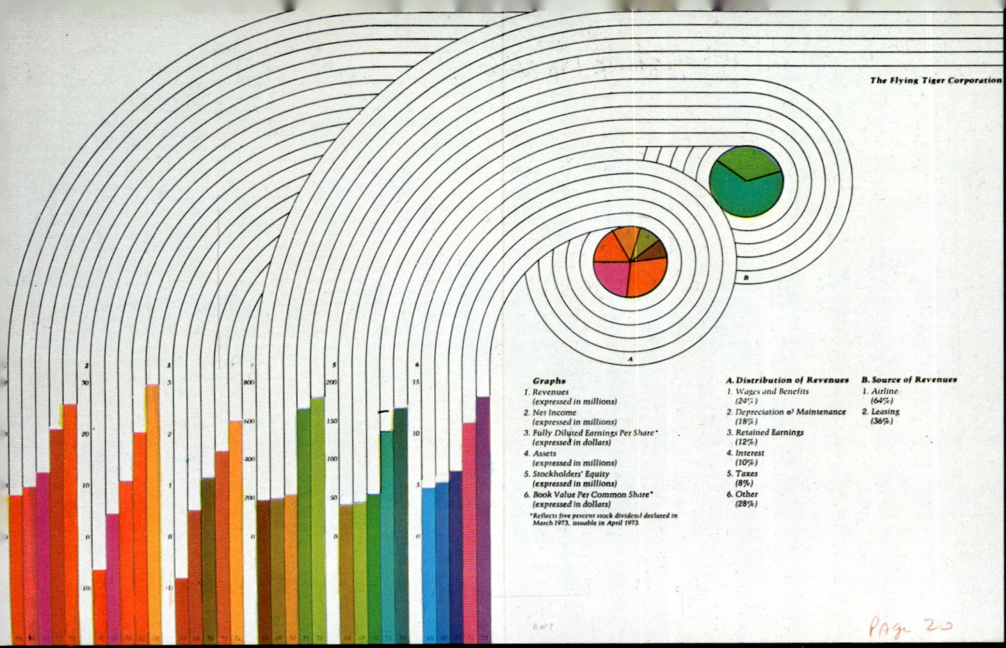
The Flying Tiger Corporation
A
B
Graphs
1. Revenues (expressed in millions)
2. Net Income (expressed in millions)
3. Fully Diluted Earnings Per Share* (expressed in dollars)
4. Assets (expressed in millions)
5. Stockholders' Equity (expressed in millions)
6. Book Value Per Common Share* (expressed in dollars)
*Reflects five percent stock dividend declared in March 1973, issuable in April 1973.
A. Distribution of Revenues
1. Wages and Benefits (24%)
2. Depreciation & Maintenance (18%)
3. Retained Earnings (12%)
4. Interest (10%)
5. Taxes (8%)
6. Other (28%)
B. Source of Revenues
1. Airline (64%)
2. Leasing (36%)

41

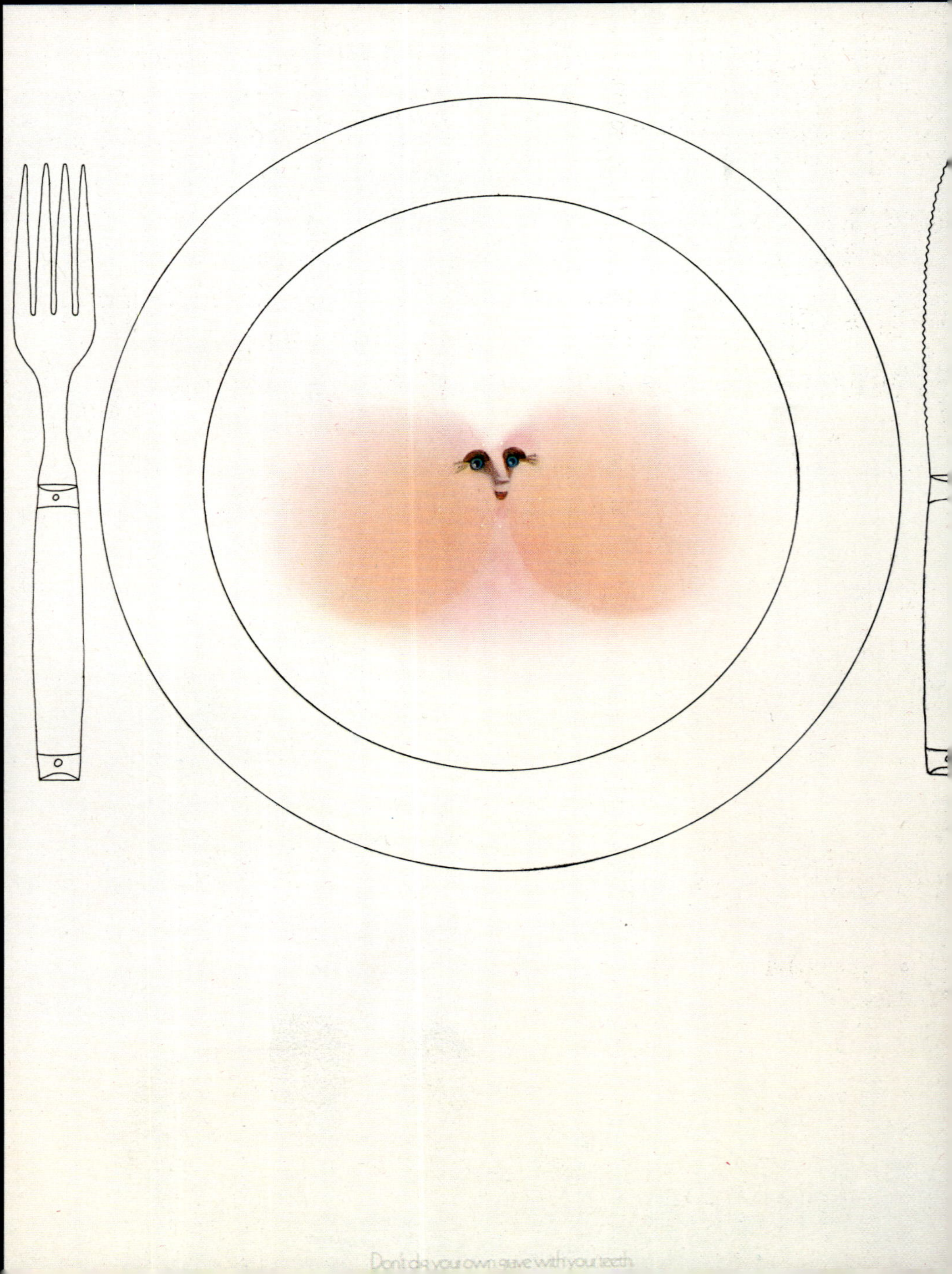
Don't dig your own grave with your teeth.

40
Robert Miles Runyan & Associates Entrant
Robert Miles Runyan Art Director
Rusty Kay Designer
Marvin Silver Photographer
Art Mochizuki Artist
The Flying Tiger Corporation Client

41
Lars Melander Entrant
Hera Anonsbyrå Agency
Tinta-Tryck Client

42
Exxon Corporation Entrant
Harry Diamond, John Conley Art Directors
Alan E. Cober Illustrator
The Lamp Magazine Client

43-45
Exxon Corporation Entrant
Harry Diamond, John Conley Art Directors
André François Illustrator
The Lamp Magazine Client

43

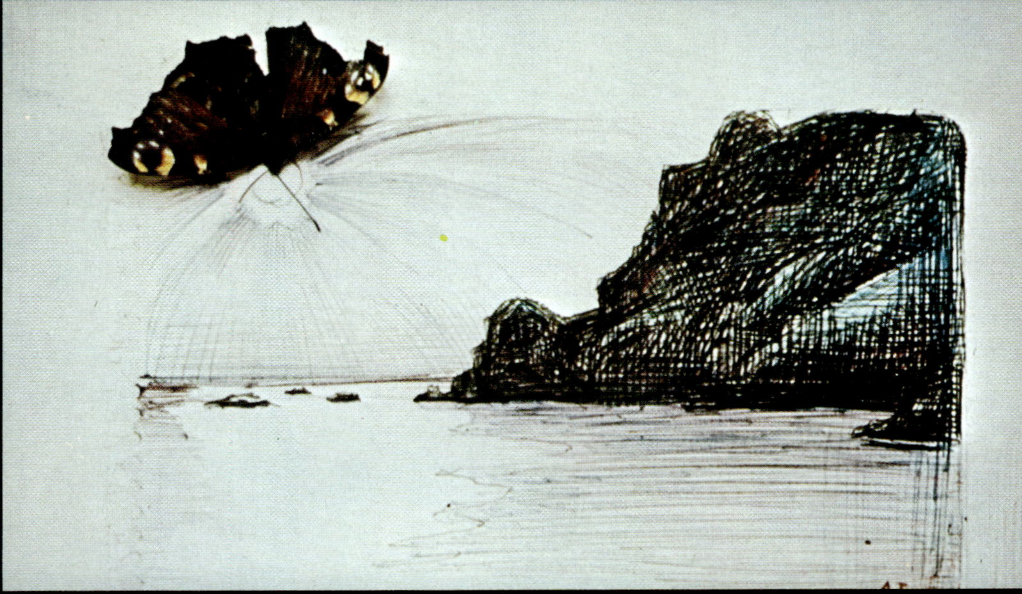

44

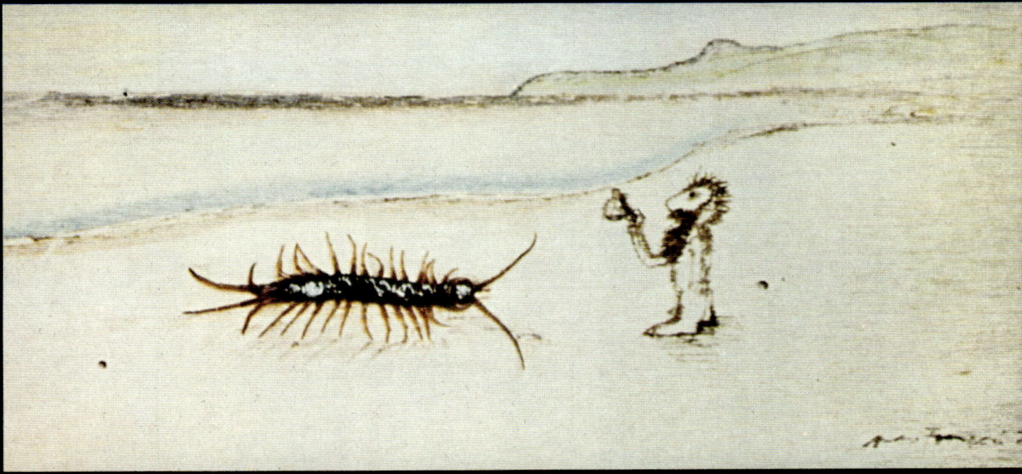

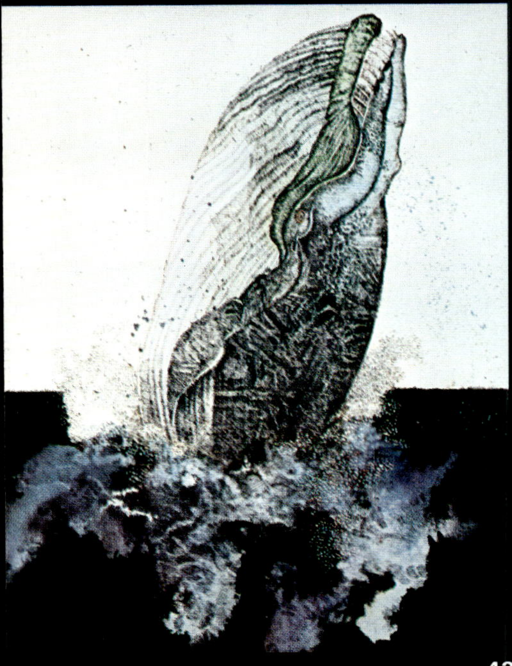

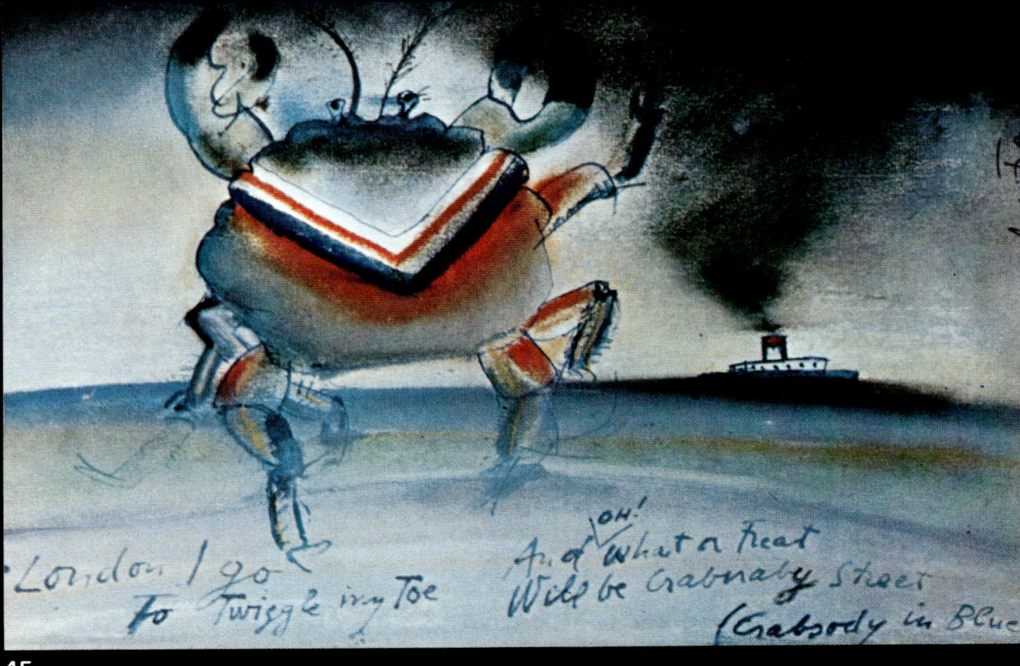
London I go
To Twiggle my Toe
And OH! What a treat
Will be Crabnaby Street
(Crabsody in Blue

42 45

46

47

48

FIREPLUG
overloaded wires result in great fires

P13N

49

Polyimide
Molding Powder

50

We're moving to a street
named after a famous purple fruit
Into a building with a very large
nut and bolt painted on the side of it
We hope to do business
with re america
The T W Ford Company
437 Plum Street Cincinnati Ohio 45202
Phone 381-1122
We do great things
in spite of it all

51

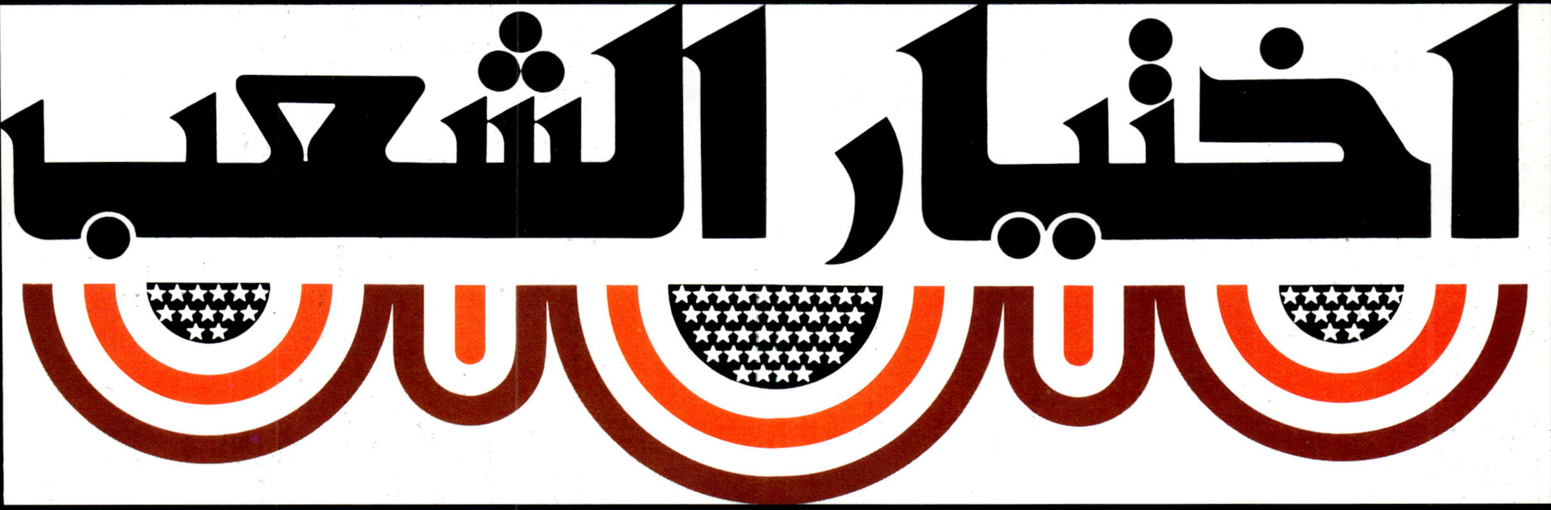
اختيار الشعب

52

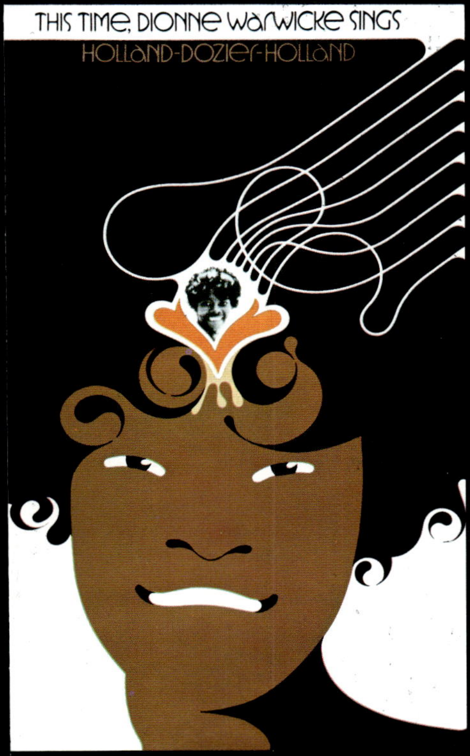
THIS TIME, DIONNE WARWICKE SINGS
HOLLAND-DOZIER-HOLLAND

53

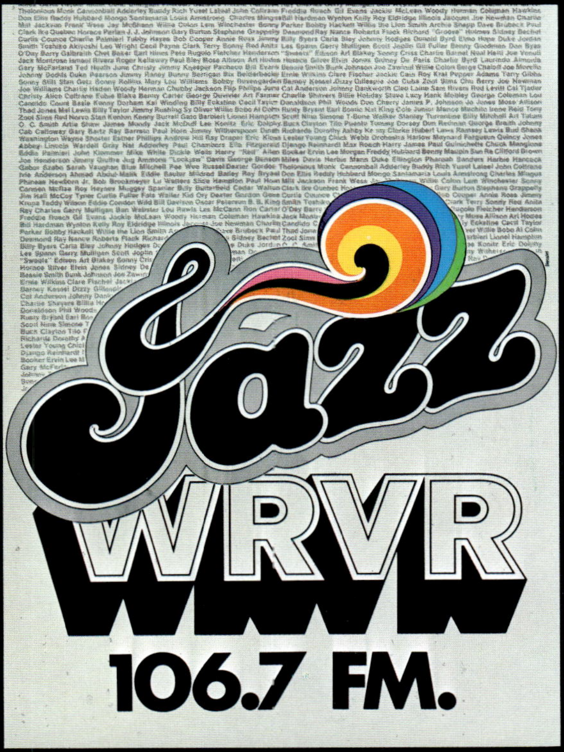
Jazz
WRVR
106.7 FM.

54

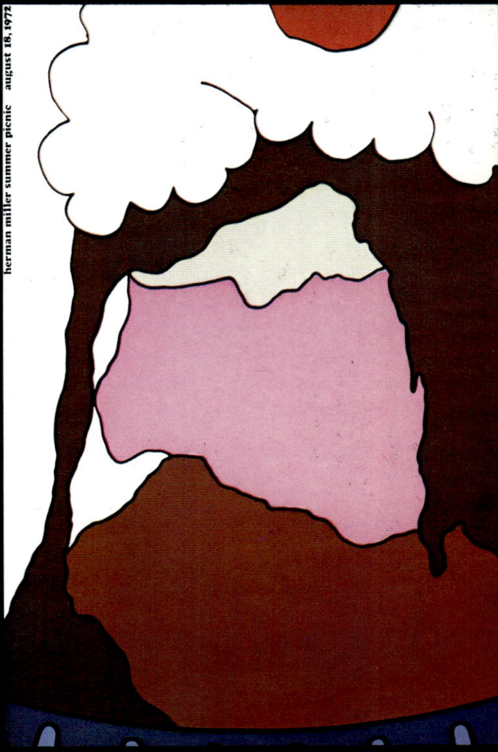
herman miller summer picnic august 18, 1972

50
Intermedia, Inc. Entrant
Bob Cosgrove Art Director
Jim Williams Illustrator
Craig Jiebel Copywriter
The Art Group Studio
J.W. Ford Co. Client

51
U.S. Information Agency Entrant
Robert Banks
Art Director
Al Majal Magazine
Client

52
Weller & Juett, Inc. Entrant
Chris Whorf
Art Director
Don Weller
Illustrator
Warner Bros. Records, Inc. Client

53
Besalel Ltd.
Entrant
Ely Besalel
Art Director
Ray Cruz
Letterer
WRVR Client

54
Herman Miller, Inc.
Entrant
Stephen Frykholm, Mark Sturzenegger
Designers

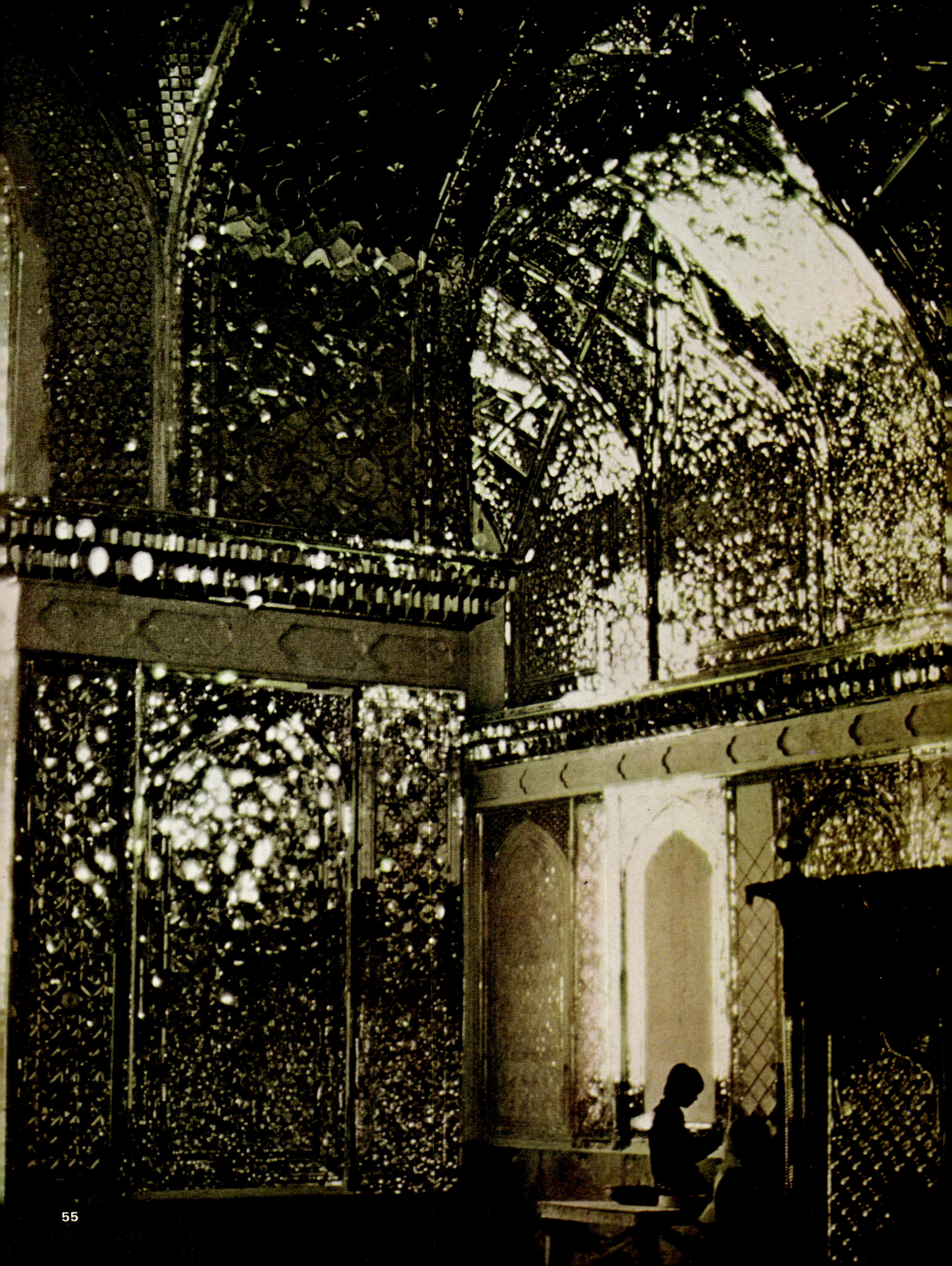

55
Jay Maisel Entrant
**Jacques Lowe, Heinz Heimann,
Nimal Jayserka** Art Directors
**Creative Communications S.A.,
Franklin Book Programs, Inc.** Clients

56
Joseph R. Palsa Entrant
Joseph R. Palsa & Assoc. Agency
Roulston & Co. Client

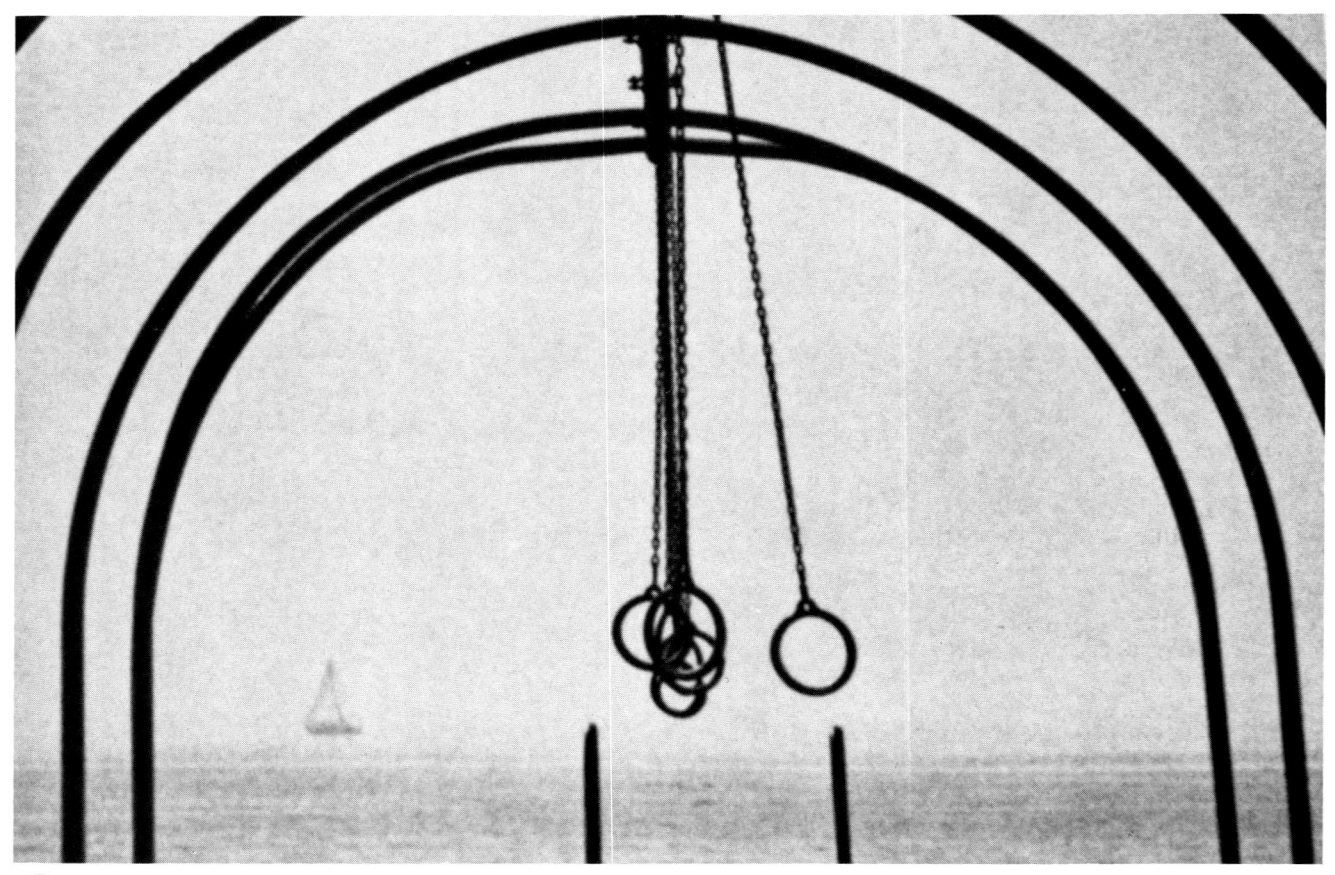

57

57
Weller & Juett Inc. Entrant
Don Weller, Dennis Juett Art Directors
Koltun Brothers Client

58
Earl Miller Entrant
John Jensen Art Director
Bernstein, Rein, & Boasberg Agency
American Stair-Glide Corp. Client

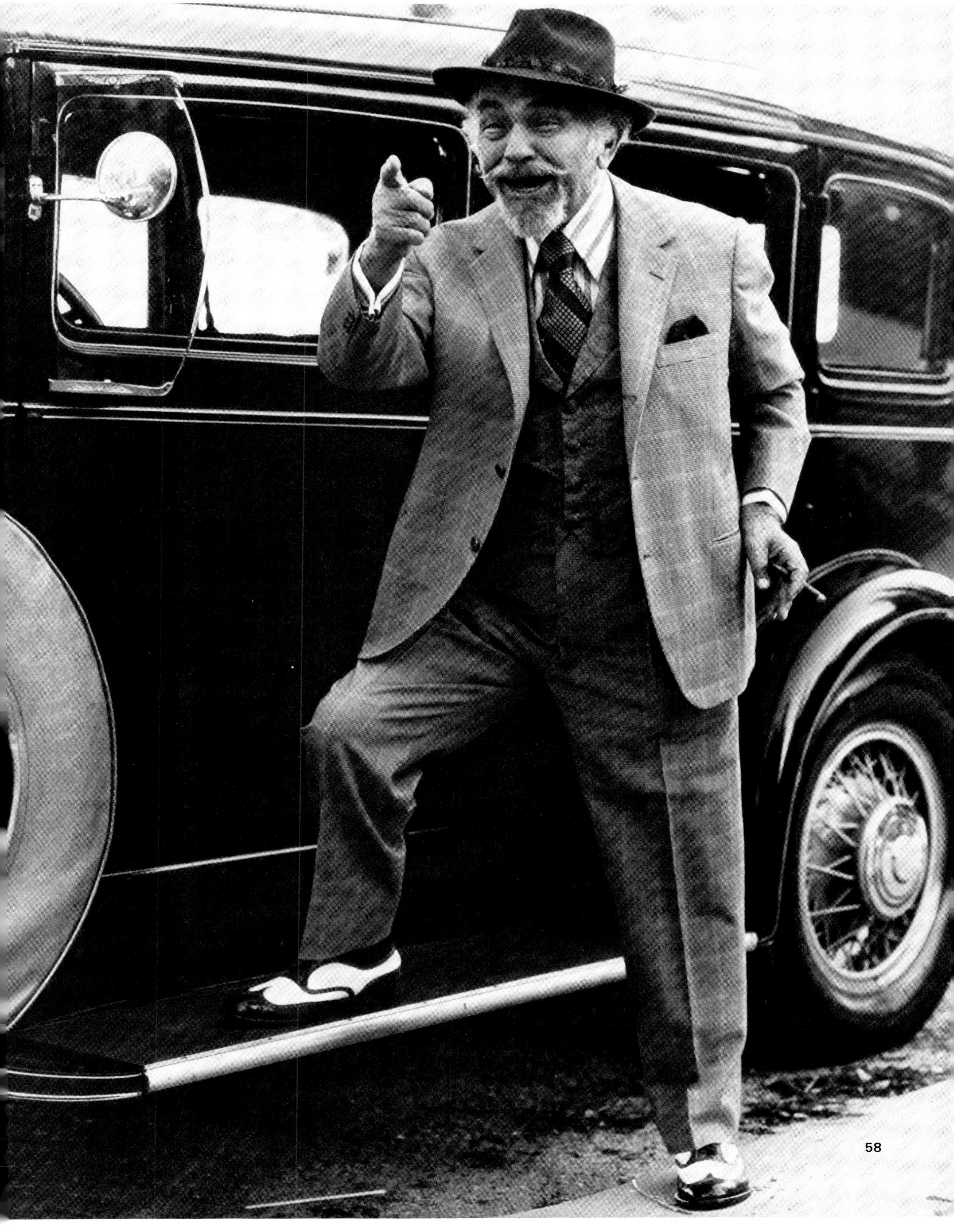

59

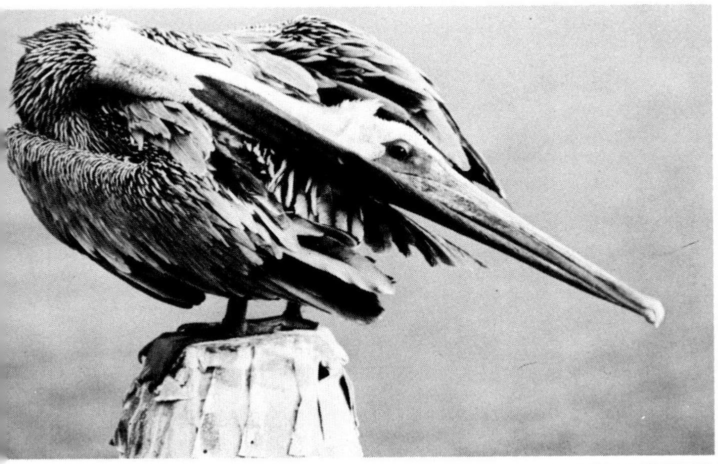

60

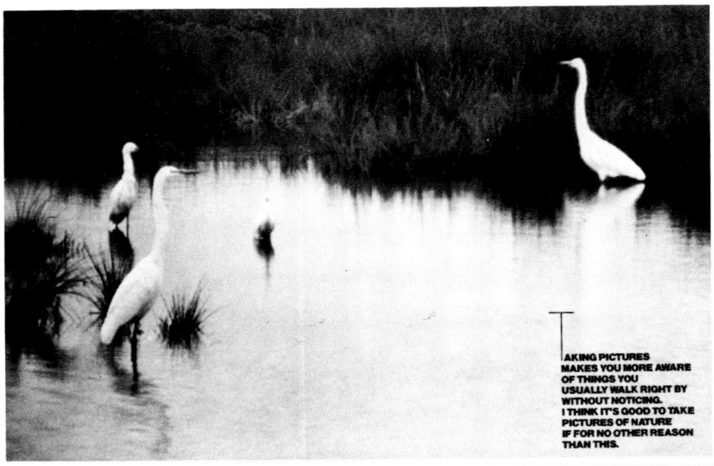
TAKING PICTURES
MAKES YOU MORE AWARE
OF THINGS YOU
USUALLY WALK RIGHT BY
WITHOUT NOTICING.
I THINK IT'S GOOD TO TAKE
PICTURES OF NATURE
IF FOR NO OTHER REASON
THAN THIS.

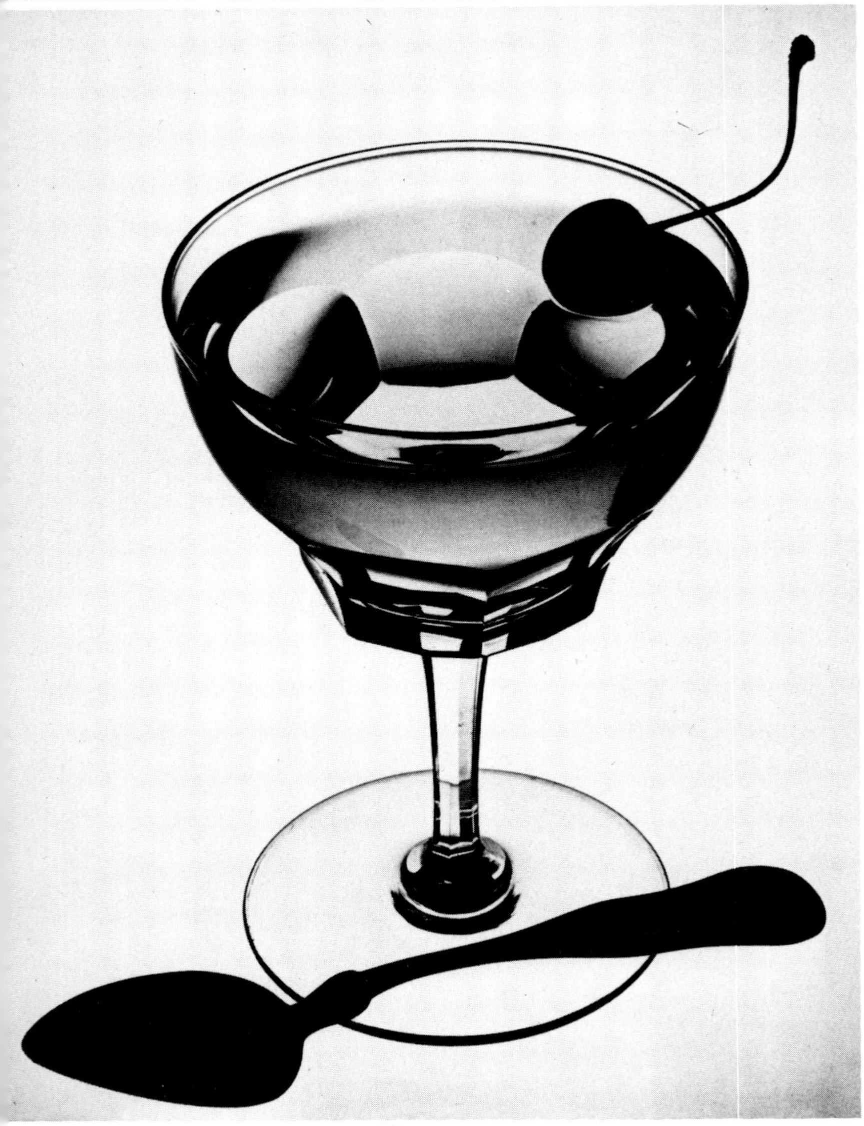

61

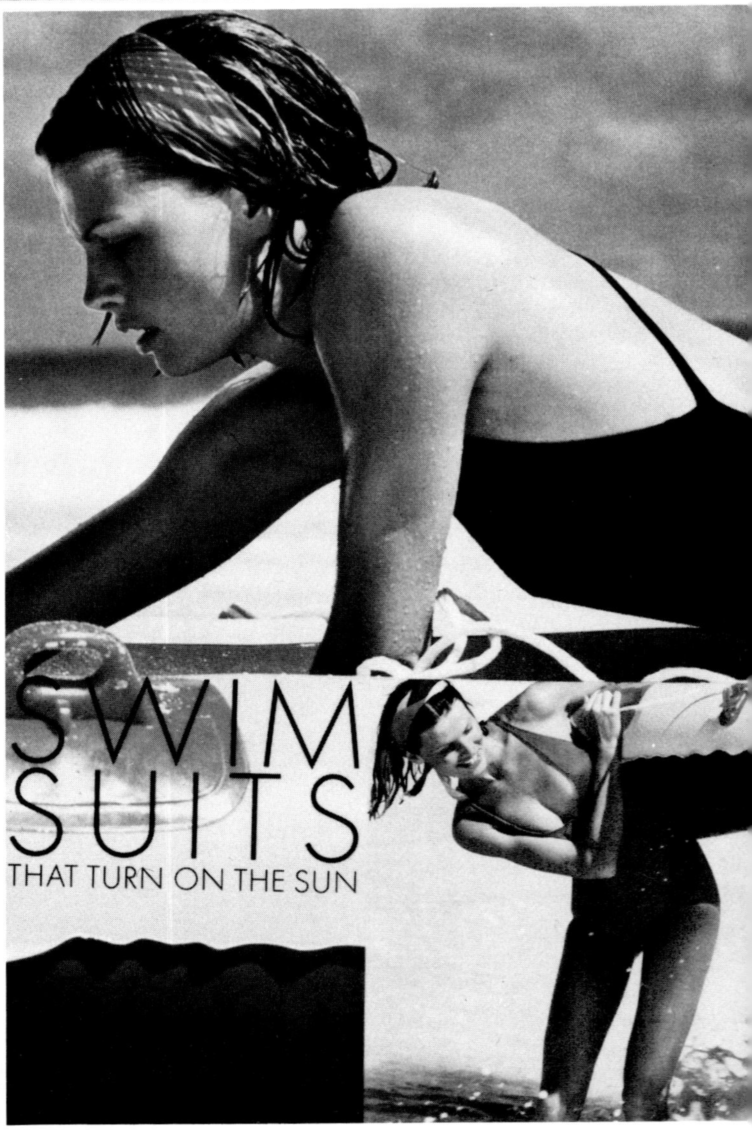
SWIM
SUITS
THAT TURN ON THE SUN

62

59
Bob Drayton Entrant
Harvard Engraving Client

60
William Kemsley Entrant
Peter J. Blank Don Menell Art Directors
William Kemsley, Ruth Smiley Photographers
WKA Corporate Graphics Agency
Backpacker Magazine Client

61
Fred Schenk Entrant
Thomas J. Knowles Art Directo
Fred Schenk Studio Studio

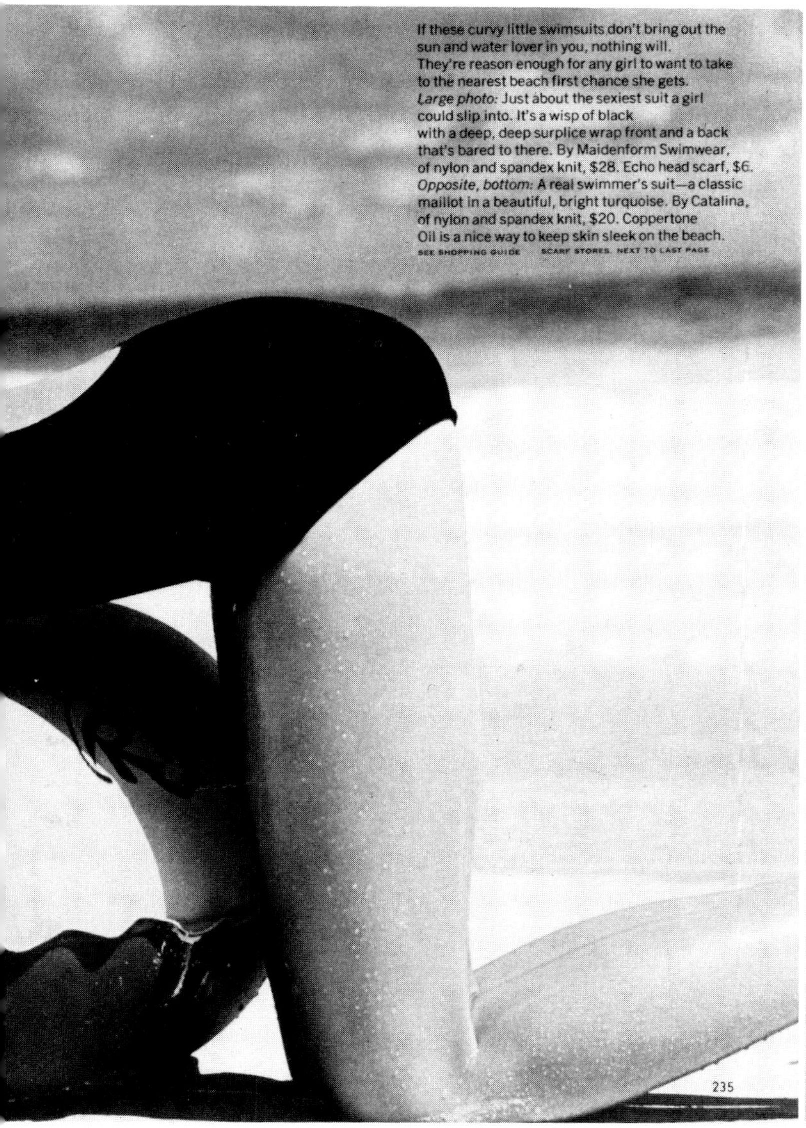

If these curvy little swimsuits don't bring out the sun and water lover in you, nothing will. They're reason enough for any girl to want to take to the nearest beach first chance she gets.
Large photo: Just about the sexiest suit a girl could slip into. It's a wisp of black with a deep, deep surplice wrap front and a back that's bared to there. By Maidenform Swimwear, of nylon and spandex knit, $28. Echo head scarf, $6.
Opposite, bottom: A real swimmer's suit—a classic maillot in a beautiful, bright turquoise. By Catalina, of nylon and spandex knit, $20. Coppertone Oil is a nice way to keep skin sleek on the beach.
SEE SHOPPING GUIDE
SCARF STORES, NEXT TO LAST PAGE
235

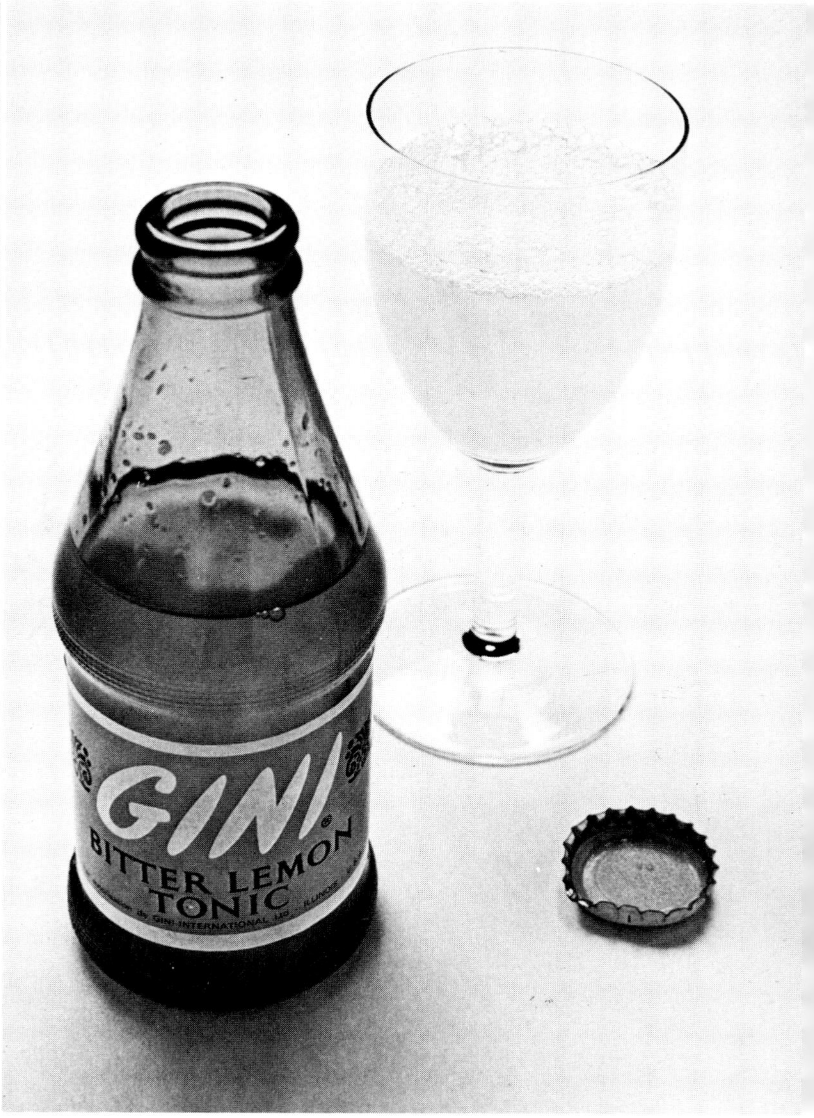

GINI
BITTER LEMON
TONIC

63

2
lamour Magazine Entrant
eorge Hartman Art Director
artick Demarchelier Photographer
onde Nast Publications Client

63
Norman Gorbaty Design Inc. Entrant
Brian Ganton Art Director
Soft Drinks Magazine Client

64
Steven Duckett Entrant
Alfred Gescheidt Photographer
Scholastic Magazines Inc. Client

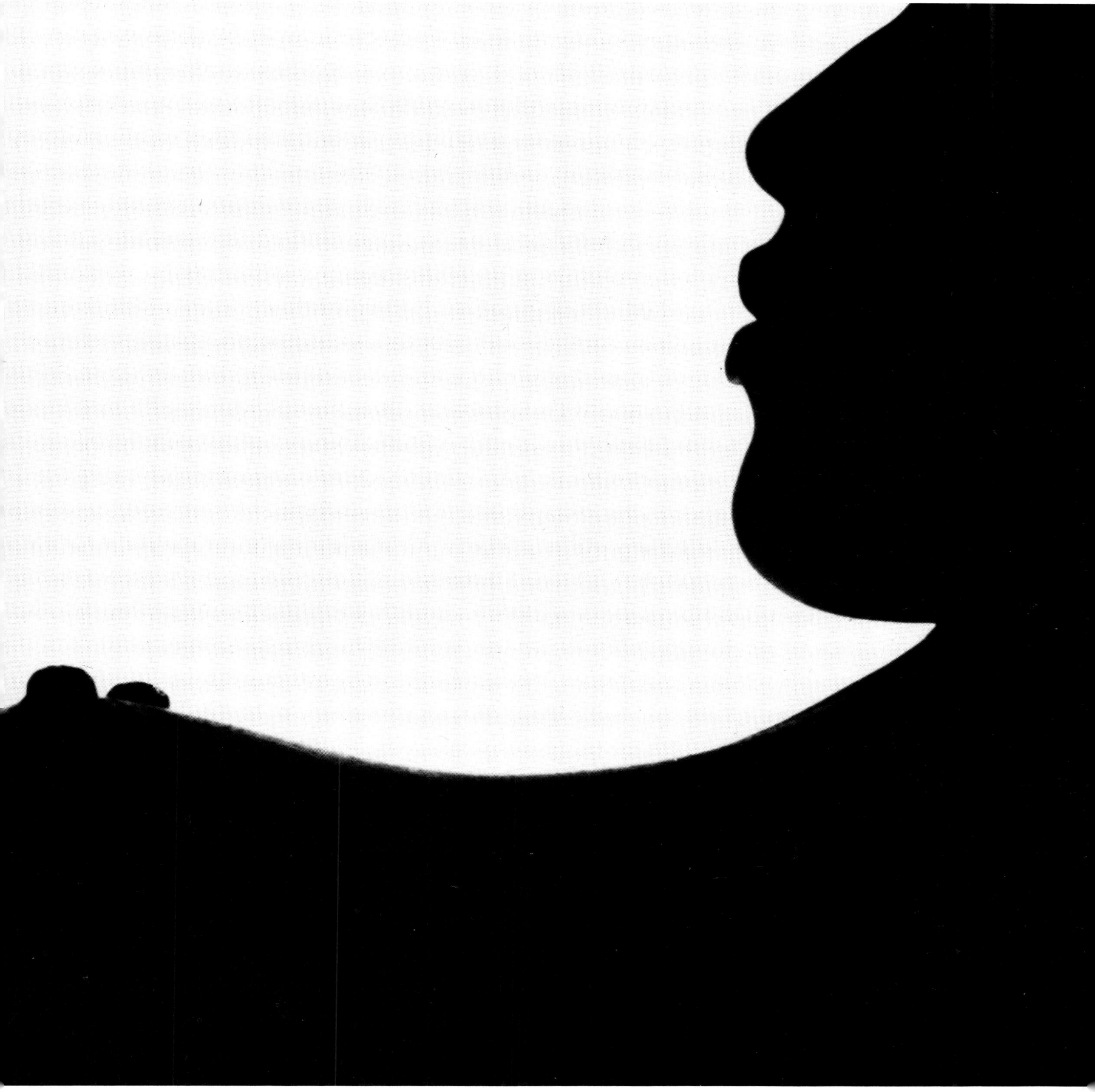

65
Bichsel Photographic Illust. Entrant
Frank Lerner Photographer

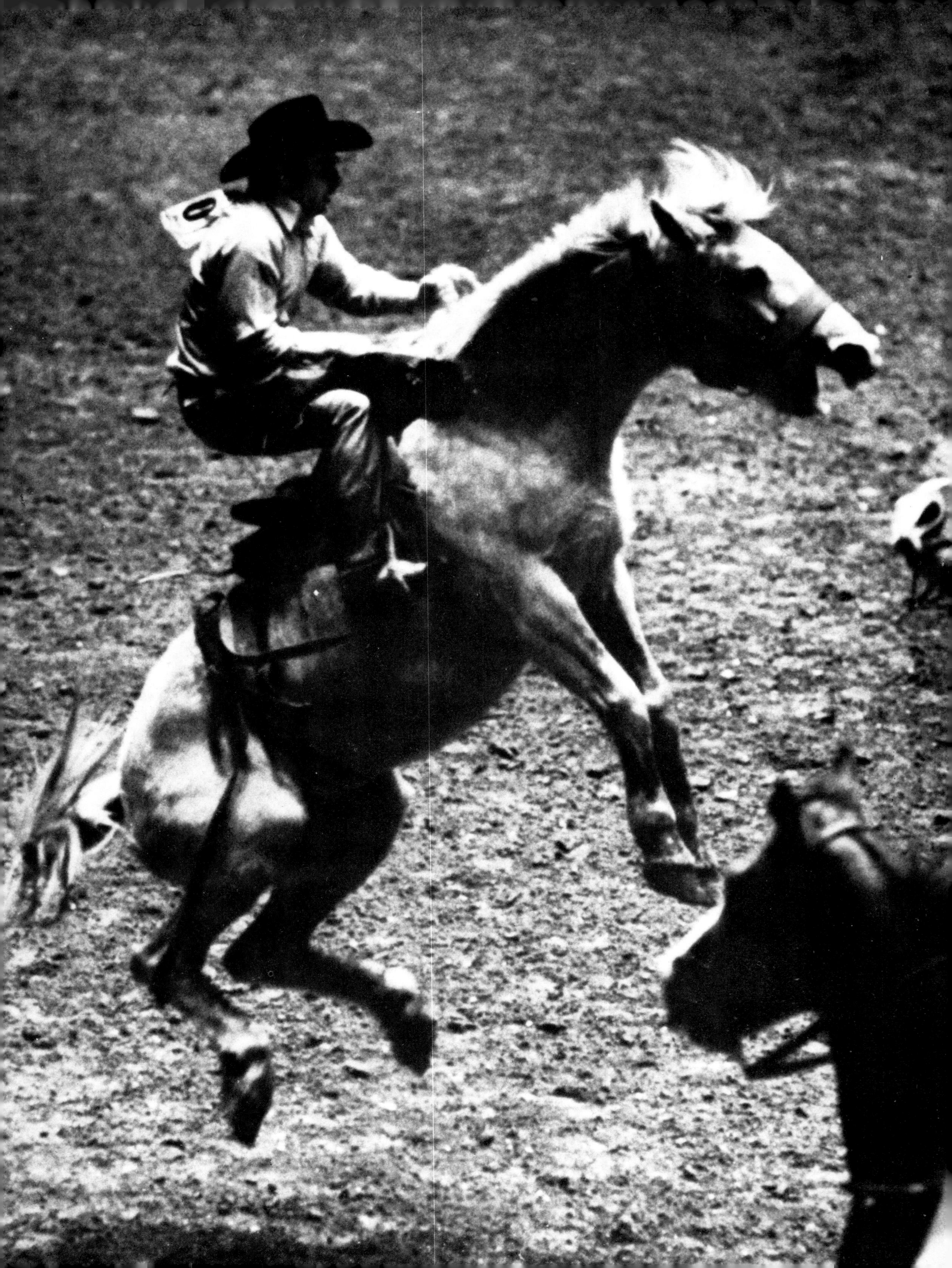

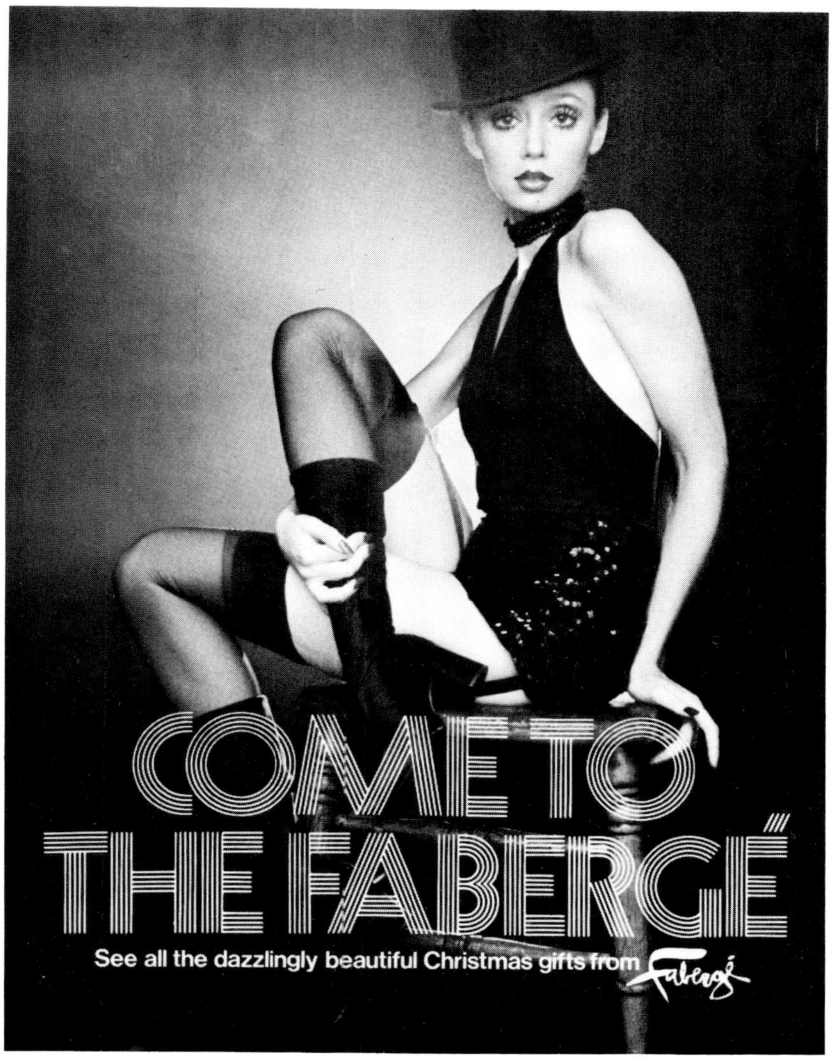
COME TO
THE FABERGÉ
See all the dazzlingly beautiful Christmas gifts from Fabergé

67

66
Sport Magazine Entrant
Al Braverman Art Director
Steve Krivisky Designer
Martin Blumenthal Photographer
Lubalin, Smith, Carnase Studio

67
Nadler & Larimer, Inc. Entrant
Irwin Goldberg Art Director
John Paul Endress Photographer
Faberge, Inc. Client

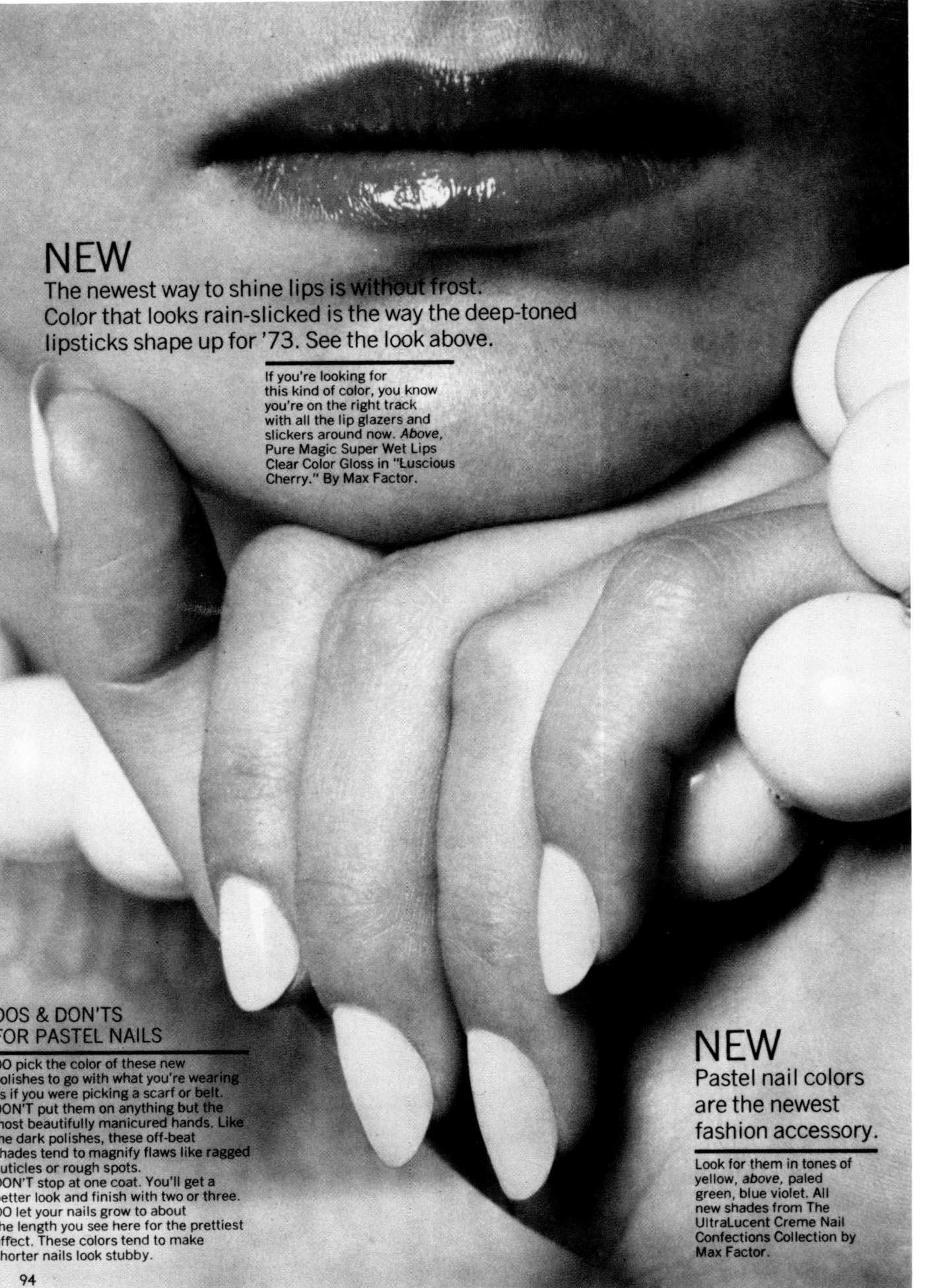

WHAT'S NEW, WHAT GOES, WHAT STAYS, WHAT'S NEW, WHAT GOES,

NEW
The newest way to shine lips is without frost. Color that looks rain-slicked is the way the deep-toned lipsticks shape up for '73. See the look above.

If you're looking for this kind of color, you know you're on the right track with all the lip glazers and slickers around now. *Above,* Pure Magic Super Wet Lips Clear Color Gloss in "Luscious Cherry." By Max Factor.

DOS & DON'TS FOR PASTEL NAILS

DO pick the color of these new polishes to go with what you're wearing as if you were picking a scarf or belt.
DON'T put them on anything but the most beautifully manicured hands. Like the dark polishes, these off-beat shades tend to magnify flaws like ragged cuticles or rough spots.
DON'T stop at one coat. You'll get a better look and finish with two or three.
DO let your nails grow to about the length you see here for the prettiest effect. These colors tend to make shorter nails look stubby.

NEW
Pastel nail colors are the newest fashion accessory.

Look for them in tones of yellow, *above,* paled green, blue violet. All new shades from The UltraLucent Creme Nail Confections Collection by Max Factor.

69

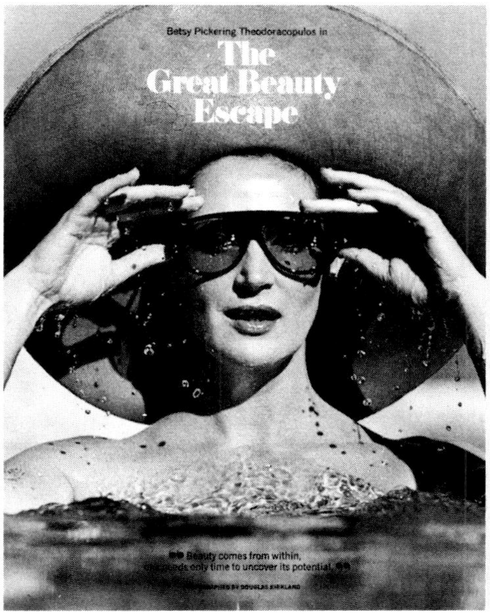

Betsy Pickering Theodoracopulos in
The Great Beauty Escape
Beauty comes from within, it needs only time to uncover its potential.

70

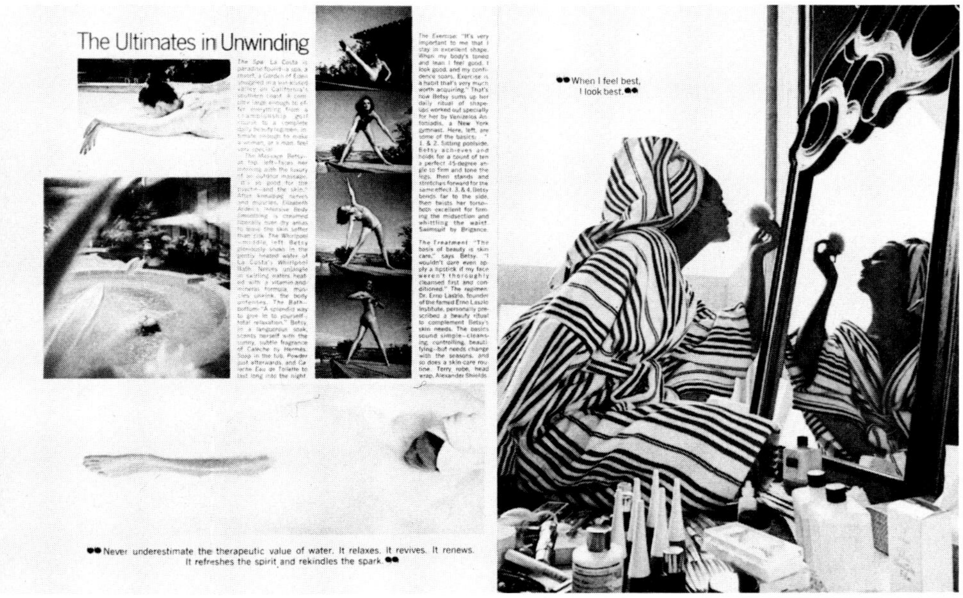

The Ultimates in Unwinding
When I feel best, I look best.
Never underestimate the therapeutic value of water. It relaxes. It revives. It renews. It refreshes the spirit and rekindles the spark.

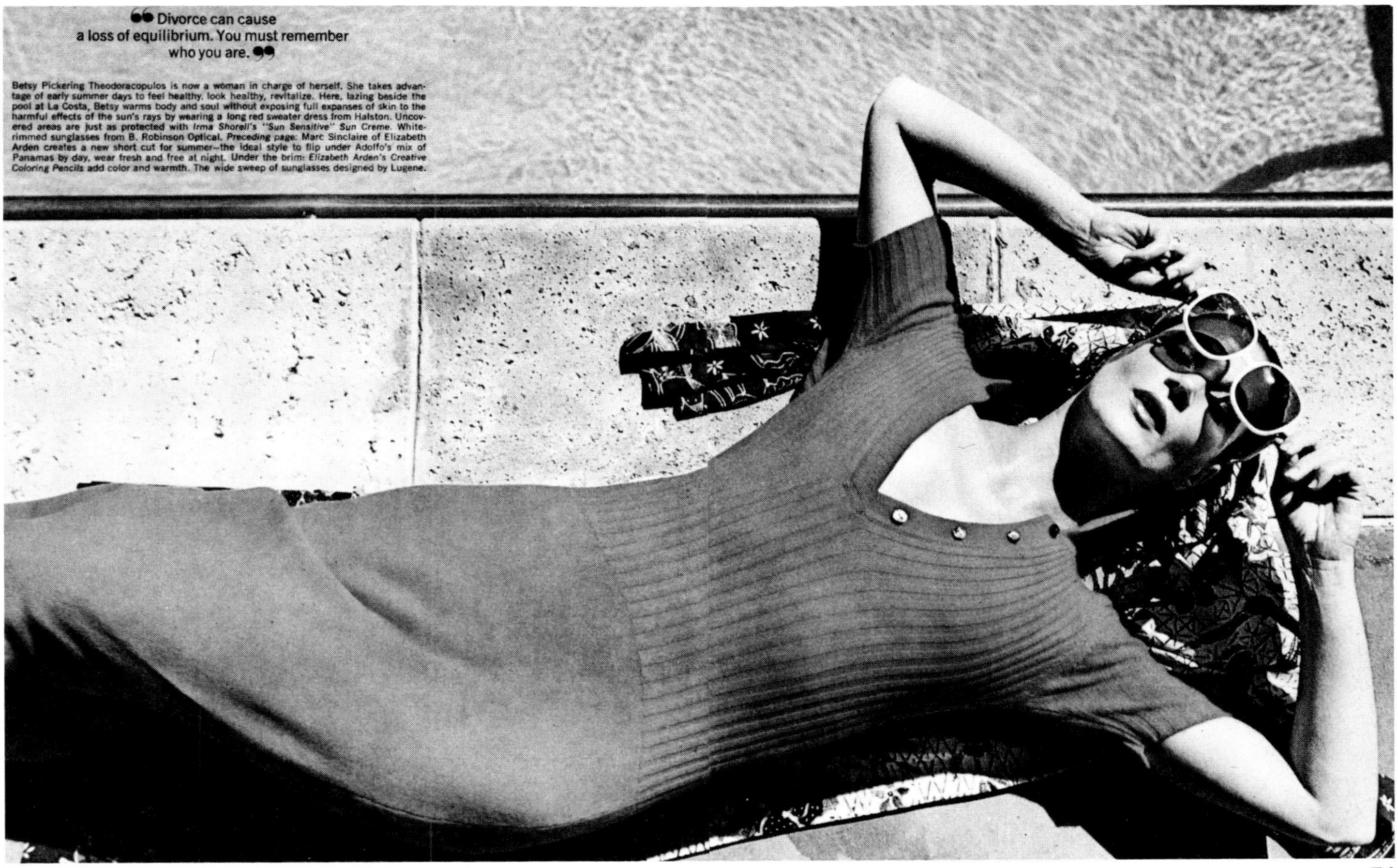

Divorce can cause a loss of equilibrium. You must remember who you are.
Betsy Pickering Theodoracopulos is now a woman in charge of herself. She takes advantage of early summer days to feel healthy, look healthy, revitalize. Here, lazing beside the pool at La Costa, Betsy warms body and soul without exposing full expanses of skin to the harmful effects of the sun's rays by wearing a long red sweater dress from Halston. Uncovered areas are just as protected with Irma Shorell's "Sun Sensitive" Sun Creme. White-rimmed sunglasses from B. Robinson Optical. Preceding page: Marc Sinclaire of Elizabeth Arden creates a new short cut for summer—the ideal style to flip under Adolfo's mix of Panamas by day, wear fresh and free at night. Under the brim: Elizabeth Arden's Creative Coloring Pencils add color and warmth. The wide sweep of sunglasses designed by Lugene.

71

68
Glamour Magazine Entrant
George Hartman Art Director
Rico Puhlmann Photographer
Conde Nast Publications Client

69-73
Town and Country Magazine Entrant
Nancy V. Kent Art Director
Douglas Kirkland Photographer

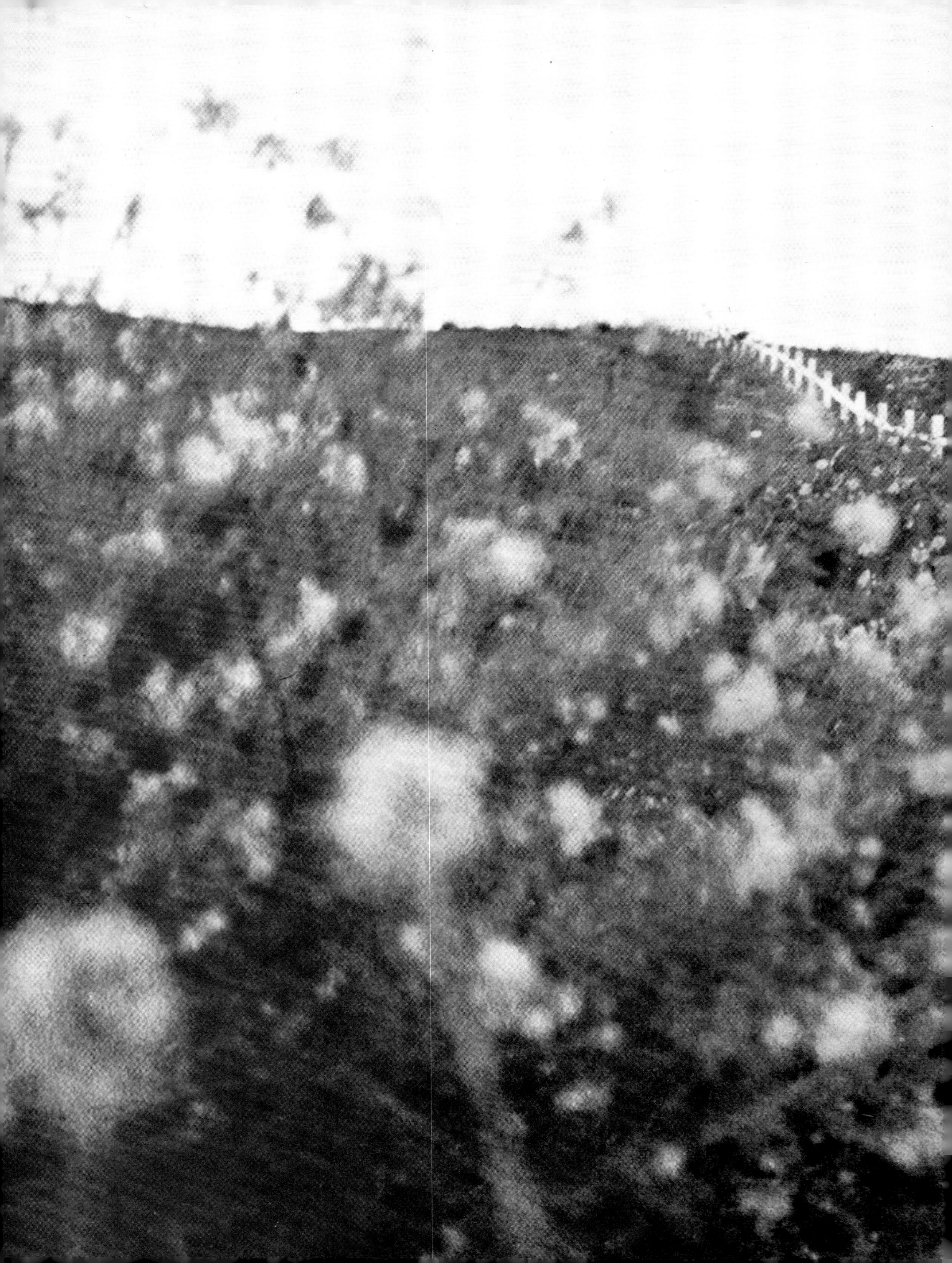

"Total solitude—a chance to rediscover, redefine. Savor the moments—when you're comfortable with life, you're comfortable with yourself."

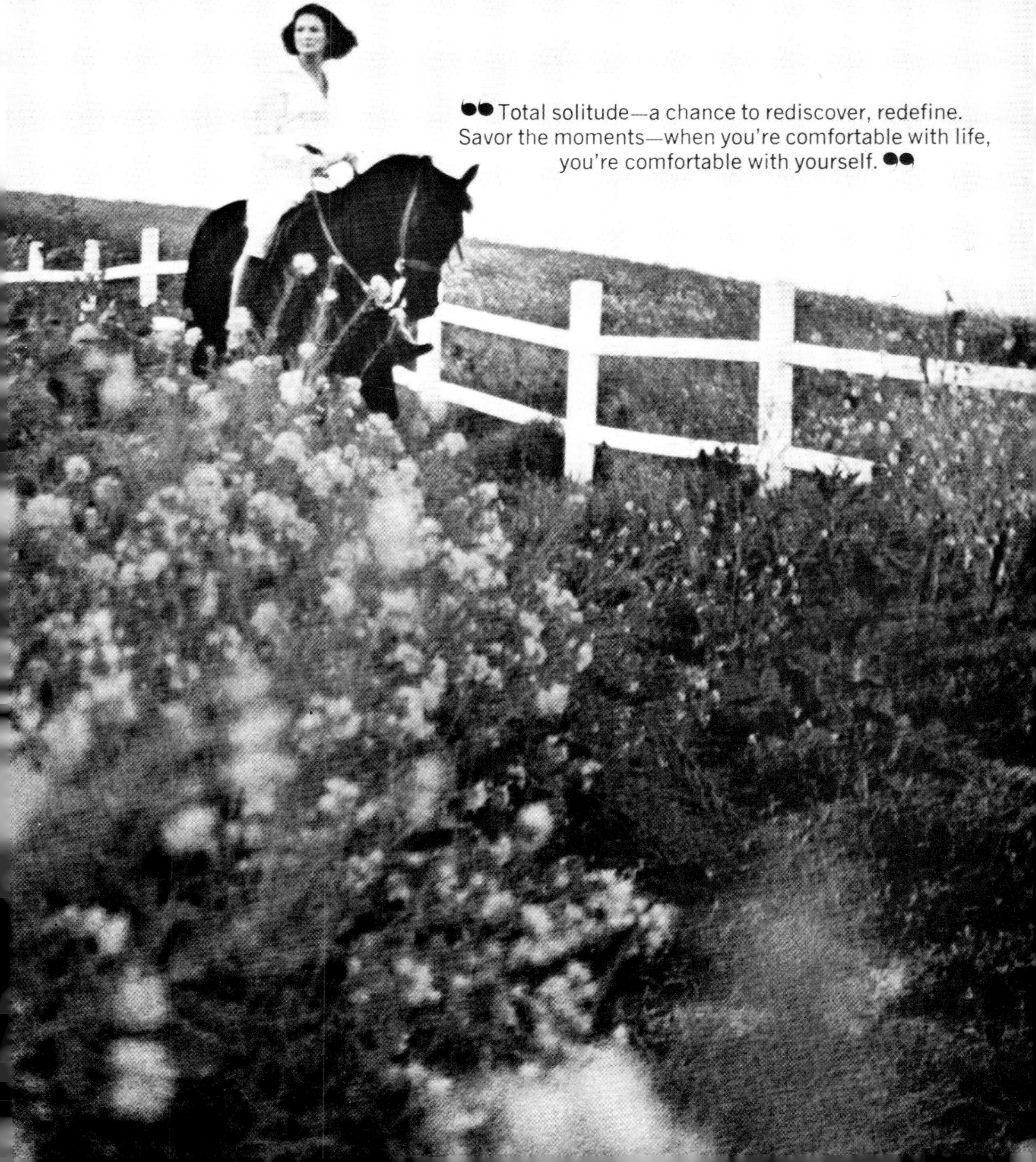

74
Henry Wolf Productions Inc. Entrant
R. Weigand Art Director
Henry Wolf Photographer
Esquire Magazine Client

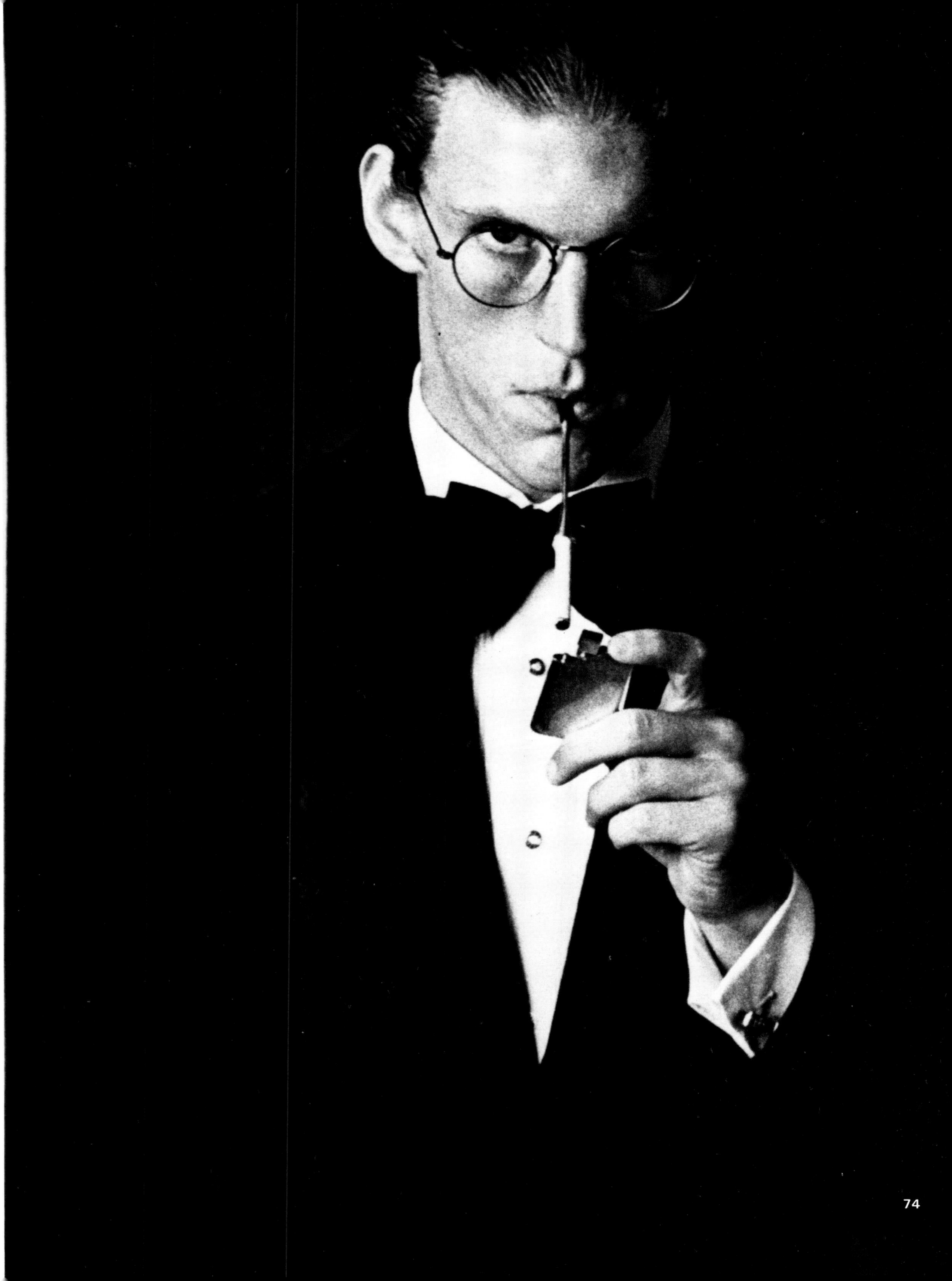

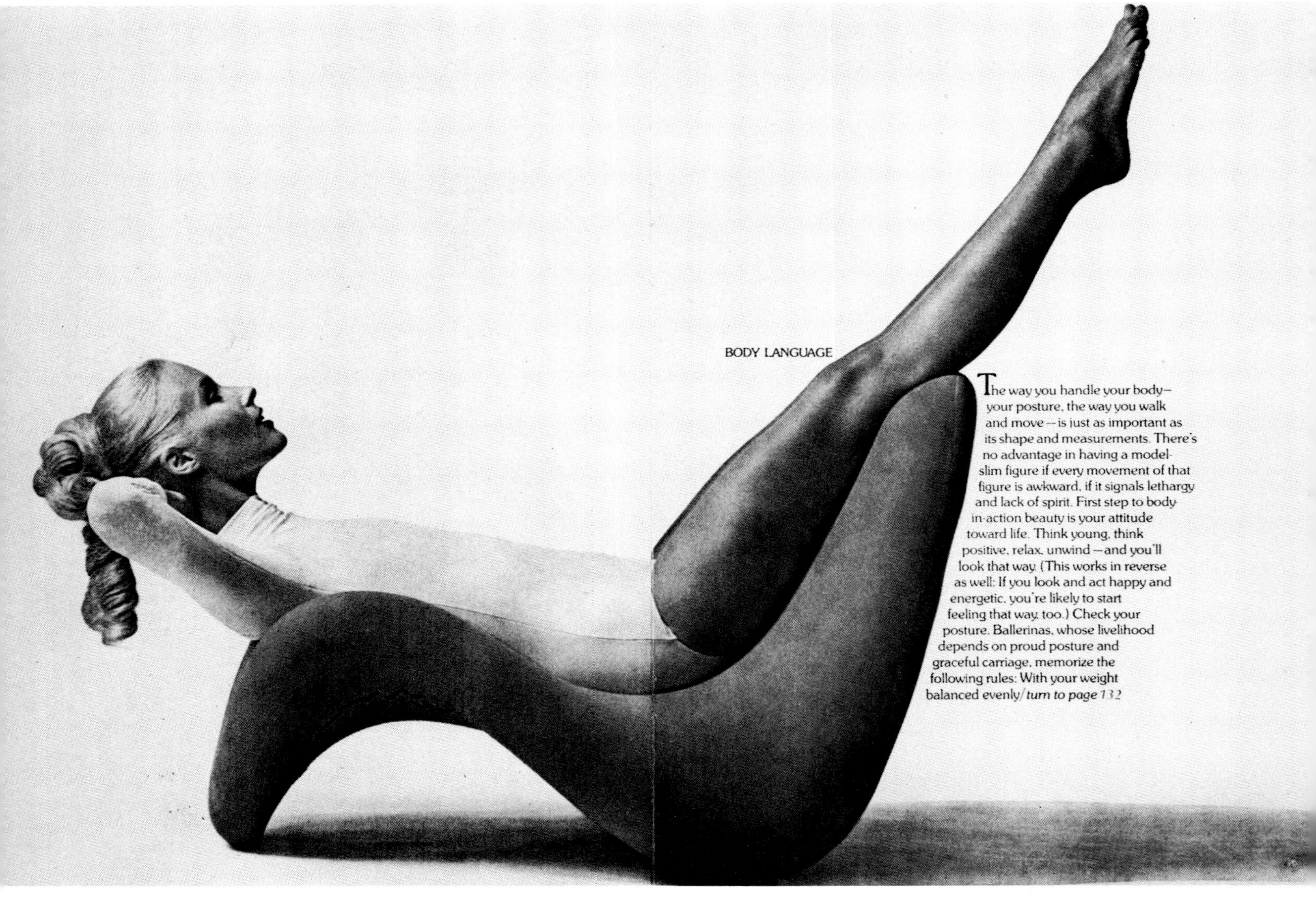

BODY LANGUAGE

The way you handle your body—your posture, the way you walk and move—is just as important as its shape and measurements. There's no advantage in having a model-slim figure if every movement of that figure is awkward, if it signals lethargy and lack of spirit. First step to body-in-action beauty is your attitude toward life. Think young, think positive, relax, unwind—and you'll look that way. (This works in reverse as well: If you look and act happy and energetic, you're likely to start feeling that way, too.) Check your posture. Ballerinas, whose livelihood depends on proud posture and graceful carriage, memorize the following rules: With your weight balanced evenly/ *turn to page 132*

75-76
Henry Wolf Productions, Inc. Entrant
Alvin Grossman Art Director
Henry Wolf Photographer
McCall's Magazine Client

*With the holidays
soon upon us, the time
to take note of your looks is
now. On these pages, the basics of
head-to-toe maintenance, plus
some quick beauty tricks for
this busy season*

HAIR GOES
NATURAL   The signals are coming through loud and
clear: The now and future direction
of hair is natural. This
doesn't mean messy or uncontrolled. You
can "go natural" and still look
as if you had just stepped out of an
expensive salon. It starts with the cut,
and the trick here is to have
your hair cut the way it wants to go.
If it's straight, choose a
flattering straight style — the sleek,
chin-length cut at right is a good
example. If it's curly, don't
fight it. Invest in a good, basic,
layered cut that works with
your hair, not against it. Maintenance
is quick and easy. With the
available profusion of gentling
shampoos and new conditioners, plus the
help of a blower-dryer, even
the woman with / *turn to page 132*

YOUR
HOLIDAY
BEAUTY
BOOK

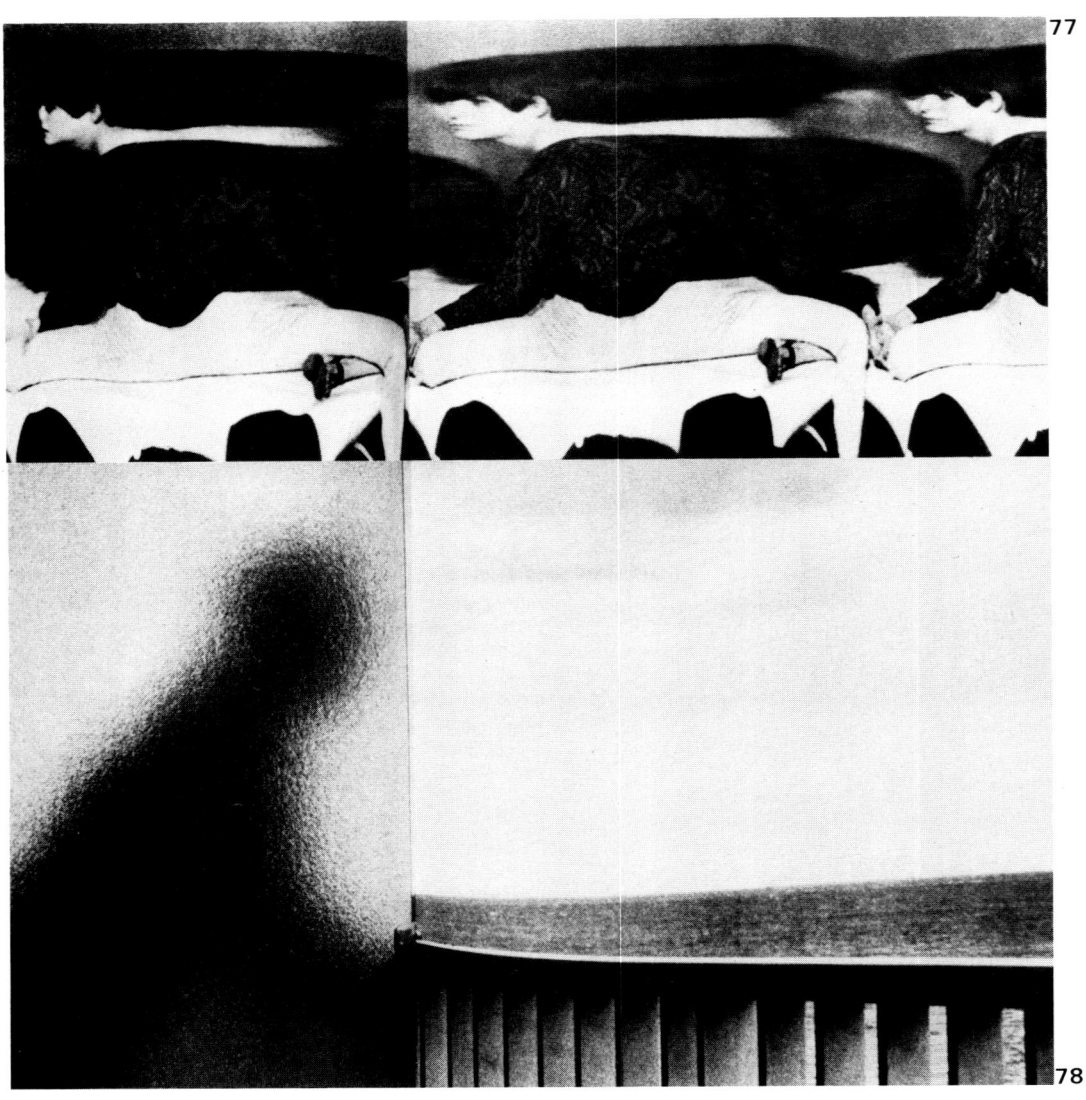

77-78
Mary Ann Lea Entrant
Hal Kearney Art Director
Naomi Savage Cover Photographer
Scott, Foresman & Co. Client

79
Exxon Corporation Entrant
Harry Diamond, John Conley Art Directors

80-81
Jerold Smokler Entrant
Nancy Kent, Ed Hamway Designers
Richard Davis Photographer
Town and Country Magazine Client

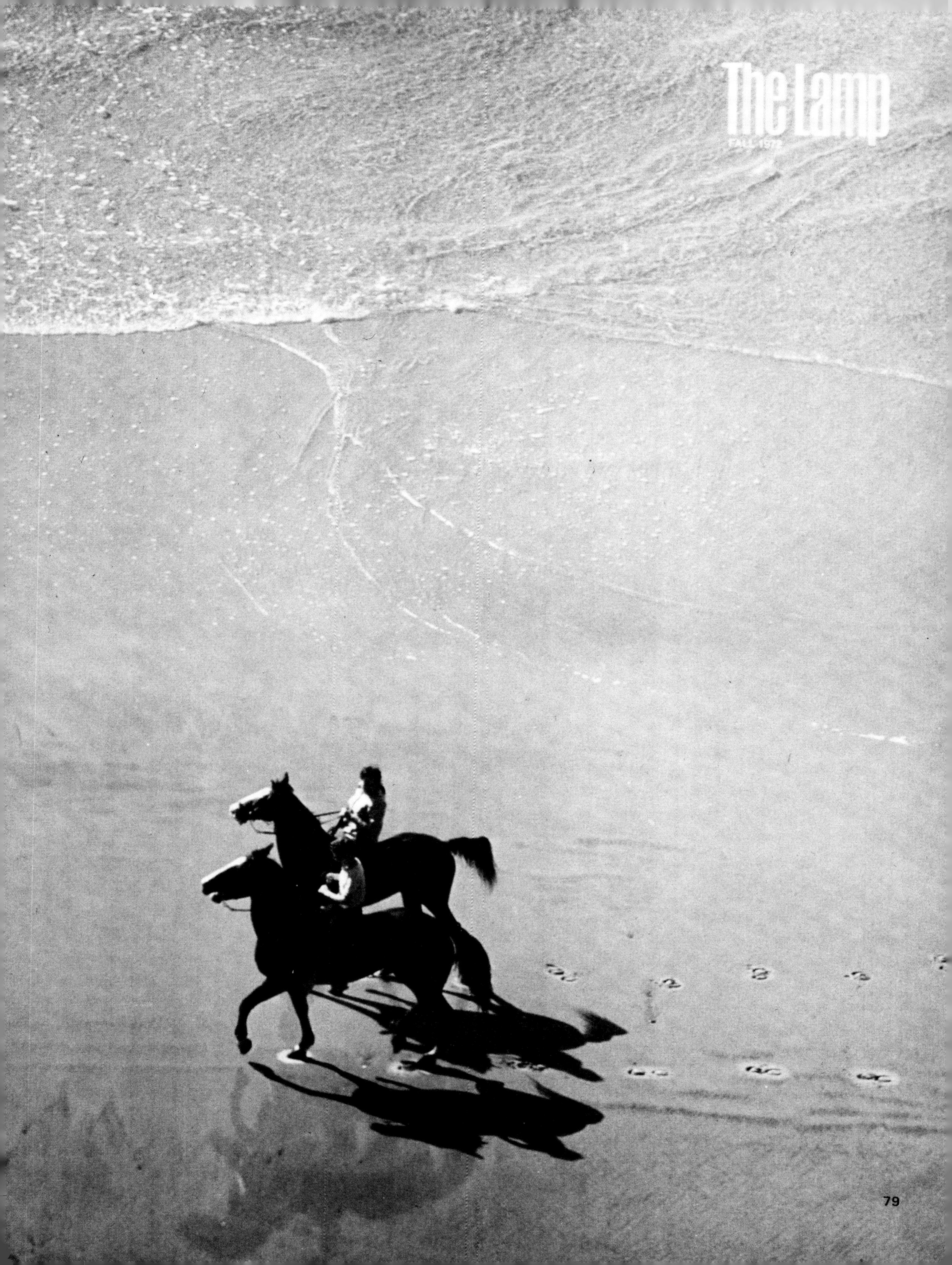
The Lamp
FALL 1972

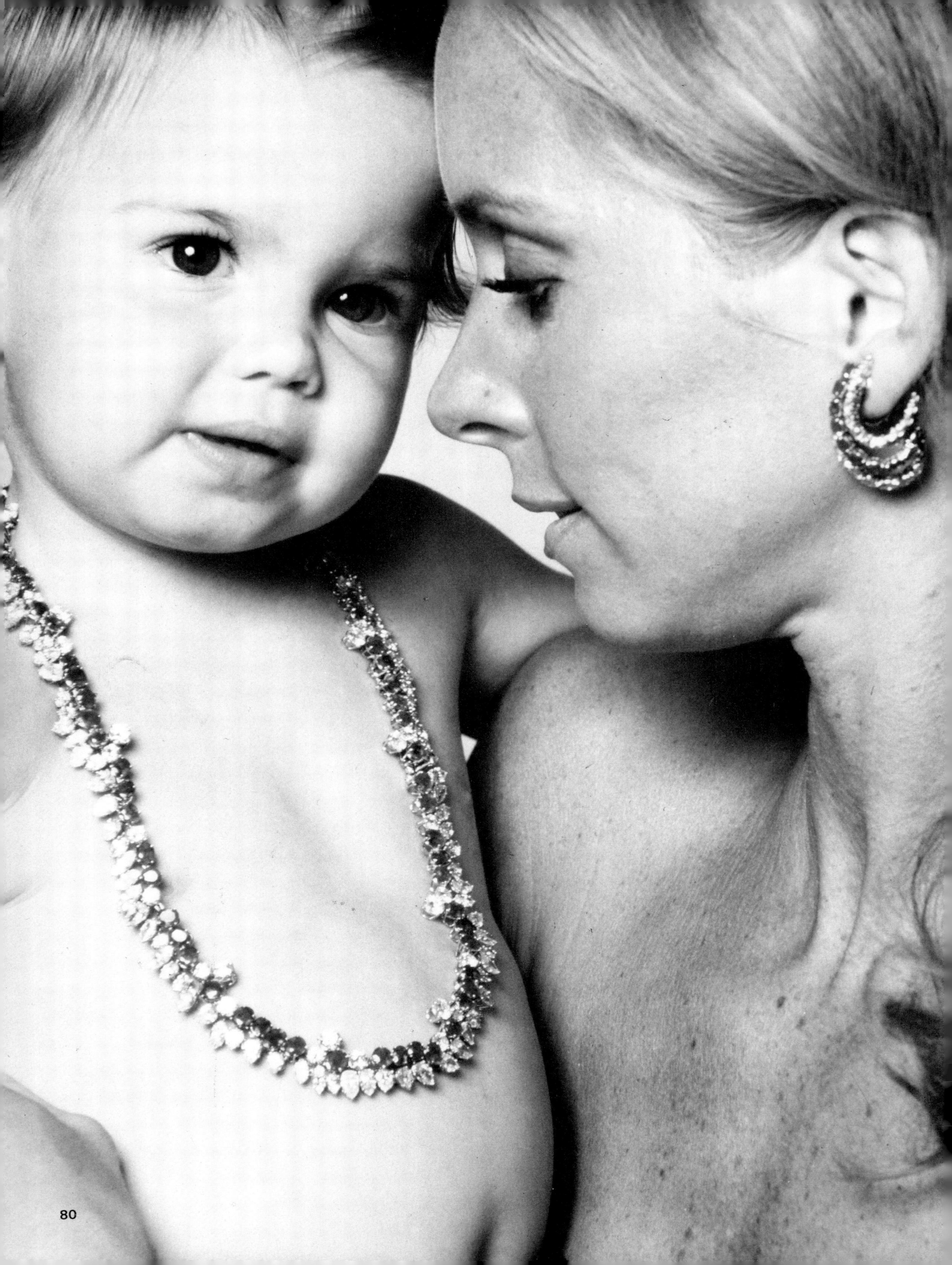

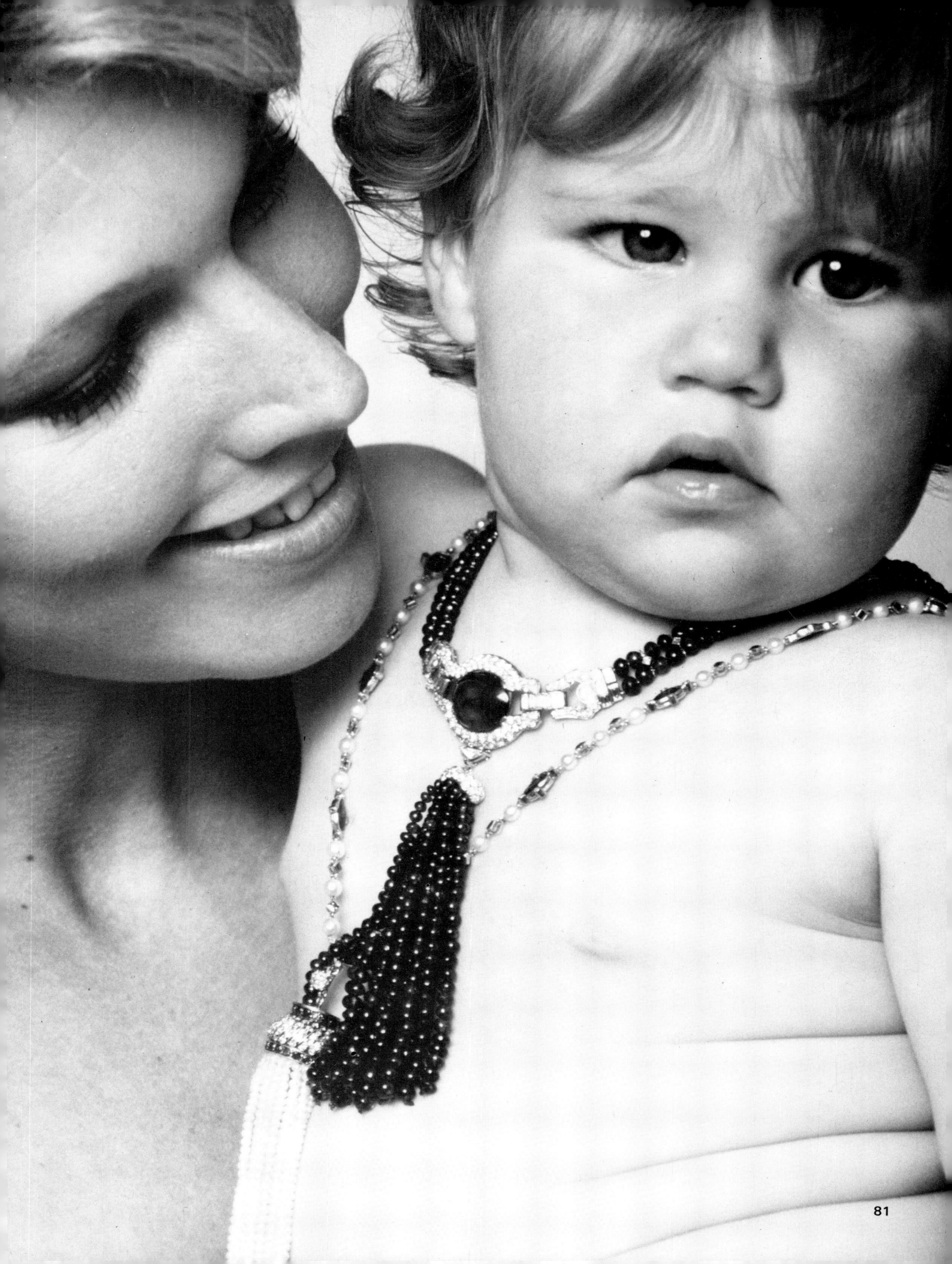

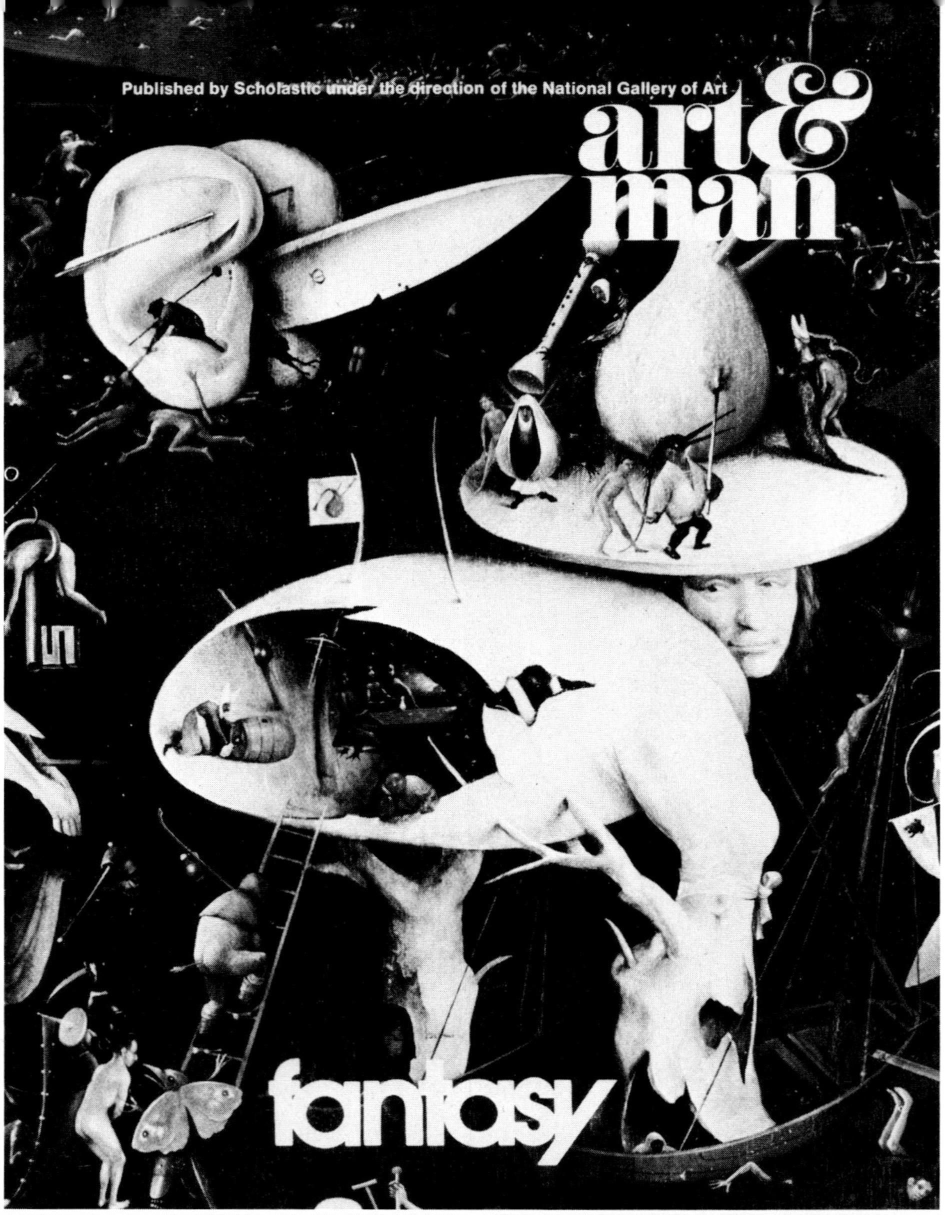
Published by Scholastic under the direction of the National Gallery of Art
art&
man
fantasy

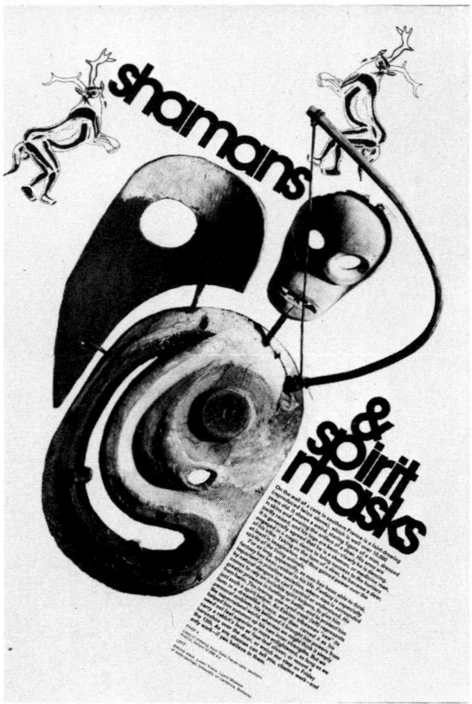
shamans
&
spirit
masks

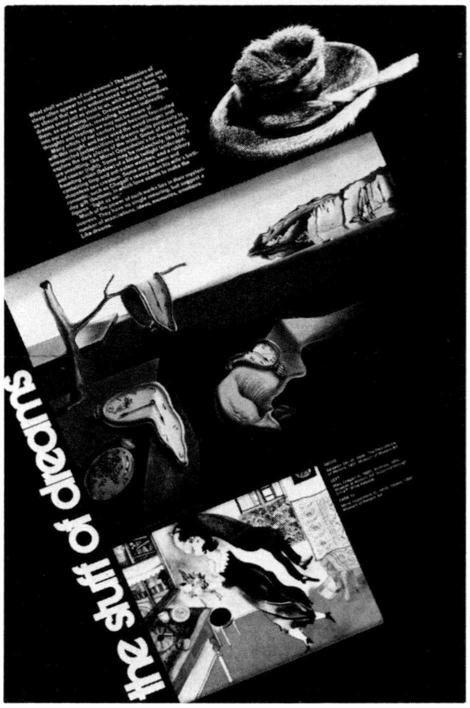
the stuff of dreams

82-84
Margaret Howlett Entrant
Scholastic Publications Client

AN OVERVIEW OF LADIES' UNDERWEAR

from bustles to step-ins to no-bra to nothing—a loving look at unmentionables through the years

PHOTOGRAPHY BY FRANK LAFFITTE AND RICHARD FEGLEY

article By WILLIAM IVERSEN

IF SHE HAD TO SPEAK of them at all, she called them her unmentionables. Of all the evasive, nice-Nelly terms that proper ladies and gentlemen once used to clothe their naked thoughts, none were more historically accurate than the coyly suggestive euphemisms for women's underwear. Throughout much of human history, female undergarments could not in truth be named—for the very good reason that they simply didn't exist.

When they did come to exist, moreover, modesty had very little to do with it. Mother Eve and her sensational little micromini fig leaf aside, modesty has, in fact, played virtually no part in the origin of any sort of human clothing—under or outer, male or female.

Modesty is born of a sense of shame. And shame concerning human nudity is a relatively late and sophisticated notion; it depends upon the communal taboos of a given time and place. "Where men and women wear only a string around the waist, their dress is decent," one pioneering student of primitive culture has observed, "but it is indecent to leave off the string."

It is from just such a primitive string, or leather thong, that our entire Western wardrobe is supposed to have evolved. So remote was the idea of concealment that the string's first apronlike appendages hung not in front but behind—to protect the seated buttocks from the damp and chilly ground.

By the time the fertility-worshiping Minoans established their civilization on the island of Crete, the original string had been expanded into a colorful, tightly laced bodice that left the breasts—the symbol of fertility—fully exposed. This pop-top Cretan creation is the ancient prototype of all the various kinds of waist cinchers members of the fair sex have worn to accentuate their natural curves.

Also more ornamental than moral was the Greek chiton, a one-piece garment that is generally considered to be the ancient forerunner of all later slips and undershirts. Its earliest styles were slung from one shoulder and left one breast exposed. Featuring a side slit that earned even the austere Spartan women a reputation as displayers of thighs, the kicky chiton was girdled with a shifty waistband called the zona—a name that gave us the English zone, now used in conjunction with such appropriate descriptives as torrid, temperate, frigid, erogenous, speed and no-parking.

According to Pearl Binder, a British student of *Muffs and Morals*, "Greek women wore no corsets during the finest epochs of Greek history, but during the time of Greek decadence they fastened themselves into corsets." A small waist "never having appealed to the Greeks at any period," the corsets were worn to emphasize the comfy amplitude of Athenian hips; many broad-beamed Greek beauties even wore their zone-huggers to bed.

Roman bosoms were generally supported by a linen underband, called a *strophium* or *mamillare*. But Messalina, the sexually insatiable wife of the Emperor Claudius, "wore a linen corset of her own design which pinched in the waist and thrust the breast outward." Messalina's come-hither corset was copied by fashionable matrons and by Roman prostitutes, who considered the empress one of the girls. It was in one of Rome's busiest brothels, Juvenal reports, that "this imperial whore" regularly "showed her golden tits . . . took the customers on, with gestures more than inviting." In her heyday—which was every day her husband took a nap—Messalina was reputed to have shucked her clever little corset and indulged in a 24-hour endurance contest, in which she outperformed "a Harlot, that was esteemed the very bravest in Love, by 25 Feats." But according to one Nicolas Venette, who wrote a circa-1740 report on the relative capabilities of famous floozies, Messalina was sexually sluggish compared with Cleopatra, who wore no corsets at all and "underwent in one Night's Time the amorous Effarts of 106 men."

Whatever the glories of ancient Egypt, female underwear wasn't one of them, and Cleopatra was the living embodiment of the human tendency to let it all hang out. She may have worn a see-through *mamillare* on occasion, but the Theda Bara breastplate usually associated with Egypt's busiest and best-known queen seems to have been more of a moviemaker's concession to 20th Century breast taboos than a bona fide fashion trademark of the Siren of the Nile.

As women's wear, robes of concealment began to appear in the Middle East during that period in history when fertility worship was on the wane and were used to promote bodily shame, rather than to ward off the elements. Concealing feminine curves from the covetous glances of male strangers was a form of birth control and robes were religiously worn in even the warmest weather.

The fact that climate was secondary is further evidenced by the Roman historian Tacitus, who tells us that women of the Germanic north wrapped themselves in sleeveless shifts. *(text continued on page 89)*

1780
Back in the late 18th Century, when a lady's bosom welled over her décolletage, high fashion called for the ensemble of whalebone-stiffened corset and puff-sleeved chemise.

1934

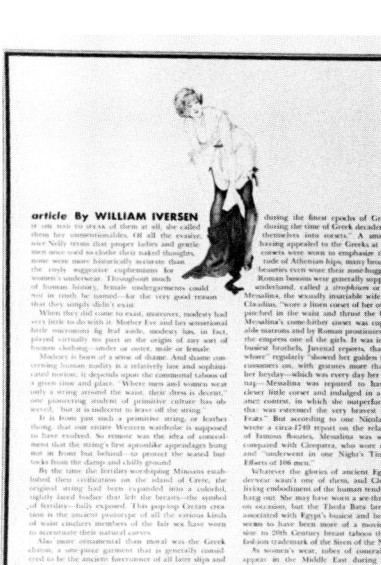

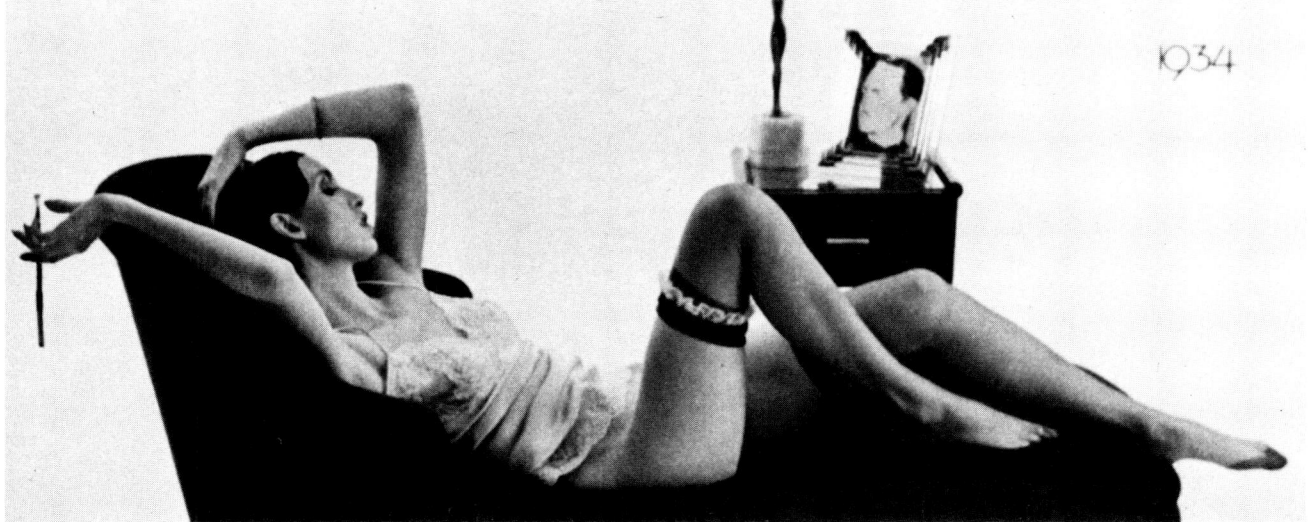

85-95
Playboy enterprises, Inc. Entrant
Arthur Paul Art Director
Frank Laffitte, Richard Fegley Photographers
Kerig Pope Designer
Playboy Magazine Client

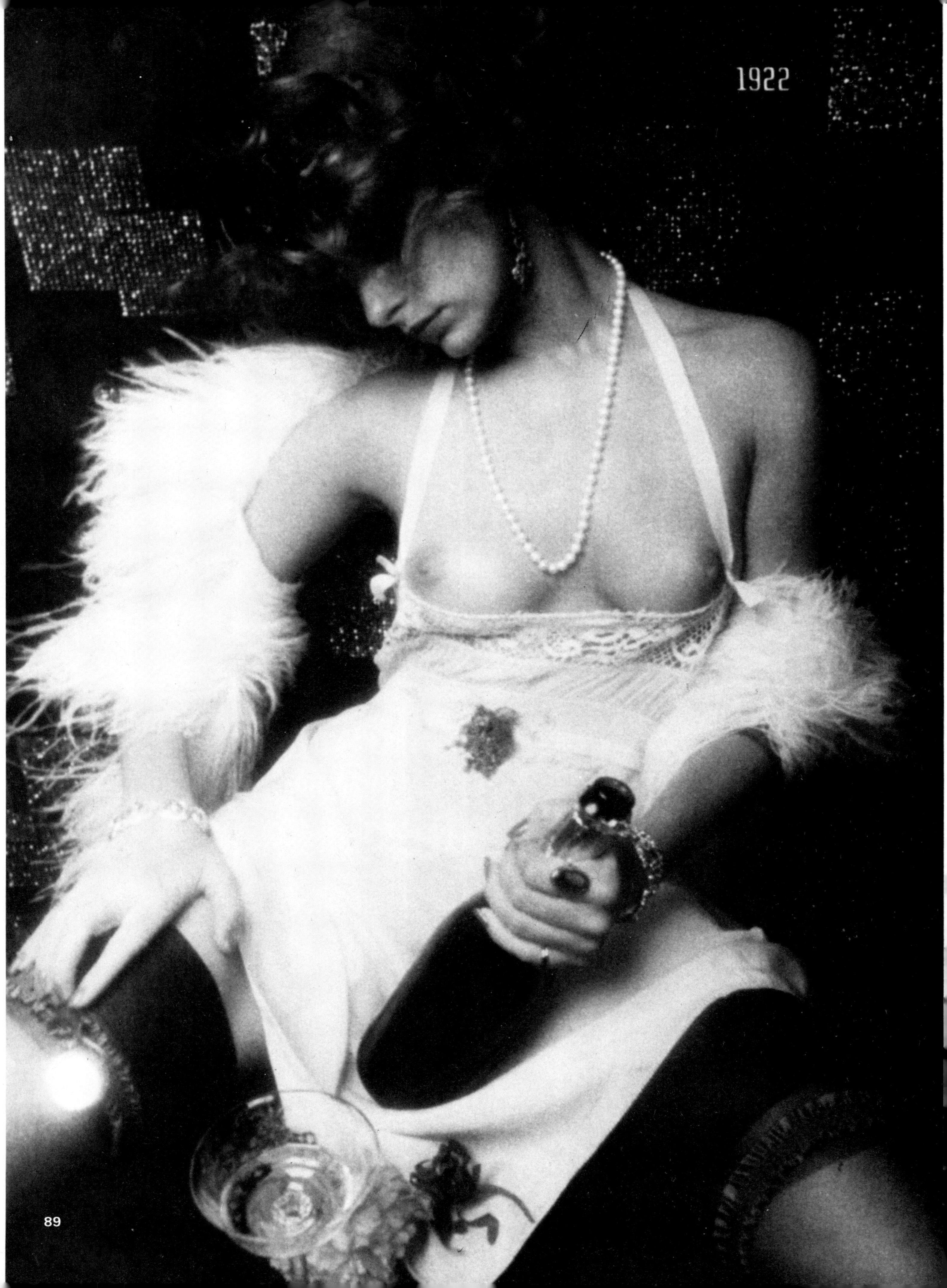
1922

90

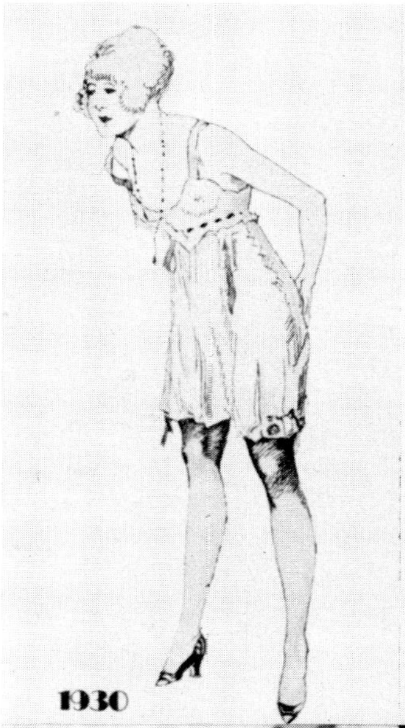
1930

91

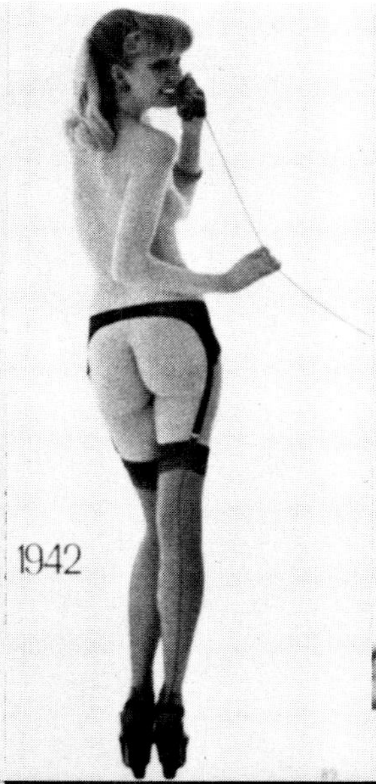
1942

92

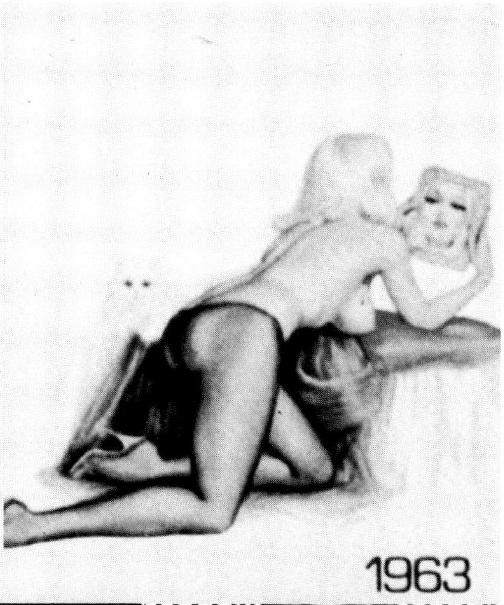
1963

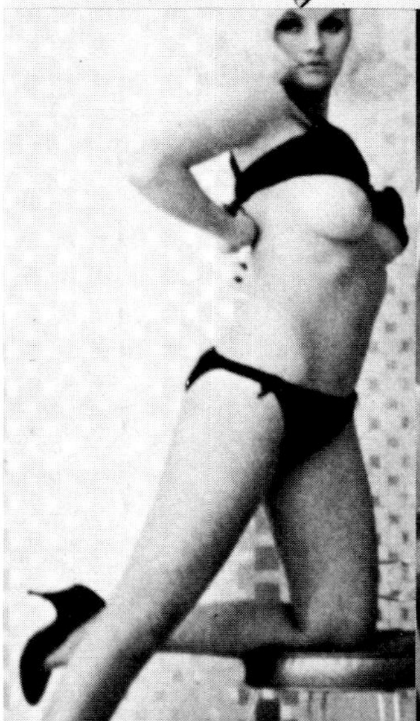

93

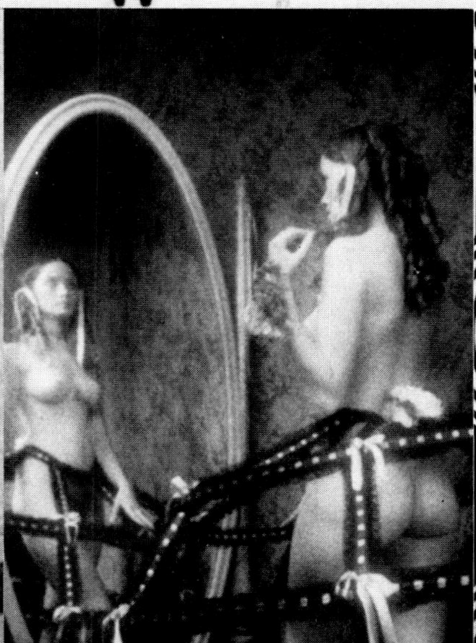

94

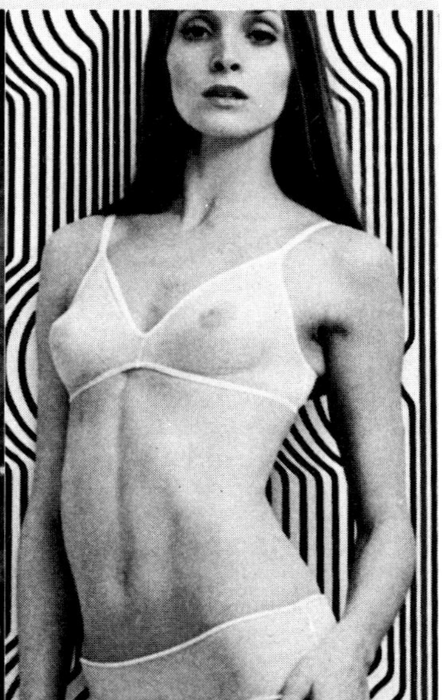

95

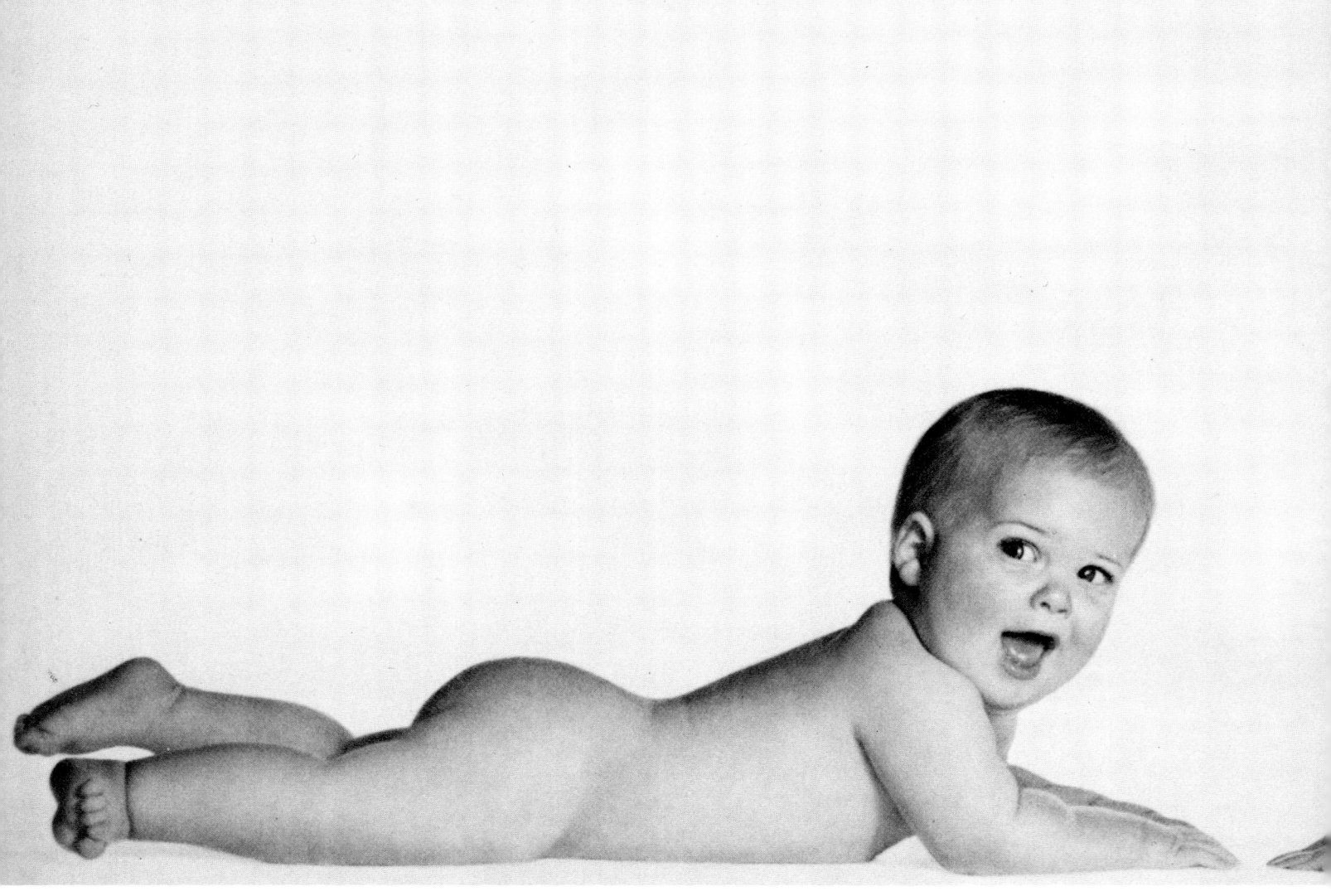

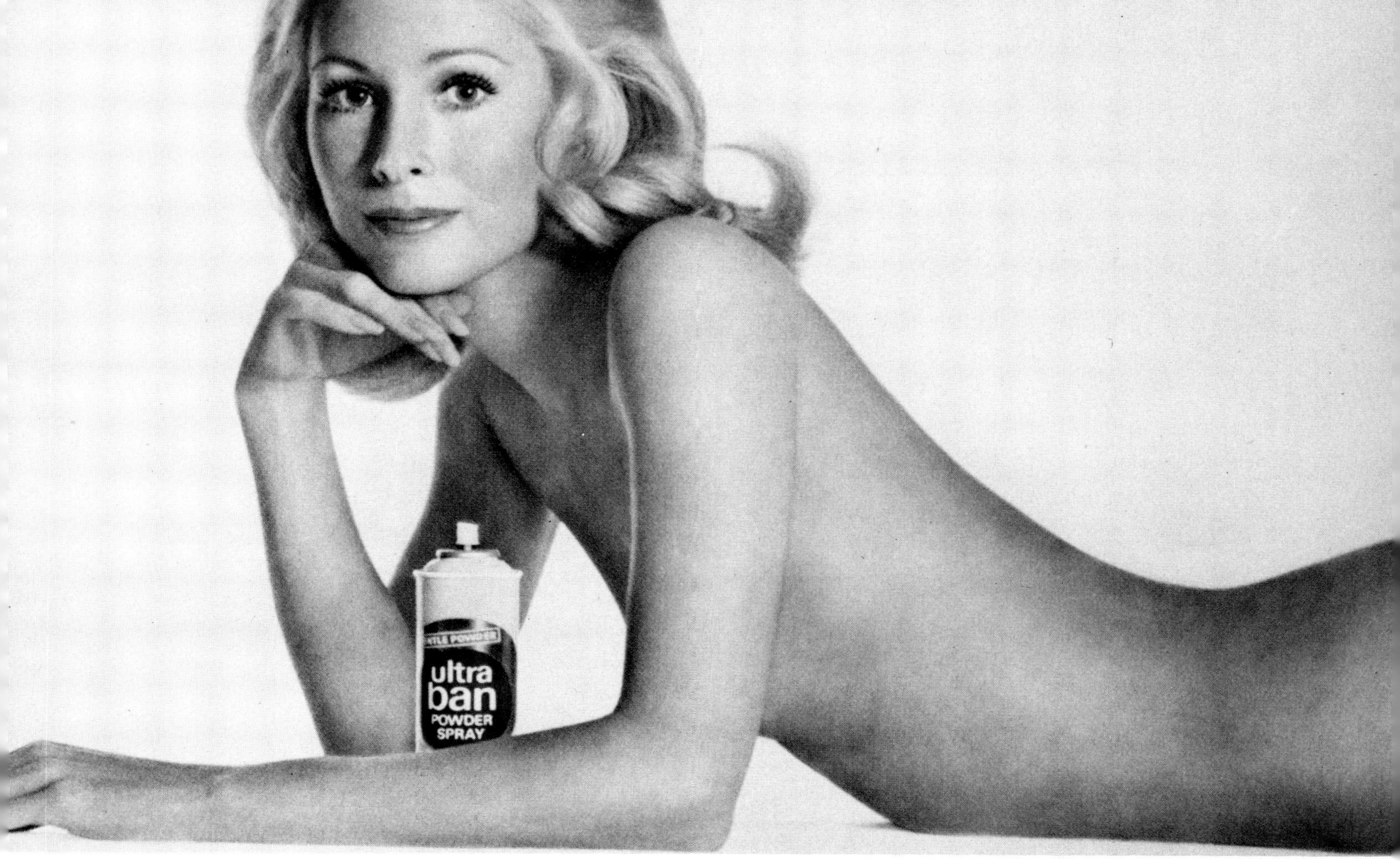
ultra
ban
POWDER
SPRAY

96
Laurence Dunst Entrant
Frank Camardella Art Director
Irving Penn Photographer
Daniel & Charles Associates, Ltd. Agency
Bristol-Myers Client

The day of the Go-Getter is here.

JAL's new Go-Getter Flight Five gives business executives more time to do business.

The 2:40 p.m.* departure from JFK gives you the full morning at the office. Or time to take care of last-minute details.

Yet you still arrive in Tokyo early enough—7:35 p.m.†—to have a bite to eat, a sauna and a solid night's sleep.

The trouble with the morning departure for Tokyo was, you *had* to finish your work at the office the night before.

Sure, you got to Tokyo in late afternoon—but you couldn't get any work done then. You had a few extra hours to kill, that's all.

Where you really need a few extra hours to relax is on the way *back*.

And here JAL has a new 10:40 a.m.* Tokyo departure for its Go-Getter Flight Six.

You get back to New York at noon instead of evening. You miss the airport crowds and rush hour traffic.

And you have an extra half day to relax with the wife and kids.

JAPAN AIR LINES

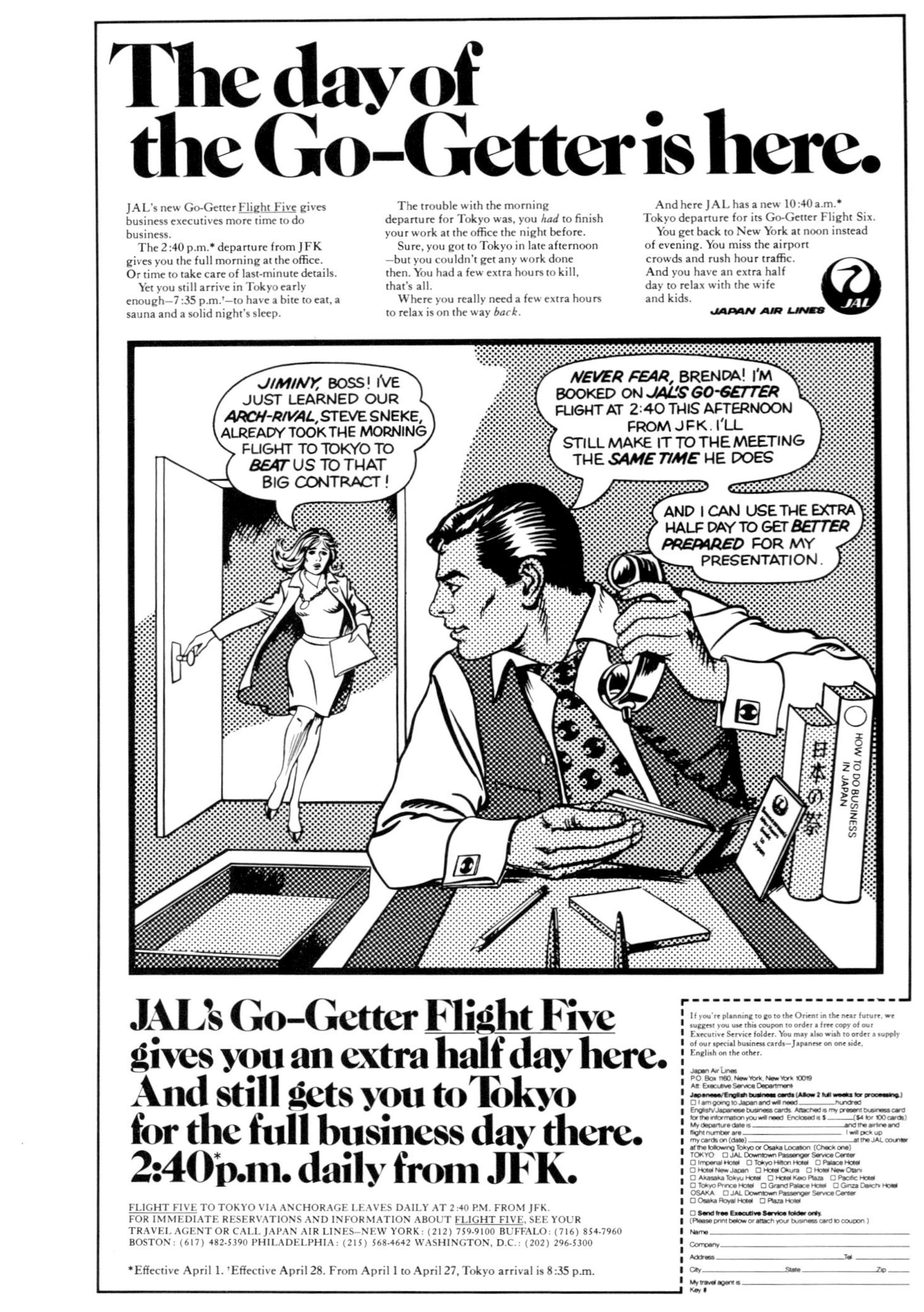
JIMINY, BOSS! I'VE JUST LEARNED OUR ARCH-RIVAL, STEVE SNEKE, ALREADY TOOK THE MORNING FLIGHT TO TOKYO TO BEAT US TO THAT BIG CONTRACT!
NEVER FEAR, BRENDA! I'M BOOKED ON JAL'S GO-GETTER FLIGHT AT 2:40 THIS AFTERNOON FROM JFK. I'LL STILL MAKE IT TO THE MEETING THE SAME TIME HE DOES
AND I CAN USE THE EXTRA HALF DAY TO GET BETTER PREPARED FOR MY PRESENTATION.
HOW TO DO BUSINESS IN JAPAN

JAL's Go-Getter Flight Five gives you an extra half day here. And still gets you to Tokyo for the full business day there. 2:40* p.m. daily from JFK.

FLIGHT FIVE TO TOKYO VIA ANCHORAGE LEAVES DAILY AT 2:40 P.M. FROM JFK. FOR IMMEDIATE RESERVATIONS AND INFORMATION ABOUT FLIGHT FIVE, SEE YOUR TRAVEL AGENT OR CALL JAPAN AIR LINES—NEW YORK: (212) 759-9100 BUFFALO: (716) 854-7960 BOSTON: (617) 482-5390 PHILADELPHIA: (215) 568-4642 WASHINGTON, D.C.: (202) 296-5300

*Effective April 1. †Effective April 28. From April 1 to April 27, Tokyo arrival is 8:35 p.m.

If you're planning to go to the Orient in the near future, we suggest you use this coupon to order a free copy of our Executive Service folder. You may also wish to order a supply of our special business cards—Japanese on one side, English on the other.

Japan Air Lines
P.O. Box 1160, New York, New York 10019
Att: Executive Service Department

Japanese/English business cards (Allow 2 full weeks for processing.)
☐ I am going to Japan and will need ________ hundred English/Japanese business cards. Attached is my present business card for the information you will need. Enclosed is $ ______ ($4 for 100 cards.) My departure date is ____________ and the airline and flight number are ____________. I will pick up my cards on (date) ____________ at the JAL counter at the following Tokyo or Osaka Location: (Check one)
TOKYO: ☐ JAL Downtown Passenger Service Center
☐ Imperial Hotel ☐ Tokyo Hilton Hotel ☐ Palace Hotel
☐ Hotel New Japan ☐ Hotel Okura ☐ Hotel New Otani
☐ Akasaka Tokyu Hotel ☐ Hotel Keio Plaza ☐ Pacific Hotel
☐ Tokyo Prince Hotel ☐ Grand Palace Hotel ☐ Ginza Daiichi Hotel
OSAKA: ☐ JAL Downtown Passenger Service Center
☐ Osaka Royal Hotel ☐ Plaza Hotel

☐ **Send free Executive Service folder only.**
(Please print below or attach your business card to coupon.)
Name ____________
Company ____________
Address ____________ Tel. ____________
City ________ State ________ Zip ______
My travel agent is ____________
Key #

97
Ketchum, MacLeod & Grove Entrant
Joseph H. Phair,
Katsuji Asada Art Directors
Arthur Tuohy, Martin Werner Copywriters
Angelo Casarola Illustrator
Japan Air Lines Client

98
GKO&S Werbeagentur GmbH & Co. KG Entrant
Ben Ojne Art Director
David Montgomery, Bob Cramp Photographers
Beiersdorf AG, Hamburg Client

100

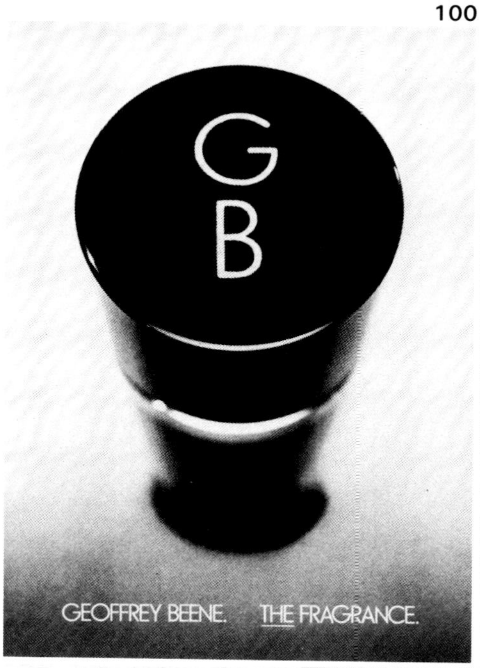

G
B
GEOFFREY BEENE. THE FRAGRANCE.

101

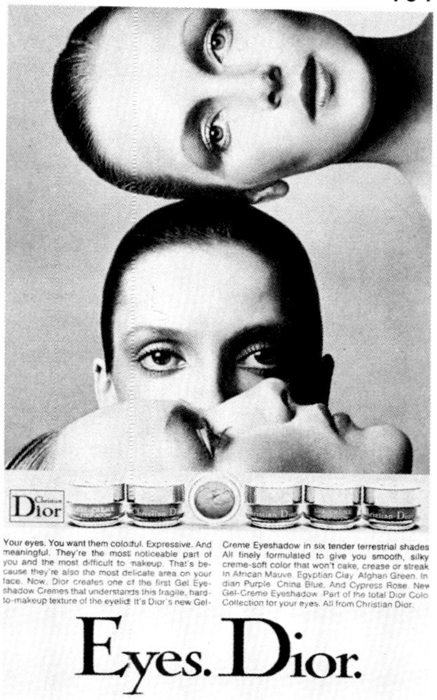

Christian Dior
Your eyes. You want them colorful. Expressive. And meaningful. They're the most noticeable part of you and the most difficult to makeup. That's because they're also the most delicate area on your face. Now, Dior creates one of the first Gel Eyeshadow Cremes that understands this fragile, hard-to-makeup texture of the eyelid. It's Dior's new Gel-Creme Eyeshadow in six tender terrestrial shades. All finely formulated to give you smooth, silky creme-soft color that won't cake, crease or streak in African Mauve. Egyptian Clay. Afghan Green. Indian Purple. China Blue. And Cypress Rose. New Gel-Creme Eyeshadow. Part of the total Dior Color Collection for your eyes. All from Christian Dior.
Eyes. Dior.

102

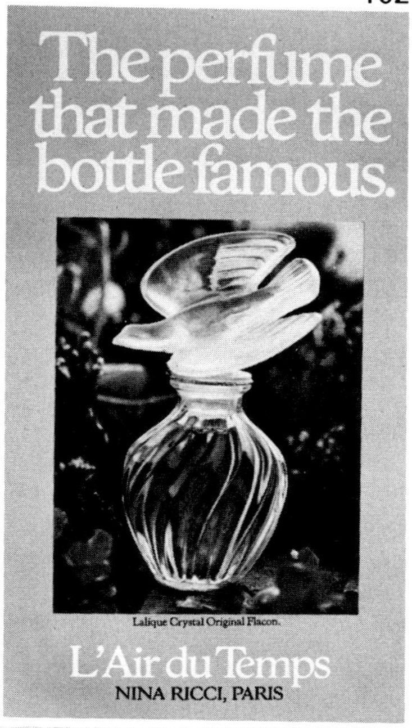

The perfume that made the bottle famous.
Lalique Crystal Original Flacon.
L'Air du Temps
NINA RICCI, PARIS

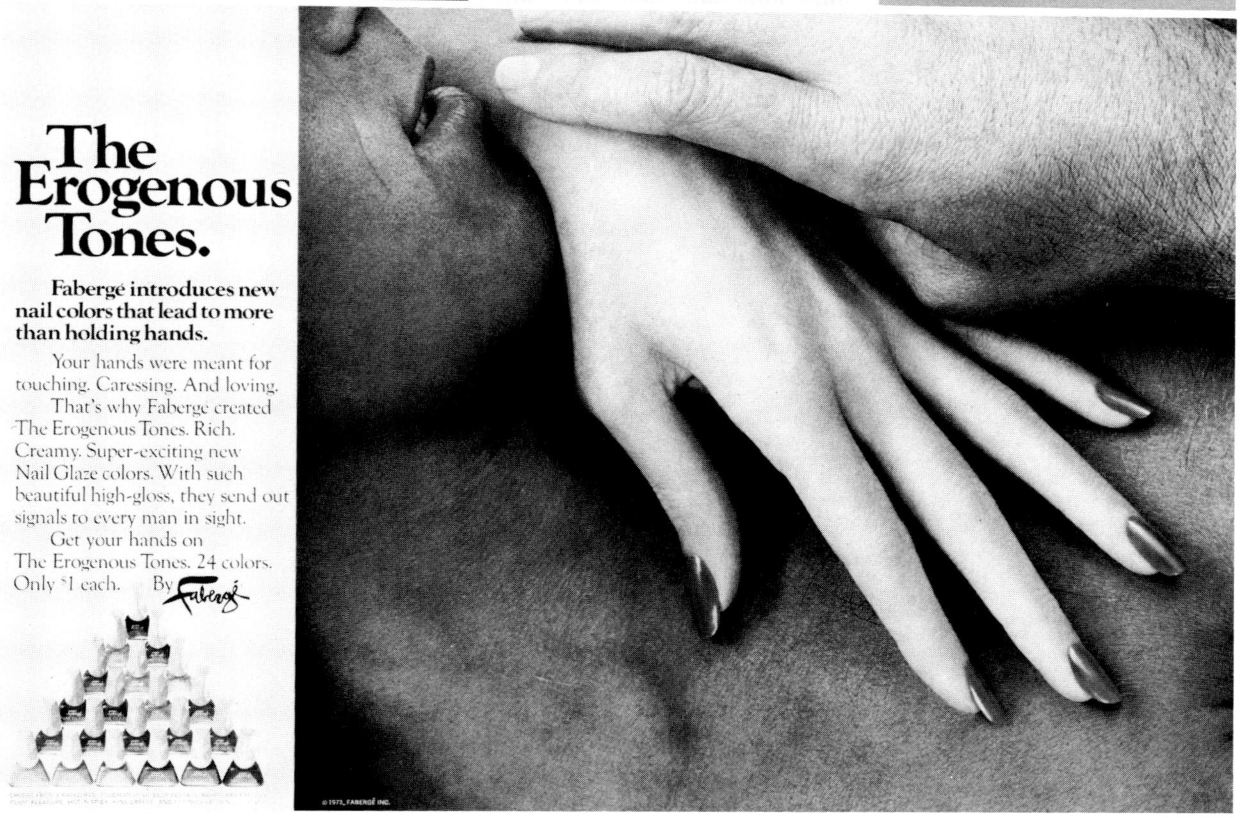

The Erogenous Tones.
Fabergé introduces new nail colors that lead to more than holding hands.
Your hands were meant for touching. Caressing. And loving.
That's why Fabergé created The Erogenous Tones. Rich. Creamy. Super-exciting new Nail Glaze colors. With such beautiful high-gloss, they send out signals to every man in sight.
Get your hands on The Erogenous Tones. 24 colors. Only $1 each. By Fabergé
© 1973, FABERGÉ INC.

103

101
Christian Dior Perfumes Ent'ant
Kuhn Caldwell Art Director
Ryszard Horowitz Photographer

102
Needham, Harper & Steers Entrant
Alley Kay Art Director
Harold Krieger Photographer
Jacqueline Cochran Client

103
Nadler & Larimer, Inc. Entrant
Irwin Goldberg Art Director
Arnold Rosenberg Photographer
Fabergé, Inc. Client

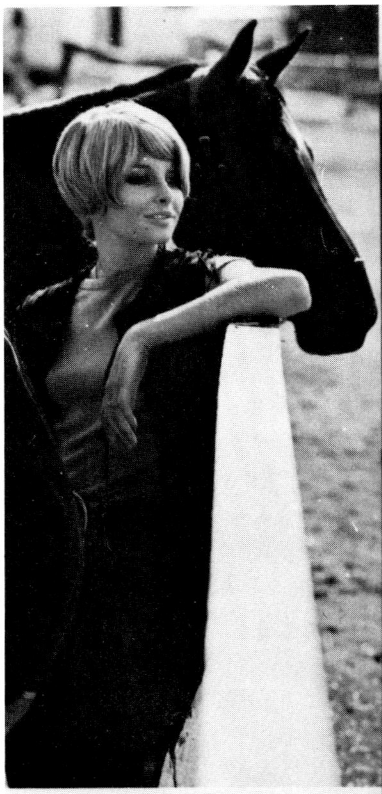

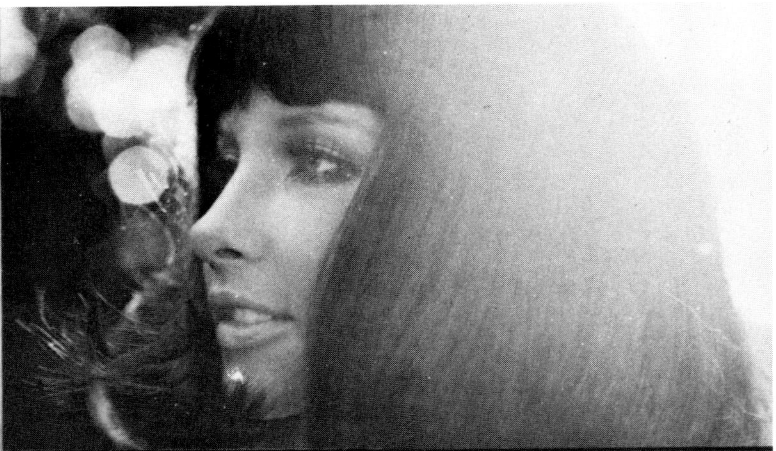

Wife swopper stopper

Pierre Kareff introduces four new instant hairstyles that transform you into five different women

With your own beautiful hair and the four Pierre Kareff wigs, you're five different women.

Yet still your same sweet self underneath it all. Just like this young house wife in these pictures. (In which picture do you think she is showing her own hair. Turn page upside down for the answer.)

So if your man's eyes begin to wander — switch. Silky-soft dyeline hair is so alive, so natural, he won't know it's not your own even when he's kissing you. You can brush it, comb it — just like your own hair. But better than your own hair, you can style it in seconds. Washing is a breeze. In lukewarm water with your usual shampoo. A shake — and the curls fall back into place. And you dry it by simply lying it on a towel.

No setting. Not even a dryer. Let your hair flick young and free on the wind. Dash through the rain. Throw yourself into life. And let your hair take care of itself.

It's easy.

A la Pierre Kareff.

Pierre Kareff

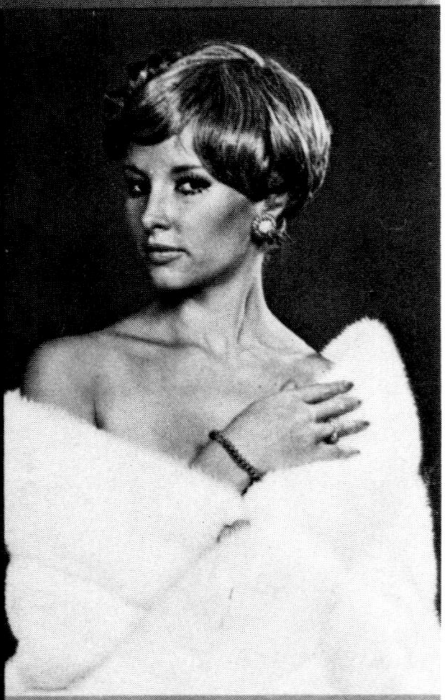

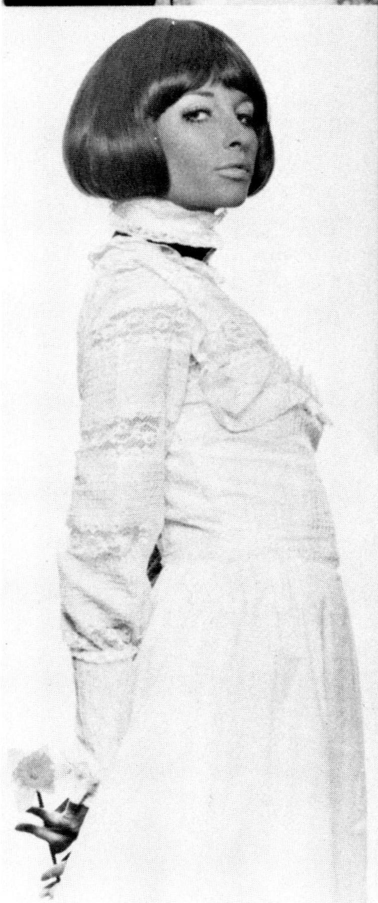

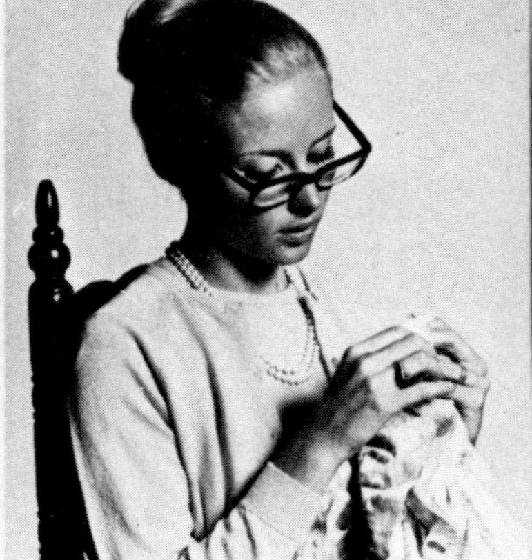

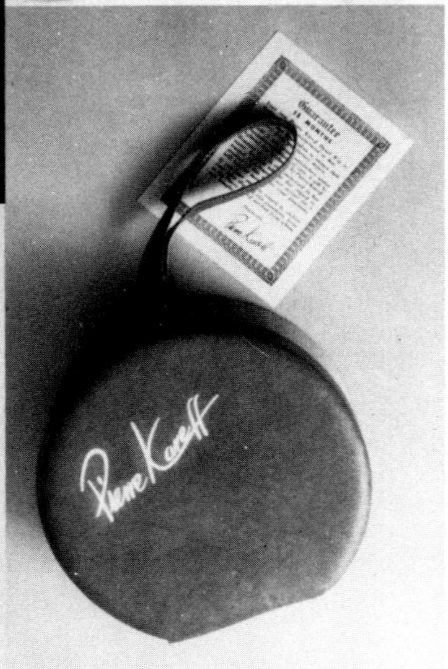
Pierre Kareff

(You'll love the tailored wig/vanity box supplied free with each wig).

100% SCOTCH WHISKIES. 86.8 PROOF. IMPORTED BY SOMERSET IMPORTERS, LTD., NEW YORK, N.Y.
Johnnie Walker
Red Label
BOTTLED IN SCOTLAND
HIGHEST AWARDS
Dear Dad...
Once I was the twinkle
in your eye.
For the next 22 years
I was the hole in your pocket.
Now that I'm earning
my own bed and board...
I hope this bottle of
Johnnie Walker Red makes
me the twinkle in your
eye again.
Your Son,
Andy

105

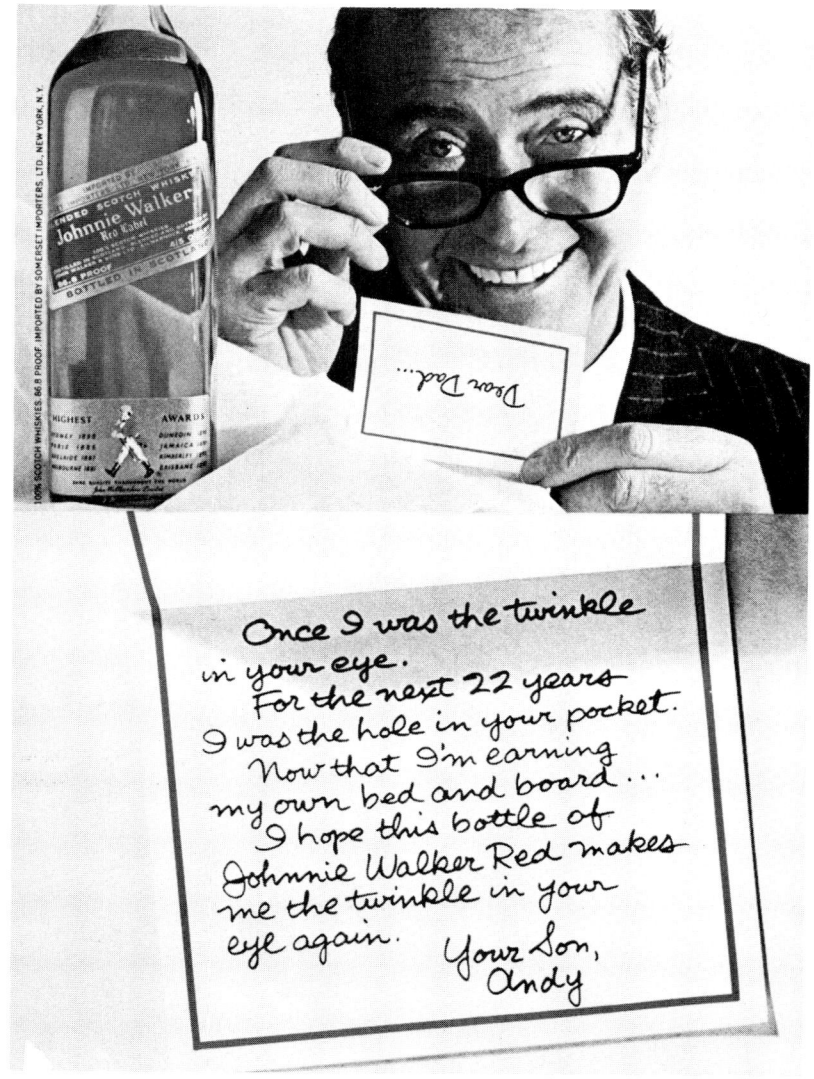

104
Lorraine & Crystal Entrants
Jacques Lorraine, Barry Crystal Art Directors
Lynton Stephenson Photographer
Twins Pharmaceuticals (Pty.) Ltd. Client

105
Needham, Harper & Steers Entrant
Phil Parker Art Director
Somerset Importers Client

106

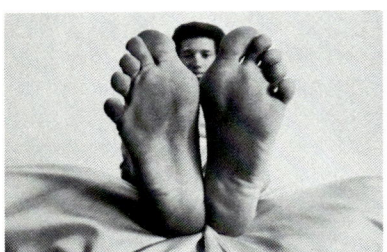

After a match, Arthur Ashe is exhausted, his arms are tired, his back aches, but at least his feet don't hurt.
AMF HEAD

107

Winter Garden
If you can afford $9.50 apiece for good seats, find a babysitter, and a cab to get you to the theater on time, you can see the biggest smash hit on Broadway this season.
Or...
You can stay home tonight and see it free on CBS.
"MUCH ADO ABOUT NOTHING" 8-11 TONIGHT CBS 2

108

It costs a lot to run a cow.
South Florida Dairy Farmers

109

Get-Away to MEXICO tonight.

Samsonite makes it tough outside.
Because we never know what's inside.
Your cargo may not be as fragile as this. But we can't take that chance. That's why we make our Silhouette cases like miniature fortresses. Mold the sides in dent-resistant Absolite. Cast the frames in super-strong magnesium. Recess the locks in a fool-proof panel. And make our handles tough enough to be guaranteed for life. We do all this because we know it's what's inside that really counts. (Shown here, Silhouette Ladies' O'Nite in Moon Glow, $38.)

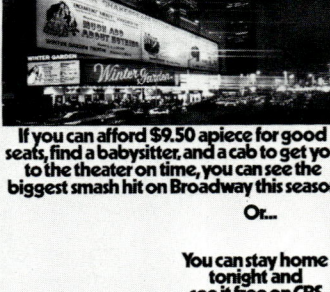

110

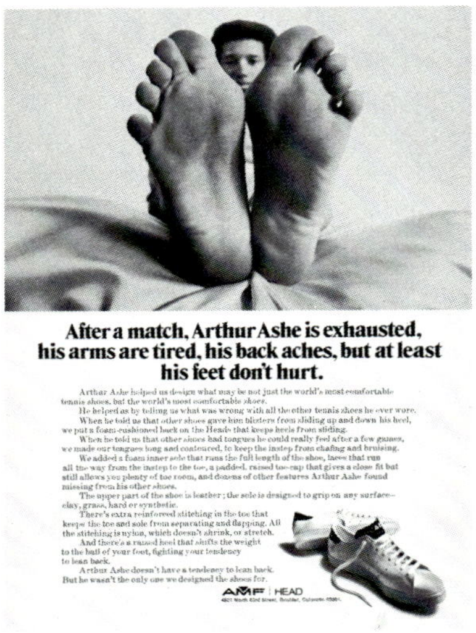

106
Muller Jordan Herrick Inc. Entrant
Mike Giaccaloni Art Director
Ken Ambrose Photographer
AMF/Head Client

107
Lou Dorfsman Entrant
CBS Television Network Client

108
Dave Romano Entrant
Bill Drier Writer
Eiger & Forer Photographers
Hume, Smith, Mickelberry Agency
South Florida Dairy Farmers Client

109
Charles Gardner Entrant
Mike Spahr Art Director
Al Swanstrom Photographer
Albert Jay Rosenthal & Co. Agency
R.J. Reynolds—Military Div. Client

110
John R. Kamerer Entrant
John Conboy Photographer
J. Walter Thompson Agency
Samsonite Luggage Client

111
Thomas J. Weisz, Ltd. Entrant
Laura Winslow Art Director
Highland National Bank of Newburgh Client

112
Dan Levin Entrant
Nigel White Art Director
Allardyce-Hampshire Ltd. Agency
Satra Motors Ltd. Client

111

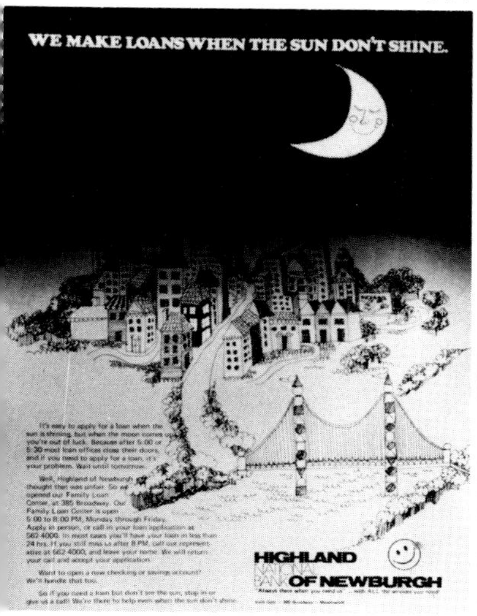

WE MAKE LOANS WHEN THE SUN DON'T SHINE.
HIGHLAND
OF NEWBURGH

112

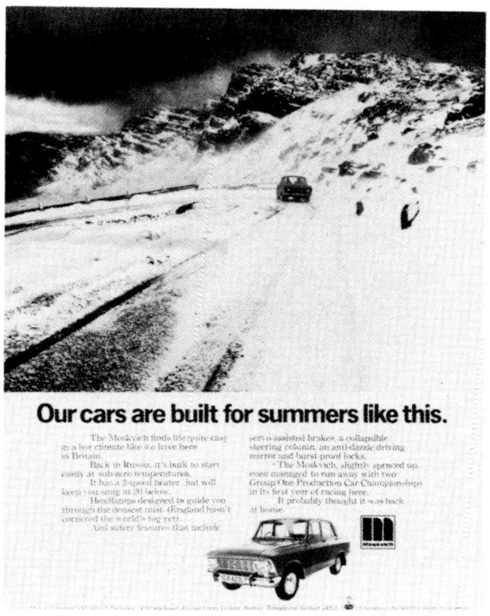

Our cars are built for summers like this.

113

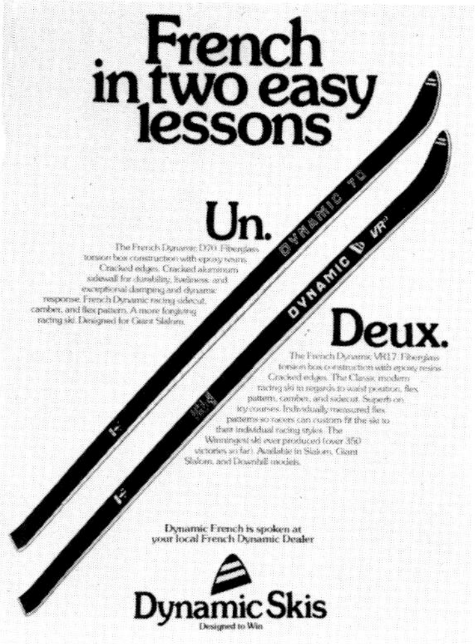

French in two easy lessons
Un.
Deux.
DYNAMIC
Dynamic French is spoken at your local French Dynamic Dealer
Dynamic Skis
Designed to Win

114

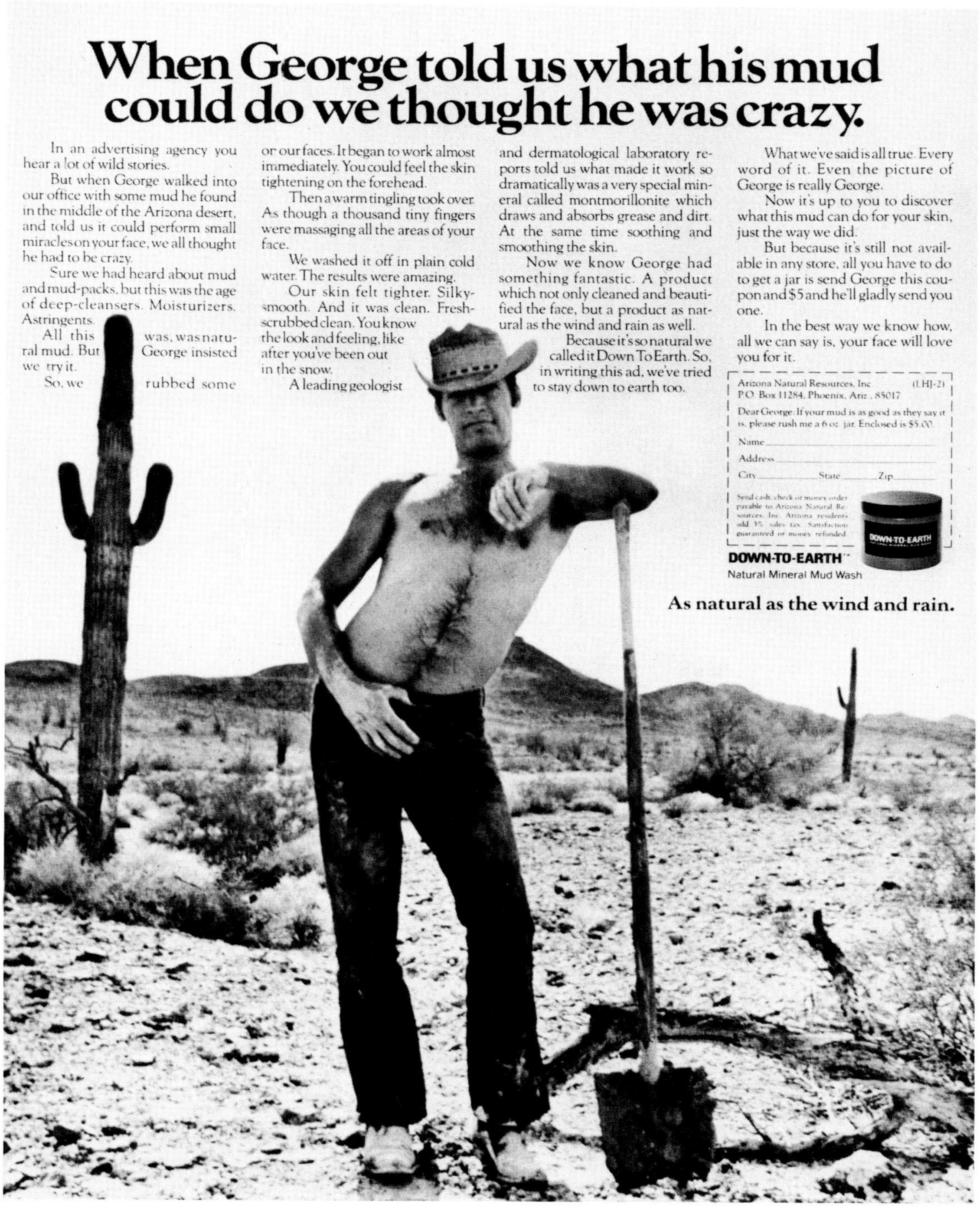

When George told us what his mud could do we thought he was crazy.
In an advertising agency you hear a lot of wild stories.
But when George walked into our office with some mud he found in the middle of the Arizona desert, and told us it could perform small miracles on your face, we all thought he had to be crazy.
Sure we had heard about mud and mud-packs, but this was the age of deep-cleansers. Moisturizers. Astringents.
All this was, was natural mud. But George insisted we try it.
So, we rubbed some on our faces. It began to work almost immediately. You could feel the skin tightening on the forehead.
Then a warm tingling took over. As though a thousand tiny fingers were massaging all the areas of your face.
We washed it off in plain cold water. The results were amazing.
Our skin felt tighter. Silky-smooth. And it was clean. Fresh-scrubbed clean. You know the look and feeling, like after you've been out in the snow.
A leading geologist and dermatological laboratory reports told us what made it work so dramatically was a very special mineral called montmorillonite which draws and absorbs grease and dirt. At the same time soothing and smoothing the skin.
Now we know George had something fantastic. A product which not only cleaned and beautified the face, but a product as natural as the wind and rain as well.
Because it's so natural we called it Down To Earth. So, in writing this ad, we've tried to stay down to earth too.
What we've said is all true. Every word of it. Even the picture of George is really George.
Now it's up to you to discover what this mud can do for your skin, just the way we did.
But because it's still not available in any store, all you have to do to get a jar is send George this coupon and $5 and he'll gladly send you one.
In the best way we know how, all we can say is, your face will love you for it.
Arizona Natural Resources, Inc (LHJ-2)
P.O. Box 11284, Phoenix, Ariz., 85017
Dear George: If your mud is as good as they say it is, please rush me a 6 oz. jar. Enclosed is $5.00.
Name
Address
City State Zip
Send cash, check or money order payable to Arizona Natural Resources, Inc. Arizona residents add 3% sales tax. Satisfaction guaranteed or money refunded.
DOWN-TO-EARTH
DOWN-TO-EARTH™
Natural Mineral Mud Wash
As natural as the wind and rain.

113
Robert Cipriani
Entrant
Don Pierce, Robert Cipriani
Art Directors
Gene Lemery
Illustrator
Gunn Associates
Studio
Dynamic Skis
Client

114
Robert Brian Advertising, Inc.
Entrant
Jerry Rosenfeld
Art Director
Vern Goldsmith
Copywriter
Les Underhill
Photographer
Arizona Natural Resources, Inc.
Client

115

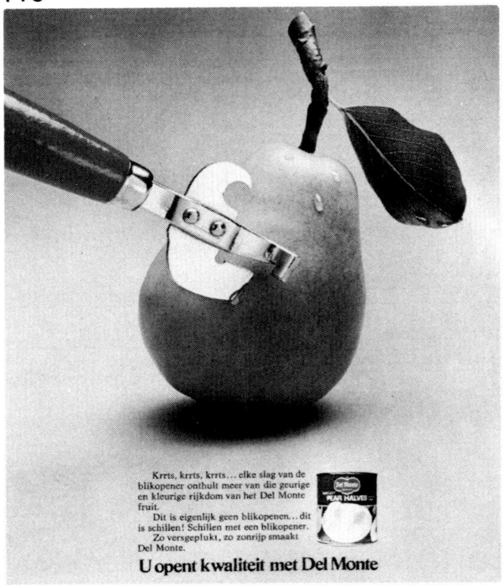
Krrts, krrts, krrts... elke slag van de blikopener onthult meer van die geurige en kleurige rijkdom van het Del Monte fruit.
Dit is eigenlijk geen blikopenen... dit is schillen! Schillen met een blikopener.
Zo versgeplukt, zo zonrijp smaakt Del Monte.
PEAR HALVES
U opent kwaliteit met Del Monte

116

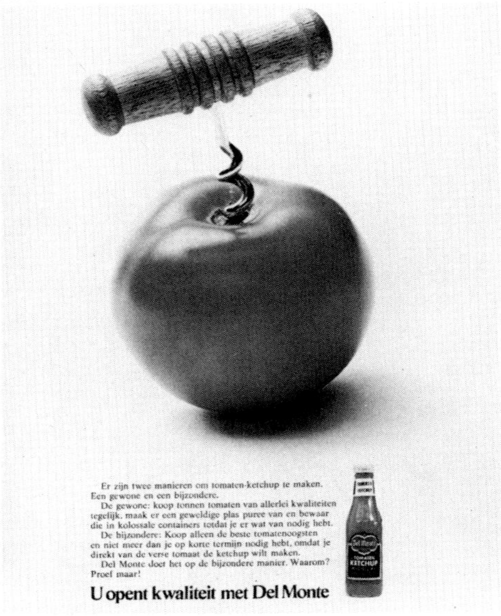
Er zijn twee manieren om tomaten-ketchup te maken. Een gewone en een bijzondere.
De gewone: koop tonnen tomaten van allerlei kwaliteiten tegelijk, maak er een geweldige plas puree van en bewaar die in kolossale containers totdat je er wat van nodig hebt.
De bijzondere: Koop alleen de beste tomatenoogsten en niet meer dan je op korte termijn nodig hebt, omdat je direkt van de verse tomaat de ketchup wilt maken.
Del Monte doet het op de bijzondere manier. Waarom? Proef maar!
KETCHUP
U opent kwaliteit met Del Monte

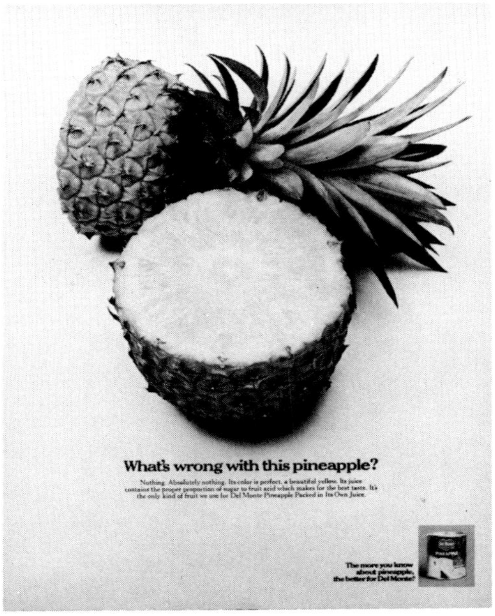
What's wrong with this pineapple?
Nothing. Absolutely nothing. Its color is perfect, a beautiful yellow. Its juice contains the proper proportion of sugar to fruit acid which makes for the best taste. It's the only kind of fruit we use for Del Monte Pineapple Packed in Its Own Juice.
The more you know about pineapple, the better for Del Monte!

117

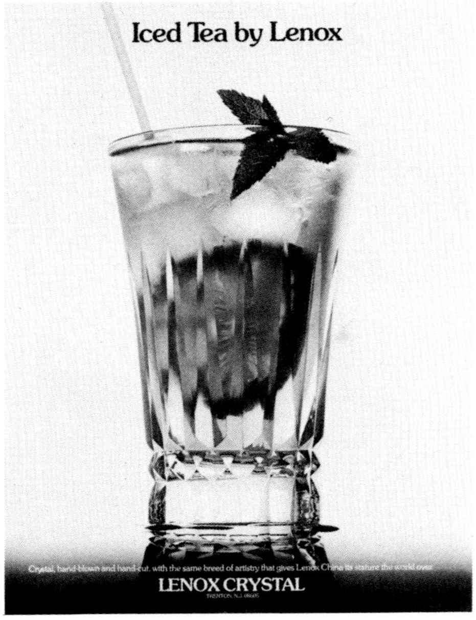
Iced Tea by Lenox
LENOX CRYSTAL
TRENTON, N.J. 08605

118

115-116
McCann-Erickson (Nederland)
Entrant
Peter Vos
Art Director
Del Monte Corp.
Client

117
Al Fessler
Entrant
Lourence Bartone
Photographer
McCann-Erickson, Inc.
Agency
Walker Engraving
Studio
Del Monte Corp.
Client

118
Craig Mierop
Entrant
Jim Vicari
Photographer
Chirurg & Cairns Advertising
Agency

119
Adolf Wirz AG Werbeberatung
Entrant
A. Bosshard Art Director
Ch. Kurz Photographer
Atlantis Hotel Client

119

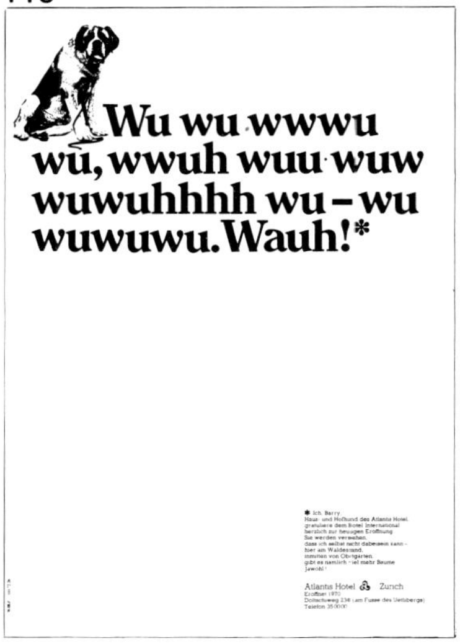

Wu wu wwwu wu, wwuh wuu wuw wuwuhhhh wu-wu wuwuwu. Wauh!*

120

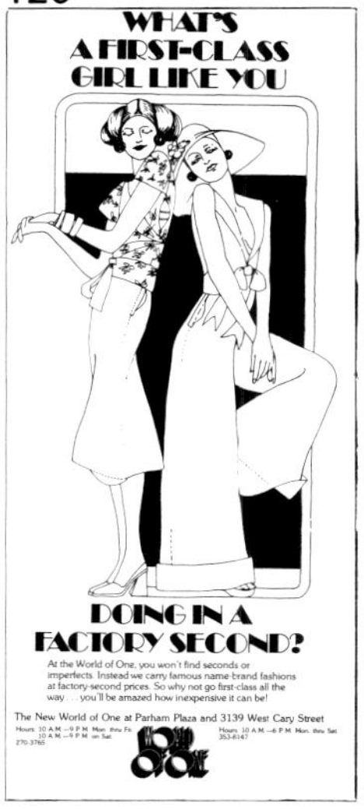

WHAT'S A FIRST-CLASS GIRL LIKE YOU
DOING IN A FACTORY SECOND?
The New World of One at Parham Plaza and 3139 West Cary Street

121

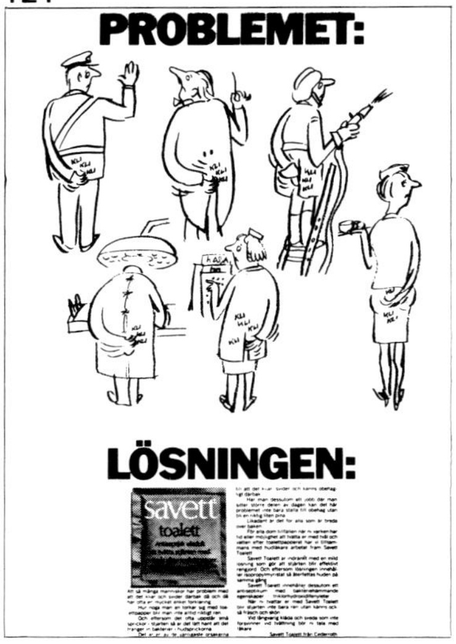

PROBLEMET:
LÖSNINGEN:
savett
toalett

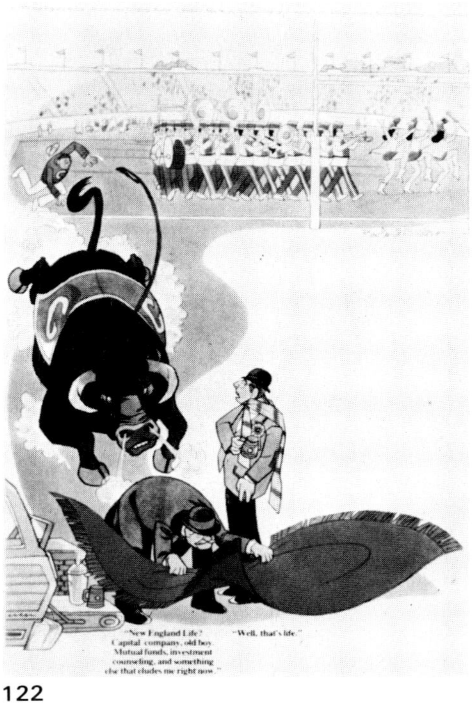

"New England Life? Capital company, old boy. Mutual funds, investment counseling, and something else that eludes me right now."
"Well, that's life."

122

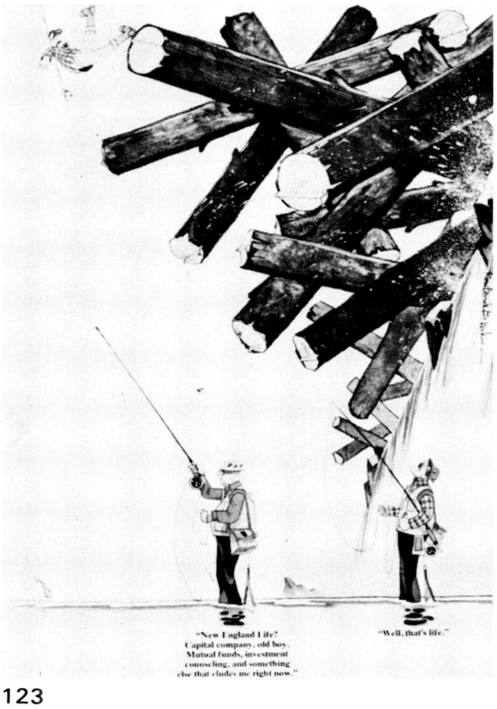

"New England Life? Capital company, old boy. Mutual funds, investment counseling, and something else that eludes me right now."
"Well, that's life."

123

120
Ernest R. Williams
Entrant
Rickie Newman Illustrator
Two One Two, Limited Studio
World of One Client

121
Ericson & Co. AB
Entrant
Advisor
Client

122-123
Hill, Holliday, Connors, Cosmopulos
Entrants
Stavros Cosmopulos, Jay Hill
Art Directors
Roland B. Wilson
Illustrator
New England Mutual Life Insurance Client

124
Charles Sawyer Entrant
Rod Capawana Art Director
Tasso Vendikos Photographer
Warner Bicking & Fenwick Agency
Ilford Inc. Client

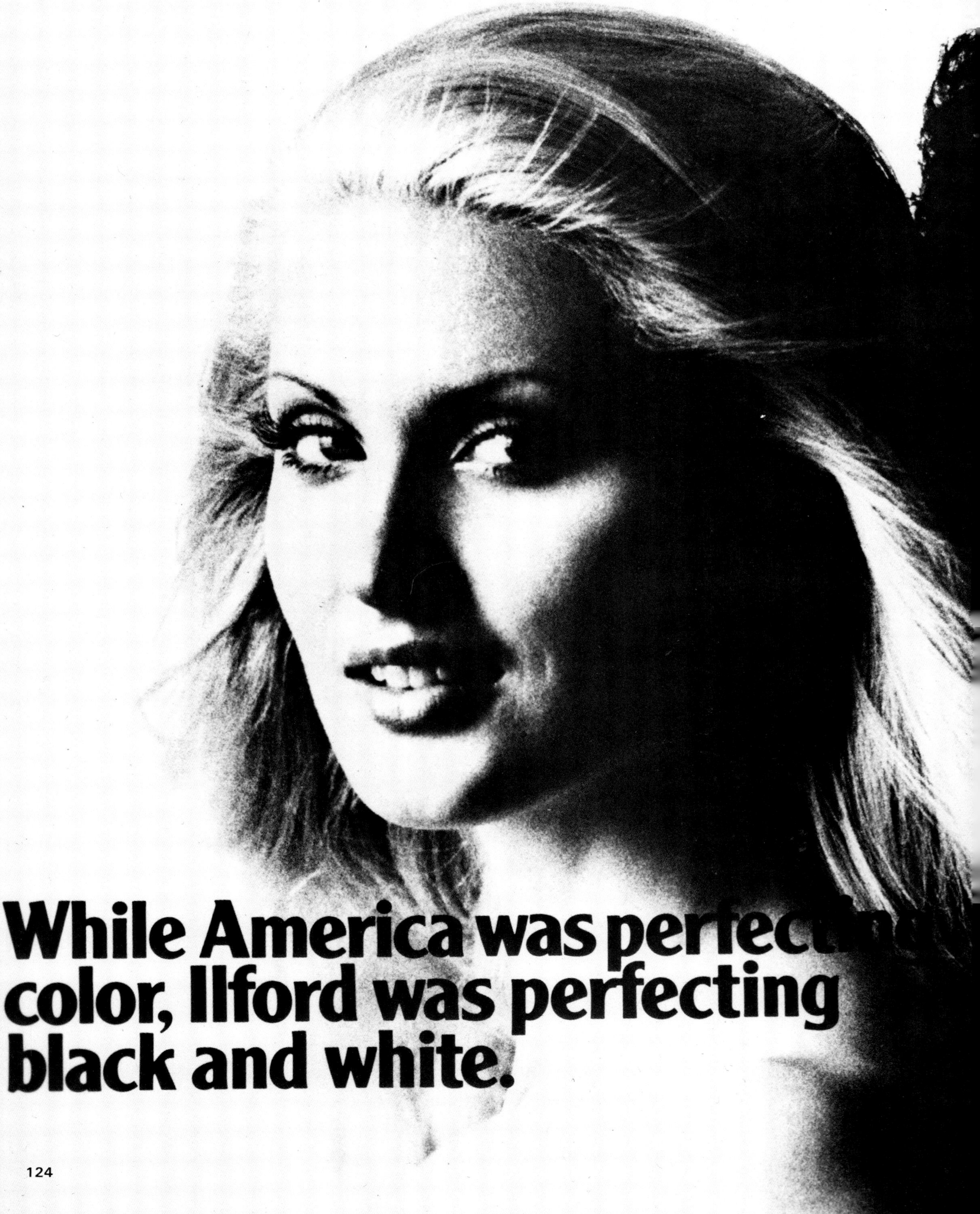
While America was perfect
color, Ilford was perfecting
black and white.

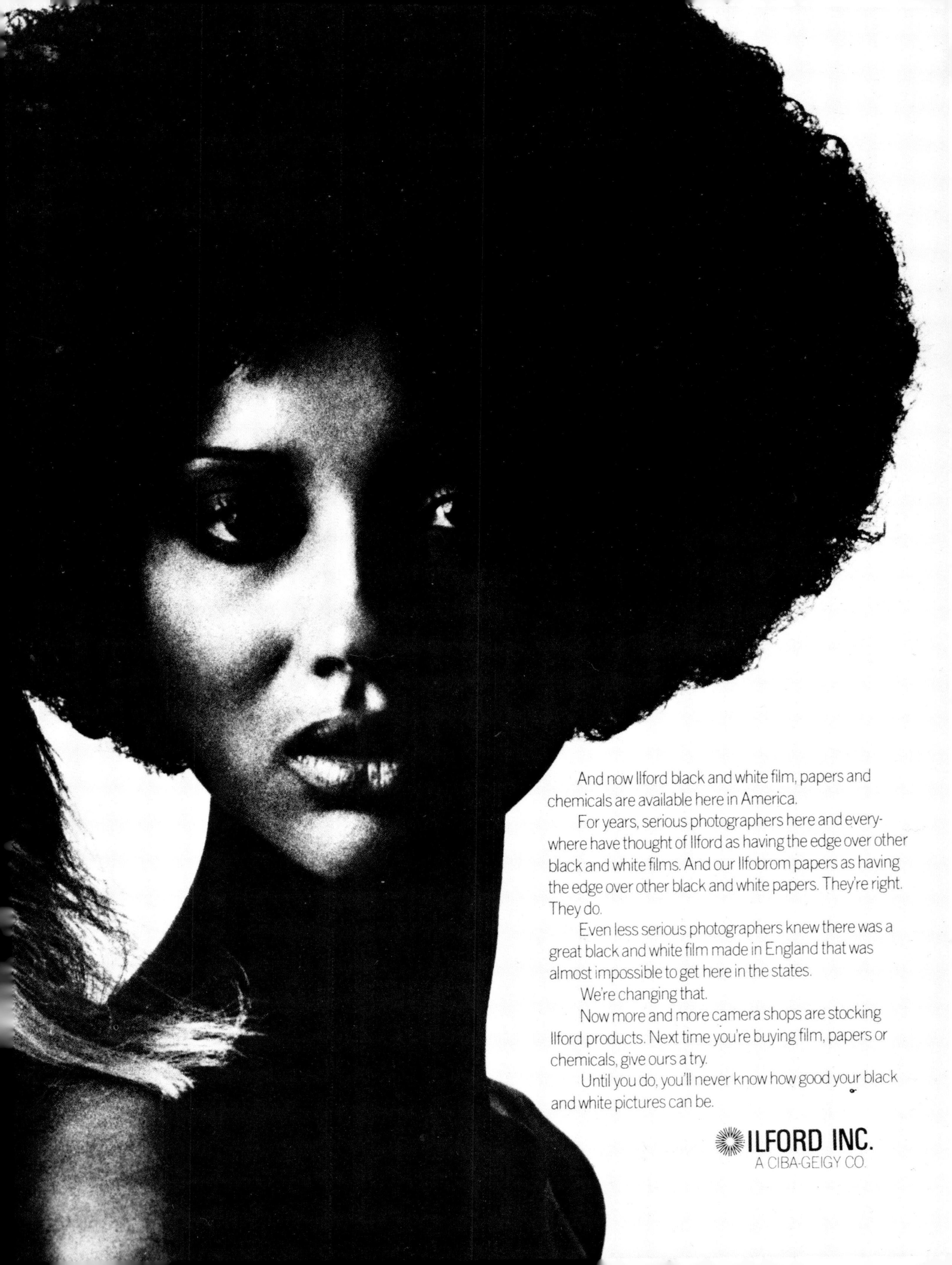
And now Ilford black and white film, papers and chemicals are available here in America.
For years, serious photographers here and everywhere have thought of Ilford as having the edge over other black and white films. And our Ilfobrom papers as having the edge over other black and white papers. They're right. They do.
Even less serious photographers knew there was a great black and white film made in England that was almost impossible to get here in the states.
We're changing that.
Now more and more camera shops are stocking Ilford products. Next time you're buying film, papers or chemicals, give ours a try.
Until you do, you'll never know how good your black and white pictures can be.
ILFORD INC.
A CIBA-GEIGY CO.

125

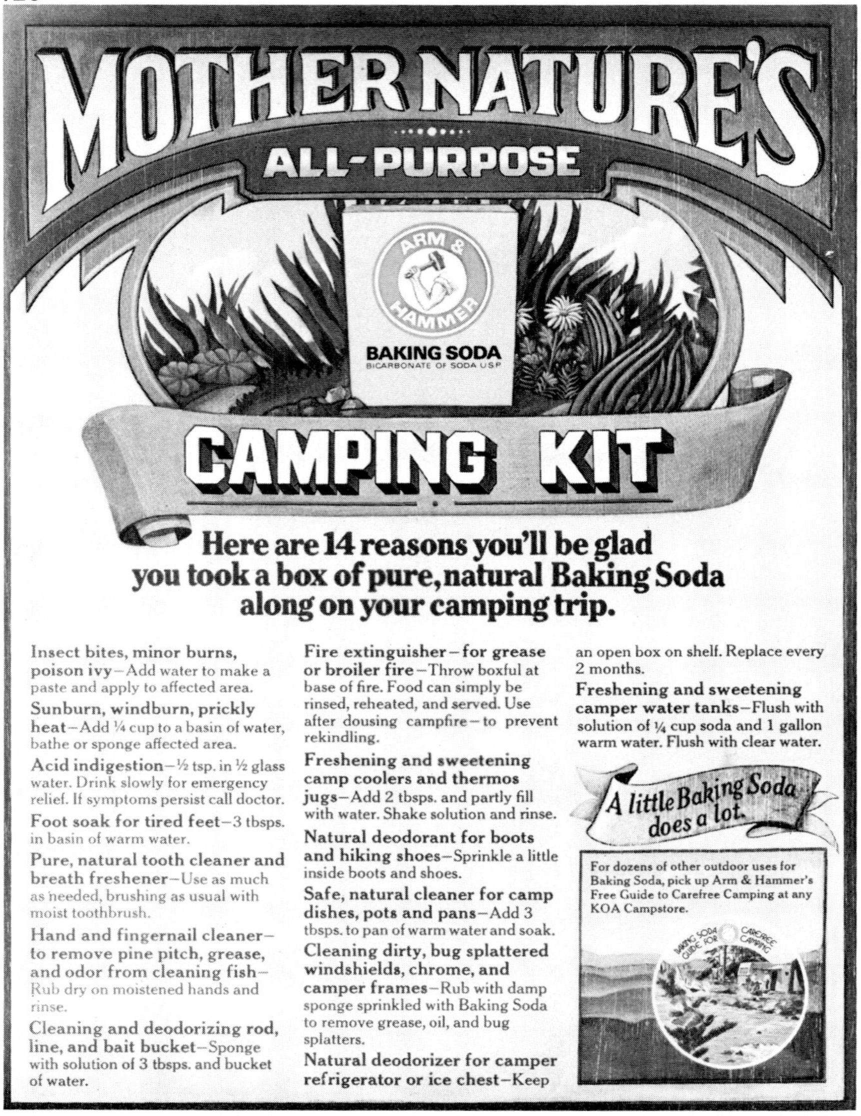
MOTHER NATURE'S
ALL-PURPOSE
ARM & HAMMER
BAKING SODA
BICARBONATE OF SODA U.S.P.
CAMPING KIT
Here are 14 reasons you'll be glad you took a box of pure, natural Baking Soda along on your camping trip.
Insect bites, minor burns, poison ivy—Add water to make a paste and apply to affected area.
Sunburn, windburn, prickly heat—Add ¼ cup to a basin of water, bathe or sponge affected area.
Acid indigestion—½ tsp. in ½ glass water. Drink slowly for emergency relief. If symptoms persist call doctor.
Foot soak for tired feet—3 tbsps. in basin of warm water.
Pure, natural tooth cleaner and breath freshener—Use as much as needed, brushing as usual with moist toothbrush.
Hand and fingernail cleaner—to remove pine pitch, grease, and odor from cleaning fish—Rub dry on moistened hands and rinse.
Cleaning and deodorizing rod, line, and bait bucket—Sponge with solution of 3 tbsps. and bucket of water.
Fire extinguisher—for grease or broiler fire—Throw boxful at base of fire. Food can simply be rinsed, reheated, and served. Use after dousing campfire—to prevent rekindling.
Freshening and sweetening camp coolers and thermos jugs—Add 2 tbsps. and partly fill with water. Shake solution and rinse.
Natural deodorant for boots and hiking shoes—Sprinkle a little inside boots and shoes.
Safe, natural cleaner for camp dishes, pots and pans—Add 3 tbsps. to pan of warm water and soak.
Cleaning dirty, bug splattered windshields, chrome, and camper frames—Rub with damp sponge sprinkled with Baking Soda to remove grease, oil, and bug splatters.
Natural deodorizer for camper refrigerator or ice chest—Keep an open box on shelf. Replace every 2 months.
Freshening and sweetening camper water tanks—Flush with solution of ¼ cup soda and 1 gallon warm water. Flush with clear water.
A little Baking Soda does a lot.
For dozens of other outdoor uses for Baking Soda, pick up Arm & Hammer's Free Guide to Carefree Camping at any KOA Campstore.
BAKING SODA GUIDE FOR CAREFREE CAMPING

125
Paul Gulotta Entrant
Richard Hess Illustrator
Kelly, Nason Inc. Agency
Church & Dwight Co., Inc. Client

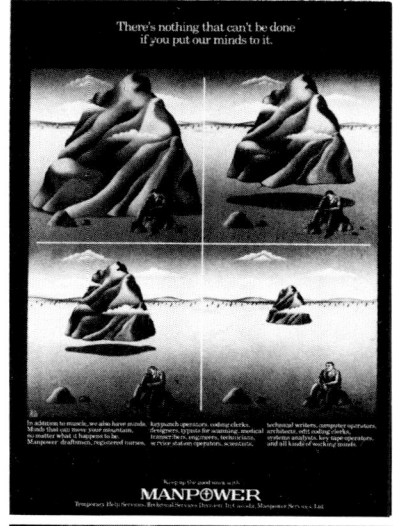

126

There's nothing that can't be done
if you put our minds to it.
MANPOWER

127

TARRA

MICHELIN:
THE OUTPERFORMER
The inside story of the world's
first Steel-Belted Radial.
The Outperformer
MICHELIN

128

126
Jeff Gorman, Lester Teich Entrants
Nader-Lief, Inc. Agency
Manpower Client

127
Muller Jordan Herrick Inc. Entrant
Edward Rostock Art Director
Harold Krieger Photographer
Tarra Hall Client

128
Henry Ries Entrant
Terry Friary Art Director
Al Paul Lefton Agency
Michelin Tires Client

"We'll show you some of the world's biggest rivers. They just don't have any water in them."

"The Henley-on-Todd Regatta has more blisters per foot than any boat race in the world, and I guess I'm responsible. I'm Reg Smith, and I run a warehouse here in Alice Springs when I'm not running regattas. Back in '62 I decided just because we're further from water than anywhere on earth was no reason to do without water sports. So every August, bottomless canoes and yachts are propelled over the Todd River's dry bed by the legs of school, club and miners' teams. There's also surf lifesaving, sand fishing for wooden fish and the Australian Cup with the *Insipid*.

"Alice's cedar-lined streets are an oasis for the Outback's stockmen and miners. And even though the Henley's insured *against* rain, there's no water shortage due to underground reserves. So when you come here, you'll stay in air-conditioned motels with swimming pools. See the Flying Doctor and School of the Air, Pitchi Ritchi Sanctuary and our Aboriginal art galleries. For dinner go to The Overland Steakhouse, owned by Dave Fisher and bartended by Tory, an ex-ringer. The Stuart Arms has dancing. There's usually folksinging somewhere. And if you're here May Day, there's the Bangtail Muster, a very western festival.

"Alice, however, is doomed to play second fiddle to geological formations. Go out to Ayers Rock, The Olgas, Ormiston Gorge, Standley Chasm, Simpson's Gap and King's Canyon. And on the way, you'll see ghost gums, kangaroos, wallabies and dingoes. Take the Did-jerri-doo, the daily mail run by small plane to cattle stations and missions. Connair's John Darmody'll fix you up. Or stay in log cabins, ride horses and throw boomerangs at Ross River cattle station.

"If you tire of the outback, drive to Adelaide for restaurants, theatres and shops. Just turn right and go down the road 1,050 miles. Or take the train, named The Ghan after the early Afghan camel drivers. By plane, the earth's red and wrinkled like a new baby. Or go to the Great Barrier Reef, the world's largest aquarium. Tasmania has history and apples. And Perth has miners and wildflowers.

"Me, I'll stay in Alice. I'm thinking of making the Henley international ever since Yale University expressed interest. Besides, where else can you get a martini and ten minutes later be on land where you can plant the first human footprint?"

See your travel agent or mail this to:
Australian Tourist Commission
1270 Ave. of the Americas, N.Y., N.Y. 10020
3550 Wilshire Boulevard, Los Angeles, Calif. 90010
111 East Wacker Drive, Chicago, Illinois 60601

☐ I'd like to challenge Reg Smith to a submarine race. Send me information on Henley-on-Todd and Alice Springs.
☐ I can't stand sand in my shoes. Send me information on the rest of Australia.

Name_____
Address_____
City & State_____ Zip_____

AUSTRALIA
Where the good old days are now.

Ted Schmitt Entrant
Elliott Irwin Photographer
Tinker Dodge & Delano Agency
Australian Tourist Commission Client

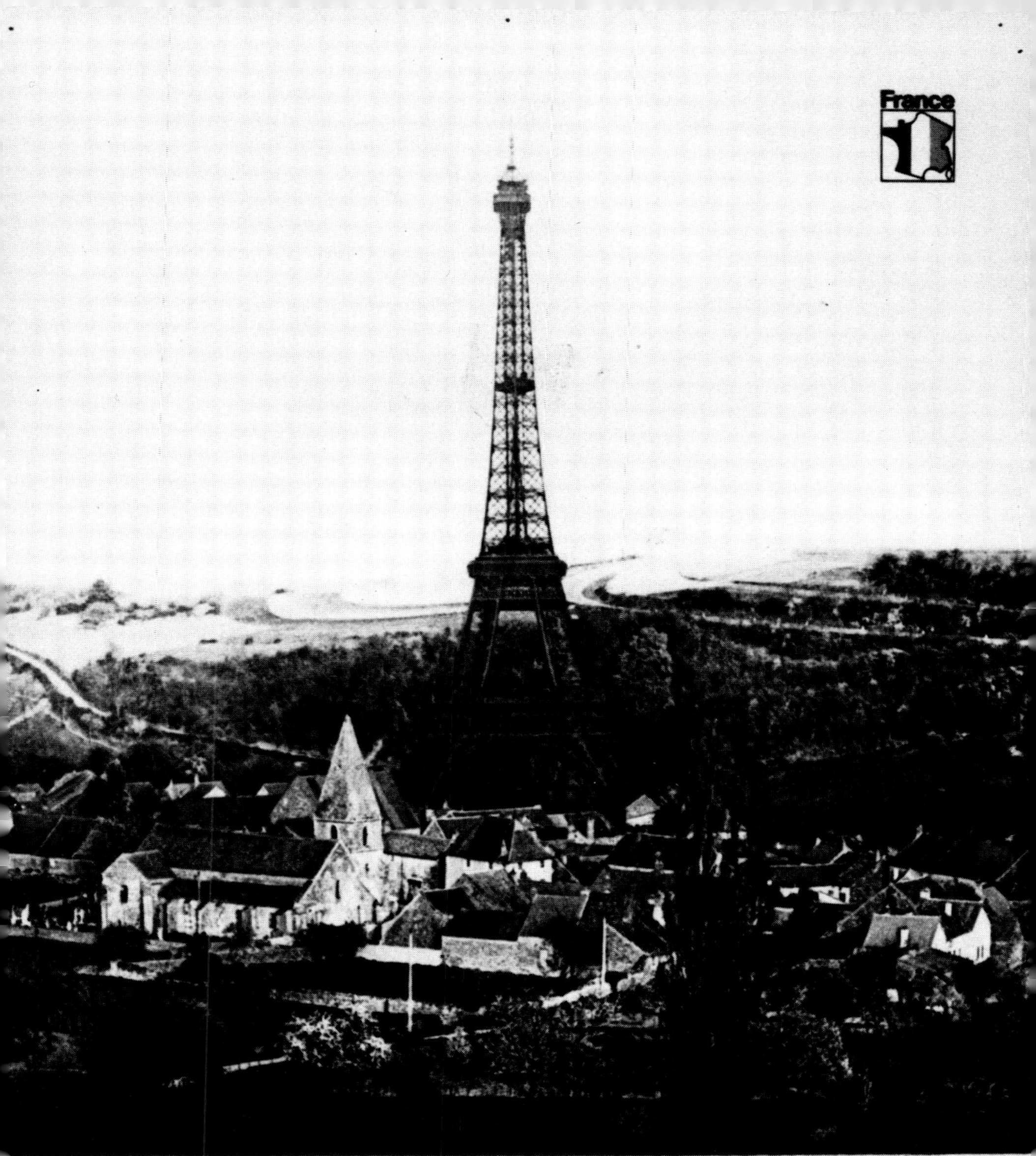
France

For a free color booklet that details the excitement of the country that surrounds Paris, see your travel agent or write: The French Government Tourist Office, Box 477, New York, N.Y. 10011.

DO WE HAVE TO PUT AN EIFFEL TOWER IN EVERY TOWN TO GET YOU TO APPRECIATE THE REST OF FRANCE?

131

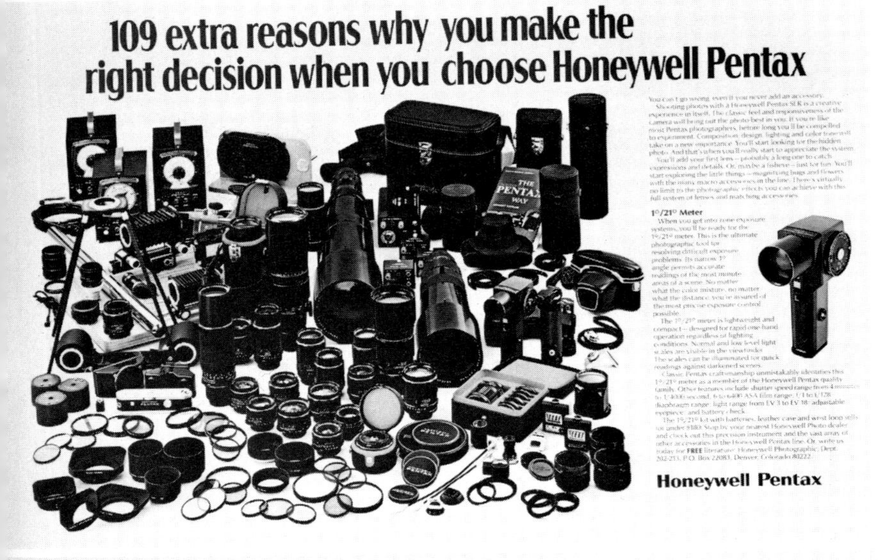
109 extra reasons why you make the right decision when you choose Honeywell Pentax
1°/21° Meter
Honeywell Pentax

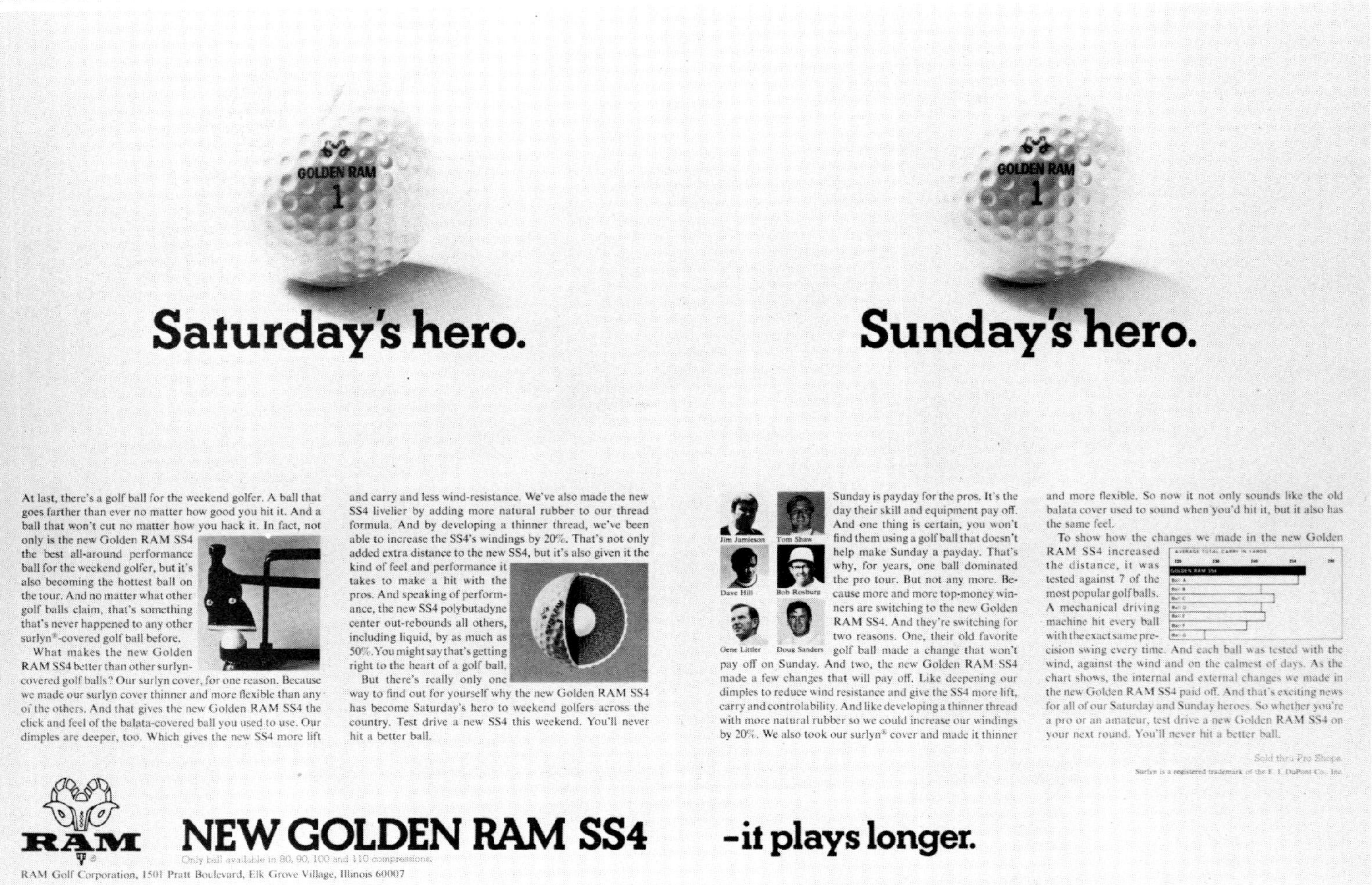
GOLDEN RAM
1
Saturday's hero.
GOLDEN RAM
1
Sunday's hero.
At last, there's a golf ball for the weekend golfer. A ball that goes farther than ever no matter how good you hit it. And a ball that won't cut no matter how you hack it. In fact, not only is the new Golden RAM SS4 the best all-around performance ball for the weekend golfer, but it's also becoming the hottest ball on the tour. And no matter what other golf balls claim, that's something that's never happened to any other surlyn®-covered golf ball before.
What makes the new Golden RAM SS4 better than other surlyn-covered golf balls? Our surlyn cover, for one reason. Because we made our surlyn cover thinner and more flexible than any of the others. And that gives the new Golden RAM SS4 the click and feel of the balata-covered ball you used to use. Our dimples are deeper, too. Which gives the new SS4 more lift and carry and less wind-resistance. We've also made the new SS4 livelier by adding more natural rubber to our thread formula. And by developing a thinner thread, we've been able to increase the SS4's windings by 20%. That's not only added extra distance to the new SS4, but it's also given it the kind of feel and performance it takes to make a hit with the pros. And speaking of performance, the new SS4 polybutadyne center out-rebounds all others, including liquid, by as much as 50%. You might say that's getting right to the heart of a golf ball.
But there's really only one way to find out for yourself why the new Golden RAM SS4 has become Saturday's hero to weekend golfers across the country. Test drive a new SS4 this weekend. You'll never hit a better ball.
Jim Jamieson
Tom Shaw
Dave Hill
Bob Rosburg
Gene Littler
Doug Sanders
Sunday is payday for the pros. It's the day their skill and equipment pay off. And one thing is certain, you won't find them using a golf ball that doesn't help make Sunday a payday. That's why, for years, one ball dominated the pro tour. But not any more. Because more and more top-money winners are switching to the new Golden RAM SS4. And they're switching for two reasons. One, their old favorite golf ball made a change that won't pay off on Sunday. And two, the new Golden RAM SS4 made a few changes that will pay off. Like deepening our dimples to reduce wind resistance and give the SS4 more lift, carry and controlability. And like developing a thinner thread with more natural rubber so we could increase our windings by 20%. We also took our surlyn® cover and made it thinner and more flexible. So now it not only sounds like the old balata cover used to sound when you'd hit it, but it also has the same feel.
To show how the changes we made in the new Golden RAM SS4 increased the distance, it was tested against 7 of the most popular golf balls. A mechanical driving machine hit every ball with the exact same precision swing every time. And each ball was tested with the wind, against the wind and on the calmest of days. As the chart shows, the internal and external changes we made in the new Golden RAM SS4 paid off. And that's exciting news for all of our Saturday and Sunday heroes. So whether you're a pro or an amateur, test drive a new Golden RAM SS4 on your next round. You'll never hit a better ball.
Sold thru Pro Shops.
Surlyn is a registered trademark of the E. I. DuPont Co., Inc.
RAM
NEW GOLDEN RAM SS4
-it plays longer.
Only ball available in 80, 90, 100 and 110 compressions.
RAM Golf Corporation, 1501 Pratt Boulevard, Elk Grove Village, Illinois 60007

132

131
Svatopluk Macha Entrant
Hakan Carheden Art Director
Campbell-Mithun, Inc. Agency
Honeywell Photographic Client

132
Kloppenburg, Switzer & Teich Entrant
Rex Teich Art Director
RAM Golf Corp. Client

133

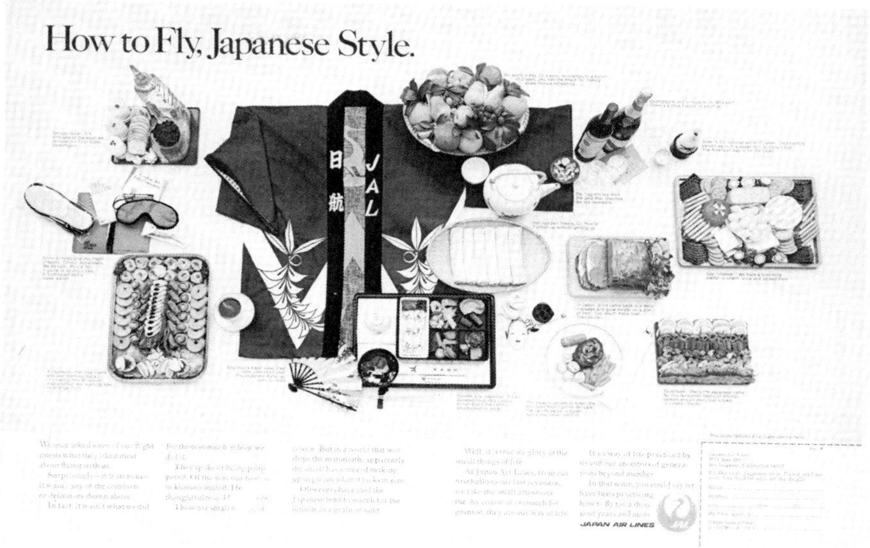
How to Fly, Japanese Style.
JAPAN AIR LINES

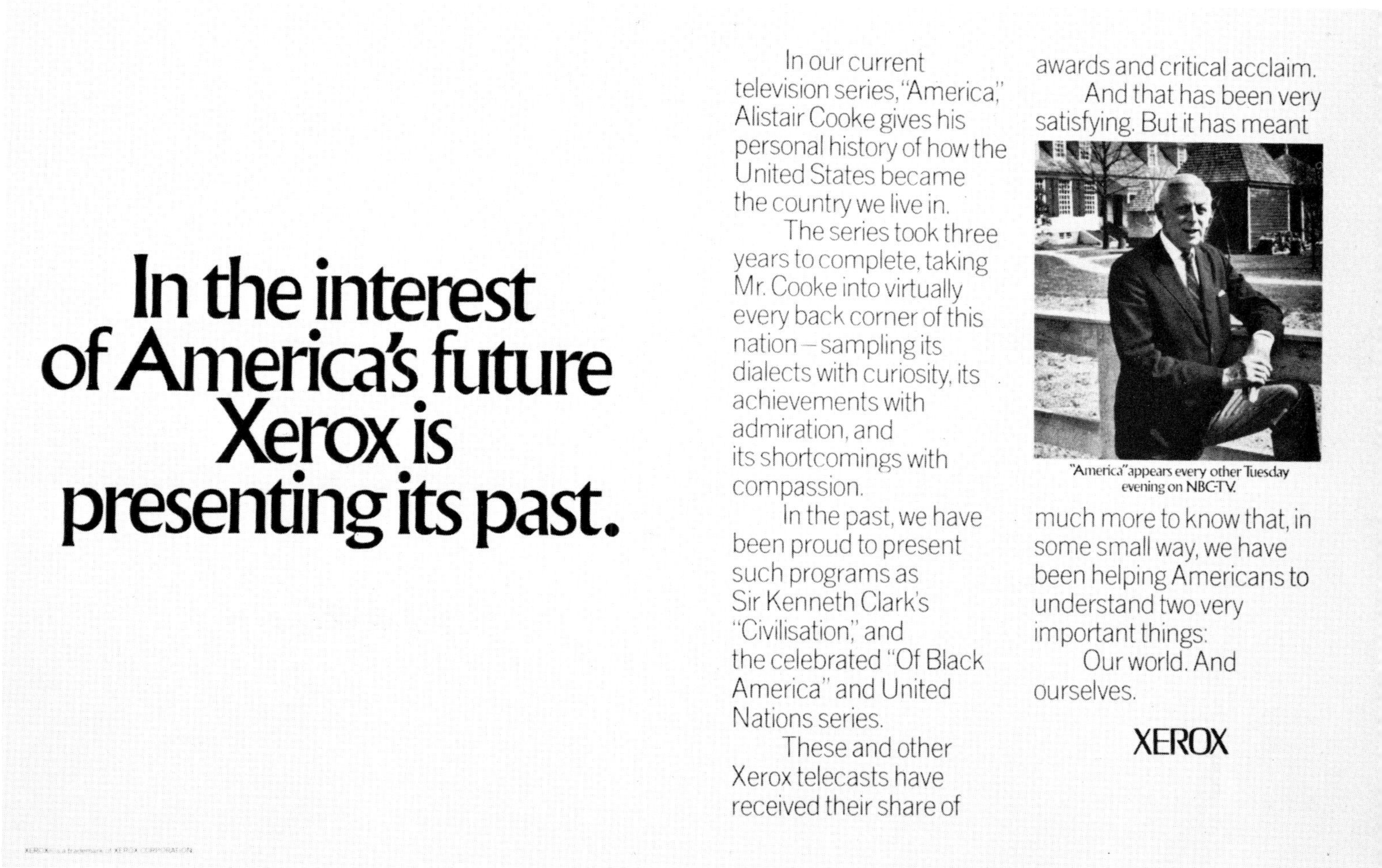
In the interest of America's future Xerox is presenting its past.
In our current television series, "America," Alistair Cooke gives his personal history of how the United States became the country we live in.
The series took three years to complete, taking Mr. Cooke into virtually every back corner of this nation—sampling its dialects with curiosity, its achievements with admiration, and its shortcomings with compassion.
In the past, we have been proud to present such programs as Sir Kenneth Clark's "Civilisation," and the celebrated "Of Black America" and United Nations series.
These and other Xerox telecasts have received their share of awards and critical acclaim.
And that has been very satisfying. But it has meant much more to know that, in some small way, we have been helping Americans to understand two very important things:
Our world. And ourselves.
"America" appears every other Tuesday evening on NBC-TV.
XEROX

134

133
Ketchum, MacLeod & Grove, Inc. Entrant
Joseph Phair Katsuji Asada Art Directors
Arthur Tuohy, Martin Werner Copywriters
Tosh Matsumoto Photographer
Japan Air Lines Client

134
Needham, Harper & Steers Entrant
Jeff Cohen Art Director
Xerox Client

THIS WEEK ON MOVIE 4
Monday "The Man With The Golden Arm" Part 1 with
FRANK SINATRA and **KIM NOVAK**
Tuesday Part 2
Wednesday "The Deadly Hunt" with
ANTHONY FRANCIOSA and **PETER LAWFORD**
Thursday "Prescription: Murder" with
PETER FALK and **GENE BARRY**
Friday "Last Train From Gun Hill" with
KIRK DOUGLAS and **ANTHONY QUINN**
4:30 on
TV4

THIS WEEK ON MOVIE 4
ARTHUR KENNEDY
and
TERESA WRIGHT
Monday in Crawlspace
HUGH O'BRIAN
Tuesday in Ten Little Indians
JERRY LEWIS
Wednesday in Visit To A Small Planet
FRED ASTAIRE
and
CYD CHARISSE
Thursday in The Band Wagon
PETER SELLERS
Friday in The Bobo
4:30 on TV4

THIS WEEK ON MOVIE 4
DEAN MARTIN and **SHIRLEY MacLAINE**
Monday in "All In A Night's Work"
LESLIE CARON and **WARREN BEATTY**
Tuesday in "Promise Her Anything"
JAMES GARNER and **ELKE SOMMER**
Wednesday in "The Art of Love"
GEORGE C. SCOTT and **TONY CURTIS**
Thursday in "Not With My Wife, You Don't"
DEBBIE REYNOLDS and **TONY CURTIS**
Friday in "Goodbye, Charlie"
4:30 on
TV4

THIS WEEK ON MOVIE 4
Monday "The Time Machine," with
YVETTE MIMIEUX ROD TAYLOR
Tuesday "Stranger On The Run," with
ANNE BAXTER HENRY FONDA
Wednesday "Arabesque," with
SOPHIA LOREN GREGORY PECK
Thursday "The Innocents," with
DEBORAH KERR MICHAEL REDGRAVE
Friday "You're A Big Boy Now," with
GERALDINE PAGE ELIZABETH HARTMAN
4:30 on
TV4

135-138
Ann Berk Entrant
Jack Jones Art Director
Al Hirschfeld Illustrator
Pictorial Powers Conway Studio
WNBC-TV Client

A-B-C
is only the beginning.

Some of our players pick horses by the alphabet. They simply play letters. It's possible to win that way. So the alphabet is okay for starters.

But to really enjoy playing you should learn to handicap a race. It's not as mysterious as it sounds. Learning to handicap is like learning to play bridge. Or checkers. You'll be surprised by how quickly you can pick up the basics. And by the fun you'll have while you learn.

Stop in and see what we mean.

I'm interested in learning about OTB. Please send me a free copy of the booklet "Everything You Always Wanted to Know about OTB".
Name:
Address:
Zip:
Send to: OTB Booklet, Box 8888, Times Square Station, New York, N.Y. 10036
5

OTB

Jim would like to make your acquaintance.

Jim Schreiber is one of our managers. Running his office takes up a big part of his day. But Jim can always find time to stop and say "hello". That's one of the reasons we made him a manager.

You see, Jim understands that OTB is a neighborhood business. So, he takes time to get to know his customers. We think that's good. For you and for us.

We have a lot of managers like Jim. One runs the office around the corner from you.

Stop in and see what we mean.

I'm interested in learning about OTB. Please send me a free copy of the booklet "Everything You Always Wanted to Know about OTB"
Name:
Address:
Zip:
Send to: OTB Booklet, Box 8888, Times Square Station, New York, N.Y. 10036
2

OTB

Our game isn't just another spectator sport.

There aren't any spectators in our game. Everybody is a player. That's what makes it fun.

Half the fun of playing is handicapping a race. There's nothing mysterious about it. Honest. Just cross off the horses you think have the least chance of winning. Keep going until you have only one left. That's your horse.

Sure. It's a challenge. But you'll be surprised by how quickly you can pick up the basics.

Stop in and see what we mean.

I'm interested in learning about OTB. Please send me a free copy of the booklet "Everything You Always Wanted to Know about OTB"
Name:
Address:
Zip:
Send to: OTB Booklet, Box 8888, Times Square Station, New York, N.Y. 10036
Q-G-4

OTB Now you can call us the N.Y. Bets

54-16 MYRTLE AVE.

Win, place and show. They're on our card too.

Nothing can replace the thrill of an afternoon or evening at the track. But when you can't get there, remember OTB.

We offer the same variety of bets as your favorite local track. Doubles, Exactas, Quinielas, Superfectas. Win, Place and Show, too. And we have the same selection of fine harness or thoroughbred horses. What's more, when the track is in New York State, our payoff price on a winning ticket is exactly the same as theirs.

We can't bring the horses to your neighborhood. We do offer you good, convenient service.

Stop in and see what we mean.

I'm interested in learning about OTB. Please send me a free copy of the booklet "Everything You Always Wanted to Know about OTB".
Name:
Address:
Zip:
Send to: OTB Booklet, Box 8888, Times Square Station, New York, N.Y. 10036
8

OTB

Picking a horse is fun. The rest is easy.

The first step in playing our game is picking your horse. You can play a hunch, take a tip from your brother-in-law, or stick pins in an entry sheet. Whatever you do, make a game of it.

Once you've picked your horse, the rest is easy. Just fill out a betting slip and take it to an OTB betting window. That's all there is.

Of course, there is one more step. Whenever you pick a winner, come back to our office to collect. That's the best step of all.

Stop in and see what we mean.

I'm interested in learning about OTB. Please send me a free copy of the booklet "Everything You Always Wanted to Know about OTB"
Name:
Address:
Zip:
Send to: OTB Booklet, Box 8888, Times Square Station, New York, N.Y. 10036

OTB

OTB

They give their winners a little extra.

The staff of the OTB office around the corner from you is so friendly that they give their winners a little extra.

Not in winnings, of course. Payoff prices on winning tickets in all our offices are the same. The "little extra" we're talking about is warm, personalized service. And, since everyone's a potential winner at OTB, everybody enjoys the same friendly treatment.

Stop in and see what we mean.

I'm interested in learning about OTB. Please send me a free copy of the booklet "Everything You Always Wanted to Know about OTB".
Name:
Address:
Zip:
Send to: OTB Booklet, Box 8888, Times Square Station, New York, N.Y. 10036
3

OTB

OFF-TRACK BETTING
OTB

On track or off, the game's the same.

Nothing can replace the thrill of an afternoon or evening at the track. But when you can't get there, remember OTB.

We offer the same selection of fine horses as your favorite local track. Harness *and* thoroughbred. We have the same variety of bets, too. And, when the track is in New York State, our payoff price on a winning ticket is exactly the same as theirs.

We can't bring the horses to your neighborhood. We do offer you good, convenient service.

Stop in and see what we mean.

I'm interested in learning about OTB. Please send me a free copy of the booklet "Everything You Always Wanted to Know about OTB".
Name:
Address:
Zip:
Send to: OTB Booklet, Box 8888, Times Square Station, New York, N.Y. 10036
7

OTB

Some people say Dolores brings them luck.

Dolores Brush is one of our most popular cashiers. Customers wait in line just for her. Why? They say it's because Dolores brings them luck. But we know better.

You see, Dolores understands that people appreciate cheerfulness. So, she treats everybody who comes to her window with a smile. For new players she always reserves a few helpful words. And they keep coming back.

We have a lot of cashiers like Dolores. Some work in the OTB office around the corner from you.

Stop in and see what we mean.

I'm interested in learning about OTB. Please send me a free copy of the booklet "Everything You Always Wanted to Know about OTB".
Name:
Address:
Zip:
Send to: OTB Booklet, Box 8888, Times Square Station, New York, N.Y. 10036

OTB

139-146
NYC Off-Track Betting Corp. Entrant
Bill O'Day Art Director
Richard Sheridan Copywriter

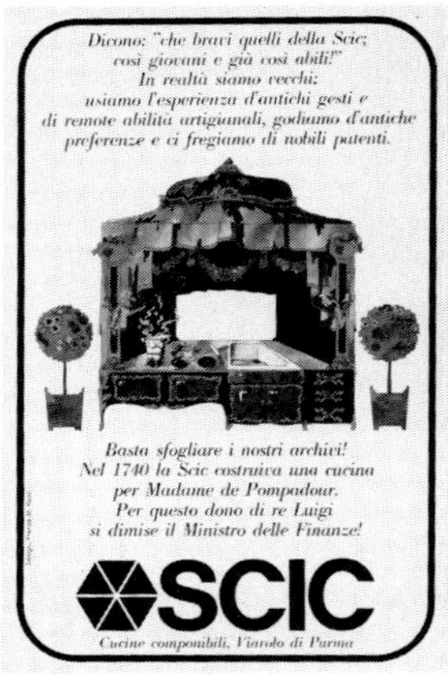
Dicono: "che bravi quelli della Scic;
così giovani e già così abili!"
In realtà siamo vecchi:
usiamo l'esperienza d'antichi gesti e
di remote abilità artigianali, godiamo d'antiche
preferenze e ci fregiamo di nobili patenti.
Basta sfogliare i nostri archivi!
Nel 1740 la Scic costruiva una cucina
per Madame de Pompadour.
Per questo dono di re Luigi
si dimise il Ministro delle Finanze!
SCIC
Cucine componibili, Viarolo di Parma

147

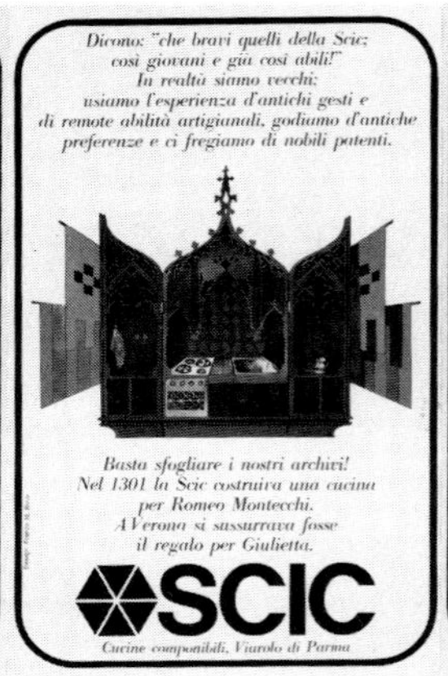
Dicono: "che bravi quelli della Scic;
così giovani e già così abili!"
In realtà siamo vecchi:
usiamo l'esperienza d'antichi gesti e
di remote abilità artigianali, godiamo d'antiche
preferenze e ci fregiamo di nobili patenti.
Basta sfogliare i nostri archivi!
Nel 1301 la Scic costruiva una cucina
per Romeo Montecchi.
A Verona si sussurrava fosse
il regalo per Giulietta.
SCIC
Cucine componibili, Viarolo di Parma

148

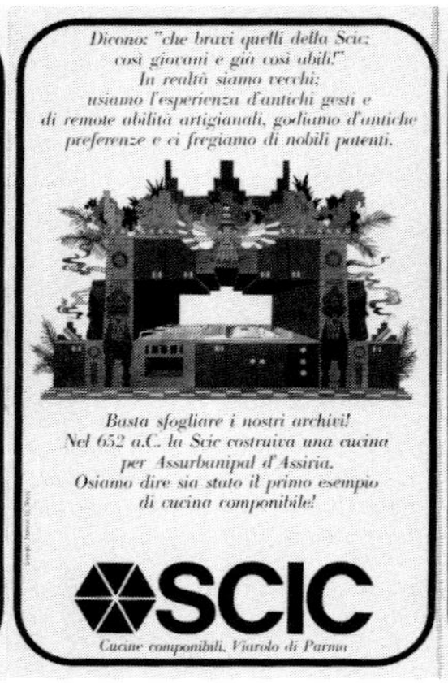
Dicono: "che bravi quelli della Scic;
così giovani e già così abili!"
In realtà siamo vecchi;
usiamo l'esperienza d'antichi gesti e
di remote abilità artigianali, godiamo d'antiche
preferenze e ci fregiamo di nobili patenti.
Basta sfogliare i nostri archivi!
Nel 652 a.C. la Scic costruiva una cucina
per Assurbanipal d'Assiria.
Osiamo dire sia stato il primo esempio
di cucina componibile!
SCIC
Cucine componibili, Viarolo di Parma

149

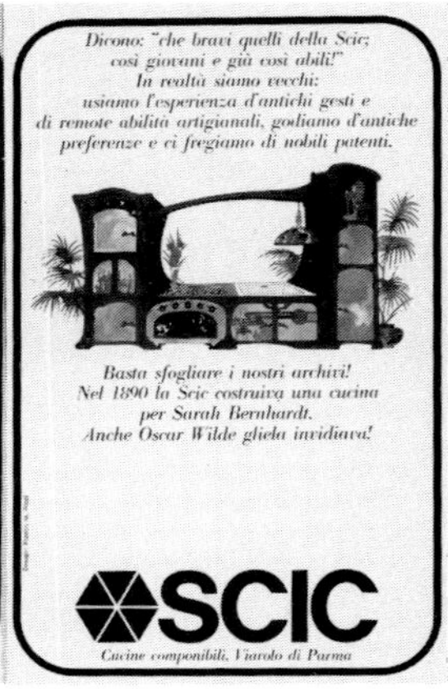
Dicono: "che bravi quelli della Scic;
così giovani e già così abili!"
In realtà siamo vecchi:
usiamo l'esperienza d'antichi gesti e
di remote abilità artigianali, godiamo d'antiche
preferenze e ci fregiamo di nobili patenti.
Basta sfogliare i nostri archivi!
Nel 1890 la Scic costruiva una cucina
per Sarah Bernhardt.
Anche Oscar Wilde gliela invidiava!
SCIC
Cucine componibili, Viarolo di Parma

150

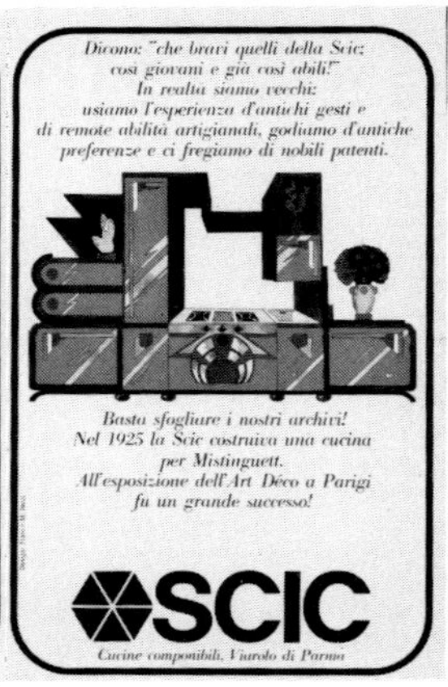
Dicono: "che bravi quelli della Scic;
così giovani e già così abili!"
In realtà siamo vecchi:
usiamo l'esperienza d'antichi gesti e
di remote abilità artigianali, godiamo d'antiche
preferenze e ci fregiamo di nobili patenti.
Basta sfogliare i nostri archivi!
Nel 1925 la Scic costruiva una cucina
per Mistinguett.
All'esposizione dell'Art Déco a Parigi
fu un grande successo!
SCIC
Cucine componibili, Viarolo di Parma

151

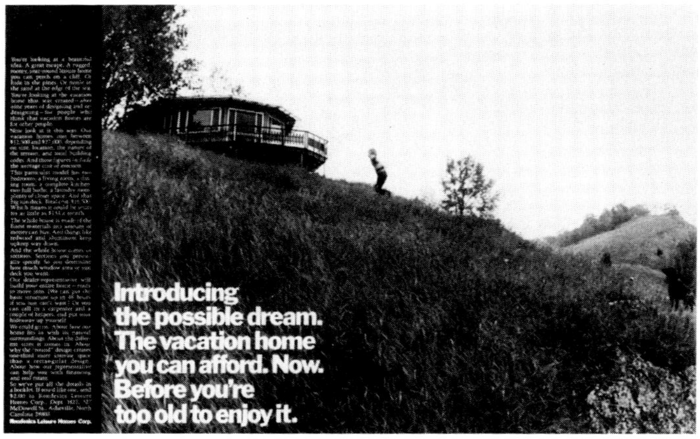
Introducing
the possible dream.
The vacation home
you can afford. Now.
Before you're
too old to enjoy it.

152

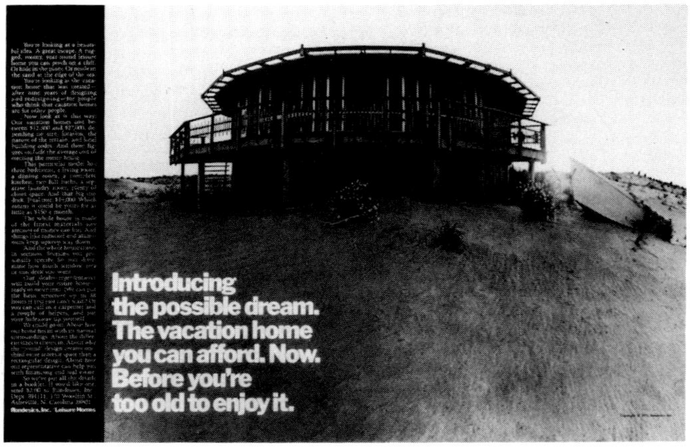
Introducing
the possible dream.
The vacation home
you can afford. Now.
Before you're
too old to enjoy it.

153

147-151
Franco Ricci Entrant
Studio Relazione Agency
SCIC Client

152-153
Jim Cole Entrant
Dick Henderson Art Director
Peter Vaeth Photographer
Cole Henderson Drake Inc. Agency
Rondesics, Inc. Client

154
Hanser, Larsson & Röstlund AB Entrant
Gunnel Westrom Art Director
Medisan AB Client

Från kinden till lilltån.

En crème som är bra, den är bra. Gör den huden mjuk och smidig pa kinden, sa händer samma sak pa halsen, armen, handen, stjärten och lilltan.

Idag finns en crème som gör huden mjuk och smidig pa ett avgjort bättre sätt än nagon annan hudcrème. HTH (Hjälper Torr Hud) heter den.

HTH innehaller bara lite, lite fett. Att den innehaller sa lite fett beror pa att man upptäckt att det som främst gör huden mjuk och smidig är fukt, inte fett! Därför finns i HTH bara precis sa mycket fett som behövs för att crèmen ska vara lätt och behaglig att använda.

Det unika med HTH är istället det aktiva, kropps-egna ämnet karbamid. Det är ett ämne som bade tillför och binder fukt i huden.

Andra crèmer, dom feta, far nöja sig med att pa sin höjd vara "fuktighetsbevarande". Men det är dom tyvärr bara sa länge fettet finns kvar pa huden. Sa om du vill fortsätta att vara mjuk och smidig, maste du smörja in dej pa nytt ganska snart.

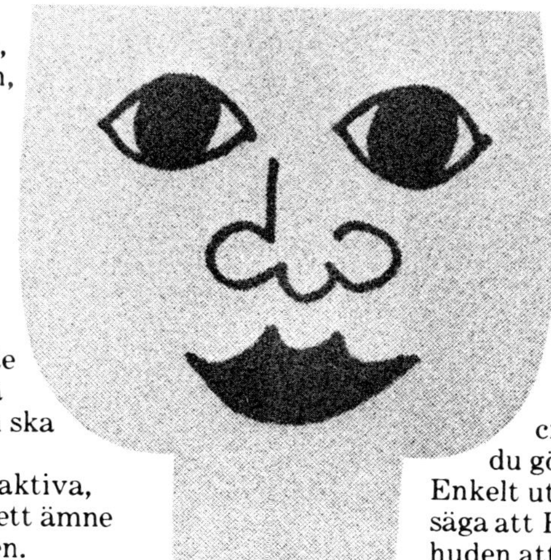

Om du väljer HTH, slipper du vara onödigt fet och kladdig i ansikte och pa händer. Och du slipper vara onödigt fet och kladdig under kläderna.

Men den kanske viktigaste skillnaden mellan HTH och feta crèmer märker du först när crèmen är "borta". För när HTH pa ett naturligt sätt torkats, nötts eller tvättats av, sa har ända ny fukt tillförts huden. Sa du behöver inte ha pa en ny klick crème det första du gör.

Enkelt uttryckt kan man säga att HTH har hjälpt huden att hjälpa sig själv.

HTH, den förnuftiga hudcrèmen.

Finns att köpa nästan överallt för bara cirka tian. Tillverkas av Medisan i Uppsala, dotterbolag till läkemedelsföretaget Pharmacia.

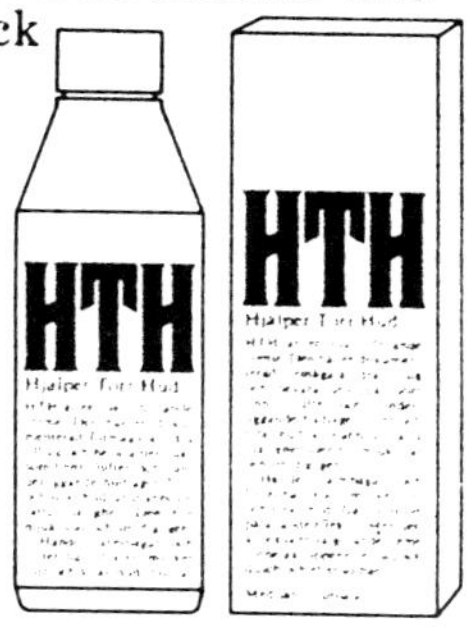
HTH
HTH

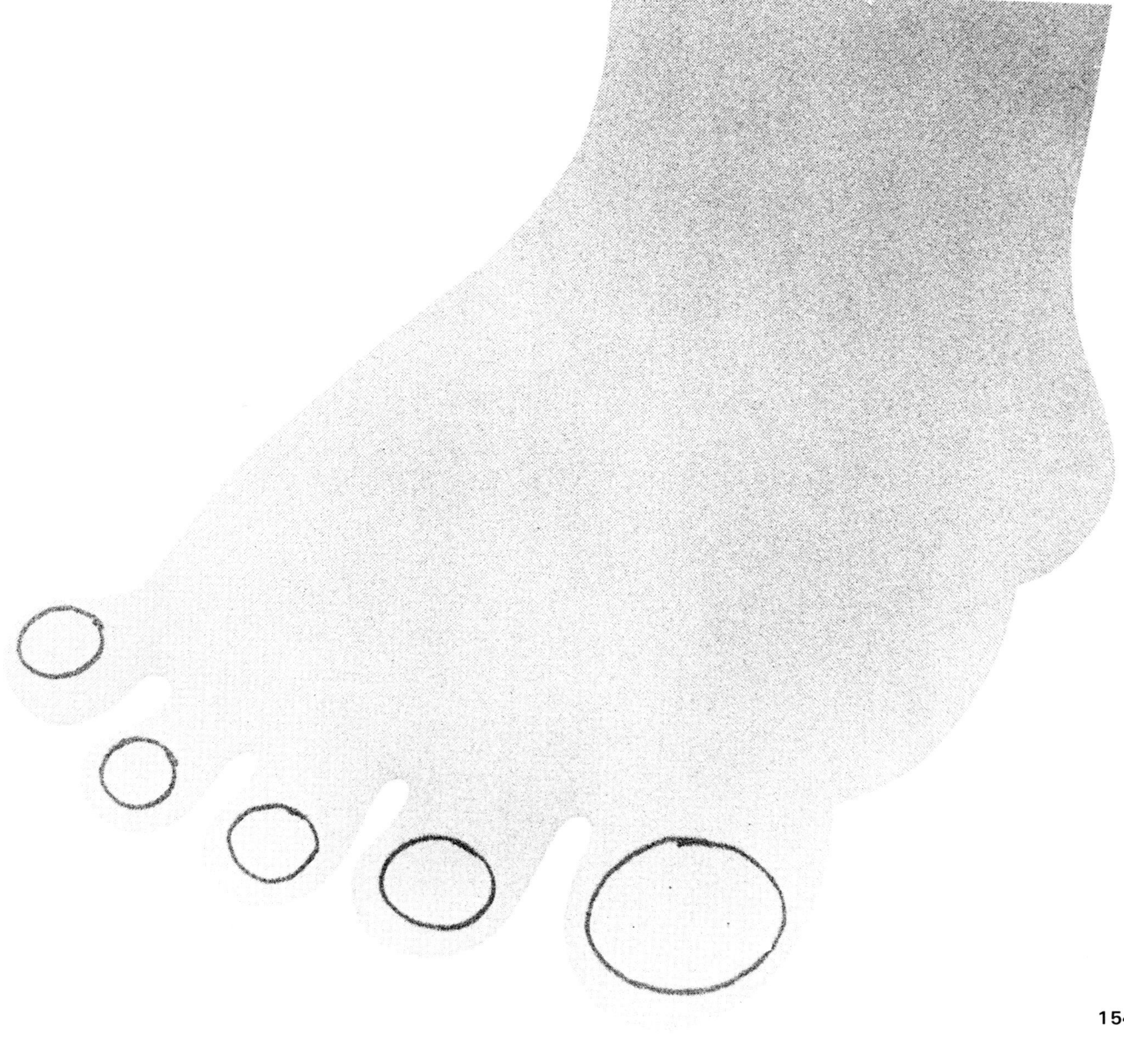

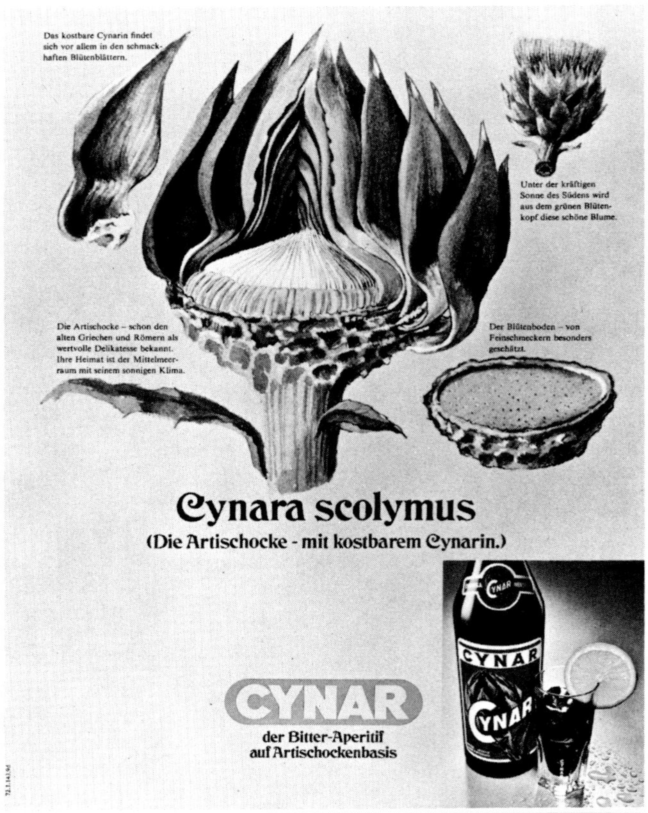
Das kostbare Cynarin findet sich vor allem in den schmackhaften Blütenblättern.
Unter der kräftigen Sonne des Südens wird aus dem grünen Blütenkopf diese schöne Blume.
Die Artischocke – schon den alten Griechen und Römern als wertvolle Delikatesse bekannt. Ihre Heimat ist der Mittelmeerraum mit seinem sonnigen Klima.
Der Blütenboden – von Feinschmeckern besonders geschätzt.
Cynara scolymus
(Die Artischocke - mit kostbarem Cynarin.)
CYNAR
der Bitter-Aperitif
auf Artischockenbasis

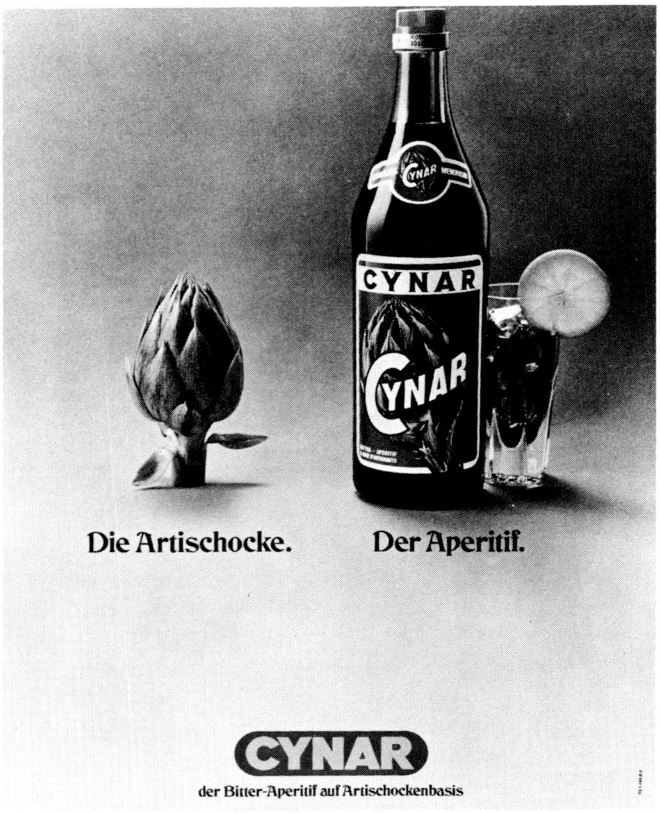
CYNAR
Die Artischocke.
Der Aperitif.
CYNAR
der Bitter-Aperitif auf Artischockenbasis

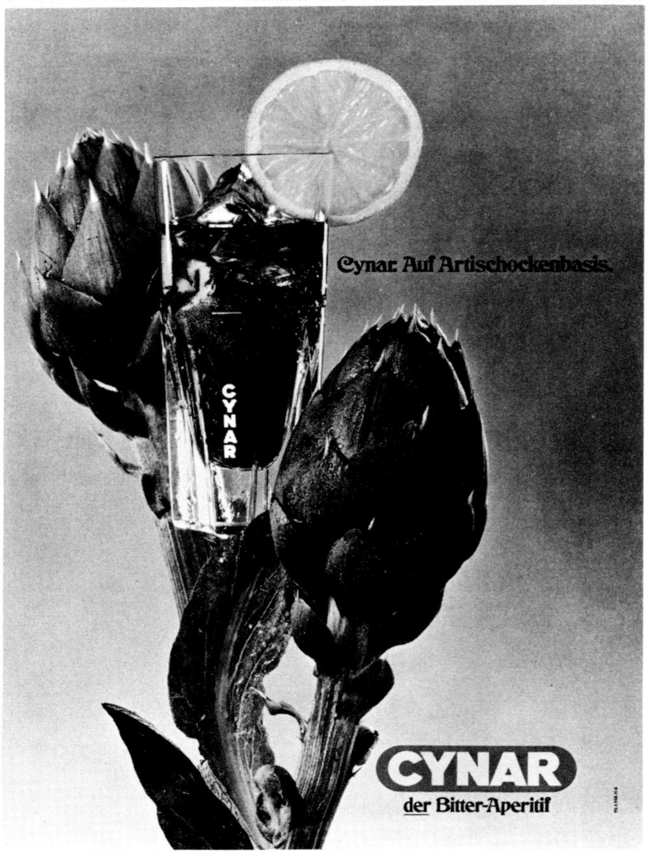
Cynar. Auf Artischockenbasis.
CYNAR
CYNAR
der Bitter-Aperitif

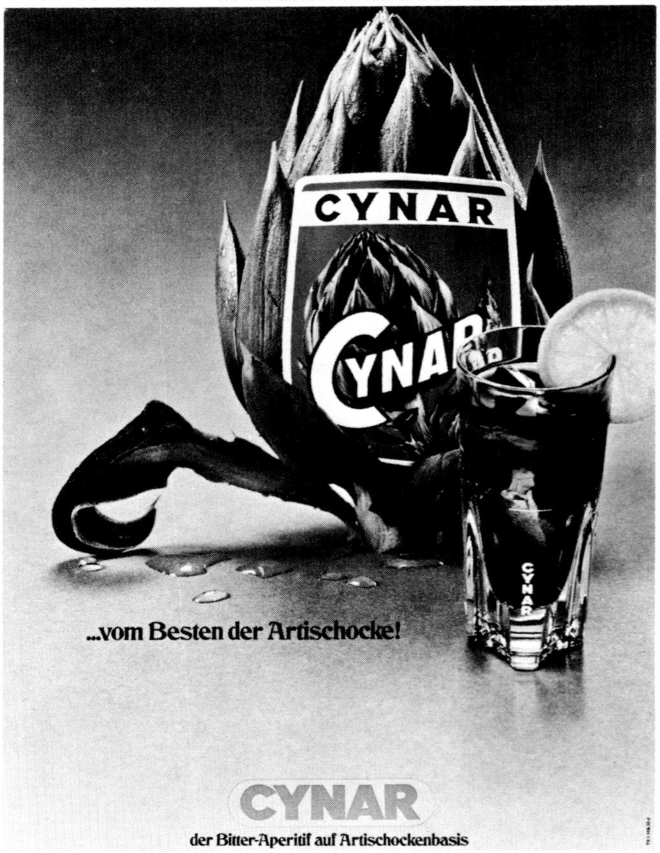
CYNAR
...vom Besten der Artischocke!
CYNAR
der Bitter-Aperitif auf Artischockenbasis

155-158
Dr. Rudolf Farner AG BSR Entrant
J. Schwerzmann Art Director
J. Tappich Photographer
Cynar S. A. Mendrisio Client

"THE BRASS MONKEY IS WORTH TWO AIRCRAFT CARRIERS IN THE CORAL SEA."
HEUBLEIN

THE BRASS MONKEY RETURNS.
The Drink That Defeated The Japanese Imperial Secret Service.
A Great Untold Story Of W.W.II.
HEUBLEIN COCKTAILS

WAS THE BRASS MONKEY A WOMAN?
LOYANA
HEUBLEIN

159-161
Stuart O. Bresner Entrant
Tony Garcia Photographer
Tinker Dodge & Delano Agency
Heublein Client

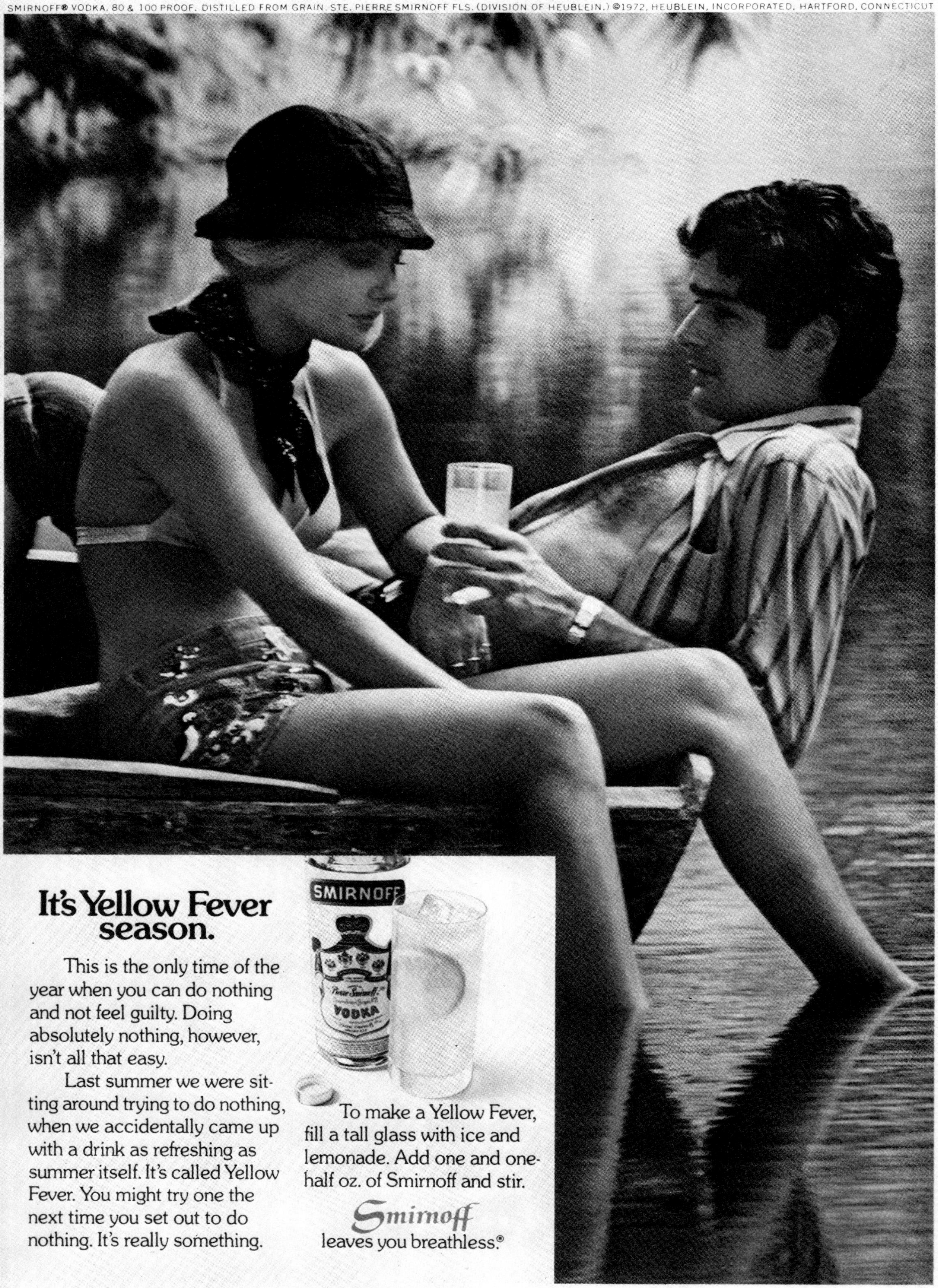
SMIRNOFF® VODKA. 80 & 100 PROOF. DISTILLED FROM GRAIN. STE. PIERRE SMIRNOFF FLS. (DIVISION OF HEUBLEIN.) ©1972, HEUBLEIN, INCORPORATED, HARTFORD, CONNECTICUT
It's Yellow Fever season.
This is the only time of the year when you can do nothing and not feel guilty. Doing absolutely nothing, however, isn't all that easy.
Last summer we were sitting around trying to do nothing, when we accidentally came up with a drink as refreshing as summer itself. It's called Yellow Fever. You might try one the next time you set out to do nothing. It's really something.
SMIRNOFF
VODKA
To make a Yellow Fever, fill a tall glass with ice and lemonade. Add one and one-half oz. of Smirnoff and stir.
Smirnoff
leaves you breathless®

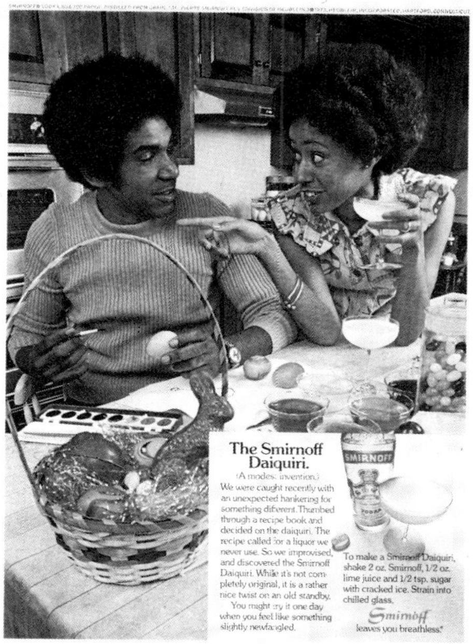

The Smirnoff Daiquiri.
(A modest invention.)
We were caught recently with an unexpected hankering for something different. Thumbed through a recipe book and decided on the daiquiri. The recipe called for a liquor we never use. So we improvised, and discovered the Smirnoff Daiquiri. While it's not completely original, it is a rather nice twist on an old standby.
You might try it one day when you feel like something slightly newfangled.
To make a Smirnoff Daiquiri, shake 2 oz. Smirnoff, 1/2 oz. lime juice and 1/2 tsp. sugar with cracked ice. Strain into chilled glass.
Smirnoff
leaves you breathless.

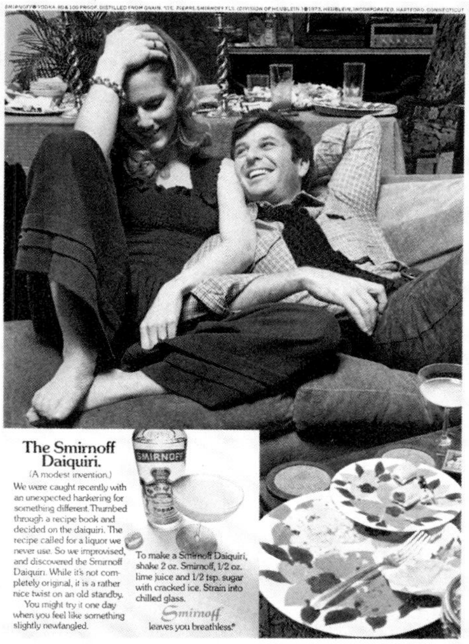

The Smirnoff Daiquiri.
(A modest invention.)
We were caught recently with an unexpected hankering for something different. Thumbed through a recipe book and decided on the daiquiri. The recipe called for a liquor we never use. So we improvised, and discovered the Smirnoff Daiquiri. While it's not completely original, it is a rather nice twist on an old standby.
You might try it one day when you feel like something slightly newfangled.
To make a Smirnoff Daiquiri, shake 2 oz. Smirnoff, 1/2 oz. lime juice and 1/2 tsp. sugar with cracked ice. Strain into chilled glass.
Smirnoff
leaves you breathless.

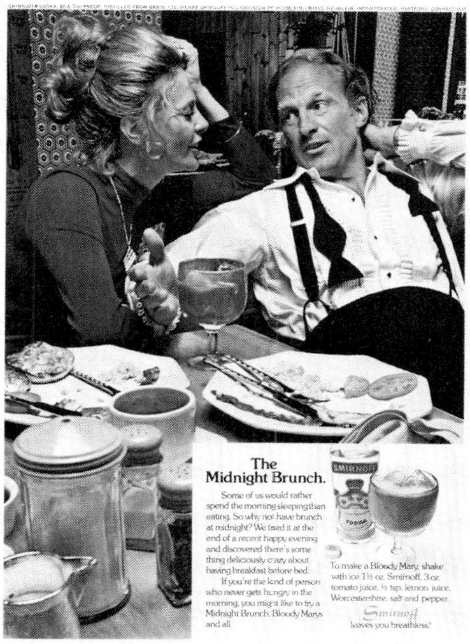

The Midnight Brunch.
Some of us would rather spend the morning sleeping than eating. So why not have brunch at midnight? We tried it at the end of a recent happy evening and discovered there's something deliciously crazy about having breakfast before bed.
If you're the kind of person who never gets hungry in the morning, you might like to try a Midnight Brunch. Bloody Marys and all.
To make a Bloody Mary, shake with ice 1½ oz. Smirnoff, 3 oz. tomato juice, ½ tsp. lemon juice, Worcestershire, salt and pepper.
Smirnoff
leaves you breathless.

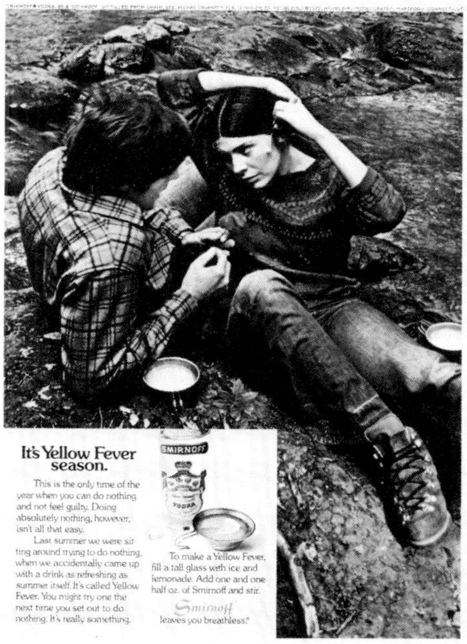

It's Yellow Fever season.
This is the only time of the year when you can do nothing and not feel guilty. Doing absolutely nothing, however, isn't all that easy.
Last summer we were sitting around trying to do nothing, when we accidentally came up with a drink as refreshing as summer itself. It's called Yellow Fever. You might try one the next time you set out to do nothing. It's really something.
To make a Yellow Fever, fill a tall glass with ice and lemonade. Add one and one half oz. of Smirnoff and stir.
Smirnoff
leaves you breathless.

162-166
Stuart O. Bresner Entrant
Bill Stettner Photographer
Tinker Dodge & Delano Agency
Heublein-Smirnoff Client

fine arts
Utica
Utica
by J.P. Stevens
fine arts
Utica
Sheets Towels Blankets
Sheets Towels Blankets

167

"Let's go take a look at the new house," your dad said.
When you got there, it didn't look like much.
You were anxious to see your bedroom.
But when your dad pointed it out to you, it was just a bunch of boards you could walk through.
Your dad was pretty excited, though.
He started explaining to you how a house was built.
It seemed to take him forever.
Probably because this workman with a funny hat on kept making silly jokes.
One time your father asked him if the shingles he ordered had come yet.
"No," the man said, "but I've got the shakes."
And they both laughed a lot.
Then your dad put his arm around you and asked if you had any questions.
"When can I go to the bathroom?" you asked.
And you'll never forget his reply.
"Can you wait about three months, son?"
Remember that day? We do.
Because in a way, we were there, too.
You see, over the years, we've helped thousands of families build their first houses.
We're the Great Savings Banks of Connecticut. 68 mutual savings banks helping people in savings and in loans, in mortgages and in life insurance.
The Great Savings Banks
For great moments, like these.

168

"Go peddle your papers, son."
You laughed.
You'd been getting up at the crack of dawn for months, trudging all over town.
And now, after putting away $14 worth of pennies, nickles and dimes in the savings account your father had opened for you, you'd finally earned it.
Your first two-wheeler.
It was bright red with balloon tires and a swell coaster brake.
Even had a neat American flag attached to the handlebars.
Your father went along with you to pick it up.
And when you pulled the wad of $1 bills out of your pocket, you don't know who was the proudest of all.
Then you finally had the bike out the door.
The old man who owned the shop walked out with you.
As you got on the bike for the first time, you heard him tell your father, "Someday that boy of yours is going to be a real wheeler-dealer."
Remember that day?
We do.
You see, in a way, we helped you get your route on the road.
We're the Great Savings Banks of Connecticut. 68 mutual savings banks helping people in savings and in loans, in mortgages and in life insurance.
LUGGAGE and BICYCLE REPAIRS
The Great Savings Banks
For great moments like these.

169

"I think you're going to like this one," he said.
"We'd better like it," you thought, as you followed your mother and father up to the front door.
It must've been the millionth house you'd seen that day.
It wasn't a bad house.
In fact, it was kind of cute.
"A perfect first home," the real estate guy called it.
You followed your parents around.
And you watched your father go through his house inspection routine.
First, he flushed all the toilets.
Then he marched down to the cellar and kicked the oil burner a couple of times.
Meanwhile, your mother was running her finger over all the sills and looking at your father.
Then you found yourself back in the living room.
The people had a fire going.
You sat there staring into it, and listened to your father talk on and on about the neighborhood, the schools, mortgages and taxes.
You were getting itchy.
You kept saying, "I want to go home."
And then all of a sudden it dawned on you… you already were.
We think we know what it was like that day.
Because in a way, we were there, too.
You see, over the years we've helped thousands of families move into their first homes, and their second homes, and their third homes for that matter.
We're the Great Savings Banks of Connecticut.
68 mutual savings banks helping people in savings and in loans, in mortgages and in life insurance.
The Great Savings Banks
For great moments, like these.

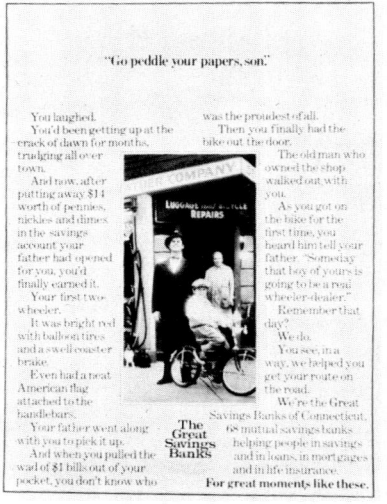

170

167
Al Margino, Lou Grasso Entrants
George Hamill Photographer
NR Promotions Agency
Foray Art Studios Studio
J. P. Stevens & Co., Inc. Client

168-170
Hill, Holliday, Connors, Cosmopulos Entrants
Dick Pantano, Stavros Cosmopulos Art Directors
Connecticut Savings Banks Client

171-174
Gennaro Trainello Entrant
Richard Hutnick Art Director
Mario Sapinaro Photographer
Waterman Advertising Agency
Sterling Regal Studio
Piedmont Industries Client

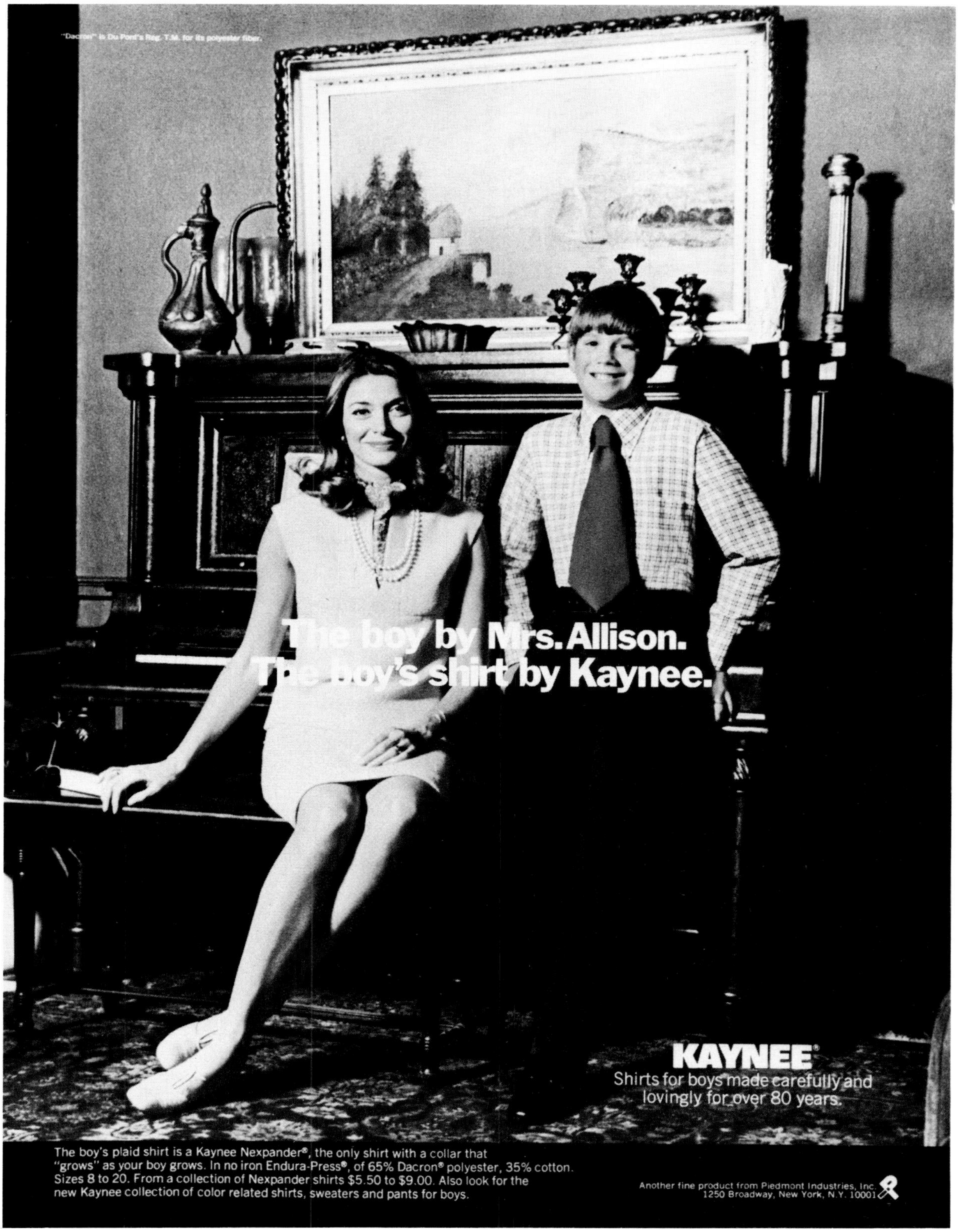
"Dacron" is Du Pont's Reg. T.M. for its polyester fiber.
The boy by Mrs. Allison.
The boy's shirt by Kaynee.
KAYNEE
Shirts for boys made carefully and lovingly for over 80 years.
The boy's plaid shirt is a Kaynee Nexpander®, the only shirt with a collar that "grows" as your boy grows. In no iron Endura-Press®, of 65% Dacron® polyester, 35% cotton. Sizes 8 to 20. From a collection of Nexpander shirts $5.50 to $9.00. Also look for the new Kaynee collection of color related shirts, sweaters and pants for boys.
Another fine product from Piedmont Industries, Inc.
1250 Broadway, New York, N.Y. 10001

171

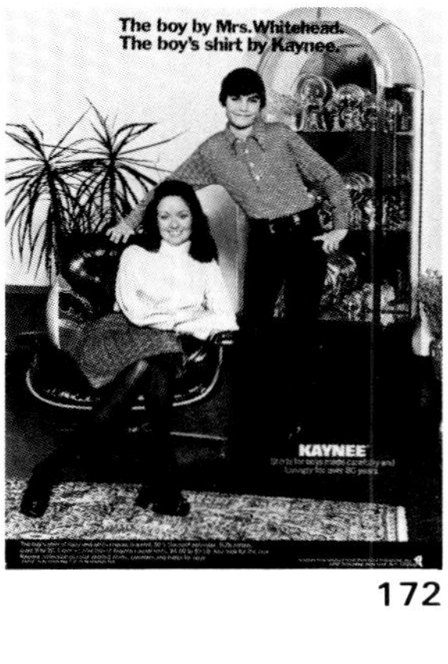
The boy by Mrs. Whitehead.
The boy's shirt by Kaynee.
KAYNEE

172

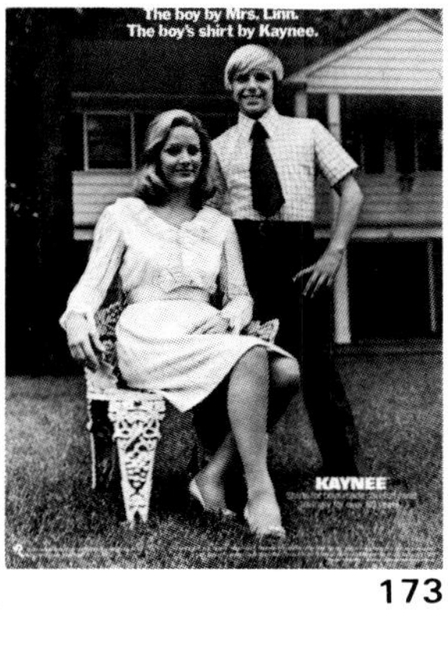
The boy by Mrs. Linn.
The boy's shirt by Kaynee.
KAYNEE

173

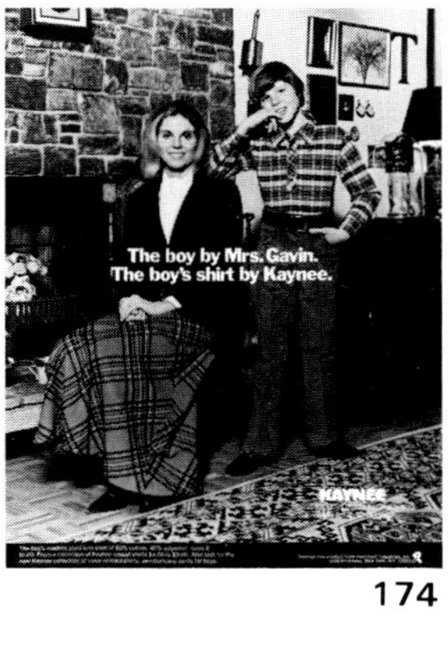
The boy by Mrs. Gavin.
The boy's shirt by Kaynee.
KAYNEE

174

175

176

GATSBY TIMES
THE ESSENCE OF THE 20'S IN SPORTSWEAR FOR THE 70'S
GATSBY

GATSBY TIMES
THE ESSENCE OF THE 20'S IN SPORTSWEAR FOR THE 70'S
GATSBY

When Ocie Durell peels them, she takes a long time.
She also pickets every 25 years.
Why do we keep her on?
Ocie Durell is our Comstock Peach lady. And she did walk out on us once. Back in the fifties, some efficiency people turned the plant upside down trying to speed things up. They didn't realize that good peach pie filling can't be rushed. But Ocie did. And that's exactly why we keep her on.
She's nobody's fool when it comes to peaches. She knows the best pie peach is the Elberta freestone. And she can spot a false blush a mile away. Because if the peach is wrinkled near the stem end, that peach was picked too green. And though a golden blush may develop, the ripe flavor never will. That might fool some folks (including those efficiency people) but not Ocie.
Anyway, getting back to those efficiency people, the young whippersnapper in charge raced around the plant so fast, Ocie suggested he get roller skates. Finally, in a last ditch effort to get our ladies going faster, he started clanging an iron pipe. That was the last straw. Our ladies got ready to walk out. Ocie, however, refused to go without finishing her peaches. Then, with the last peach, she picked up a picket sign and led the ladies out.
It wasn't long before the fruit piled up, and it was plain to see that the efficiency people were better talkers than peelers. They cleared out, lock, stock and pipe-clanger, and we pleaded with Ocie and her friends to come back. Thank goodness they agreed.
Our recipe for peach pie is on the label. And here are some of Ocie's secrets for our pie filling:
1. Add vinegar and glaze a bird, ham or leg of lamb.
2. Heat with maple syrup and top pancakes or french toast.
3. Mash with sweet potatoes, cinnamon and bake.
4. Add to diced chicken and almonds and spoon over rice.
5. Pour over a sponge cake for ice-box cake.
6. Mix with tapioca and orange rind and pour into pastry tarts.
7. Make an upside-down cake.
The only way we could wangle these ideas out of Ocie was to promise her some new ones. So please send your favorite recipe for using peach pie filling to Comstock, Box 267, Newark, N.Y. We'll gather them all together (giving credit where it's due) and send you a copy.
We also make apple, blueberry, and cherry pie fillings. They're not in Ocie's department, but they each have a persnickety old lady of their own keeping an eye on things. And, these ladies sell more pie fillings than anybody else.
We're grateful to them. Especially to Ocie. Who, to this day, keeps that piece of iron pipe hanging on the wall. Just to remind us who knows what.
Comstock
peach
PIE FILLING
BORDEN
Comstock. The pie filling made by persnickety old ladies.

Comstock Cherry Pie Filling has more cherry per ounce than the other two leading brands.*
But Harriet Foster says that's only half the story.
29¢
OFF ANY CAN OF COMSTOCK'S PIE FILLING
cherry
PIE FILLING
BORDEN
Comstock. The pie filling made by persnickety old ladies.

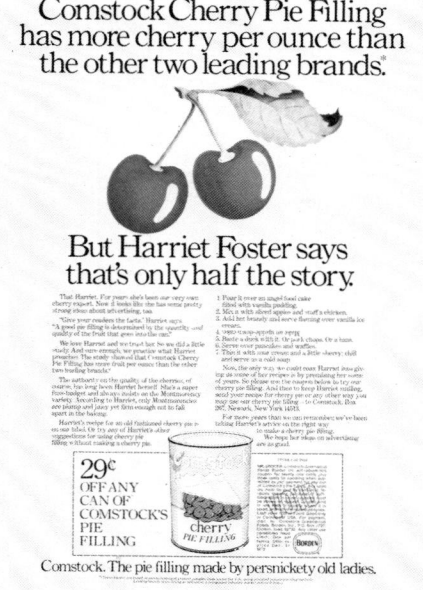

177

178

175-176
Graphics Group, Inc. Entrant
Larry Alten Art Director
Alten, Cohen, Naish Agency
Gatsby Mens Wear Client

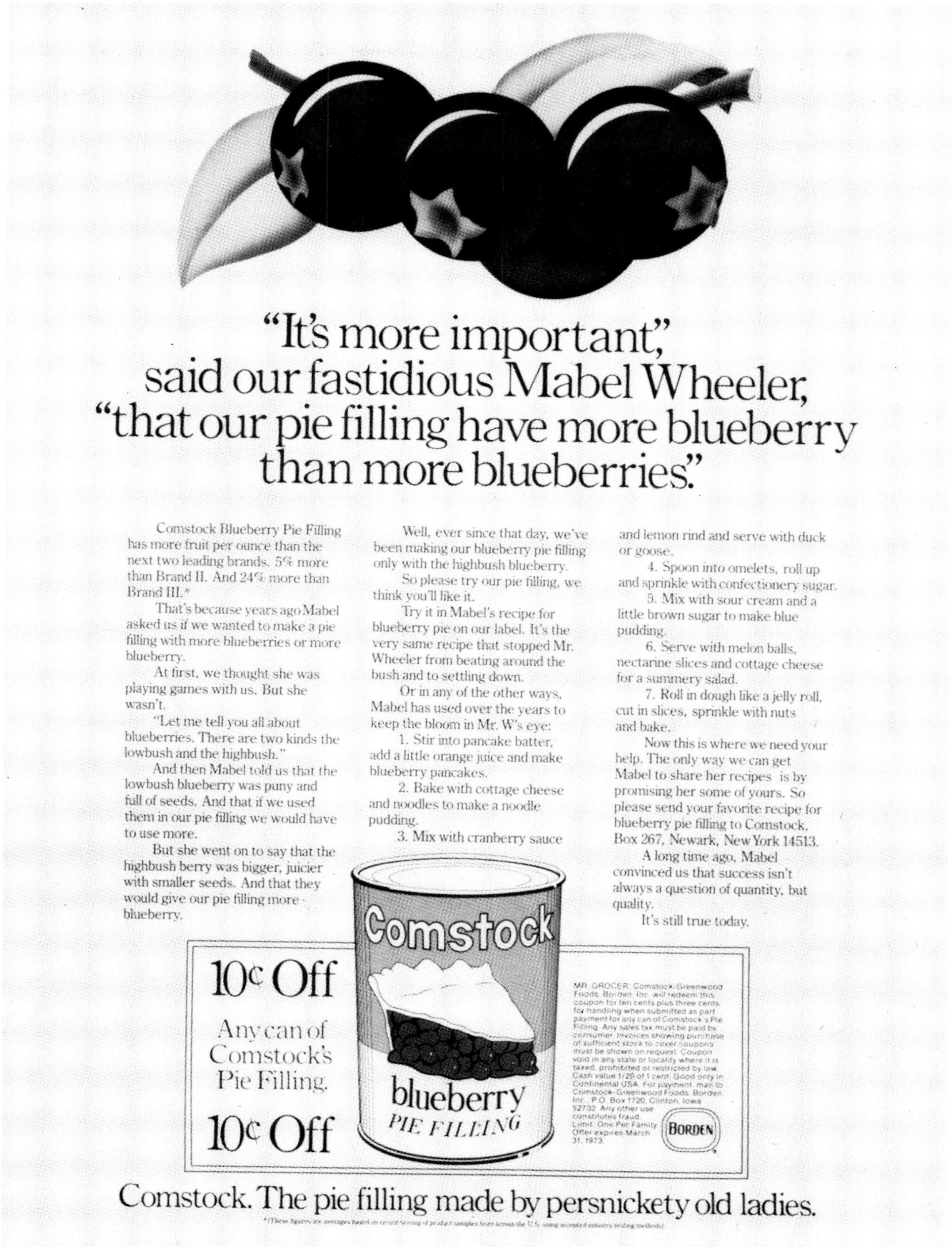

"It's more important," said our fastidious Mabel Wheeler, "that our pie filling have more blueberry than more blueberries."
Comstock Blueberry Pie Filling has more fruit per ounce than the next two leading brands. 5% more than Brand II. And 24% more than Brand III.*
That's because years ago Mabel asked us if we wanted to make a pie filling with more blueberries or more blueberry.
At first, we thought she was playing games with us. But she wasn't.
"Let me tell you all about blueberries. There are two kinds the lowbush and the highbush."
And then Mabel told us that the lowbush blueberry was puny and full of seeds. And that if we used them in our pie filling we would have to use more.
But she went on to say that the highbush berry was bigger, juicier with smaller seeds. And that they would give our pie filling more blueberry.
Well, ever since that day, we've been making our blueberry pie filling only with the highbush blueberry.
So please try our pie filling, we think you'll like it.
Try it in Mabel's recipe for blueberry pie on our label. It's the very same recipe that stopped Mr. Wheeler from beating around the bush and to settling down.
Or in any of the other ways, Mabel has used over the years to keep the bloom in Mr. W's eye:
1. Stir into pancake batter, add a little orange juice and make blueberry pancakes.
2. Bake with cottage cheese and noodles to make a noodle pudding.
3. Mix with cranberry sauce and lemon rind and serve with duck or goose.
4. Spoon into omelets, roll up and sprinkle with confectionery sugar.
5. Mix with sour cream and a little brown sugar to make blue pudding.
6. Serve with melon balls, nectarine slices and cottage cheese for a summery salad.
7. Roll in dough like a jelly roll, cut in slices, sprinkle with nuts and bake.
Now this is where we need your help. The only way we can get Mabel to share her recipes is by promising her some of yours. So please send your favorite recipe for blueberry pie filling to Comstock, Box 267, Newark, New York 14513.
A long time ago, Mabel convinced us that success isn't always a question of quantity, but quality.
It's still true today.
10¢ Off
Any can of Comstock's Pie Filling.
10¢ Off
Comstock
blueberry
PIE FILLING
MR. GROCER: Comstock-Greenwood Foods, Borden, Inc. will redeem this coupon for ten cents plus three cents for handling when submitted as part payment for any can of Comstock's Pie Filling. Any sales tax must be paid by consumer. Invoices showing purchase of sufficient stock to cover coupons must be shown on request. Coupon void in any state or locality where it is taxed, prohibited or restricted by law. Cash value 1/20 of 1 cent. Good only in Continental USA. For payment, mail to Comstock-Greenwood Foods, Borden, Inc., P.O. Box 1720, Clinton, Iowa 52732. Any other use constitutes fraud. Limit: One Per Family. Offer expires March 31, 1973.
BORDEN
Comstock. The pie filling made by persnickety old ladies.
*(These figures are averages based on recent testing of product samples from across the U.S. using accepted industry testing methods).

177-179
Allan Kaufman Entrant
Gayle Gleckler Art Director
Sagebrush Studio Illustrator
Tinker Dodge & Delano Agency
Borden: Comstock Client

ARM YOURSELF WITH SOMETHING LESS THAN IBM.
LESS COST.
LESS BULK.
LESS HEAT.
LESS WORK.
ITEL
CORPORATION

LET US REFRESH YOUR MEMORY.
ITEL
CORPORATION

WHEN THE OBVIOUS MOVE IS IBM, THE SMART MOVE IS ITEL.
ITEL
CORPORATION

HOW ITEL BECAME ONE OF IBM'S
BIGGEST CUSTOMERS
When it comes to building computers, nobody can beat IBM.
But when it comes to marketing these computer mainframes in the most financially attractive package, ITEL is the winner by a technical knockout. Because only ITEL can offer you a complete computer package including IBM System/370 with our technologically advanced peripherals. And here's the clincher:
ITEL lease terms range from 3 to 8 years, and savings can be as great as 60% of IBM rental.
Such savings typify our leasing expertise, which covers more than $1 billion of capital equipment, including railroad rolling stock, truck trailers, containers, tankers, 747 aircraft, and some $100 million in IBM 370s.
So, when you want advanced computer equipment on the best terms, call the Data Products Group at ITEL—the financial alternative to IBM.
ITEL
CORPORATION
One Embarcadero Center
San Francisco, California 94111
Phone: (415) 989-4220
...AND TOUGHEST COMPETITORS.

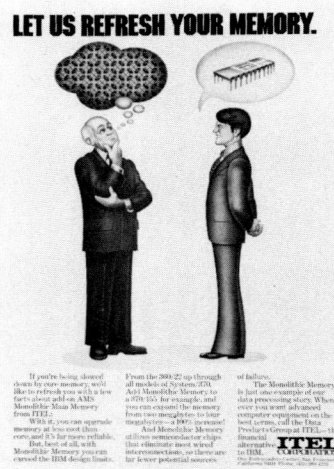

180-183
Forrest L. Sigwart Entrant
Ignacio Gomez Illustrator
Itel Corporation Client

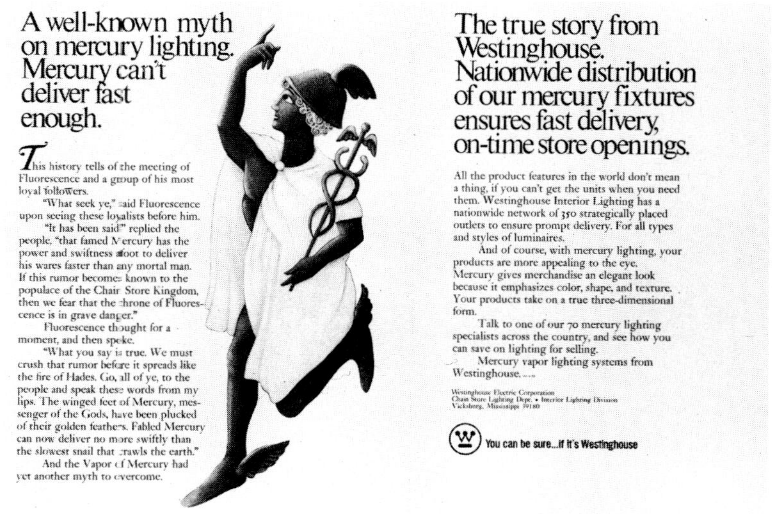

A well-known myth on mercury lighting. Mercury can't deliver fast enough.
This history tells of the meeting of Fluorescence and a group of his most loyal followers.
"What seek ye," said Fluorescence upon seeing these loyalists before him.
"It has been said," replied the people, "that famed Mercury has the power and swiftness afoot to deliver his wares faster than any mortal man. If this rumor becomes known to the populace of the Chain Store Kingdom, then we fear that the throne of Fluorescence is in grave danger."
Fluorescence thought for a moment, and then spoke.
"What you say is true. We must crush that rumor before it spreads like the fire of Hades. Go, all of ye, to the people and speak these words from my lips. The winged feet of Mercury, messenger of the Gods, have been plucked of their golden feathers. Fabled Mercury can now deliver no more swiftly than the slowest snail that crawls the earth."
And the Vapor of Mercury had yet another myth to overcome.
The true story from Westinghouse. Nationwide distribution of our mercury fixtures ensures fast delivery, on-time store openings.
All the product features in the world don't mean a thing, if you can't get the units when you need them. Westinghouse Interior Lighting has a nationwide network of 350 strategically placed outlets to ensure prompt delivery. For all types and styles of luminaires.
And of course, with mercury lighting, your products are more appealing to the eye. Mercury gives merchandise an elegant look because it emphasizes color, shape, and texture. Your products take on a true three-dimensional form.
Talk to one of our 70 mercury lighting specialists across the country, and see how you can save on lighting for selling.
Mercury vapor lighting systems from Westinghouse.
Westinghouse Electric Corporation
Chain Store Lighting Dept. • Interior Lighting Division
Vicksburg, Mississippi 39180
You can be sure...if it's Westinghouse

A well-known myth on mercury lighting. You need the Midas touch to pay for its high cost.
And it came to pass, that in his quest to protect his throne against the famed Vapor of Mercury, Fluorescence spoke to the people of the Land of the Chain Stores.
"Beware," he said, "of rash adventures among the mercury lights. For they will burden your hard-earned treasures with their high costs. It would surely take the golden touch of Midas, to meet the golden cost of Mercury."
And the people, fearful of losing their wealth, listened and believed. And, with the sun of each new day, this great Mercury Myth prevailed.
The true story from Westinghouse. Mercury saves you as much as 50%.
It takes only one-third as many mercury lamps to provide the same light levels as fluorescents. So, even though the initial cost of mercury units may be slightly higher, fewer lamps mean fewer luminaires, less installation. And added savings. Plus, mercury lamps last as much as 10,000 hours longer.
Our studies show that a 400-watt deluxe mercury system costs the same as a cool white fluorescent system of two-lamp heavy-duty *strip* luminaires. But the mercury system provides a far superior color quality to the products it is illuminating. To match the color quality of mercury, a CWX fluorescent system is needed. The cost of this system is 50 percent higher than mercury.
And mercury lighting makes products more appealing. It gives them an elegant look, because it emphasizes shape, color, and texture. And when the long lines of fluorescents are removed, emphasis is put on merchandise, not the ceiling.
Talk to one of our 70 mercury lighting specialists across the country and see how you can save on lighting for selling. Mercury vapor lighting systems from Westinghouse.
Westinghouse Electric Corporation
Chain Store Lighting Dept. • Interior Lighting Division
Vicksburg, Mississippi 39180
You can be sure...if it's Westinghouse

A well-known myth on mercury lighting. The Cyclops look. One style. No variety.
Long ago, in the great Land of the Chain Stores, Fluorescence, ruler and mortal among mortals, grew fearful of losing his crown to the famed Vapor of Mercury.
It seems that Mercury, long on the outside of the Chain Store Kingdom, yearned to spread his light within. And the followers of Fluorescence, hearing marvelous stories about Mercury, were restless.
"The wind," they said, "has whispered tales of the plentiful selection and styles of fixtures Mercury has to offer them."
They desired to see this great variety. But Fluorescence eased their doubts with words as soft and shining as satin.
"Hear not what the wind whispers," soothed the mortal ruler. "It is merely fantasy from the wanderer of wanderers. Let the truth be known. Mercury experiences no greater variety than the awesome Cyclops, who has but one single shape and appearance."
And the first of many Mercury myths was born.
The true story from Westinghouse. We offer designers a choice with our wide variety of luminaires.
Design possibilities with mercury are virtually limitless. The reduced number of lights creates a less cluttered ceiling. When the long lines of fluorescents are removed, ceilings appear higher, stores larger and more airy, and emphasis is put on the merchandise, not up toward the ceiling.
Westinghouse manufactures a complete line of fixtures for mercury vapor. The many styles to choose from include mercury rounds, squares, stockroom units, and recessed deep reveals for dramatic effect. As well as mercury lighting for parking areas, malls, and unloading docks.
And mercury lighting makes products more appealing. It gives them an elegant look, because it highlights shape and texture.
Talk to one of our 70 mercury lighting specialists across the country, and see how you can save on lighting for selling. Mercury vapor lighting systems from Westinghouse.
Westinghouse Electric Corporation
Chain Store Lighting Dept. • Interior Lighting Division
Vicksburg, Mississippi 39180
You can be sure...if it's Westinghouse

184-186
Marini, Climes & Guip, Inc. Entrant
Hugo DiZinno Art Director
Jackie Geyer Illustrator
Ketchum, MacLeod & Grove, Inc. Agency
Westinghouse Electric Corp. Client

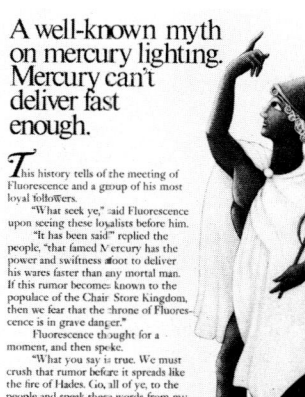

187

Plot Your Project-
From the Bottom Up
EAI makes your data do more. Because we've got a great new computer-controlled graphics system plus the software to make it work. Just feed your project information into the EAI 930 Graphics System and take your choice of a variety of special-purpose plots.
You can start, for instance, with contour plotting, based on surface variables. Then three-dimensionalize it for a perspective view. And go on to map out the entire tract.
Your plots are complete. A tract map, for instance, includes boundaries, line labels, bearing lines, distances and bearings . . . including the calculations. You can even have street names printed out.
Because there's a DATAPLOTTER® at the output end of the system, you get high-speed plotting. Variable, up to 16 inches per second. Even on curves. All in smooth, continuous lines with no "sawtooth" effect.
Built-in error detection protects your plot. Tape noise, dropouts, static electricity . . . anything that might generate errors stops the system. Until corrected.
You can play with the plot. Shrink it, stretch it or rotate it around any point you choose. Or do the same with any area inside the plot. It's yours to command.
Plot on a multitude of materials with a variety of instruments. You have complete flexibility—from your systems and software to your peripheral equipment. Our EAI 930 Graphics System delivers total computer-aided drafting. And now a quick note or phone call will bring you the whole picture. From the bottom up.
Electronic Associates, Inc.
185 Monmouth Parkway
West Long Branch, New Jersey 07764
(201) 229-1100

188

The Plotter With an Eagle Eye.
It Stops Errors Dead.
The unique DATAPLOTTER 430®. It's truly the only plotter that spots and stops drawing errors before they're made. Because it's the single plotter with an eagle-eyed predetector.
When our machine senses an anomaly coming up—say, some hash or a bit of bit drop-out—the pen lifts. Everything comes to a dead halt. Even physical disturbances and bothersome static electricity are caught before they are committed to paper. All automatically.
Then, when you're ready to start again, you just back up to the trouble spot. The DATAPLOTTER 430 picks up from there. You won't be able to tell where the retracing began. And you've saved your drawing, your manpower plus your computer time, something you couldn't possibly do on any other plotter.
This predetector is just one feature that engineers find valuable in applications such as mapping, subdivision platting, topo and contour drawing. Even on linen or for direct reproduction masters. Needless to say, we have program packages ready and waiting for these and other applications.
So we think it might just prove your foresight to learn about all the other advanced features we've built into the DATAPLOTTER 430. For instance, resolution to .001 inches, smooth-line curve-tracing speeds of 16 ips, compatibility with a wide variety of computer systems, not to mention new EAI computer-based civil-engineering systems. And we could go on, but that's what brochures are for. Write for ours. Or better yet, why don't you telephone us for more information today.
Electronic Associates, Inc.
185 Monmouth Parkway
West Long Branch, New Jersey 07764
(201) 229-1100

189

How to Deal a Straight Hand
With a Crooked Deck
Use one of EAI's new card readers. We have three that will accept and process cards that would jam most other readers.
Our readers use a "vacuum finger" that can pick even a badly damaged card off the bottom of the stack and feed it to the friction transport system. Which, in turn, moves it at a constant speed past the read station.
And there our synchronous logic data sensing and verification method ensures accurate reading of card information that's misregistered by up to half a column.
Fiber-optics light distribution at the read station makes the readers even more accurate. Light from the single light source is channeled to all parts of the card uniformly, so all the photo-transistor sensing elements receive light of precisely the same intensity. This also makes it possible to provide self-diagnosing circuitry, so maintenance problems are simplified immeasurably.
The three EAI card readers are the CR-300, the CR-600, and the MR-300. The first two read punched cards only (at 300 and 600 cards per minute). The MR-300 Optical Mark Reader reads punched *and* pencil-marked cards—in any order. Mix them up—it's all the same to the MR-300. What's more, it can look at an erasure and ignore it, while correctly registering a weak little pencil mark. Smudges don't bother it, nor does any variation in card color.
Incidentally, if the description of these readers seems familiar, it may be because you recognize the GDI reader line. We took over that line, added our own touch of engineering finesse, and we now bring the readers to you under our own name.
For the straight story on the good deal in card reading, please write or phone us today.
Electronic Associates, Inc.
185 Monmouth Parkway
West Long Branch, New Jersey 07764
(201) 229-1100.

John isn't a squealer.
John had a real racket going for him. And what an operator. He never missed a chance to leak, squeak, whistle or squeal.
Preliminary investigation uncovered his toilet tank and the incriminating evidence. It was a routine case of an out-dated ball cock, corroded and leaking.
When Fluidmaster arrived on the scene, John immediately quieted down. Because unlike old-fashioned ball cocks with tank float and arm, Fluidmaster controls toilet tank water hydraulically. Working with water pressure, instead of against it. So shut-off is fast and positive. No leaks. No squeaks. No whistles.
Write today for full details. Before your John is found guilty of disturbing the peace.
FLUIDMASTER, INC.
1800 Via Burton
Anaheim, Calif. 92805
Manufacturer of the Model 100, 200 and 400.

190

FLUIDMASTER
Give old John something to shut him up.
Leaks. Squeaks. Whistles.
Chances are, your toilet is trying to tell you it has a serious problem. Simple, but serious. An out-dated, corroded ball cock that leaks.
There are different ways to deal with toilet noise. Pretend to ignore it. Have some sleepless nights. Fuss and cuss a lot (not recommended where children are present).
Or, stop toilet noise once and for all. With Fluidmaster.
Fluidmaster eliminates the old-fashioned tank float and arm. And, because Fluidmaster operates hydraulically, it works with water pressure, for fast, positive shut-off.
Write today for full details. And give John the silent treatment.
FLUIDMASTER, INC.
1800 Via Burton
Anaheim, Calif. 92805
Manufacturer of the Model 100, 200 and 400.

191

John doesn't say much anymore.
John used to be pretty obnoxious. He'd leak, squeak and sometimes even whistle.
He never knew when to shut up. Or shut off, for that matter. John had no self-control.
Finally, someone got smart and looked into his toilet tank. The problem was obvious. John's insides consisted of an ancient ball cock, rod arm and float ball. Complete with corrosion and leaks.
Once rid of those, John got what was coming to him: a Fluidmaster. The simple hydraulic device that eliminates old-fashioned rod arm, float ball, and other corrosive parts. To work with water pressure, instead of against it. For fast, positive shut-offs. And no leaks, squeaks, or whistles.
Write today for full details. And change your John into the strong, silent type.
FLUIDMASTER, INC.
1800 Via Burton
Anaheim, Calif. 92805
Manufacturer of the Model 100, 200 and 400.

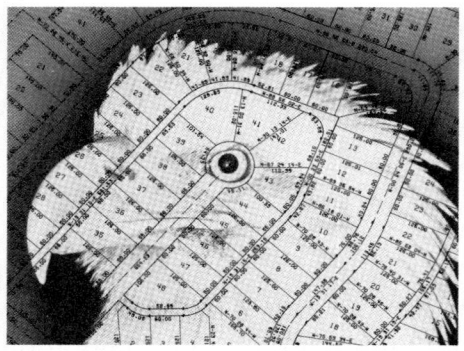

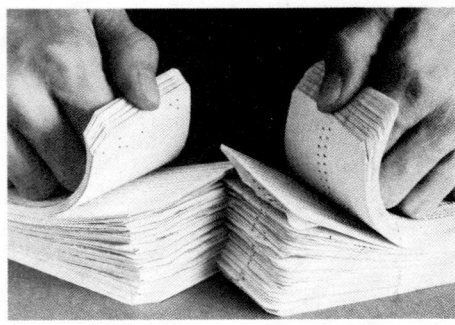

192

187-189
Gerald Clarke, Inc. Entrant
Arthur Celedonia Art Director
Gerald Kraus Photographer
Electronic Associates, Inc. Client

190-192
Cochrane Chase & Co. Entrant
Bill Fortune, Don Stone, Ralph Lenac Art Directors
Fluidmaster, Inc. Client

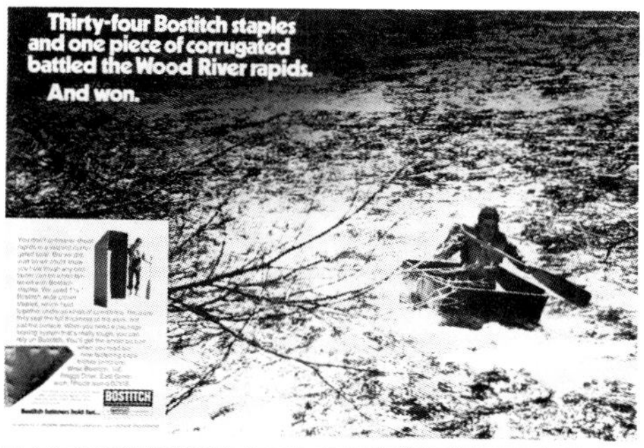

Thirty-four Bostitch staples and one piece of corrugated battled the Wood River rapids.
And won.
BOSTITCH

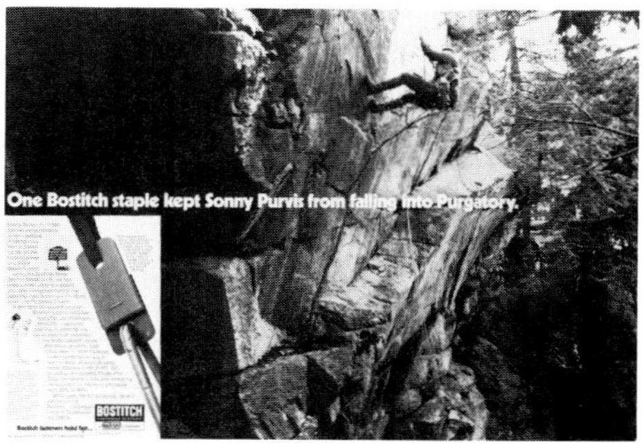

One Bostitch staple kept Sonny Purvis from falling into Purgatory.
BOSTITCH

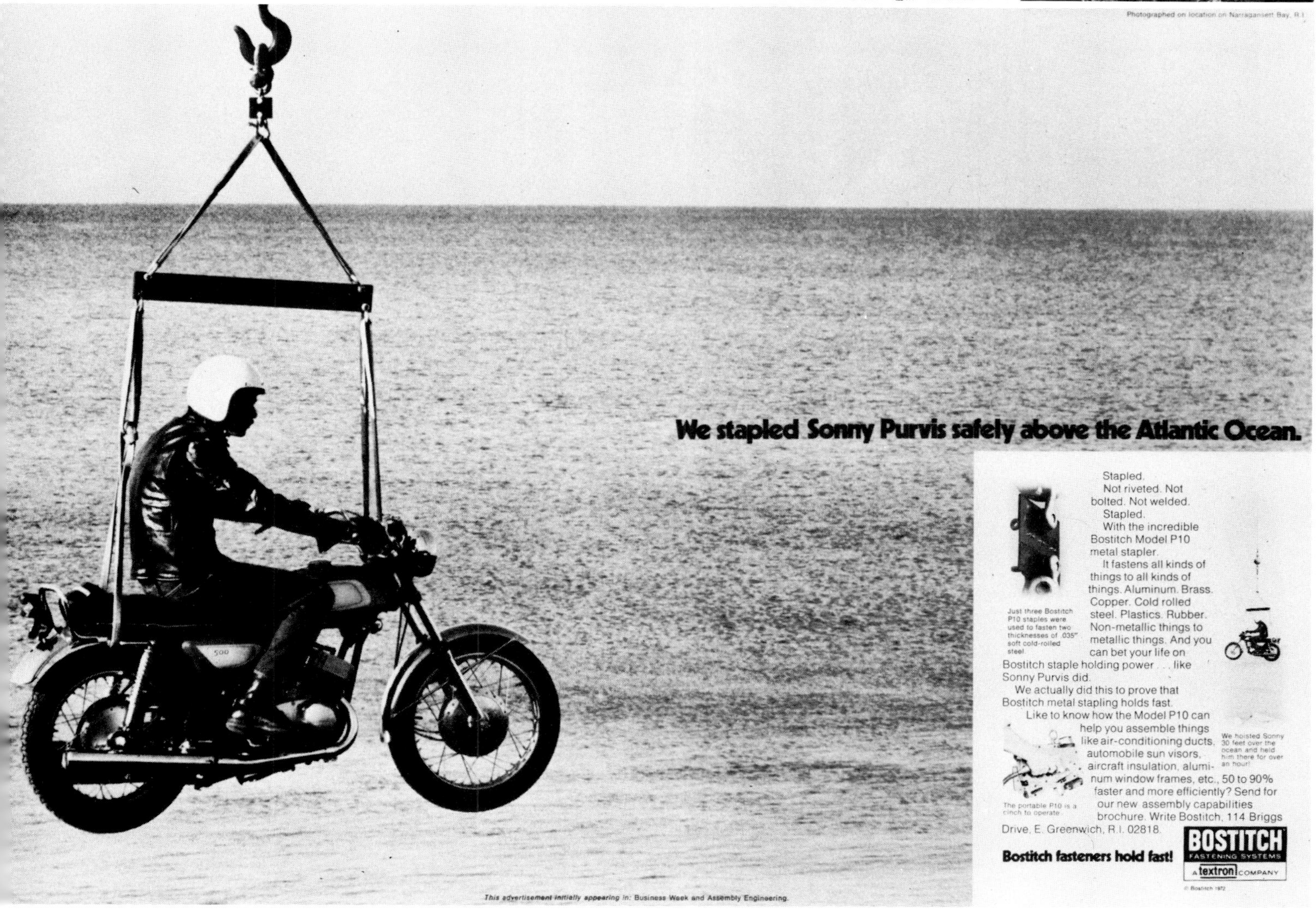

Photographed on location on Narragansett Bay, R.I.
We stapled Sonny Purvis safely above the Atlantic Ocean.
Stapled.
Not riveted. Not bolted. Not welded.
Stapled.
With the incredible Bostitch Model P10 metal stapler.
It fastens all kinds of things to all kinds of things. Aluminum. Brass. Copper. Cold rolled steel. Plastics. Rubber. Non-metallic things to metallic things. And you can bet your life on Bostitch staple holding power . . . like Sonny Purvis did.
We actually did this to prove that Bostitch metal stapling holds fast.
Like to know how the Model P10 can help you assemble things like air-conditioning ducts, automobile sun visors, aircraft insulation, aluminum window frames, etc., 50 to 90% faster and more efficiently? Send for our new assembly capabilities brochure. Write Bostitch, 114 Briggs Drive, E. Greenwich, R.I. 02818.
Just three Bostitch P10 staples were used to fasten two thicknesses of .035" soft cold-rolled steel.
We hoisted Sonny 30 feet over the ocean and held him there for over an hour!
The portable P10 is a cinch to operate.
Bostitch fasteners hold fast!
BOSTITCH
FASTENING SYSTEMS
A textron COMPANY
© Bostitch 1972
This advertisement initially appearing in: Business Week and Assembly Engineering.

193-195
Creamer, Trowbridge, Case & Basford Entrant
Tyler Smith Art Director
John Swanberg Photographer
Bostitch Inc. Client

196 197 198

199 200 201

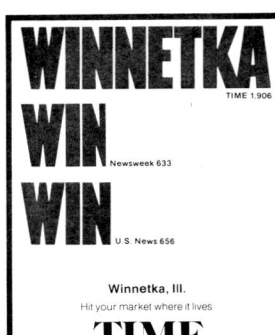

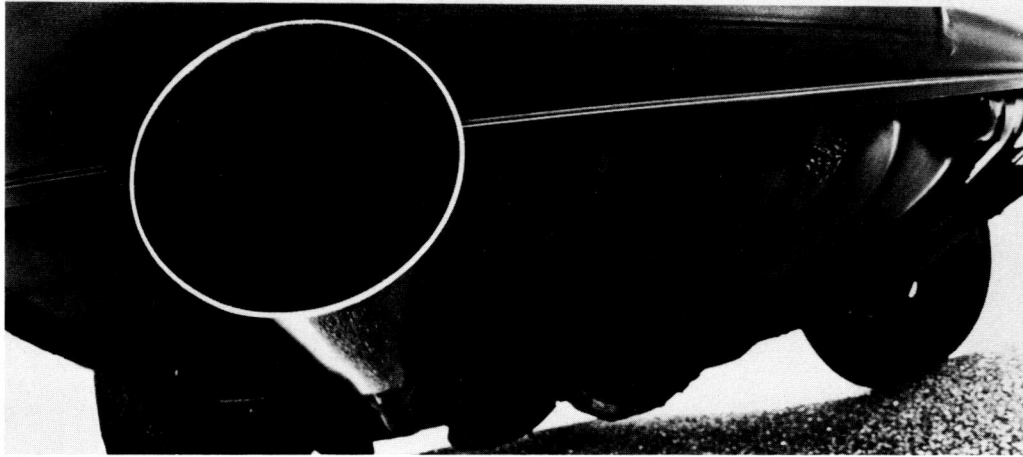

SUMMIT
TIME 1,793
SUM
Newsweek 750
SU
U.S. News 492
Summit, N.J.
Hit your market where it lives
TIME

WINNETKA
TIME 1,906
WIN
Newsweek 633
WIN
U.S. News 656
Winnetka, Ill.
Hit your market where it lives
TIME

WILMETTE
TIME 2,673
WIL
Newsweek 851
WI
U.S. News 766
Wilmette, Ill.
Another example of circulation concentration where it counts.
TIME

LOSALTOS
TIME 2,695
LOSA
Newsweek 1,078
LOS
U.S. News 887
Los Altos, Calif.
Another example of circulation concentration where it counts.
TIME

WESTPORT
TIME 2,539
WEST
Newsweek 1,105
WE
U.S. News 627
Westport, Conn.
Another example of circulation concentration where it counts.
TIME

PALOALTO
TIME 6,577
PALO
Newsweek 3,168
PA
U.S. News 1,682
Palo Alto, Calif.
Another example of circulation concentration where it counts.
TIME

Under the octane gun.
The first step, and beyond. How we can help.
Despite the recent spate of lead-free and low-lead gasolines, nobody knows at this point exactly what the octane numbers and composition of future gasolines will be.
Especially for the markets in the mid-1970's.
Should your basic gasoline production method put the emphasis on catalytic reforming, alkylation, or isomerization? Or some combination of them?
Nobody knows definitely. But refiners must evaluate all of the alternatives now.
We think we can help.
Out of our experience with virtually every refinery process, we've developed the Foster Wheeler refinery optimization method, using our IBM 360/50.
With it we investigate alternatives quickly and exhaustively. Focus on the really important aspects. Study the effect of various combinations. And from the almost infinite number of possibilities pick *the* optimum scheme.
But our refinery optimization method is only the beginning.
Nobody else has the across-the-board evaluation capabilities that we have in-house. Which includes our fully-integrated fired heater and equipment divisions.
It means we can plug in up-to-the-minute labor, material and operating costs for all your calculations. Which means you get realistic investment and operating costs on which to base your decision.
And of course our people have the experience to take your project through to completion without interruption. From process search through plant startup.
It all adds up to true single source capability, a guarantee of confidentiality, and fast delivery. So that you can be producing your new gasoline months earlier.
The octane gun.
Perhaps we can help you get out from under it, sooner.
Foster Wheeler Corporation, 666 Fifth Avenue, New York, N.Y. 10019
FOSTER WHEELER

202

We've developed a certain sensitivity to NOx emissions.

203

196-201
Walter Lefmann Entrant
Time, Inc. Client

202-204
Ian Gunn Entrant
Ray Fedynak Art Director
Ken Ambrose Photographer
Muller Jordan Herrick Inc. Agency
Foster Wheeler Corporation Client

205

Container Corporation of America
Situation/Need
Optimization
Product-Packaging-Consumer Linkup
Beyond Packaging

CS-72-28
ss a result, purchasers of the newest
'oster Wheeler boilers are a lot less
ensitive on the subject of pollution.
' wasn't easy. And we didn't do it
vernight.
n fact, when we began our NOx in-
estigations some years ago, there
as no satisfactory mobile system
or sniffing out the kind of informa-
on we needed.
we worked with instrument makers
develop one that could help us
uild an inventory of reliable field
ata, based on continuous flue gas
nalysis.
date, NOx tests have been run on
over 50 different steam generators, our own and others. Units ranging up to 850 MW, firing a variety of fuels under varying operating conditions.
To this information, we've added extensive data generated in combustion test facilities in the U.S., Europe and the Far East. Where we're able to vary an infinite number of air-fuel-temperature ratios. All carefully correlated to our field experience.
From the results of all these tests, we now know how to accurately predict the amount of NOx for any given plant design.
And, more importantly, how to reduce it substantially.
This knowledge can be applied to your existing boiler. Or if you're adding capacity, it can come already designed into your new Foster Wheeler unit.
Either way, we can help eliminate one of the more noxious things in your life.
Foster Wheeler Corporation, 666 Fifth Avenue, New York, N.Y. 10019
FOSTER WHEELER

CS-72-22
American Electric Power puts on the fifth of the world's largest double reheat boilers.
It's the Appalachian Power Company's Unit No. 2 at the John E. Amos plant, West Virginia.
This makes five Foster Wheeler coal-fired, 800 MW once-through boilers AEP has put in service since 1969.
They're the five largest units of their kind. And a lot more.
Each of the boilers was delivered and started up on time, and has achieved some remarkable availability records.
For example, Unit No. 1 at the Amos plant (the most recent to complete a year of service) has racked up a boiler operating availability record of over 96% in its first year of operation.
This kind of success is largely the result of Foster Wheeler's design approach.
Like the way we design our multiple series passes to limit super-critical fluid enthalpy inbalance.
It's done by frequent mixing between passes. Which results in furnace circuits that are extremely stable and insensitive to heat absorption upsets.
Small wonder that on initial start-up, AEP's Amos #1 ramped up to full load without delay.
And after coming down only for turbine strainer removal, it immediately went back on line and operated for 120 consecutive days at full power.
Quite a break-in record. And even then, it took a bolt of lightning to shut it down.
Makes us proud to be an American Electric Power supplier.
Foster Wheeler Corporation, 666 Fifth Avenue, New York, NY 10019
FOSTER WHEELER

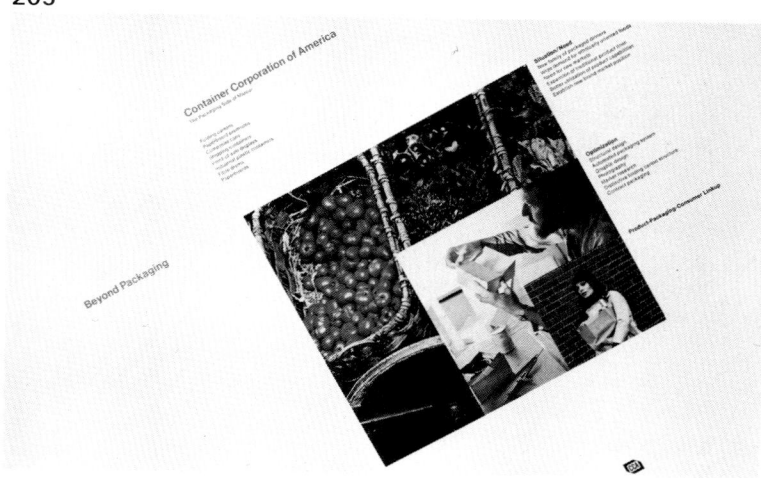

204

205
Container Corp. of America Entrant
Robert Loth, Bill Bonnell III Art Directors
Rudy Jansu, Tony Kelly, Rhodes Patterson Photographers

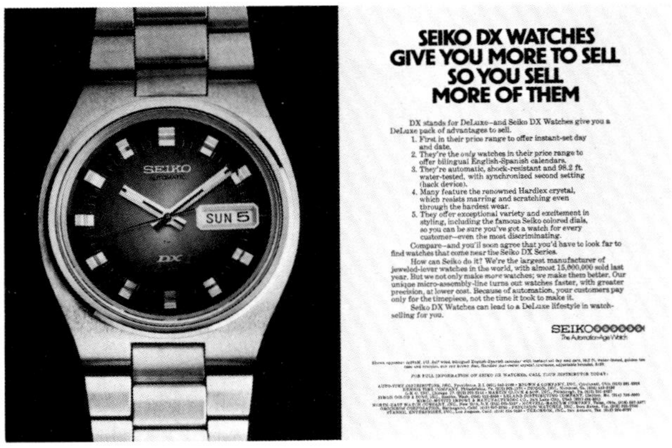
SEIKO DX WATCHES
GIVE YOU MORE TO SELL
SO YOU SELL
MORE OF THEM
DX stands for DeLuxe—and Seiko DX Watches give you a DeLuxe pack of advantages to sell.
1. First in their price range to offer instant-set day and date.
2. They're the only watches in their price range to offer bilingual English-Spanish calendars.
3. They're automatic, shock-resistant and 98.2 ft. water-tested, with synchronized second setting (hack device).
4. Many feature the renowned Hardlex crystal, which resists marring and scratching even through the hardest wear.
5. They offer exceptional variety and excitement in styling, including the famous Seiko colored dials, so you can be sure you've got a watch for every customer—even the most discriminating.
Compare—and you'll soon agree that you'd have to look far to find watches that come near the Seiko DX Series.
How can Seiko do it? We're the largest manufacturer of jeweled-lever watches in the world, with almost 15,000,000 sold last year. But we not only make more watches; we make them better. Our unique micro-assembly-line turns out watches faster, with greater precision, at lower cost. Because of automation, your customers pay only for the timepiece, not the time it took to make it.
Seiko DX Watches can lead to a DeLuxe lifestyle in watch-selling for you.
SEIKO
The Automation-Age Watch

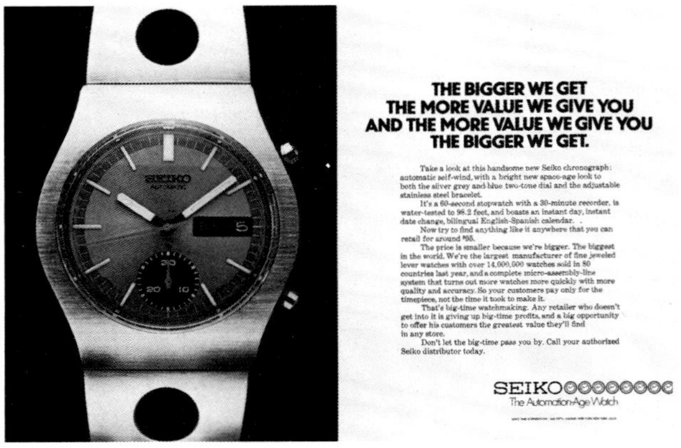
THE BIGGER WE GET
THE MORE VALUE WE GIVE YOU
AND THE MORE VALUE WE GIVE YOU
THE BIGGER WE GET.
Take a look at this handsome new Seiko chronograph: automatic self-wind, with a bright new space-age look to both the silver grey and blue two-tone dial and the adjustable stainless steel bracelet.
It's a 60-second stopwatch with a 30-minute recorder, is water-tested to 98.2 feet, and boasts an instant day, instant date change, bilingual English-Spanish calendar.
Now try to find anything like it anywhere that you can retail for around $95.
The price is smaller because we're bigger. The biggest in the world. We're the largest manufacturer of fine jeweled lever watches with over 14,000,000 watches sold in 80 countries last year, and a complete micro-assembly-line system that turns out more watches more quickly with more quality and accuracy. So your customers pay only for the timepiece, not the time it took to make it.
That's big-time watchmaking. Any retailer who doesn't get into it is giving up big-time profits, and a big opportunity to offer his customers the greatest value they'll find in any store.
Don't let the big-time pass you by. Call your authorized Seiko distributor today.
SEIKO
The Automation-Age Watch

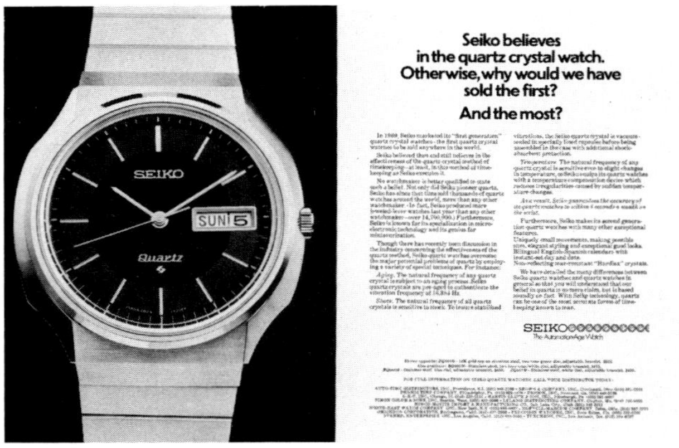
Seiko believes
in the quartz crystal watch.
Otherwise, why would we have
sold the first?
And the most?
SEIKO
The Automation-Age Watch

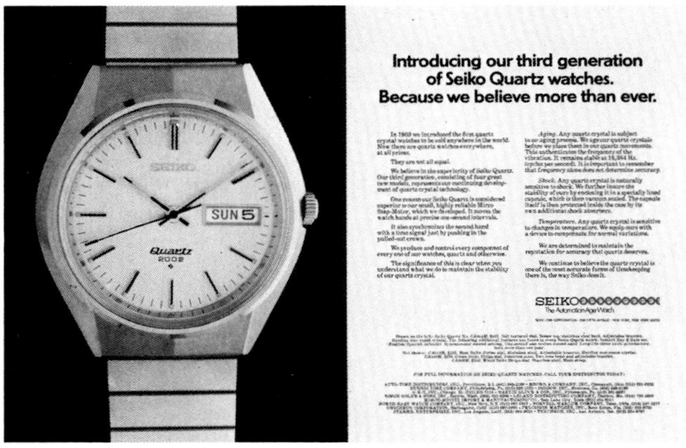
Introducing our third generation
of Seiko Quartz watches.
Because we believe more than ever.
SEIKO
The Automation-Age Watch

206-209
David Wenman Entrant
Jay Irving Photographer
AC&R Advertising Agency
Seiko Watches Client

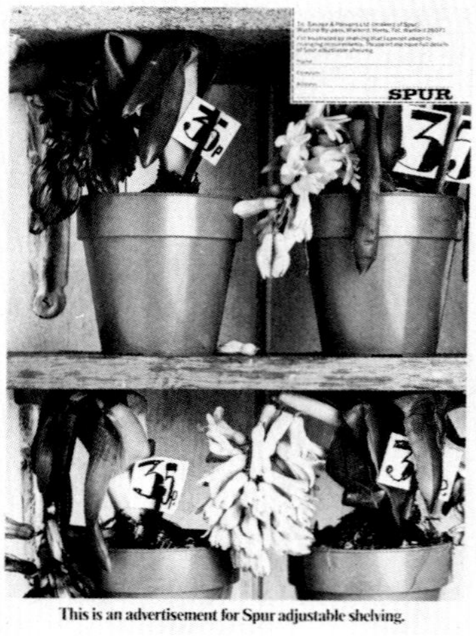
SPUR
This is an advertisement for Spur adjustable shelving.

210-211
Roger Deakin Entrant
Nigel Hemsley Art Director
David Cripps Photographer
Interlink Advertising Ltd. Agency
Savage & Parsons Ltd. Client

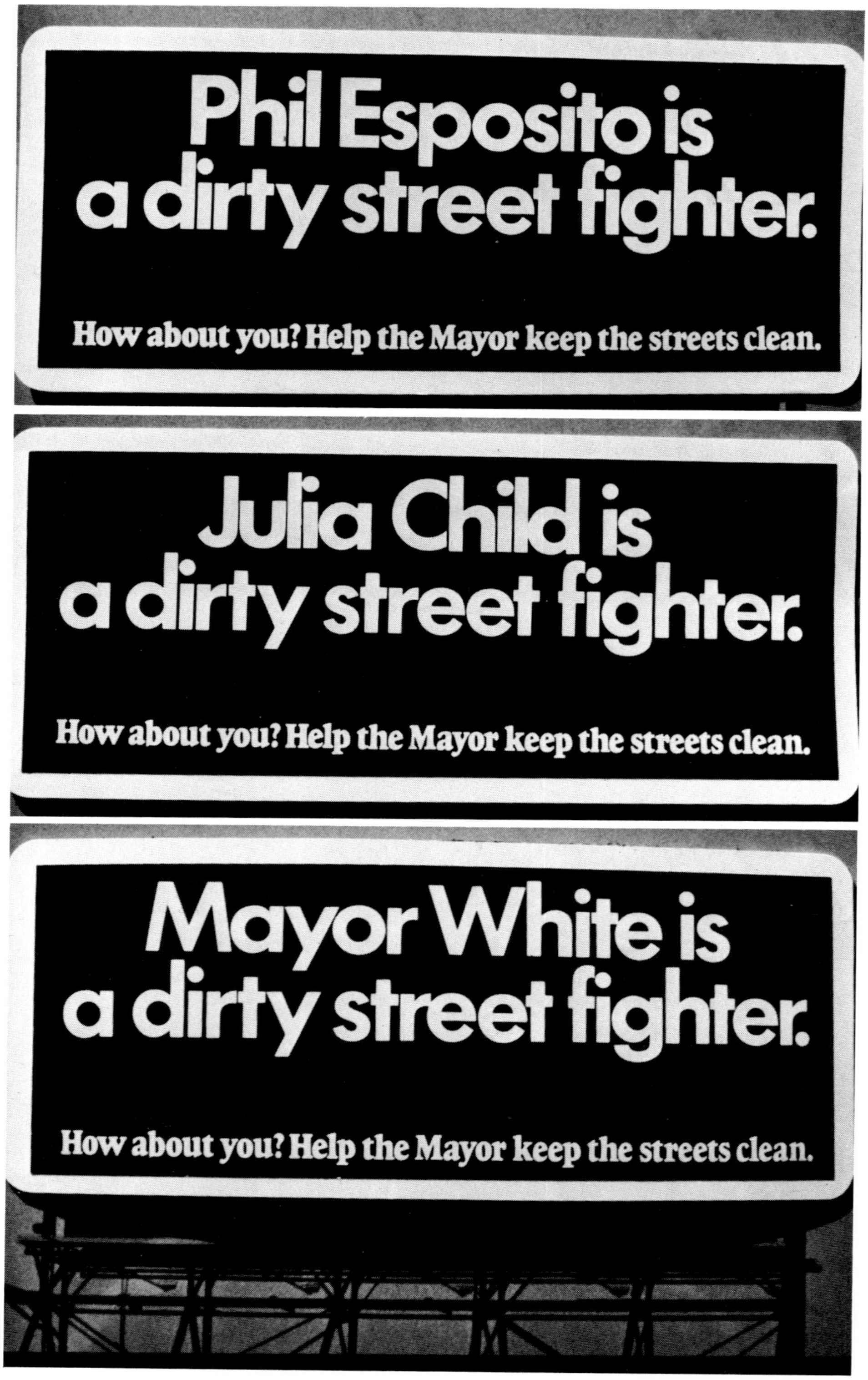
Phil Esposito is a dirty street fighter.
How about you? Help the Mayor keep the streets clean.
Julia Child is a dirty street fighter.
How about you? Help the Mayor keep the streets clean.
Mayor White is a dirty street fighter.
How about you? Help the Mayor keep the streets clean.

212-214
Hill, Holliday, Connors, Cosmopulos Entrants
Stavros Cosmopulos, Dick Pantano Art Directors
City of Boston Client

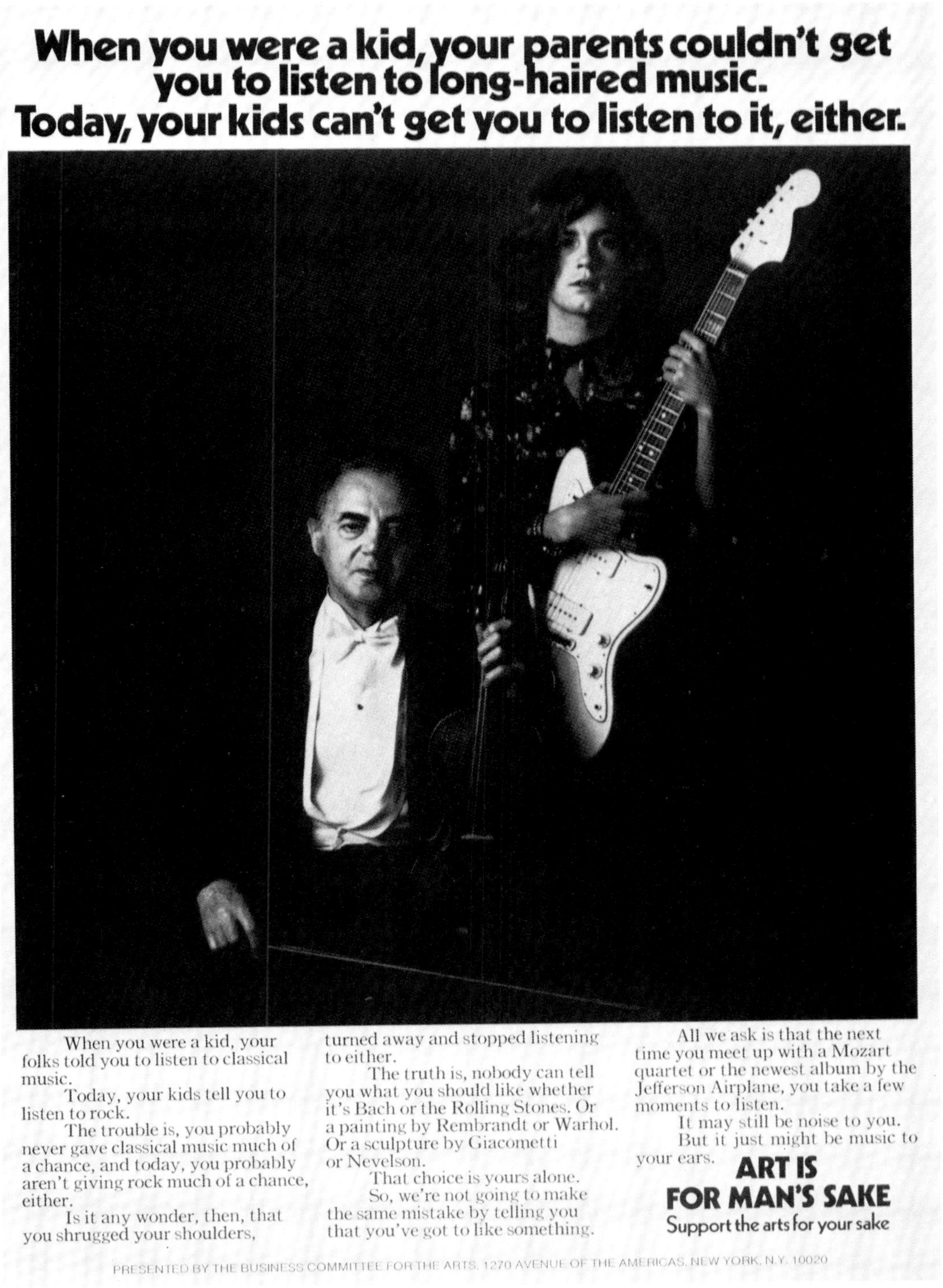
When you were a kid, your parents couldn't get you to listen to long-haired music.
Today, your kids can't get you to listen to it, either.
When you were a kid, your folks told you to listen to classical music.
Today, your kids tell you to listen to rock.
The trouble is, you probably never gave classical music much of a chance, and today, you probably aren't giving rock much of a chance, either.
Is it any wonder, then, that you shrugged your shoulders, turned away and stopped listening to either.
The truth is, nobody can tell you what you should like whether it's Bach or the Rolling Stones. Or a painting by Rembrandt or Warhol. Or a sculpture by Giacometti or Nevelson.
That choice is yours alone.
So, we're not going to make the same mistake by telling you that you've got to like something.
All we ask is that the next time you meet up with a Mozart quartet or the newest album by the Jefferson Airplane, you take a few moments to listen.
It may still be noise to you.
But it just might be music to your ears.
ART IS FOR MAN'S SAKE
Support the arts for your sake
PRESENTED BY THE BUSINESS COMMITTEE FOR THE ARTS, 1270 AVENUE OF THE AMERICAS, NEW YORK, N.Y. 10020

215
Frank McCallum Entrant
Norman Kantor Writer
Arnold Beckerman Photographer
Lee King & Partners Agency
Business Committee for the Arts Client

216

217

Påsen.
Får vi presentera Påsen – en skräppåse som du kan ha i båten.
Påsar, den här eller vilken som helst, är nämligen bra att ta med sig skräp i medan man åker omkring i vår ömtåliga skärgård. Det gäller faktiskt bara att skaffa några innan man ger sig ut.
Och det är mycket svårt att komma ihåg.
Det vill säja, om man inte hör till dom tusentals människor som redan skurit sig i foten på glasskärvor.
Eller är en av alla dom som fått böta några hundra kronor för nerskräpning. (All nerskräpning, även obetydlig, är straffbar.)
Eller helt enkelt är en vanlig skattebetalare. (Renhållningen i Sverige går löst på hundratals skattemiljoner om året.)
För dom människorna är det rena barnleken att komma ihåg att lägga med några tompåsar i matsäcken för en båtutflykt.
När vi nu ändå är i farten – tänk också på några andra saker: Stör inte häckande fågel, håll hunden kopplad när du går iland. Var försiktig med eld och gör inte upp brasor på släta fina klipphällar (berget spricker och blir fult). Sköt om skärgården, så sköter skärgården om dig.
Och framför allt. Släng inget skräp i havet. Havet har det svårt nog ändå.
Släng skräpet i Påsen. På nästa sida kan du läsa om var du enklast blir av med den.
Tänk på att täta påsar kan vara farliga för barn.
Håll Skärgården Ren

218

219

IF
a Legislator
really cares
about
you...
He'll fight
for you!
T. C. YIM
CARES!

Treasure

220

Conspiracy

221

Celebration
175

222

Summit meeting

223

Easter parade

224

Action play

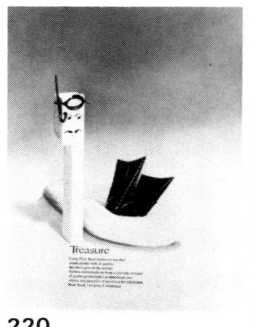

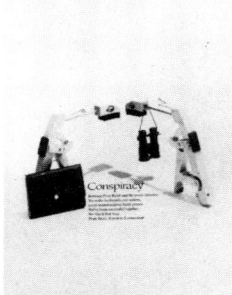

225

216-217
Hera Annonsbyrå AB Entrant
Lars Melander Art Director
Keep the Archipelago Clean Committee Client

218-219
David Reed Entrant
Reed/Kaina Adv. Inc. Agency
Rep. T.C. Yim Client

220-225
Marc Dorian, Inc. Entrant
Marc Dorian Art Director
Dick Ross Photographer
Pratt-Read Client

226

FLY POEM
FLIES
SPREAD
DISEASE
KEEP YOURS DONE UP
Stephen Morris

THE
STORY
OF
THE
FLORIDA
BAR

227

MR. ERNEST.
En komedi av Oscar Wilde
FOLKAN

228

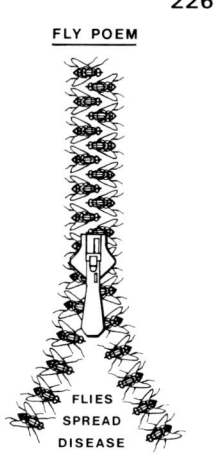

226
Stephen Morris
Entrant

227
Robert L. Foss Entrant
Sam Westbrook Art Director
Marta Legeckis Illustrator
Ampersand Studios Studio
The Florida Bar Client

228
Lars Melander
Entrant
Folkan
Client

Wat gaan we zeggen?

Wat gaan we zeggen als de baby's van nu ons over 20 jaar vragen: Vader, moeder, waarom hebben jullie ons in godsnaam op deze wereld gezet... op deze kapotgemaakte, onbewoonbaar geworden wereld waarvan de grond vergiftigd is, waarvan water en lucht verpest zijn, waar groen en bloemen vervangen zijn door beton en asfalt, waar we samen moeten leven in propvolle steden, vol vuil en stank en lawaai...

Wat gaan we dan zeggen?

Zo hebben wij het niet gewild?

Nee, maar we hebben het wèl zo gemaakt.

Door teveel te willen èn door met tevelen te zijn.

Door steeds maar meer kinderen geboren te laten worden, die we straks afschepen met een uitzichtloze toekomst.

Laten we beginnen met kleine gezinnen als een noodzaak te zien.

Misschien, heel misschien dat we dan ooit uit de problemen komen.

Prof. Dr. J. A. C. de Kock van Leeuwen
directeur Nederlands Instituut
voor praeventieve geneeskunde TNO

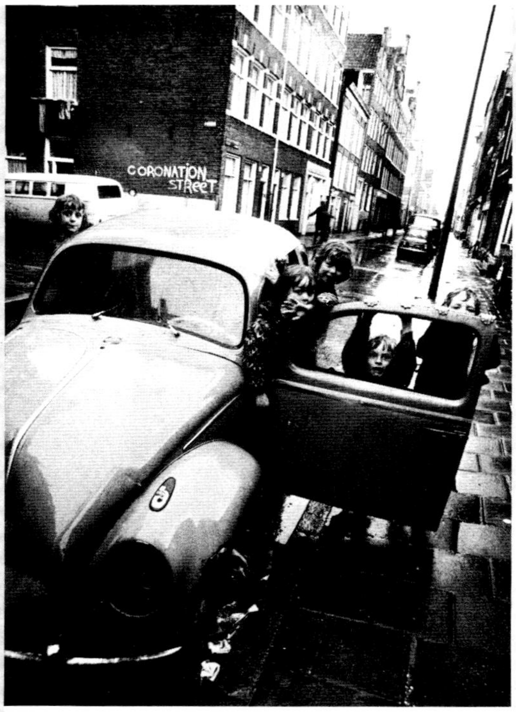
CORONATION STREET

**Veel te veel kinderen krijgen straks geen leven.
Geboortenbeperking is noodzaak.**

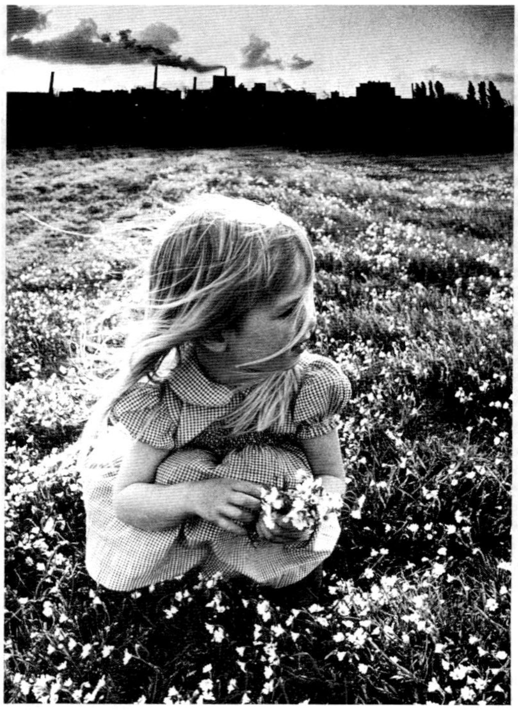

Zou niet ieder kind het (voor)recht moeten hebben madelieven te kunnen plukken, blij als dit meisje?

Maar als onze bevolking blijft doorgroeien, bloeien er straks alleen nog bloemen in de middenberm van autobanen.

Geboortenregeling is dan ook nodig.

En in elk gezin mogelijk.

Geen enkel kind behoeft meer een ongewild kind te zijn.

Wanneer ieder kind als gewenst kind ter wereld komt zijn we al op de goede weg.

Wanneer de bevolking niet gestabiliseerd wordt, zodat er een evenwicht ontstaat tussen geboorten- en sterftecijfers, worden de ontplooiingsmogelijkheden minder.

In de milieuhygiëne is nu reeds zichtbaar dat de grens aan het vermogen van de aarde om mensen een bestaan te verzekeren bereikt gaat worden.

Het twee-kinderengezin zal meer regel dan uitzondering moeten gaan worden.

Het bevolkingsvraagstuk moet nú worden opgelost.

Voor het welzijn van onze kinderen en hun kinderen.

Prof. Dr. A. A. Haspels
hoogleraar in de verloskunde en gynaecologie

**Veel te veel kinderen krijgen straks geen leven.
Geboortenbeperking is noodzaak.**

Onze generatie heeft enorme problemen te verwerken, problemen die we met ons allen onder ogen zullen moeten zien.

Ook problemen die we met ons allen zullen moeten oplossen, willen we nog een toekomst hebben.

Maar dan moeten we wèl één ding goed beseffen: al die problemen als natuurvernietiging, milieuafbraak, uitputting van grondstoffen, enz. worden oneindig veel zwaarder, zolang er steeds meer mensen bijkomen op deze wereld.

Dan moeten we tegelijkertijd goed beseffen dat méér dan twee kinderen per gezin het steeds moeilijker maken oplossingen te vinden, oplossingen die dringend noodzakelijk zijn, willen onze kinderen en kleinkinderen nog een menswaardig bestaan krijgen.

Twee kinderen per gezin is een grens, een evenwicht.

Alleen als wij nú dat evenwicht kunnen vinden, kan de volgende generatie weer vooruit.

Paula Wassen-van Schaveren
lid Eerste Kamer D'66

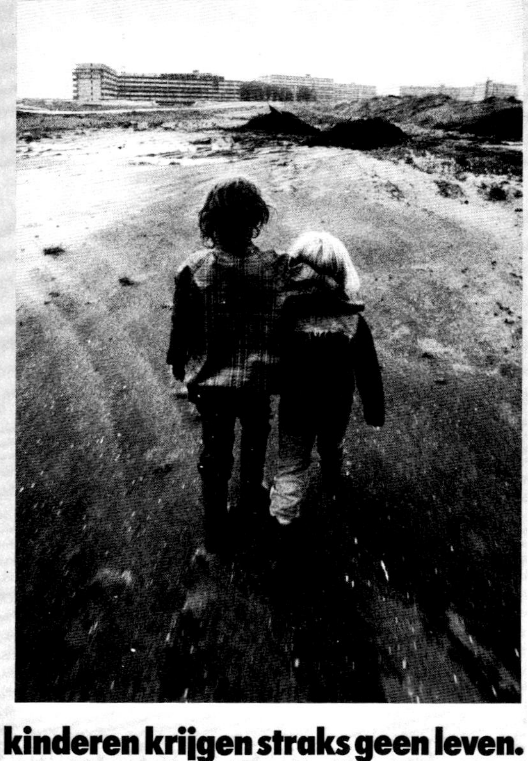

**Veel te veel kinderen krijgen straks geen leven.
Geboortenbeperking is noodzaak.**

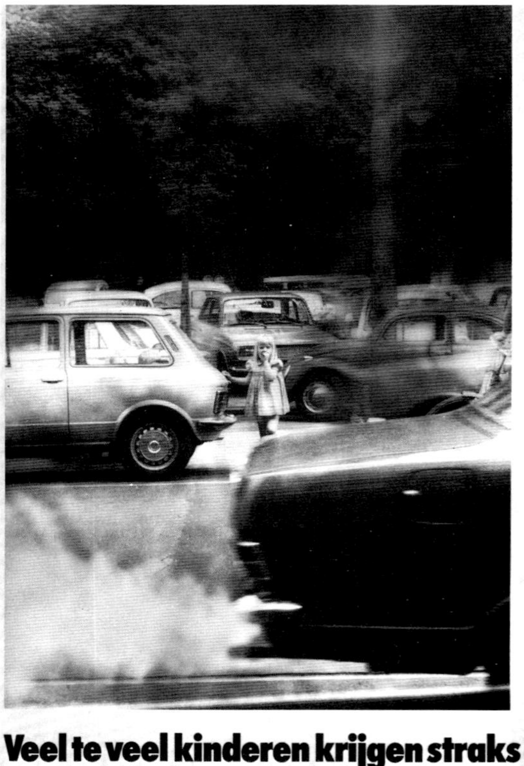

De plichten van de ouders vormen de grondslag voor de rechten van de mens.

In de universele verklaring van de rechten van de mens staat geschreven, dat de mens niet alleen recht heeft op leven, doch ook op gezondheid en welzijn.

Gezondheid betekent naast lichamelijk welzijn ook geestelijk welbevinden.

Voorwaarde voor geestelijk welbevinden vormt het leefmilieu van de mens.

De gezondheid van het leefmilieu wordt bepaald door ruimte-rust-reinheid.

Ruimte-rust-reinheid worden verstoord door steeds toenemende bevolkingsdichtheid.

Plicht van de ouders is het daarom door geboortenbeperking mede te werken aan het afremmen van de bevolkingsgroei en daarmee aan het scheppen van menselijke rechten voor de komende generatie.

Prof. Dr. P. Muntendam
oud - Directeur - Generaal van de Volksgezondheid
oud - hoogleraar in de sociale geneeskunde
voorzitter Staatscommissie Bevolkingsvraagstuk.

**Veel te veel kinderen krijgen straks geen leven.
Geboortenbeperking is noodzaak.**

229-232
McCann-Erickson (Nederland) BV
Frans Hettinga Art Director
Rob van Booren, Philip Mechanicus Photographers
Sire Client

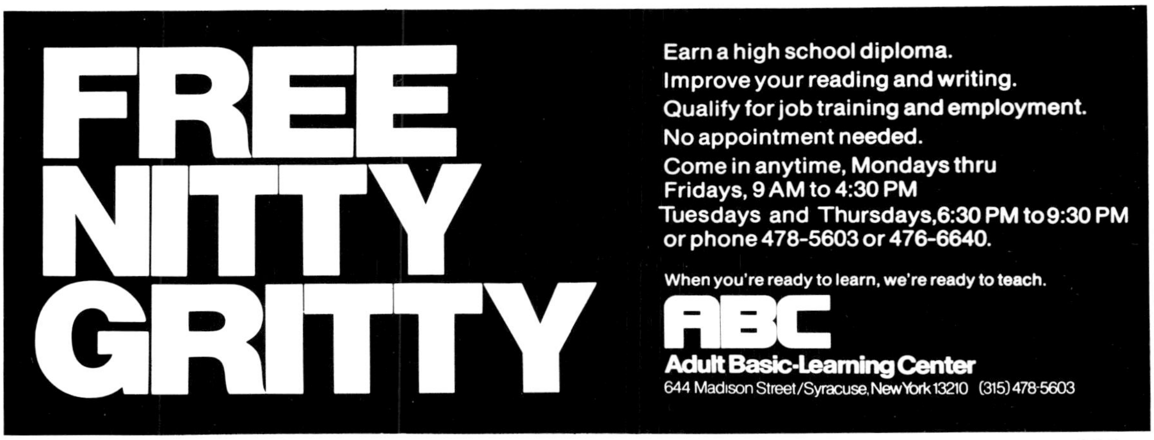
FREE NITTY GRITTY
Earn a high school diploma.
Improve your reading and writing.
Qualify for job training and employment.
No appointment needed.
Come in anytime, Mondays thru Fridays, 9 AM to 4:30 PM
Tuesdays and Thursdays, 6:30 PM to 9:30 PM
or phone 478-5603 or 476-6640.
When you're ready to learn, we're ready to teach.
ABC
Adult Basic-Learning Center
644 Madison Street/Syracuse, New York 13210 (315) 478-5603

233

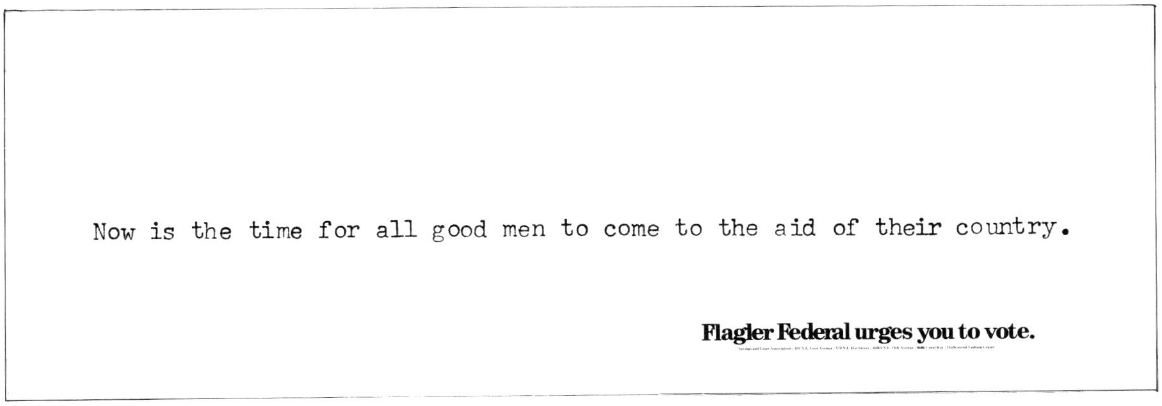
Now is the time for all good men to come to the aid of their country.
Flagler Federal urges you to vote.

234

233
Jacqueline Dedell Entrant
Adult Basic Learning Center Client

234
Caravetta Allen Kimbrough Inc. Entrant
Fred Caravetta Art Director
Flagler Federal Savings & Loan Association Client

McGraphic.

PUBLISHED BY GRAPHIC ARTISTS AND WRITERS FOR McGOVERN/SHRIVER, 19 EAST 53RD STREET, NEW YORK, N.Y. 10022

NIXON REVEALED!

The funniest show ever.
High jinks in high places!
The cows come home to roost!
I.T.T. picks up a tab!
The Bashful Benefactors!
The Watergate caper!

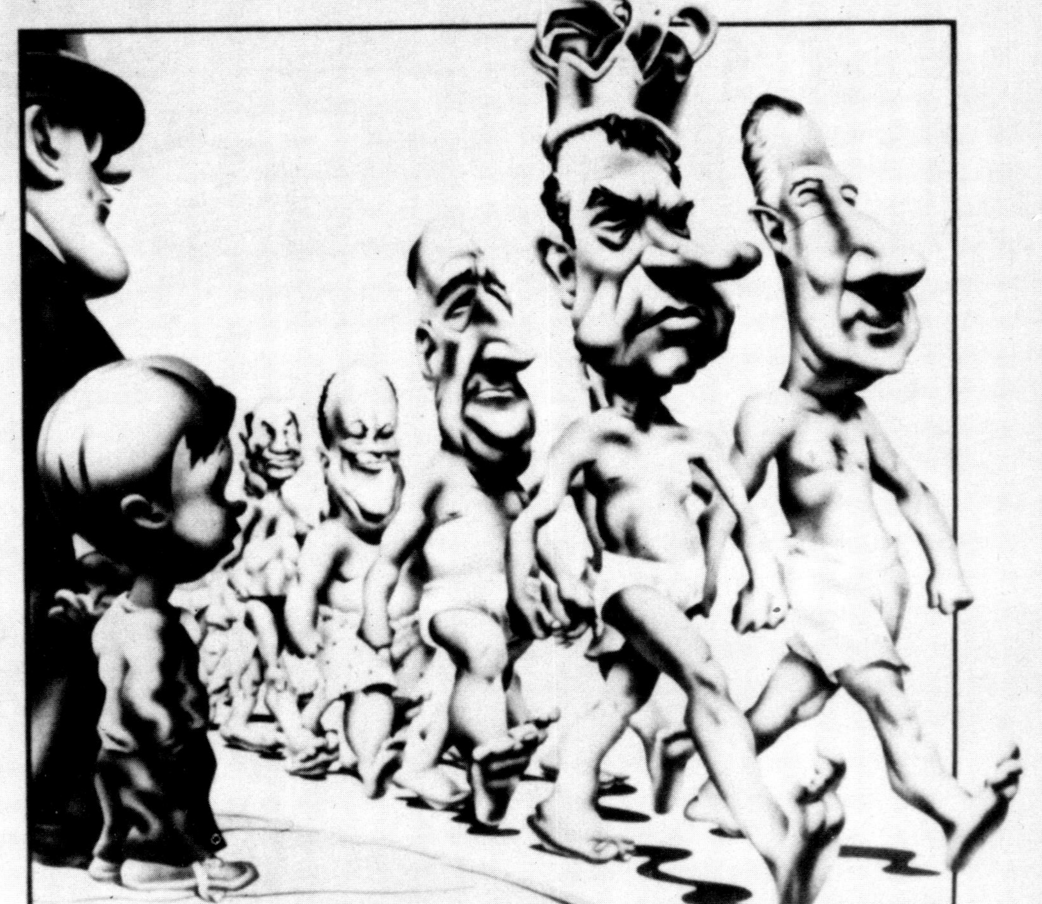

235

235
Lubalin, Smith, Carnase Entrant **Herb Lubalin** Art Director
Seymour Chwast, Bill Maloney, Ellen Shapiro Designers & Editors
Marshall Arisman, Jules Feiffer, Paul Giovanopoulos,
Norman Green, Robert Grossman, David Levine, Ed Renfr
James McMullan, Burt Silverman, Edward Sorel Illustrator
Citizens Committe for McGovern/Shriver Client

Shoplifting is easy... but there's a catch.
The crackdown on shoplifters has begun in earnest. Retailers refuse to stand by while national losses from stealing in stores cost billions in lost revenue. Plain-clothes security men and women are on the payroll of every store of size. Special detectors in many stores can pick up merchandise that hasn't had the code removed by authorized sales clerks. Hidden video cameras record unguarded store areas. In short, the odds that shoplifters (thieves) will be caught and prosecuted are getting shorter and shorter all the time. And once caught, the consequences are severe. First time offenders can get a fine of $300 or six months imprisonment. Once convicted, offenders lose their right to hold public office, to hold a job requiring bonding, to work for the government at any level, to enter many colleges and universities... and they find employment anywhere difficult to obtain. Even this is sometimes less difficult to face than one's self. The tarnish of one's reputation can permanently damage a person's future quest for happiness. Sure, It's easy to shoplift. But what could one possibly steal that would be worth the consequences?
Published as a public service by The Miami Herald

236

236
The Miami Herald Entrant
Dave Cross Art Director
Bill Sanders Photographer
Greater Miami Retailers Assoc. Client

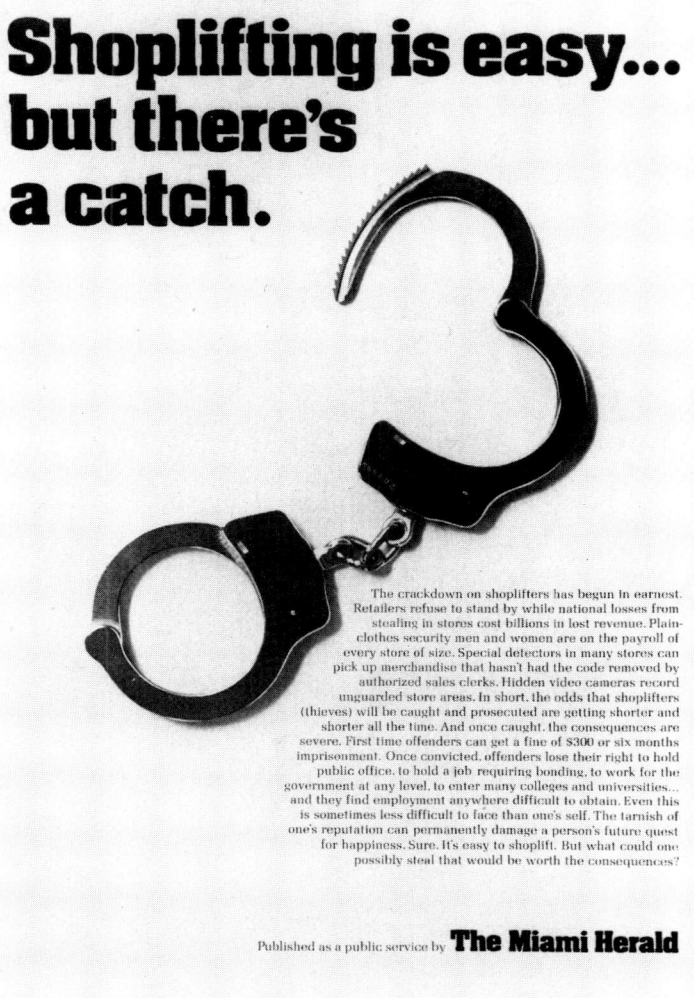

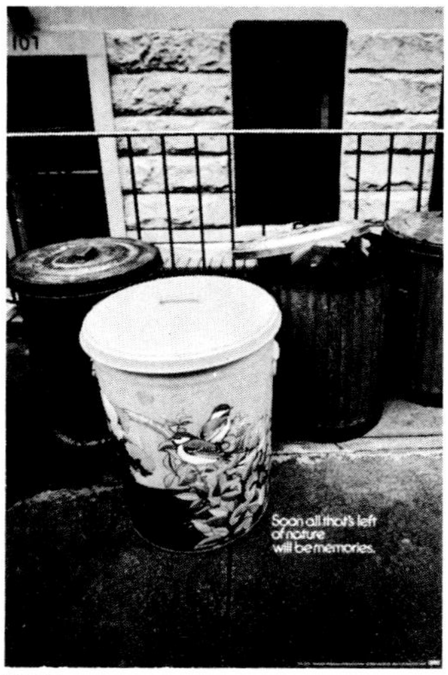
Soon all that's left
of nature
will be memories.

237

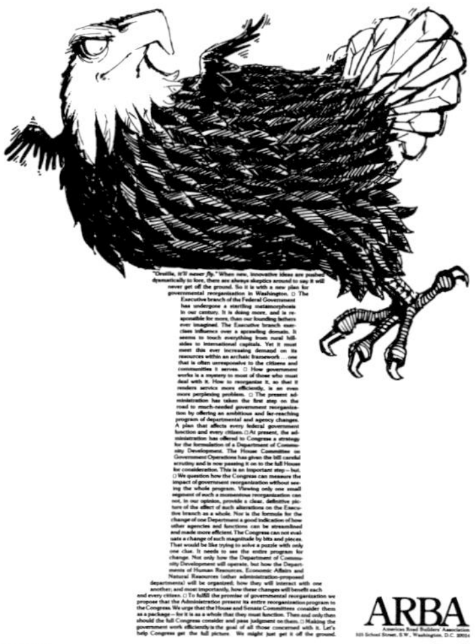
ARBA

238

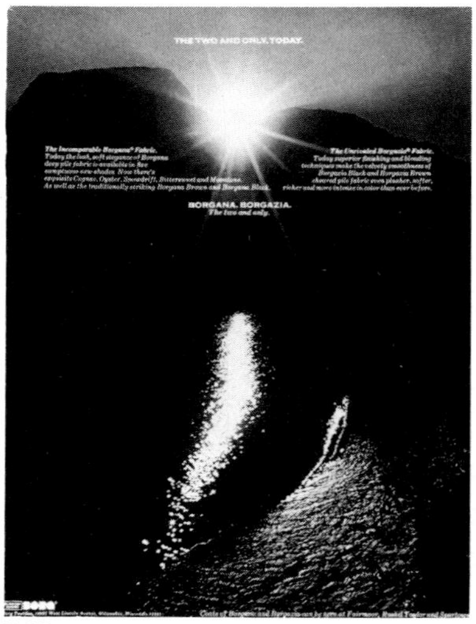
THE TWO AND ONLY. TODAY.
BORGANA. BORGAZIA.

240

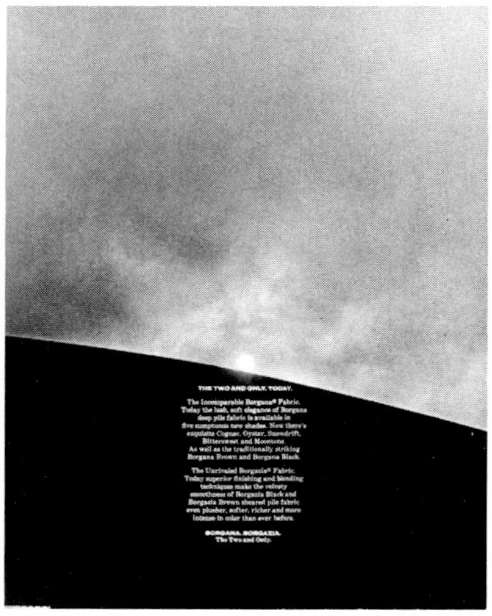
THE TWO AND ONLY. TODAY.

241

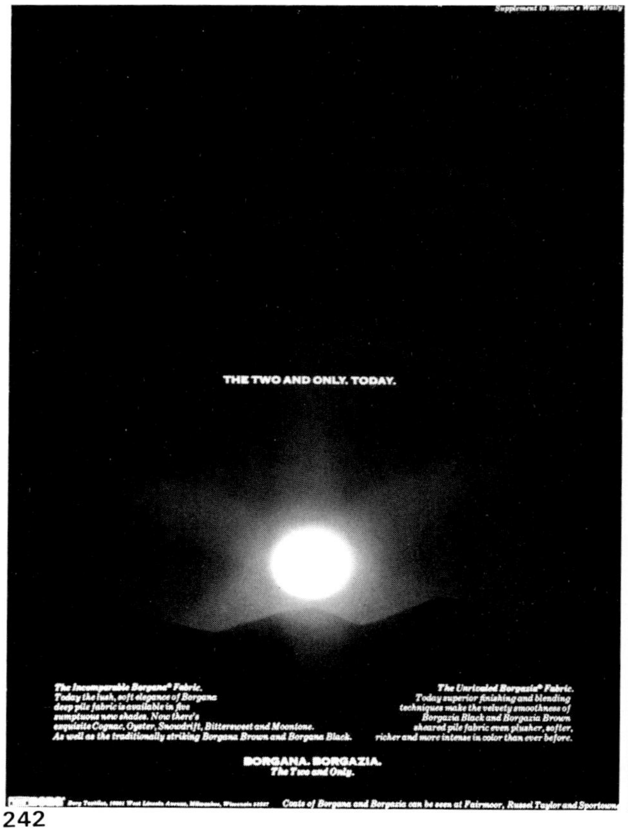
Supplement to Women's Wear Daily
THE TWO AND ONLY. TODAY.
The Incomparable Borgana® Fabric.
Today the lush, soft elegance of Borgana
deep pile fabric is available in five
sumptuous new shades. Now there's
exquisite Cognac, Oyster, Snowdrift, Bittersweet and Moontone.
As well as the traditionally striking Borgana Brown and Borgana Black.
The Unrivaled Borgazia® Fabric.
Today superior finishing and blending
techniques make the velvety smoothness of
Borgazia Black and Borgazia Brown
sheared pile fabric even plusher, softer,
richer and more intense in color than ever before.
BORGANA. BORGAZIA.
The Two and Only.
Coats of Borgana and Borgazia can be seen at Fairmoor, Russel Taylor and Sportown

242

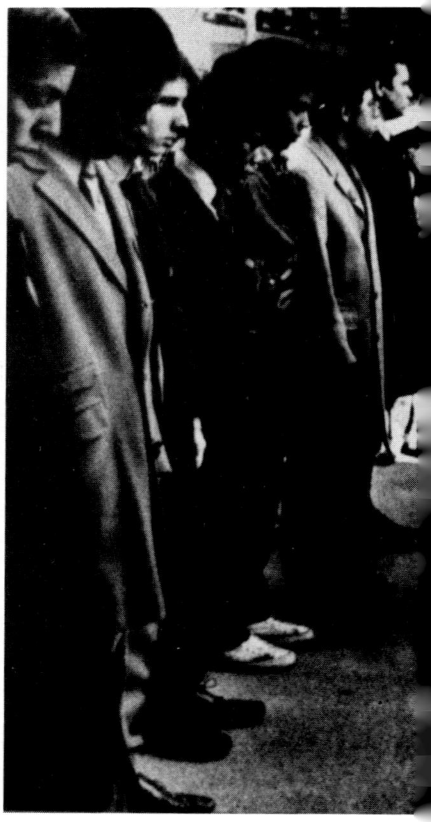

237
Bonnie Bishop Entrant
Sal Catalano Illustrator
Jeremiah Bean Photographer
Scholastic Books Inc. Client

238
Jim Morrison Entrant
Hugh Frost Art Director
Kal, Merrick & Salan, Inc. Agency
American Road Builders Assn. Client

239
Edwin Williamson Entrant
Bob Crawford Photographer
Brand-Edmonds-Packett Agency
Tap Manpower Client

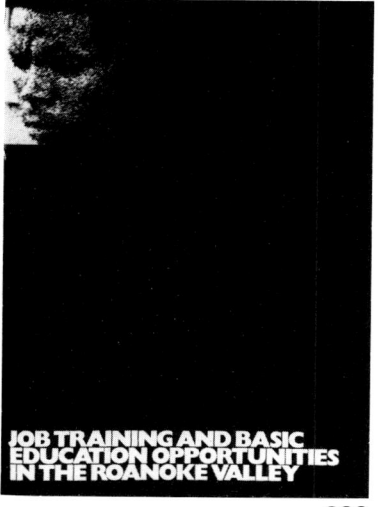

JOB TRAINING AND BASIC
EDUCATION OPPORTUNITIES
IN THE ROANOKE VALLEY

239

Jose
Delacruz
1957-1971
Drugs kill.
Odyssey House
treats young
addicts
who need help.
Now we need
your help.
Send any
amount to:
Garden State
Odyssey House
61 Lincoln Park
Newark

243

240-242
Gennaro Trainello Entrant
Ernst Haas Photographer
Waterman Advertising Agency
Borg Textiles Client

243
Bob Salpeter Entrant
Lopez Salpeter Inc. Agency
Odyssey House Client

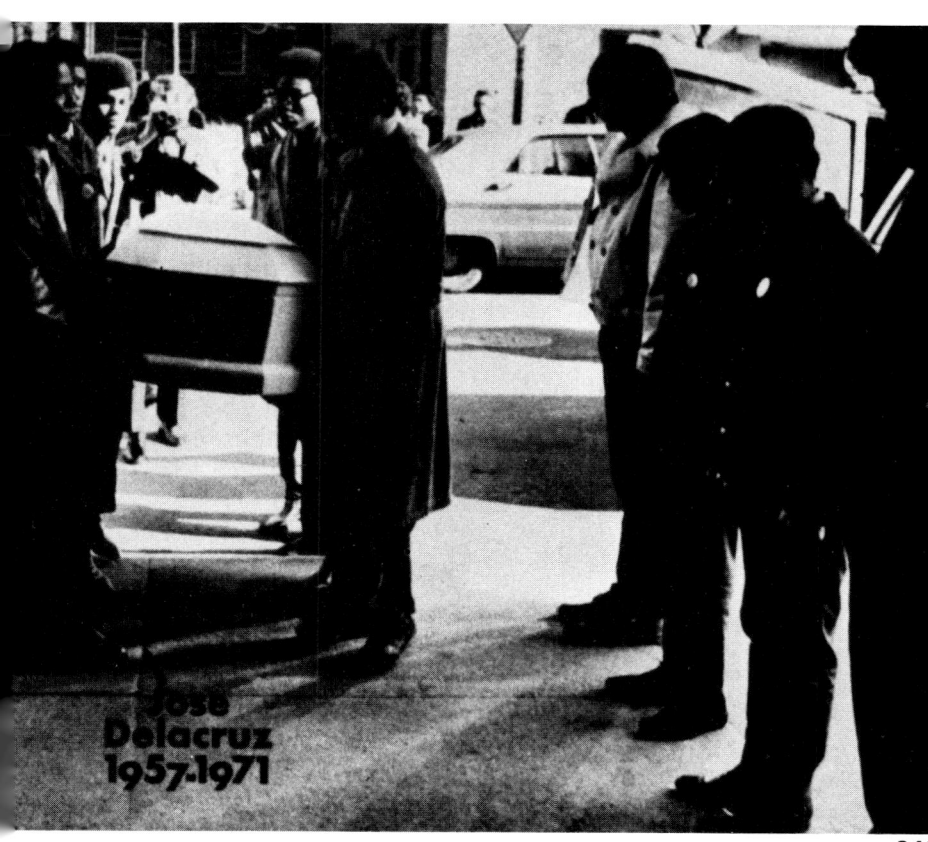

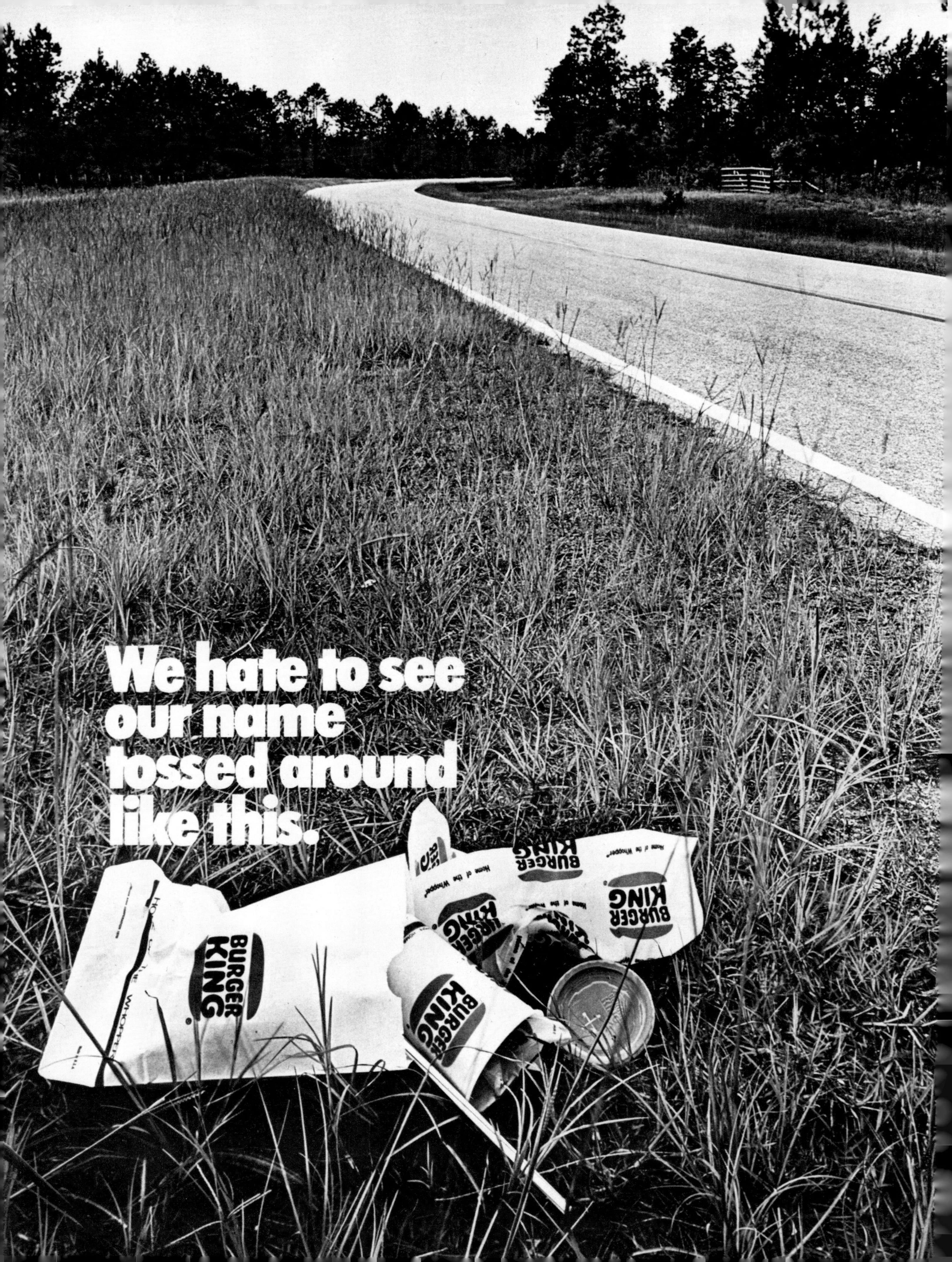
We hate to see our name tossed around like this.
BURGER KING
Home of the Whopper

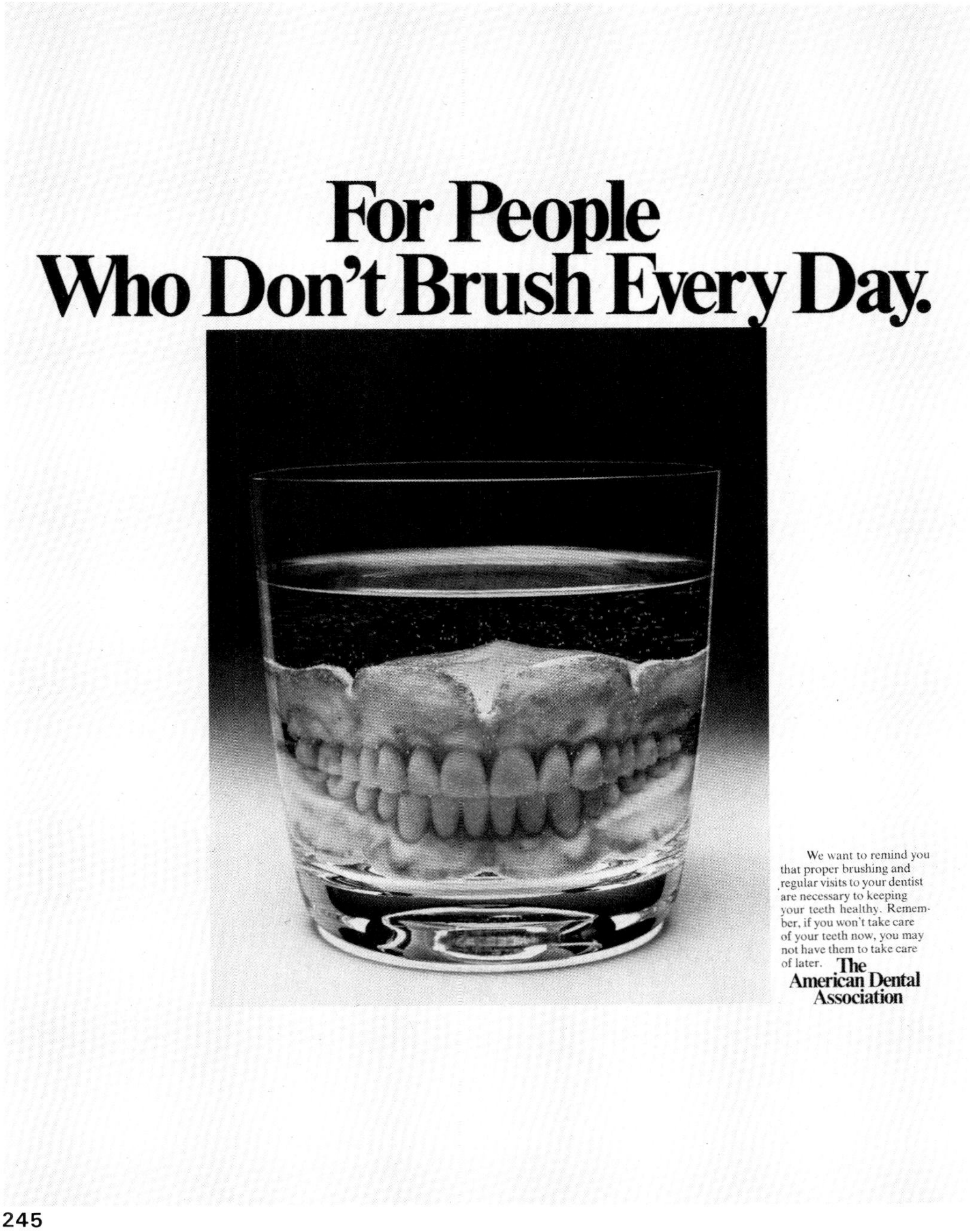
For People
Who Don't Brush Every Day.
We want to remind you that proper brushing and regular visits to your dentist are necessary to keeping your teeth healthy. Remember, if you won't take care of your teeth now, you may not have them to take care of later.
The American Dental Association

245

244
Caravetta Allen Kimbrough Inc. Entrant
Fred Caravetta Art Director
Robert Panuska Photographer
Burger King Corp. Client

245
Richard Brown Entrant
Shelley Isaacs, Richard Brown Copywriters
Joe Morello Photographer
The American Dental Association Client

246

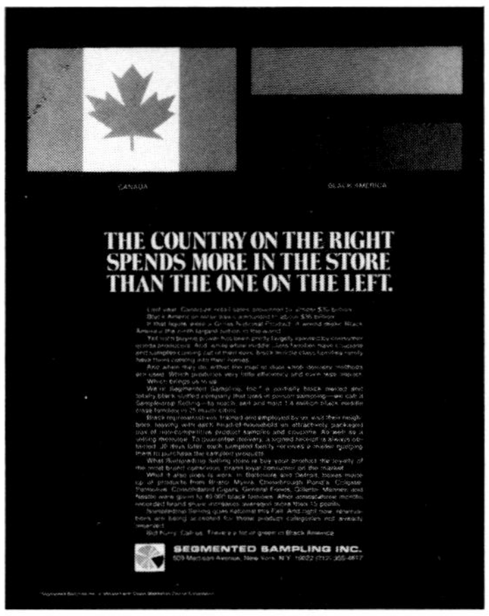
THE COUNTRY ON THE RIGHT SPENDS MORE IN THE STORE THAN THE ONE ON THE LEFT.
SEGMENTED SAMPLING INC.

247

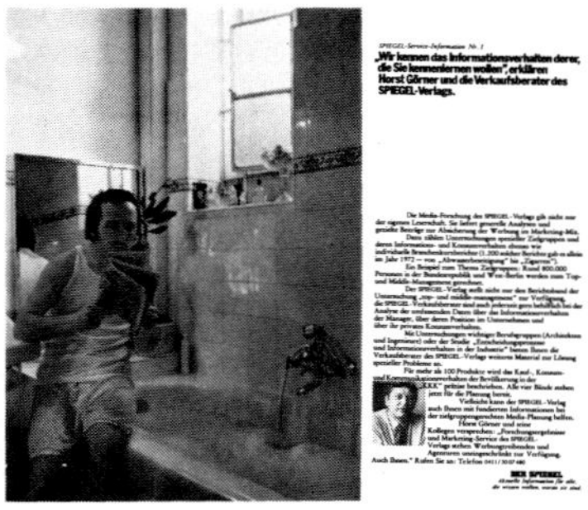

248

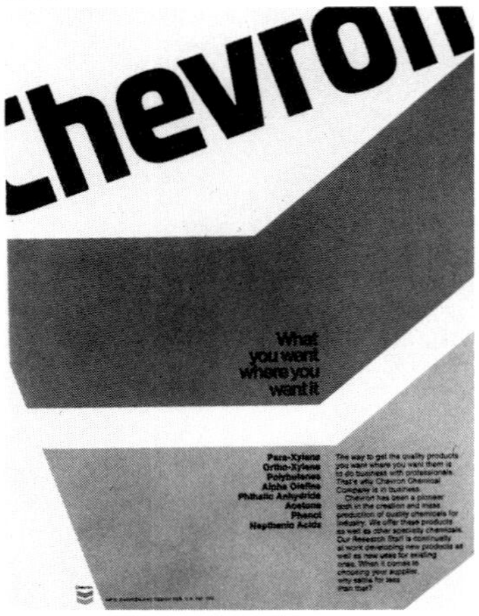
What you want where you want it

249

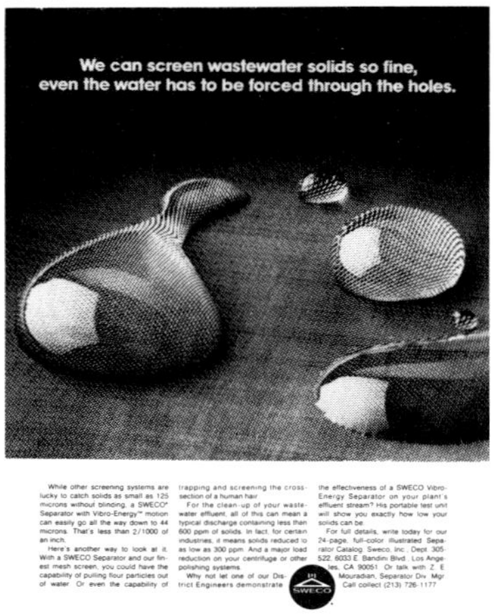
We can screen wastewater solids so fine, even the water has to be forced through the holes.

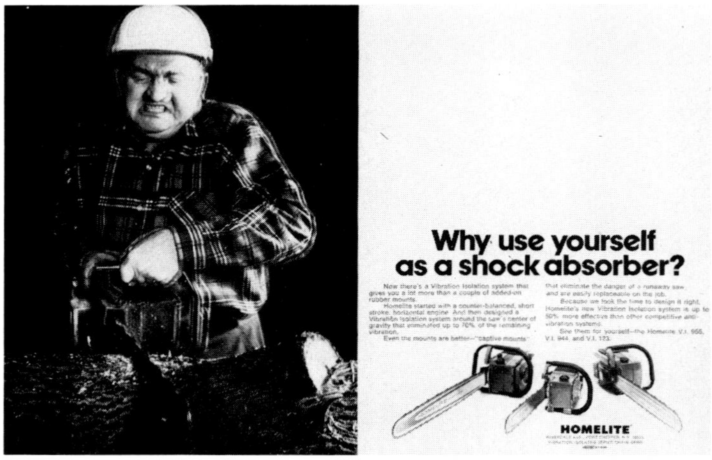
Why use yourself as a shock absorber?
HOMELITE

250

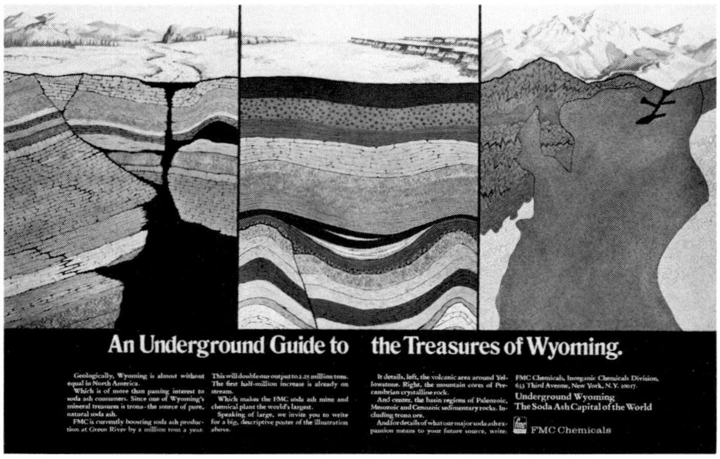
An Underground Guide to the Treasures of Wyoming.
FMC Chemicals

25

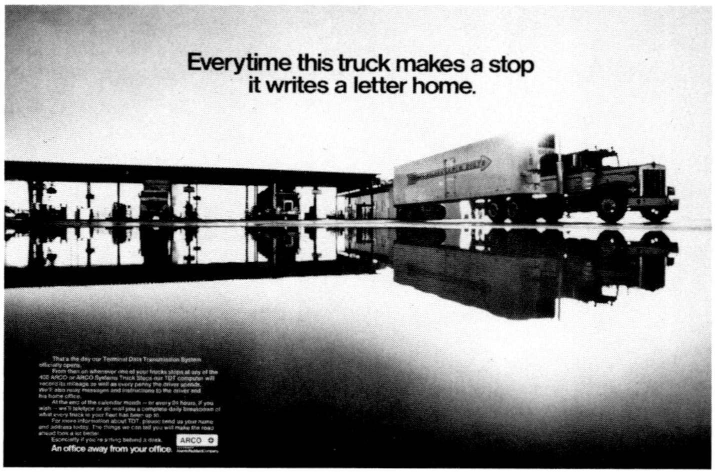
Everytime this truck makes a stop it writes a letter home.
An office away from your office.

252

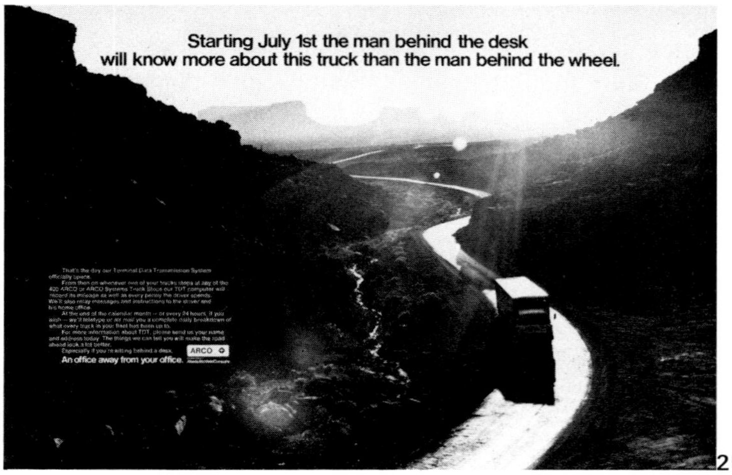
Starting July 1st the man behind the desk will know more about this truck than the man behind the wheel.
An office away from your office.

25

246
Courtland Thomas White Entrant
Courtland Thomas White, Inc. Agency
Segmented Sampling Inc. Client

247
GKO&S Werbeagentur GmbH & Co. KG Entrant
Ben Ojne Art Director
Spiegel-Verlag, Hamburg Client

248
Al Fessler Entrant
McCann-Erickson, Inc. Agency
Walker Engraving Studio
Chevron Chemical Co. Client

249
Cochrane Chase & Co. Entrant
Ralph Lenac, Bill Fortune Art Directors
SWECO, Inc. Client

250
Richard Brown
Joe Morello Entrants
Richard Brown Art Directo
Jim Souffle Writer
Joe Morello Photographer
Needham, Harper & Steer Agency
Homelite Client

The Sandelman File.

One of advertising's best kept secrets.

This is Bob Sandelman.

For 17 years he's been one of advertising's best kept secrets.

The "man who never was" who created some of advertising's biggest and most successful ideas but never took credit for them.

The man who solved the problems the agencies couldn't.

The man you came to when your product was in trouble.

The man everyone knew but didn't dare talk about.

Sound like a book or a movie? It's not. Maybe you've heard the talk.

The stories whispered in the posh corridors of Madison Avenue.

About the small office in an Eastside brownstone. The hushed phone calls. The late-night meetings in out-of-the-way places.

The who's who of industry.

And the silent conversations about escalating shares of market. Runaway sales and profits.

They're all true.

Because in 17 years, Sandelman never had a single failure.

How did he do it? What was it he knew that no one else seemed to know?

To begin with, he didn't think or work the way traditional agencies work.

They believe you've got to write ads to get sales moving. He doesn't. He believes ads are only part of what it takes to turn sales around.

Secondly, traditional agencies base their strategies on what's right about a product.

He goes much further. He bases his strategies not just on what's right about a product, but on what's *wrong* as well.

You might call him a problem solver. But problem finder would be more correct.

Because that's what he does. He digs deep for the problem.

The real problem. Not the obvious, surface problem, but the deep-down problem.

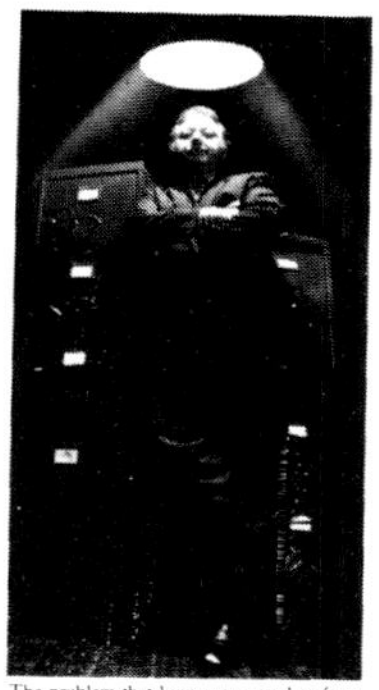

The problem that keeps your product from really taking off.

Where does he dig?

In places traditional agencies never dreamed of looking.

At your whole company. In the field. With your sales force. With your distributors. In your factory. At production. Shipping. Inventory. R & D.

Aside from the normal areas of consumer research, marketing and the product itself.

But *how* he looks is what makes his story even more unusual.

How, disguised as a truckdriver, he found the solution that sent a well-known oil company's sales skyrocketing.

How, posing as a salesman, he created the national campaign which made sales for a leading cigarette soar.

How, as a department store demonstrator, he found the answer which not only helped a national home cleaning product company get out of the red but pushed it all the way into first place.

How, as a salesman, he discovered the problem that went unsolved for 41 years and helped one of the nation's leading corporations' least profitable divisions show *a rise in profit of over 400% in just 60 days.*

Those are just some of the stories in the file. Today they can be told.

Because today, the man who solved the problems the agencies couldn't is there to help you solve yours.

Because today, Bob Sandelman is president of his own advertising agency. An agency staffed with unusually talented people, all committed to the same philosophies which proved so successful in the past.

An agency dedicated to finding and resolving your problems before putting your commercials on the air or your ads in print.

An agency dedicated to what's wrong with your product as well as what's right with it.

Therefore, a whole new kind of agency, unlike any agency before. An agency which invites you to measure its results.

If you're a company president, its director of marketing, or advertising manager, and you've got a problem no agency's ever been able to solve, come talk to Bob Sandelman.

Come let us show you why we're the people who can solve it for you.

Come hear Bob Sandelman and the story of his secret file.

Robert Brian Advertising
107 East 38th St., New York, New York 10016
532-2600

LIQUITEX MODULAR COLORS. SO YOU CAN SPEND MORE TIME PAINTING. NOT MIXING.

Every painter we've ever known wants to paint, wants to get to his canvas and work on the idea in his head. He doesn't want to spend so much of his time just mixing paints.

That's why we created LIQUITEX MODULAR colors. An entirely new range of 35 acrylic colors. All with the remarkable ability to mix and form related color groups. In virtually no time at all. And with an exactness you just may have trouble believing.

So you can forget about time-taking hit-and-miss mixing. And you can forget about mud.

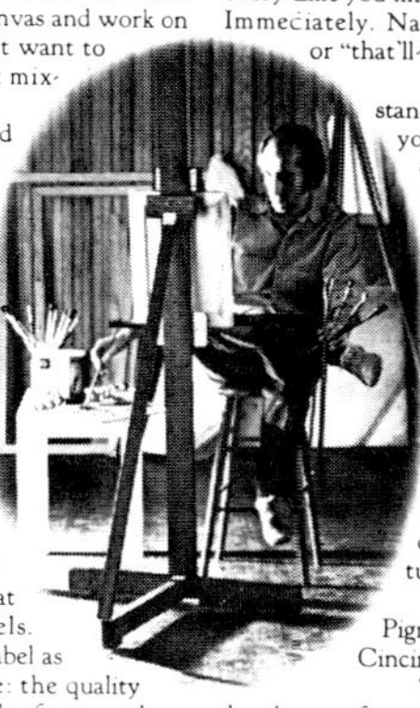

LIQUITEX MODULAR colors end all that because they're colors scientifically measured to equal values. And at unusually high chroma levels. Colors identified right on the label as to hue, value and chroma. (Hue: the quality by which we distinguish one color from another. Value: the lightness or darkness of the hue. Chroma: the intensity or grayness of the hue). So every time you mix, you get the color you want. Immediately. Naturally. With no off-shades or "that'll-have-to-do" colors.

And if you're currently using standard LIQUITEX® acrylic colors you'll find them compatible with our new LIQUITEX MODULAR colors. Both are available in tubes or jars.

Why not send for our full-color, illustrated booklet that gives you the whole story. It's free and you can get one by simply writing to us. Or, if you include just $5.95 (check or money order) we'll send you the free booklet plus our special LIQUITEX MODULAR color set containing twelve 3/4 fl. oz. tubes.

Write to Permanent Pigments, 2700 Highland Avenue, Cincinnati, Ohio 45121.

Thousands of painters have already sent for our set and free booklet. These people want to paint. Not mix.

How about you?

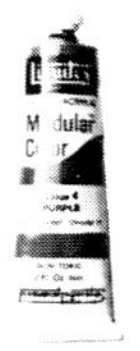

LIQUITEX MODULAR COLORS
By Permanent Pigments, Inc.

251
Muller Jordan Herrick Inc. Entrant
Robert Martin Art Director
Rudy Spinoza Illustrator
FMC Chemicals Client

252-253
Richard Brown Entrant
Alan Frazier Writer
Robert Philips Photographer
Needham, Harper & Steers Agency
Atlantic Richfield Co. Client

254
Robert Brian Advertising Inc. Entrant
Jerry Rosenfeld Art Director
Vern Goldsmith Copywriter
Bill Stettner Photographer

255
Mark Miller Entrant
Jim Vicari Photographer
Chirurg & Cairns Advertising Agency
Permanent Pigments Client

256

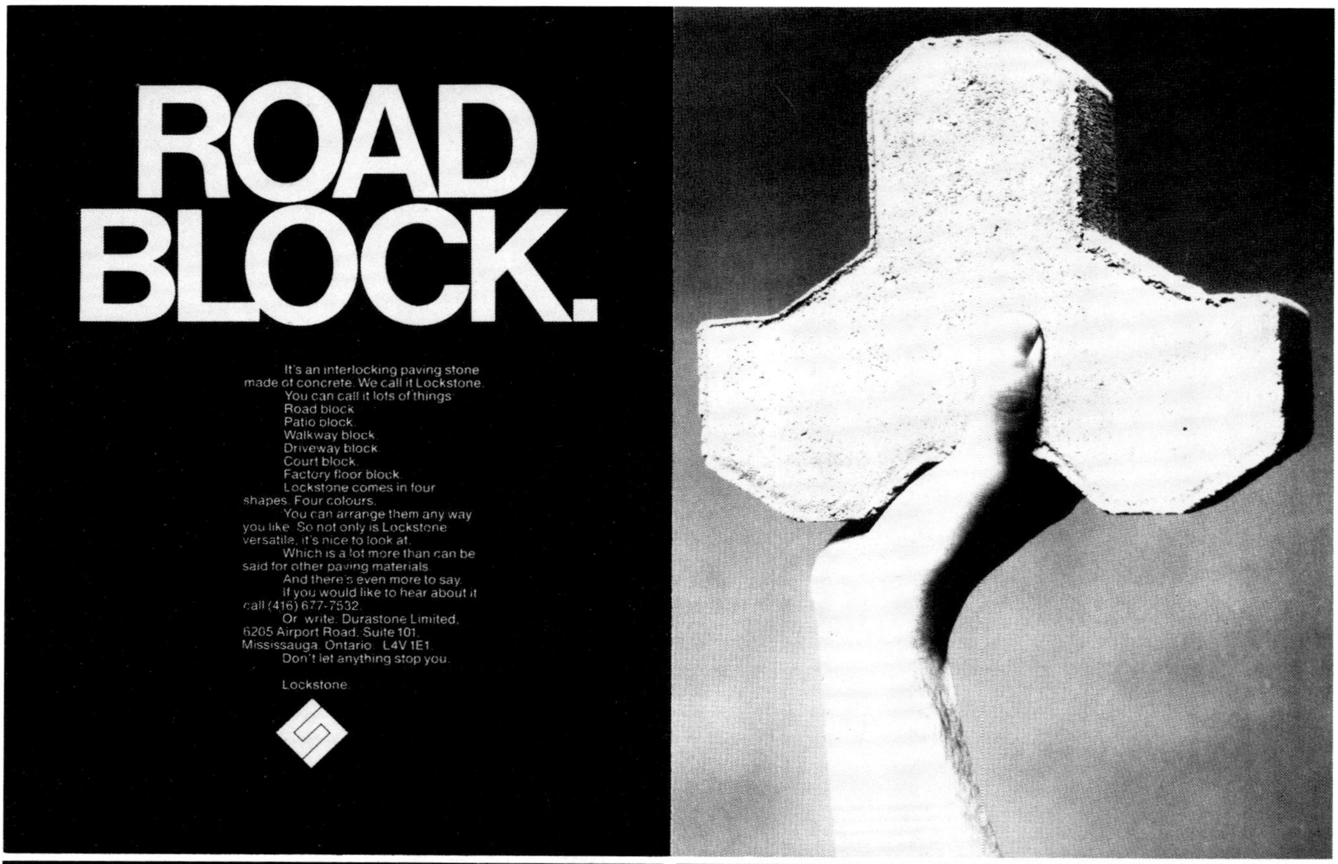
ROAD
BLOCK.
It's an interlocking paving stone made of concrete. We call it Lockstone.
You can call it lots of things:
Road block.
Patio block.
Walkway block.
Driveway block.
Court block.
Factory floor block.
Lockstone comes in four shapes. Four colours.
You can arrange them any way you like. So not only is Lockstone versatile, it's nice to look at.
Which is a lot more than can be said for other paving materials.
And there's even more to say.
If you would like to hear about it call (416) 677-7532.
Or write: Durastone Limited, 6205 Airport Road, Suite 101, Mississauga, Ontario. L4V 1E1.
Don't let anything stop you.
Lockstone.

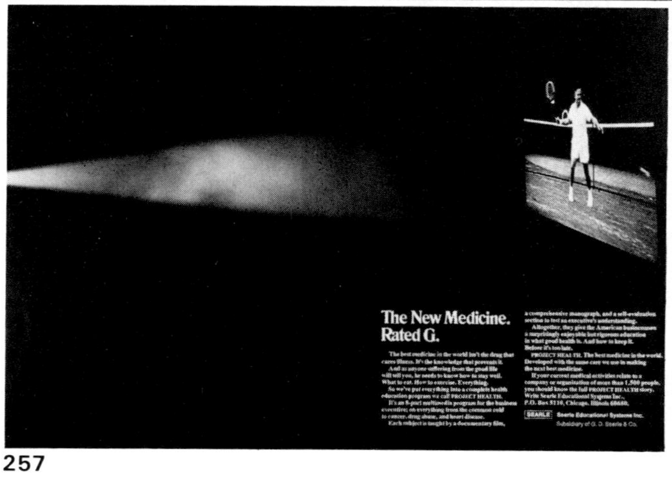
The New Medicine.
Rated G.
SEARLE
Searle Educational Systems Inc.

257

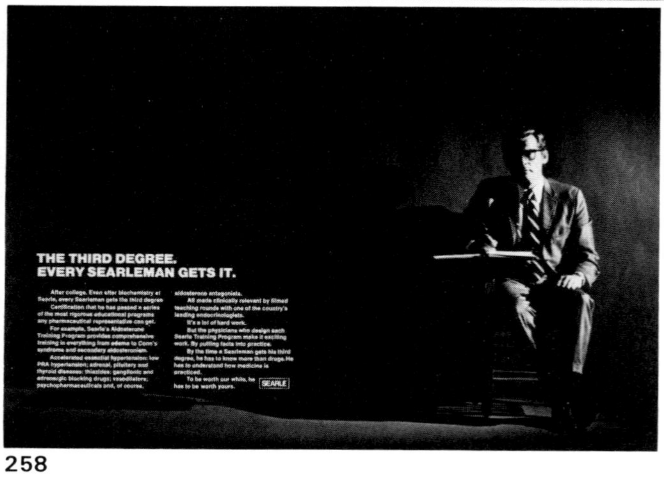
THE THIRD DEGREE.
EVERY SEARLEMAN GETS IT.
SEARLE

258

256
Raymond Lee & Assoc., Ltd.
Entrant
Raymond Lee Art Director
Cy Beard Photographer
Durastone Limited (Lockstone)
Client

257-258
Medcom, Inc. Entrant
Richard Nathan
Art Director
Irv Bahrt Photographer
G.D. Searle & Co. Client

259

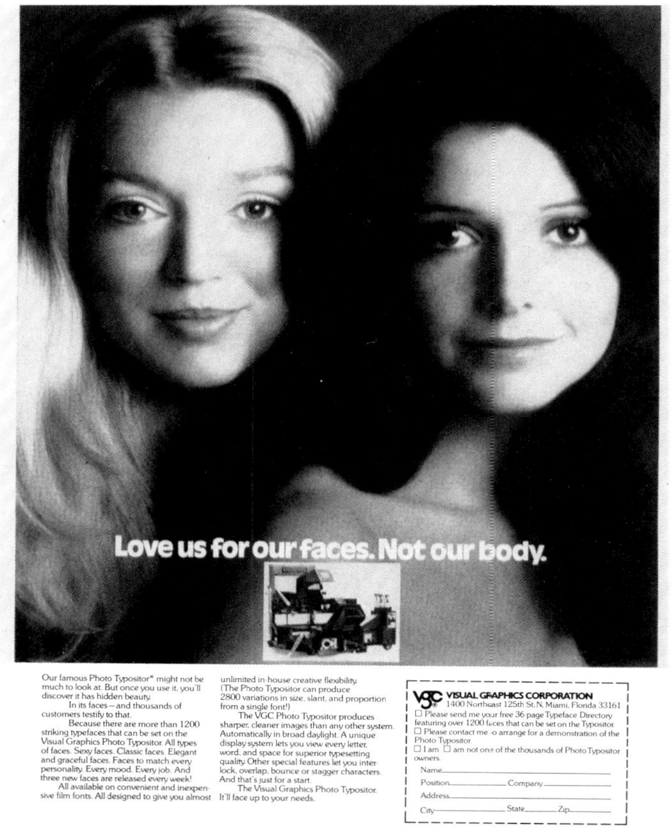
Love us for our faces. Not our body.
Our famous Photo Typositor* might not be much to look at. But once you use it, you'll discover it has hidden beauty.
In its faces—and thousands of customers testify to that.
Because there are more than 1200 striking typefaces that can be set on the Visual Graphics Photo Typositor. All types of faces. Sexy faces. Classic faces. Elegant and graceful faces. Faces to match every personality. Every mood. Every job. And three new faces are released every week!
All available on convenient and inexpensive film fonts. All designed to give you almost unlimited in-house creative flexibility. (The Photo Typositor can produce 2800 variations in size, slant, and proportion from a single font!)
The VGC Photo Typositor produces sharper, cleaner images than any other system. Automatically in broad daylight. A unique display system lets you view every letter, word, and space for superior typesetting quality. Other special features let you interlock, overlap, bounce or stagger characters. And that's just for a start.
The Visual Graphics Photo Typositor. It'll face up to your needs.
VGC VISUAL GRAPHICS CORPORATION
1400 Northeast 125th St. N. Miami, Florida 33161
☐ Please send me your free 36-page Typeface Directory featuring over 1200 faces that can be set on the Typositor.
☐ Please contact me to arrange for a demonstration of the Photo Typositor.
☐ I am ☐ am not one of the thousands of Photo Typositor owners.
Name
Position Company
Address
City State Zip

260

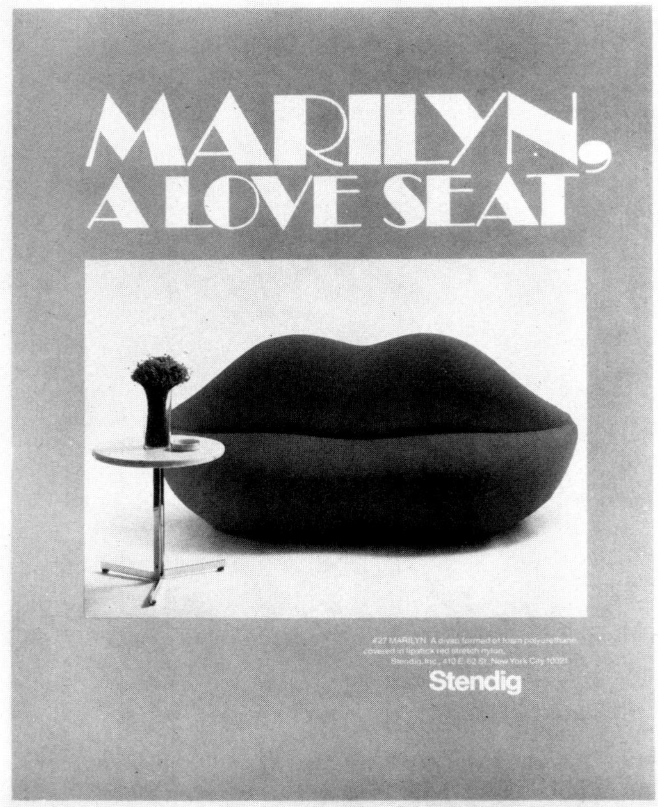
MARILYN,
A LOVE SEAT
Stendig

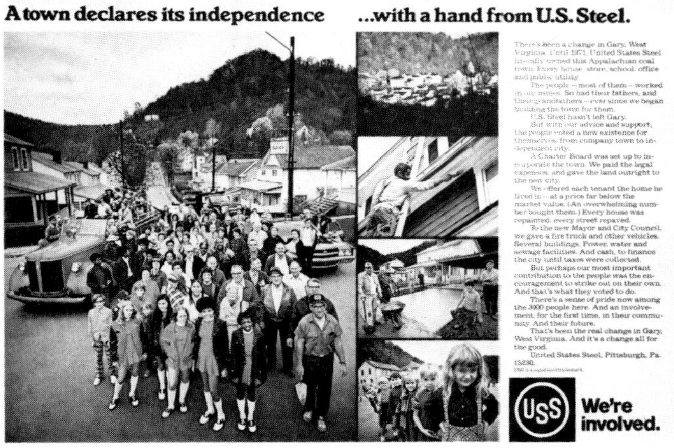
A town declares its independence ...with a hand from U.S. Steel.
There's been a change in Gary, West Virginia. Until 1971, United States Steel literally owned this Appalachian coal town. Every house, store, school, office and public utility.
The people—most of them—worked in our mines. So had their fathers, and their grandfathers—ever since we began building the town for them.
U.S. Steel hasn't left Gary.
But with our advice and support, the people voted a new existence for themselves, from company town to independent city.
A Charter Board was set up to incorporate the town. We paid the legal expenses, and gave the land outright to the new city.
We offered each tenant the home he lived in—at a price far below the market value. (An overwhelming number bought them.) Every house was repainted, every street repaved.
To the new Mayor and City Council, we gave a fire truck and other vehicles. Several buildings. Power, water and sewage facilities. And cash, to finance the city until taxes were collected.
But perhaps our most important contribution to the people was the encouragement to strike out on their own. And that's what they voted to do.
There's a sense of pride now among the 3000 people here. And an involvement, for the first time, in their community. And their future.
That's been the real change in Gary, West Virginia. And it's a change all for the good.
United States Steel, Pittsburgh, Pa. 15230.
USS We're involved.

261

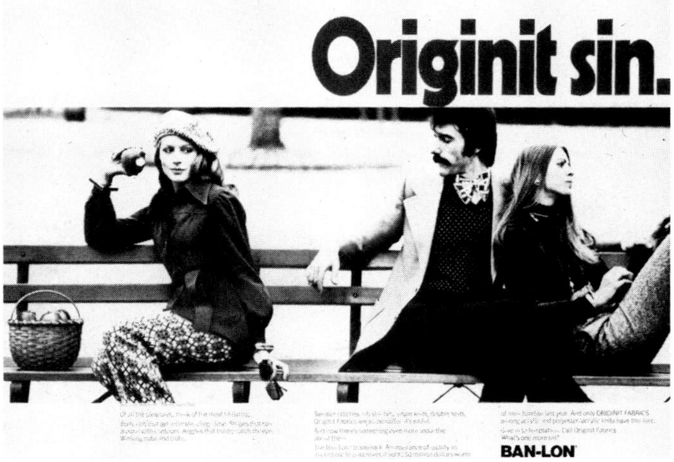
Originit sin.
BAN-LON

262

259
Louis Bolanos Entrant
Bob Gelberg Photographer
Lando/Bishopric
Advertising Agency
Visual Graphics Corp.
Client

260
Appelbaum & Curtis
Entrant
Burt Hillebrand
Photographer
Ed Reder Advertising
Agency
Stendig, Inc. Client

261
John Olivo
Entrant
Peter White
Art Director
Compton Advertising
Agency
United States Steel
Client

262
Don Wise Co.
Entrant
Richard Trask
Art Director
Art Barclay
Photographer
Ban-Lon Client

263

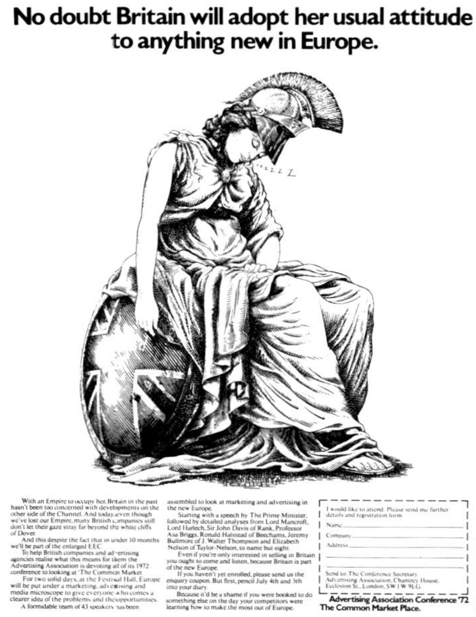
No doubt Britain will adopt her usual attitude to anything new in Europe.
Advertising Association Conference '72
The Common Market Place.

264

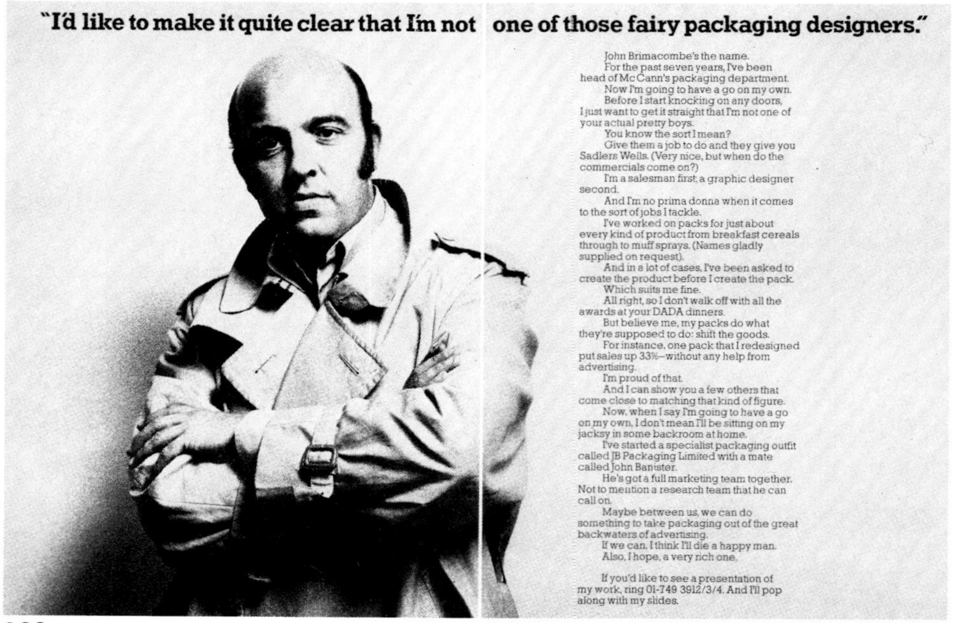
"I'd like to make it quite clear that I'm not one of those fairy packaging designers."
John Brimacombe's the name.
For the past seven years, I've been head of McCann's packaging department.
Now I'm going to have a go on my own.
Before I start knocking on any doors, I just want to get it straight that I'm not one of your actual pretty boys.
You know the sort I mean?
Give them a job to do and they give you Sadlers Wells. (Very nice, but when do the commercials come on?)
I'm a salesman first, a graphic designer second.
And I'm no prima donna when it comes to the sort of jobs I tackle.
I've worked on packs for just about every kind of product from breakfast cereals through to muff sprays. (Names gladly supplied on request).
And in a lot of cases, I've been asked to create the product before I create the pack.
Which suits me fine.
All right, so I don't walk off with all the awards at your DADA dinners.
But believe me, my packs do what they're supposed to do: shift the goods.
For instance, one pack that I redesigned put sales up 33%—without any help from advertising.
I'm proud of that.
And I can show you a few others that come close to matching that kind of figure.
Now, when I say I'm going to have a go on my own, I don't mean I'll be sitting on my jacksy in some backroom at home.
I've started a specialist packaging outfit called JB Packaging Limited with a mate called John Banister.
He's got a full marketing team together. Not to mention a research team that he can call on.
Maybe between us, we can do something to take packaging out of the great backwaters of advertising.
If we can, I think I'll die a happy man.
Also, I hope, a very rich one.
If you'd like to see a presentation of my work, ring 01-749 3912/3/4. And I'll pop along with my slides.

265

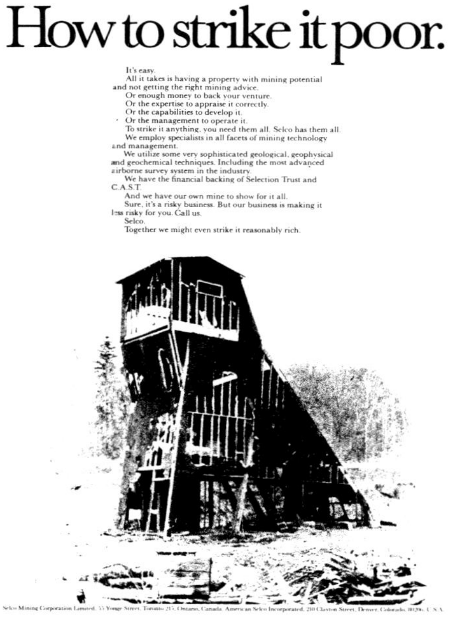
How to strike it poor.
It's easy.
All it takes is having a property with mining potential and not getting the right mining advice.
Or enough money to back your venture.
Or the expertise to appraise it correctly.
Or the capabilities to develop it.
Or the management to operate it.
To strike it anything, you need them all. Selco has them all.
We employ specialists in all facets of mining technology and management.
We utilize some very sophisticated geological, geophysical and geochemical techniques. Including the most advanced airborne survey system in the industry.
We have the financial backing of Selection Trust and C.A.S.T.
And we have our own mine to show for it all.
Sure, it's a risky business. But our business is making it less risky for you. Call us.
Selco.
Together we might even strike it reasonably rich.

266

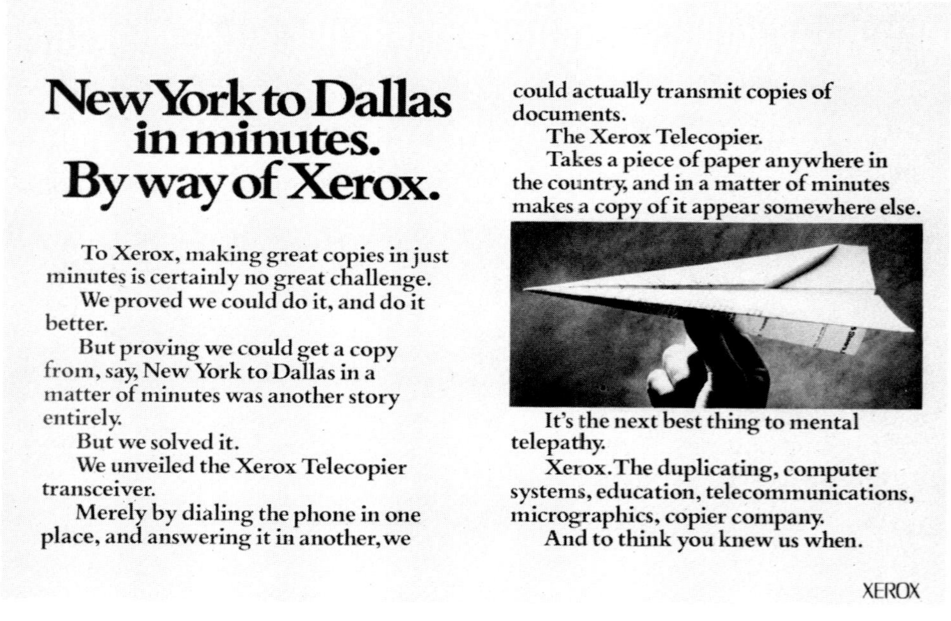
New York to Dallas in minutes. By way of Xerox.
To Xerox, making great copies in just minutes is certainly no great challenge.
We proved we could do it, and do it better.
But proving we could get a copy from, say, New York to Dallas in a matter of minutes was another story entirely.
But we solved it.
We unveiled the Xerox Telecopier transceiver.
Merely by dialing the phone in one place, and answering it in another, we could actually transmit copies of documents.
The Xerox Telecopier.
Takes a piece of paper anywhere in the country, and in a matter of minutes makes a copy of it appear somewhere else.
It's the next best thing to mental telepathy.
Xerox. The duplicating, computer systems, education, telecommunications, micrographics, copier company.
And to think you knew us when.
XEROX

263
Euro Advertising Ltd. Entrant
Barry Craddock Illustrator
Robin Wight Copywriter
Derrick Hass Art Director
Advertising Association Client

264
Euro Advertising Ltd. Entrant
Derrick Hass Art Director
John Claridge Photographer
David Brown Copywriter
J.B. Packaging Client

265
Raymond Lee & Assoc., Ltd. Entrant
Raymond Lee Art Director
Selco Mining Corporation Ltd. Client

266
Needham, Harper, & Steers Entrant
Allen Kay Art Director
Stephen Steigman Photographer
Xerox Client

267
Nadler & Larimer, Inc. Entrant
Irwin Goldberg Art Director
John Paul Eudress Photographer
Austin, Nichols (Wild Turkey) Client

268
Editorial America S.A. Entrant
Emilio Rodriguez Jr. Art Director
Mauricio Mendoza Photographer
Cosmopolitan en Español Magazine Client

270

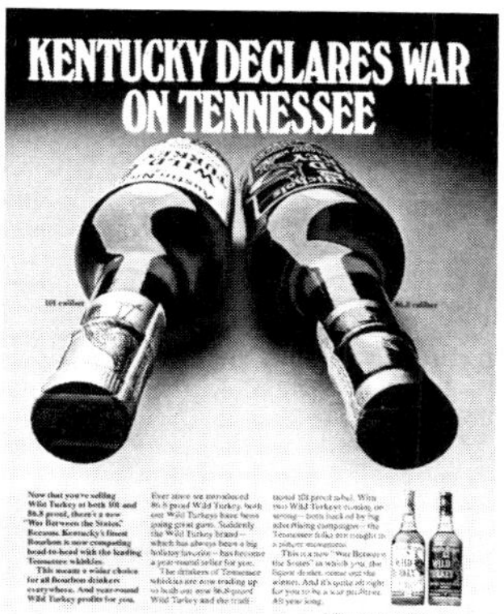
KENTUCKY DECLARES WAR ON TENNESSEE

267

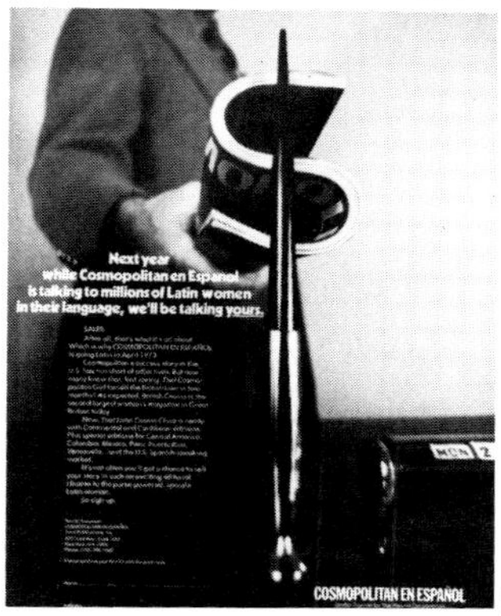
Next year
while Cosmopolitan en Español
is talking to millions of Latin women
in their language, we'll be talking yours.
COSMOPOLITAN EN ESPAÑOL

268

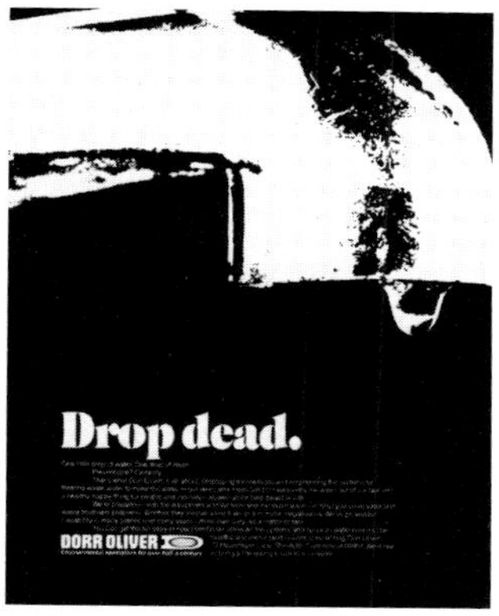
Drop dead.
DORR OLIVER

269

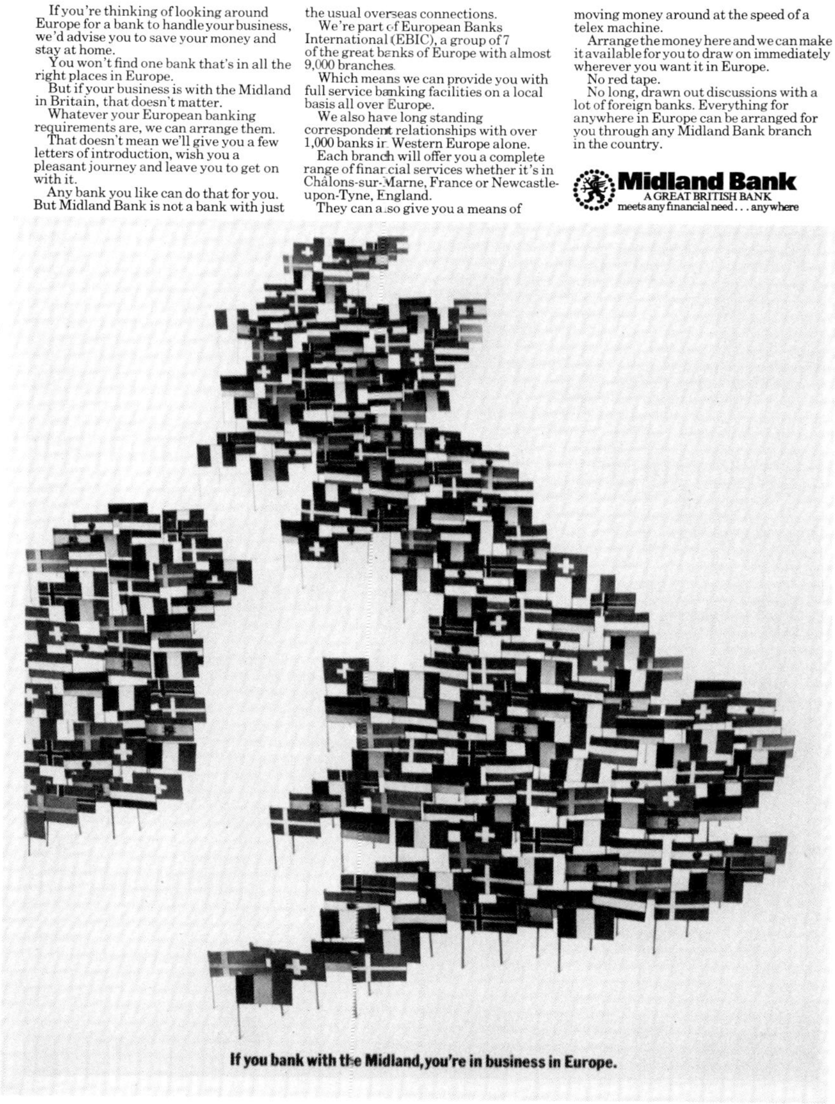
If you're thinking of looking around Europe for a bank to handle your business, we'd advise you to save your money and stay at home.
You won't find one bank that's in all the right places in Europe.
But if your business is with the Midland in Britain, that doesn't matter.
Whatever your European banking requirements are, we can arrange them.
That doesn't mean we'll give you a few letters of introduction, wish you a pleasant journey and leave you to get on with it.
Any bank you like can do that for you. But Midland Bank is not a bank with just the usual overseas connections.
We're part of European Banks International (EBIC), a group of 7 of the great banks of Europe with almost 9,000 branches.
Which means we can provide you with full service banking facilities on a local basis all over Europe.
We also have long standing correspondent relationships with over 1,000 banks in Western Europe alone.
Each branch will offer you a complete range of financial services whether it's in Châlons-sur-Marne, France or Newcastle-upon-Tyne, England.
They can also give you a means of moving money around at the speed of a telex machine.
Arrange the money here and we can make it available for you to draw on immediately wherever you want it in Europe.
No red tape.
No long, drawn out discussions with a lot of foreign banks. Everything for anywhere in Europe can be arranged for you through any Midland Bank branch in the country.
Midland Bank
A GREAT BRITISH BANK
meets any financial need . . . anywhere
If you bank with the Midland, you're in business in Europe.

271

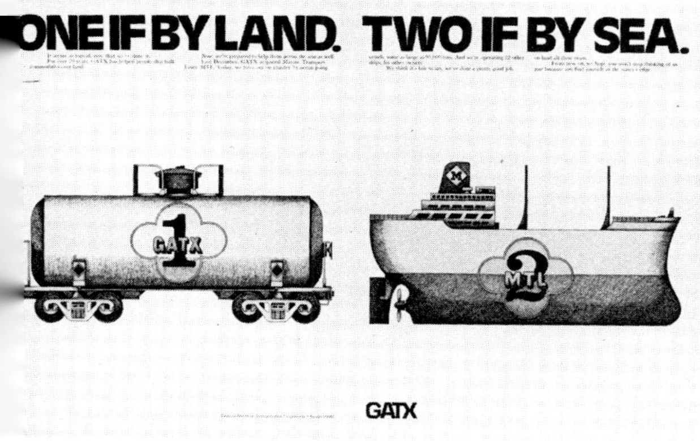
ONE IF BY LAND. TWO IF BY SEA.
GATX
1
2
GATX

272

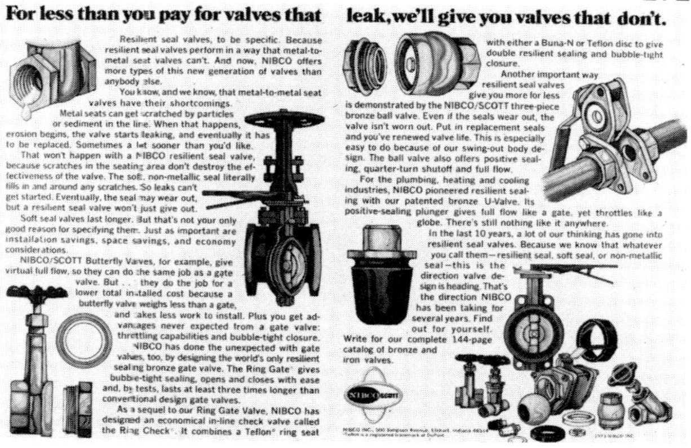
For less than you pay for valves that leak, we'll give you valves that don't.
NIBCO

269
Rich St. Vincent
Entrant
St. Vincent/ Chew/Milone, Inc.
Agency
Dorr Oliver Inc.
Client

270
Nigel Hensley
Entrant
Bernard Phillips
Photographer
McCormack Hensley Palmer Ltd. Agency
Midland Bank
Client

271
Eric Lob Entrant
Ray Nyquist Art Director
Mabey/Trousdell, R. Grossman, R. Searle Illustrator
Lee King & Partners Agency
General American Trans. Corp. Client

272
Dan A. Bixler
Entrant
Slug Signorino
Illustrator
Juhl Advertising Agency Agency
Nibco, Inc.
Client

273

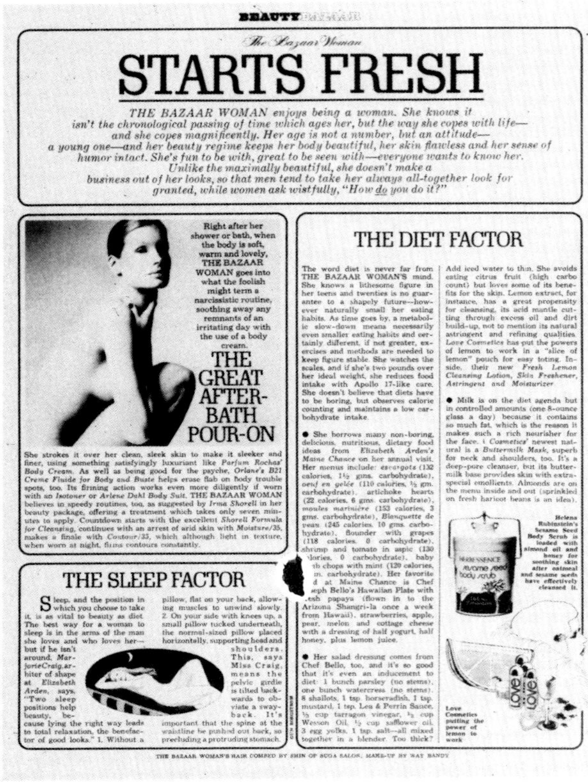
BEAUTY BAZAAR

The Bazaar Woman

STARTS FRESH

THE BAZAAR WOMAN enjoys being a woman. She knows it isn't the chronological passing of time which ages her, but the way she copes with life—and she copes magnificently. Her age is not a number, but an attitude—a young one—and her beauty regime keeps her body beautiful, her skin flawless and her sense of humor intact. She's fun to be with, great to be seen with—everyone wants to know her. Unlike the maximally beautiful, she doesn't make a business out of her looks, so that men tend to take her always all-together look for granted, while women ask wistfully, "How do you do it?"

Right after her shower or bath, when the body is soft, warm and lovely, THE BAZAAR WOMAN goes into what the foolish might term a narcissistic routine, soothing away any remnants of an irritating day with the use of a body cream.

THE GREAT AFTER-BATH POUR-ON

THE DIET FACTOR

THE SLEEP FACTOR

THE BAZAAR WOMAN'S HAIR COMBED BY SHIN OF SUGA SALON. MAKE-UP BY WAY BANDY

274

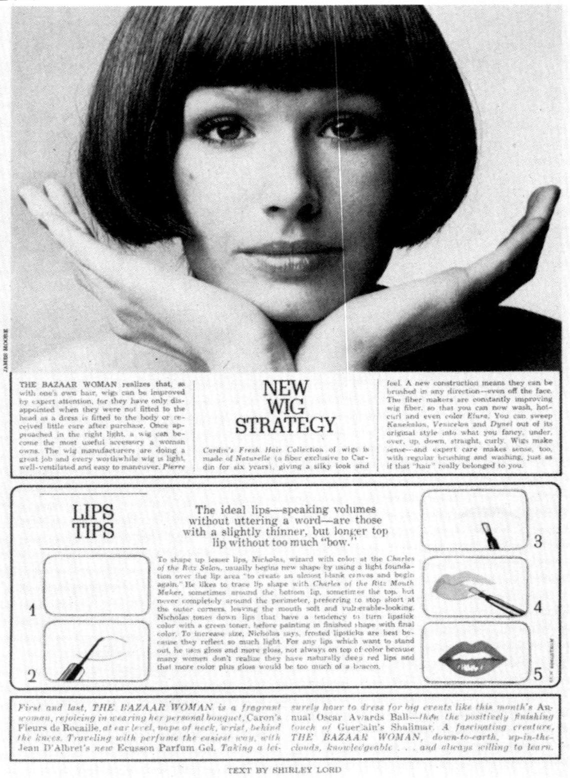
NEW WIG STRATEGY

LIPS TIPS

The ideal lips—speaking volumes without uttering a word—are those with a slightly thinner, but longer top lip without too much "bow."

1 2 3 4 5

TEXT BY SHIRLEY LORD

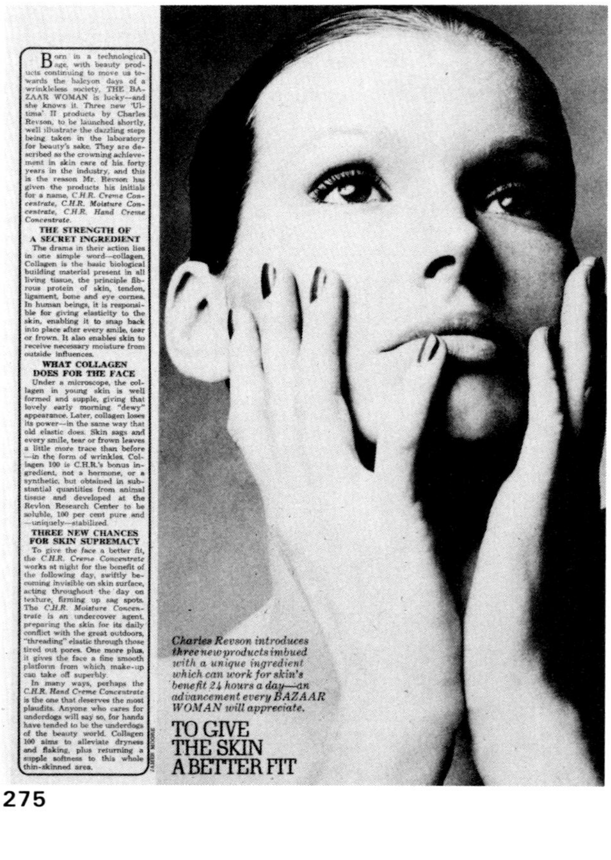
Charles Revson introduces three new products imbued with a unique ingredient which can work for skin's benefit 24 hours a day—an advancement every BAZAAR WOMAN will appreciate.

TO GIVE THE SKIN A BETTER FIT

275

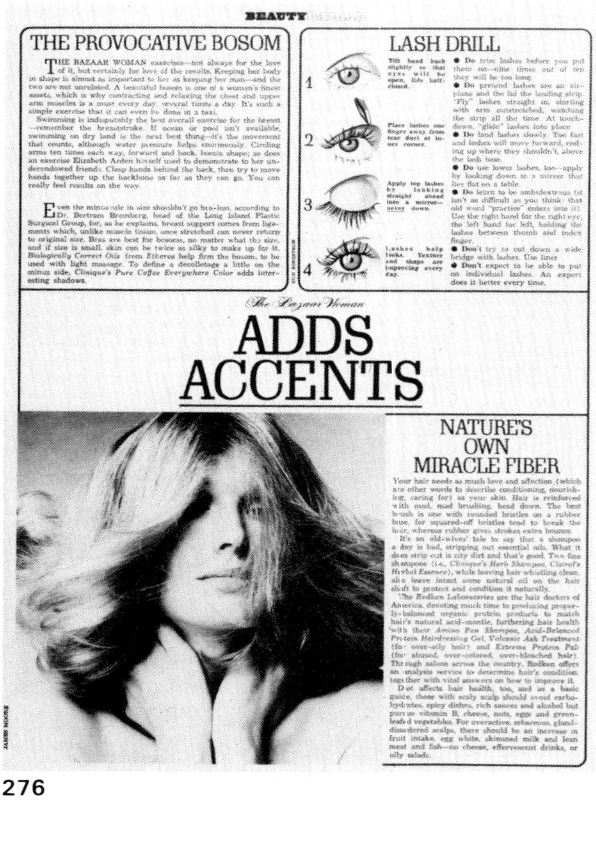
BEAUTY BAZAAR

THE PROVOCATIVE BOSOM

LASH DRILL

1 2 3 4

The Bazaar Woman

ADDS ACCENTS

NATURE'S OWN MIRACLE FIBER

276

273-277
Jerold Smokler Entrant
Jade Albert Designer
Gun Borgstrom Illustrator
James Moore Photographer
Harper's Bazaar Client

278
Emergency Medicine Entrant
Ira Silberlicht Art Director
Laszlo Hege Photographer

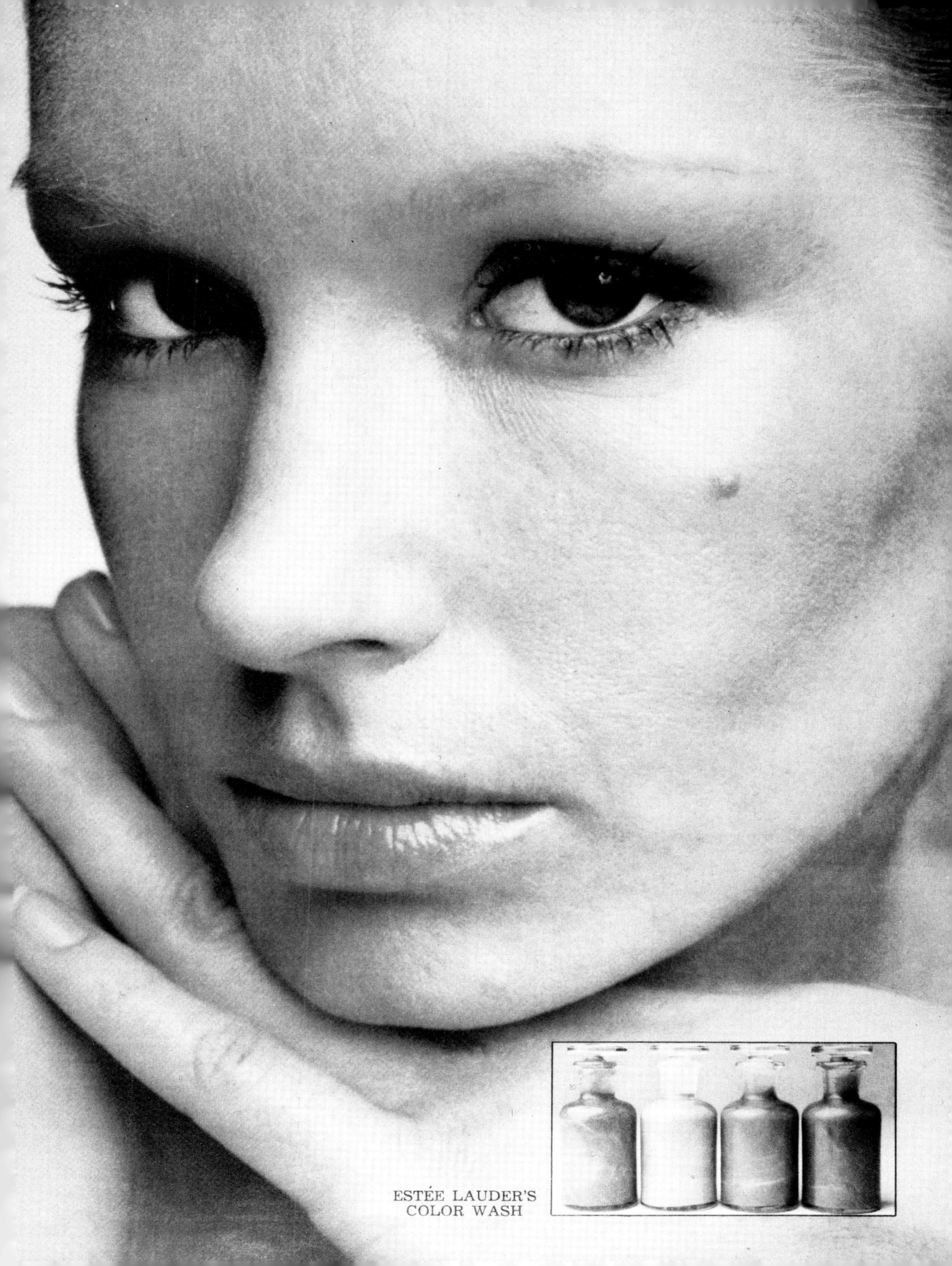

ESTÉE LAUDER'S
COLOR WASH

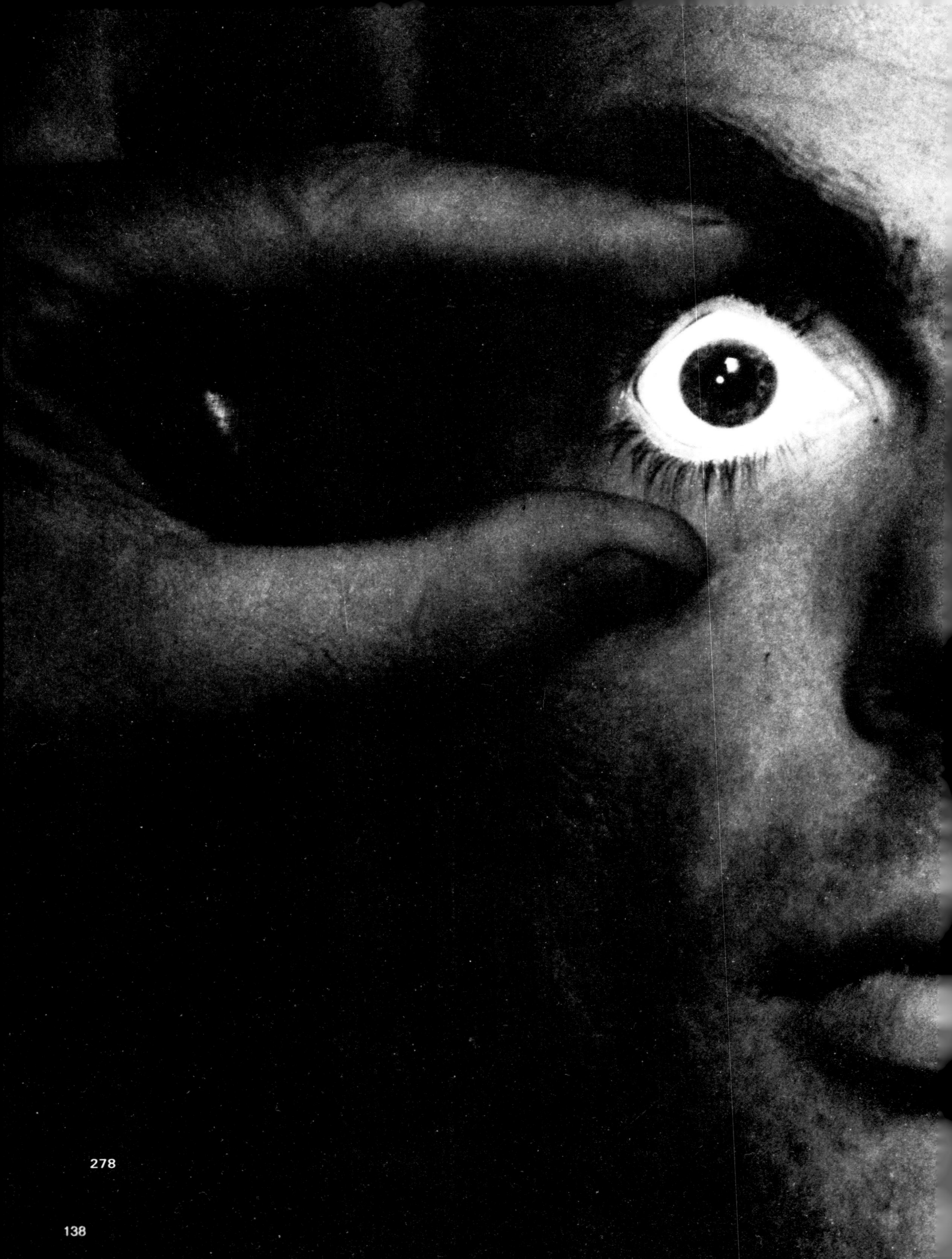

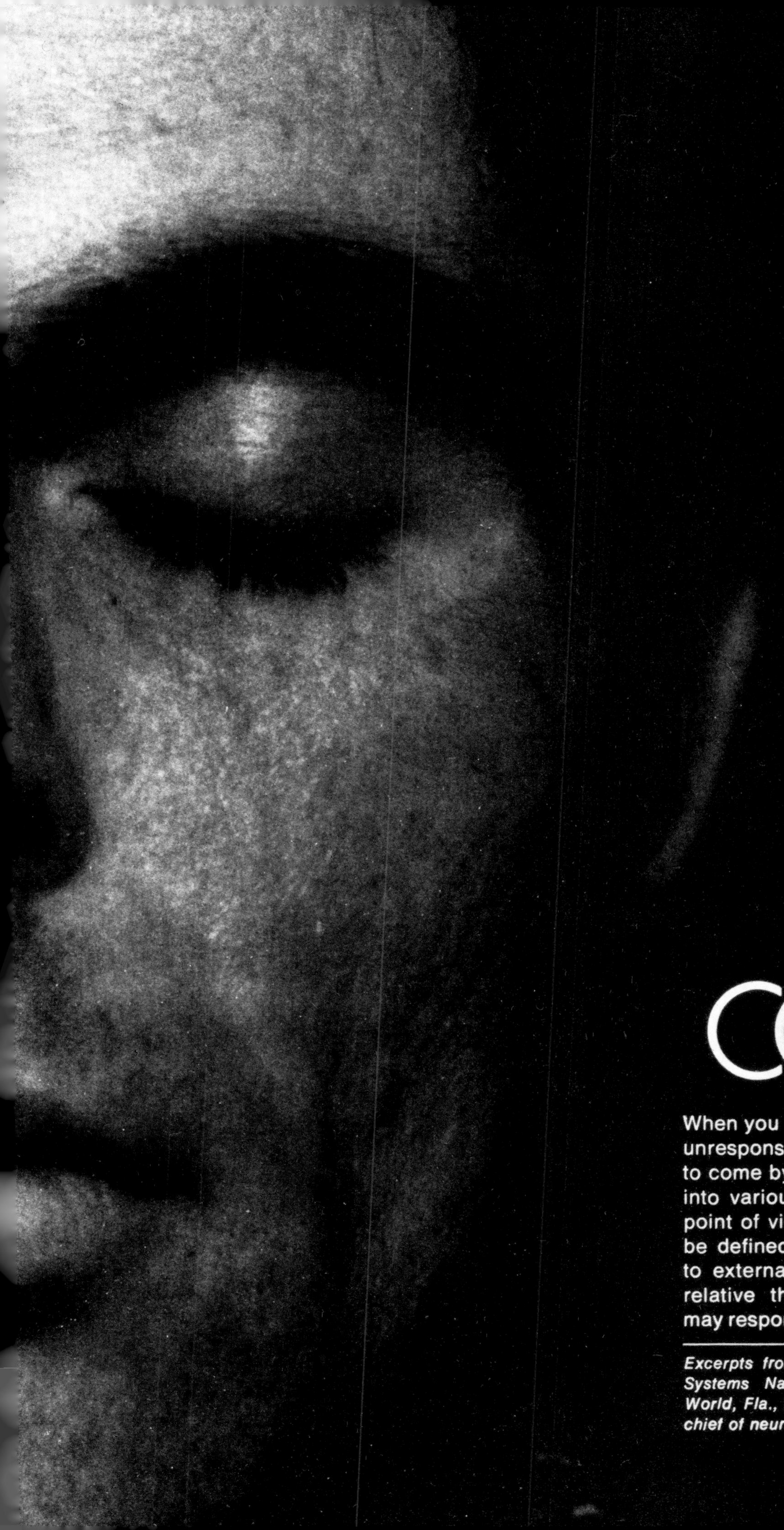

ON COMA

When you talk about the comatose or the unresponsive patient, definitions are hard to come by unless you break them down into various categories. From a clinical point of view, the comatose patient may be defined as one who is unresponsive to external stimuli. Obviously, this is a relative thing, because some patients may respond to severe tactile *continued*

Excerpts from a talk at the Emergency Medical Systems National Symposium at Walt Disney World, Fla., by Melvin Greer, M.D., professor and chief of neurology at the University of Florida.

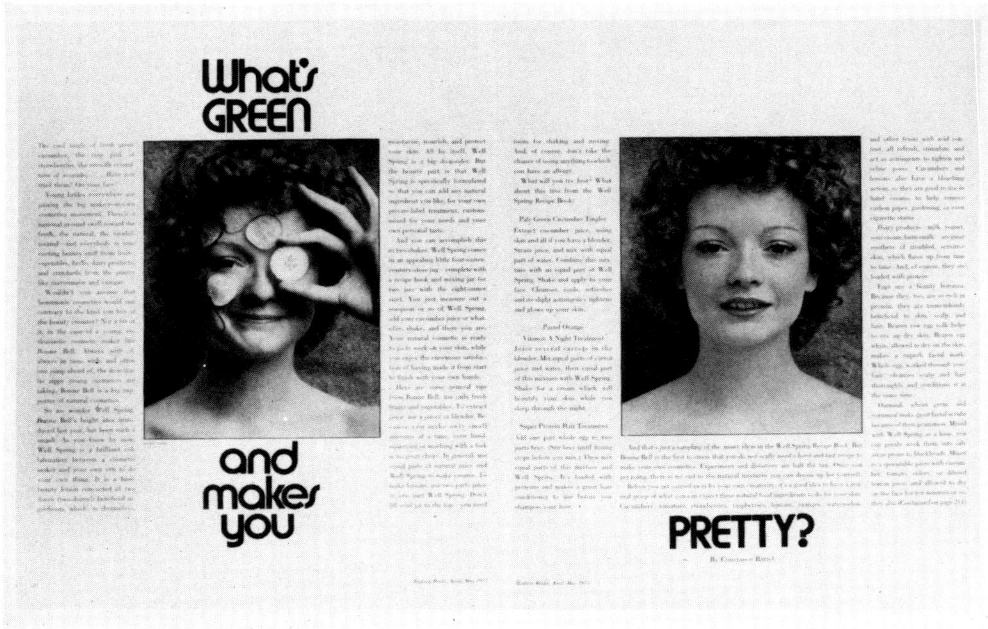
What's
GREEN
and
makes
you
PRETTY?

279

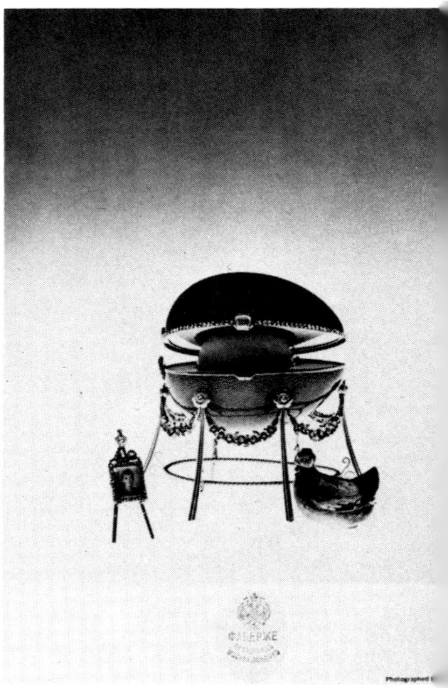

280

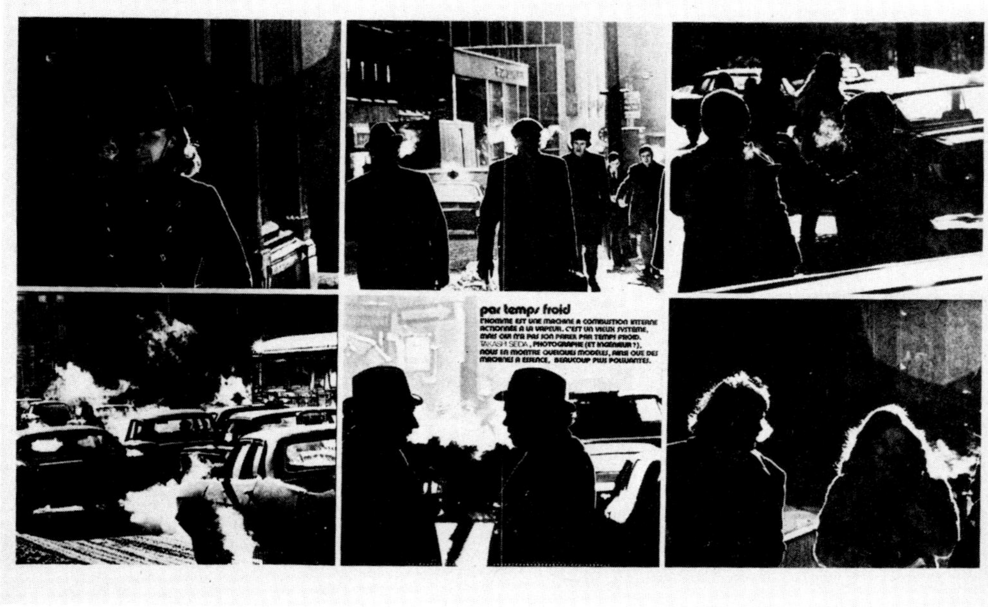
par temps froid

281

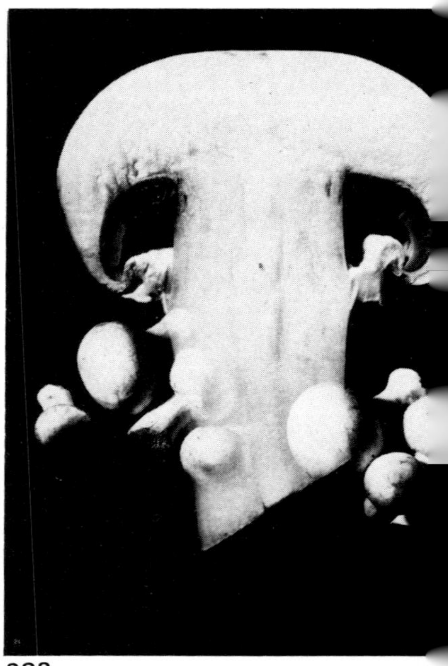

282

279
Modern Bride Entrant
Robin Rule Art Director
Kenn Mori Photographer
Ziff-Davis Publishing Co. Client

280
Henry Wolf Productions Inc. Entrant
Richard Weigand Art Director
Henry Wolf Photographer
Esquire Magazine Client

281
Perspectives Inc. Entrant
Gilles Daigneault Art Director
Takashi Seida Photographer
Perspectives Inc. Studio

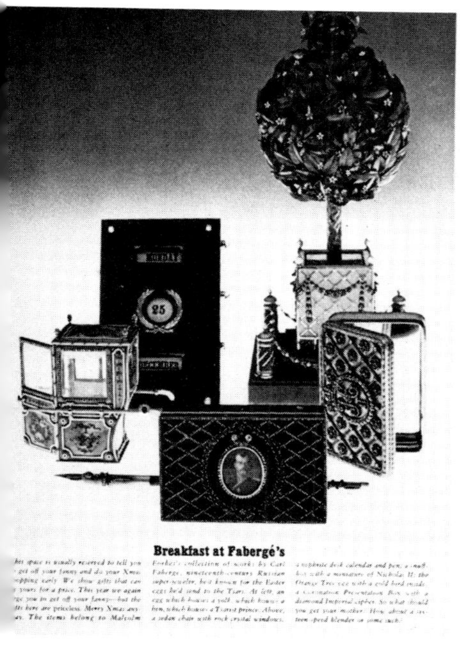
Breakfast at Fabergé's

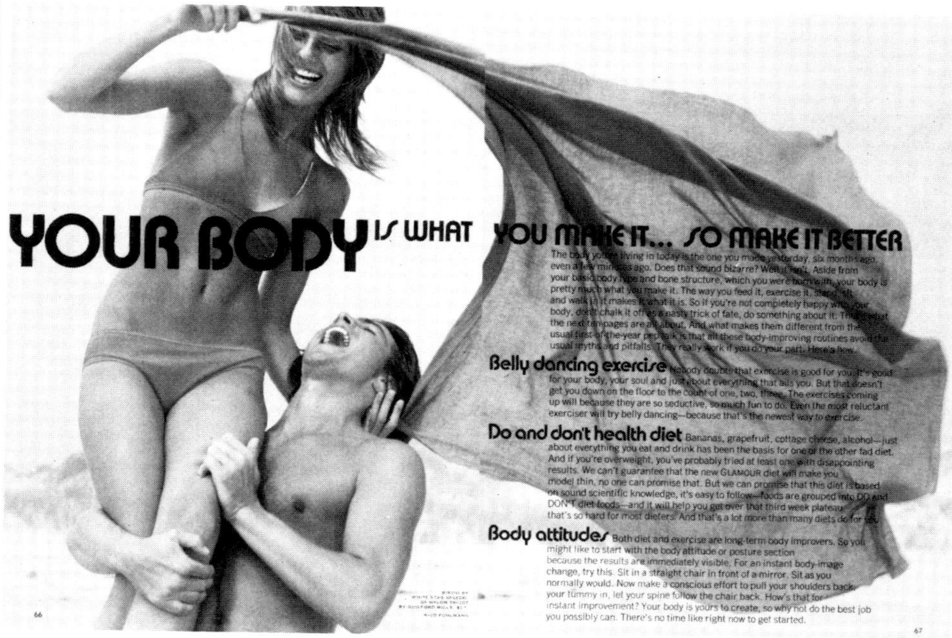
YOUR BODY IS WHAT YOU MAKE IT... SO MAKE IT BETTER
Belly dancing exercise
Do and don't health diet
Bananas, grapefruit, cottage cheese, alcohol—just about everything you eat and drink has been the basis for one or the other fad diet. And if you're overweight, you've probably tried at least one with disappointing results. We can't guarantee that the new GLAMOUR diet will make you model thin, no one can promise that.
Body attitudes
Both diet and exercise are long-term body improvers. So you might like to start with the body attitude or posture section because the results are immediately visible. For an instant body-image change, try this. Sit in a straight chair in front of a mirror. Sit as you normally would. Now make a conscious effort to pull your shoulders back, your tummy in, let your spine follow the chair back. How's that for instant improvement? Your body is yours to create, so why not do the best job you possibly can. There's no time like right now to get started.
66
67

283

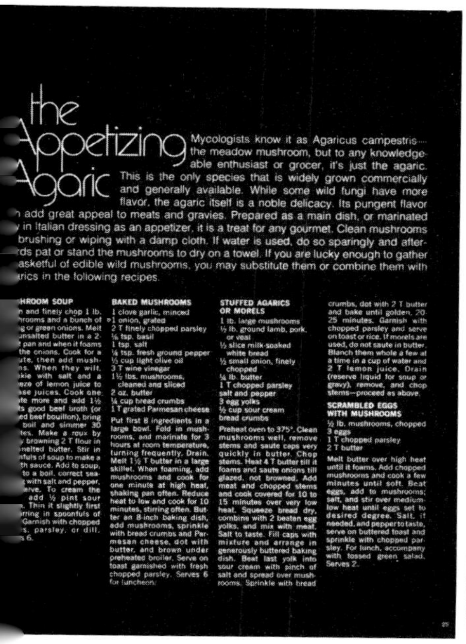
the Appetizing Agaric
Mycologists know it as Agaricus campestris—the meadow mushroom, but to any knowledgeable enthusiast or grocer, it's just the agaric. This is the only species that is widely grown commercially and generally available. While some wild fungi have more flavor, the agaric itself is a noble delicacy. Its pungent flavor
BAKED MUSHROOMS
STUFFED AGARICS OR MORELS
SCRAMBLED EGGS WITH MUSHROOMS

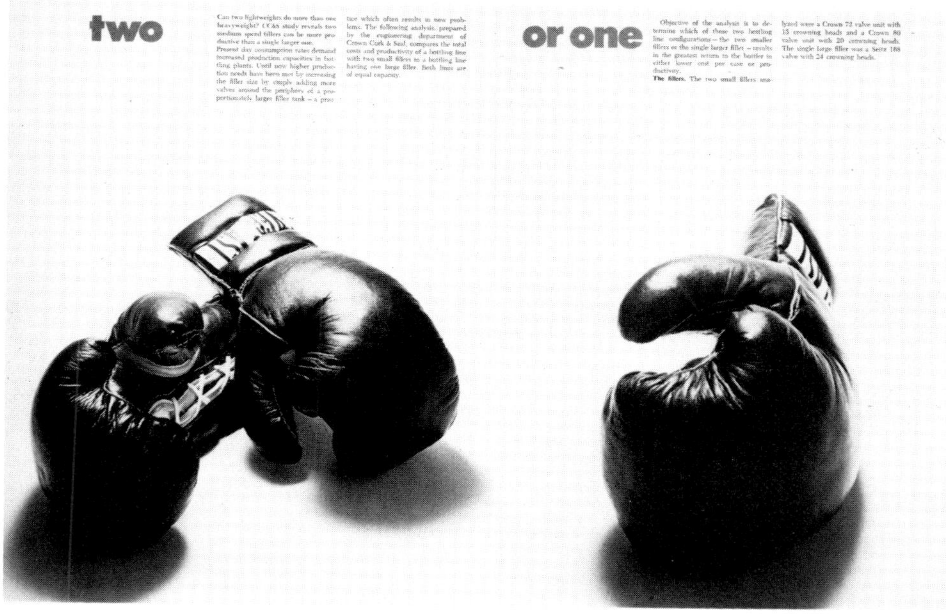
two
or one

284

282
Herman Duerr Entrant
Robert E. Smallman Photographer
Ceco Publishing Company Agency
Chevrolet Client

283
Glamour Magazine Entrant
George Hartman Art Director
Rico Puhlmann Photographer
Conde Nast Publications Client

284
Norman Gorbaty Design Entrant
Brian Ganton Art Director
Soft Drinks Magazine Client

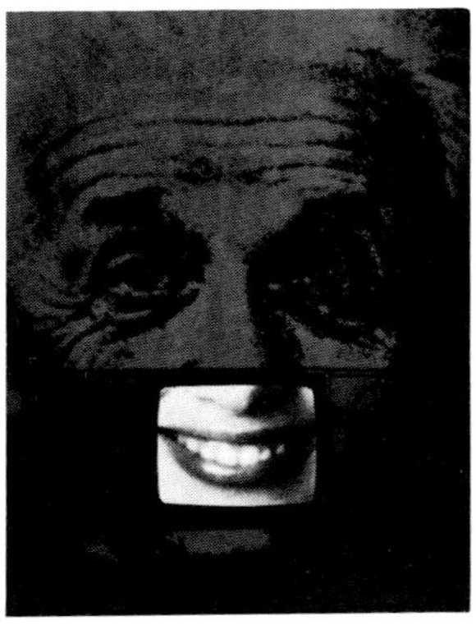

285

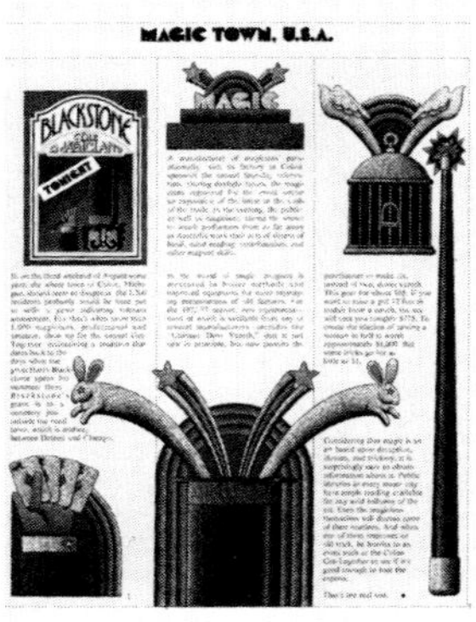
MAGIC TOWN, U.S.A.

286

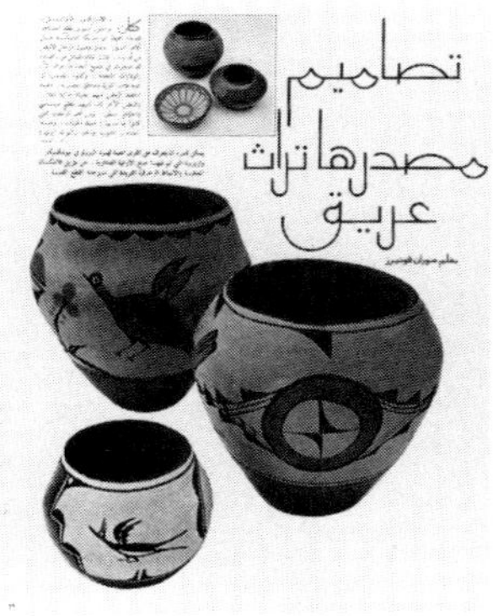
تصاميم
مصدرها تراث
عريق

287

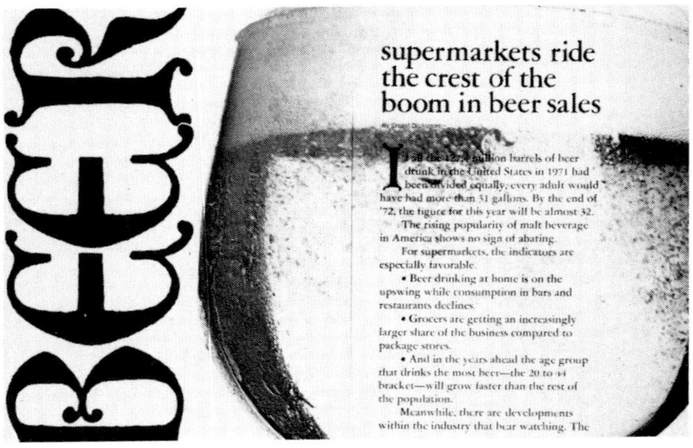
BEER
supermarkets ride the crest of the boom in beer sales

288

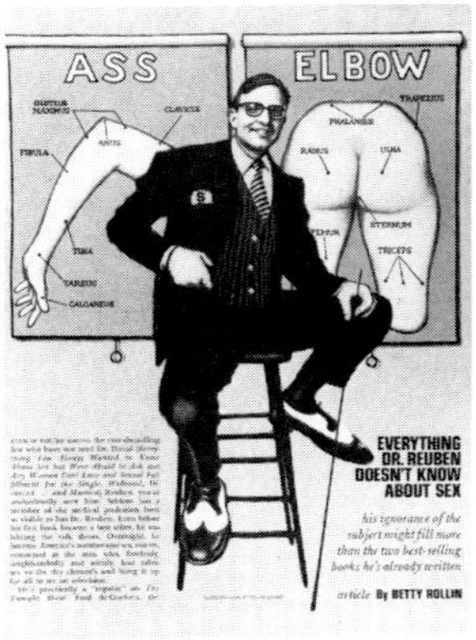
ASS
ELBOW
EVERYTHING DR. REUBEN DOESN'T KNOW ABOUT SEX

289

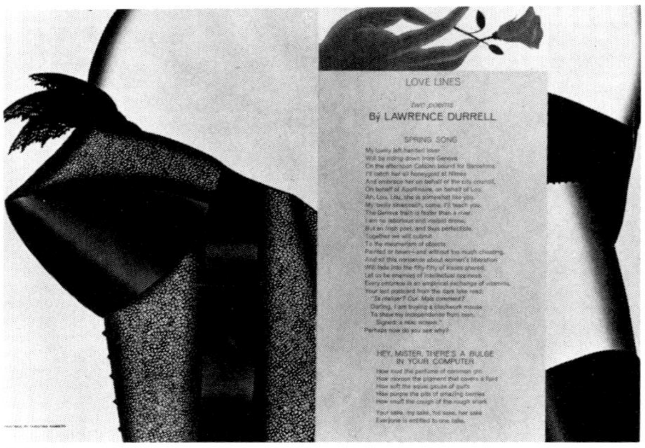
LOVE LINES
By LAWRENCE DURRELL

290

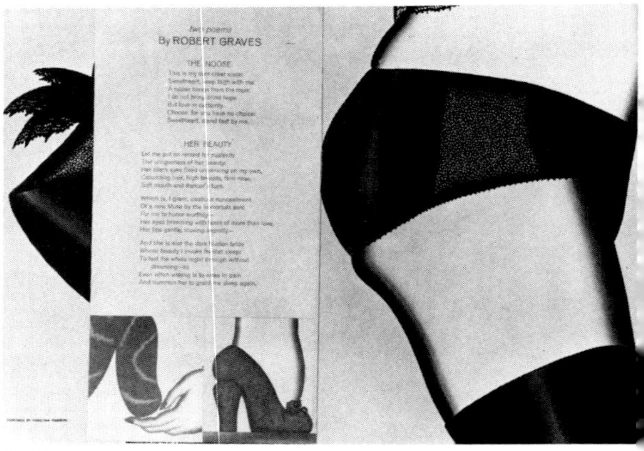
By ROBERT GRAVES

291

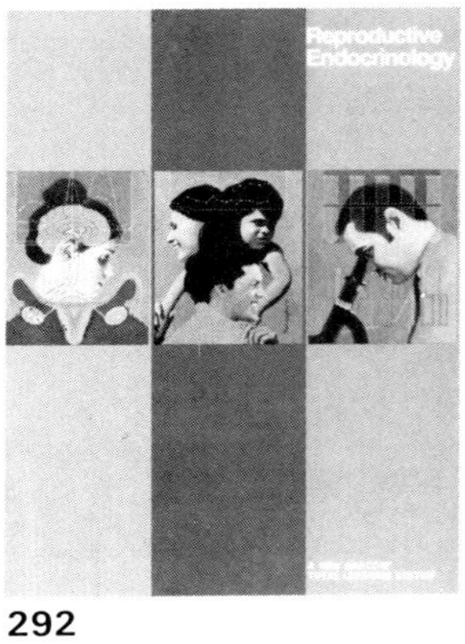
Reproductive Endocrinology

292

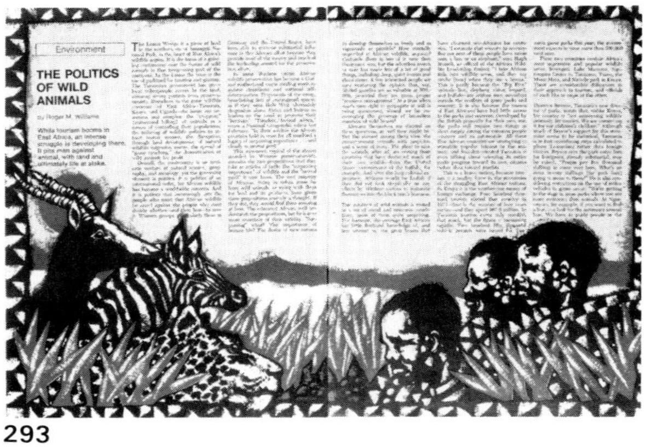
Environment
THE POLITICS OF WILD ANIMALS

293

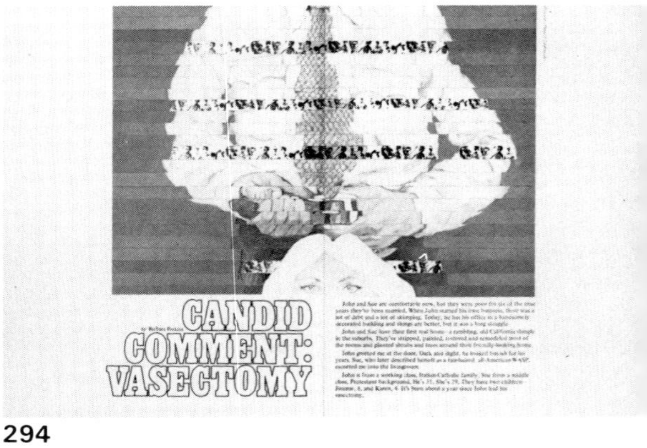
CANDID COMMENT: VASECTOMY

294

285
Henry Wolf Productions Inc. Entrant
Henry Wolf Art Director
Audience Magazine Client

286
George Watson Entrant
Patti Churchill Illustrator
Ceco Publishing Co. Agency
Inner Circle Magazine, United Delco Division G.M. Corp. Client

287
U.S. Information Agency Entrant
Robert Banks Art Director
Sam Burlockoff Designer
Richard Noble Photographer
Al Majal Magazine Client

288
Jeff Babitz Entrant
Bruce Nemeth Photographer
A.I.M.S. Agency
Supermarketing Client

289
Playboy Enterprises, Inc. Entrant
Arthur Paul Art Director
Ed Paschke Artist
Alfred Zelcer Designer
Playboy Magazine Client

290-291
Playboy Enterprises, Inc. Entrant
Arthur Paul Art Director
Christina Ramberg Illustrator
Kerig Pope Designer
Playboy Magazine Client

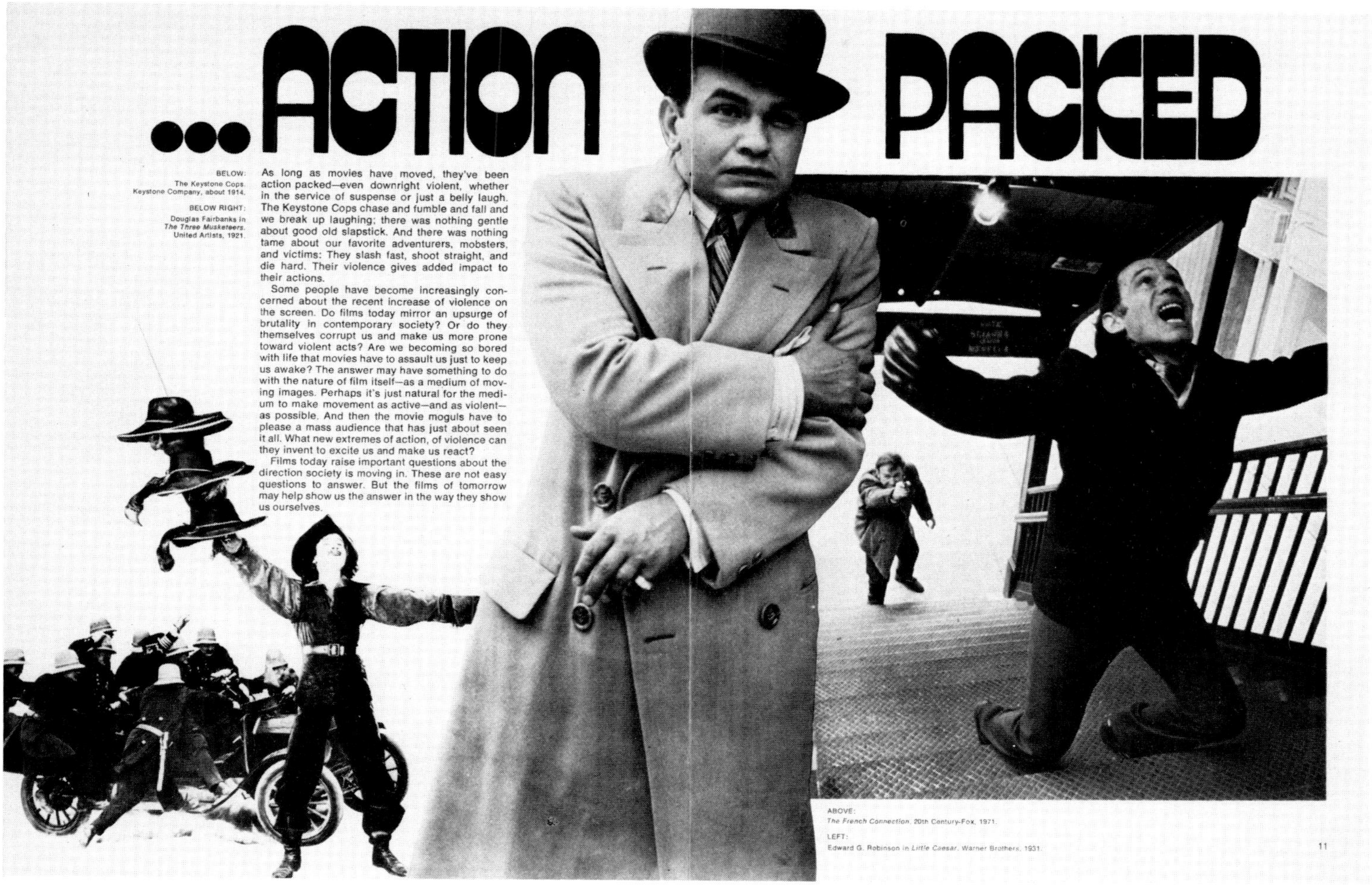

...ACTION PACKED

BELOW:
The Keystone Cops. Keystone Company, about 1914.

BELOW RIGHT:
Douglas Fairbanks in *The Three Musketeers*. United Artists, 1921.

As long as movies have moved, they've been action packed—even downright violent, whether in the service of suspense or just a belly laugh. The Keystone Cops chase and fumble and fall and we break up laughing; there was nothing gentle about good old slapstick. And there was nothing tame about our favorite adventurers, mobsters, and victims: They slash fast, shoot straight, and die hard. Their violence gives added impact to their actions.

Some people have become increasingly concerned about the recent increase of violence on the screen. Do films today mirror an upsurge of brutality in contemporary society? Or do they themselves corrupt us and make us more prone toward violent acts? Are we becoming so bored with life that movies have to assault us just to keep us awake? The answer may have something to do with the nature of film itself—as a medium of moving images. Perhaps it's just natural for the medium to make movement as active—and as violent—as possible. And then the movie moguls have to please a mass audience that has just about seen it all. What new extremes of action, of violence can they invent to excite us and make us react?

Films today raise important questions about the direction society is moving in. These are not easy questions to answer. But the films of tomorrow may help show us the answer in the way they show us ourselves.

ABOVE:
The French Connection. 20th Century-Fox, 1971.

LEFT:
Edward G. Robinson in *Little Caesar*. Warner Brothers, 1931.

11

295

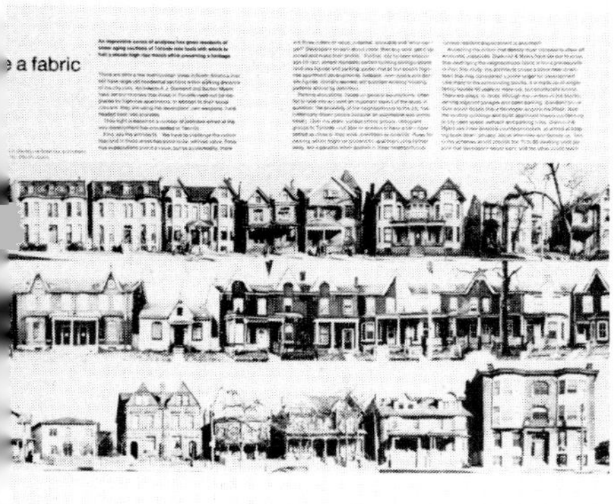

a fabric

296

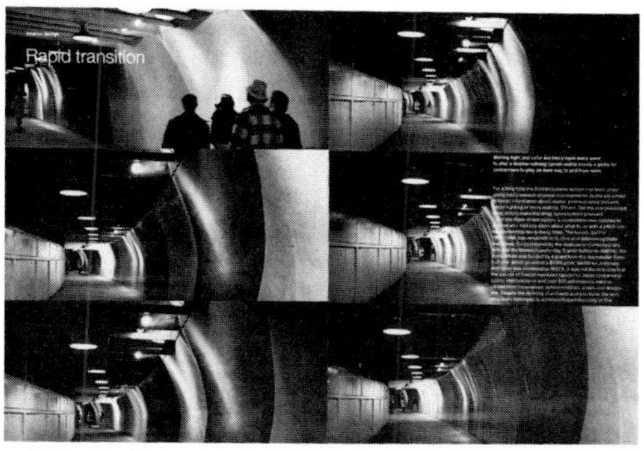

Rapid transition

297

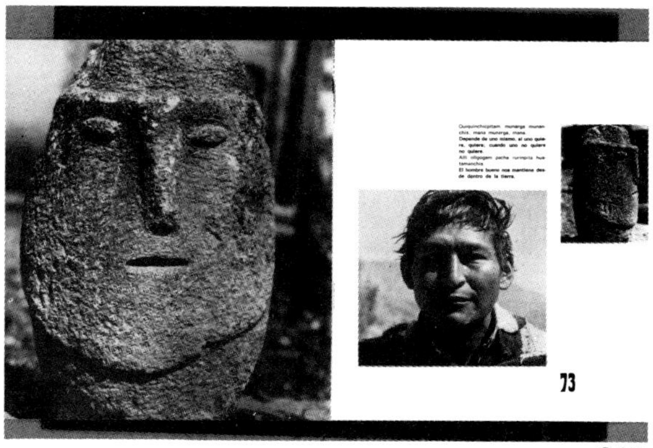

298

292
Arthur Beckenstein
Entrant
Medcom Inc.
Agency
Alex Guidziejko
Illustrator
Wyeth Laboratories
Client

293
World Magazine
Entrant
Judith Adel
Art Director
Marcia McElrath
Designer
Miriam Schottland
Illustrator

294
Steven Jacobs Design, Inc.
Entrant
Steve Jacobs
Art Director
Dennis Ziemienski
Illustrator
California Girl Magazine
Client

295
Margaret Howlett
Entrant
Scholastic Publications
Client

296
Reinhold Publishing Co. Entrant
Joel Petrower
Art Director
Joseph Bower
Photographer
Progressive Architecture
Client

297
Reinhold Publishing Co. Entrant
Joel Petrower
Art Director
Sharon Lee Ryder
Photographer
Progressive Architecture
Client

298
Claude Dieterich
Entrant
Associacion de Artes y Estudios Experimentales Lima, Peru
Client

299

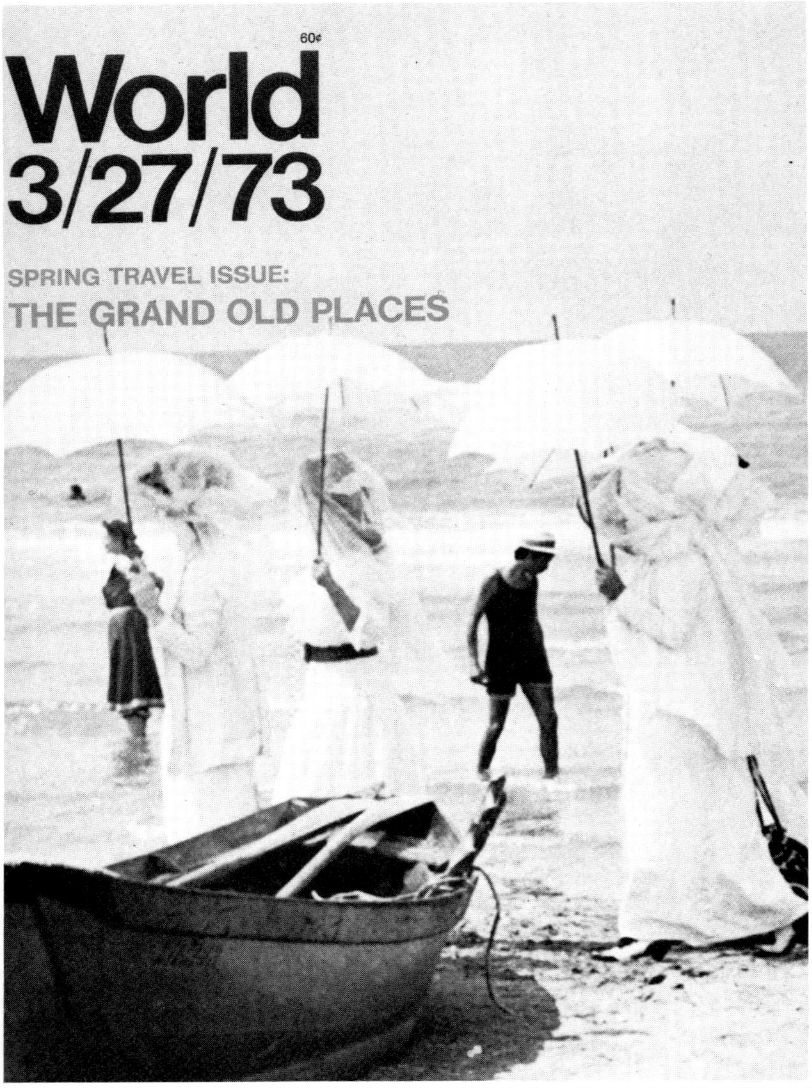
60¢
World
3/27/73
SPRING TRAVEL ISSUE:
THE GRAND OLD PLACES

300

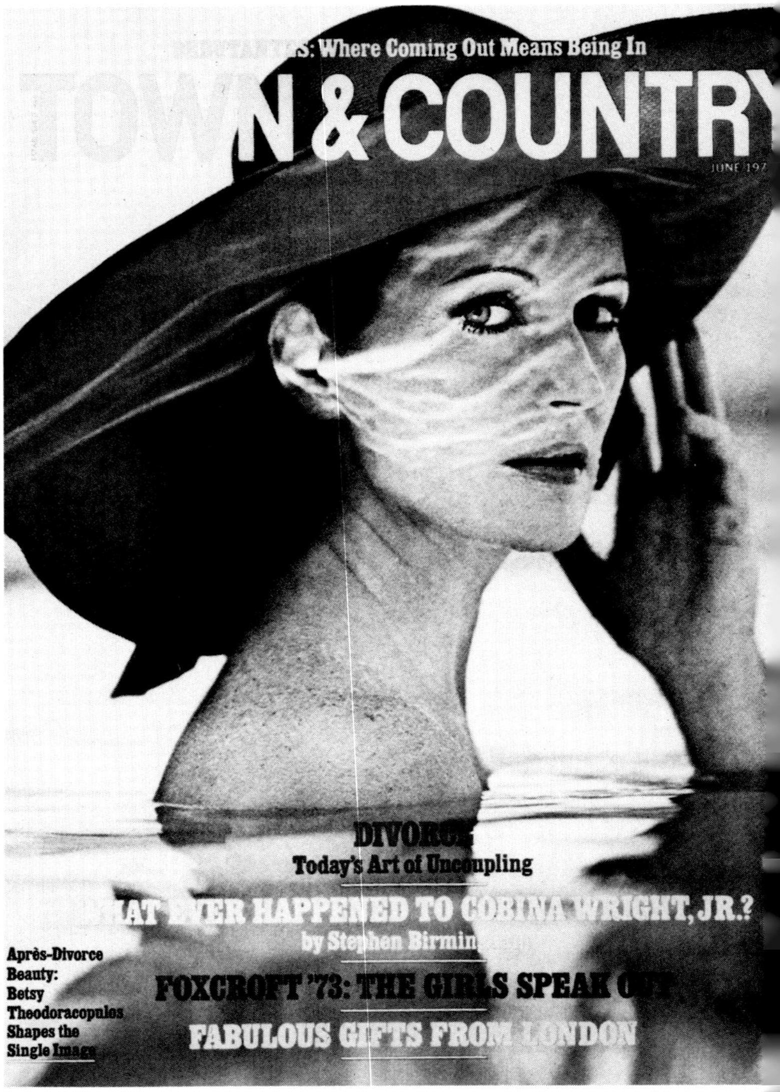
Where Coming Out Means Being In
N & COUNTRY
Today's Art of Uncoupling
Après-Divorce Beauty: Betsy Theodoracopulos Shapes the Single Image

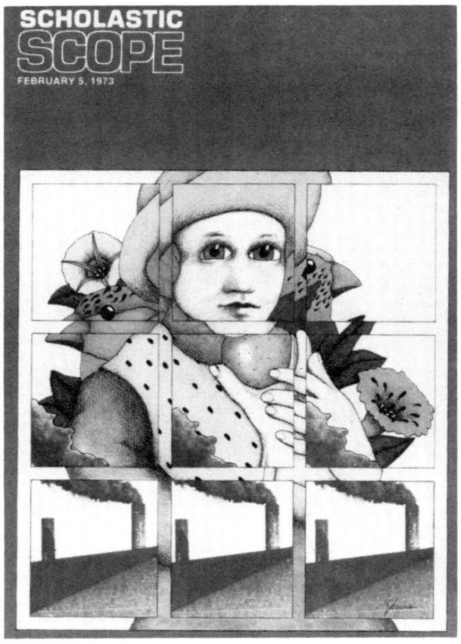
SCHOLASTIC
SCOPE
FEBRUARY 5, 1973

301

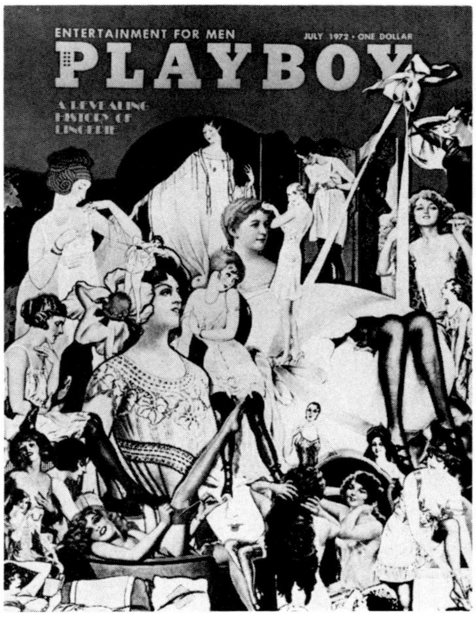
ENTERTAINMENT FOR MEN
JULY 1972 • ONE DOLLAR
PLAYBOY

302

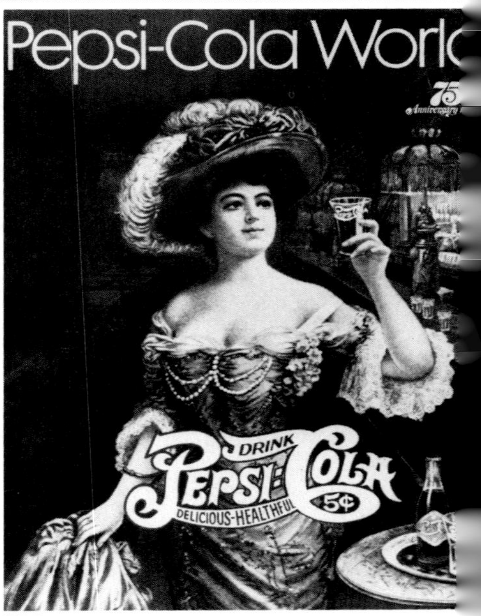
Pepsi-Cola Worl
DRINK
PEPSI-COLA
DELICIOUS-HEALTHFUL
5¢

303

299
World Magazine
Entrant
Judith Adel
Art Director

300
Town & Country Magazine
Entrant
Nancy V. Kent
Art Director
Douglas Kirkland
Photographer

301
Frank Rothman
Entrant
Russell D'Anna
Art Director
Doug Gervasi
Illustrator
Scholastic Magazines Inc. Studio

302
Playboy Enterprises Inc. Entrant
Arthur Paul
Art Director
Tom Tomc Illustrator
Kerig Pope Designer
Playboy Magazine
Client

303
Eiseman and Enock Inc. Entrant
PepsiCo Inc.
Client

304

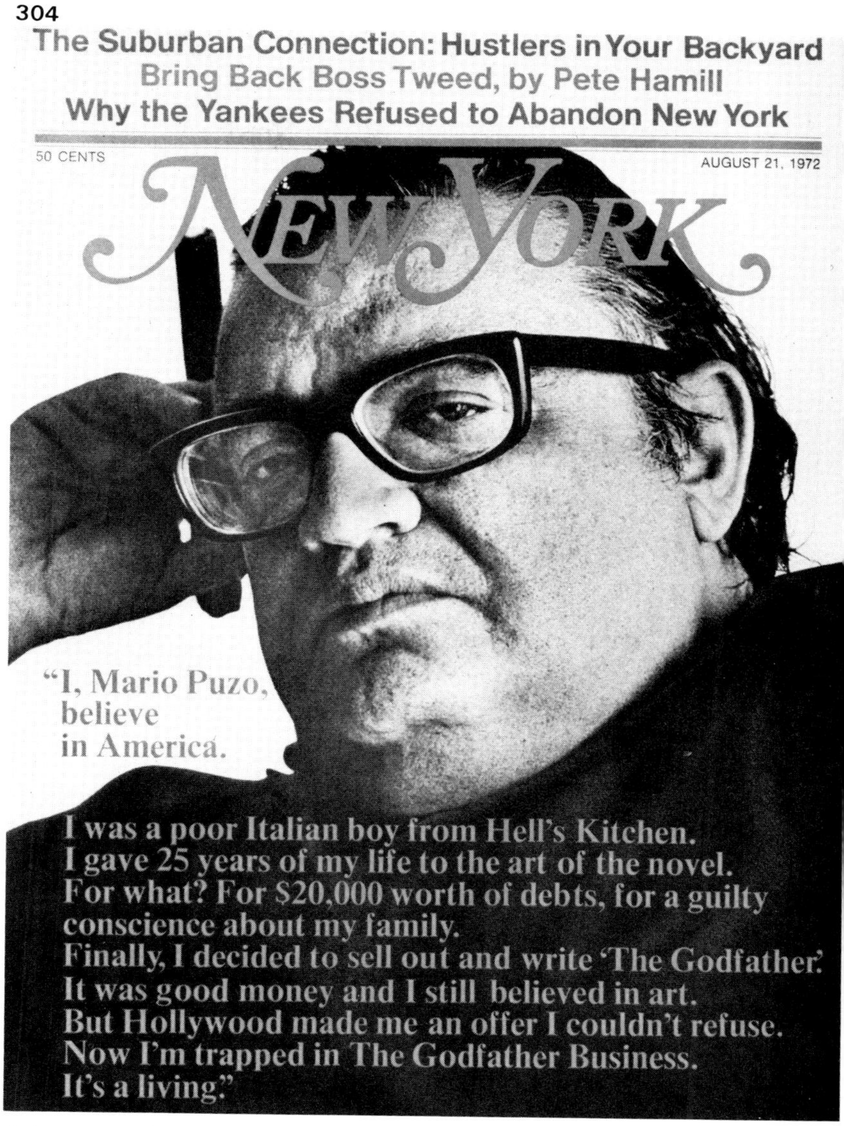
The Suburban Connection: Hustlers in Your Backyard
Bring Back Boss Tweed, by Pete Hamill
Why the Yankees Refused to Abandon New York
50 CENTS
AUGUST 21, 1972
NEW YORK
"I, Mario Puzo, believe in America.
I was a poor Italian boy from Hell's Kitchen.
I gave 25 years of my life to the art of the novel.
For what? For $20,000 worth of debts, for a guilty conscience about my family.
Finally, I decided to sell out and write 'The Godfather.'
It was good money and I still believed in art.
But Hollywood made me an offer I couldn't refuse.
Now I'm trapped in The Godfather Business.
It's a living."

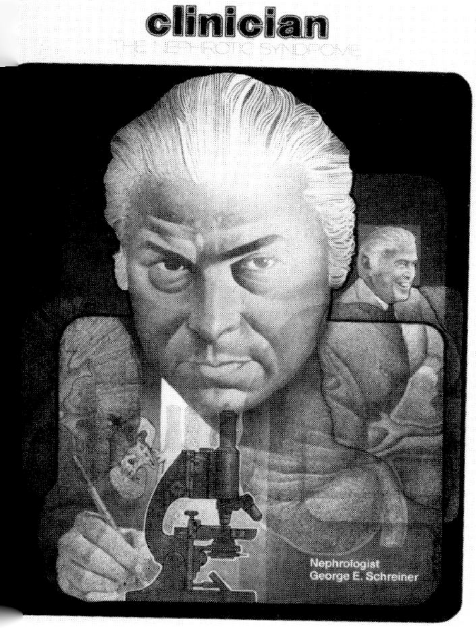
clinician
THE NEPHROTIC SYNDROME
Nephrologist
George E. Schreiner

305

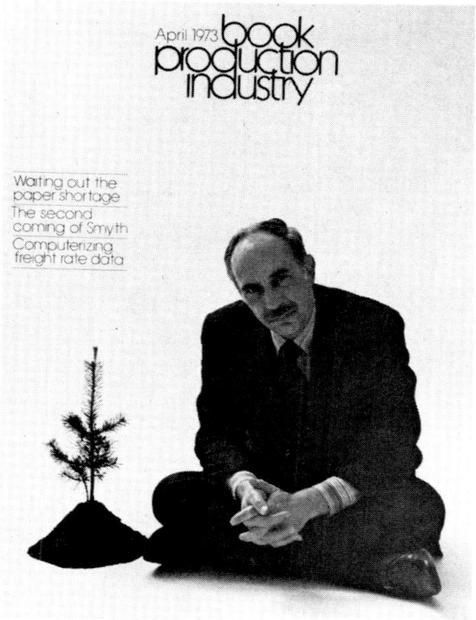
April 1973 book production industry
Waiting out the paper shortage
The second coming of Smyth
Computerizing freight rate data

306

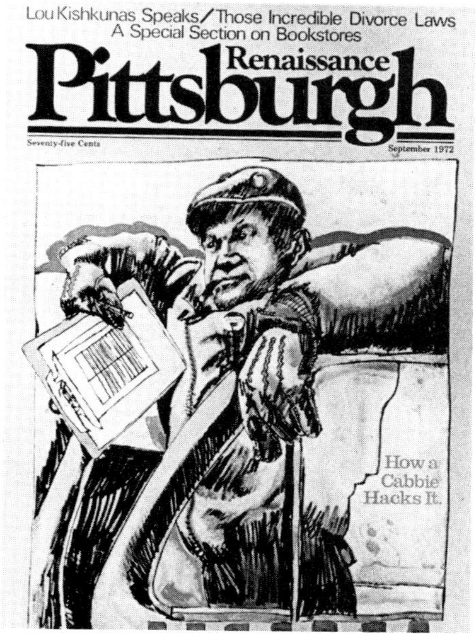
Lou Kishkunas Speaks/Those Incredible Divorce Laws
A Special Section on Bookstores
Renaissance
Pittsburgh
Seventy-five Cents
September 1972
How a Cabbie Hacks It.

307

304
Daniel Kramer
Entrant
Walter Bernard
Art Director
New York Magazine
Client

305
Gary N. Olivo
Entrant
Medcom Inc.
Agency
Mark English
Illustrator
Searle & Co.
Client

306
Book Production Industry Entrant
William W. Demlin
Art Director
Jack Elness
Photographer

307
J.M. Essex/Design Center Entrant
J. Michael Essex
Art Director
Ed Zelinsky
Illustrator
WQED/Design Center
Agency
Metropolitan Pittsburgh Public Broadcasting
Client

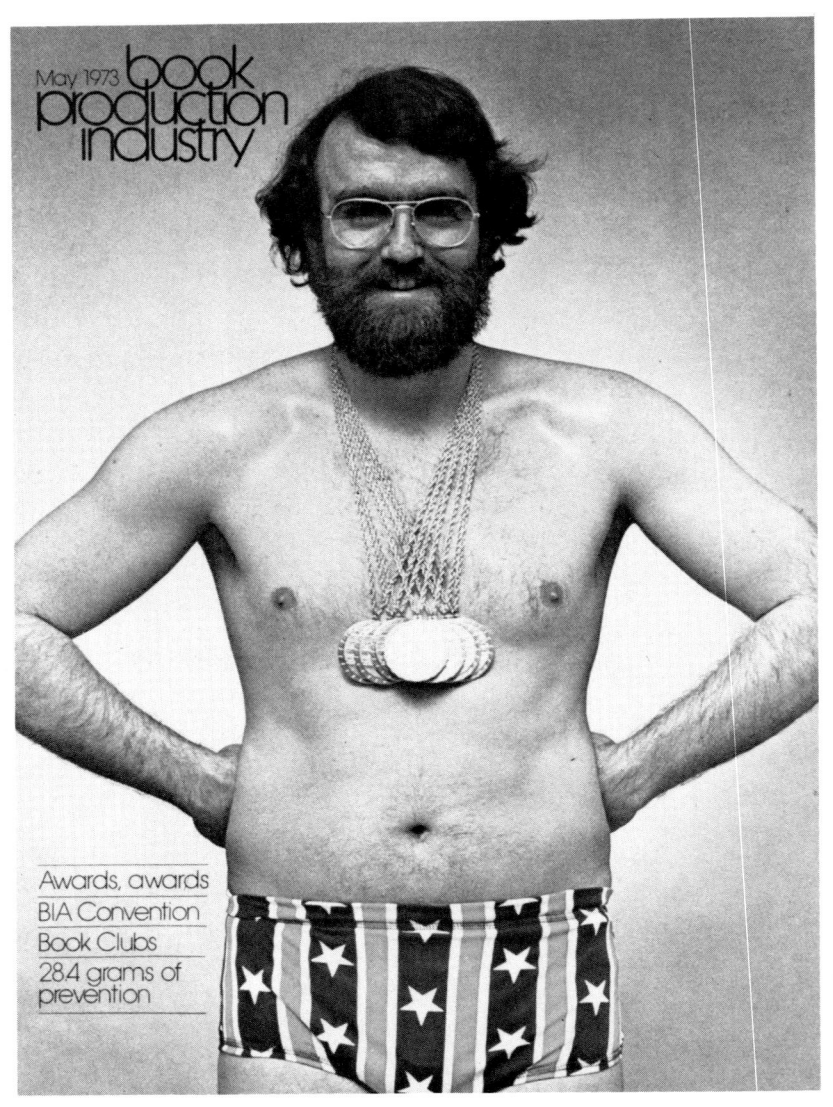

May 1973
book production industry
Awards, awards
BIA Convention
Book Clubs
28.4 grams of prevention

308
Book Production Industry Entrant
William W. Demlin Art Director
Jack Elness Photographer

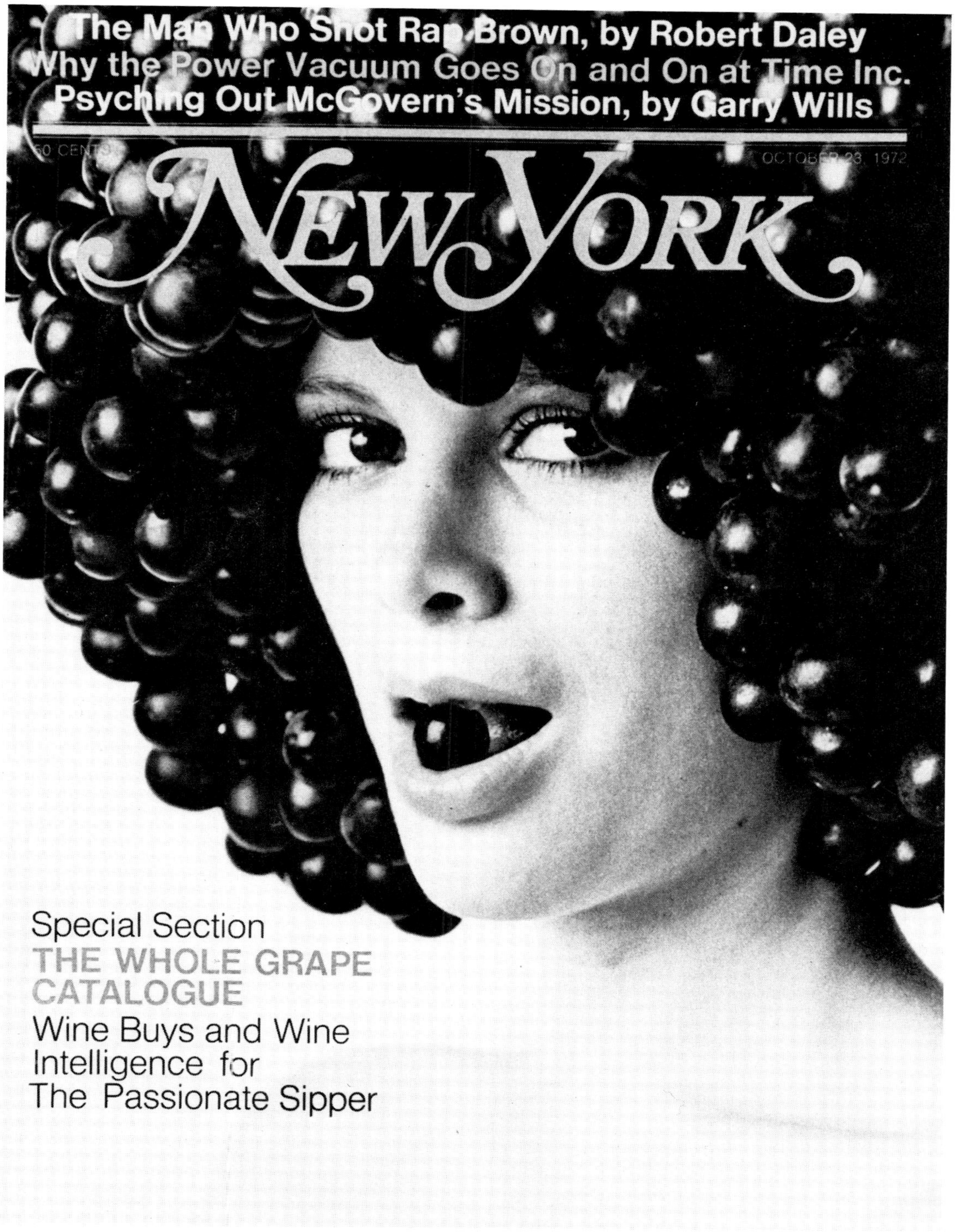
The Man Who Shot Rap Brown, by Robert Daley
Why the Power Vacuum Goes On and On at Time Inc.
Psyching Out McGovern's Mission, by Garry Wills
50 CENTS
OCTOBER 23, 1972
NEW YORK
Special Section
THE WHOLE GRAPE CATALOGUE
Wine Buys and Wine Intelligence for The Passionate Sipper

309
Henry Wolf Productions, Inc. Entrant
Walter Bernard Art Director
New York Magazine Client

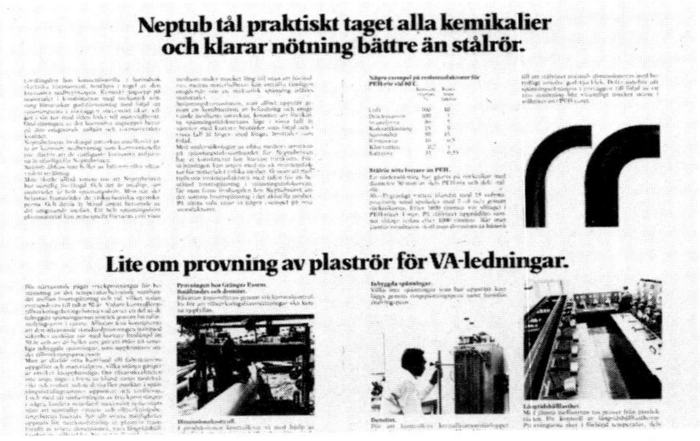
Neptub tål praktiskt taget alla kemikalier
och klarar nötning bättre än stålrör.
Lite om provning av plaströr för VA-ledningar.

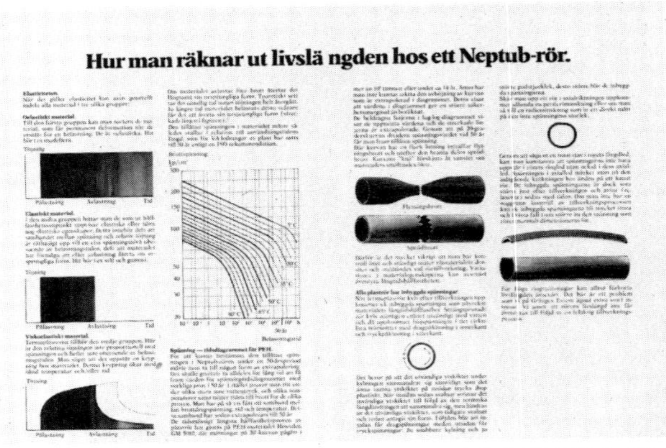
Hur man räknar ut livslä ngden hos ett Neptub-rör.

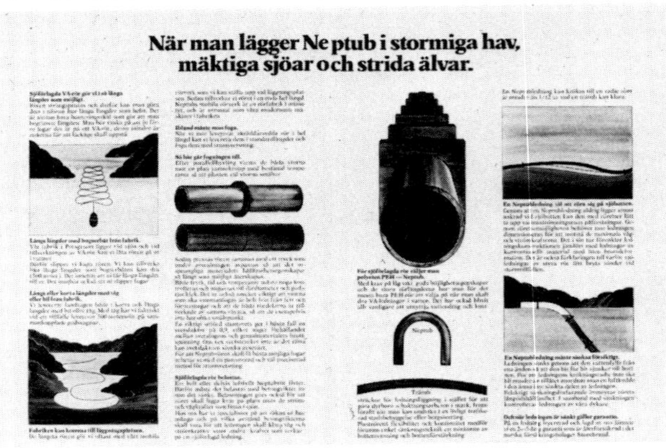
När man lägger Ne ptub i stormiga hav,
mäktiga sjöar och strida älvar.

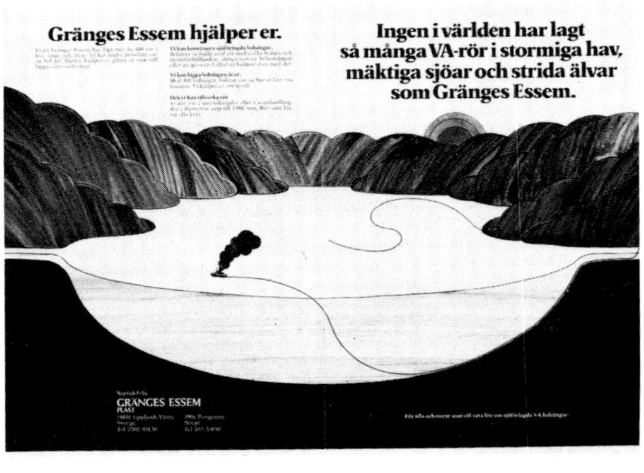
Gränges Essem hjälper er.
Ingen i världen har lagt
så många VA-rör i stormiga hav,
mäktiga sjöar och strida älvar
som Gränges Essem.
GRÄNGES ESSEM

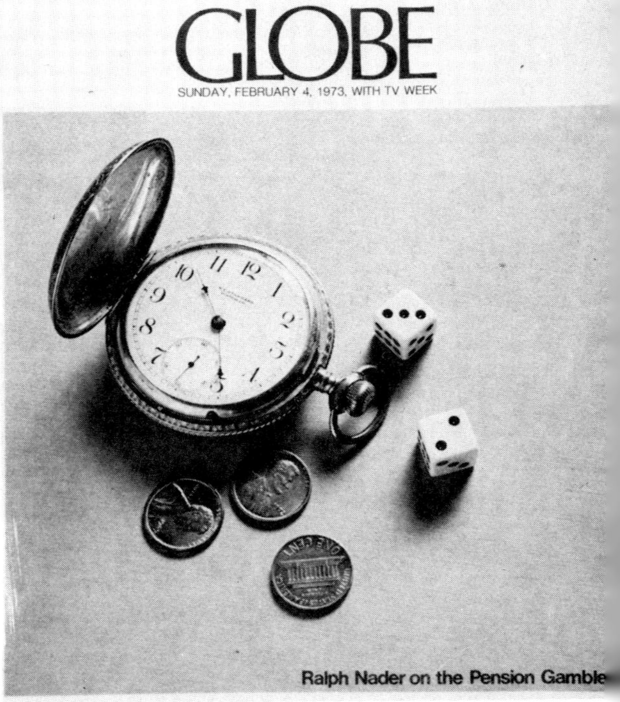
GLOBE
SUNDAY, FEBRUARY 4, 1973, WITH TV WEEK
Ralph Nader on the Pension Gamble

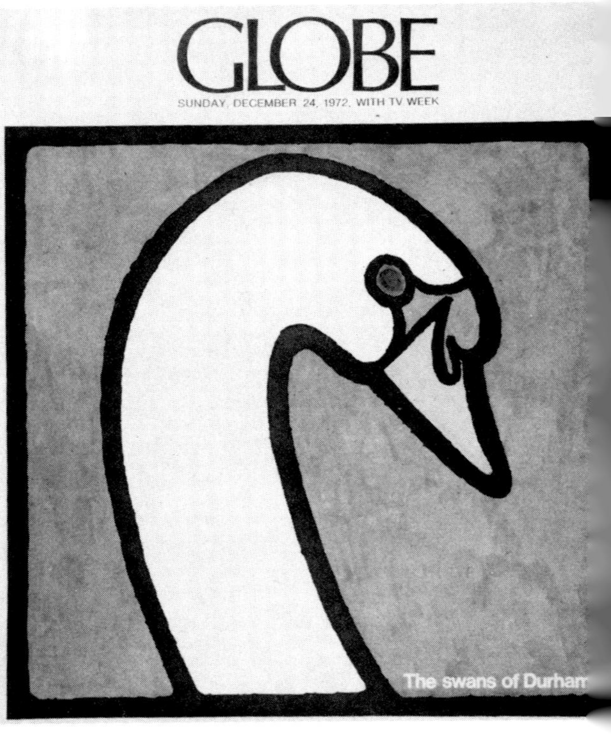
GLOBE
SUNDAY, DECEMBER 24, 1972, WITH TV WEEK
The swans of Durham

310-313
Sven O. Blomquist Annonsbyrå AB Entrant
Par Friden Art Director
Gränges Essem Plast. Upplands Vasby. Client

314-315
The Boston Globe Entrant
Herbert Rogalski Art Director

316

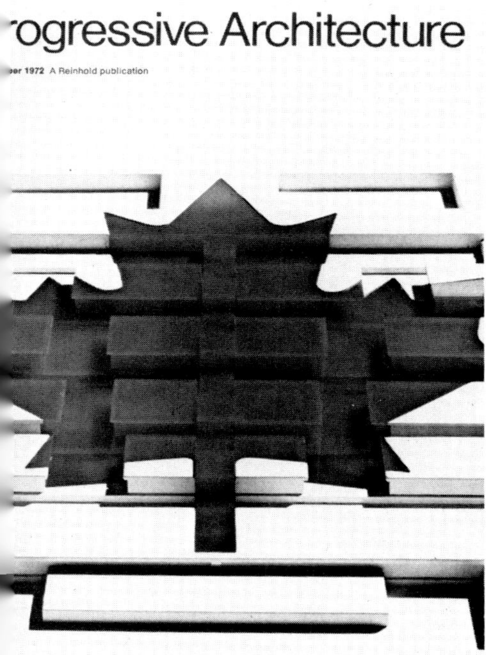
rogressive Architecture
A Reinhold publication

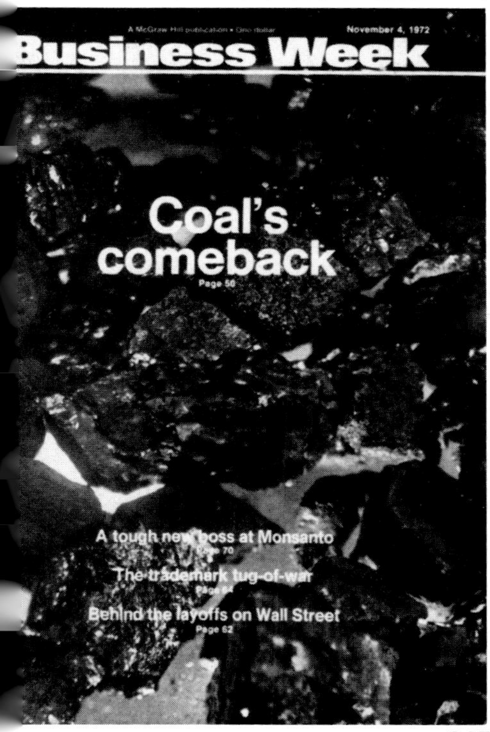
November 4, 1972
Business Week
Coal's comeback
A tough new boss at Monsanto
The trademark tug-of-war
Behind the layoffs on Wall Street

317

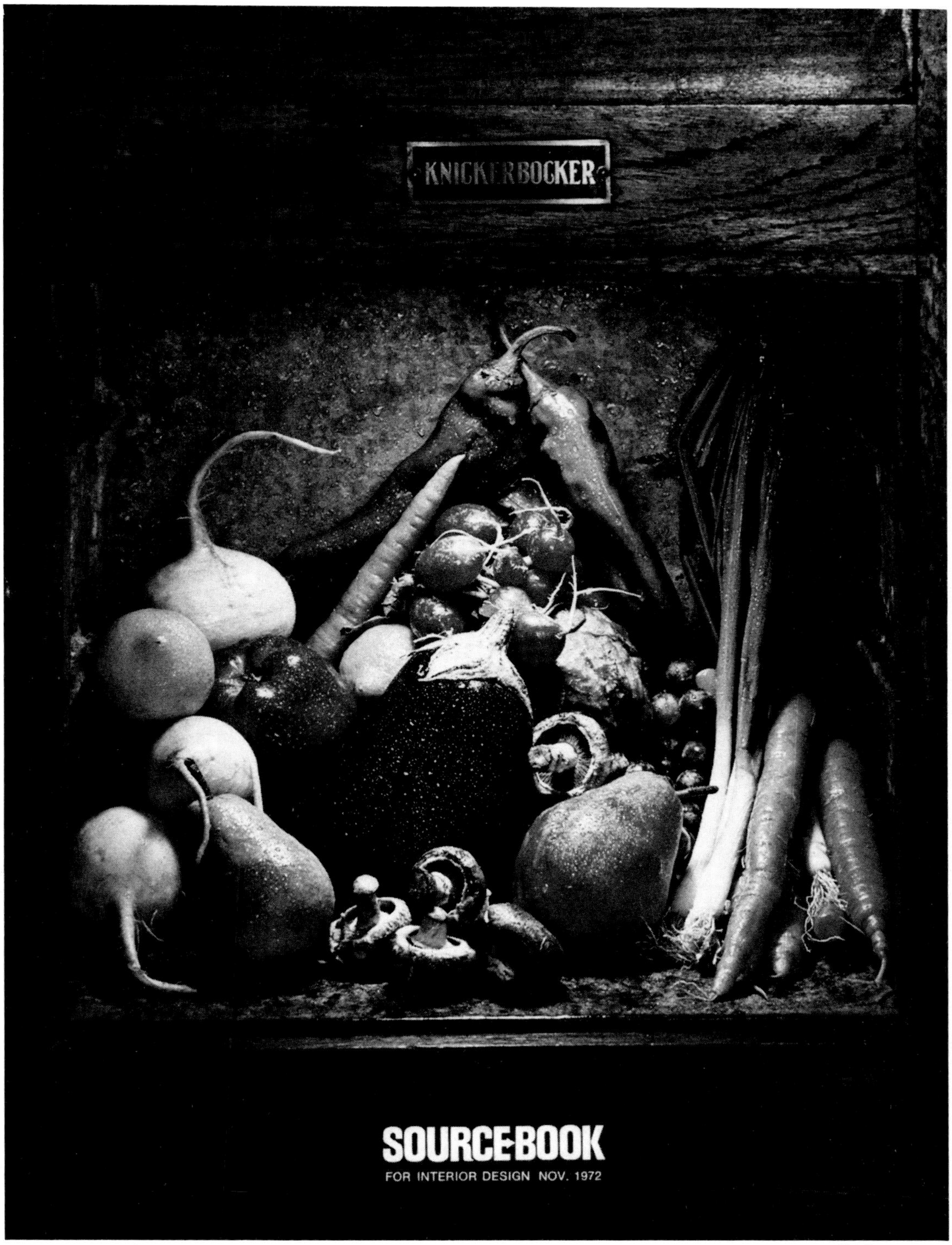
KNICKERBOCKER
SOURCEBOOK
FOR INTERIOR DESIGN NOV. 1972

318

316
Reinhold Publishing Co. Entrant
Joel Petrower Art Director
Bradbury-McCormick Photographers
Cappabianca Displays Studio
Progressive Architecture Client

317
Business Week Magazine Entrant
Robert N. Essman Art Director
Richard Knapp Photographer

318
John Cahoon Photography Entrant
Rex Goode Editor
Sourcebook Magazine Client

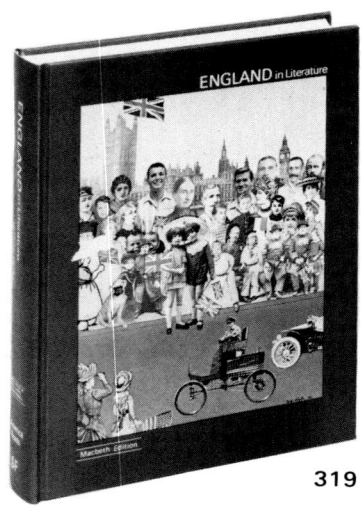

ENGLAND in Literature
Macbeth Edition

319

The UNITED STATES in Literature
The Glass Menagerie Edition

320

Safety Manual

321

Eye Protection
15
The wearing of eye protection is mandatory in certain designated areas of our manufacturing buildings and laboratories. Typical eye protection equipment consists of goggles, safety glasses, and face shields. Your supervisor will instruct you as to which operations require use of this equipment.
Avoid eye injuries by preventing splashes, particles, or irritating vapors from entering the eye. Care must be taken not to rub or wipe the eye with hands or shirt sleeves that may be dirty or contaminated.
In removing safety goggles, bend the head over and remove the goggles in an upward sweep to avoid contaminating the eye area.
Keep your eye protection devices clean and give them reasonable care. In turn, they will protect your eyes.
ersonal Cleanliness
16
Soap and water is the Safety equipment you use to prevent skin irritation or dermatitis.
It is an excellent idea to wash your hands, arms, and face thoroughly after working with chemicals to remove all traces. This is especially important before you eat or smoke.
The Company provides protective Safety equipment to help prevent contact with chemicals. The equipment should be washed thoroughly after use to remove irritating substances.
By keeping your clothing, yourself, and the equipment with which you work clean, you will be helping to curb skin problems.

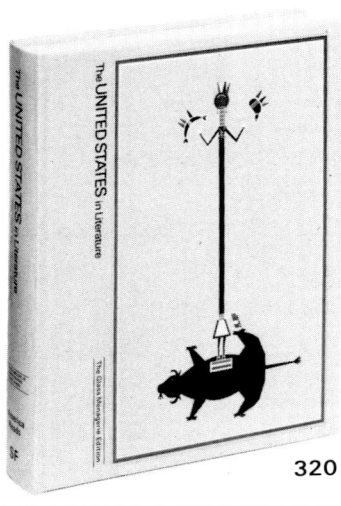

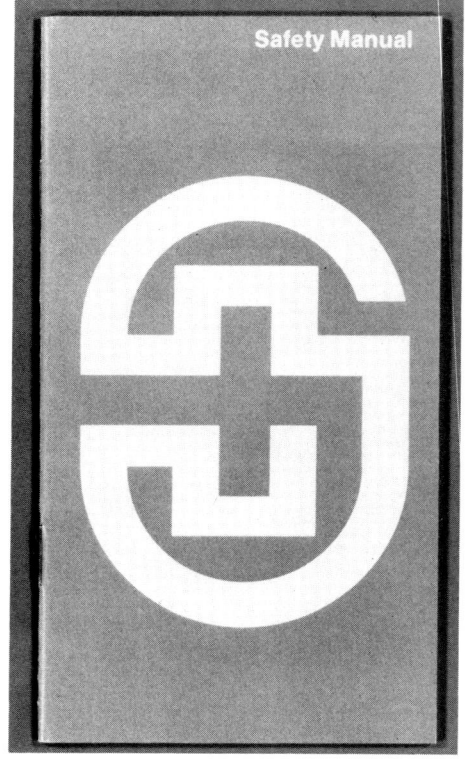

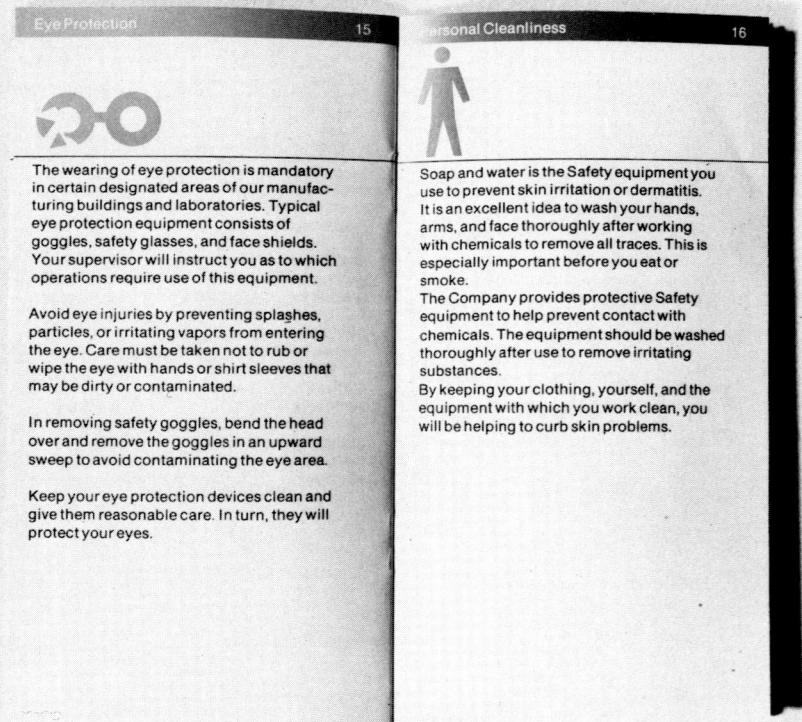

322

319-320
Robert Amft Entrant
Hal Kearney Art Director
Scott, Foresman Client

321-322
Markus J. Low Entrant
Stan Baker, Otto Daeppen Art Directors
Ciba-Geigy Corporation Client

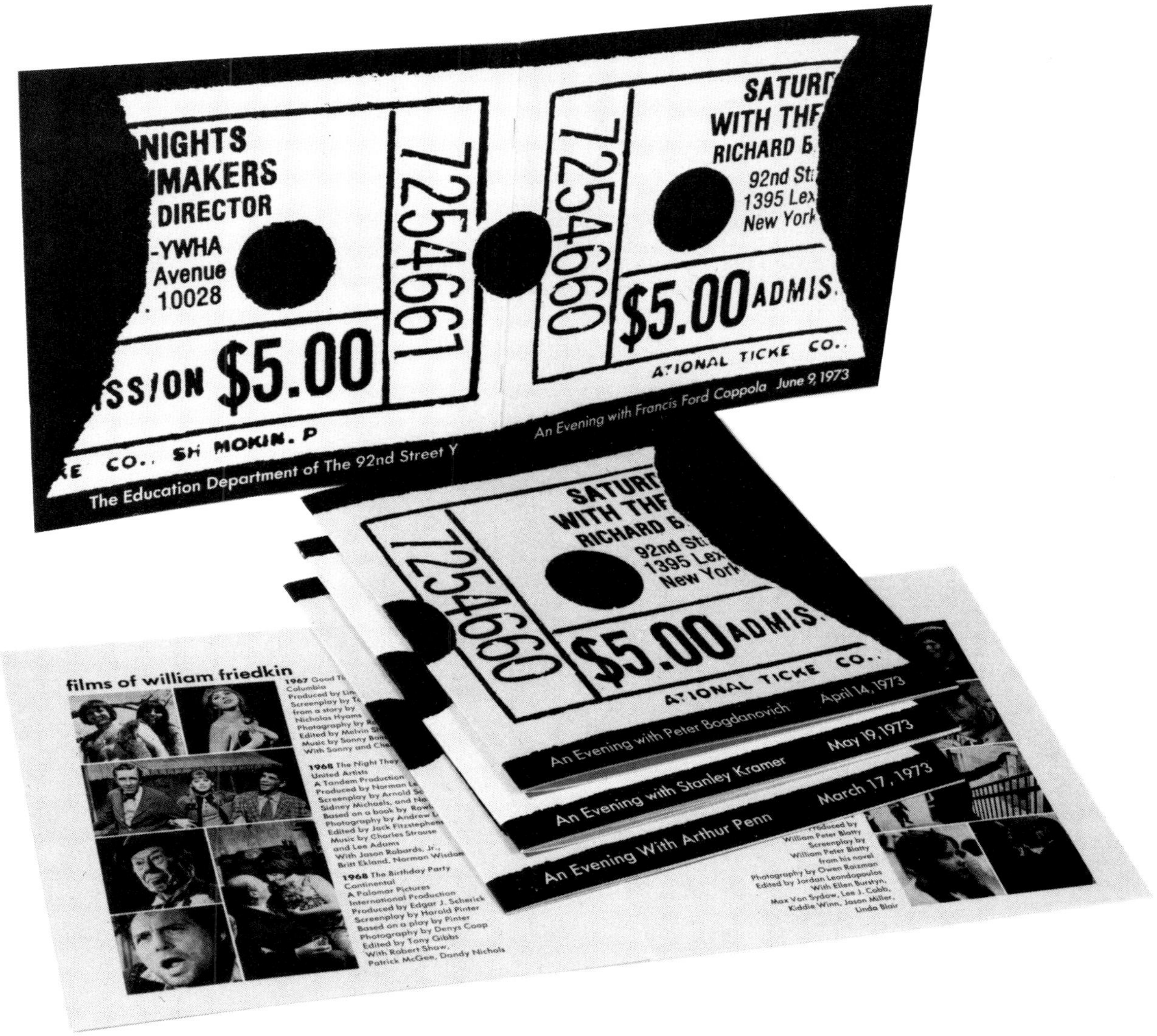

NIGHTS
MAKERS
DIRECTOR
-YWHA
Avenue
. 10028
7254661
SSION $5.00
CO.. SH MOKIN, P
The Education Department of The 92nd Street Y
SATURD
WITH THE
RICHARD B.
92nd St
1395 Lex
New York
7254660
$5.00 ADMIS.
ATIONAL TICKE CO..
An Evening with Francis Ford Coppola June 9, 1973
An Evening with Peter Bogdanovich April 14, 1973
An Evening with Stanley Kramer May 19, 1973
An Evening With Arthur Penn March 17, 1973
films of william friedkin

323
Marty Davidson, Doris Maltz Entrant
Richard Brown—YMHA Client

324

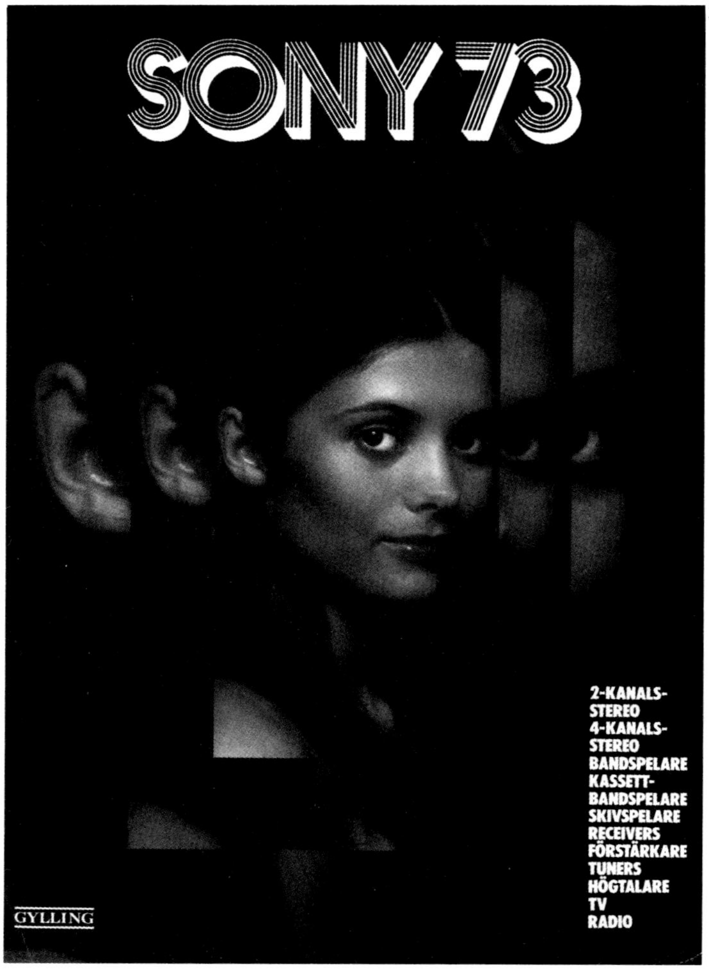
SONY 73
2-KANALS-
STEREO
4-KANALS-
STEREO
BANDSPELARE
KASSETT-
BANDSPELARE
SKIVSPELARE
RECEIVERS
FÖRSTÄRKARE
TUNERS
HÖGTALARE
TV
RADIO
GYLLING

325

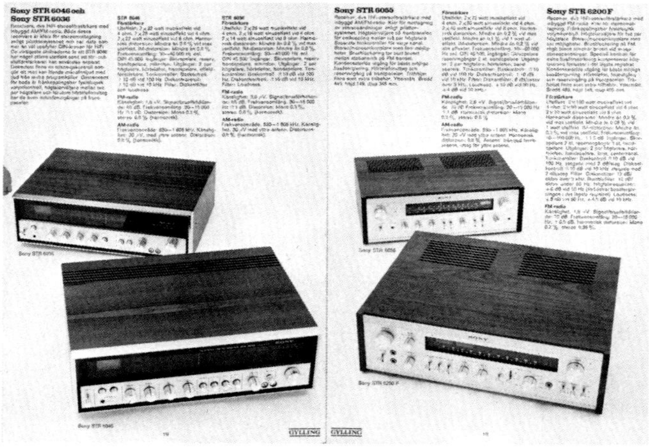

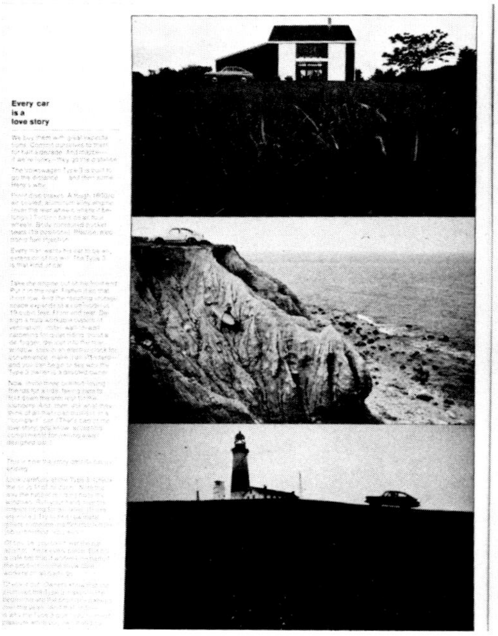
Every car
is a
love story

326

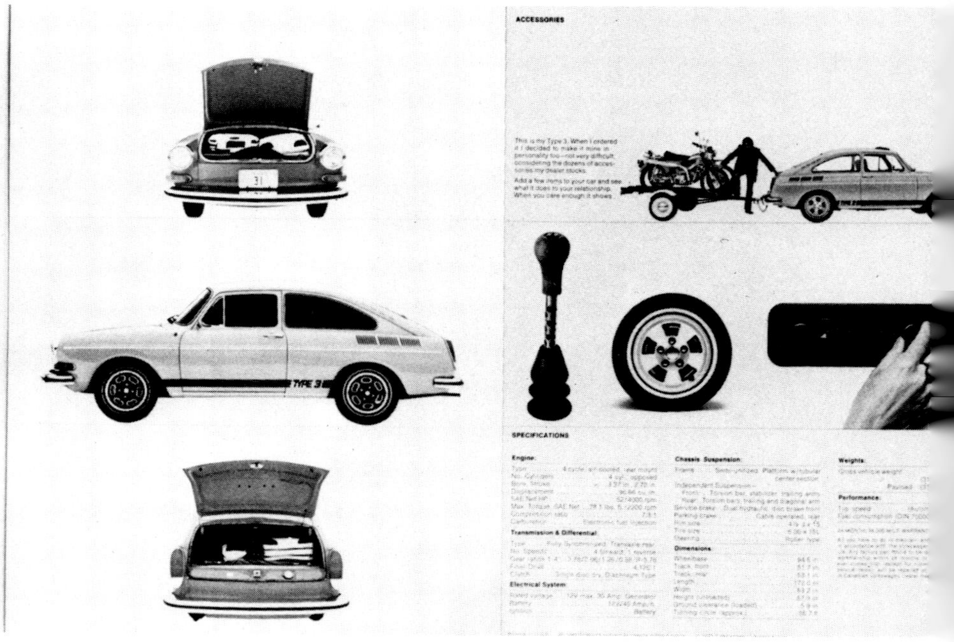
ACCESSORIES
SPECIFICATIONS

327

324-325
Marknads Kommunikation AB Entrant
Jorma Kosunen Art Director
Jan Bengtsson Photographer
Gylling (Sony) Client

326-328
B. Martin Pedersen Entrant
Pete Turner Photographer
Pedersen Design Inc. Studio
Volkswagen of America, Inc. Client

329

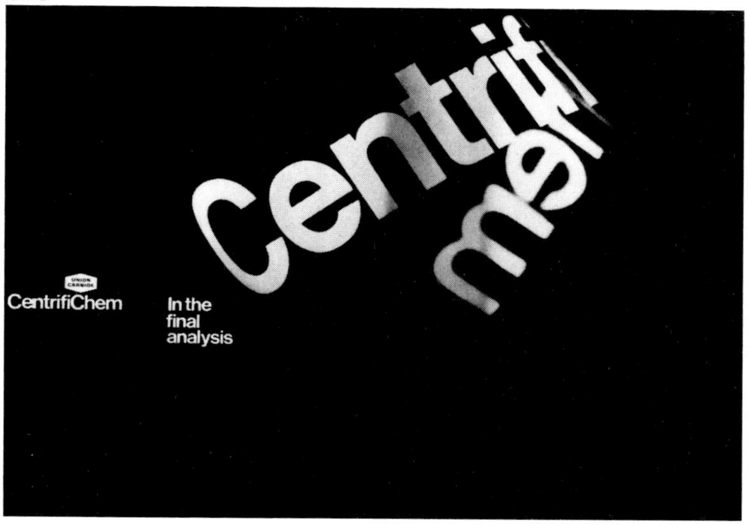
Centrifi
CentrifiChem
In the
final
analysis

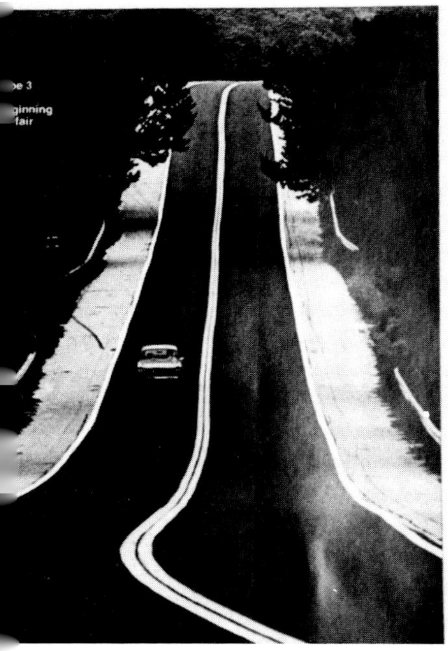

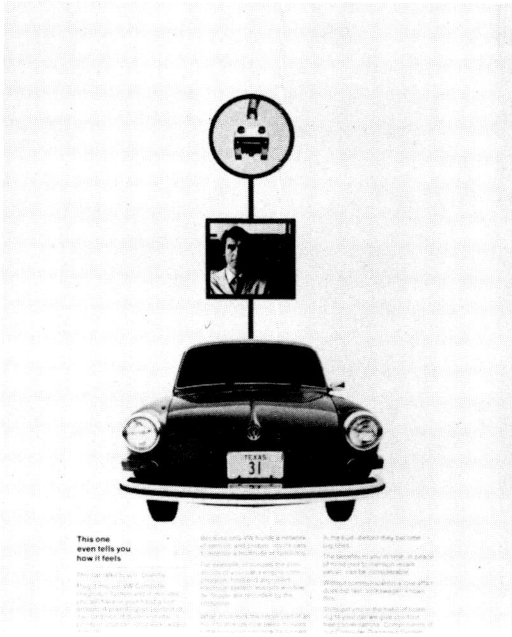
TEXAS
31
This one
even tells you
how it feels

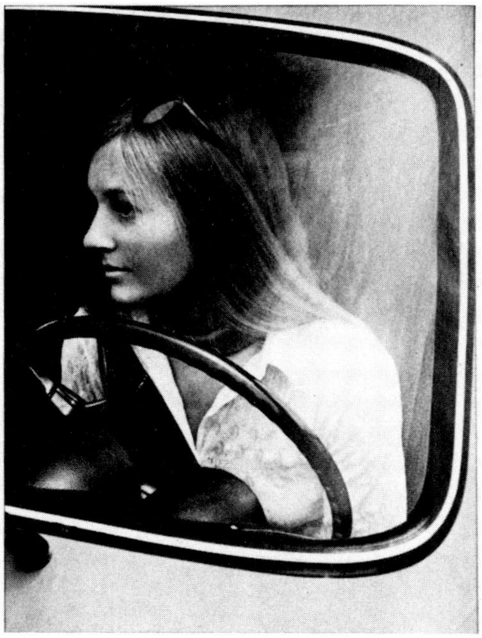

328

329
Ted Colangelo Entrant
George Bradbury Photographer
Singer & Cole Agency
Ted Colangelo Assoc. Studio
Union Carbide Client

330

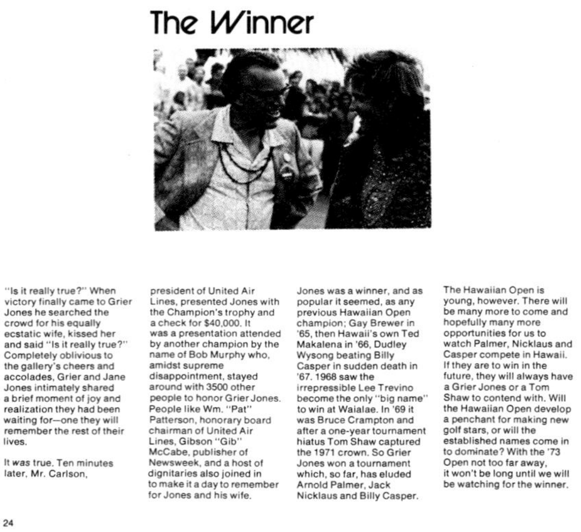

The Winner
"Is it really true?" When victory finally came to Grier Jones he searched the crowd for his equally ecstatic wife, kissed her and said "Is it really true?" Completely oblivious to the gallery's cheers and accolades, Grier and Jane Jones intimately shared a brief moment of joy and realization they had been waiting for—one they will remember the rest of their lives.
It *was* true. Ten minutes later, Mr. Carlson, president of United Air Lines, presented Jones with the Champion's trophy and a check for $40,000. It was a presentation attended by another champion by the name of Bob Murphy who, amidst supreme disappointment, stayed around with 3500 other people to honor Grier Jones. People like Wm. "Pat" Patterson, honorary board chairman of United Air Lines, Gibson "Gib" McCabe, publisher of Newsweek, and a host of dignitaries also joined in to make it a day to remember for Jones and his wife.
Jones was a winner, and as popular it seemed, as any previous Hawaiian Open champion; Gay Brewer in '65, then Hawaii's own Ted Makalena in '66, Dudley Wysong beating Billy Casper in sudden death in '67. 1968 saw the irrepressible Lee Trevino become the only "big name" to win at Waialae. In '69 it was Bruce Crampton and after a one-year tournament hiatus Tom Shaw captured the 1971 crown. So Grier Jones won a tournament which, so far, has eluded Arnold Palmer, Jack Nicklaus and Billy Casper.
The Hawaiian Open is young, however. There will be many more to come and hopefully many more opportunities for us to watch Palmer, Nicklaus and Casper compete in Hawaii. If they are to win in the future, they will always have a Grier Jones or a Tom Shaw to contend with. Will the Hawaiian Open develop a penchant for making new golf stars, or will the established names come in to dominate? With the '73 Open not too far away, it won't be long until we will be watching for the winner.
24

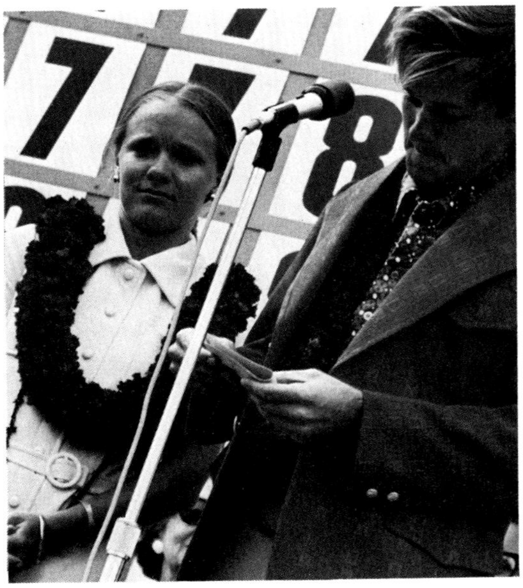

339

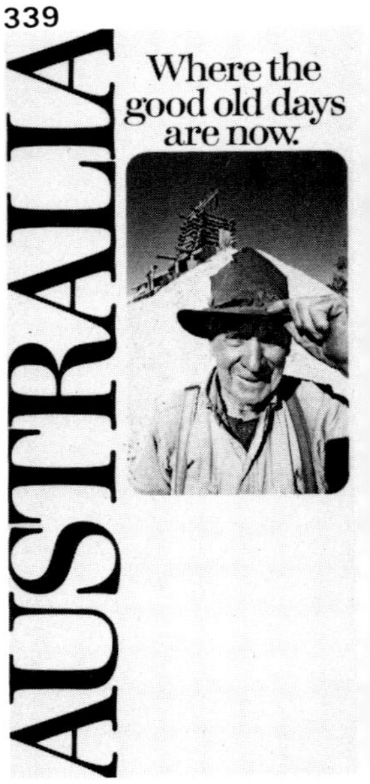

AUSTRALIA
Where the good old days are now.

331

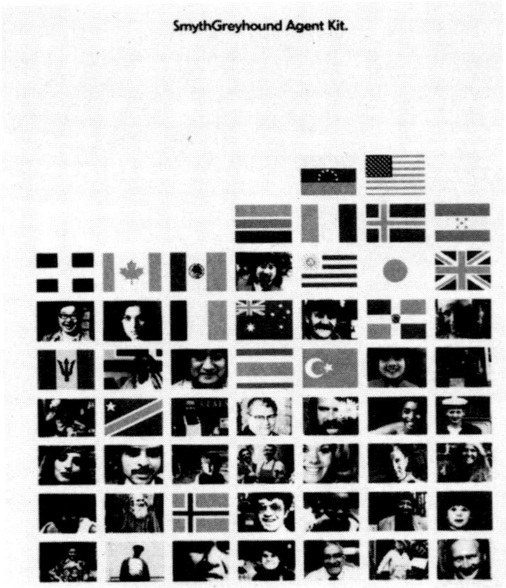

SmythGreyhound Agent Kit.

332

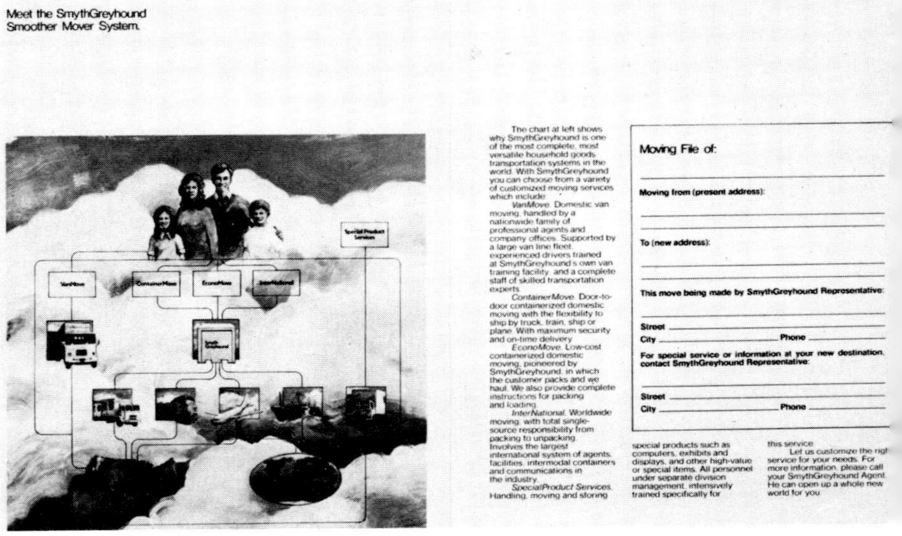

Meet the SmythGreyhound Smoother Mover System.
The chart at left shows why SmythGreyhound is one of the most complete, most versatile household goods transportation systems in the world. With SmythGreyhound you can choose from a variety of customized moving services which include:
VanMove. Domestic van moving, handled by a nationwide family of professional agents and company offices. Supported by a large van line fleet, experienced drivers trained at SmythGreyhound's own van training facility, and a complete staff of skilled transportation experts.
ContainerMove. Door-to-door containerized domestic moving with the flexibility to ship by truck, train, ship or plane. With maximum security and on-time delivery.
EconoMove. Low-cost containerized domestic moving, pioneered by SmythGreyhound, in which the customer packs and we haul. We also provide complete instructions for packing and loading.
InterNational. Worldwide moving, with total single-source responsibility from packing to unpacking. Involves the largest international system of agents, facilities, intermodal containers and communications in the industry.
SpecialProduct Services. Handling, moving and storing special products such as computers, exhibits and displays, and other high-value or special items. All personnel under separate division management, intensively trained specifically for this service.
Let us customize the right service for your needs. For more information, please call your SmythGreyhound Agent. He can open up a whole new world for you.
Moving File of:
Moving from (present address):
To (new address):
This move being made by SmythGreyhound Representative:
Street
City
Phone
For special service or information at your new destination, contact SmythGreyhound Representative:
Street
City
Phone

333

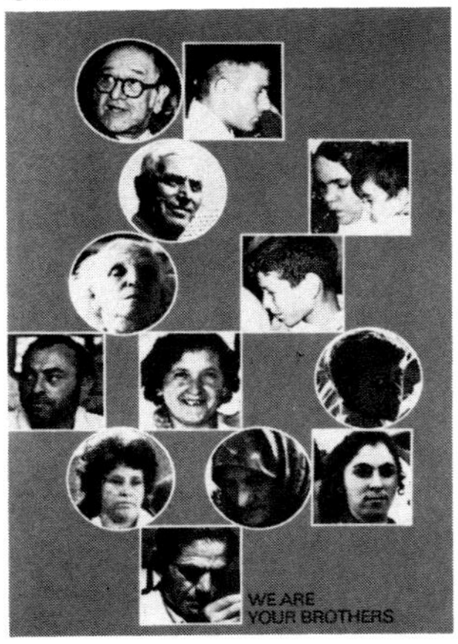

WE ARE YOUR BROTHERS

334

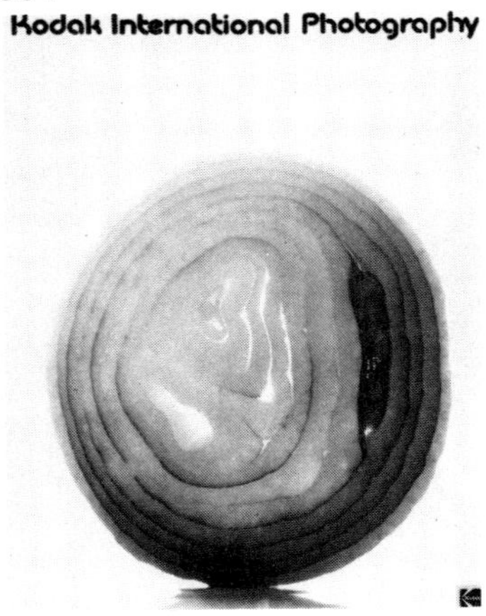

Kodak International Photography

335

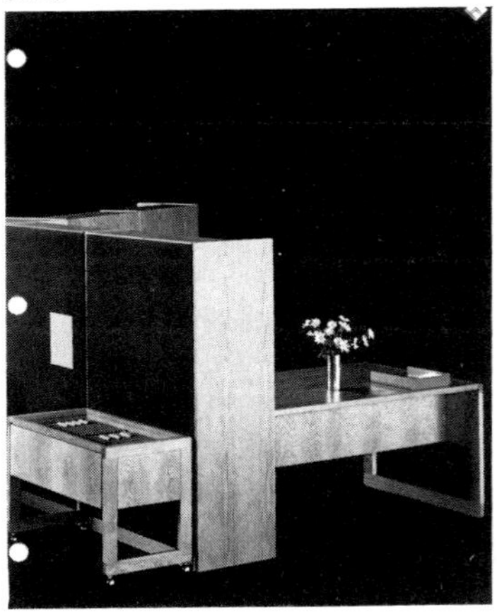

336

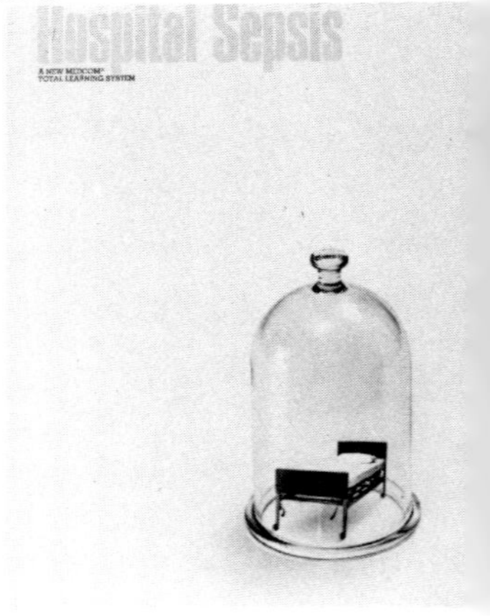

Hospital Sepsis
A NEW MEDCOM TOTAL LEARNING SYSTEM

330
Jack O'Grady Studios Inc. Entrant
John Grember Art Director
Fred Baldwin, Bill Cornelia Photographers
United Air Lines Client

331-332
Richardson Seigle Rolfs & McCoy Inc. Entrant
Bob Billings, Vic Warren Art Directors
Fred Thomas Illustrator
Roy Robinson Photography Photographers
Smyth Greyhound Client

333
Nanette Hucknall Entrant
Leni Sonnenfeld and others Photographers
United Jewish Appeal of New York Client

334
Kenn Jacobs Entrant
Kevin Miller Art Director
Rumrill-Hoyt Agency
Eastman Kodak Company Client

335
Center for Advanc Research Design Entrant
John Massey, Tomoko Miho Art Director
Hardwood House Client

338

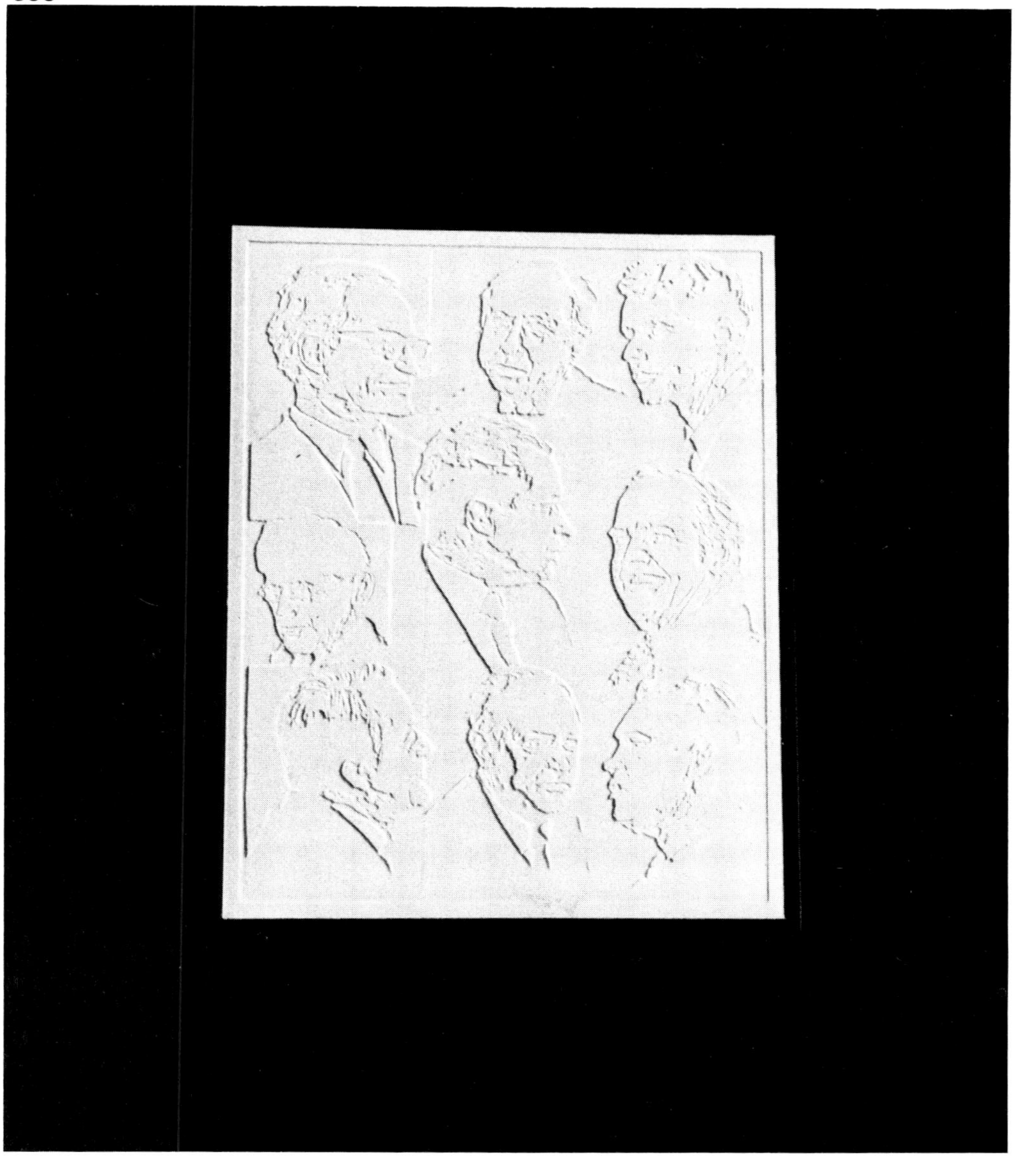

337

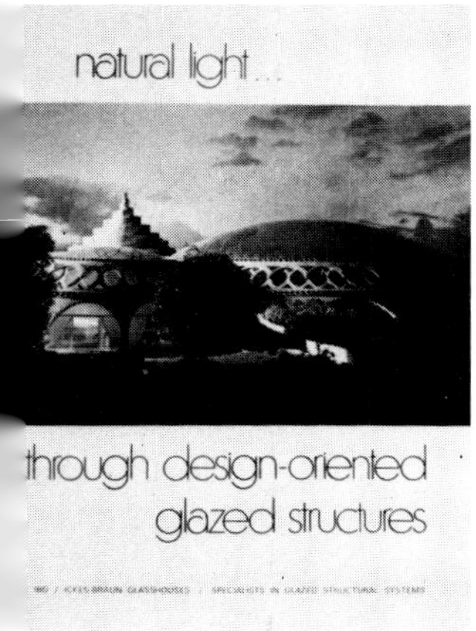
natural light...
through design-oriented
glazed structures

340

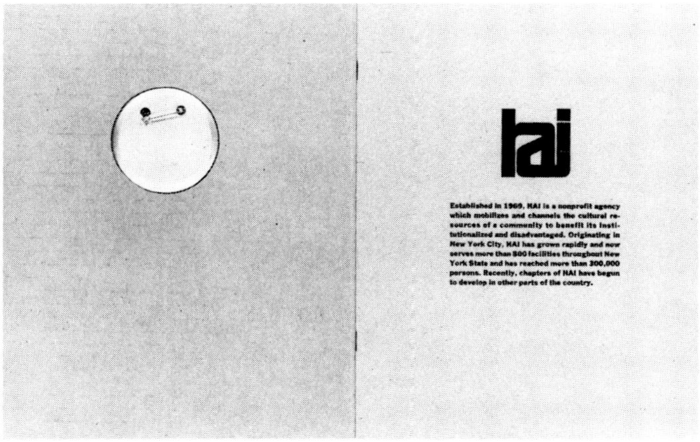
hai

341

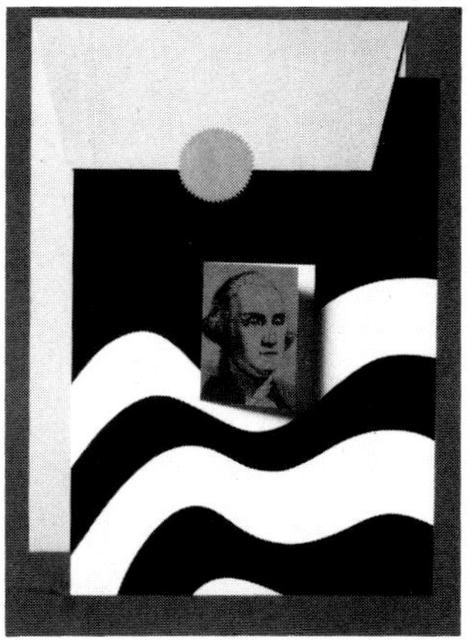

6
dcom Inc.
rant
hard Nathan
Director
ng Bahrt
ver Photographer
venol Laboratories
ent

337
Sweet's Div., McGraw-Hill Information Systems Co. Entrant
Ed Dann
Art Director
Ickes Braun Client

338
William Duevell
Entrant
William Duevell
H. Epstein Art Directors
Robert Cunningham
Illustrator
ABC News
Client

339
Ted Schmitt
Entrant
Elliott Irwin Photographer
Tinker Dodge & Delano Agency
Australian Tourist Commission Client

340
Exxon Corp.
Entrant
John J. Conley
Art Director
Hospital Audiences Inc.
Client

341
W. Chris Gorman
Entrant
W. Chris Gorman Associates Studio
Alliance One
Client

342

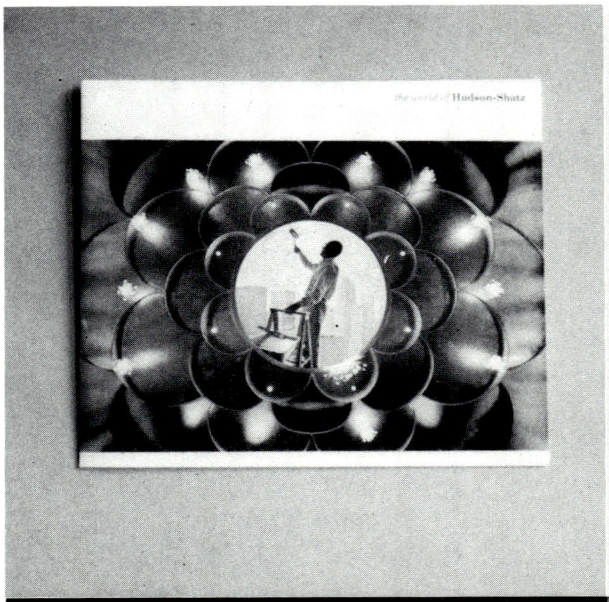
the world of Hudson-Shatz

343

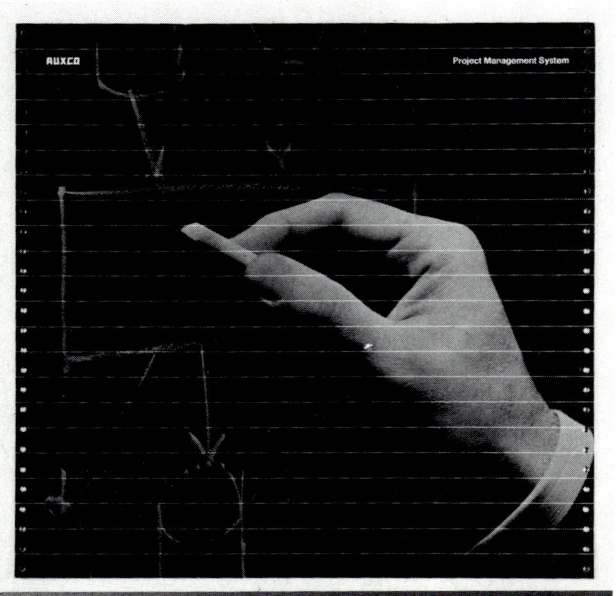
AUXCO
Project Management System

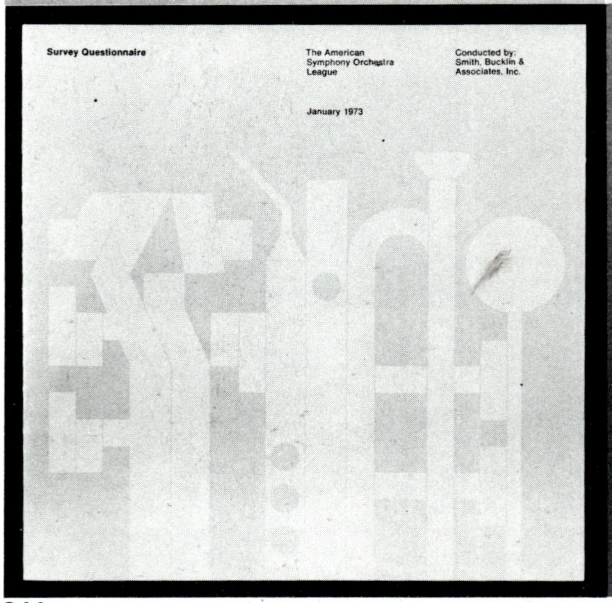
Survey Questionnaire
The American Symphony Orchestra League
Conducted by: Smith, Bucklin & Associates, Inc.
January 1973

344

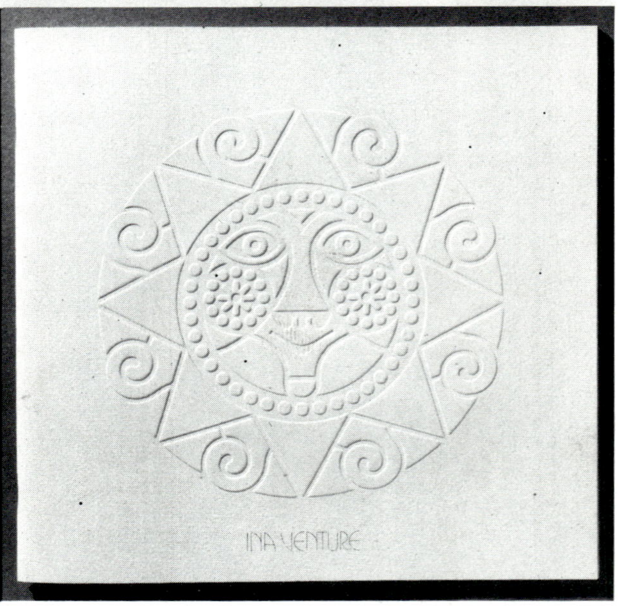
INA VENTURE

345

342
Graphics Institute, Inc. Entrant
Martin A. Miller Art Director
Richard Litwin Photographer
Case-Hoyt Studio
Hudson Shatz Painting Company Client

343
Ford, Byrne & Associates Entrant
Auxco Client

344
Sanders & Noe Inc. Entrant
Bernard B. Sanders Art Director
Smith, Bucklin & Assoc., Inc. Agency
David M. Seager Illustrator
American Symphony Orchestra League Client

For his leadership, his wisdom, his devotion to the objectives of the American democratic society; for his tenacity, boldness and courage in furthering broadcasting's capacity to achieve those objectives; and for his uncompromising rejection of encroachments upon radio and television's freedom and capacity to advance the greater public interest, the National Association of Broadcasters proudly pays tribute unprecedented in our history to our valiant colleague.

**FRANK STANTON:
WE CITE YOU, SIR, FOR
HIGHEST ACHIEVEMENT IN THE
PUBLIC INTEREST AND IN THE FORWARD PROGRESS
OF THE BROADCAST MEDIA.**

In particular, we identify you with the words of the eminent Chief Justice John Marshall, recalled by you in your landmark defence of the First Amendment on June 24, 1971: "The genius of the constitution, and the opinions of the people of the United States, cannot be overruled by those who administer the Government. Among those principles deemed sacred in America; among those sacred rights considered as forming the bulwark of their liberty, which the Government contemplates with awful reverence, and would approach only with the most cautious circumspection, there is no one of which the importance is more deeply impressed on the public mind than the liberty of the press. That this liberty is often carried to excess; that it has sometimes degenerated into licentiousness, is seen and lamented; but the remedy has not yet been discovered. Perhaps it is an evil inseparable from the good with which it is allied; perhaps it is a shoot which cannot be stripped from the stalk, without wounding vitally the plant from which it is torn. However desirable those measures might be which might correct without enslaving the press, they have never yet been devised in America."—John Marshall, 1798, American State Papers, Vol. II, Foreign Relations, p. 193.

The central act of a democracy is the choice, by the people, of its leadership. The essential ingredient in the electoral process, an informed electorate, became increasingly difficult to achieve as our nation expanded across a continent, as it grew towards a population of over 200 million, as its internal character and external relationships became infinitely more complex and its destiny was caught up in a speed of events that vastly reduced tolerable margins of error. Moreover, many of the old limitations of our political procedures became more hazardous — convention decisions made far from the sight and hearing of voters in the secrecy of smoke-filled rooms, for example, and candidates who were seen or heard during campaigns by only the tiny sprinkling of voters before whom they could appear in person.

More than any other factor, broadcasting, with its directness, its immediacy and its ubiquity, changed all that. The electorate could be witnesses at nominating conventions. The voters could hear and, later, see for themselves the candidates seeking their votes. When radio began covering the conventions in 1924, the nominating process was released from the private domain of the political operators; a million and a quarter receiving sets all across the land were tuned in directly to the convention halls. From that point, the people were no longer dependent on what they were told about the proceedings; the people could hear for themselves, and they could make their decisions based upon direct access to the events and personalities of the campaign.

Slogans and hearsay gave way to direct exposure of candidates to the electorate, with a significance that is easily gauged. In the last election before the dawning of the broadcast era, in 1920, only 43.5 percent of eligible voters went to the polls, as compared to 64 percent in 1960, when suspension of the equal-time restrictions to permit the Kennedy-Nixon debates made possible the fullest use of broadcasting as yet in history.

But the effect of broadcasting upon the democratic experience has gone far beyond elections. The monumental events of this century — depression, wars, uneasy peace, the birth of more new nations in two decades than had occurred before in two centuries, undreamed of scientific breakthroughs, profound social revolution — all these were made immediate intimate realities to Americans through, first, the ears of radio and, later, the eyes of television. No longer were the decisions of the American people made in an information vacuum, as they witnessed the towering events of their time that were bound to have incisive political repercussions.

As broadcasters we can take pride in the role we have played in all this. We have not been blind to our responsibilities. Even our severest critics must concede that. Each of the broadcast media became, within the first generation of its existence, the first source of news to most of our countrymen. It has been this freedom from government intervention or control that has made possible the monumental achievement of U.S. broadcast journalism and is the primary condition of its survival.

Survival of broadcast freedom is not so often a matter of dramatic resistance as it is of constant watchfulness and quiet determination. The threat is not always direct or frontal. No one proclaims himself for government control of program content, whether news, entertainment or advertising. In fact, we have all come to recognize, as the first sign of proposals that would have the ultimate effect of government control, the protesting words from the proposer: "I am against censorship, I am against government control, *but…*"

You are familiar with the current inventory of existing and proposed restrictions on the freedom of broadcasting to do its job — which is to serve the American people in the same context

---

345
Ford, Byrne & Associates Entrant
INA Corp. Client

346
Lou Dorfsman Entrant
Lou Dorfsman, Ted Andresakes Designers
Columbia Broadcasting System, Inc. Client

Fragrance. Dior.
347

Nails. Dior.
348

Skin. Dior.
349

Lips. Dior.
350

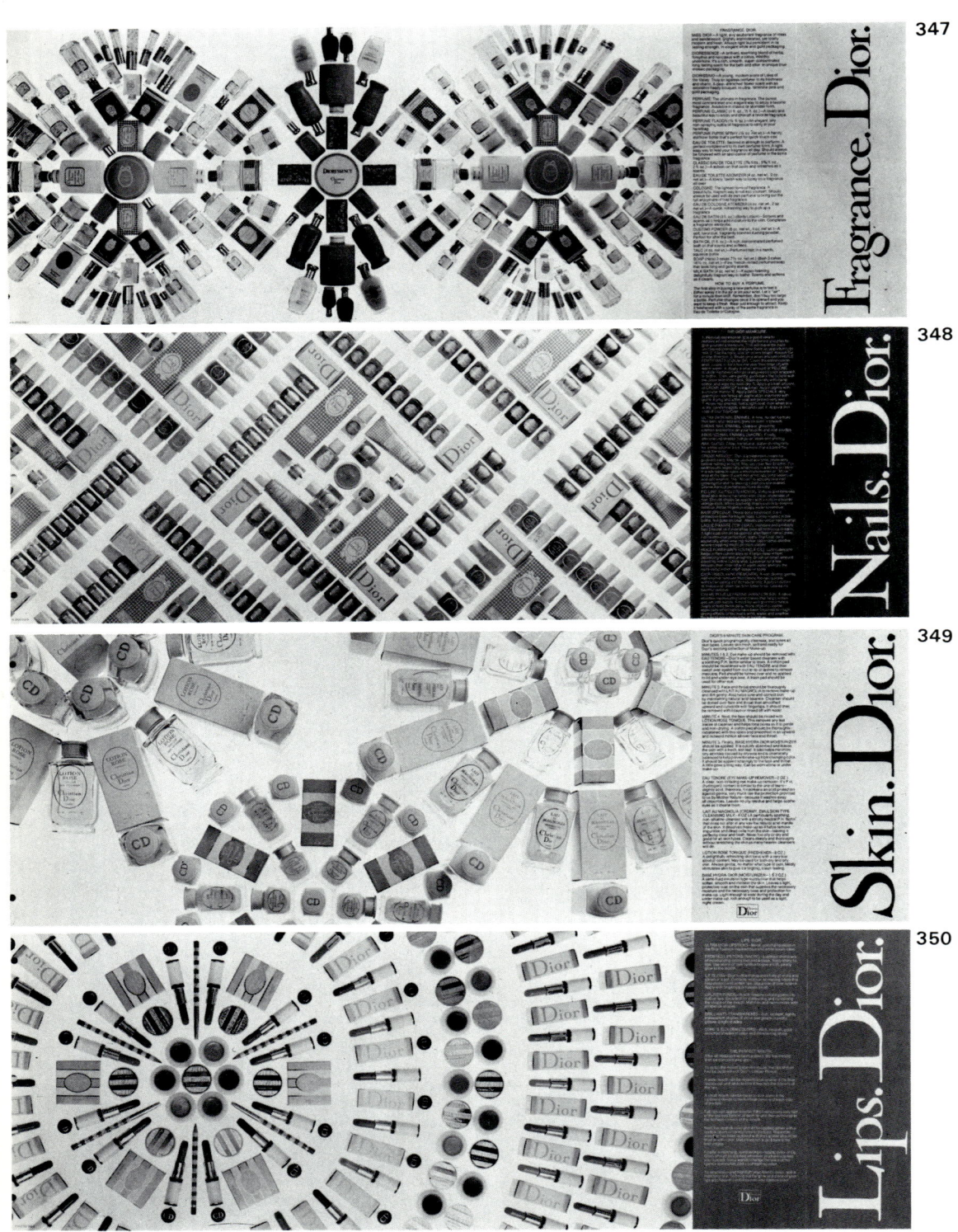

347-350
Christian Dior Perfumes
Kuhn Caldwell Art Director
Tosh Matsumoto Photographer

351
Schumaker Deur Designers Entrant
Bob Schumaker Art Director
Bill Andrews Photographer
Wolverine World Wide, Inc. Client

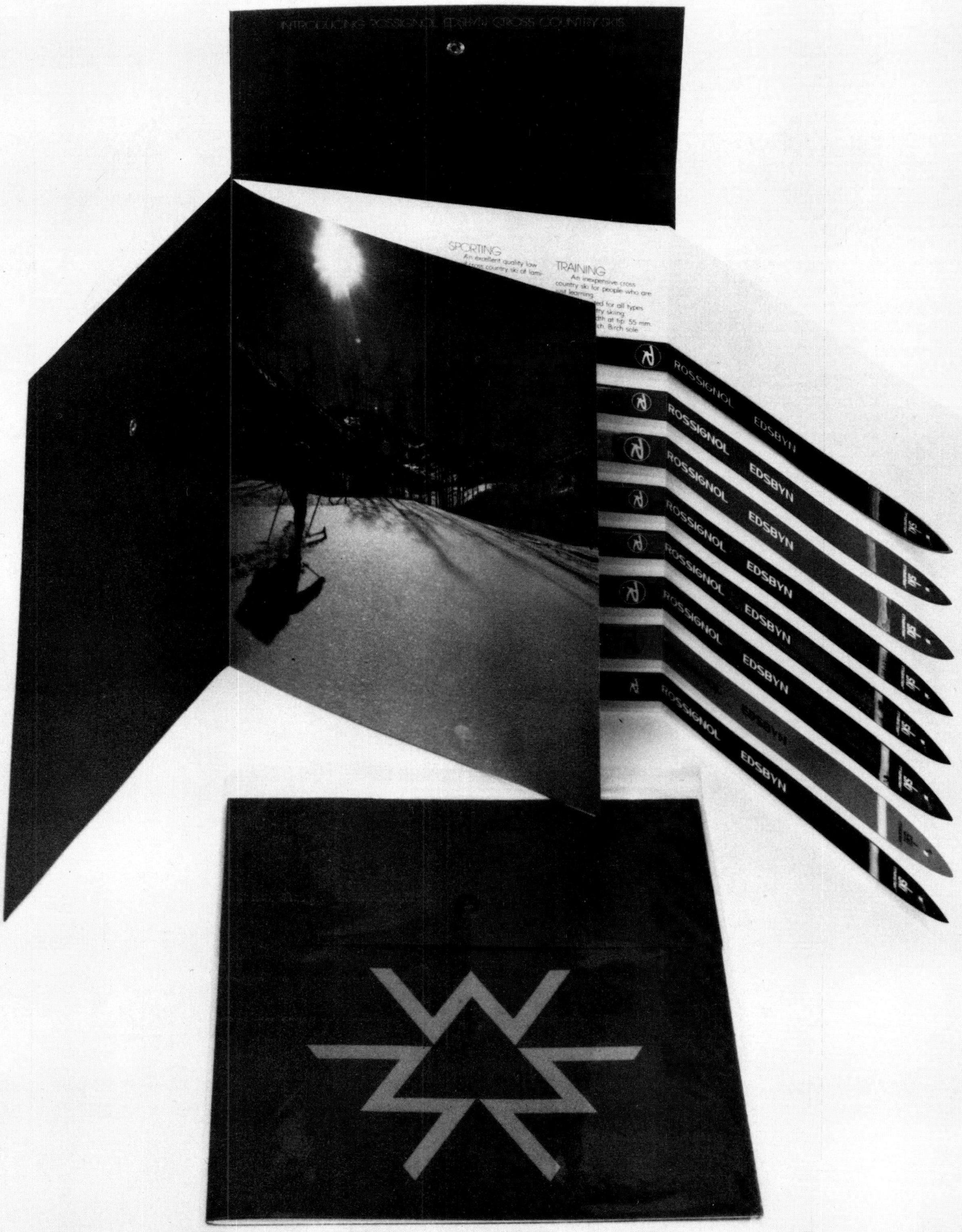
INTRODUCING ROSSIGNOL EDSBYN CROSS COUNTRY SKIS
SPORTING
TRAINING
An inexpensive cross
country ski for people who are
ROSSIGNOL
EDSBYN

352

Graphic Art Products
Catalog
Letraset usa

354

Odell Hardware Co.

353

358

duPont Glore Forgan

359

"...male and female He created them.
And God blessed them, saying: increase
and multiply, and fill the earth and
subdue it..."
Genesis
A Population Attitudes Study Commissioned by WNBC TV4

355

Bread winners of America. You are earning more today than ever before. However, with the continual rise in the cost of living you are getting less & less for your hard earned dollar.
At last help has come! The all purpose consumer economy card is here! Now
Not a credit card - but a savers card. It's simple. Just present your American Savers Card to any of the participating merchants and you'll save a minimum of 10 percent on everything you buy.
Take a vacation - or put a pool in your back yard. Buy a new car or get automobile parts and service. How about a new washing machine? The American Savers Card will save you cash on just about anything. You'll even save when you bank with your American Savers Card.
The American Savers Card can save you hundreds of dollars the first year you have one. Apply today and start saving tomorrow.
FIDO
The American Savers Card is here!

356

AMERICAN GREETINGS
introduces
Kewpies from Yesterday
for People Today

357

Baltimore
is alive and well
and living In-town

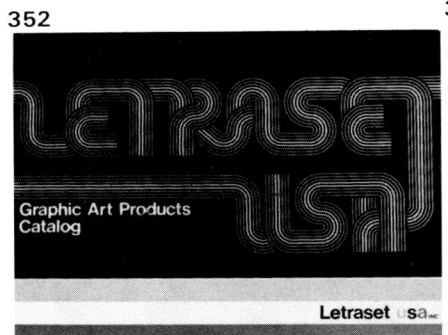

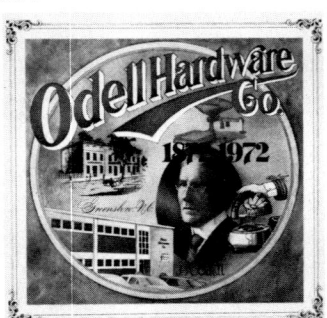

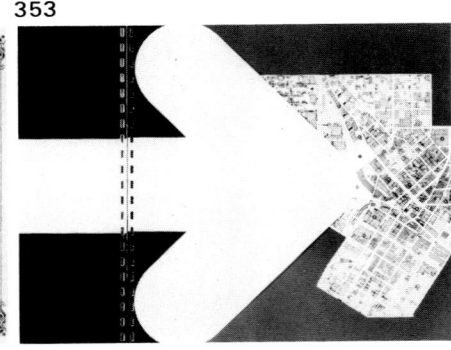

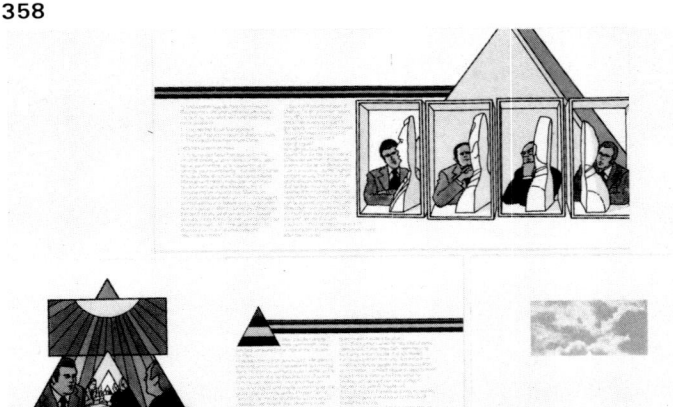

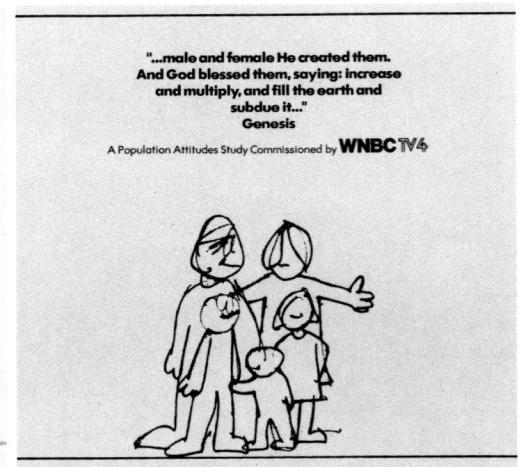

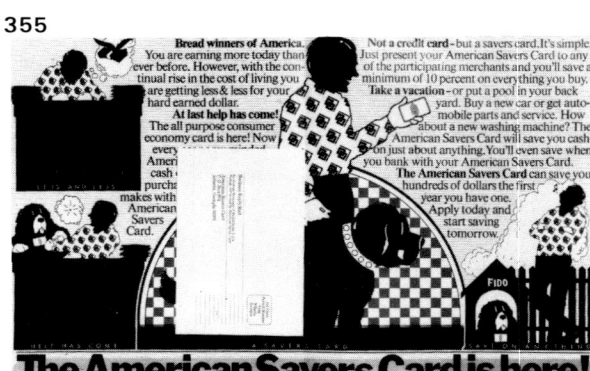

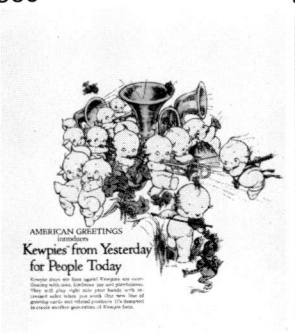

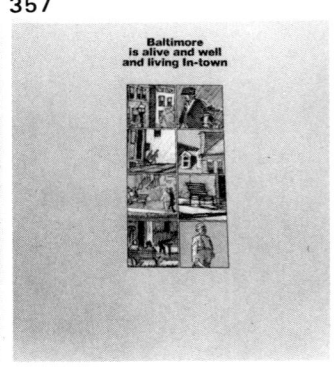

352
Letraset USA Inc. Entrant
Val C. Florio Art Director
Rumford Press Production

353
Jim Cole Entrant
Dick Henderson, Tom Wood Art Directors
Richard Hoflich Photographer
Cole Henderson Drake Inc. Agency
International City Corporation Client

354
The Paper Prism Entrant
Mike Carrier Art Director
Fisher-Harrison Printing Co. Production
Odell Hardware Co. Client

355
Graphicsgroup, Inc. Entrant
Ken Thompson Art Director
American Savers Club Client

356
Carlton Faughender Entrant
Grant Ichida Designer
Visual Design Studio
American Greetings Corporation Client

There is a children's riddle about a pond and some water lilies. The lilies are doubling in size every day; in 30 days they will cover the entire pond and kill all the creatures living in it. The owner does not want that to happen, but being busy with other things, he decides to postpone cutting back the plants until they cover half the pond. The question is, on what day will the lilies cover half the pond? The answer is, on the twenty-ninth day. On that day, the owner will have one day left to save his pond.

347
The Dombrosky/
Peck Coalition Inc.
Entrant
Bill Wilson
Art Director
The In-Town
Living Council
Client

358
Century Expanded
Entrant
George McCathern
Art Director
Arno Sternglas
Illustrator
duPont Glore Forgan
Client

359
Ann E. Berk Entrant
William Rodriguez
Art Director
Raleigh Lithograph
Production
WNBC-TV
Client

360
A. Norman Law
Entrant
Arthur D. Little, Inc.
Client

361

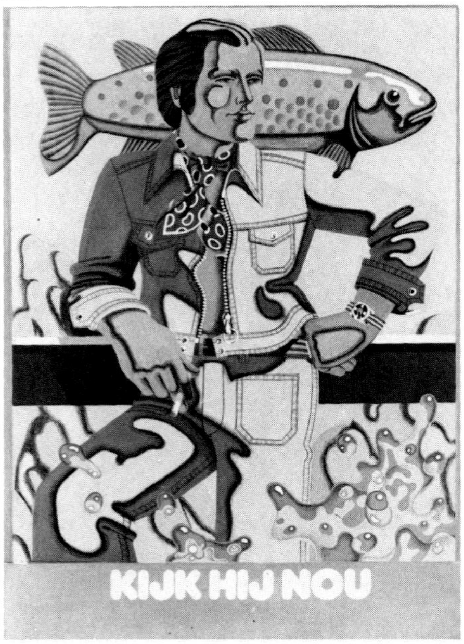
KIJK HIJ NOU

362

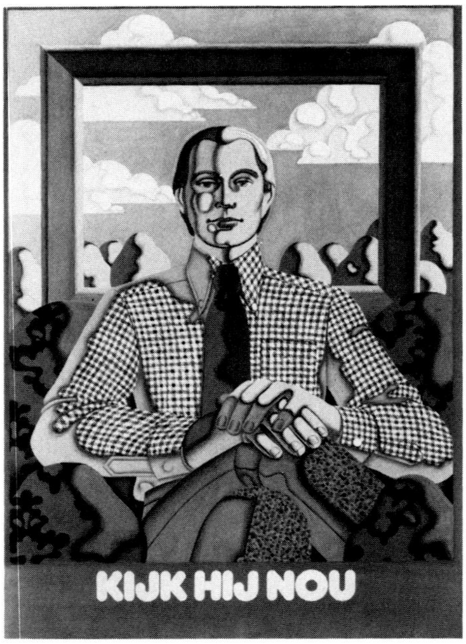
KIJK HIJ NOU

363

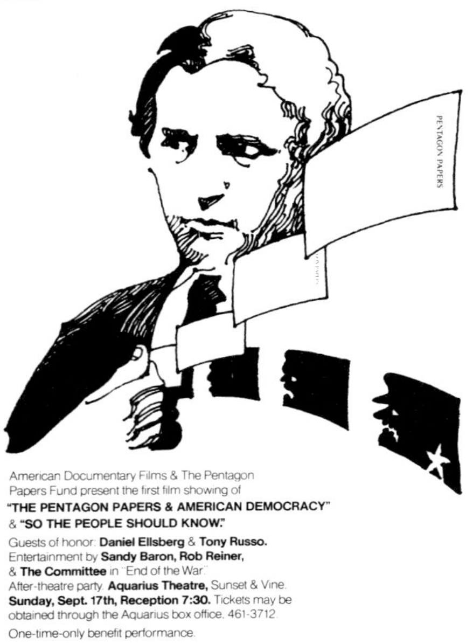
PENTAGON PAPERS
American Documentary Films & The Pentagon Papers Fund present the first film showing of
"THE PENTAGON PAPERS & AMERICAN DEMOCRACY"
& "SO THE PEOPLE SHOULD KNOW."
Guests of honor: Daniel Ellsberg & Tony Russo.
Entertainment by Sandy Baron, Rob Reiner,
& The Committee in "End of the War."
After-theatre party. Aquarius Theatre, Sunset & Vine.
Sunday, Sept. 17th, Reception 7:30. Tickets may be obtained through the Aquarius box office. 461-3712.
One-time-only benefit performance.

364

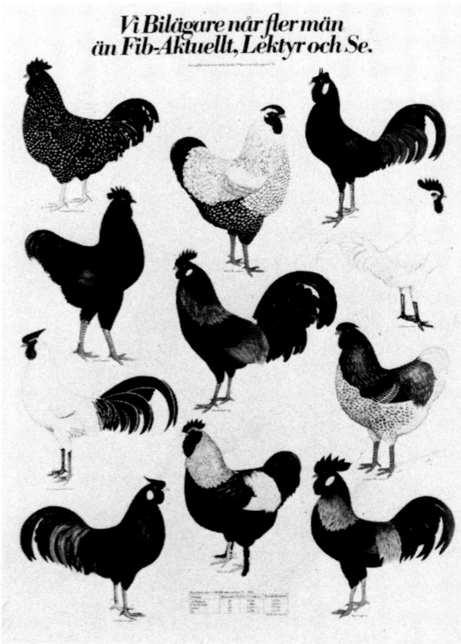
Vi Bilägare når fler män
än Fib-Aktuellt, Lektyr och Se.

365

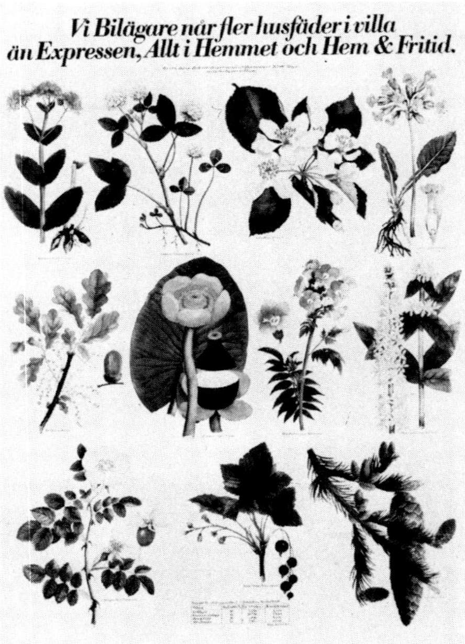
Vi Bilägare når fler husfäder i villa
än Expressen, Allt i Hemmet och Hem & Fritid.

366

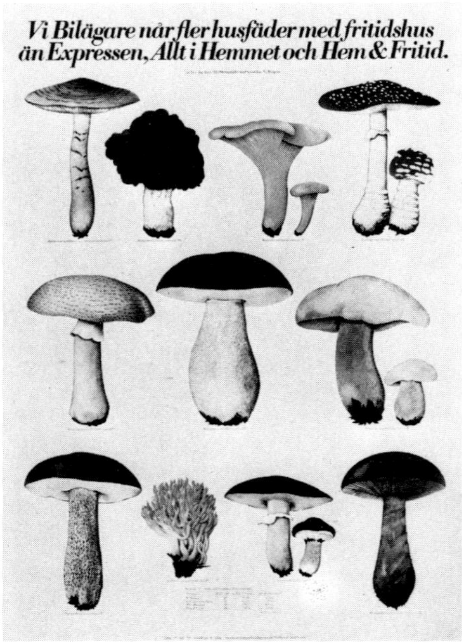
Vi Bilägare når fler husfäder med fritidshus
än Expressen, Allt i Hemmet och Hem & Fritid.

361-362
J. Walter Thompson Entrant
Lysander Apol Art Director
Studio White Studio
Hij Herenmode Client

363
Weller & Juett, Inc. Entrant
Don Weller Art Director
American Documentary Films Client

364-366
Ericson & Co. AB Entrant
Vi Bilagare Client

367
Bill Gold Entrant
Tal Stubis Art Director
Bill Teason Illustrator
Universal Pictures Client

368
Graphicsgroup, Inc. Entrant
Gene Wilkes Art Director

369
Intermedia, Inc. Entrant
Bob Cosgrove Art Directo
Jim Williams Illustrator
Craig Jiebel Copywriter
The Art Group Studio
J.W. Ford Co. Client

367

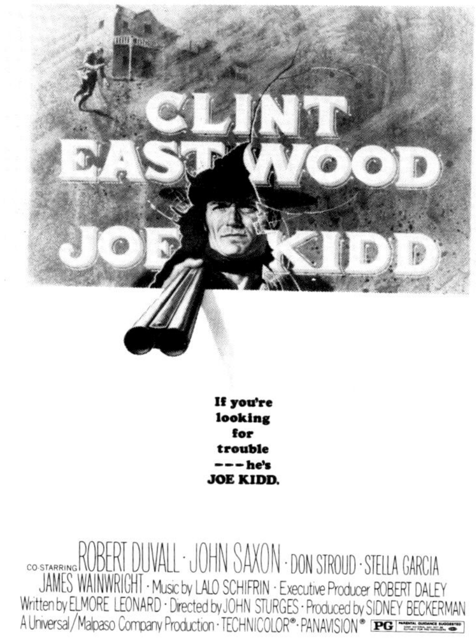
CLINT EASTWOOD
JOE KIDD
If you're looking for trouble ---he's JOE KIDD.
CO STARRING ROBERT DUVALL · JOHN SAXON · DON STROUD · STELLA GARCIA
JAMES WAINWRIGHT · Music by LALO SCHIFRIN · Executive Producer ROBERT DALEY
Written by ELMORE LEONARD · Directed by JOHN STURGES · Produced by SIDNEY BECKERMAN
A Universal/Malpaso Company Production · TECHNICOLOR® · PANAVISION® PG

368

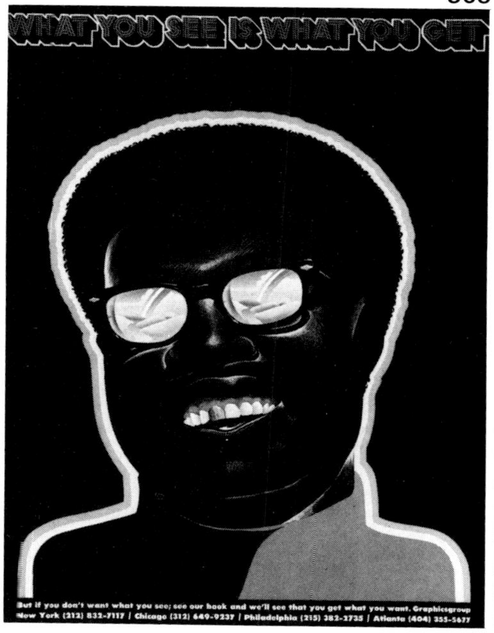
WHAT YOU SEE IS WHAT YOU GET
But if you don't want what you see; see our book and we'll see that you get what you want. Graphicsgroup

369

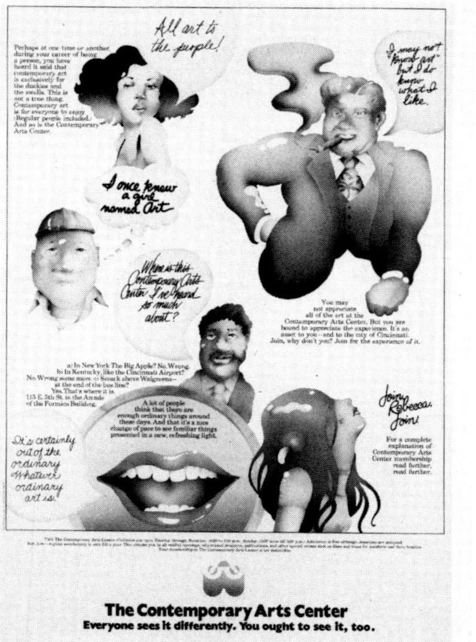
All art to the people!
I once knew a girl named Art
The Contemporary Arts Center
Everyone sees it differently. You ought to see it, too.

370

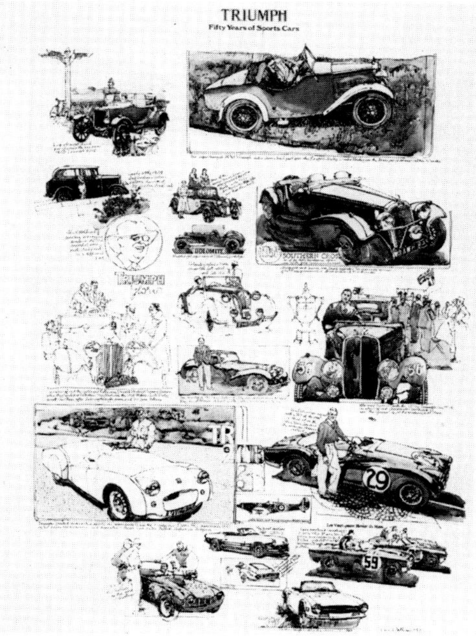
TRIUMPH
Fifty Years of Sports Cars

371

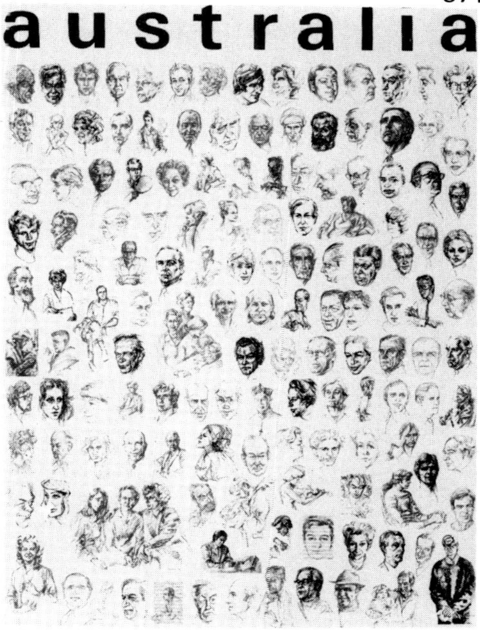
australia

372

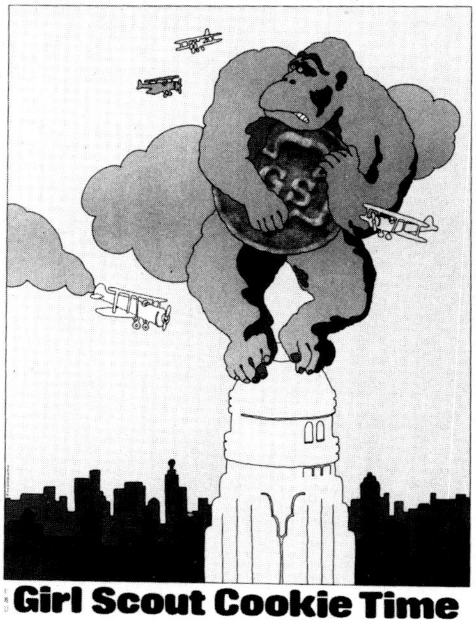
Girl Scout Cookie Time

370
Brian O'Neill Entrant
John Dugdale Art Director
Ken Dallison Illustrator
British Leyland Motors, Inc. Client

371
Peter Wittman, Champion International Entrant
James Miho Art Director
Louis Kahan Illustrator
Miho Inc. Studio
Champion International Client

372
Saul Bass & Associates Inc. Entrant
Arthur Goodman Art Director
John Wanek Illustrator
Burry's Div., Quaker Oats Client

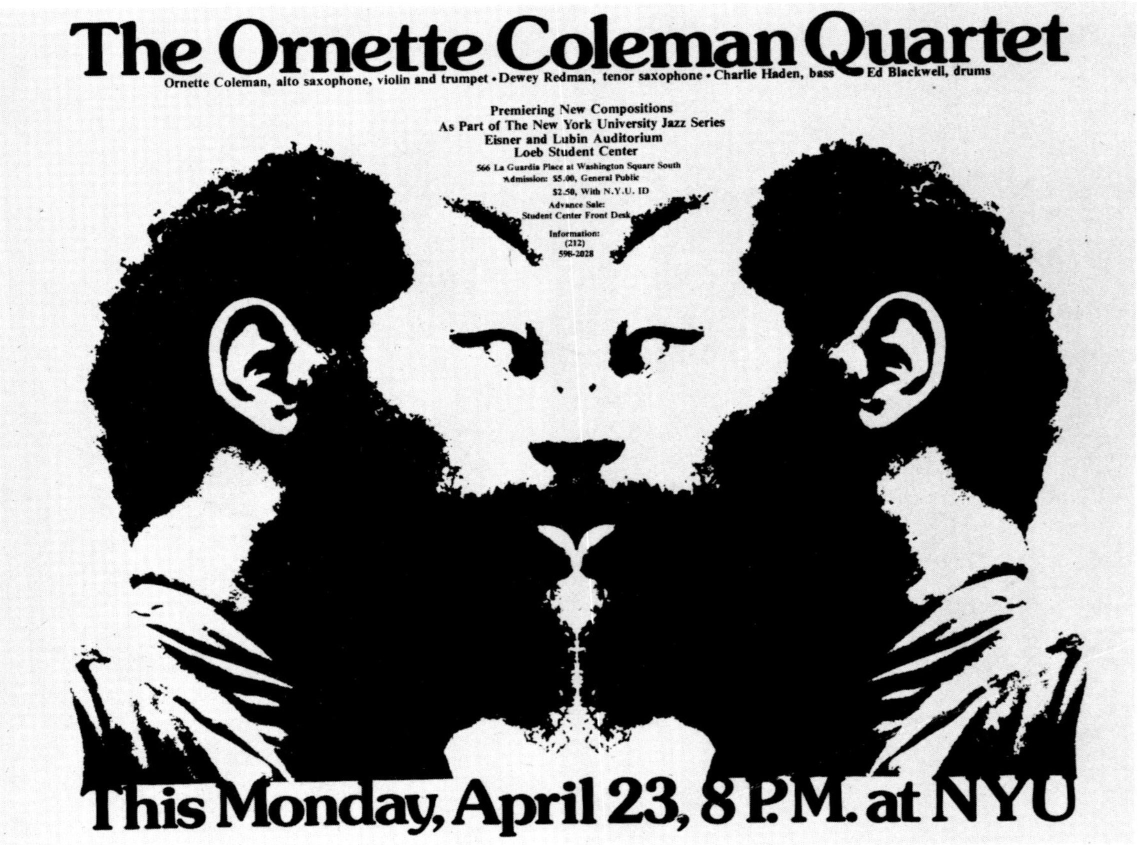
The Ornette Coleman Quartet
Ornette Coleman, alto saxophone, violin and trumpet • Dewey Redman, tenor saxophone • Charlie Haden, bass
Ed Blackwell, drums
Premiering New Compositions
As Part of The New York University Jazz Series
Eisner and Lubin Auditorium
Loeb Student Center
566 La Guardia Place at Washington Square South
Admission: $5.00, General Public
$2.50, With N.Y.U. ID
Advance Sale:
Student Center Front Desk
Information:
(212)
598-2028
This Monday, April 23, 8 P.M. at NYU

373

374

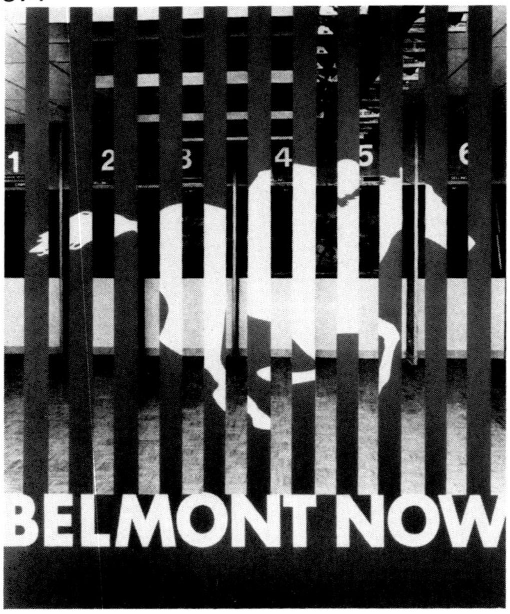
1
2
3
4
5
6
BELMONT NOW

375

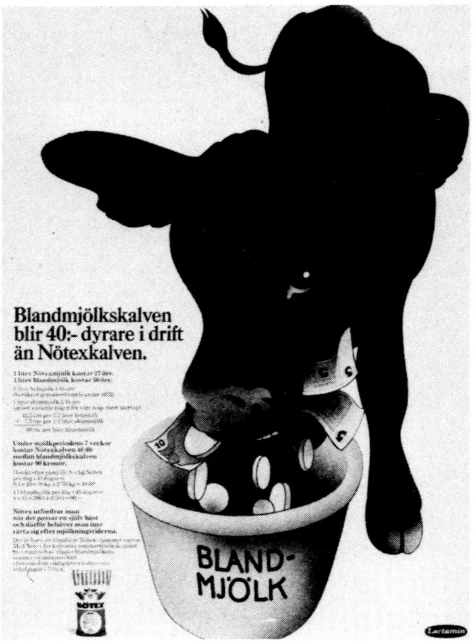
Blandmjölkskalven blir 40:- dyrare i drift än Nötexkalven.
BLAND-
MJÖLK

373
NYU Publications Bureau
Entrant
Hector Perez
Art Director
Jose A. Perez
Designer
Loeb Program Board
Client

374
NYC Off-Track Betting Corp.
Entrant
Bill O'Day
Art Director
Robert Negrin
Designer

375
Törnbloms
Entrant
Claes Bergquist
Art Director
Ericson & Co. AB
Agency

380

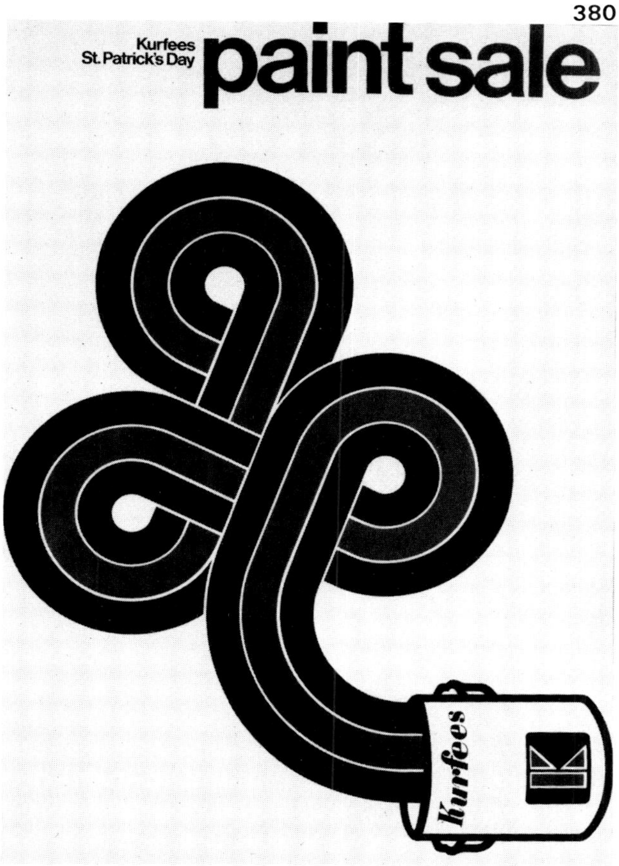
Kurfees
St. Patrick's Day
paint sale
Kurfees

379

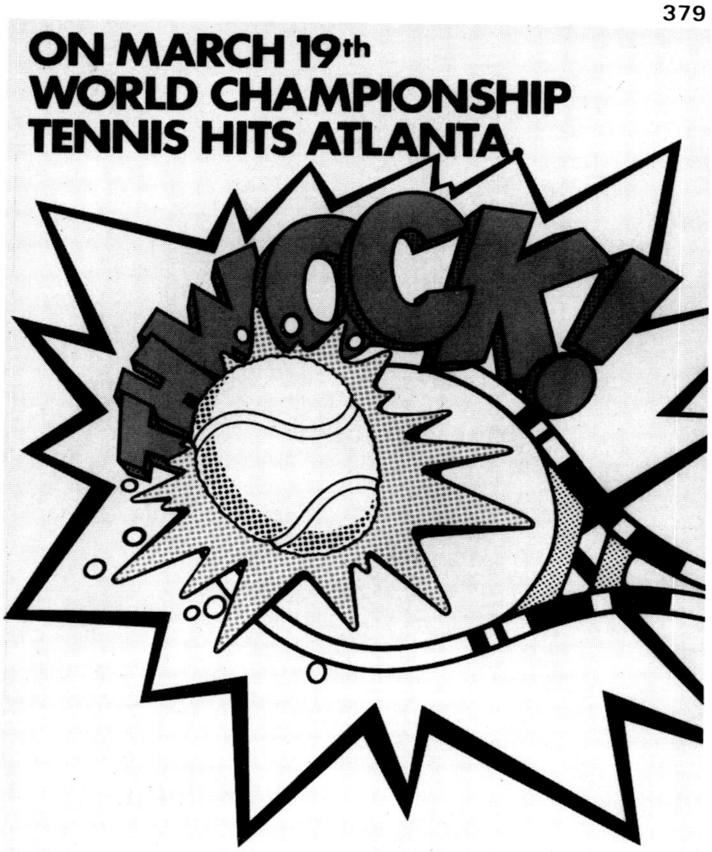
ON MARCH 19th
WORLD CHAMPIONSHIP
TENNIS HITS ATLANTA.
THWOCK!

376

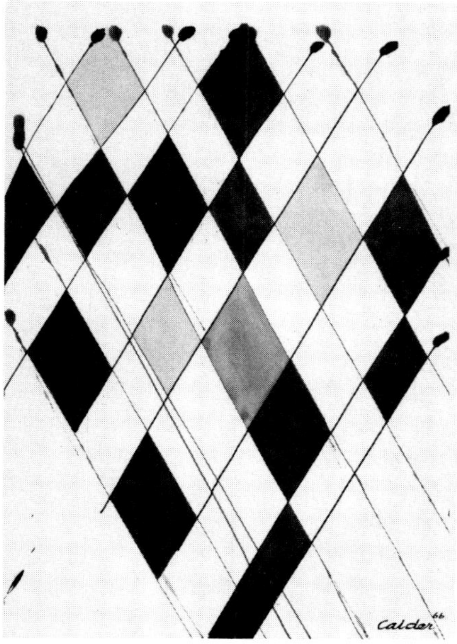
Calder 66

377

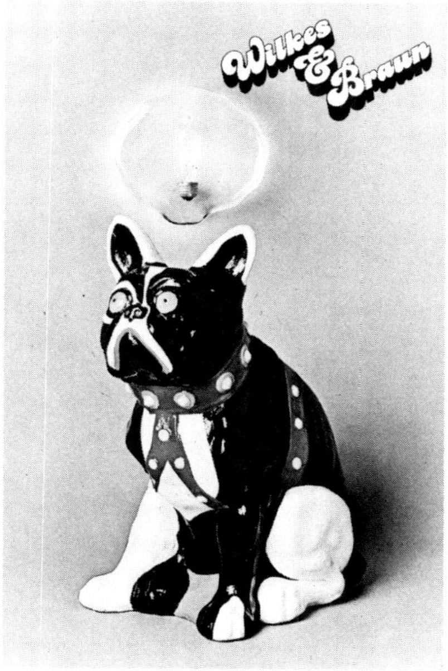
Wilkes & Braun

378

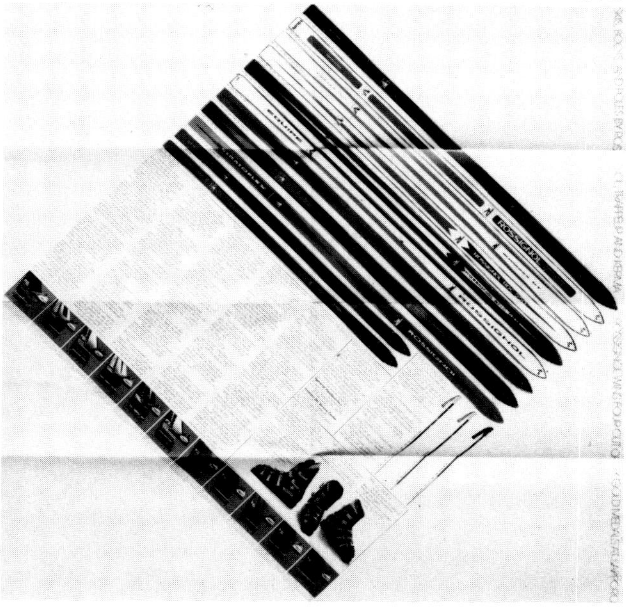

376
Peter Wittman
Entrant
James Miho
Art Director
Alexander Calder
Illustrator
Miho, Inc.
Studio
Champion International
Client

377
Wilkes & Braun Inc.
Entrant
Tom Wilkes
Art Director
Jim McCrary
Photographer

378
Schumaker Deur
Designers Entrant
Paul Deur
Art Director
Shorty Wilcox
Photographer
Wolverine World
Wide, Inc. Client

379
Jim Cole Entrant
Jerry Sullivan
Art Director
Gene Wilkes Illustrator
Cole Henderson
Drake, Inc. Agency
Peachtree Corners
Client

380
Designers Ross
Stewart & Winner
Entrants
Frank Ross, Harriet Winner,
Dan Stewart
Art Directors
Kurfees Paint
Company Client

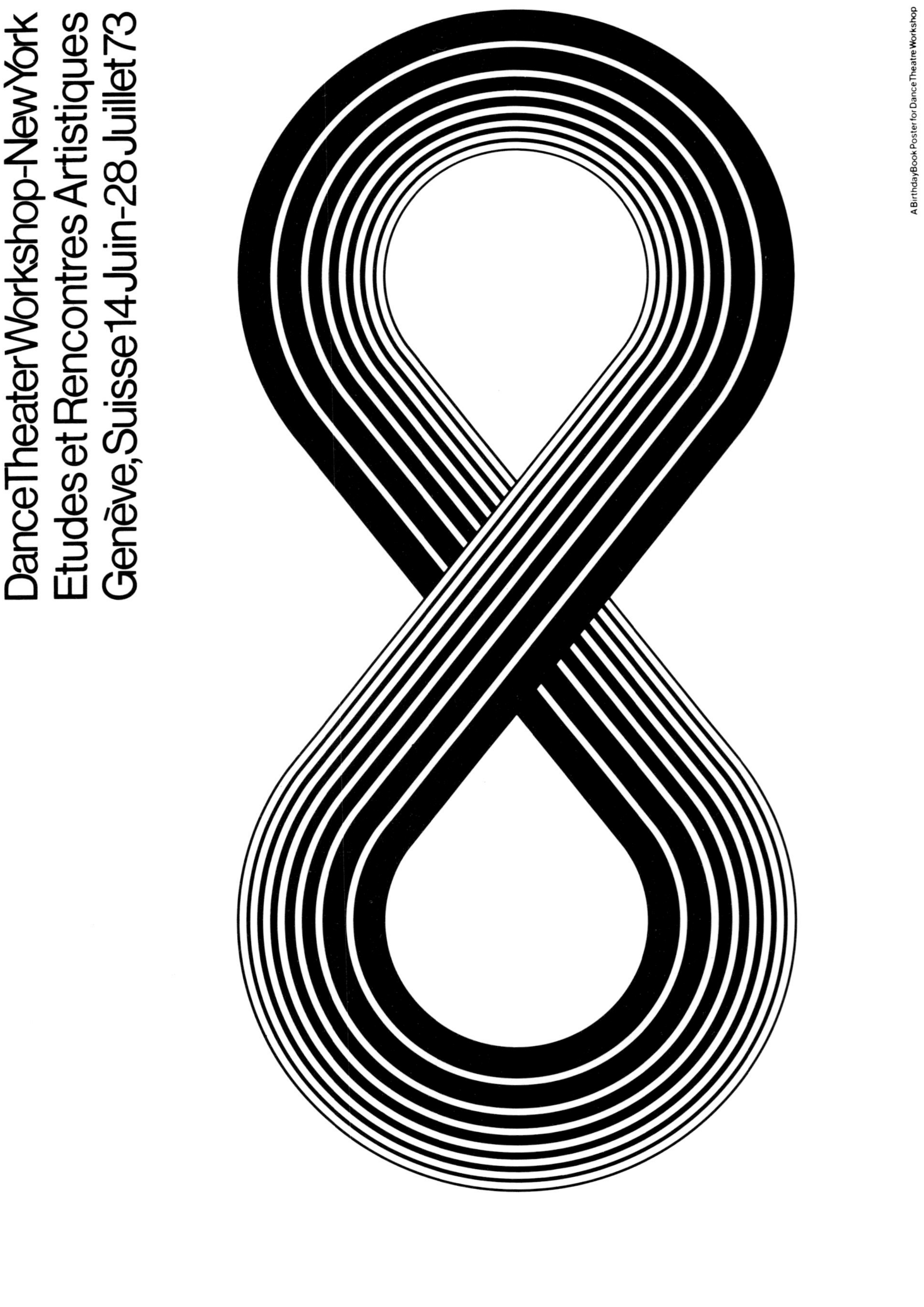

DanceTheaterWorkshop-NewYork
Etudes et Rencontres Artistiques
Genève, Suisse 14 Juin-28 Juillet 73
A Birthday Book Poster for Dance Theatre Workshop

382
Birthday Book Entrant
William R. Tobias Art Director
Dance Theater Workshop of N.Y. Client

American-Type Sculpture: Part 1
Opening March 20th 5 30 PM-7 30 PM Gallery Hours Monday hrough Thursday 10 00 AM to 5 00 PM, and 6 30 PM to 9 00 PM Friday, 10 00 AM to 4 00 PM Closed Saturdays and Sundays
Design by B. Martin Pedersen
avid Smith Seymour Lipton Herbert Ferber David Hare Louise Bourgeois Isamu Noguchi Ibram Lassaw March 20 April 13 Guest Director Phyllis Tuchman

381
B. Martin Pederson Entrant
Pederson Design Inc. Studio
Visual Arts Gallery Client

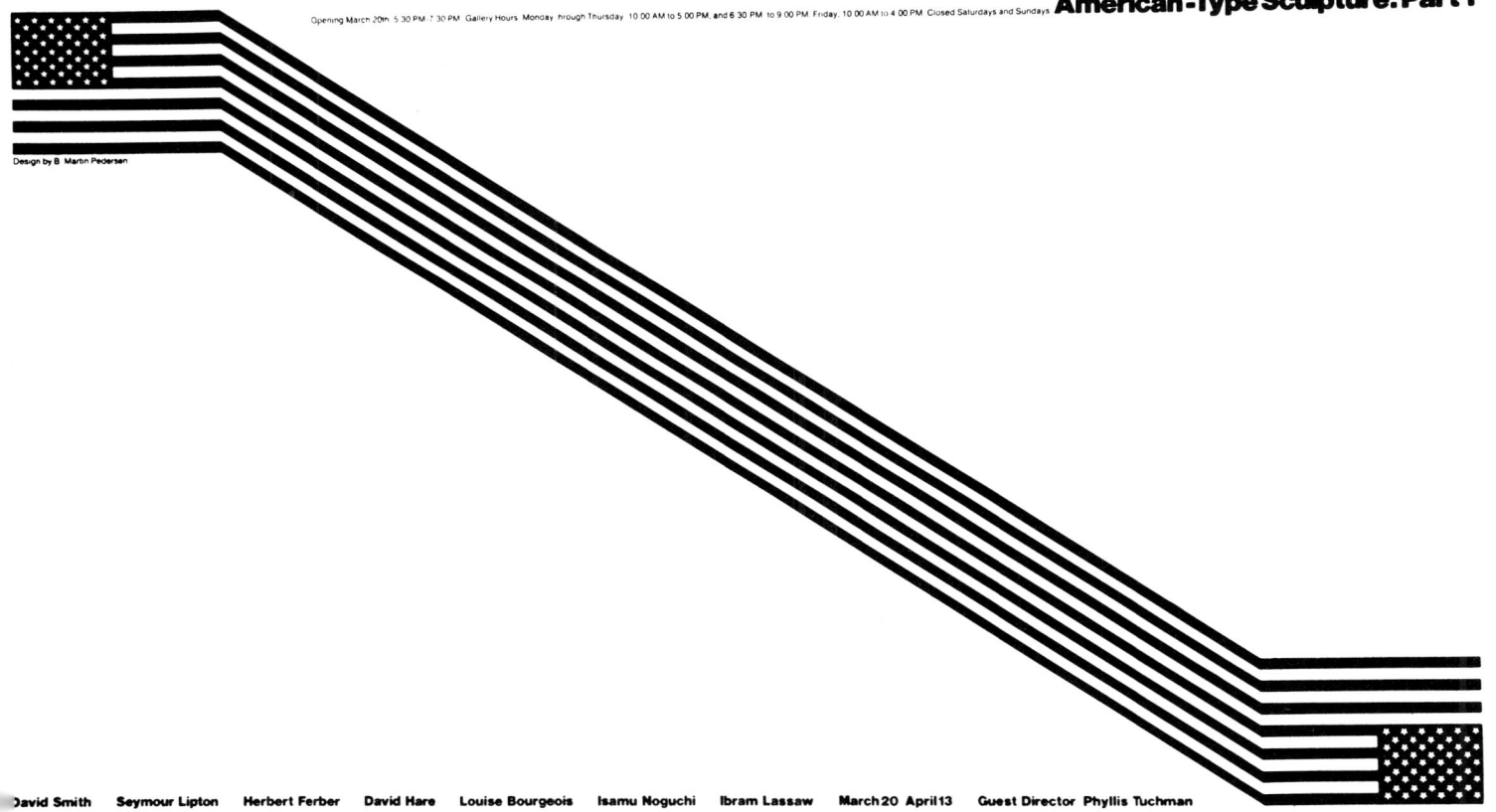

acupuncture

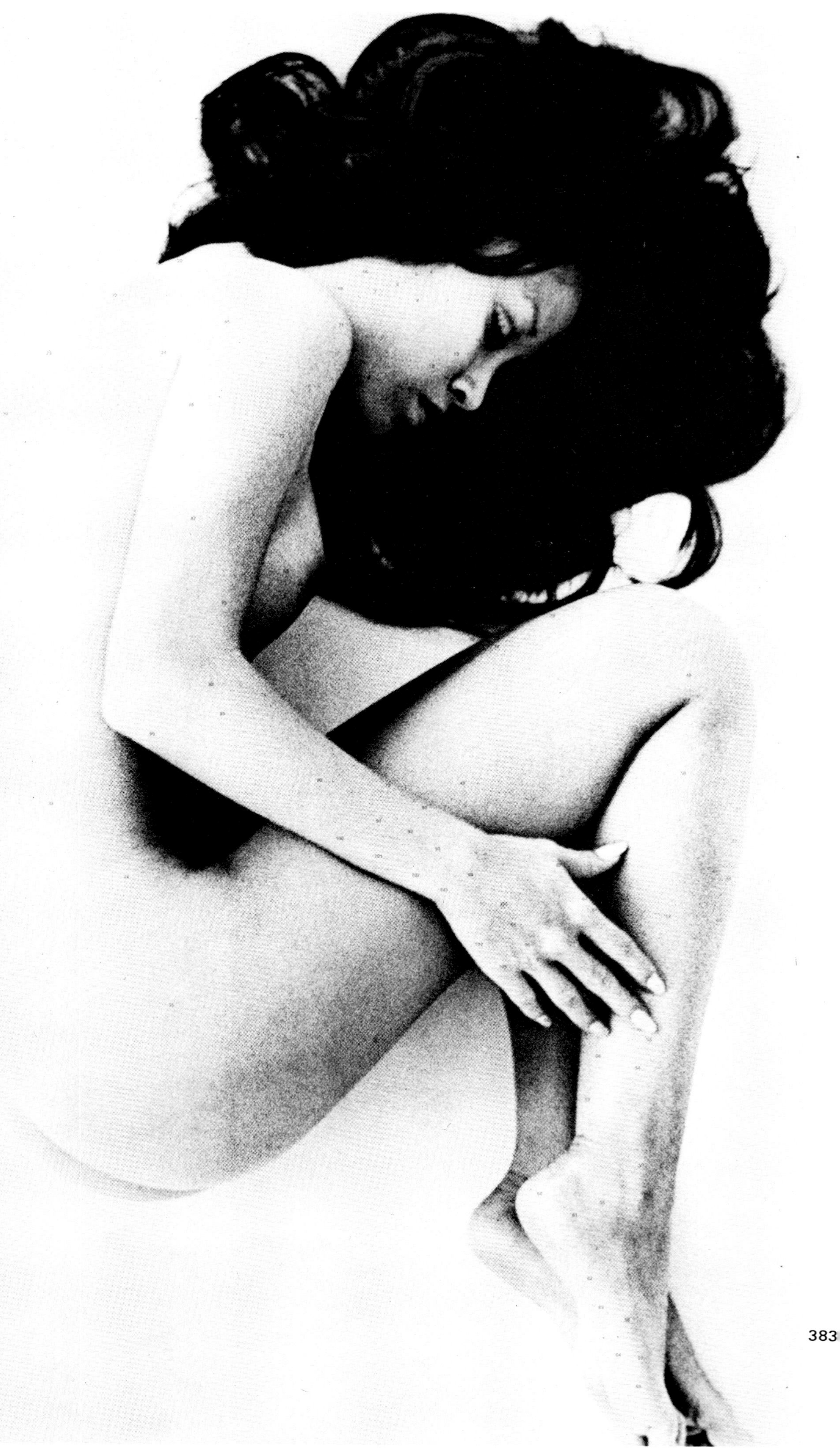

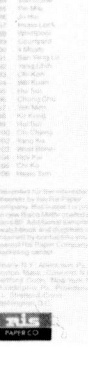

384

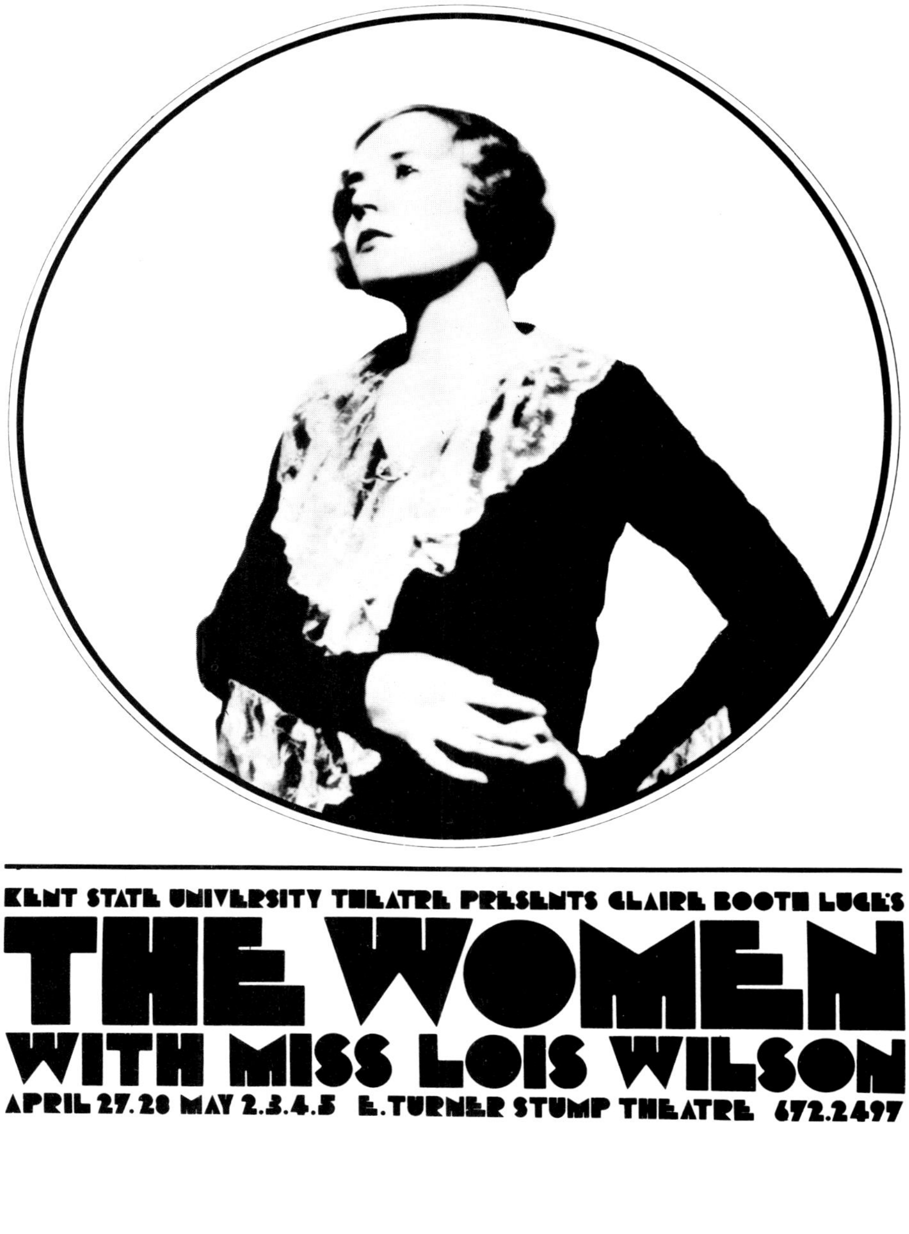
KENT STATE UNIVERSITY THEATRE PRESENTS CLAIRE BOOTH LUCE'S
THE WOMEN
WITH MISS LOIS WILSON
APRIL 27.28 MAY 2.3.4.5 E.TURNER STUMP THEATRE 672.2497

383
Intercept Entrant
Philip Gips Art Director
Lock Huey Photographer
Ris Paper Company Client

384
J. Charles Walker, J. Brett Buchanan Entrants
Tarragon Graphics Agency
University Theater, Kent State Univ. Client

385

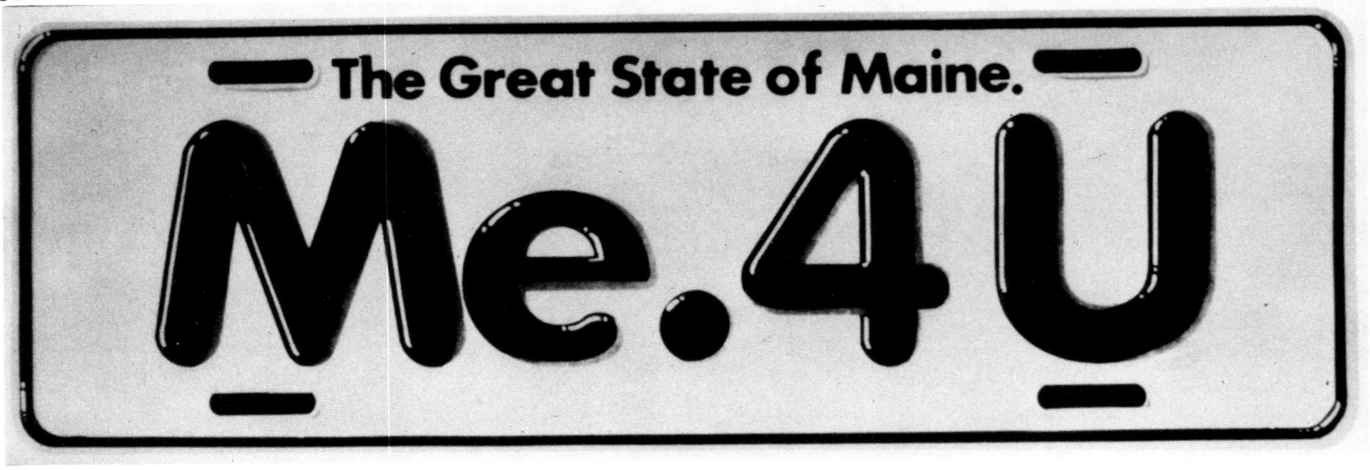
The Great State of Maine.
Me.4U

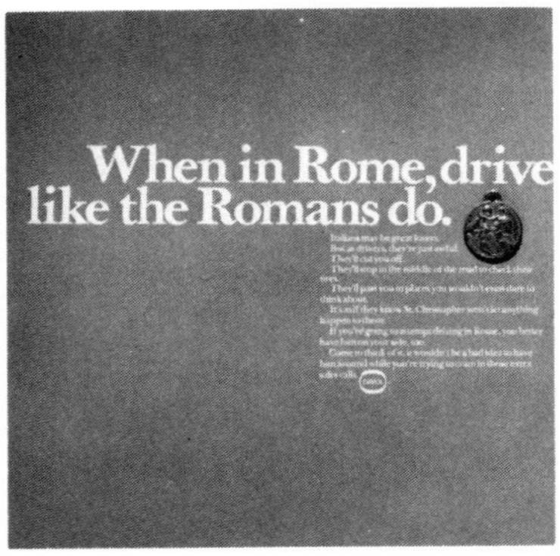
When in Rome, drive like the Romans do.

386

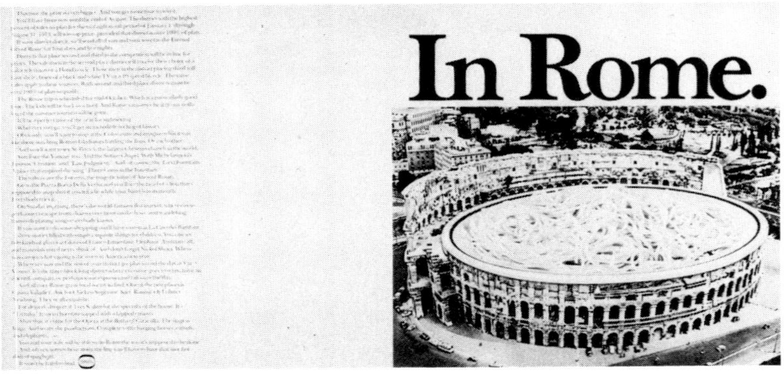
In Rome.

387

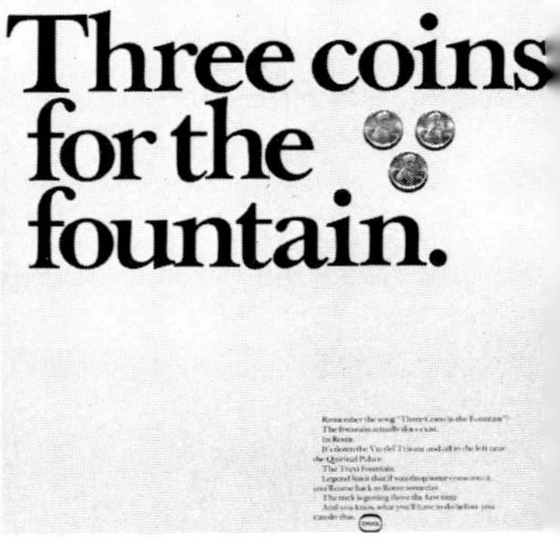
Three coins for the fountain.

388

391

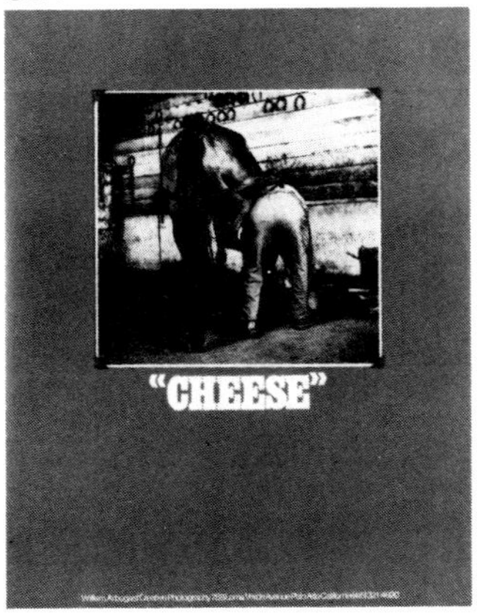
"CHEESE"

392

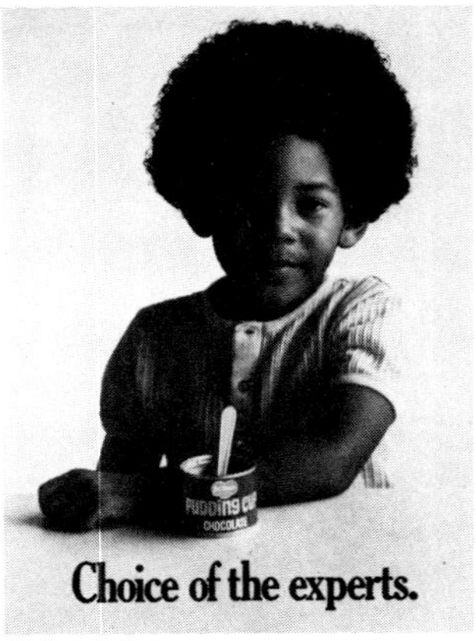
Choice of the experts.

393

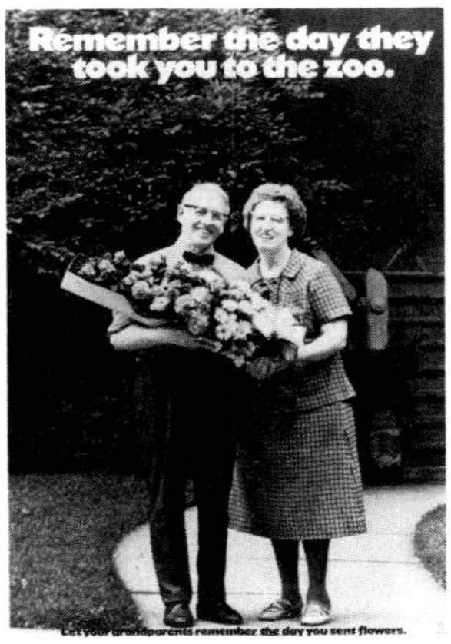
Remember the day they took you to the zoo.
Let your grandparents remember the day you sent flowers.

394

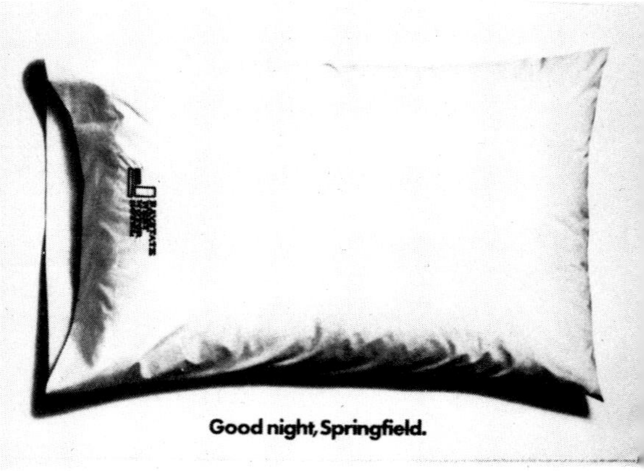
Good night, Springfield.

385
Hill, Holliday, Connors, Cosmopulos Entrants
Stavros Cosmopulos Art Director
State of Maine Client

386-390
Creamer, Trowbridge, Case & Basford Entrant
Tyler Smith Art Director
Frank Eck, Myron Taplin Photographers
Davol Inc. Client

391
Steven Jacobs Design, Inc. Entrant
Steve Jacobs Art Director
Bill Arbogast Photographer
Arbogast Photography Client

392
Al Fessler Entrant
Lynn McCarthy Photographer
McCann-Erickson Inc. Agency
Del Monte Corp. Client

393
Albert Jay Rosenthal & Co. Entrant
Jerry Roach Art Director
Burt Harris Photographer
Florafax Client

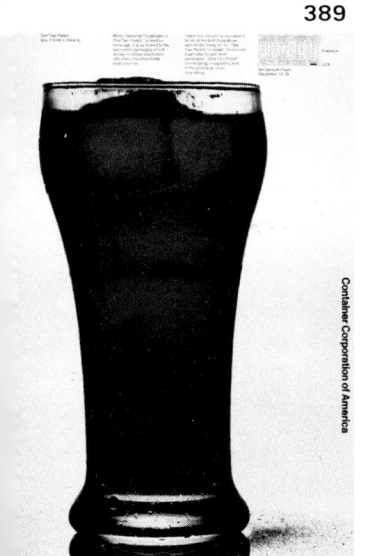

389

See Rome as the Romans do.

390

395

397

396

394	395	396	397
Hill, Holliday, Connors, Cosmopulos Entrants	Ketchum, MacLeod & Grove Entrant	Container Corp. of America Entrant	Dr. Rudolf Farner AG BSR Entrant
Stavros Cosmopulos, Dick Pantano Art Directors	Walter Kaprielian Art Director	Bill Bonnell Art Director	G. Wyland Art Director
Baystate West Motor Hotel Client	Gordon Smith Photographer	Conrad Bailey Photographer	J. Tappich Photographer
	Air Jamaica Client		Cynar S.A. Mendrisio Client

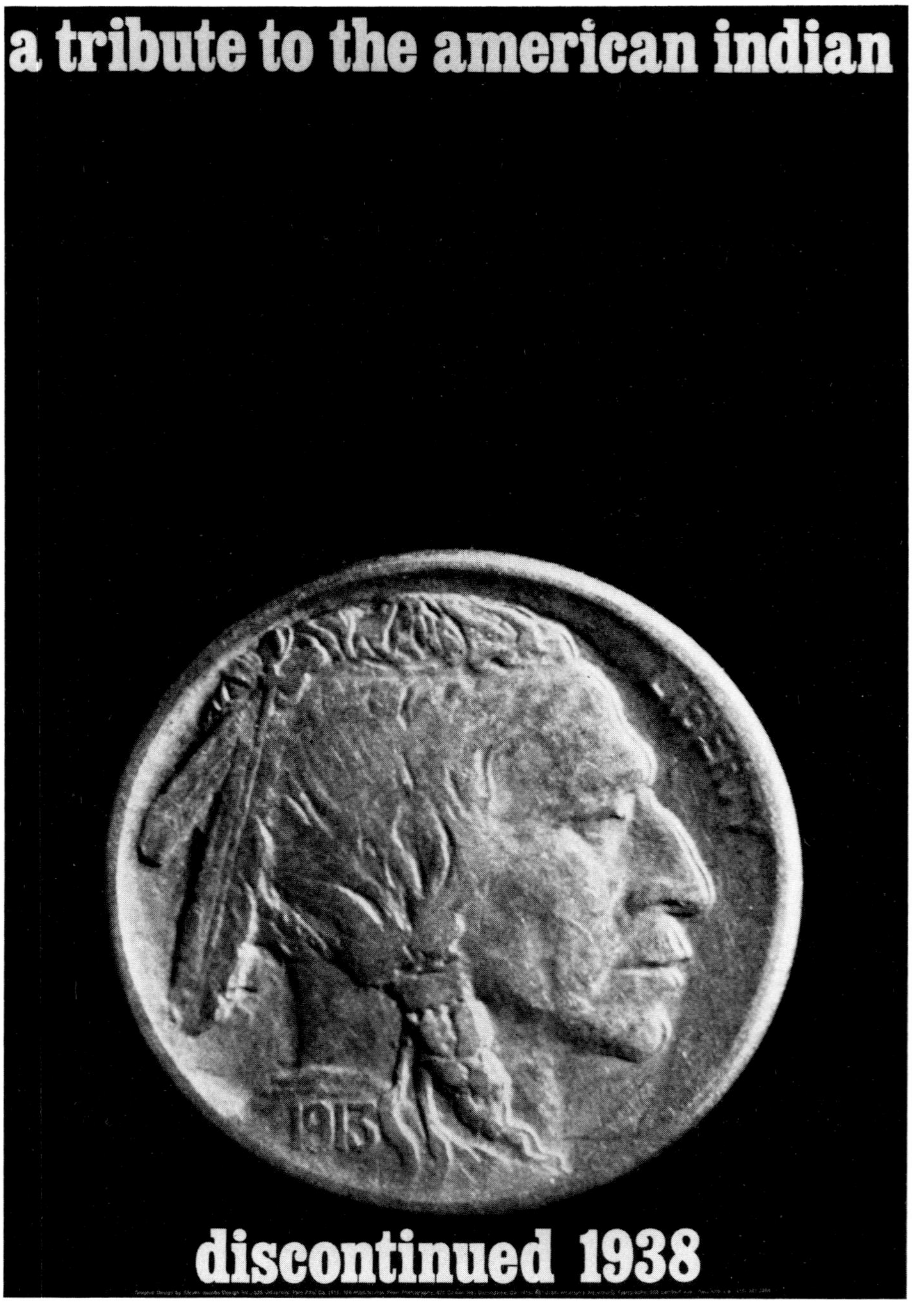
a tribute to the american indian
discontinued 1938

398

398
Steven Jacobs Design, Inc. Entrant
Steve Jacobs Art Director
Norton Pearl
Photographer

399
The Dombrosky/Peck Coalition Entrant
Bill Wilson, Joe Herrick Art Directors
Michael Friedman Photographer

How'd you like a fat wallet?

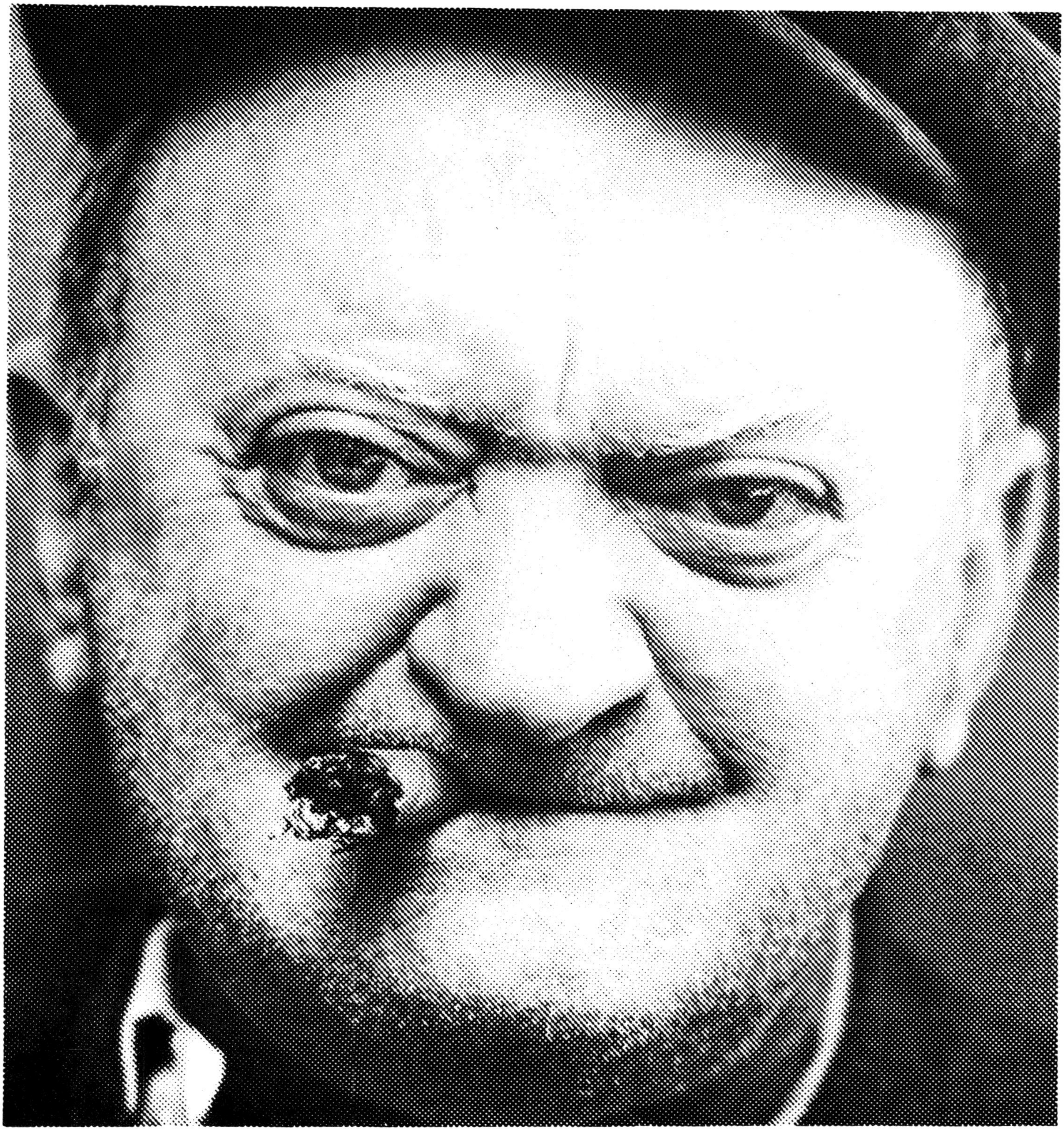

How'd you like your wallet thicker because you came to Hobelmann Volkswagen for your car?

AUTHORIZED DEALER

399

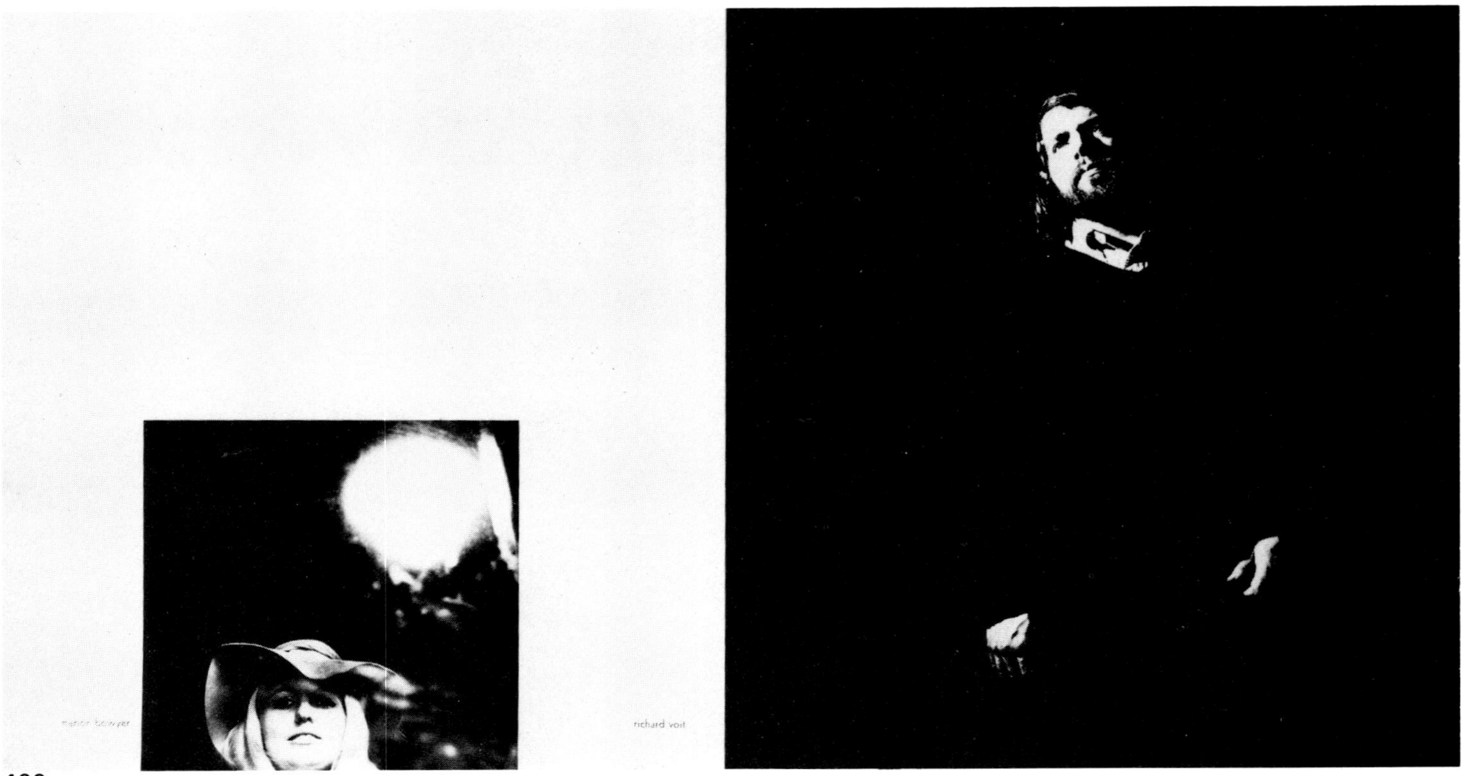
richard voit

400

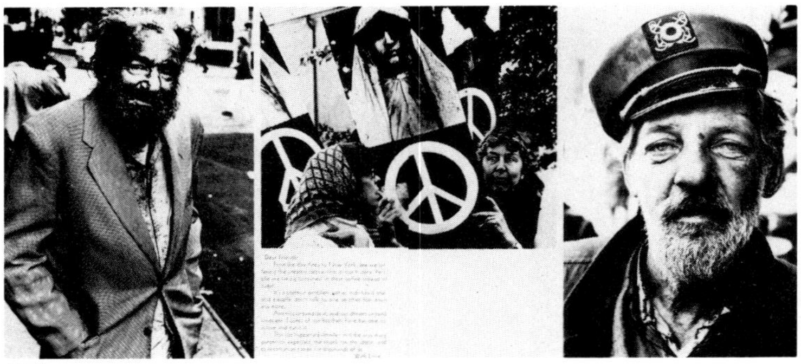

401

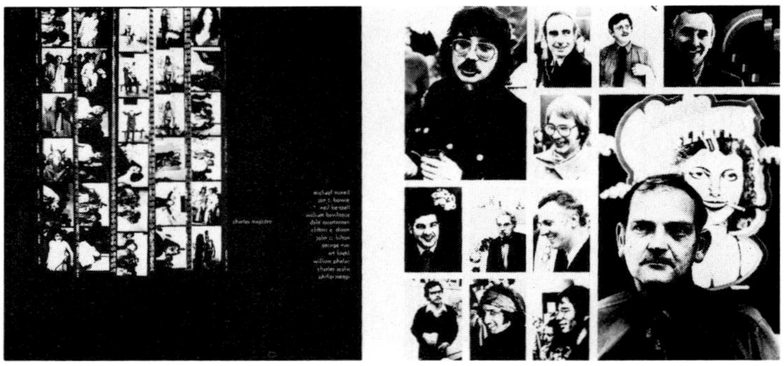

402

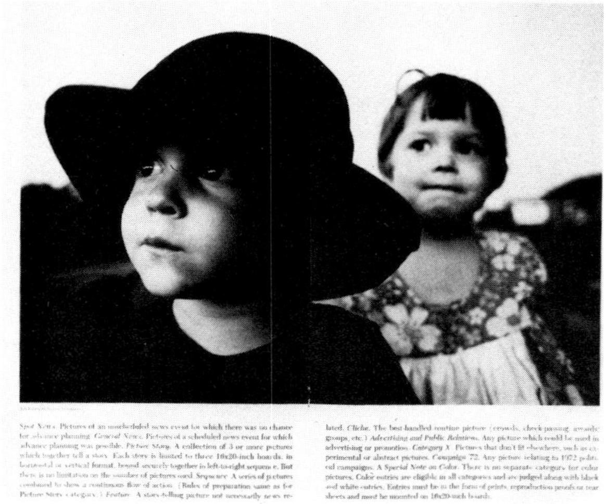
Spot News. Pictures of an unscheduled news event for which there was no chance for advance planning. General News. Pictures of a scheduled news event for which advance planning was possible. Picture Story. A collection of 3 or more pictures which together tell a story. Each story is limited to three 16x20-inch boards, in horizontal or vertical format, bound securely together in left-to-right sequence. But there is no limitation on the number of pictures used. Sequence. A series of pictures combined to show a continuous flow of action. (Rules of preparation same as for Picture Story category.) Feature. A story-telling picture not necessarily news related. Cliche. The best handled routine picture (crowds, check-passing, awards groups, etc.) Advertising and Public Relations. Any picture which could be used in advertising or promotion. Category X. Pictures that don't fit elsewhere, such as experimental or abstract pictures. Campaign 72. Any picture relating to 1972 political campaigns. A Special Note on Color. There is no separate category for color pictures. Color entries are eligible in all categories and are judged along with black and white entries. Entries must be in the form of prints, reproduction proofs or tear sheets and must be mounted on 16x20-inch boards.

403

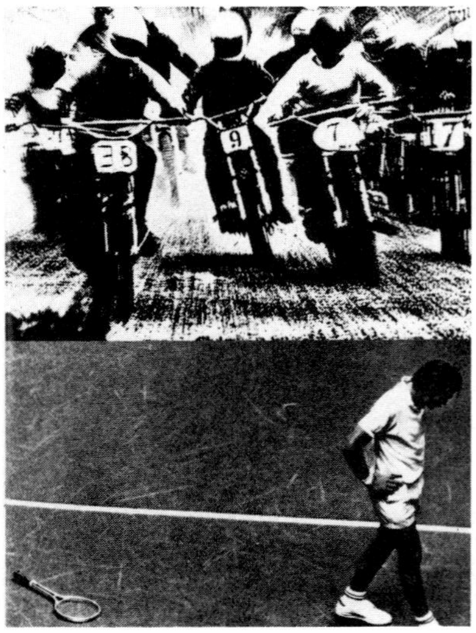

404

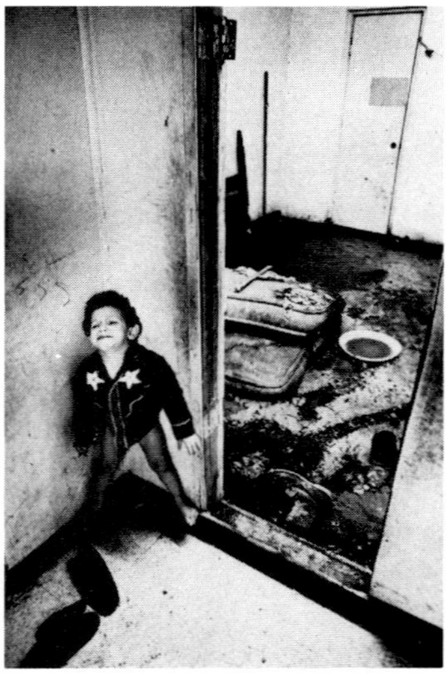

405

400-402
Joel Vann Fuller Entrant
Joel Fuller, Chuck Deafenbaugh, Claude Skelton, Brownie Harris Illustrators
Gibbs Assoc., The Design Group Agency
Virginia Commonwealth University Client

403-405
Joel Vann Fuller Entrant
Gibbs Assoc., The Design Group Agency
Southern Short Course in News Photography Client

406

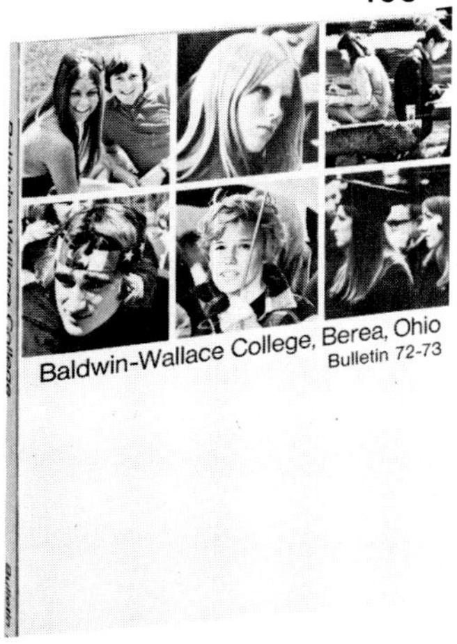
Baldwin-Wallace College, Berea, Ohio
Bulletin 72-73

407

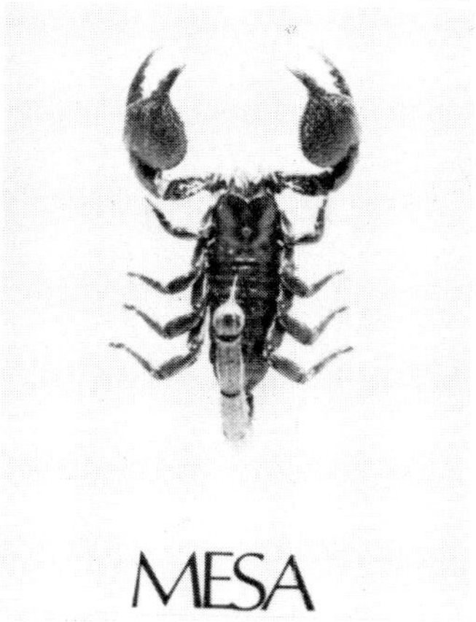
MESA

408

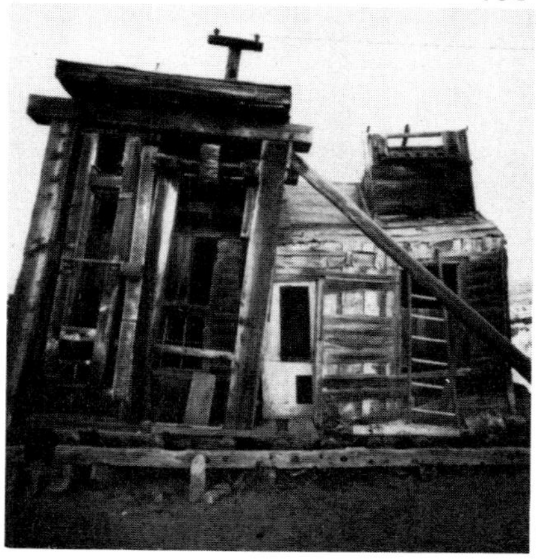

409

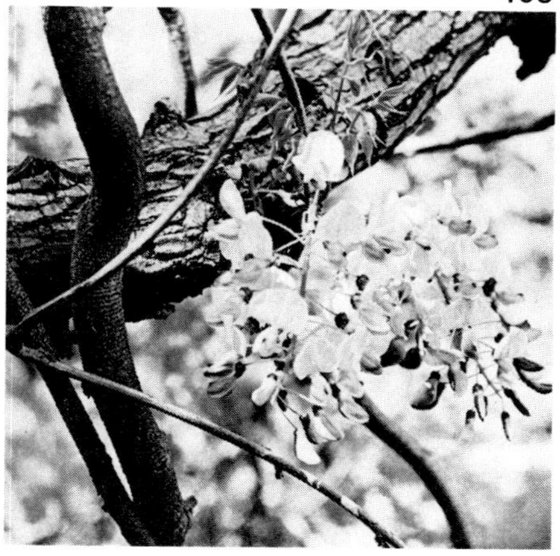

410

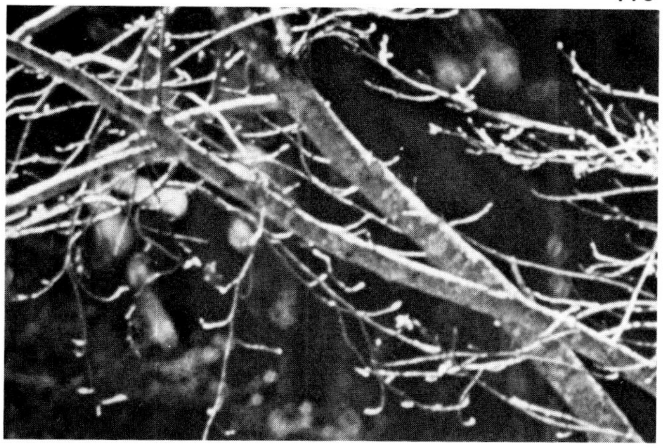

411

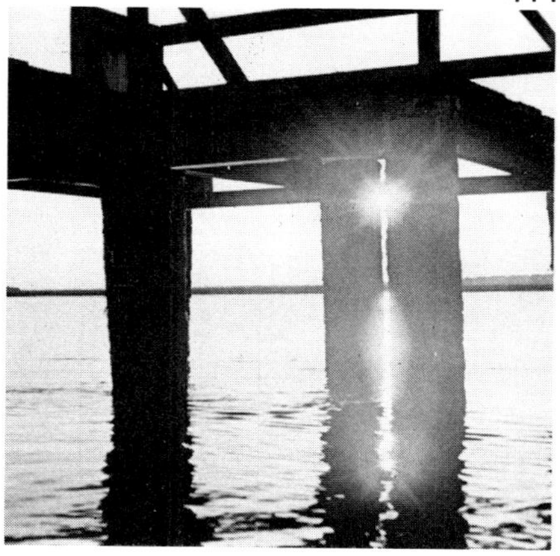

412

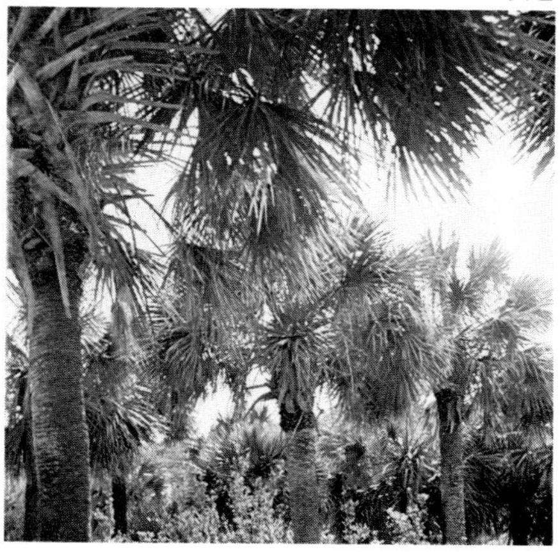

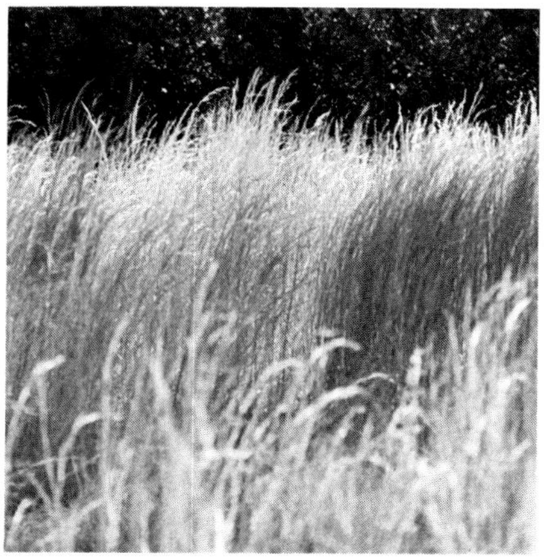

413

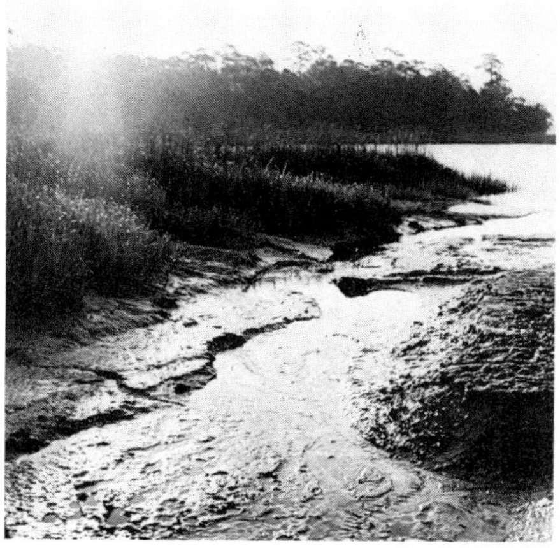

414

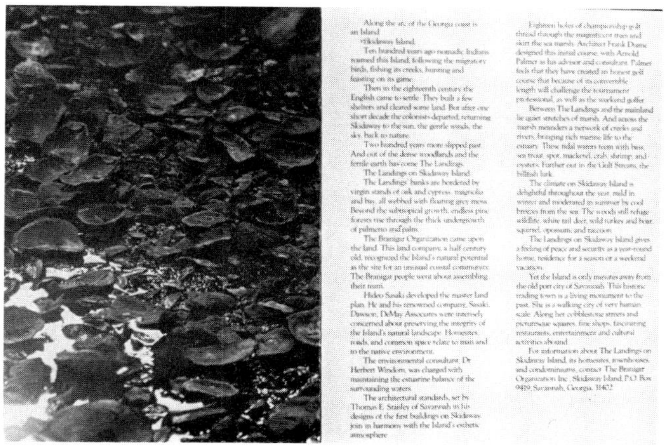

415

406
Marlin Bush Entrant
Will Richmond Photographer
Baldwin-Wallace College Client

407-408
Steven Jacobs Design, Inc. Entrant
Steve Jacobs Art Director
Robert Isaacs, Bill Arbogast Photographers
Simpson Lee Paper Company Client

409-415
Cunningham, Tallman, Pennington Entrant
Ewen Pennington Art Director
The Landings on Skidaway Island Client

416

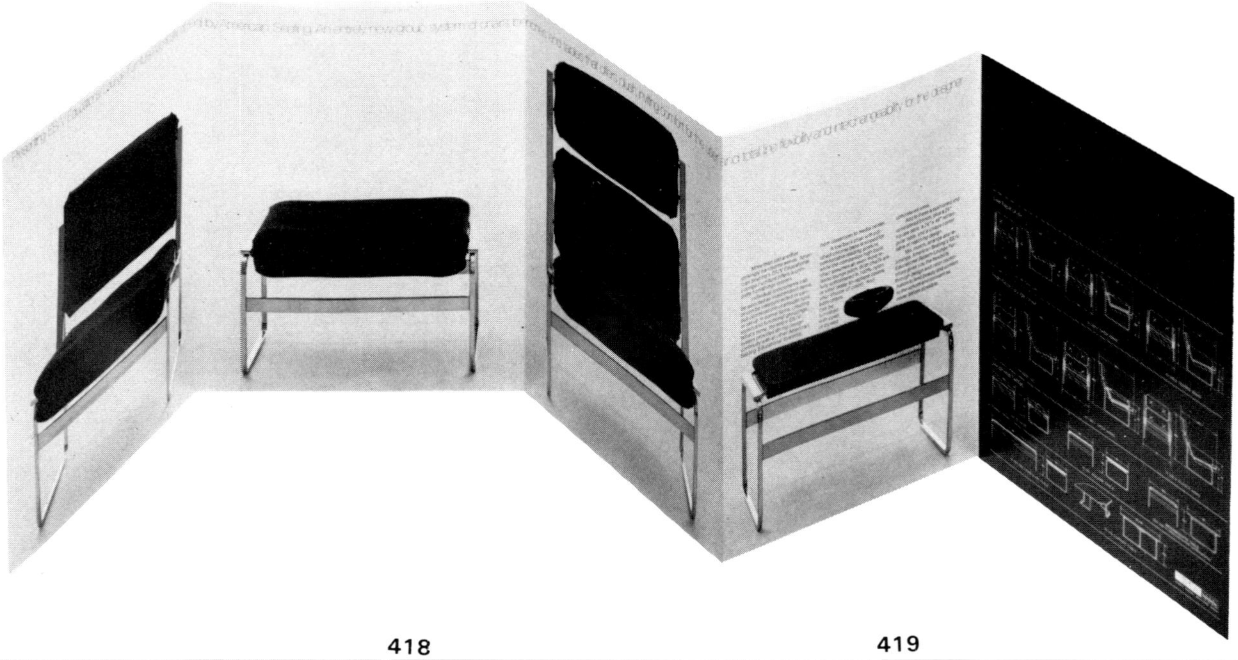

417

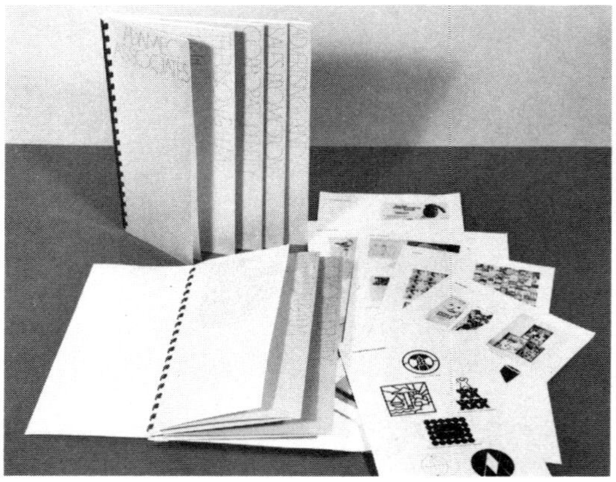

418

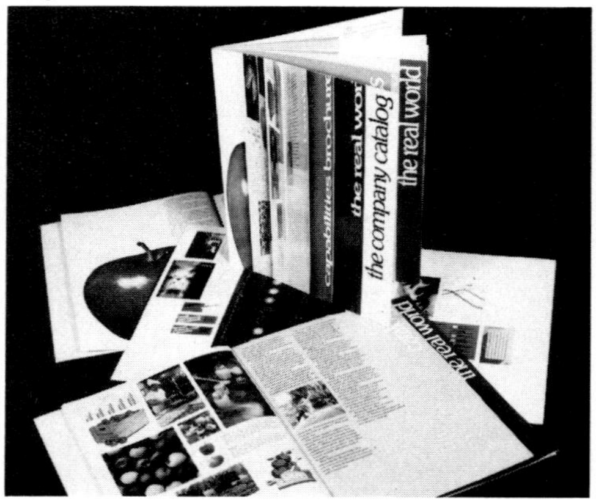
capabilities brochure
the real world
the company catalog
the real world

419

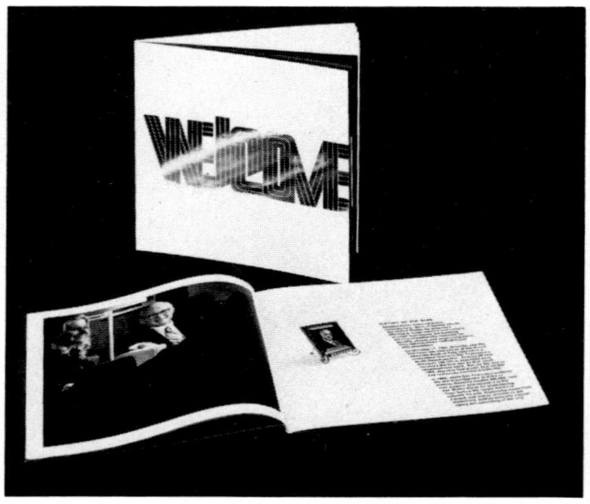
WELCOME

420

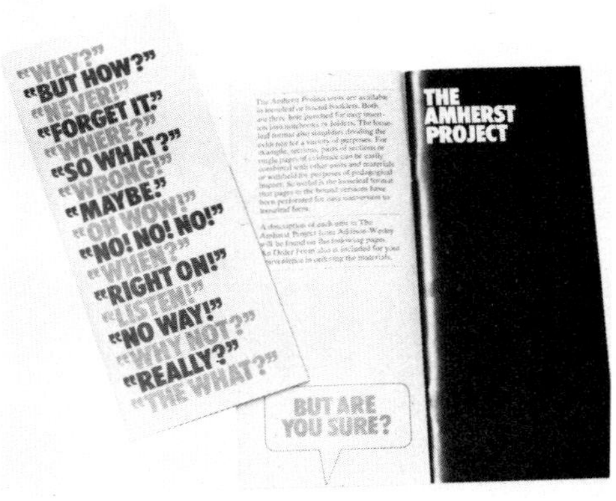
"WHY?"
"BUT HOW?"
"NEVER!"
"FORGET IT!"
"WHERE?"
"SO WHAT?"
"WRONG!"
"MAYBE."
"OH WOW!"
"NO! NO! NO!"
"WHEN?"
"RIGHT ON!"
"LISTEN!"
"NO WAY!"
"WHY NOT?"
"REALLY?"
"THE WHAT?"
BUT ARE YOU SURE?
THE AMHERST PROJECT

421

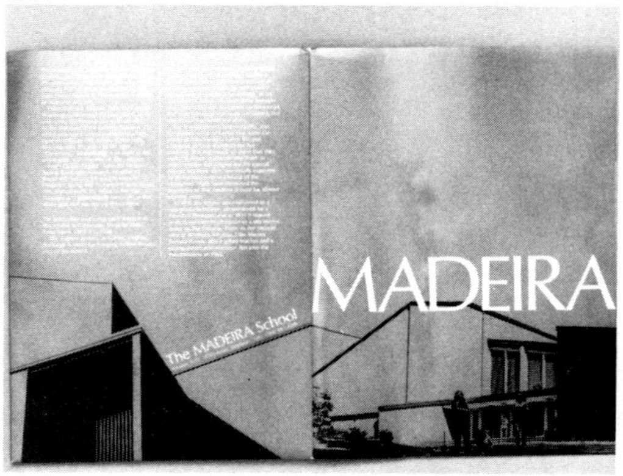
MADEIRA
The MADEIRA School

422

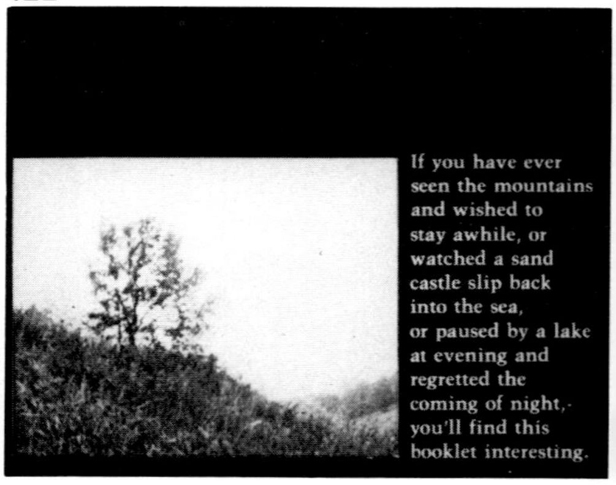
If you have ever seen the mountains and wished to stay awhile, or watched a sand castle slip back into the sea, or paused by a lake at evening and regretted the coming of night,- you'll find this booklet interesting.

417
Adamec Assoc. Entrant
Donald A. Adamec Art Director

418
Robert Cipriani-Gunn Assoc. Entrant
Robert Cipriani Art Director
David Niles, Gene Lemery, Mark Bellerose Illustrators
Ozzie Sweet, Holmes Hurll Photographers
Gunn Associates Studio
S.D. Warren Co. Client

419
Thom LaPerle Entrant
Paul Chan Photographer
Graphic Communications Center Agency
Bank of America Client

420
Paul Sinn Entrant
Sam Smidt Assoc. Agency
Addison Wesley Publishing Co. Client

423

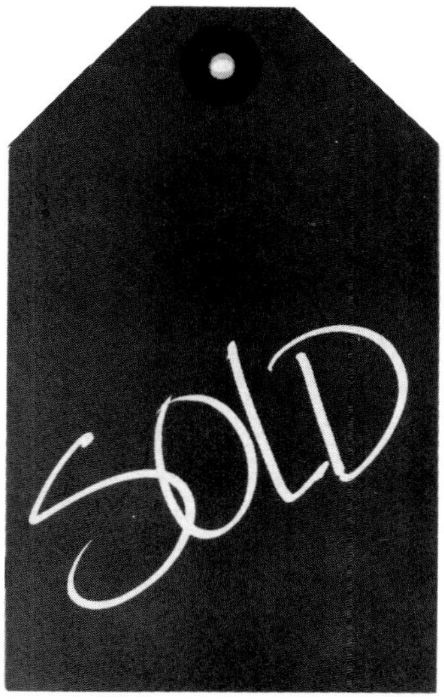
SOLD

424

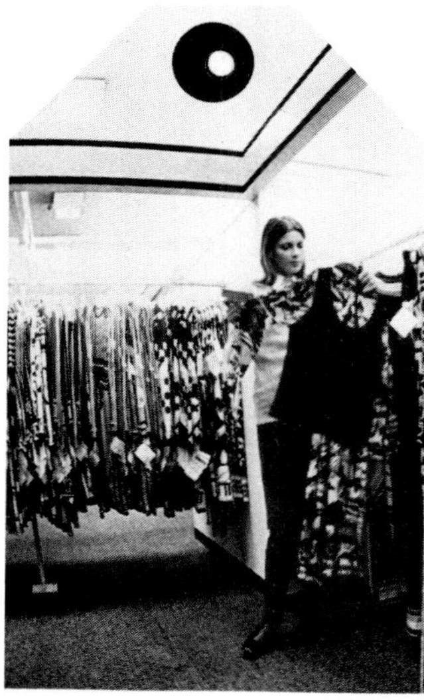

425

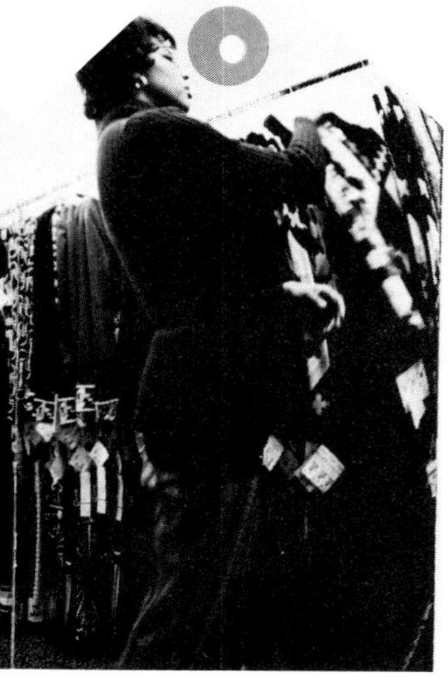

426

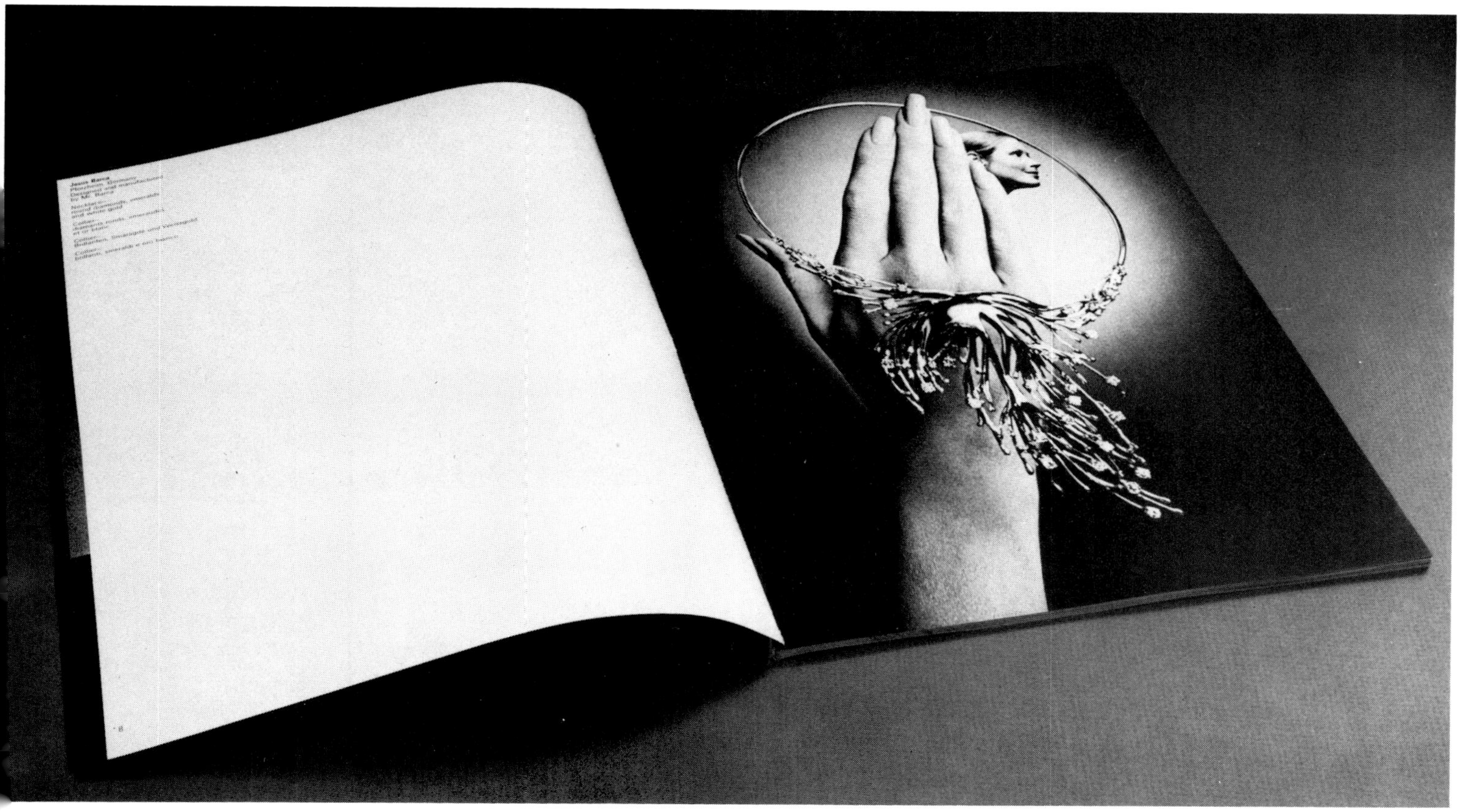

421
Graphics 4 Inc.
Entrant
John S. Corrao
Art Director
The Madeira School
Client

422
Jim Cole Entrant
Dick Henderson
Art Director
Peter Vaeth
Photographer
Cole Henderson Drake Inc. Agency
Rondesics Client

423-425
R.V. Paganucci
Entrant
IBM
Client

426
Howard Grant
Entrant
Howard Grant, Richard Ritter
Designers
Ryzard Horowitz
Photographer
Ayer Design
Agency
De Beers Consolidated Mines, Ltd.
Client

427

JAMAICA
A LAND OF CONTRAST

428

Residential
Commercial

429

One Federal Street

430

A regular way to learn the conjugations of irregular French verbs.

431

French Verb Handbook simplifies irregular verb conjugations. Two key charts form the foundation for the verb system. Chart A contains the endings for regular and most irregular verbs. Chart B shows how to form the stems of irregular verbs. After a student memorizes these key charts, he learns only the irregular parts of sixty basic irregular verbs. The blank spaces on the conjugation charts are "regular" with respect to Charts A and B. Every irregular verb in the French language fits one of these sixty basic models and can be learned by using the appropriate conjugation chart.
Harold W. Lee originated the method in view of the difficulty his students experienced in mastering French verbs. In his several years of language instruction at Stanford and at Brigham Young University, Dr. Lee had seen students repeatedly use French verb dictionaries without learning the verb conjugations. French Verb Handbook now makes verb mastery simple.
In addition to serving as chairman of the language department at Brigham Young University, Harold Lee has twice served as section chairman for the Rocky Mountain Modern Language Association. He has spent eight years in residence in France, two summers as director of the University of Paris summer school, and two semesters as director of the BYU Semester Abroad program at the University of Grenoble. Dr. Lee's extensive language background well qualifies him to author this language teaching methods book.

432

Chart A
List of the Common French Irregular Verbs
"Dr. Harold Lee's method of learning irregular verbs is a revolutionary new approach. I found that French irregular verbs are not as difficult and numerous as I had imagined. I didn't think it was possible to conjugate by memory until I was introduced to this method. French Verb Handbook has helped me understand and remember the different conjugations in all tenses and cases."
Lee J. Westover
Third-year French Student
"I found the verb charts in French Verb Handbook very worthwhile. They have helped me organize the different verb tenses in my mind so at last they make sense. Until now the various tenses have been one mass of confusion, but with the charts, each one has its own place. When I need a verb in a particular tense, I can picture the chart in my mind and easily pick out the appropriate ending or endings."
Kathy Kellough
Third-year French Student
"Dr. Lee's verb book is the best method to learn verbs that I have encountered in the United States or in France. It is concise and easy to understand. This productive method remains clear and usable in my mind. It has taken the pain out of learning verbs. I regret I didn't have access to it earlier.
George R. Nackos
Third-year French Student

433

BRIGHAM YOUNG UNIVERSITY BULLETIN
GAME OF COLLEGE
SUITABLE FOR UP TO 25000 PLAYERS

434

START
So you want to play the game of college?
That's good. But let's get one thing straight:
College isn't a game — it's very serious business.
The reason we're presenting this introduction
in game form is simply to help you enjoy getting
acquainted with Brigham Young University.
Once you're here, you won't need a game
to help you enjoy our style of college life.
You'll enjoy it because of its unique
challenge and unique advantage.

435

WIN
30

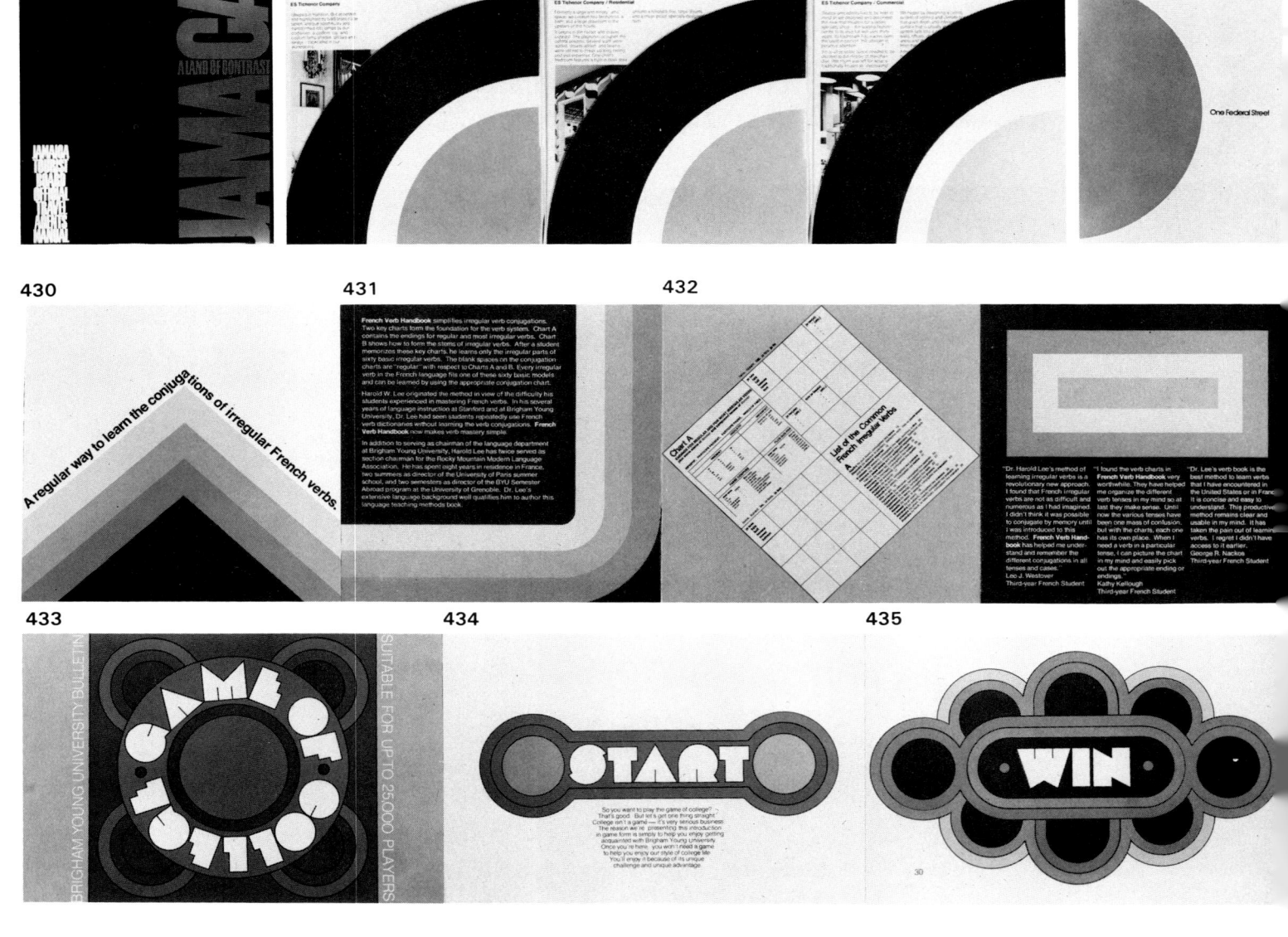

427
Lubalin, Smith, Carnase Entrant
Herb Lubalin Art Director
Joe Veno Illustrator
Bernard Wolf, Deidi von Schaewen Photographers
Jamaica Tourist Board Client

428
Designers Ross Stewart & Winner Entrant
Frank Ross, Dan Stewart Art Directors
Ray Schuhmann Photography Inc. Photographers
E.S. Tichenor Co. Client

429
Giardini/Russell, Inc. Entrant
Robert H. Russell Art Director
Arthur Monks Assoc. Client

430-432
McRay Magleby Entrant
Fay Ping Andrus Art Director
Graphic Communications Studio
Brigham Young University Client

433-435
McRay Magleby Entrant
McRay Magleby
Julie Fuhrimann Illustrators

437

436

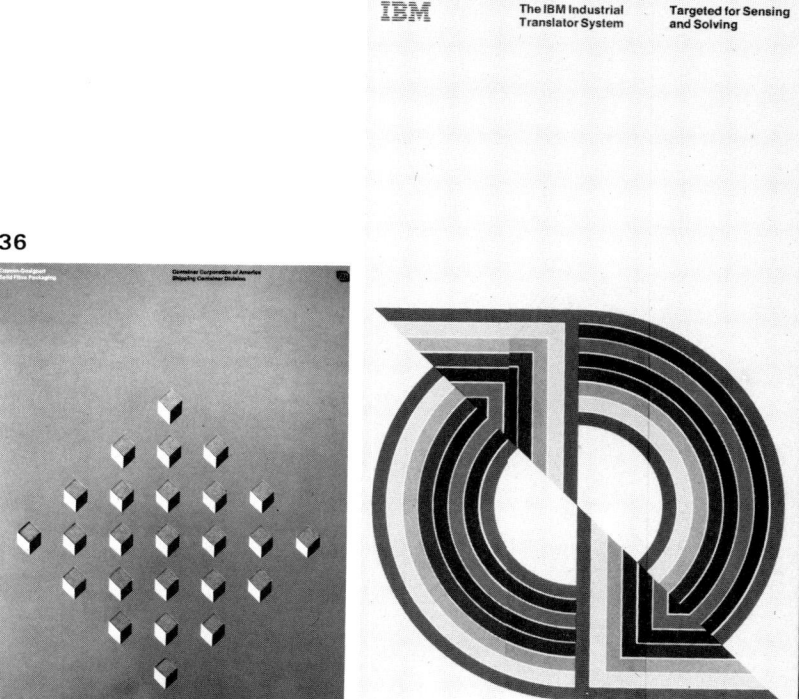

438

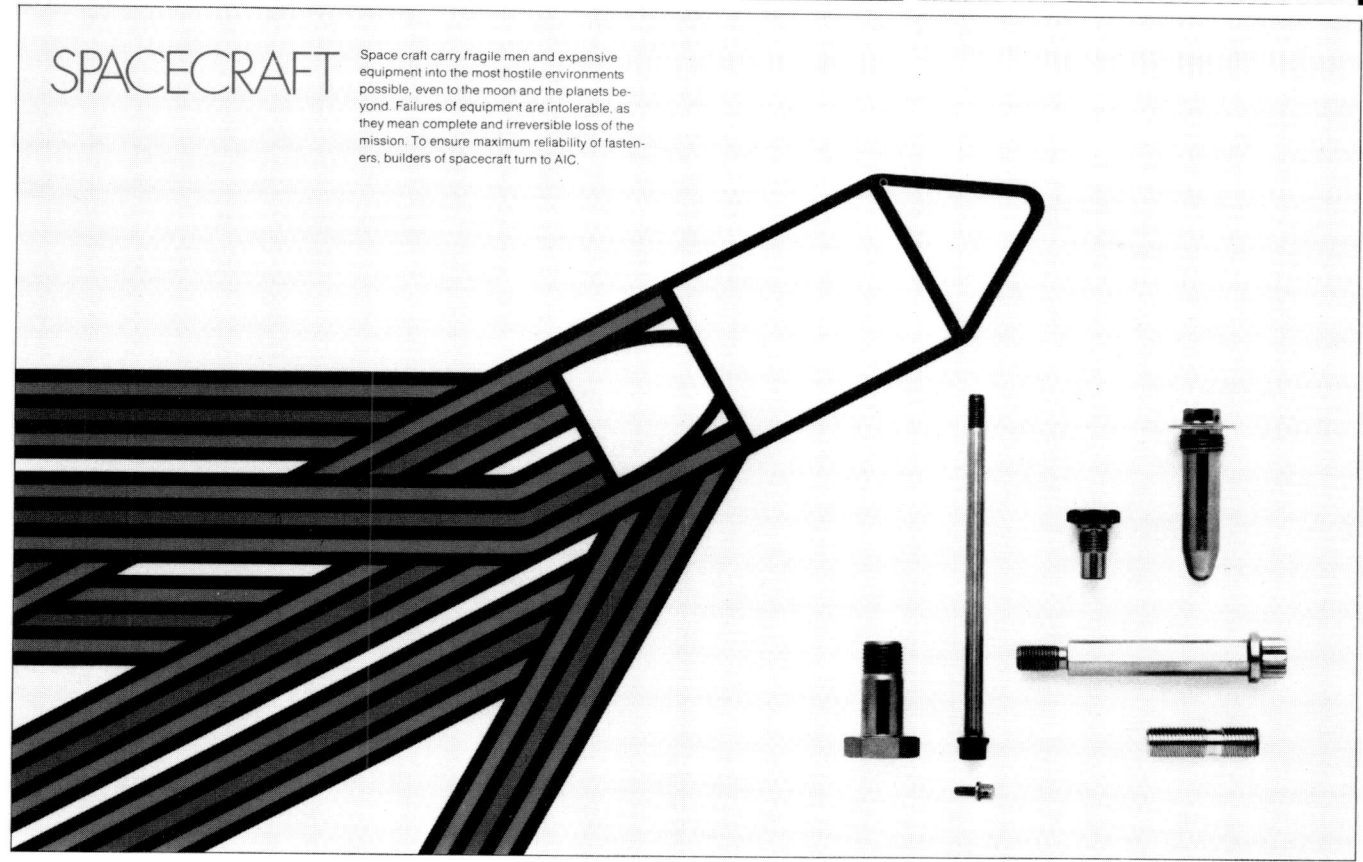

	436	437	438	
aphic Communications dio gham Young iversity nt	R.E. Loth Entrant Bill Bonnell, Bob Loth Art Directors Container Corp. of America Client	R. V. Paganucci Entrant J. Mancini Designer IBM Client	Robert Miles Runyan & Associates Entrant Robert Miles Runyan Art Director Jim Guerard Designer	Steve Kahn, Robert Stevens Photographers Karyl Sisson, Art Mochizoki Artists Air Industries Corporation Client

439

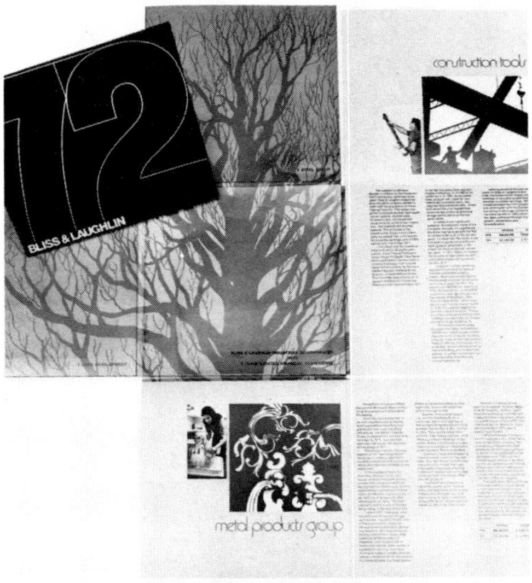
72
BLISS & LAUGHLIN
construction tools
metal products group

440

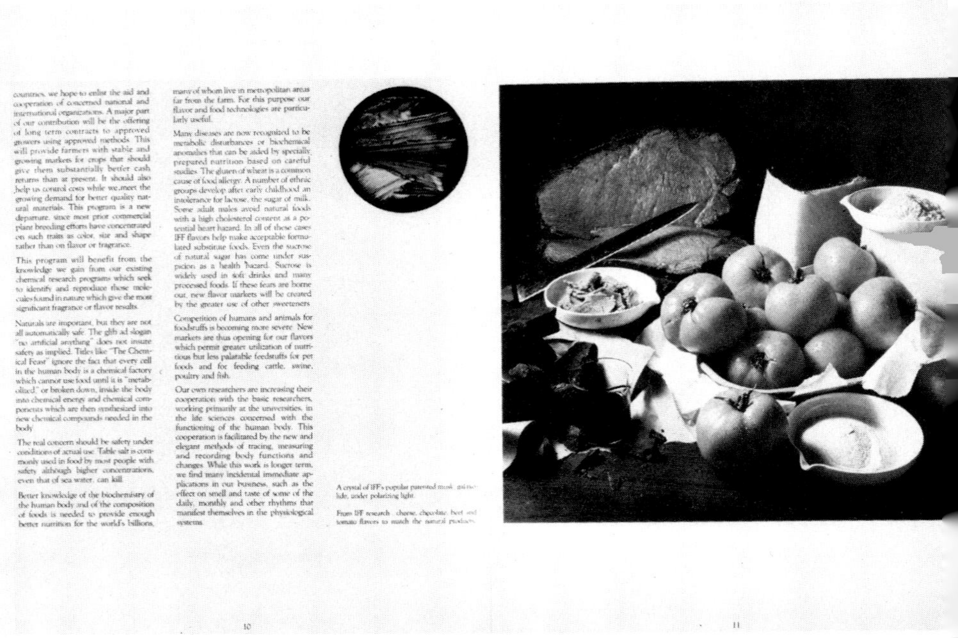

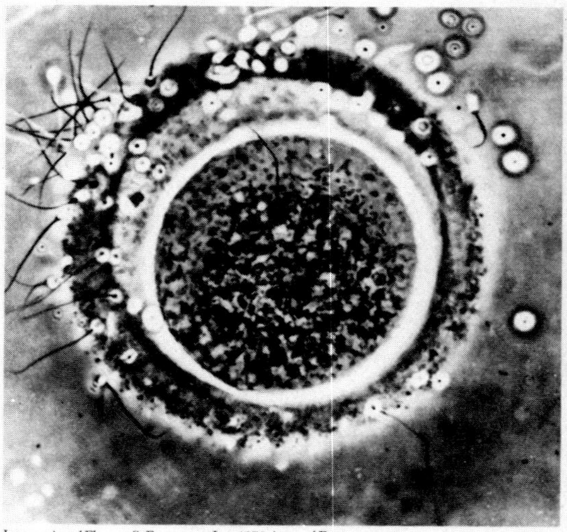

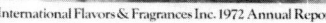

International Flavors & Fragrances Inc. 1972 Annual Report

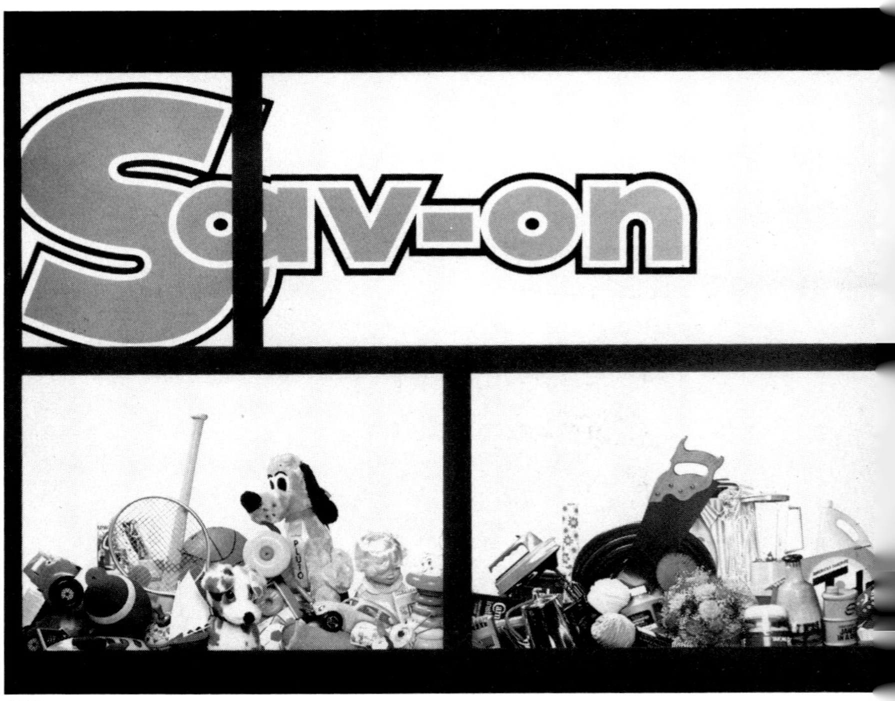
Sav-on

441

442

439
Scott Bivans Entrant
Nader-Lief, Inc. Agency
Bliss & Laughlin Client

440-441
Brian O'Neill Entrant
Tom McCarthy, Alan Vogel, Nick Samardge Photographers
Davis-Delaney-Arrow Agency
International Flavors & Fragrances Inc. Client

442
John Anselmo Entrant
John Anselmo Design Assoc., Ltd. Studio
John Anselmo, Thomas Bloch Designers
Allan D. Walker Photographer
Sav-On Drugs, Inc. Client

444

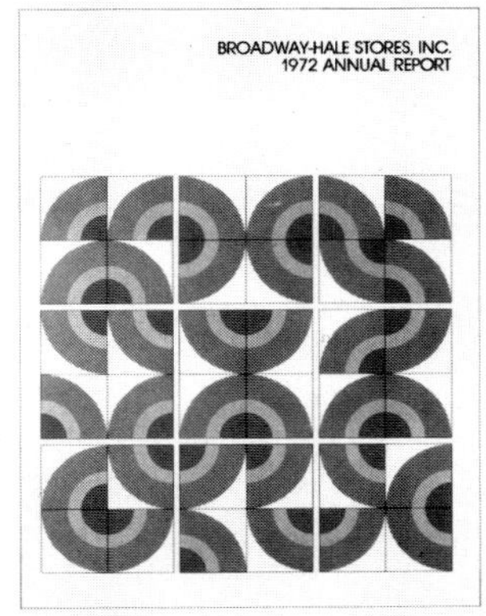

BROADWAY-HALE STORES, INC.
1972 ANNUAL REPORT

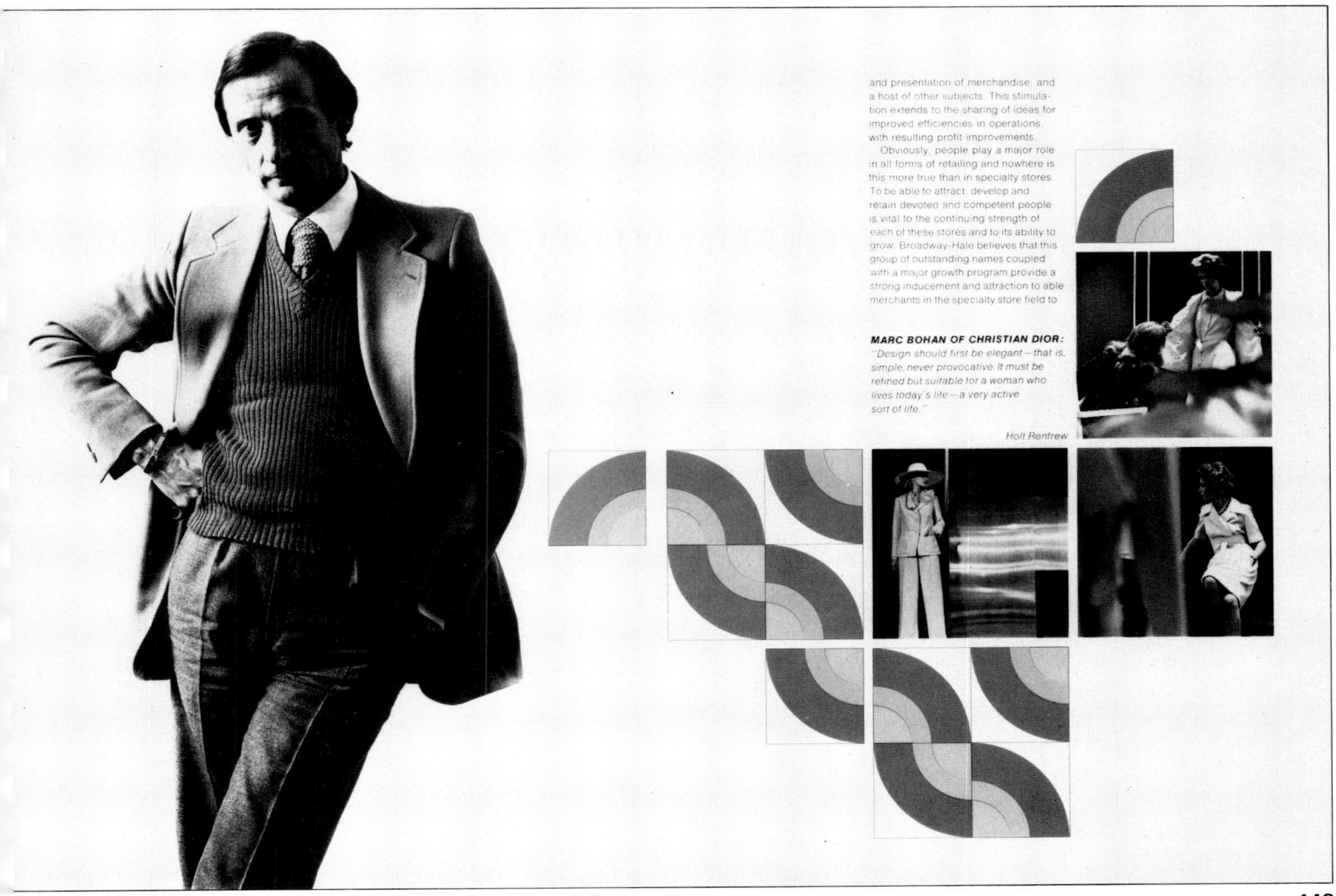

and presentation of merchandise, and a host of other subjects. This stimulation extends to the sharing of ideas for improved efficiencies in operations, with resulting profit improvements.

Obviously, people play a major role in all forms of retailing and nowhere is this more true than in specialty stores. To be able to attract, develop and retain devoted and competent people is vital to the continuing strength of each of these stores and to its ability to grow. Broadway-Hale believes that this group of outstanding names coupled with a major growth program provide a strong inducement and attraction to able merchants in the specialty store field to

MARC BOHAN OF CHRISTIAN DIOR:
"Design should first be elegant—that is, simple, never provocative. It must be refined but suitable for a woman who lives today's life—a very active sort of life."

Holt Renfrew

443

443-444
Robert Miles Runyan & Associates Entrant
Robert Miles Runyan Art Director
Gary Hinsche Designer
Marvin Silver Photographer
Karyl Sisson, Birgitta Forsman, Art Mochizoki Artists
Broadway-Hale Stores, Inc. Client

445

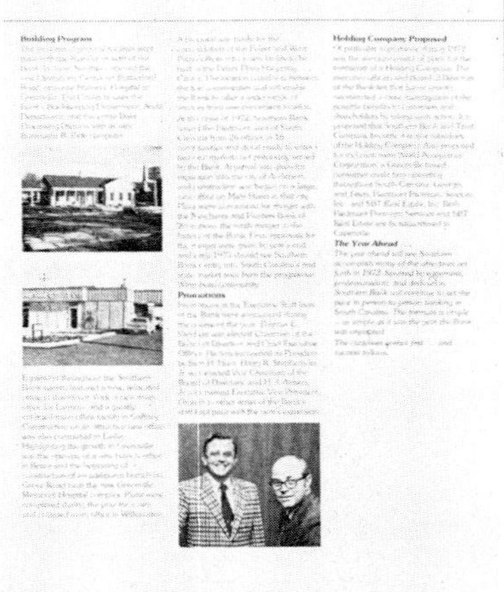

446

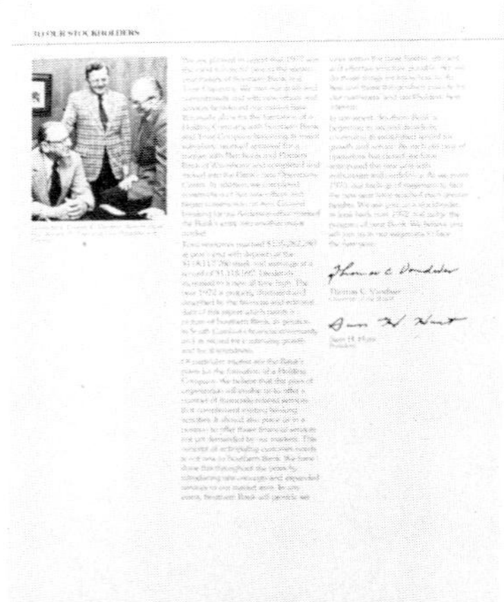

447

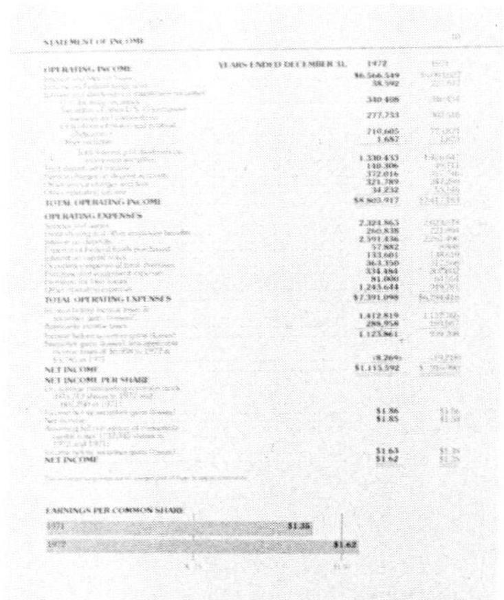

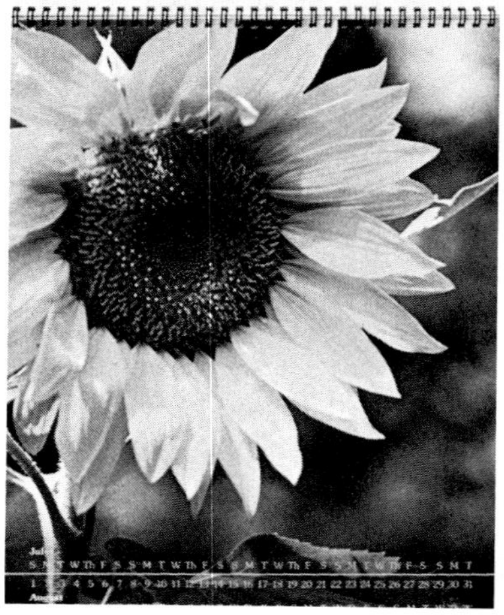

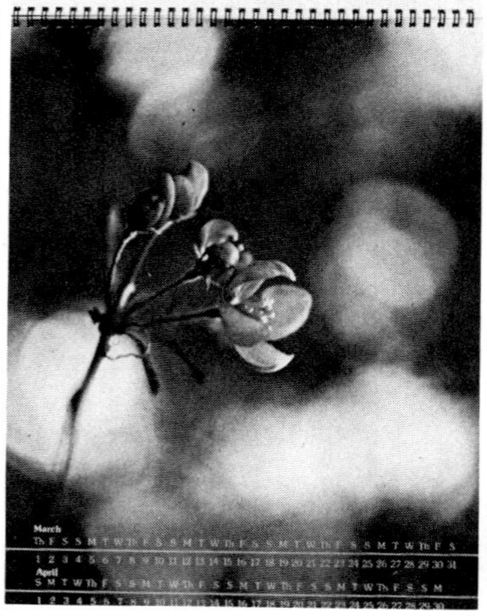

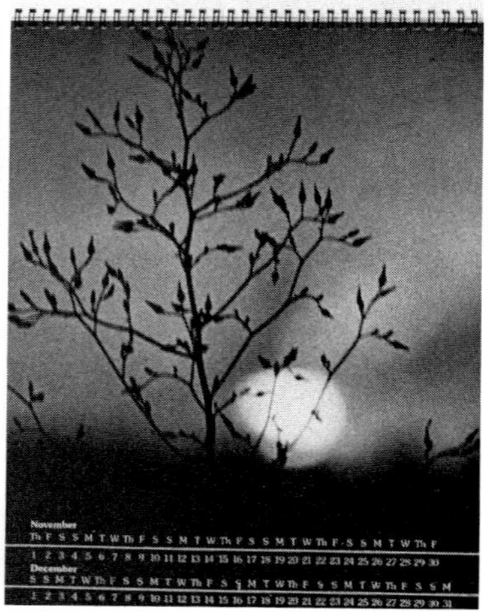

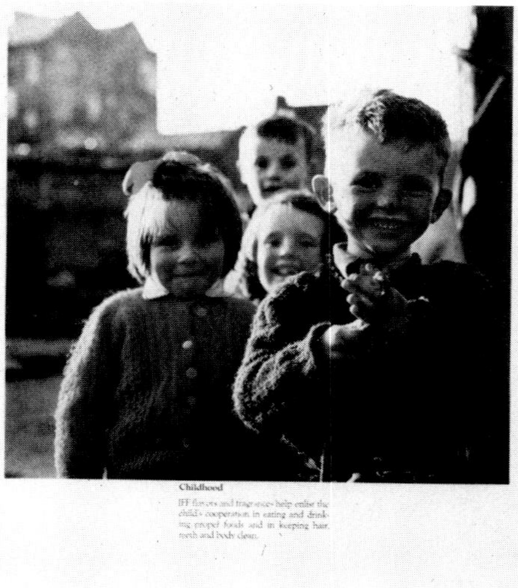
Childhood

449

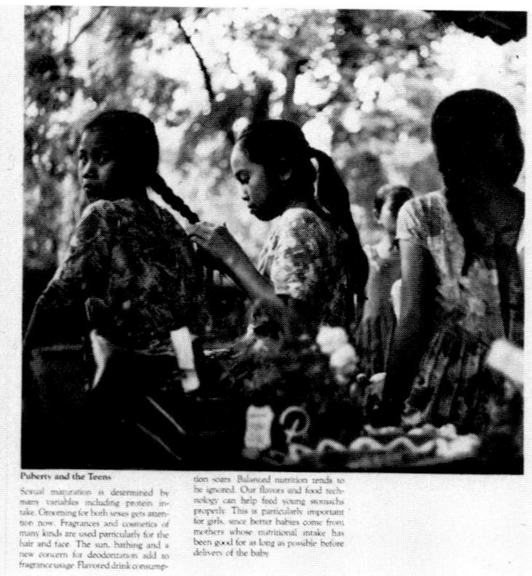
Puberty and the Teens

450

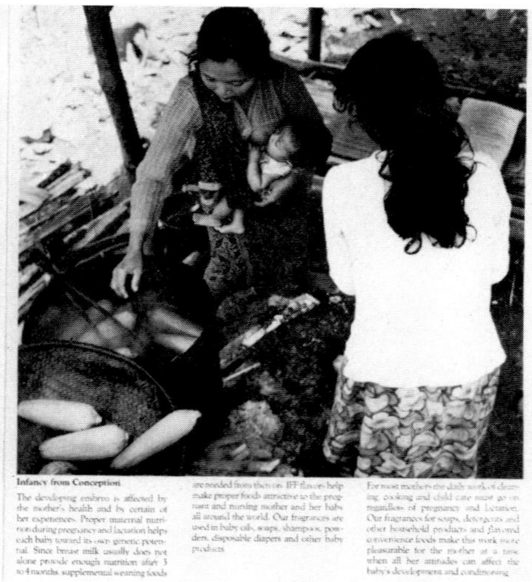
Infancy from Conception

451

449-451
Brian O'Neill Entrant
Tom McCarthy, Alan Vogel, Nick Samardge Photographers
Davis-Delaney-Arrow Agency
International Flavors & Frangrances Inc. Client

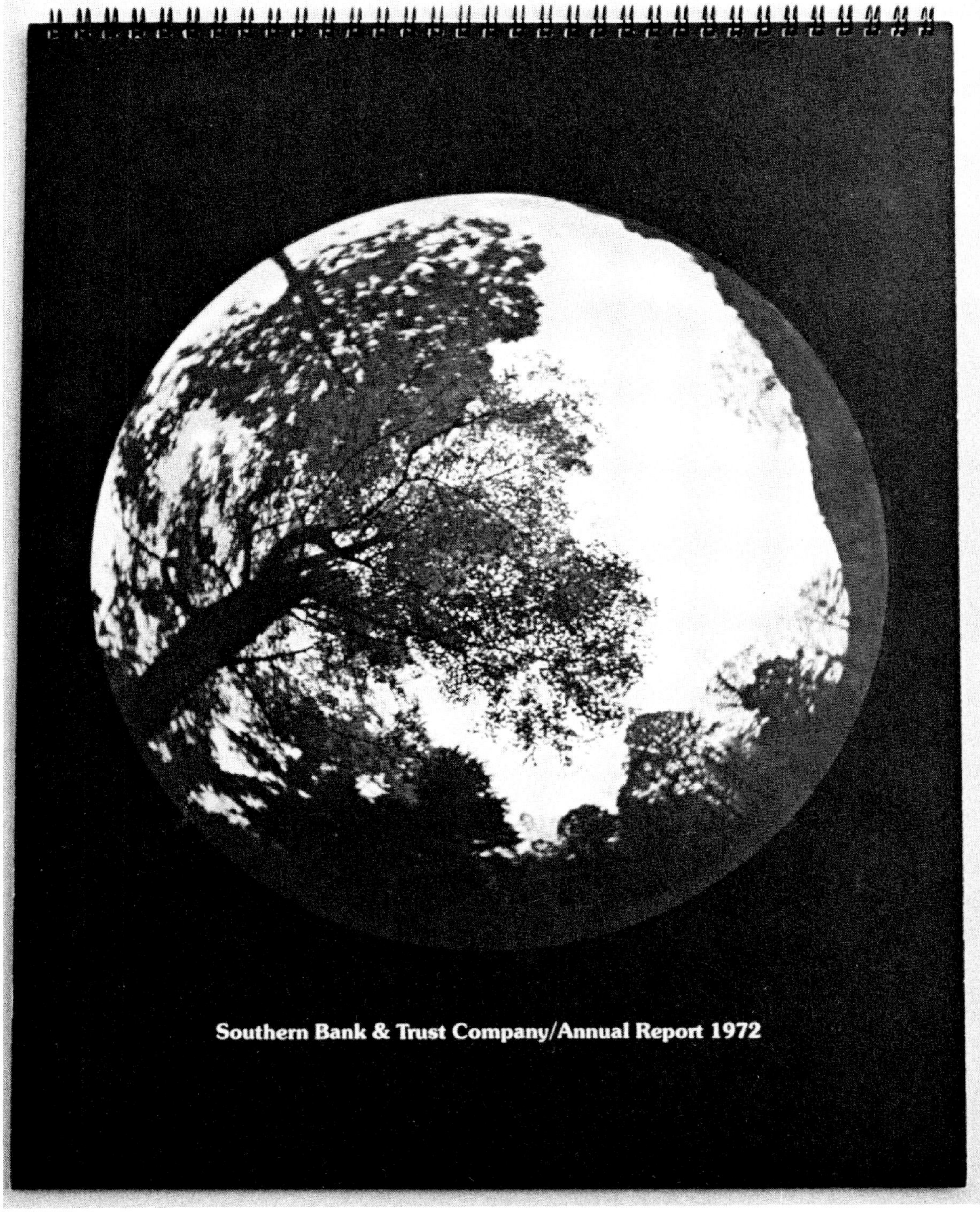
Southern Bank & Trust Company/Annual Report 1972

448

445-448
S.T. Schuett Entrant
Russell/Nicholson Photographers
Leslie Advertising Agency Agency
Southern Bank & Trust Client

452

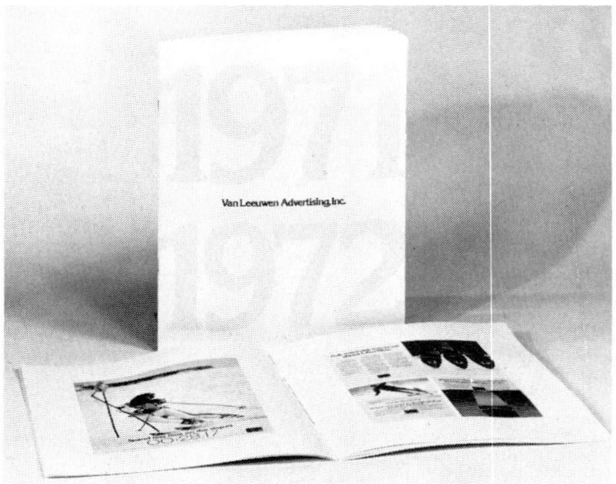
1971
Van Leeuwen Advertising, Inc.
1972

453

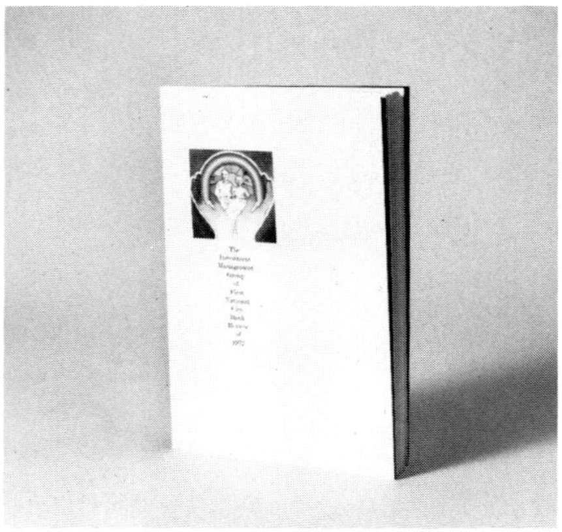

454

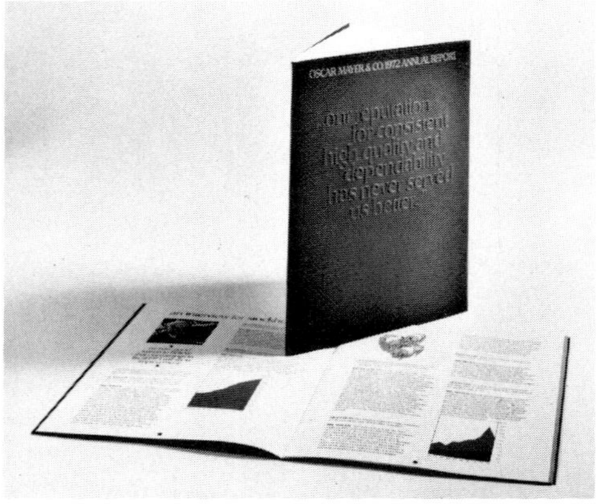

455

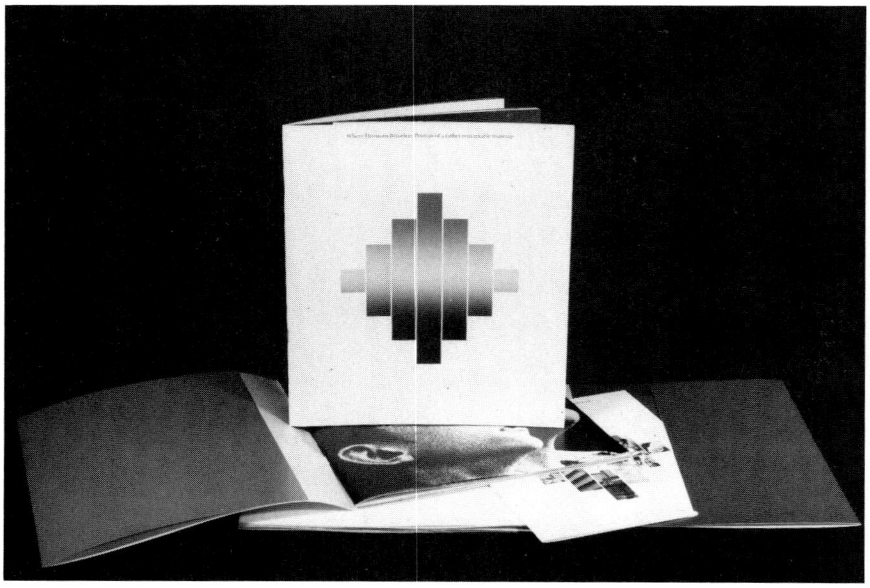

456

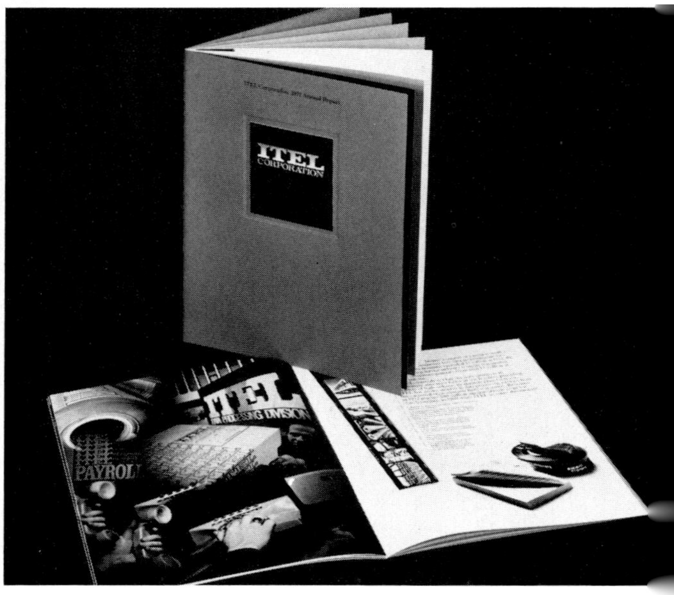
ITEL
CORPORATION
PAYROLL

452
Van Leeuwen Advertising Entrant
Ed Israel Art Director

453
Odette Associates Inc. Entrant
Jack Odette Art Director
Bob Pepper Illustrator
Investment Management Group of First National City Bank Of N. Y. Client

454
Marshall Smith & Associates Entrant
Nicholas Warrillow Art Director
Paul Tofte Artist
Wetzel Brothers, Inc. Studio
Oscar Mayer & Co. Client

455
Robert Cipriani Entrant
George Dow, Stavros Cosmopolous, John Glynn Photographers
Guan Associates Studio
Museum of Science Client

456
Thom LaPerle Entrant
Herb Finger, Thom LaPerle Art Directors
Larry Keenan, Jr. Photographer
Graphic Communicatior Center Studio
Itel Corp. Client

457

458 459

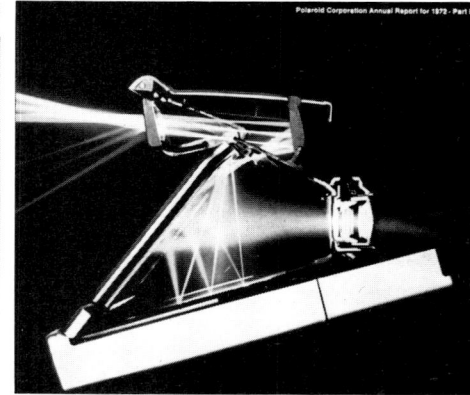

460   462   461

457	458	459	460	461	462
rrie White & Assoc. Entrant Lienhart Designer hard Frybarger Director chie Lieberman Others Photographers ere & Company ent	Michael McCarty Entrant John Kelly Photographer Communigraphics Studio Pima College Client	Fred Barrett Entrant Bryan Donaldson Photographer Promotion Graphics Studio Deltona Corp. Client	NYC Off-Track Betting Corp. Entrant Bill O'Day Art Director	Nicholas Zarkades Doug French, Steve Long Photographers The Gillette Company Client	Polaroid Corporation Entrant William Field Art Director Stan Malcolm Adv. Art. Studio

463

William M. Witter
Chairman
of the Board
and Chief
Executive Officer

TO OUR FELLOW SHAREHOLDERS:

It is indeed a pleasure to welcome our new shareholders in this our first Annual Report since we became a publicly held company. The fiscal year just ended produced record earnings and revenues. This marks our 48th consecutive year of profitability since the firm began in 1924. Without the capital contributed by our shareholders, the continued support of our clients, and the high performance of our employees, this record would not have been possible.

Our initial public offering of 1,250,000 shares of stock was made in early February. One month later our stock was listed on the New York and Pacific Coast stock exchanges. Our capital account is now $84 million, one of the largest in the industry. This offering was significant for the $28 million it raised and for facilitating the transition to a permanent capital structure.

As we plan for the future this new capital provides us additional flexibility. We are continuing our efforts to improve our profit margin and increase our market share, pursuing economies in operation wherever they are compatible with our commitment to excellence in serving our clients.

Planning in our industry is a challenge accentuated by volatility in revenues. In addition, we see increased competition from both within and outside our industry as the battle for the consumers' investment dollar intensifies. Coming regulatory developments may well create a substantially different marketplace.

It is our intention to approach these and other challenges with the same adaptability and dedication that has enabled our firm to be profitable throughout our history, which includes the Great Depression, World War II, and the period of turmoil in our industry in recent years.

We are impressed with the growth potential we see ahead of us. Increased capital requirements to sustain industrial growth, and changing demographic trends indicating an increased proportion of our population moving into age categories favoring our business, promise significant opportunities for revenue and profit building in the years ahead.

William M. Witter

Chairman of the Board and Chief Executive Officer

5

464

465

463
Logan Carey & Rehag Entrant
Ronald Rampley Art Director
Don Shapero Photographer
Dean Witter & Co., Inc. Client

464-465
Robert Miles Runyan & Assoc. Entrant
Robert Miles Runyan Art Director
Fred C. Kidder Designer
Jim Walden Photographer
Birgitta Forsman Artist
National General Corporation Client

466
Logan Carey & Rehag Entrant
Ronald Rampley Art Director
Dean Witter & Co., Inc. Client

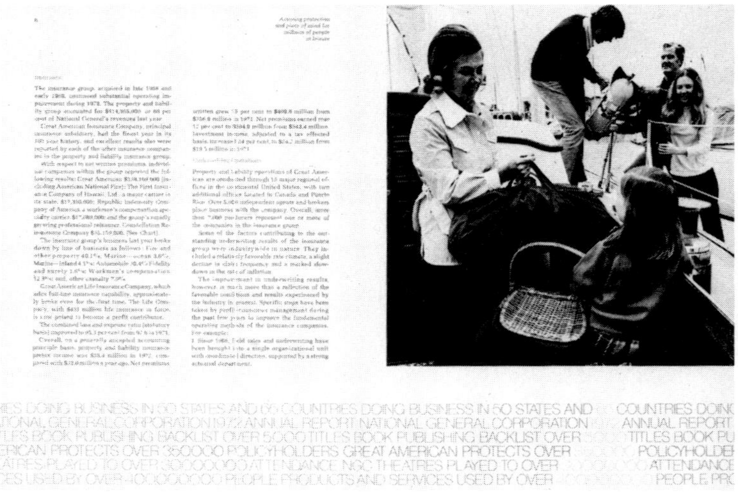

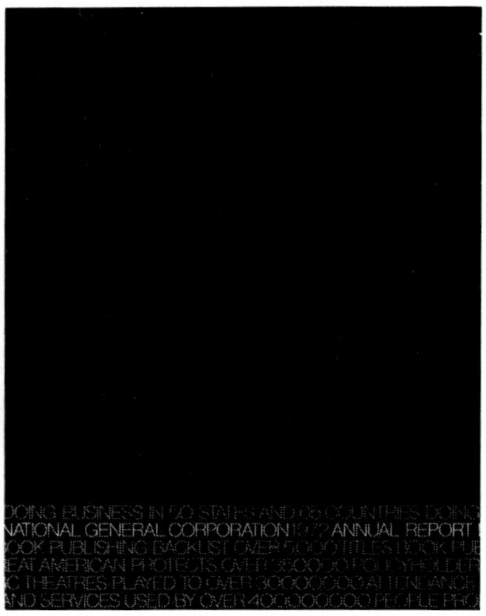

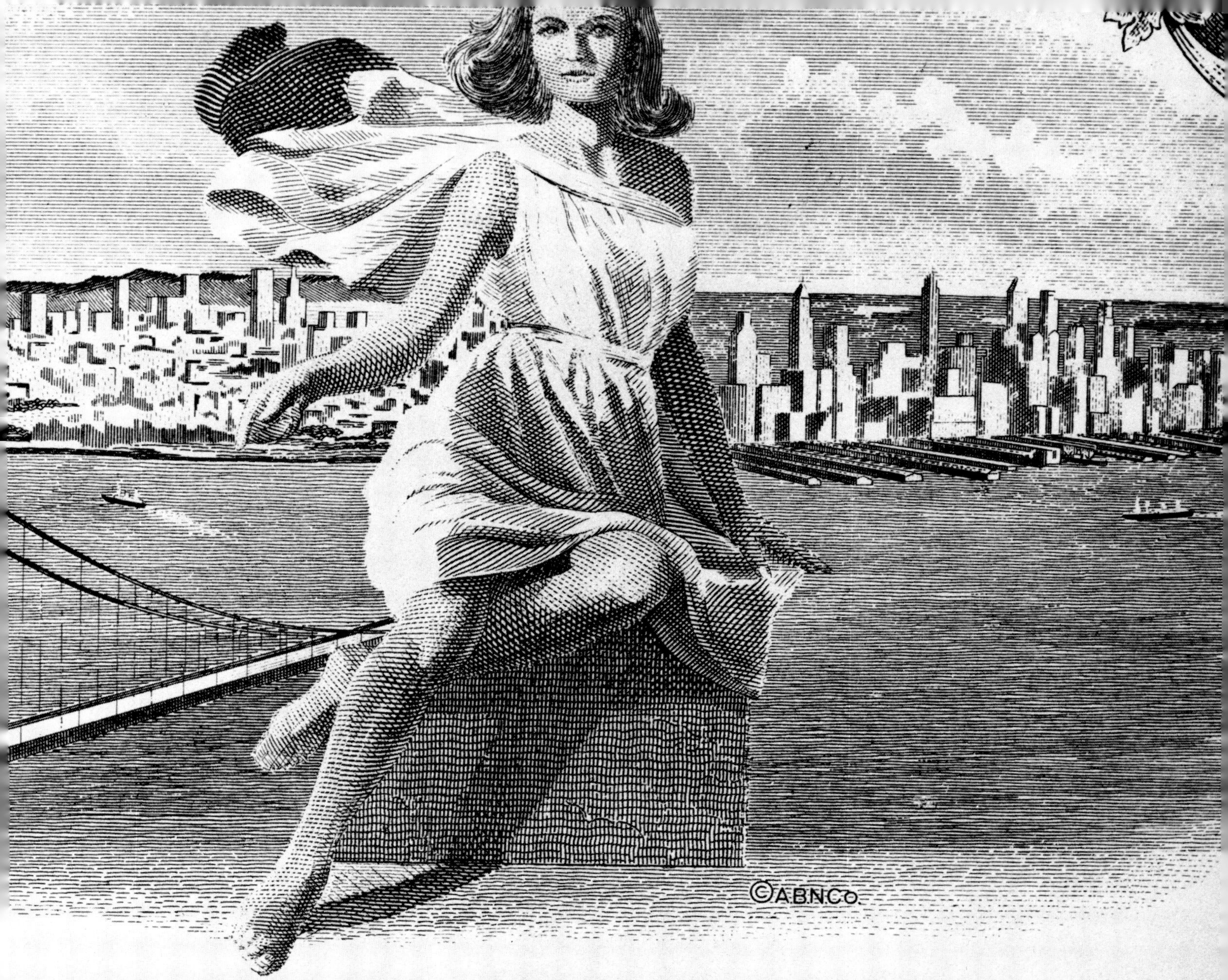
©ABNCo.

AN WITTER & C

INCORPORATED

TIFICATE IS TRANSFERABLE IN SAN FRANCISCO OR IN THE CITY OF NEW YORK

The Dean Witter 1972 Annual Report

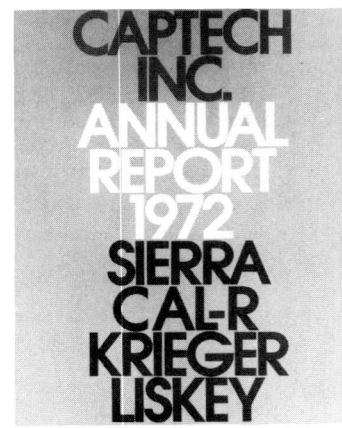

CAPTECH
INC.
ANNUAL
REPORT
1972
SIERRA
CAL-R
KRIEGER
LISKEY

467

SIERRA

468

COLLINS FOODS INTERNATIONAL, INC.
1972 ANNUAL REPORT

469

KENTUCKY FRIED CHICKEN RETAIL STORES*
$36.00 1972
$30.26 1971
$26.85 1970
$19.61 1969
$13.28 1968
KENTUCKY FRIED CHICKEN DIVISION

470

Foster Grant Co.,Inc. Annual Report 1972
"Our 1972 fiscal year was the most dynamic, most profitable, most innovative year in the history of Foster Grant– a real milestone."

471

Monomer
Output Triples

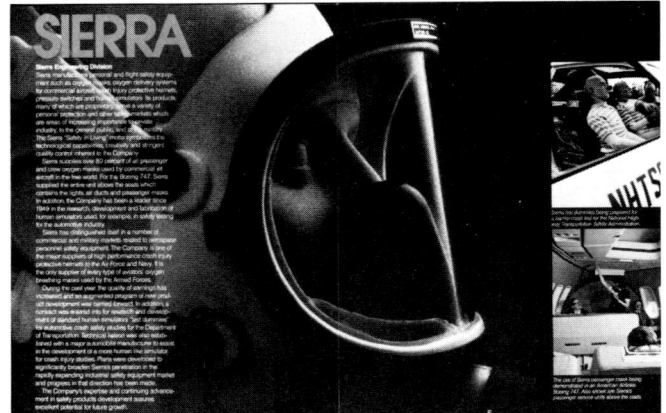

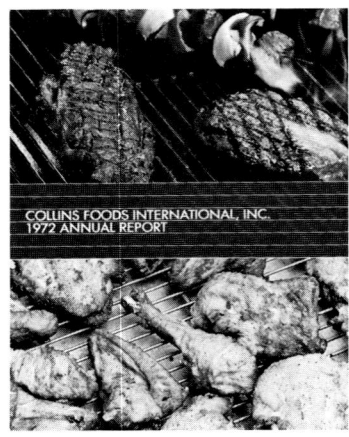

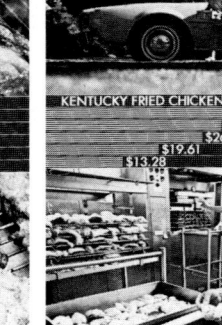

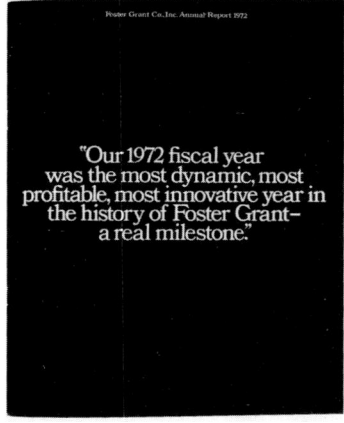

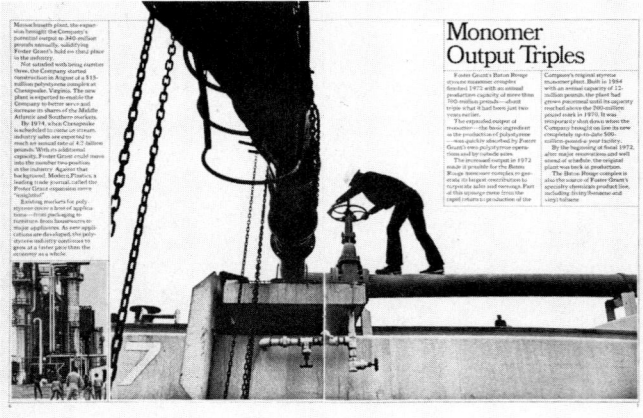

472

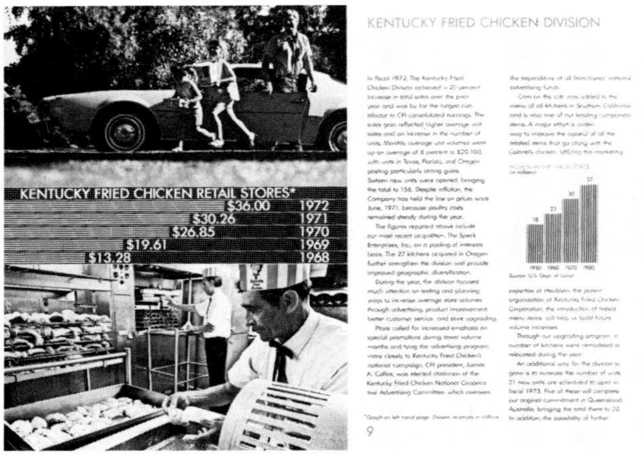

467-468
Finlay Kaiser Inc. Entrant
Michael Kaiser Art Director
CapTech Inc. Client

469-470
Finlay Kaiser Inc. Entrant
Michael Kaiser Art Director
George Meinzinger Photographer
Collins Foods International, Inc. Client

471-472
Hinrichs Design Assoc. Entrant
Kit Hinrichs Art Director
Foster Grant AR Client

473

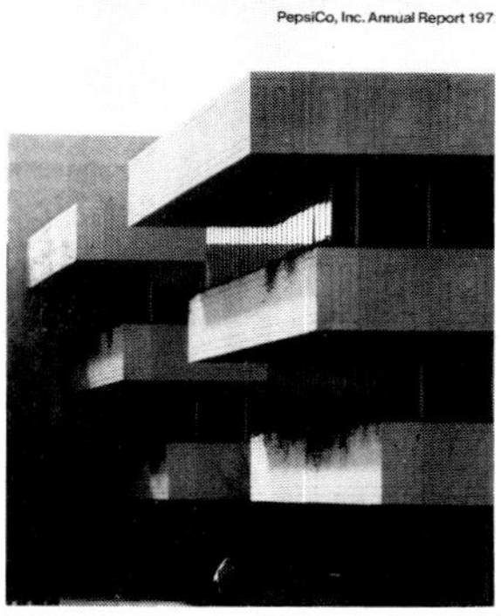
PepsiCo, Inc. Annual Report 197

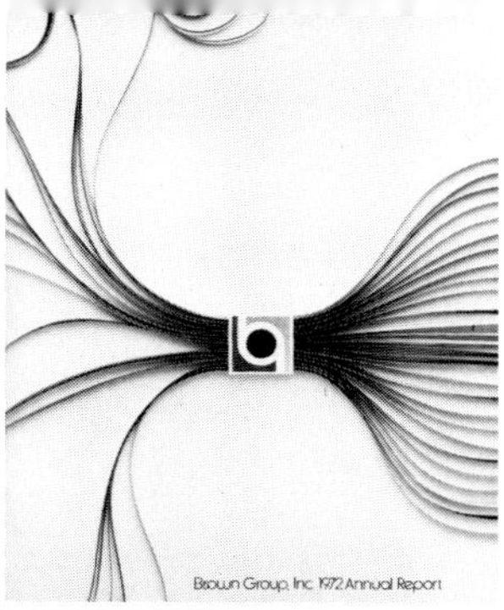
Brown Group, Inc. 1972 Annual Report

474

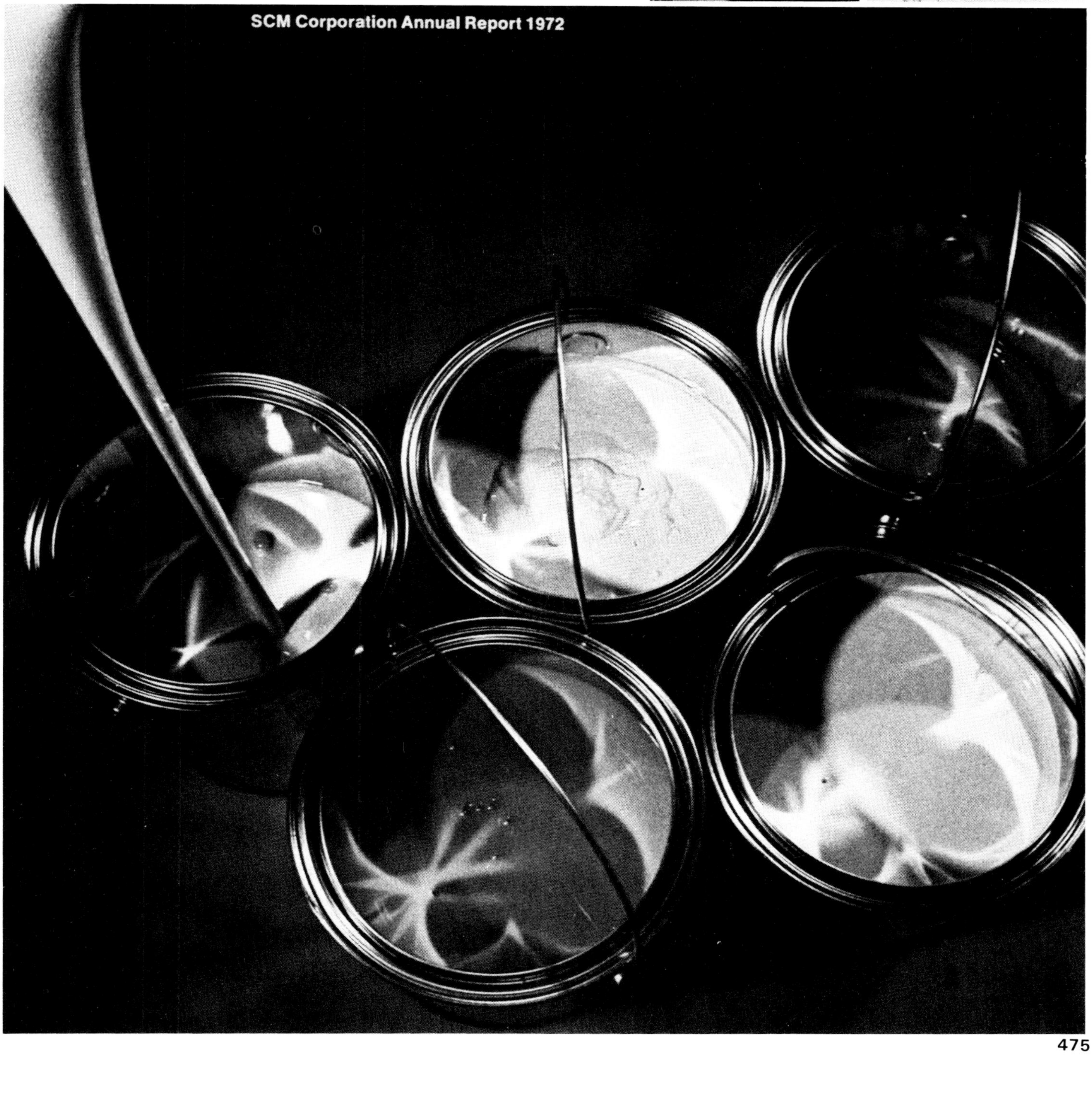
SCM Corporation Annual Report 1972

475

473
Eisenman and Enock Inc. Entrant
Burt Glinn Photographer
PepsiCo, Inc. Client

474
Goldsholl Associates Entrant
Morton Goldsholl Art Director
Tom Freese Photographer
Wright-Manning Co. Client

475
Peter Harrison Associates, Inc. Entrant
Wolf von dem Bussche Photographer
SCM Corporation Client

476

Research
SYNTEX: THE SUM OF ITS PEOPLE
Annual Report 1972

477

To Our Shareholders:

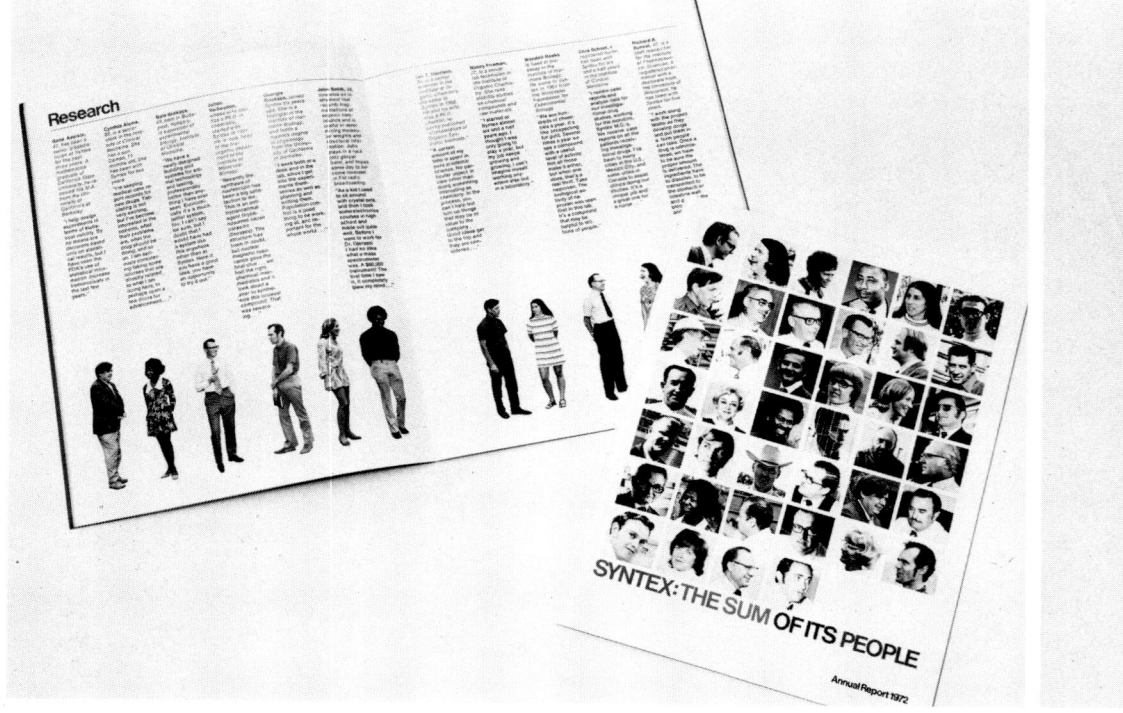

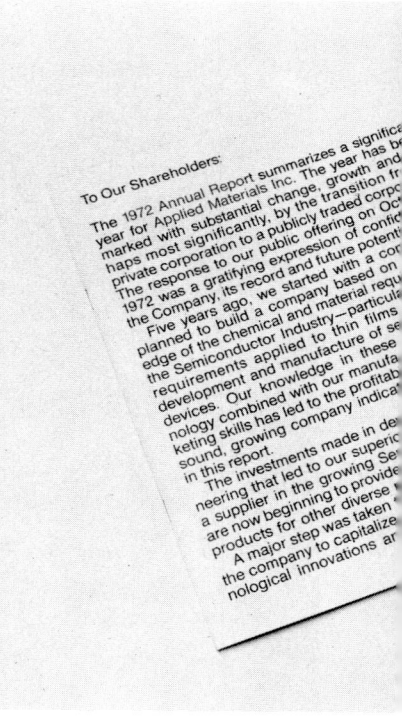

476
Art Kirsch Entrant
Art Kirsch, Paul Sinn Art Directors
Sam Smidt Assoc. Agency
Syntex Corporation Client

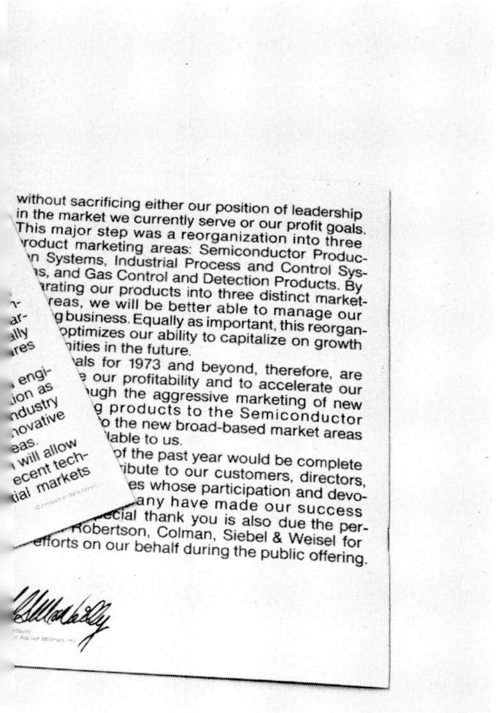

without sacrificing either our position of leadership
in the market we currently serve or our profit goals.
This major step was a reorganization into three
roduct marketing areas: Semiconductor Produc-
n Systems, Industrial Process and Control Sys-
s, and Gas Control and Detection Products. By
rating our products into three distinct market-
reas, we will be better able to manage our
g business. Equally as important, this reorgan-
optimizes our ability to capitalize on growth
nities in the future.
als for 1973 and beyond, therefore, are
e our profitability and to accelerate our
ugh the aggressive marketing of new
g products to the Semiconductor
o the new broad-based market areas
lable to us.
of the past year would be complete
ibute to our customers, directors,
es whose participation and devo-
any have made our success
pecial thank you is also due the per-
Robertson, Colman, Siebel & Weisel for
efforts on our behalf during the public offering.

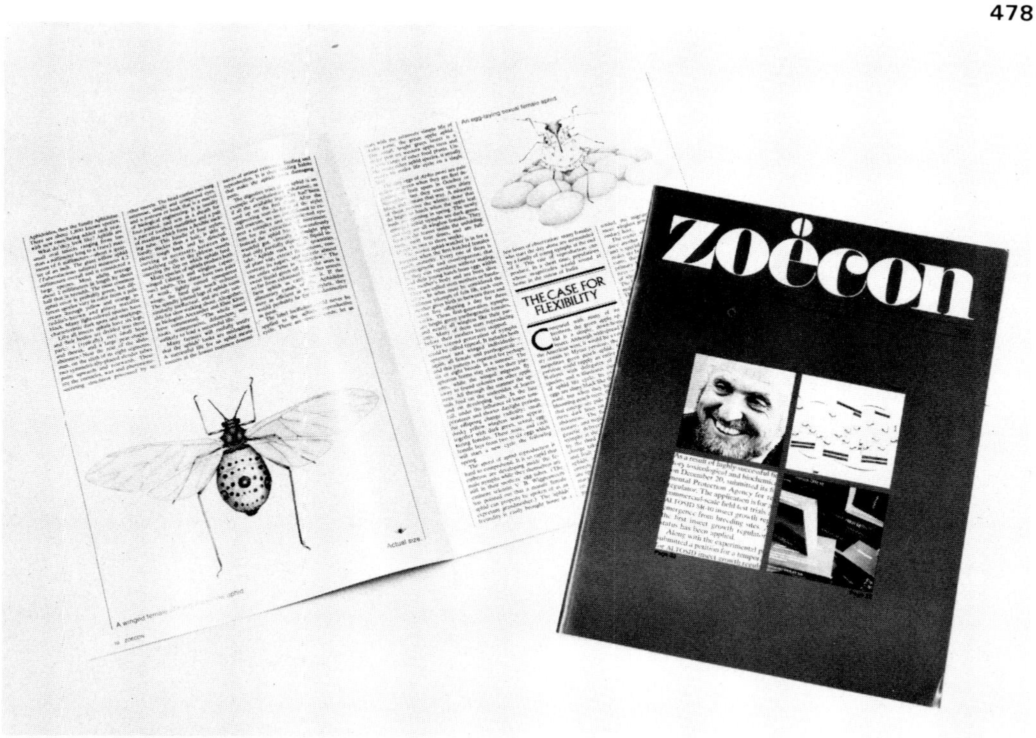

THE CASE FOR FLEXIBILITY
zoëcon

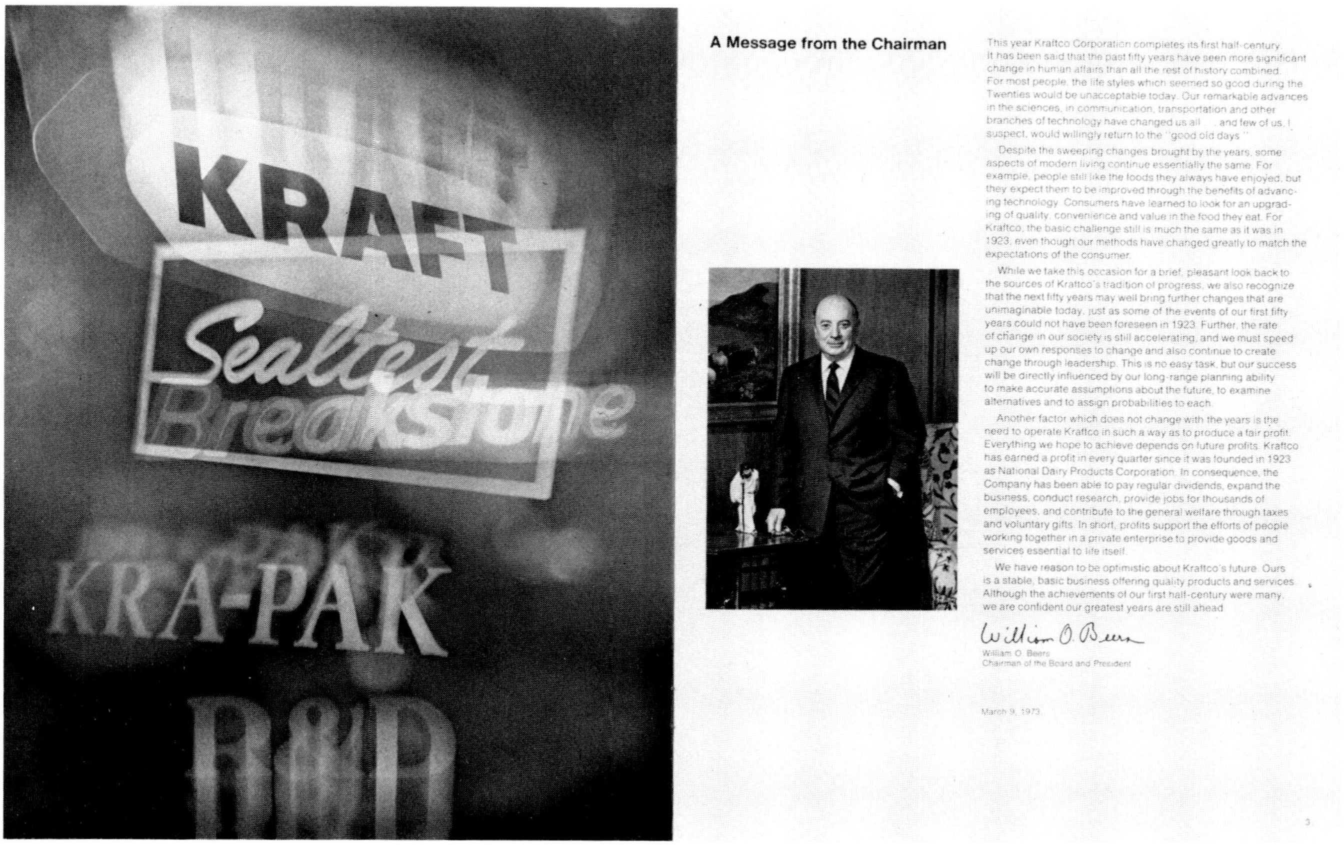

KRAFT
Sealtest
Breakstone
KRA-PAK
R&D
A Message from the Chairman
This year Kraftco Corporation completes its first half-century. It has been said that the past fifty years have seen more significant change in human affairs than all the rest of history combined. For most people, the life styles which seemed so good during the Twenties would be unacceptable today. Our remarkable advances in the sciences, in communication, transportation and other branches of technology have changed us all . . . and few of us, I suspect, would willingly return to the "good old days."
Despite the sweeping changes brought by the years, some aspects of modern living continue essentially the same. For example, people still like the foods they always have enjoyed, but they expect them to be improved through the benefits of advancing technology. Consumers have learned to look for an upgrading of quality, convenience and value in the food they eat. For Kraftco, the basic challenge still is much the same as it was in 1923, even though our methods have changed greatly to match the expectations of the consumer.
While we take this occasion for a brief, pleasant look back to the sources of Kraftco's tradition of progress, we also recognize that the next fifty years may well bring further changes that are unimaginable today, just as some of the events of our first fifty years could not have been foreseen in 1923. Further, the rate of change in our society is still accelerating, and we must speed up our own responses to change and also continue to create change through leadership. This is no easy task, but our success will be directly influenced by our long-range planning ability to make accurate assumptions about the future, to examine alternatives and to assign probabilities to each.
Another factor which does not change with the years is the need to operate Kraftco in such a way as to produce a fair profit. Everything we hope to achieve depends on future profits. Kraftco has earned a profit in every quarter since it was founded in 1923 as National Dairy Products Corporation. In consequence, the Company has been able to pay regular dividends, expand the business, conduct research, provide jobs for thousands of employees, and contribute to the general welfare through taxes and voluntary gifts. In short, profits support the efforts of people working together in a private enterprise to provide goods and services essential to life itself.
We have reason to be optimistic about Kraftco's future. Ours is a stable, basic business offering quality products and services. Although the achievements of our first half-century were many, we are confident our greatest years are still ahead.
William O. Beers
Chairman of the Board and President
March 9, 1973

479

477
Sue Wilson Entrant
Lars Speyer, Ronald Turner Photographers
Sam Smidt Assoc. Agency
Applied Materials Inc. Client

478
Paul Sinn Entrant
Nancy Lawton Illustrator
Sam Smidt Assoc. Agency
Zoëcon Client

479
Ong & Associates, Inc. Entrant
James Ong Art Director
Pablo Rivera Photographer
Kraftco Corporation Client

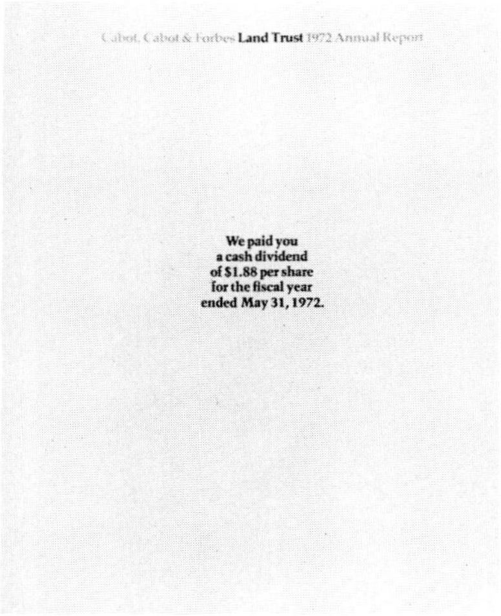
Cabot, Cabot & Forbes Land Trust 1972 Annual Report
We paid you
a cash dividend
of $1.88 per share
for the fiscal year
ended May 31, 1972.
480

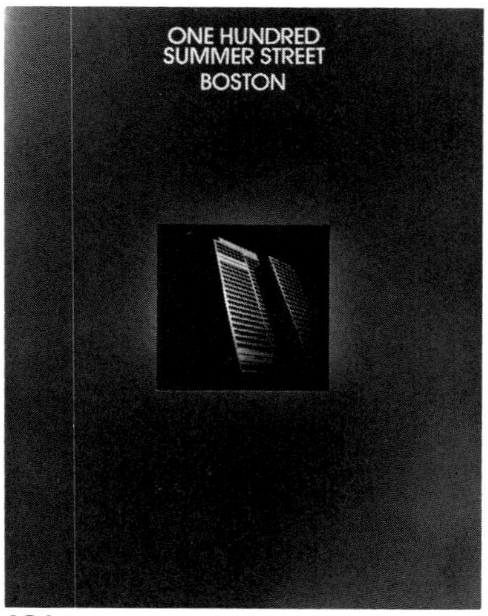
ONE HUNDRED
SUMMER STREET
BOSTON
481

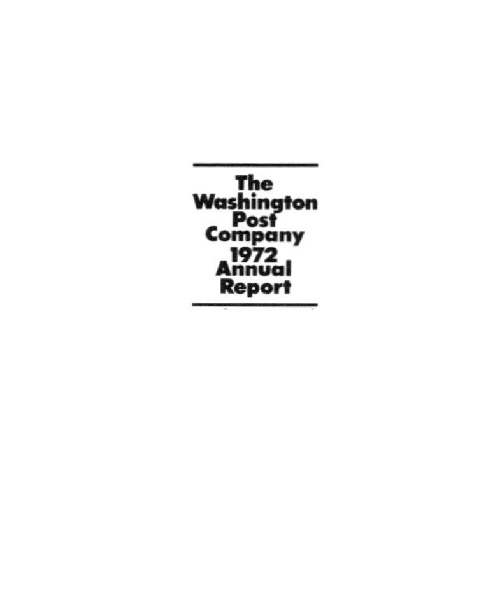
The
Washington
Post
Company
1972
Annual
Report
482

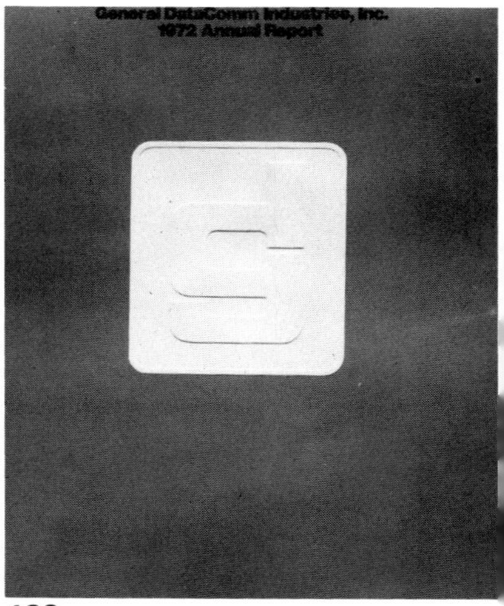
General DataComm Industries, Inc.
1972 Annual Report
483

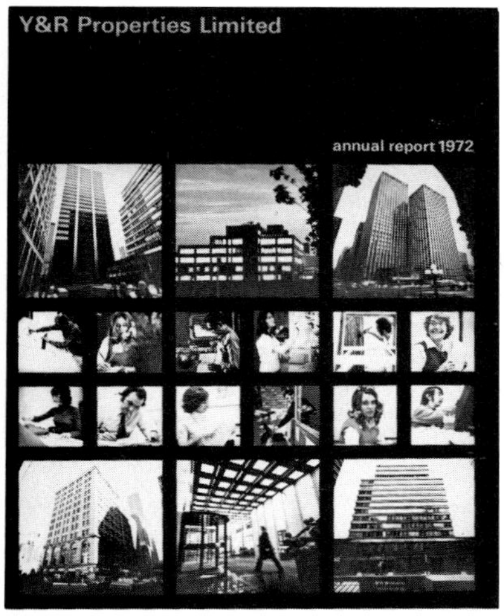
Y&R Properties Limited
annual report 1972
484

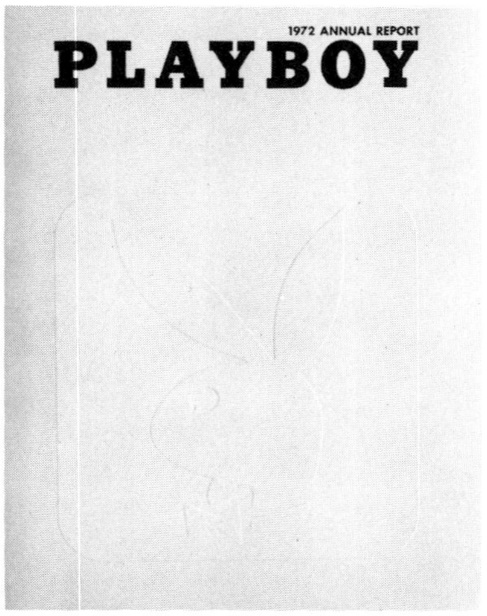
1972 ANNUAL REPORT
PLAYBOY
485

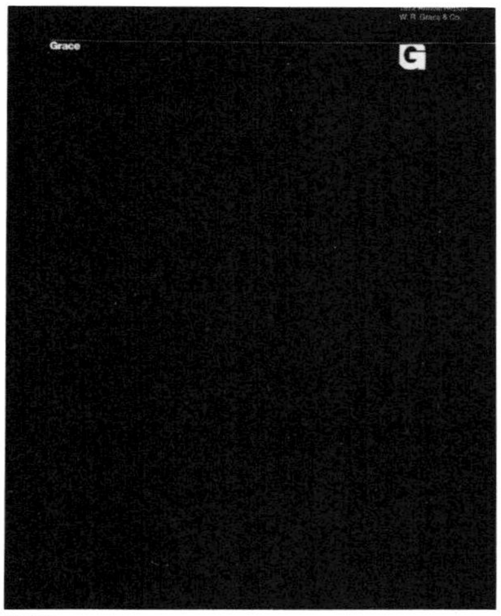
Grace
G
486

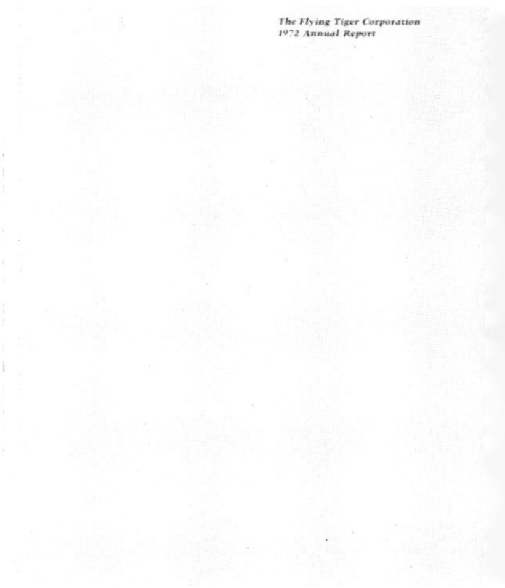
The Flying Tiger Corporation
1972 Annual Report
487

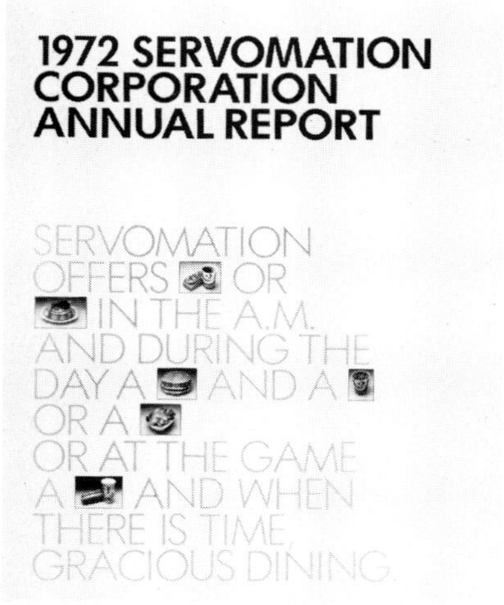
1972 SERVOMATION
CORPORATION
ANNUAL REPORT
SERVOMATION
OFFERS OR
IN THE A.M.
AND DURING THE
DAY A AND A
OR A
OR AT THE GAME
A AND WHEN
THERE IS TIME,
GRACIOUS DINING.
488

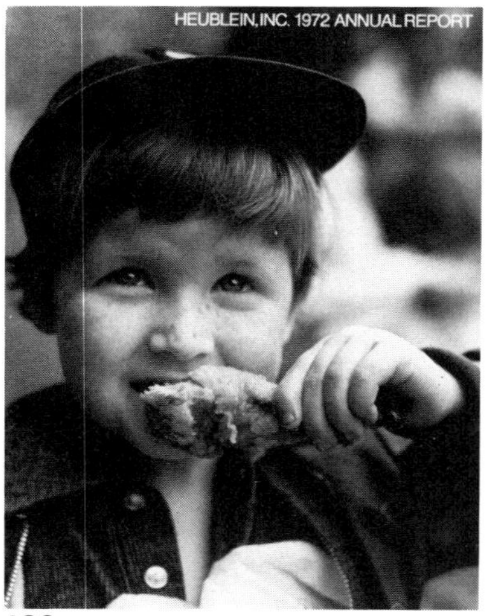
HEUBLEIN, INC. 1972 ANNUAL REPORT
489

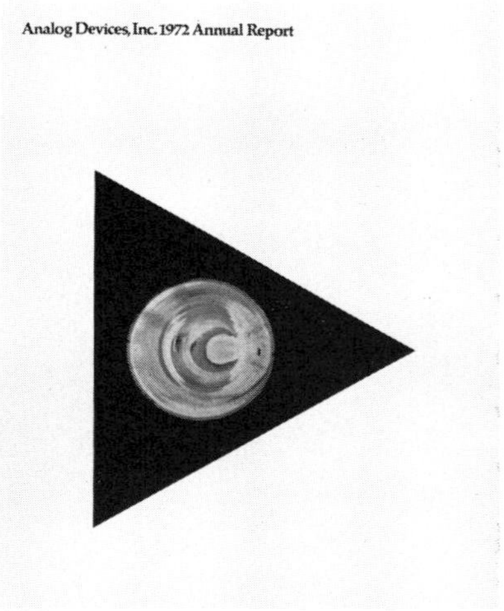
Analog Devices, Inc. 1972 Annual Report
490

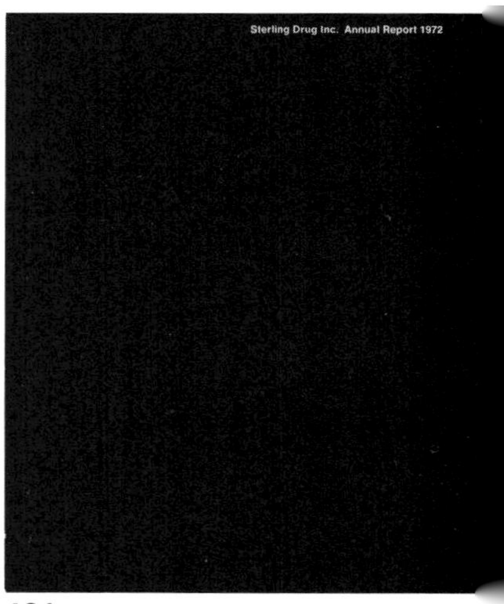
Sterling Drug Inc. Annual Report 1972
491

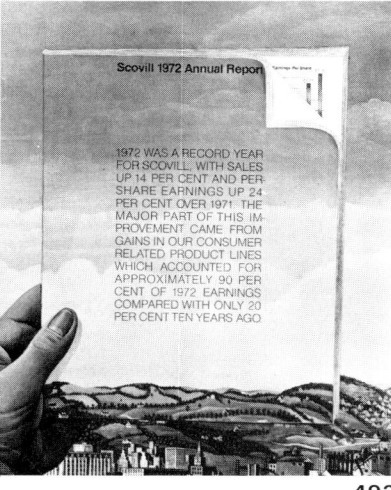

Scovill 1972 Annual Report
1972 WAS A RECORD YEAR FOR SCOVILL, WITH SALES UP 14 PER CENT AND PER SHARE EARNINGS UP 24 PER CENT OVER 1971. THE MAJOR PART OF THIS IMPROVEMENT CAME FROM GAINS IN OUR CONSUMER RELATED PRODUCT LINES WHICH ACCOUNTED FOR APPROXIMATELY 90 PER CENT OF 1972 EARNINGS COMPARED WITH ONLY 20 PER CENT TEN YEARS AGO.

492

FUQUA

493

1972 ANNUAL REPORT LOWE'S COMPANIES, INC.
LOWE'S

494

COMBUSTION ENGINEERING, INC.
19 72 ANNUAL REPORT TO INVESTORS

495

AMERICAN CAN COMPANY ANNUAL REPORT 1972

496

KraftcoCorporation
1972
50th Anniversary
1923

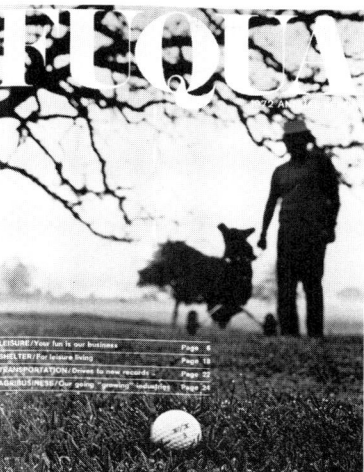

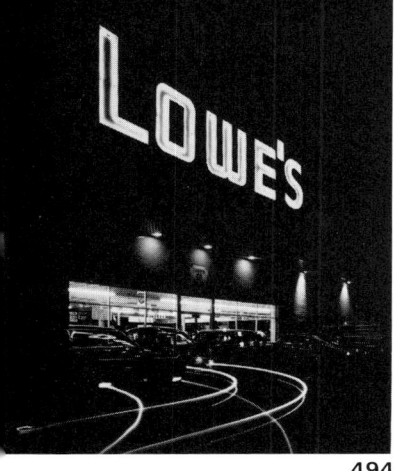

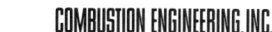

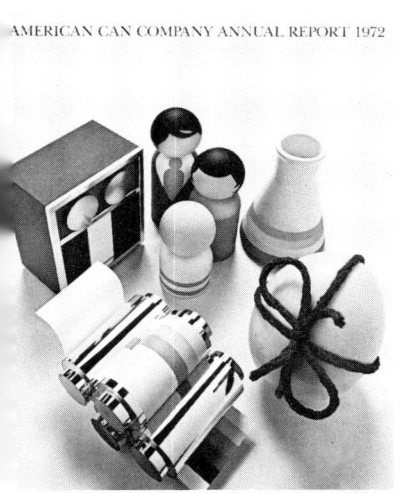

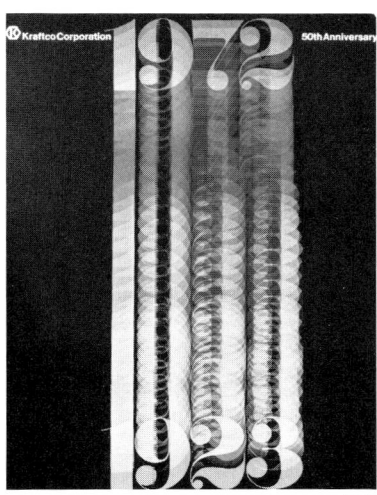

497

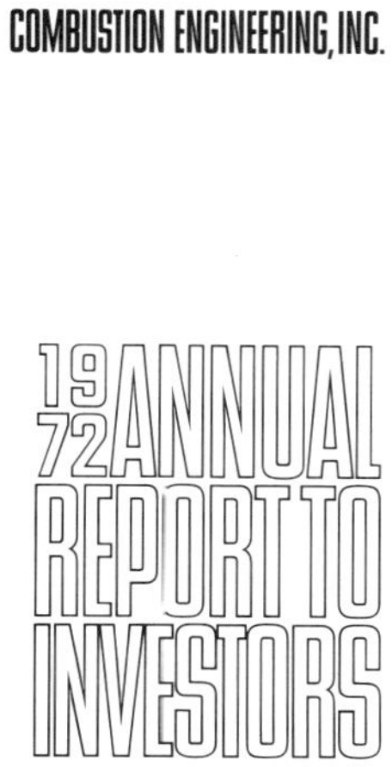

480-481
Richard Stack
Entrant
Robert Russell, Patricia Zwisler
Photographers
Giardini/ Russell Inc.
Agency
Cabot, Cabot & Forbes Land Trust Client

482
William Kemsley
Entrant
Peter J. Blank
Art Director
Richard Alcorn
Photographer
WKA Corporate Graphics, Inc.
Agency
Washington Post Company
Client

483
Ted Colangelo
Entrant
Sandor Acs
Photographer
General DataComm Client

484
A.L. Pollock-Southam Murray
Entrant
Paul Crouch
Art Director
Y & R Properties Limited Client

485
Playboy Enterprises, Inc. Entrant
Helga Aktipis, John Dixon
Art Directors

486
Corporate Annual Reports Entrant
Leslie Segal
Art Director
Jay Maisel
Photographer
W.R. Grace & Co. Client

487
Robert Miles Runyan & Associates
Entrant
Robert Miles Runyan
Art Director
Rusty Kay
Designer
Marvin Silver
Photographer
Art Mochizuki
Artist
The Flying Tiger Corporation
Client

488
William Kemsley
Entrant
Peter J. Blank, Don Menell
Art Directors
Charles Gold
Photographer
WKA Corporate Graphics, Inc.
Agency
Servomation Corporation
Client

489
Matt Klim & Assoc. Inc.
Entrant
Matt Klim
Art Director
Carroll Seghers II
Photographer
Heublein Inc.
Client

490
Giardini/ Russell, Inc.
Entrant
Robert H. Russell
Art Director
Patricia Zwisler
Photographer
Analog Devices, Inc. Client

491
Corporate Annual Reports
Entrant
Len Fury
Art Director
Marvin Koner
Illustrator
Sterling Drug Inc. Client

492
Corporate Annual Reports
Entrant
Leslie Segal
Art Director
Richard Hess
Illustrator
Scovill Manfacturing Co.
Client

493
Stein Printing Co.
Entrant
Bob Bragg
Art Director
Chuck Rogers
Photographer
Fuqua Industries, Inc.
Client

494
Stein Printing Co.
Entrant
Bob Bragg
Art Director
Bob Special and Jerry Drown
Photographers
Lowe's Industries, Inc.
Client

495
Corporate Annual Reports
Entrant
Robert Nemser
Art Director
George Haling
Photographer
Combustion Engineering, Inc.
Client

496
Norman Gorbaty Design Inc.
Entrant
Norman Gorbaty
Art Director
Brian Ganton
(Cover and Products),
Phil Marco
(Theme Shots),
Claude Chassagne
(Portraits and Supermarkets)
Photographers
American Can Company
Client

497
Ong & Associates, Inc.
Entrant
James Ong
Art Director
Kraftco Corporation
Client

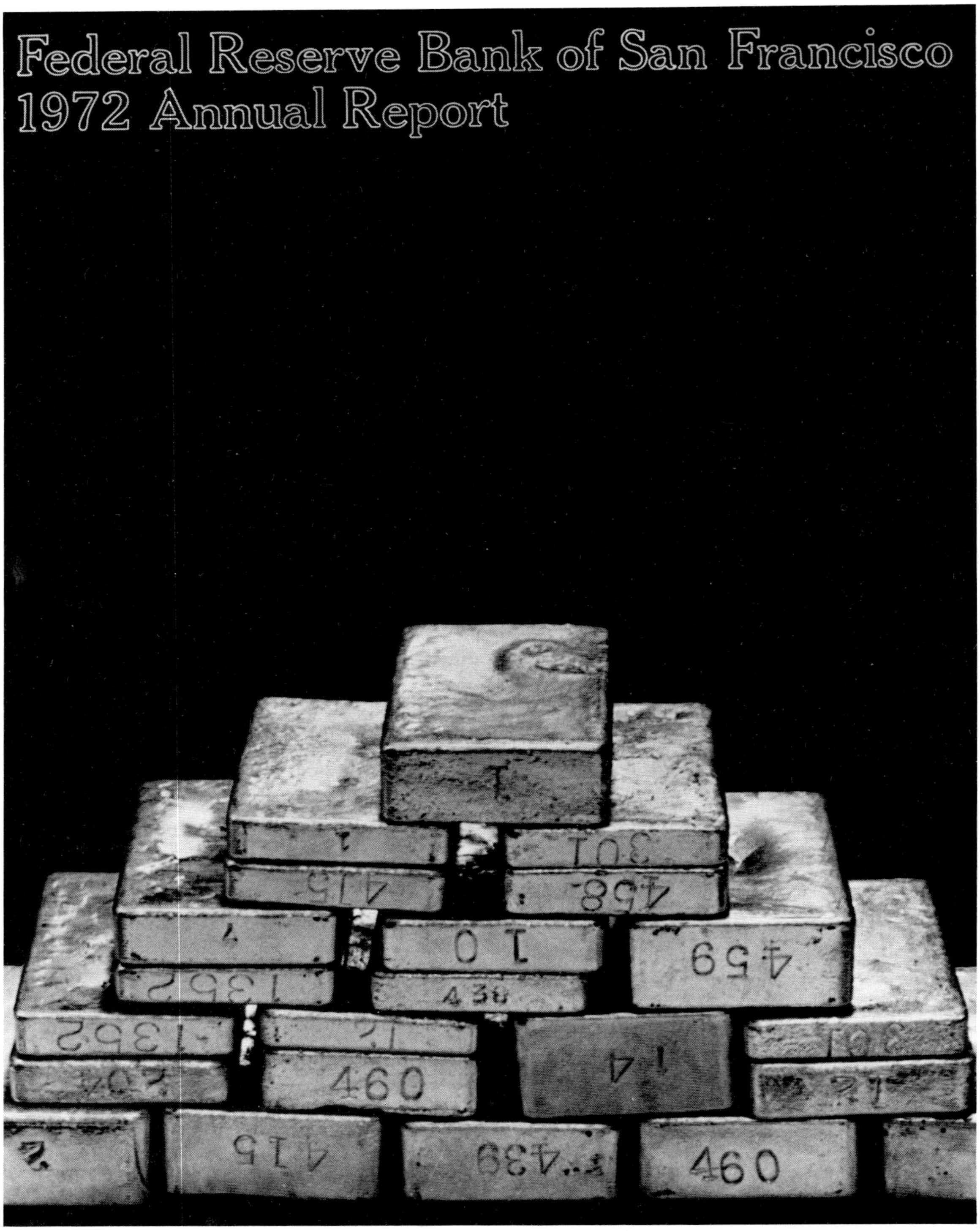
Federal Reserve Bank of San Francisco
1972 Annual Report

498
Karen B. Rusk Entrant
Janis Wilson Chartist
Thomas Moulin Photographer
Federal Reserve Bank of San Francisco Client

Schlumberger 1972 Annual Report

In Brief:	1972
Revenues	$812.062.000
Net Income	$70.233.000
Net Income Per Share	$1.44
Dividends paid Per Share	$0.49

*Before extraordinary items

499
Lubalin, Smith, Carnase Entrant
Herb Lubalin Art Director
Schlumberger Ltd. Client

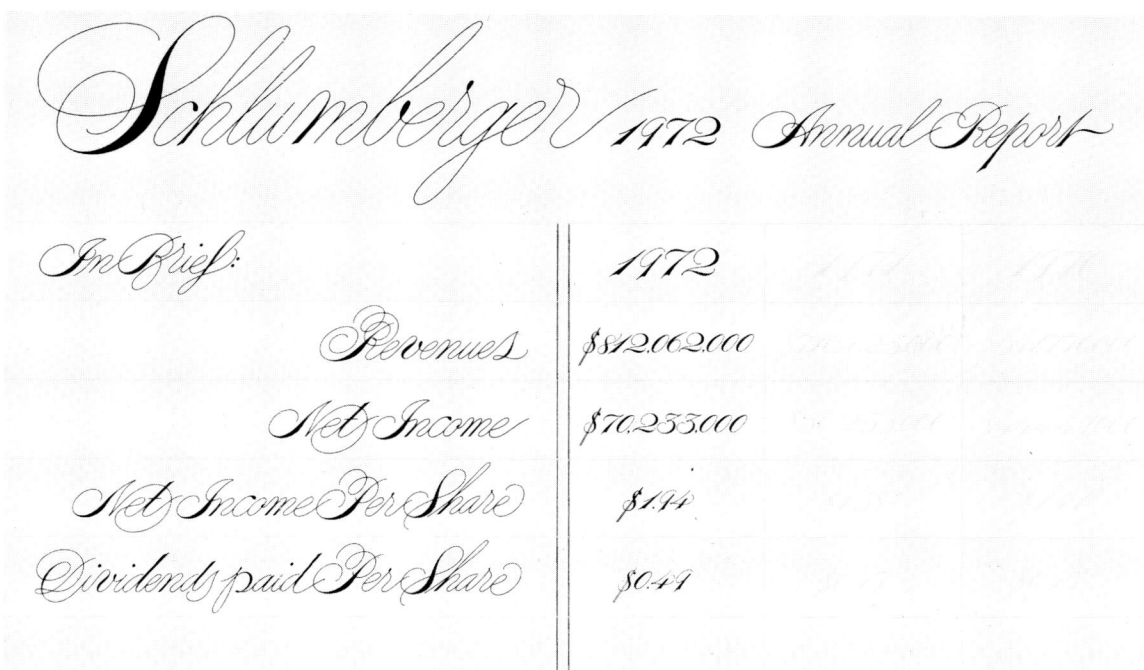

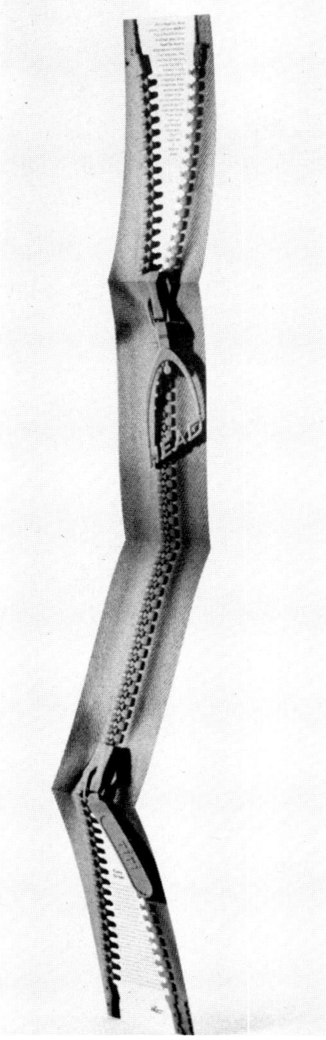

500

schools. To be sure, many law schools are already experimenting with clinical approaches and new curriculum. But only the Antioch School of Law has created a totally new educational institution for training legal professionals. Antioch will be:

-- the first and only law school in the U.S. built around a teaching law firm which will provide students with day-by-day opportunities to work with real clients under the supervision of experienced practitioners on the faculty. This teaching law firm is analagous to the teaching hospital of the medical field.

-- the first and only law school to train Certified Legal Technicians. These paraprofessionals will be able to handle many of the functions now performed by lawyers, thus freeing lawyers from many time-consuming tasks and helping to ease the critical legal manpower shortage. The services provided by these legal paraprofessionals are akin to those provided by nurses and paramedics in the medical field.

THE DISENCHANTED CONSUMERS

The need for Antioch's first-hand clinical approach sounds loud and clear from the disenchanted "consumers" of the law school's product. Private firms report that the graduate fresh from law school is largely useless, a loss to be written off. Judges continually voice concern at the amount of incompetence parading through the courts. Because of his lack of "on-the-job training," the typical law graduate:

-- doesn't know how to talk to or listen to clients.

-- doesn't know his way to or around a courtroom.

3

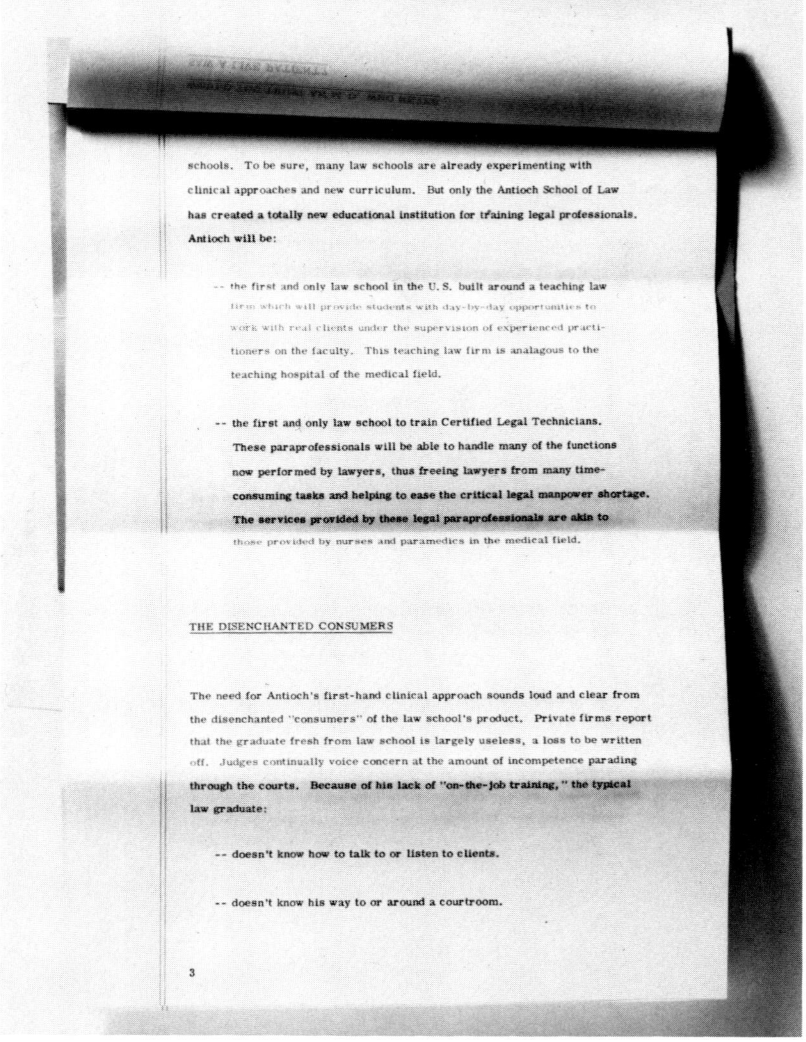

504

501

502

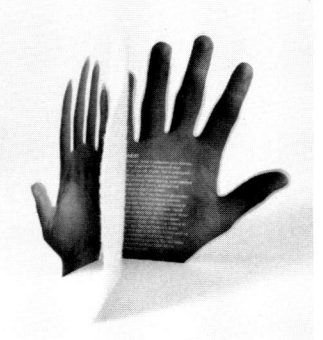

503

500-503
Odette Associates, Inc. Entrant
Rex Wilson, Valrie Lieberman Art Directors
Bernard Lawrence Photographer
Head Ski and Sportswear Client

504-505
Odette Associates, Inc. Entrant
Jack Odette, Valrie Lieberman Art Directors
Sidney Green Associates Agency
The Antioch School of Law Client

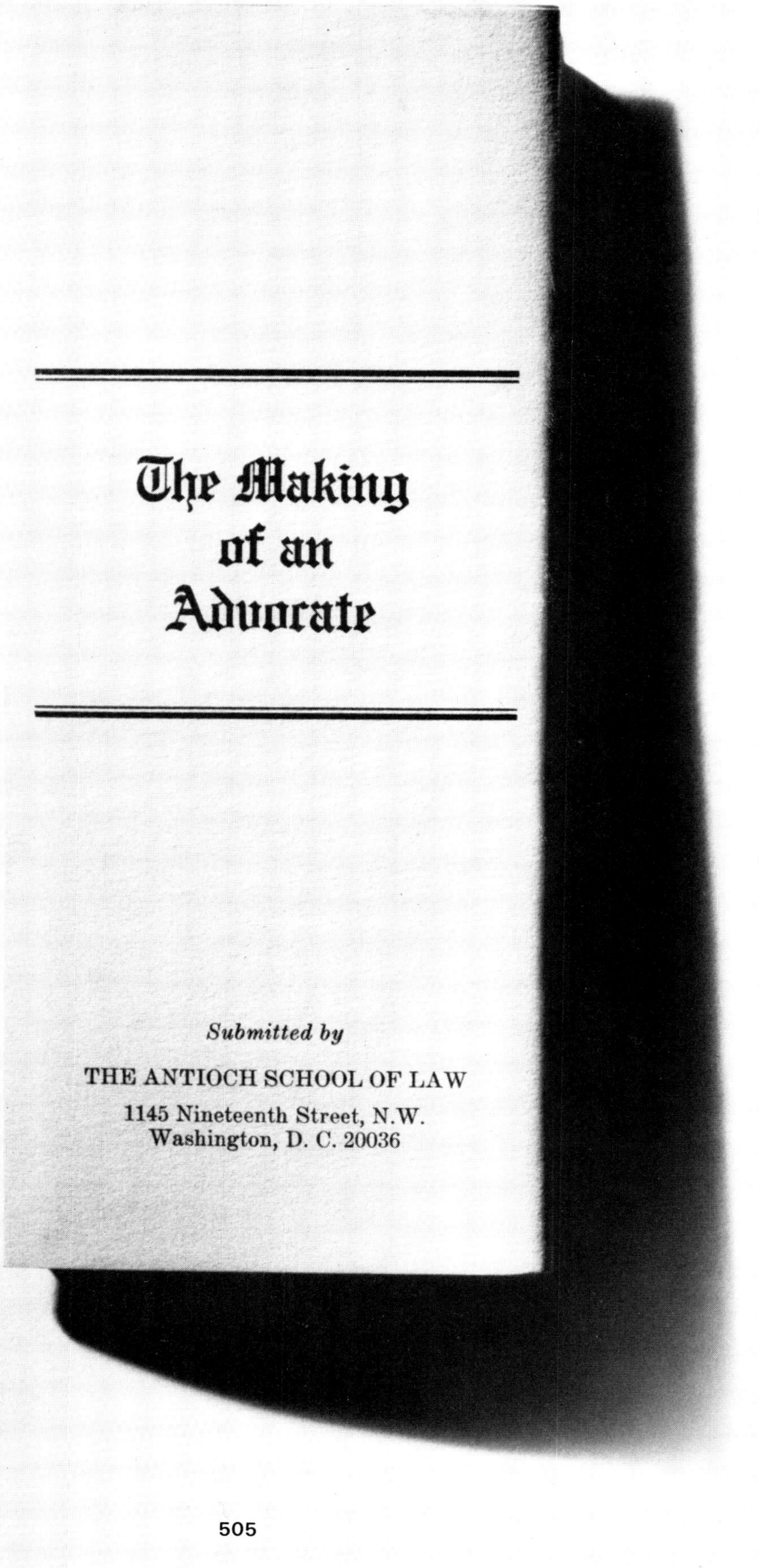
The Making of an Advocate
Submitted by
THE ANTIOCH SCHOOL OF LAW
1145 Nineteenth Street, N.W.
Washington, D. C. 20036

Alaska
Alaska
Alaska
Alaska

506

507

digital
TYPESET-10

508

THE AUDACITY OF DESPAIR

509

FOLIO 60

Murder Ink.
THE MYSTERY BOOKSTORE

510

Group Therapy.

511

JANUARY
DECEMBER

512

506
Richardson Seigle Rolfs & McCoy Inc.
Entrant
Vic Warren
Art Director
Alaska Airlines
Client

507
Digital Equipment Corp.
Entrant
David Raymond
Art Director

508
Donald Baird
Entrant
Thomas Cocozza
Art Director
Abbey, Hansard Advertising
Agency
Banner Press
Studio
Merck, Sharp Dohme
Client

509
J.M. Essex/ Design Center
Entrant
J. Michael
Art Director
Cary Cochrane
Illustrator
John Bilecky
Photographer
WQED/ Design Center
Agency
Earthrise Design Inc.
Client

510
Herb Passberger
Entrant
PKL Advertising Inc.
Agency
Murder Ink
Client

511
Graphics Group, Inc.
Entrant
Steve Foster, Don Gill
Art Directors
McDonald & Little Advertising
Agency
Six Flags over Georgia
Client

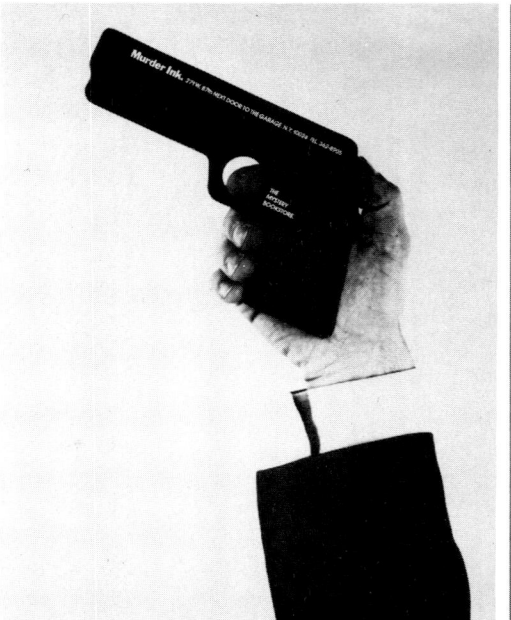

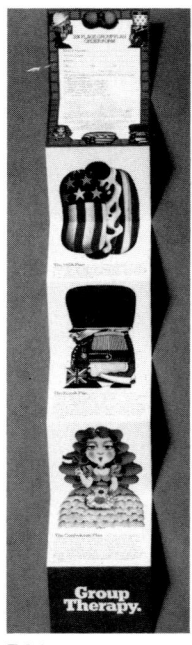

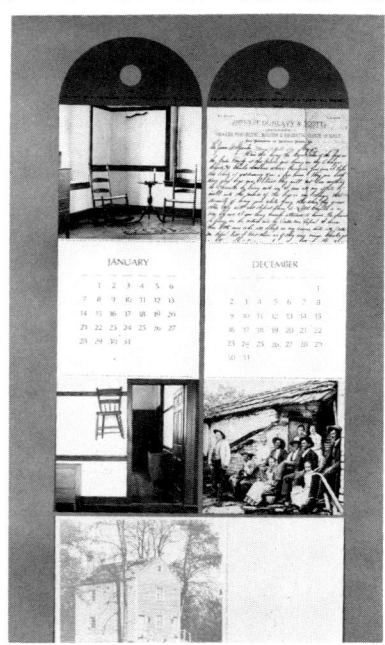

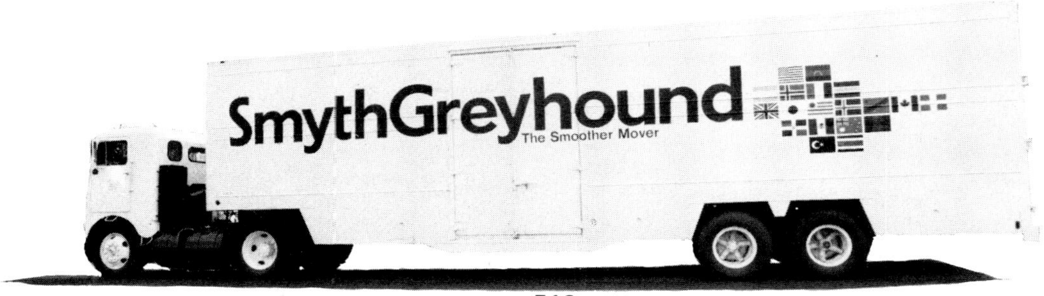
SmythGreyhound
The Smoother Mover

513

512

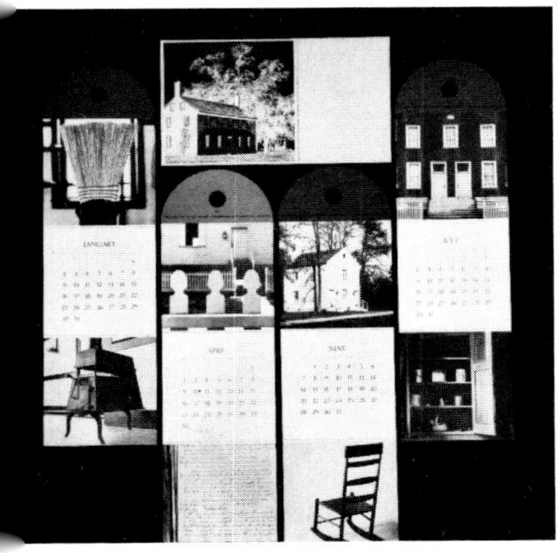

514

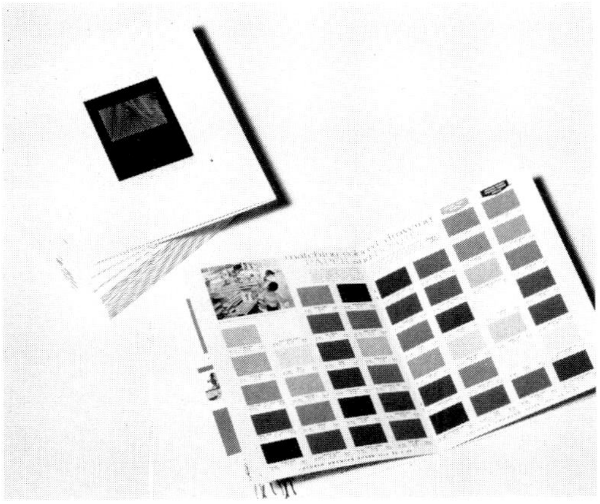

515

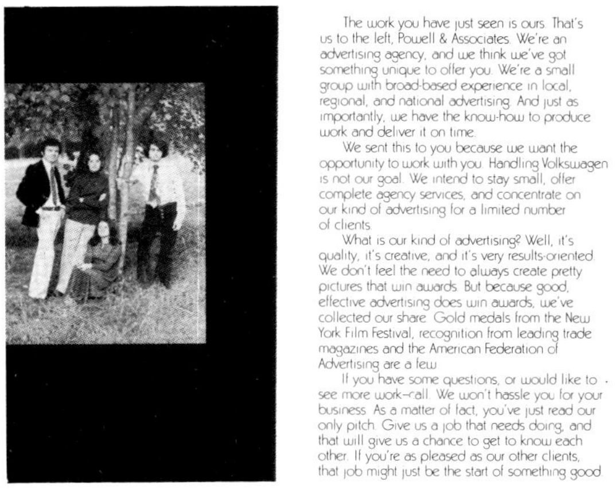
The work you have just seen is ours. That's us to the left, Powell & Associates. We're an advertising agency, and we think we've got something unique to offer you. We're a small group with broad-based experience in local, regional, and national advertising. And just as importantly, we have the know-how to produce work and deliver it on time.
We sent this to you because we want the opportunity to work with you. Handling Volkswagen is not our goal. We intend to stay small, offer complete agency services, and concentrate on our kind of advertising for a limited number of clients.
What is our kind of advertising? Well, it's quality, it's creative, and it's very results-oriented. We don't feel the need to always create pretty pictures that win awards. But because good, effective advertising does win awards, we've collected our share. Gold medals from the New York Film Festival, recognition from leading trade magazines and the American Federation of Advertising are a few.
If you have some questions, or would like to see more work–call. We won't hassle you for your business. As a matter of fact, you've just read our only pitch. Give us a job that needs doing, and that will give us a chance to get to know each other. If you're as pleased as our other clients, that job might just be the start of something good.

517

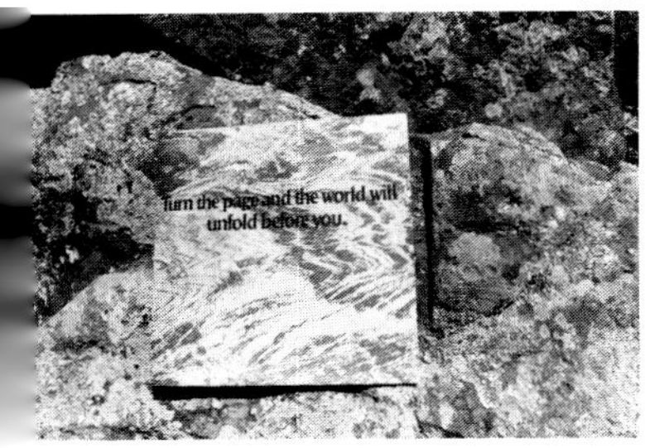
Turn the page and the world will unfold before you.

516

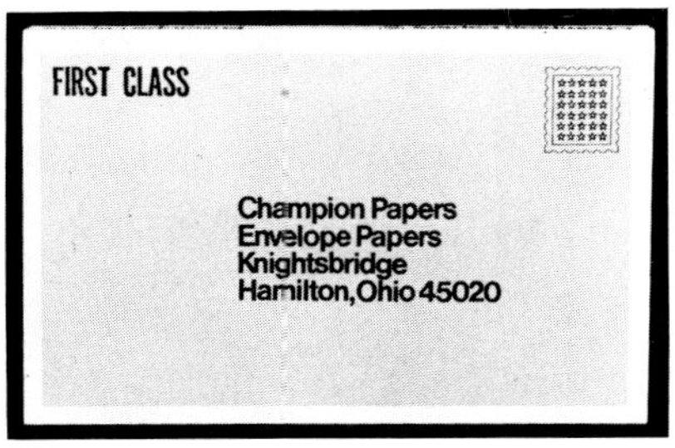
FIRST CLASS
Champion Papers
Envelope Papers
Knightsbridge
Hamilton, Ohio 45020

518

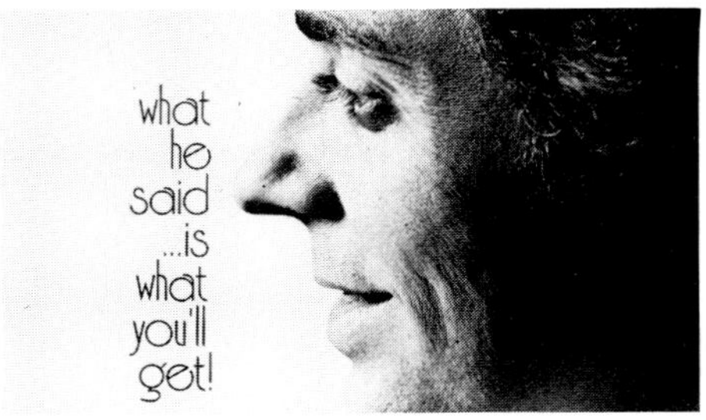
what he said ...is what you'll get!

519

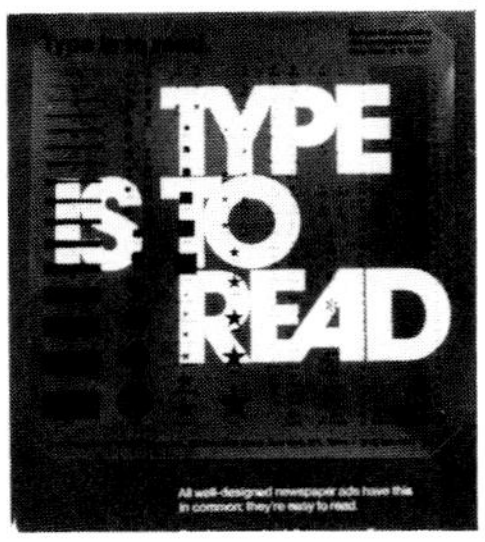
TYPE IS TO READ

2
san
ckson Keig
trant
mes L.
llard
otographer
akertown
Pleasant
l, Ky.
ent

513
Richardson Seigle Rolfs & McCoy
Entrant
Vic Warren, Bob Billings
Art Directors
Weisz Decal Inc.
Studio
Bob Billings
Illustrator
Smyth Greyhound
Client

514
Barry Johnson Studio
Entrant
Barry Johnson
Art Director
Crescent Cardboard Co.
Client

515
Powell & Associates
Entrant
Bill Powell
Art Director

516
Peter Wittman
Entrant
James Miho
Art Director
Miho Inc.
Studio
Champion Papers
Client

517
CRM Books
Entrant
Paul Slick
Art Director
Frank Armitage
Illustrator
Payson Stevens
Map Concept
Richard Carter, Kurt Kolbe
Map Production

518
Michael Tedesco
Entrant
Gil Trevino
Photographer
Francis & Shaw Inc.
Agency
Sony Corporation Of America
Client

519
Tom Clemente
Entrant
John McInnes
Designer
Dick Dorne
Copywriter
Tri-Arts Press
Production
Daily Newspapers U.S. & Canada
Client

520

An apple a day...

521

The egg has been called Nature's most perfect package. Which may have been true in a world of soft grasses and slow paces when the chicken and the consumer often lived on the same farm and neither was in a hurry. But when 520 million eggs per week have to be hustled from henhouse through high speed sorting, packaging, hauling, and the bustling supermarket cycle — well then Nature's perfect package needs a little help. Then the egg becomes just another of the marvelous inventions — possibly including some of yours — which need extra protection to prevent a great deal of grief both for the consumer and the seller. That's one of the reasons we sell so much Dylite foam plastic for packaging. This expandable polystyrene is shock resistant, so it cushions fragile items. It's almost infinitely moldable, so it easily forms compartments for products that need the sorting or separation. And it makes an attractive showcase to give
PROGRESS REPORT ON THE PERFECT PACKAGE
retail products more appeal to the consumer. Dylite is used to package such critical cargo as crystal goblets, wine bottles, sensitive seismic and electronic components, and blood serum vials, yet it's inexpensive enough to be practical for eggs. At the Lamirada, California, plant of Sinclair-Koppers, we extrude Dylite sheet in white and in bright colors for egg cartons. The cartons have even become an advertising medium: companies who use coupon or direct mail advertising can have their messages affixed to the inside cover — for millions of consumers to see and possibly to send. As for the eggs enclosed here, they didn't really need Dylite packaging, but they seemed to deserve it. They're candy — rather good candy — and hollow, with some novelty surprises inside. They would make a big hit at a children's party or a light, harmless hit at a political rally. But do consider tossing one to your top man on packaging.
KOPPERS

PAPER POWER
How to plug your products by mixing or matching Hammermill Cover & Textopaque.

522

november 1973
Z 4 11 18 25
M 5 12 19 26
D 6 13 20 27
W 7 14 21 28
D 1 8 15 22 29
V 2 9 16 23 30
Z 3 10 17 24

523

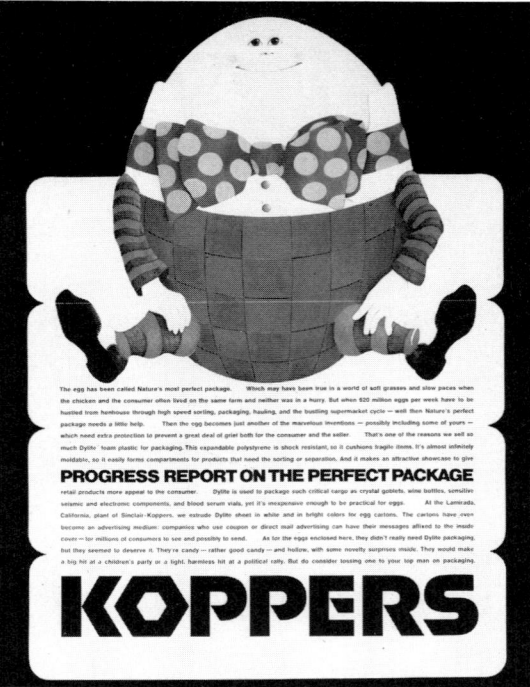

520
Redbook Magazine
Entrant
Valerie Kleckner
Art Director
Jim Luft
Illustrator
Gordon Smith
Photographer

521
Larry Marini Entrant
Rick Horton Art Director
Jackie Geyer Illustrator
Van Dine Horton Agency
Marini, Climes & Guip Inc.
Studio
Koppers Client

522
Thomas Lowes Associates
Entrant
James G. Halt
Art Director
Hammermill Paper Company
Client

523
Studio Wortel & Delaere
Entrant
Van Gelder Papier—Holland
Client

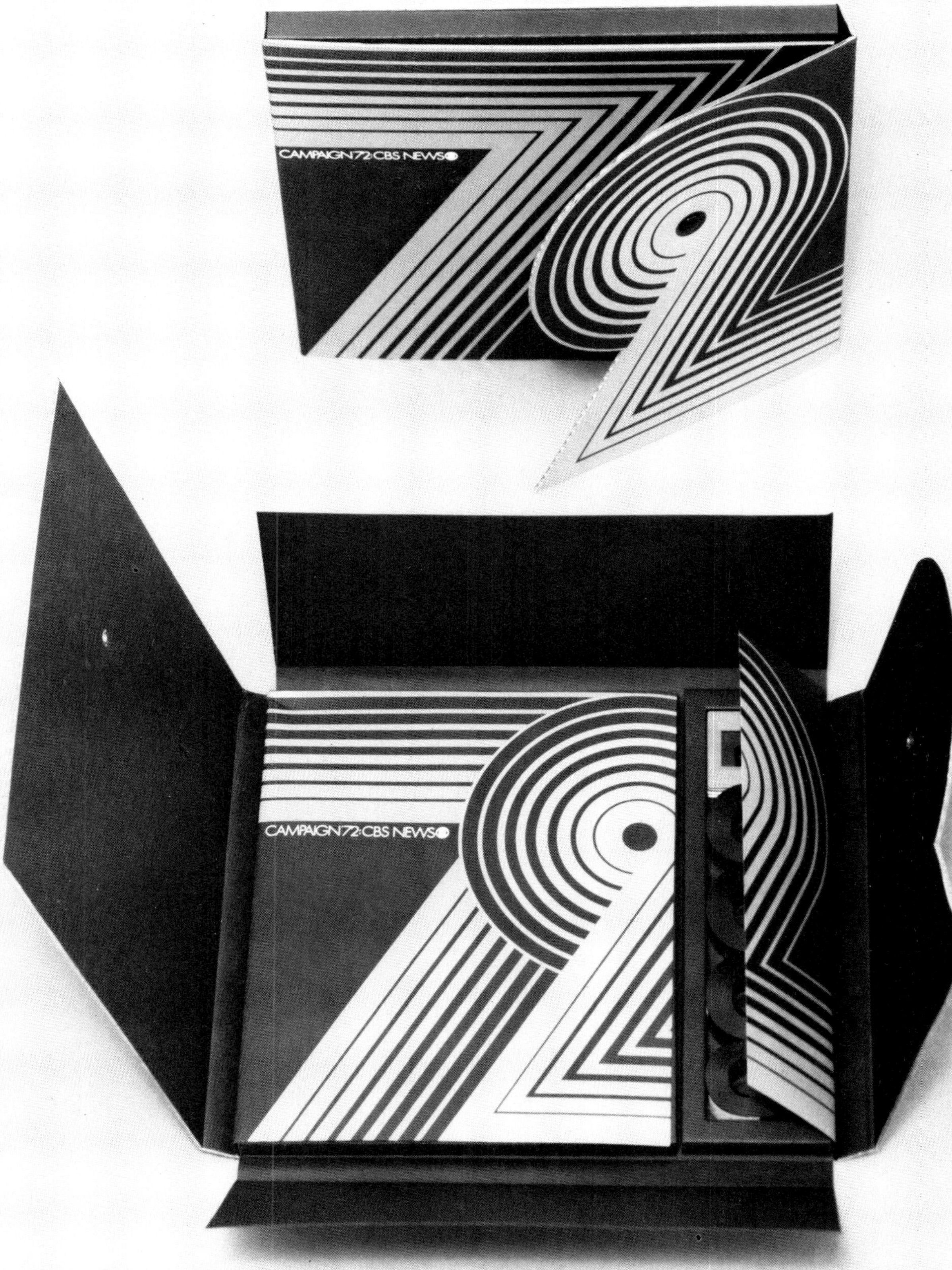
CAMPAIGN72:CBS NEWS
CAMPAIGN72:CBS NEWS

524
Lou Dorfsman
Entrant
Lou Dorfsman,
Ted Andresakes
Designers
CBS/Broadcast Group
Agency
CBS News Client

525

The Diabetic Gourmet
by Angela Bowen, M.D.

526

The Diabetic Gourmet
by Angela Bowen, M.D.

527

THE CASE FOR PROSPECTON
Guide to Prospecton Industrial Lots
Prospecton

528

Cut your own Christmas tree this year
Cut your own Christmas tree this year...

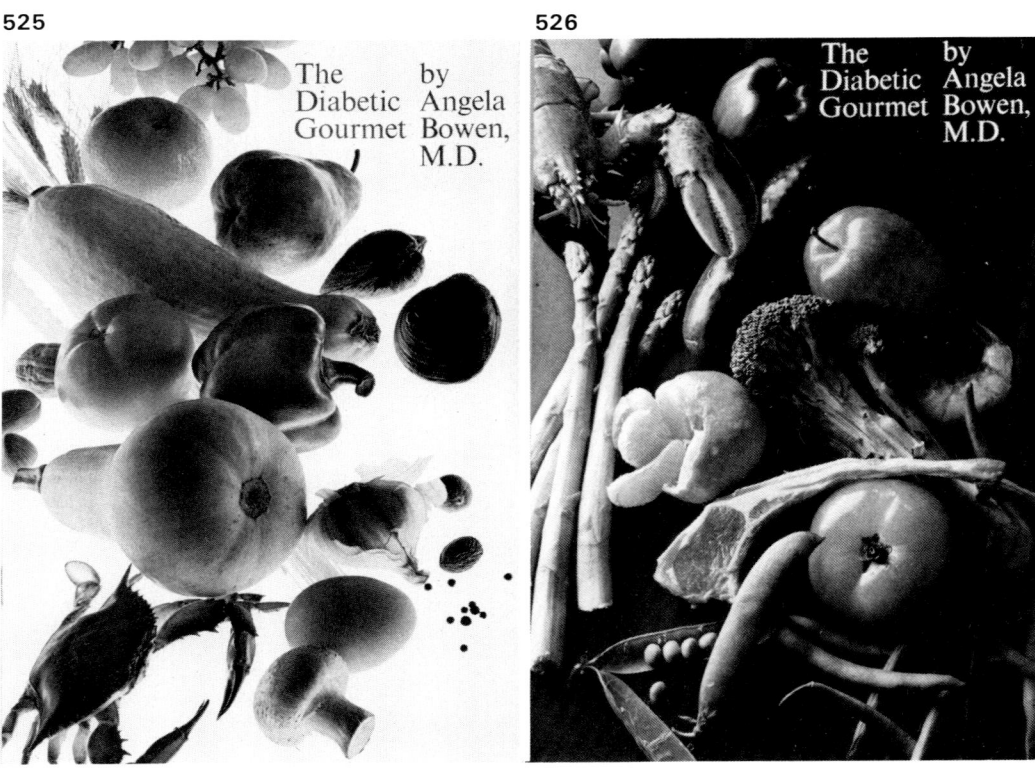

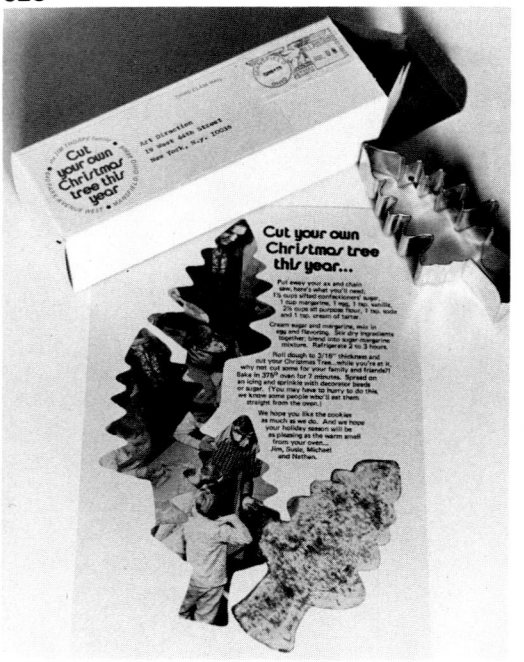

525-526
Geigy Pharmaceuticals Entrant
John de Cesare Art Director
Henry Sandbank Photographer
Mago Inforna Studio

527
Lorraine & Crystal Entrant
Barry Crystal Art Director
Kiley Baker Plastics Studio
Awolo American Client

528
Jim Thorpe Entrant

529

530

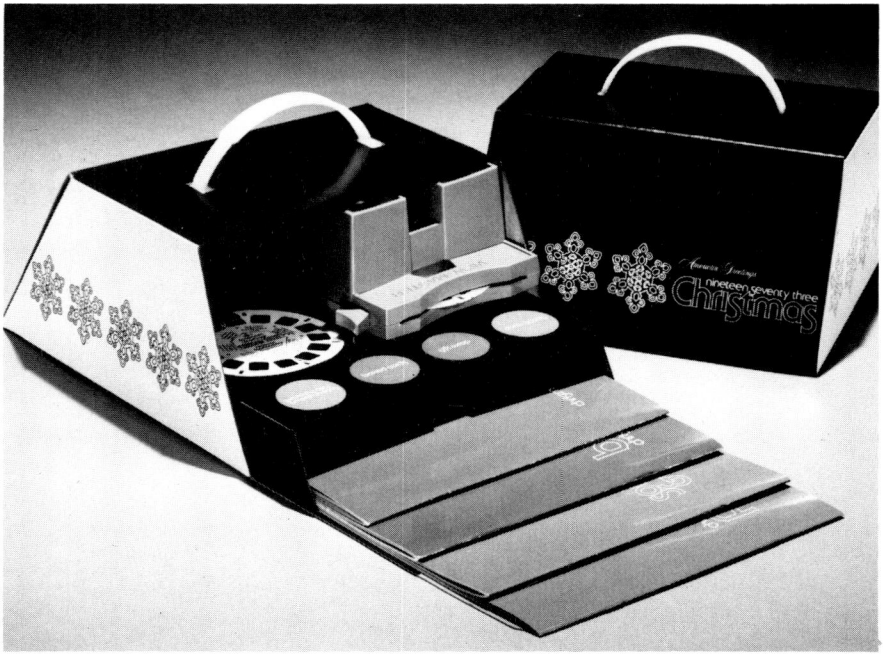

Seasons
Greetings
Makers of
appetizing, tasteful
films.

531

nineteen seventy three
Christmas

529
Century Expanded Entrant
George McCathern Art Director
Alan Breslau Photographer
American Dietaids Client

530
Steve Sohmer Inc. Entrant
Steve Sohmer Art Director

531
Carlton Faughender Entrant
Pam Stuermer Designer
Visual Design Studio
American Greetings Corporation Client

532

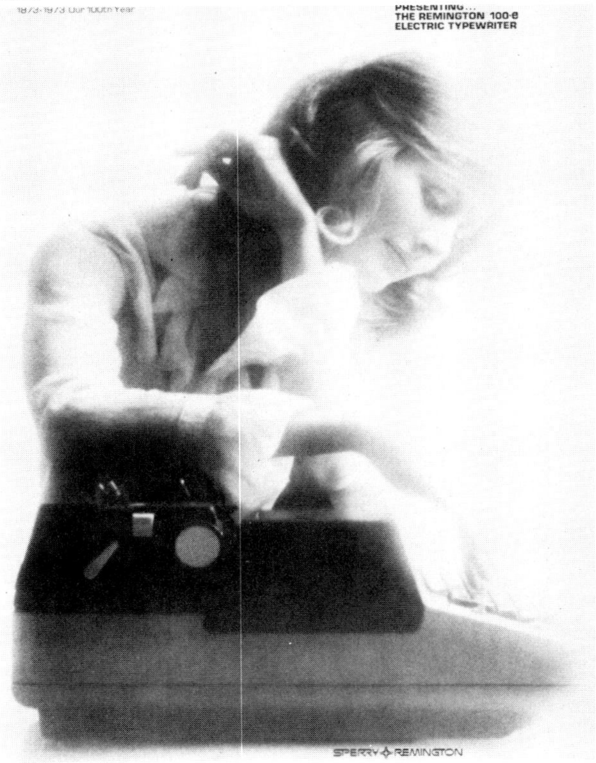
1873-1973 Our 100th Year
PRESENTING...
THE REMINGTON 100-e
ELECTRIC TYPEWRITER
SPERRY REMINGTON

533

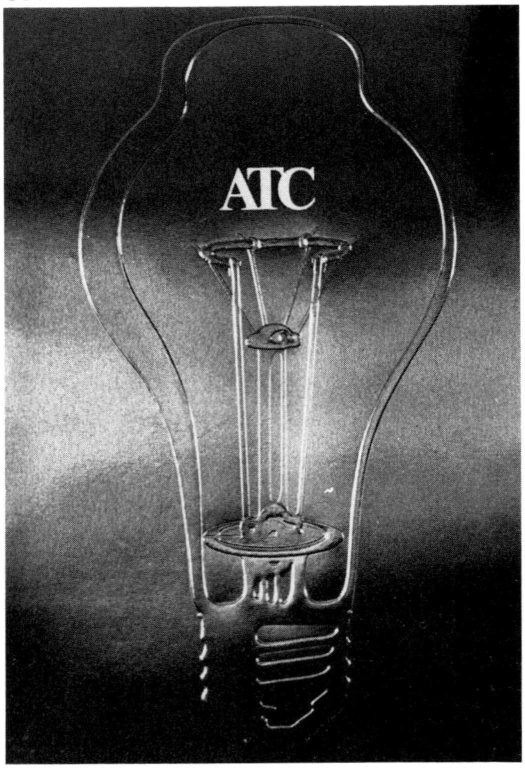
ATC

534

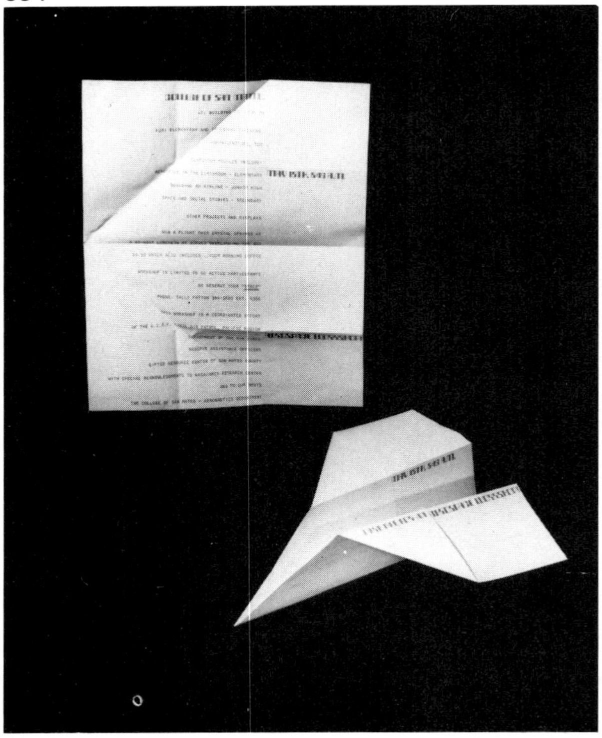

535

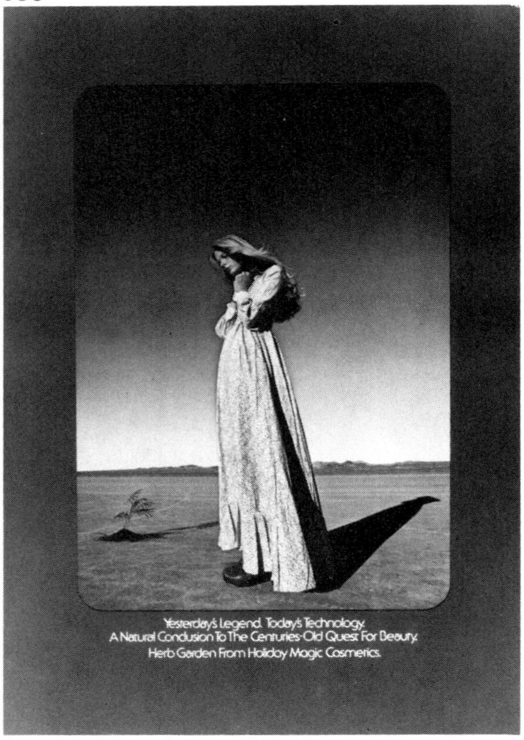
Yesterday's Legend. Today's Technology.
A Natural Conclusion To The Centuries-Old Quest For Beauty.
Herb Garden From Holiday Magic Cosmetics.

532
Ford, Byrne & Brennan Entrant
Sperry-Remington Client

533
Hinrichs Design Associates Entrant
Kit Hinrichs, J. Wright Art Directors
Durotest Corporation Client

534
Ed Jung Entrant
Gifted Resource Center Client

535
Donald Faia Entrant
Ron Thal Photographer
The Taylor Agency Agency
Holiday Magic Cosmetics Client

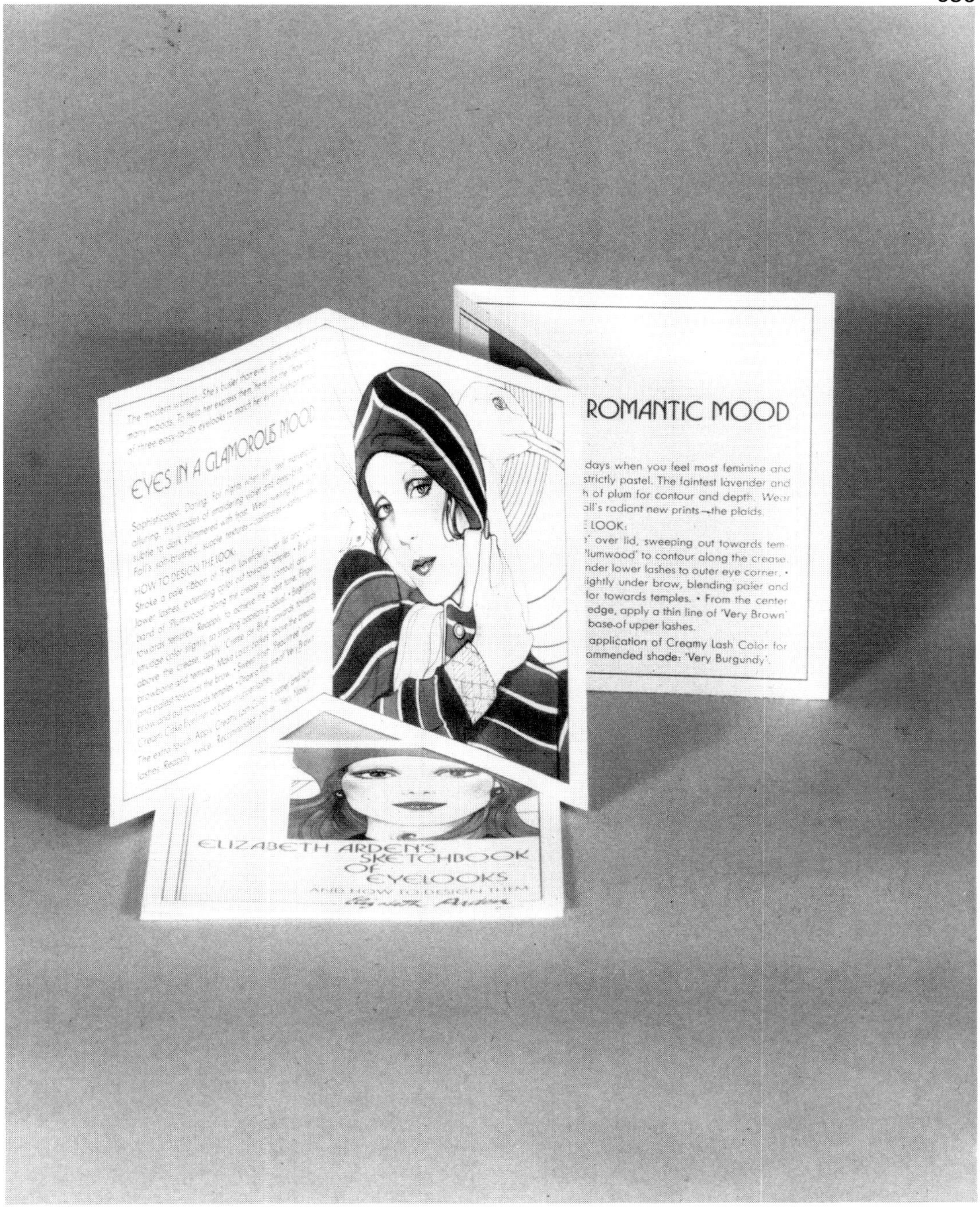
ROMANTIC MOOD
days when you feel most feminine and
strictly pastel. The faintest lavender and
h of plum for contour and depth. Wear
all's radiant new prints—the plaids.
LOOK:
' over lid, sweeping out towards tem
'Plumwood' to contour along the crease.
nder lower lashes to outer eye corner. •
lightly under brow, blending paler and
lor towards temples. • From the center
edge, apply a thin line of 'Very Brown'
base of upper lashes.
application of Creamy Lash Color for
ommended shade: 'Very Burgundy'.
EYES IN A GLAMOROUS MOOD
HOW TO DESIGN THE LOOK:
ELIZABETH ARDEN'S
SKETCHBOOK
OF
EYELOOKS
AND HOW TO DESIGN THEM

536
Elizabeth Arden Inc.
Entrant
Jean Ansado
Art Director

GO TEAM
This is what your prospects will be reading the next few months.

537

How to make him believe what you told him.

538

The Job

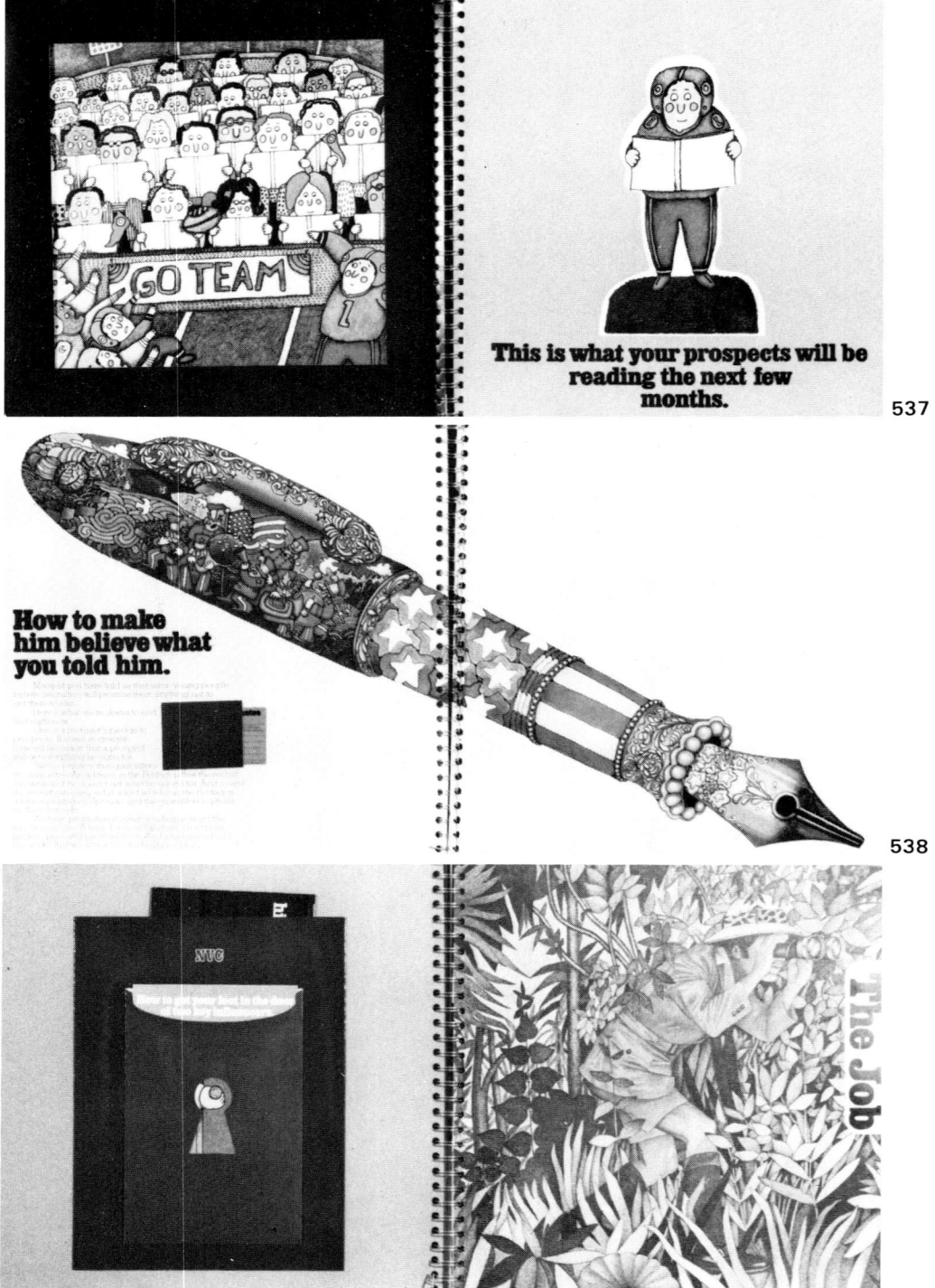

537-538
Mickey Tender Entrant
Mabey Trousdell Illustrators
Cailor/Resnick Photographers
N.W. Ayer—Philadelphia Agency
U.S. Army Client

539

STUDENT UNION
The Most Colorful Change in the Beetle Since 1948

540

541

542

543

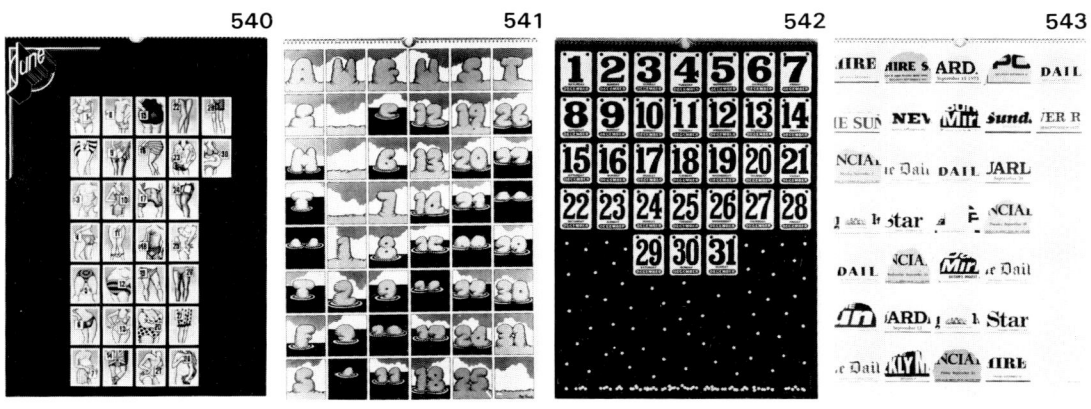

539
Charles E. Bird, Inc. Entrant
Joe Iwanaga Art Director
Dick Sakahara Illustrator
House of Design Production House

540-543
Jonathan d Morgan Entrant
Jonathan d Morgan, John Gorham, Chris Broughton, Anita Kwan, Adrian Williamson, Pete Beard, Mike Warwick, Chris Smosarski, Mike Gregory Illustrators
Typographic Workshop Studio
Leeds Polytechnic Client

544

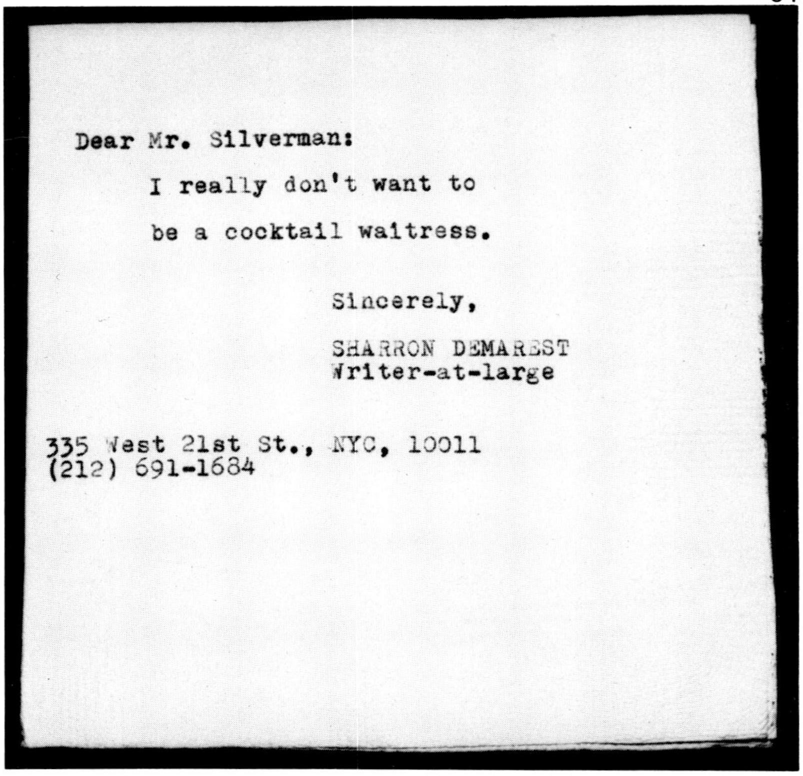

Dear Mr. Silverman:

I really don't want to be a cocktail waitress.

Sincerely,

SHARRON DEMAREST
Writer-at-large

335 West 21st St., NYC, 10011
(212) 691-1684

545

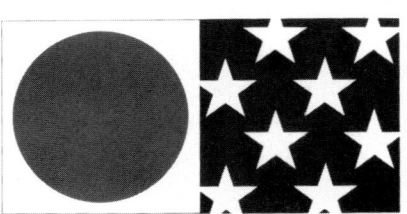

1973
KENNETH WALKER

546

TIME SURVEY 1973: JAPAN/U.S.A.

547

JELL-O
BRAND GELATIN
The Dessert America Grew Up With Serves You An Exciting New Opportunity.

544
Sharron Demarest Entrant

546
Kenneth Walker Entrant

545
Seldon Dix Entrant
Walter Lefmann Art Director
Time, Inc. Client

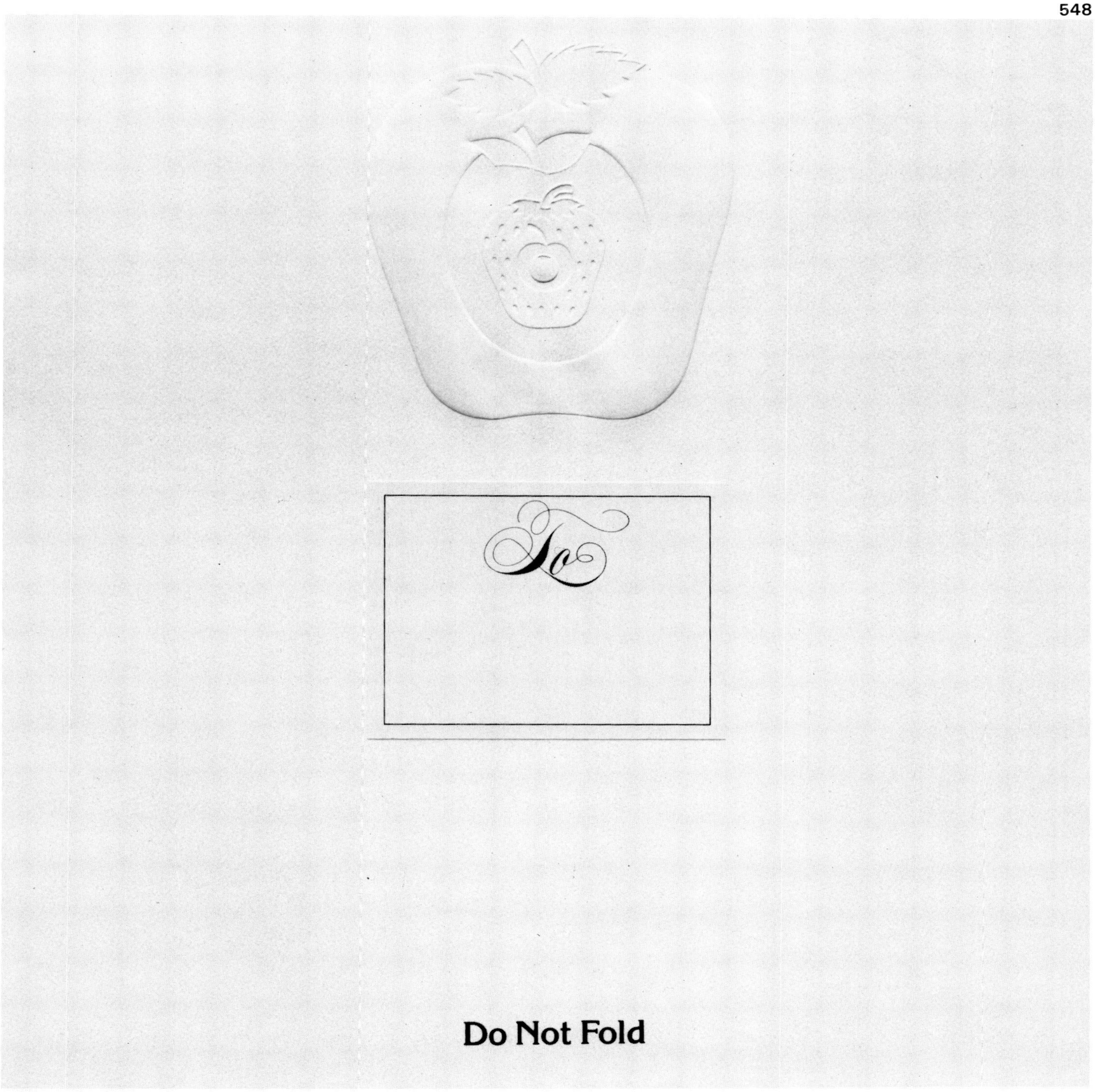
To
Do Not Fold

547-548
Ketchum, MacLeod & Grove Entrant
Walter Kaprielian Art Director
Walter Kaprielian, Hal Florian, Joel Benay Designers
Push Pin Studios Illustrator
General Foods Corp. Client

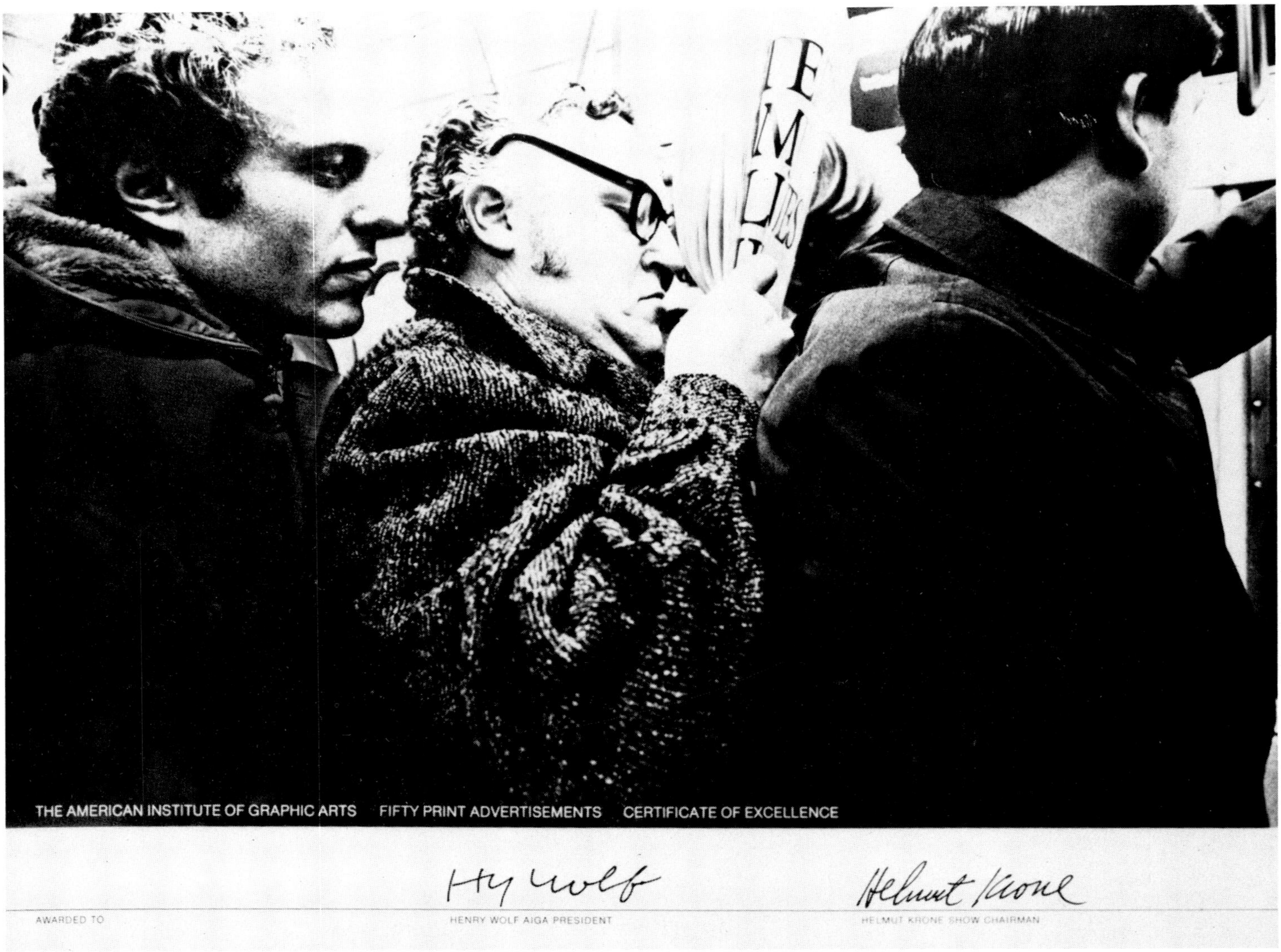
THE AMERICAN INSTITUTE OF GRAPHIC ARTS
FIFTY PRINT ADVERTISEMENTS
CERTIFICATE OF EXCELLENCE
Hy Wolf
Helmut Krone
AWARDED TO
HENRY WOLF AIGA PRESIDENT
HELMUT KRONE SHOW CHAIRMAN

549
Bob Salpeter Entrant
Lopez Salpeter Inc. Agency
Larry Sillen Photographer
American Institute of Graphic Arts Client

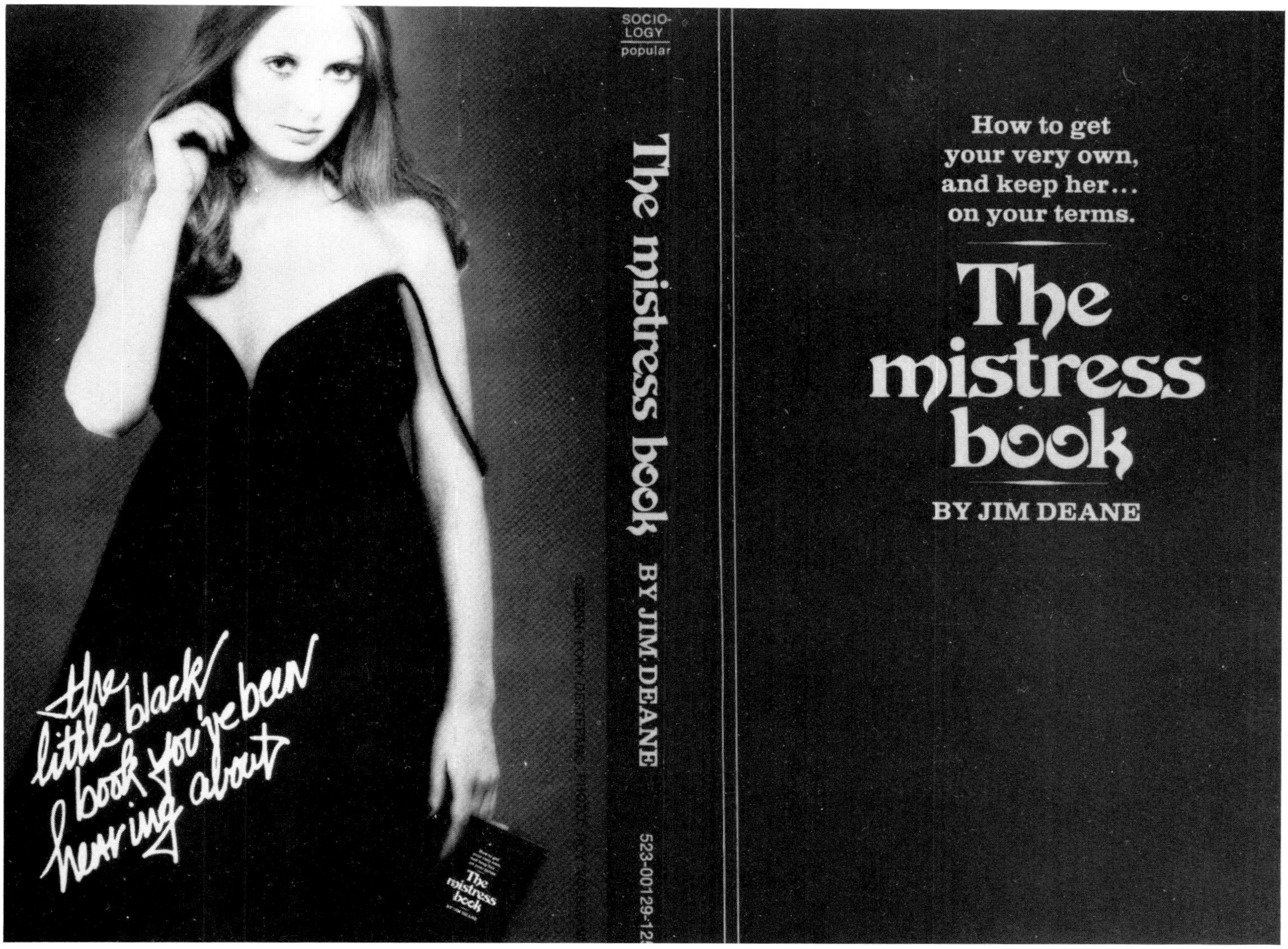
SOCIO-
LOGY
popular
The mistress book
BY JIM DEANE
the little black book you've been hearing about
How to get
your very own,
and keep her...
on your terms.
The
mistress
book
BY JIM DEANE

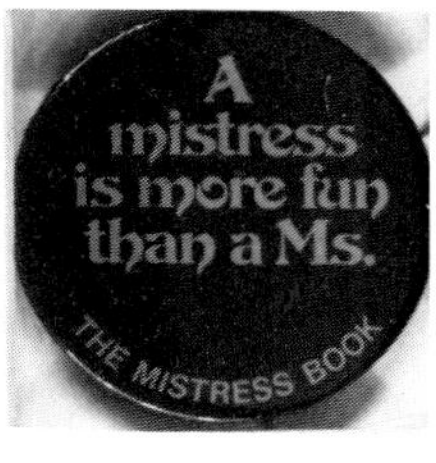
A
mistress
is more fun
than a Ms.
THE MISTRESS BOOK

550-551
Tony Destefano Entrant
Roy Volkman Photographer
Pinnacle Books Inc. Client

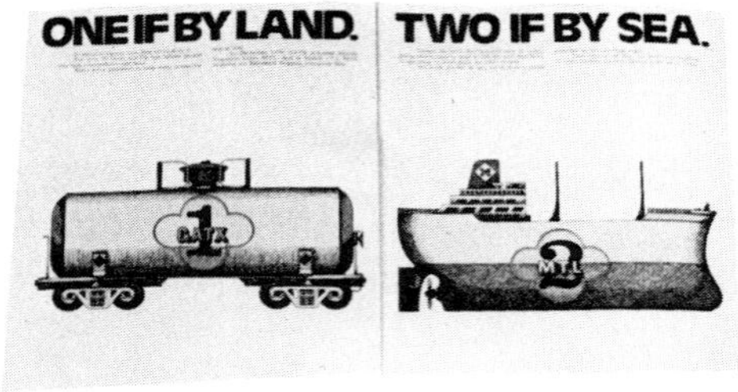
ONE IF BY LAND.
TWO IF BY SEA.

552

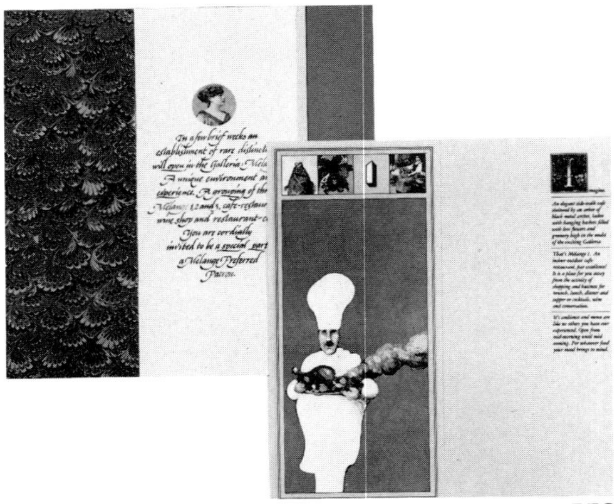

553

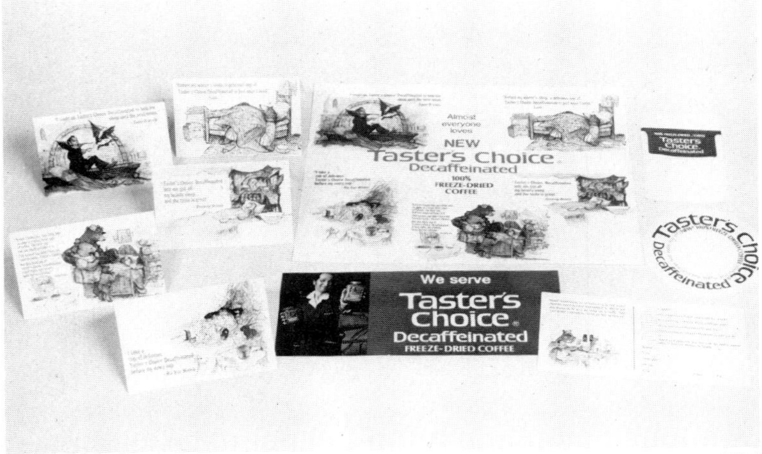
Almost everyone loves
NEW
Taster's Choice
Decaffeinated
100%
FREEZE-DRIED
COFFEE
We serve
Taster's Choice
Decaffeinated
FREEZE-DRIED COFFEE

554

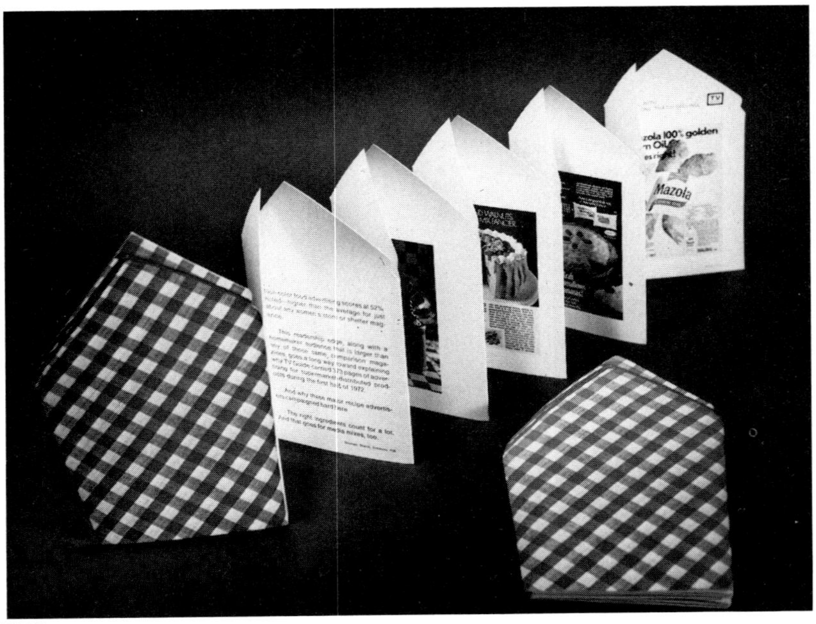
Mazola

555

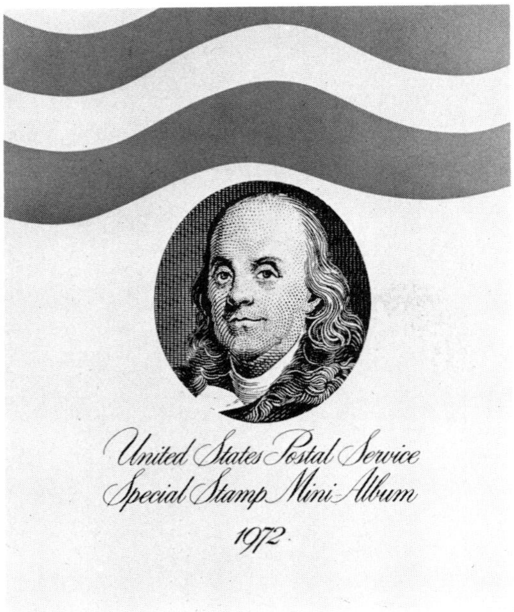
United States Postal Service
Special Stamp Mini Album
1972

556

552
Eric Lob Entrant
Ray Nyquist Art Director
Mabey Trousdell, Gib Foster Illustrators
Lee King & Partners Agency
General American Trans Client

553
Jerry Herring Entrant
Jerry Jennard Illustrator
Kelvin Group Part. Studio
Melange Client

554
Food Graphics Inc. Entrant
Ted Bobetski, Don Axelrod Art Directors
John Bobbish Illustrator
Nestle Client

555
TV Guide Entrant
John Brown Art Director
Fred Rosato Designer
William Grant Photographer

dynamo

557

Some very important things you shouldn't forget

558

Don't forget to brush your teeth
before going out with Raquel Welch.

559

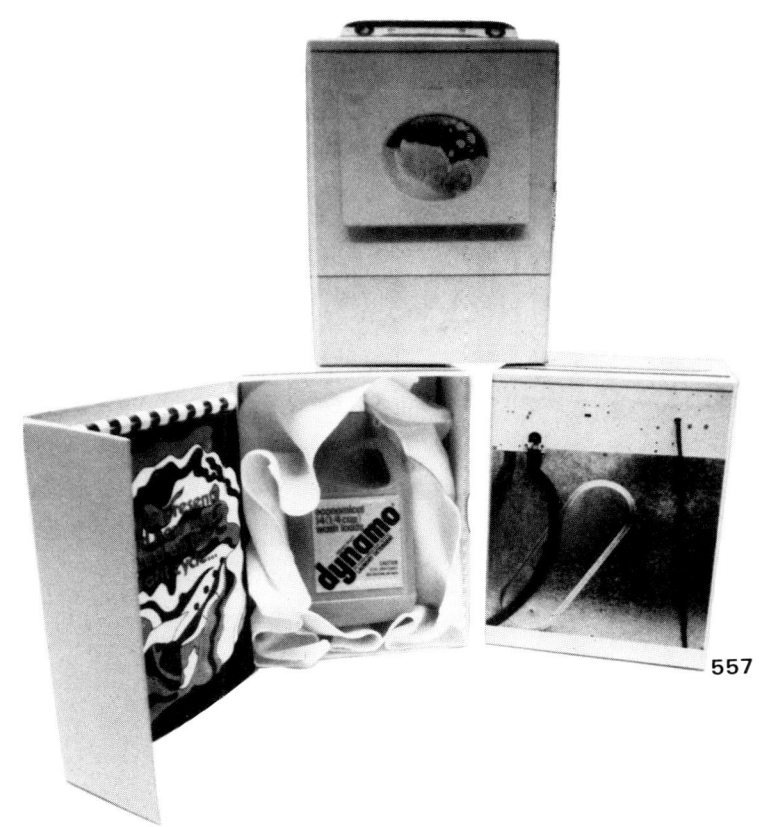

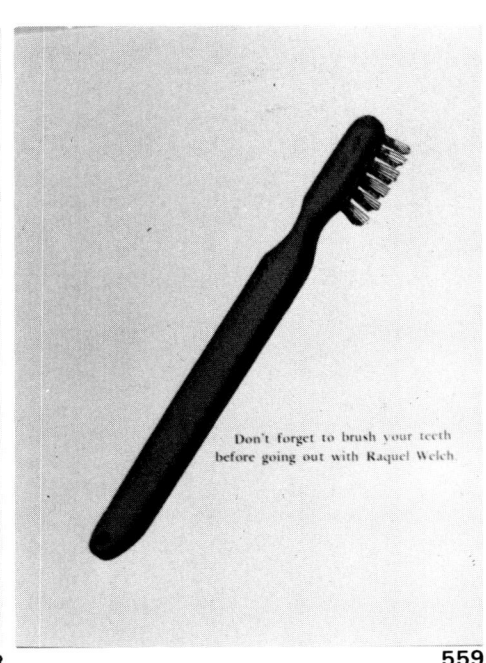

556
U.S. Postal Service Entrant
David Foote Art Director
Creative Services Agency
Harry Knox & Assoc. Studio

557
Century Expanded Entrant
George McCathern Art Director
Alan Breslau Photographer
Colgate-Palmolive Client

558-559
David E. Carter Entrant
Charles Buell Illustrator
Kentucky Electric Steel Co. Client

560

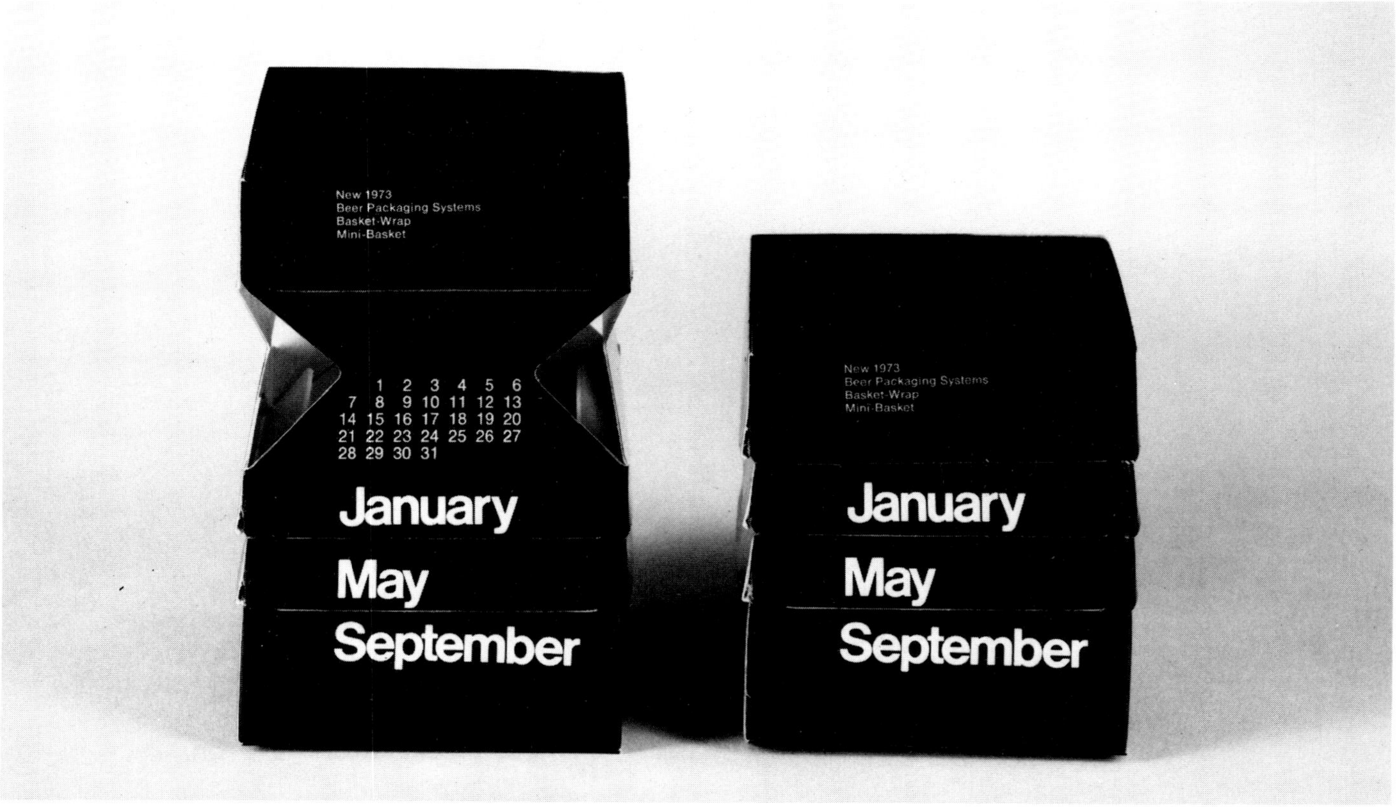
New 1973
Beer Packaging Systems
Basket-Wrap
Mini-Basket
1 2 3 4 5 6
7 8 9 10 11 12 13
14 15 16 17 18 19 20
21 22 23 24 25 26 27
28 29 30 31
January
May
September
New 1973
Beer Packaging Systems
Basket-Wrap
Mini-Basket
January
May
September

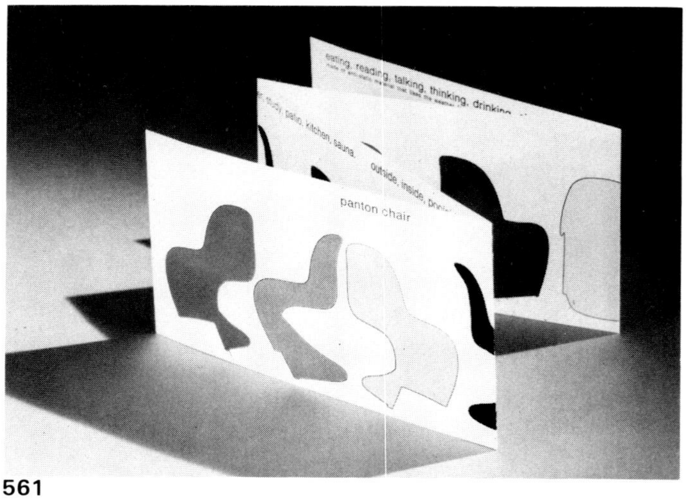
panton chair

561

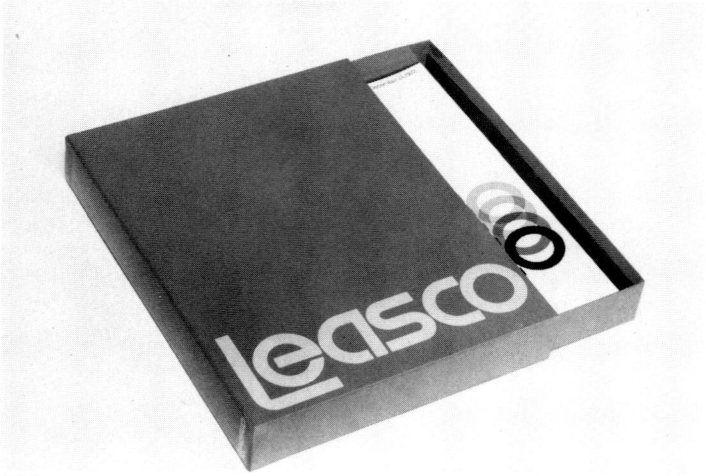
Leasco

562

562
SCI. Stanley Church Inc. Entrant
Stanley Church Art Director
Ray Barker Type Designer
Leasco Corp. Client

561
Herman Miller Inc. Entrant
Stephen Frykholm,
Mark Sturzenegger Designers

560
Container Corporation of America Entrant
Bill Bonnell Art Director

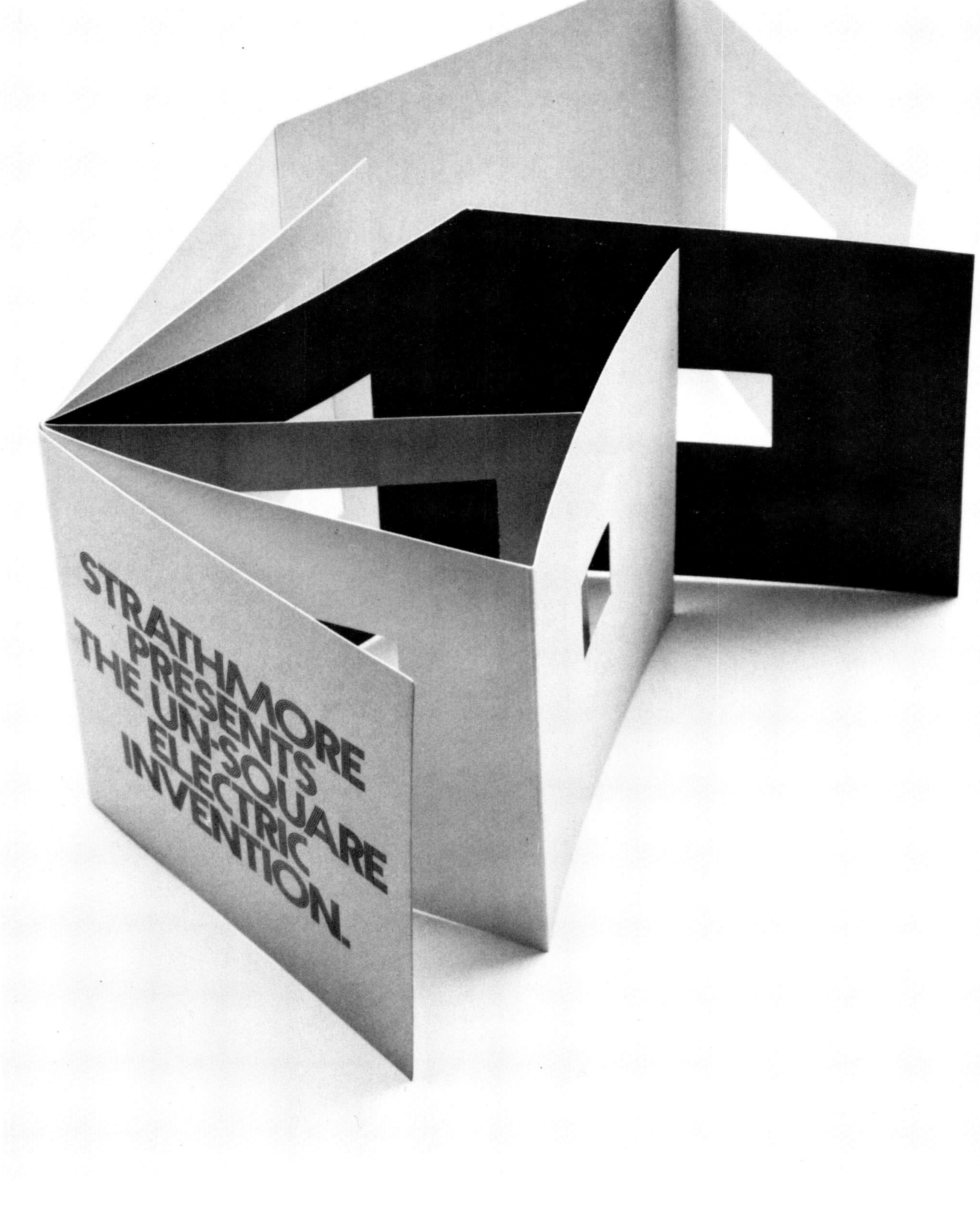
STRATHMORE
PRESENTS
THE UN-SQUARE
ELECTRIC
INVENTION.

563
Creamer, Trowbridge, Case & Basford Entrant
Paul Langmuir Art Director
Strathmore Paper Company Client

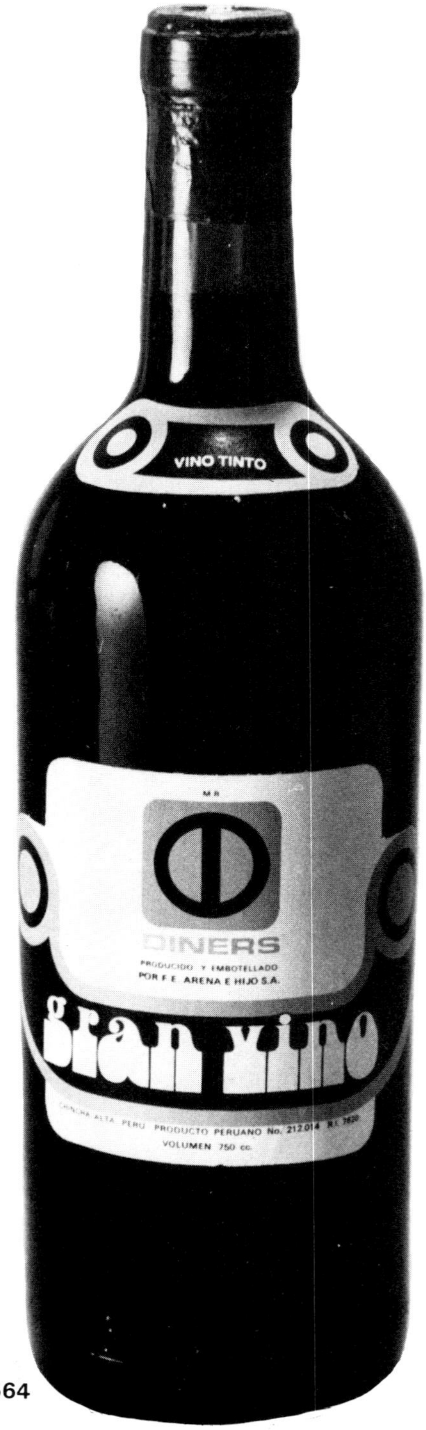
VINO TINTO
DINERS
PRODUCIDO Y EMBOTELLADO
POR F.E. ARENA E HIJO S.A.
gran vino
VOLUMEN 750 cc.

564

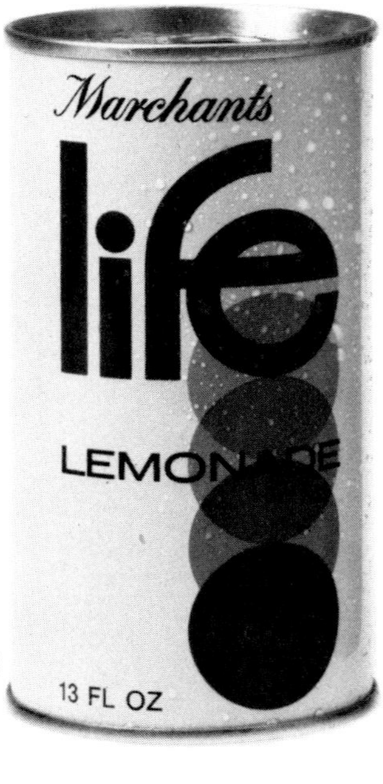
Marchants
life
13 FL OZ

565

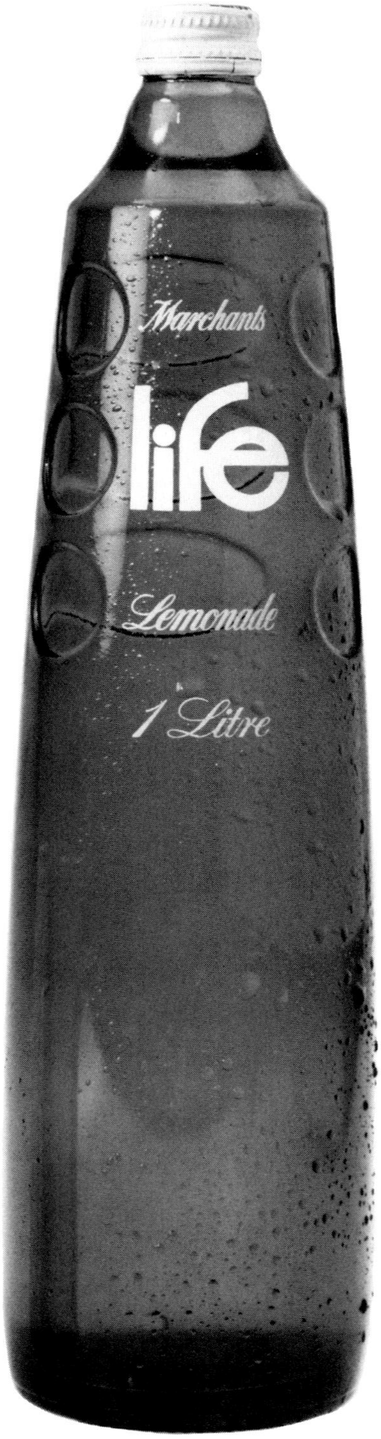
Marchants
life
Lemonade
1 Litre

566

564
Claude Dieterich Entrant
Diners Club, Lima, Peru Client

565-566
Gould & Assoc. Entrant
Jerome Gould, Ray Wood Art Directors
A.P.D./British Tobacco Client

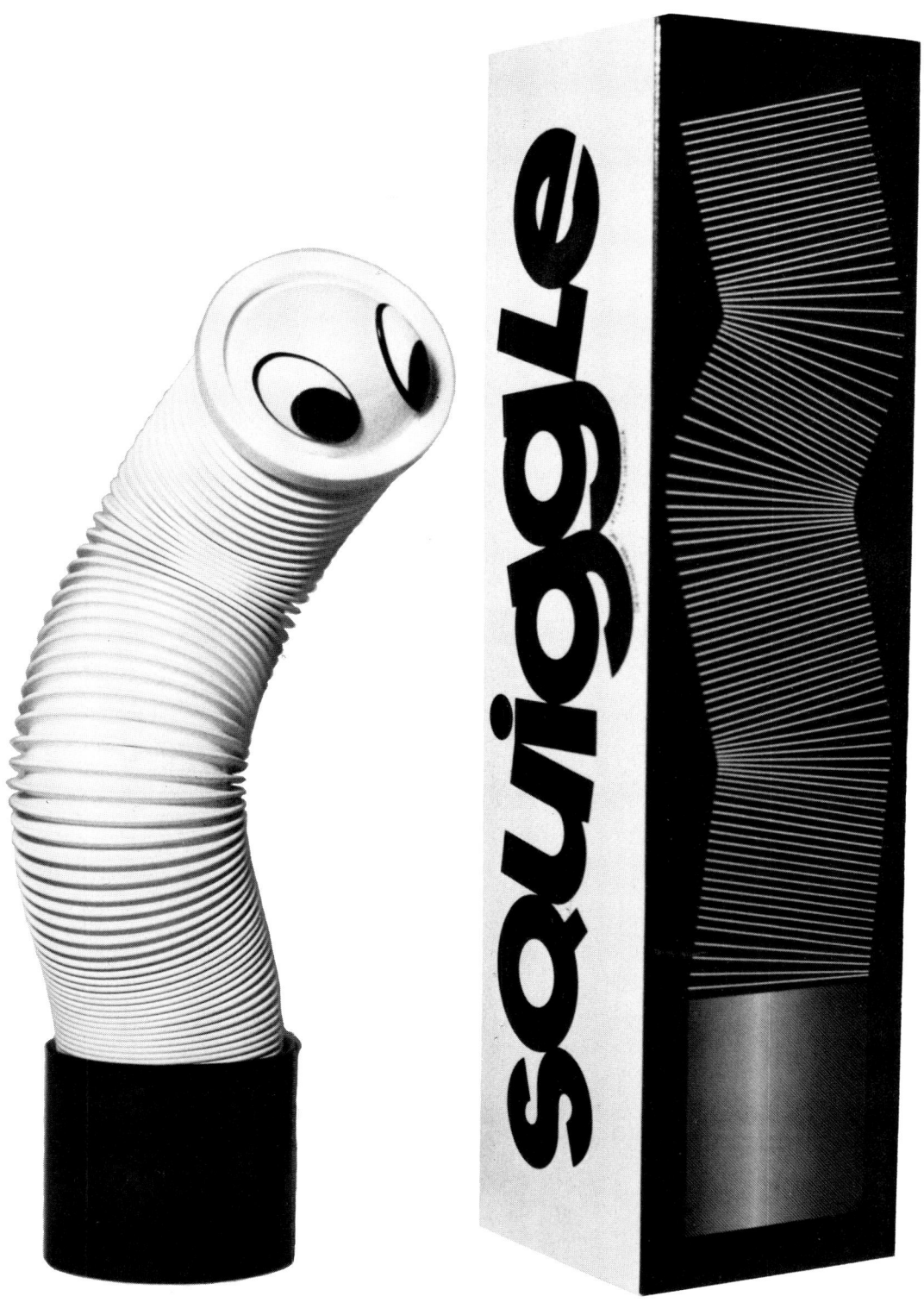

567
William Weaver Entrant
Kindley-Lenowitz Design Associates Studio
Designsense, Inc. Client

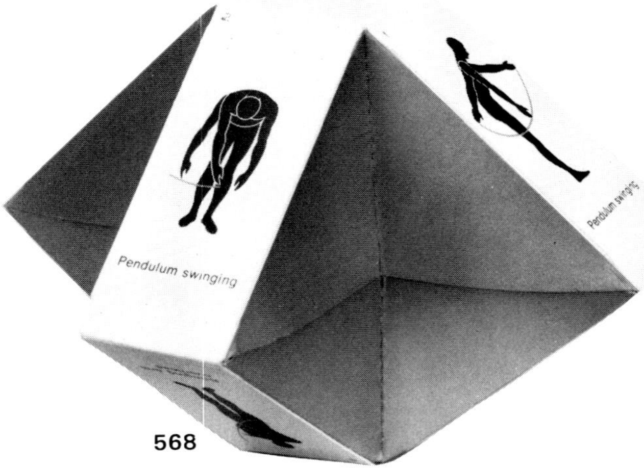
Pendulum swinging
Pendulum swinging

568

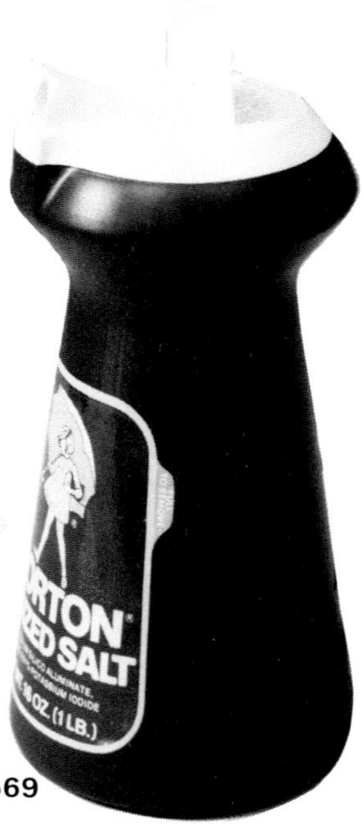

569

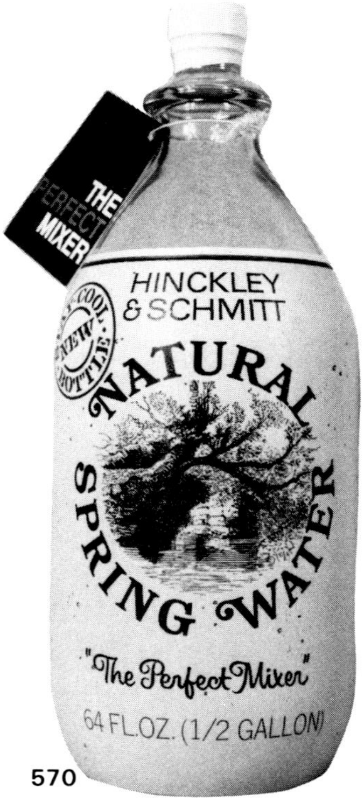
THE PERFECT MIXER
HINCKLEY & SCHMITT
NATURAL SPRING WATER
"The Perfect Mixer"
64 FL.OZ. (1/2 GALLON)

570

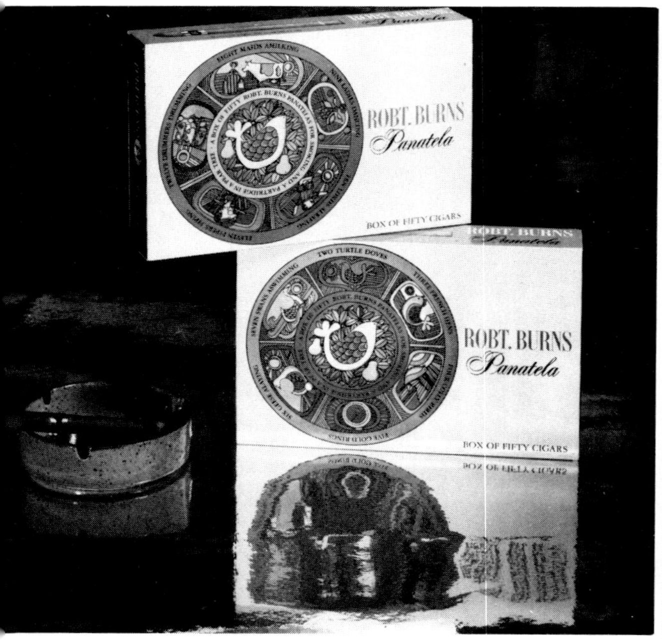
ROBT. BURNS
Panatela
BOX OF FIFTY CIGARS
ROBT. BURNS
Panatela
BOX OF FIFTY CIGARS

571

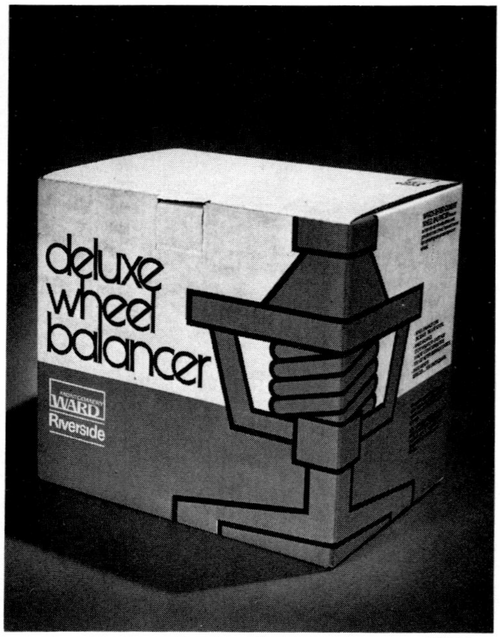
deluxe wheel balancer
WARD
Riverside

572

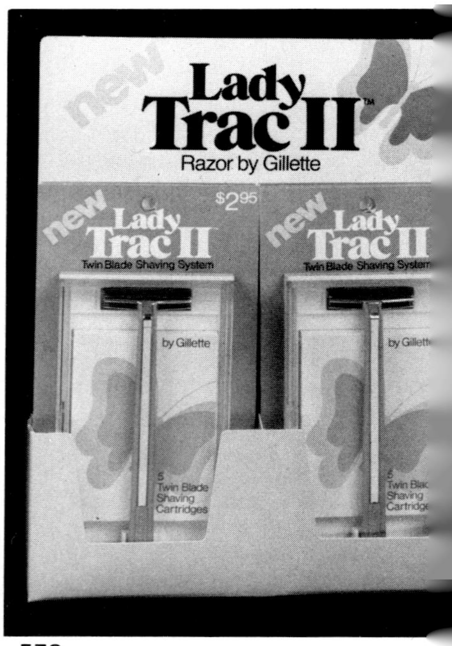
new
Lady Trac II™
Razor by Gillette
$2.95
new Lady Trac II
Twin Blade Shaving System
new Lady Trac II
Twin Blade Shaving System
by Gillette
5 Twin Blade Shaving Cartridges

573

568
Geigy Pharmaceuticals
Entrant
Joe Fazio
Art Director
Ken Jordan, Ron Vareltzis
Photographers

569
Gould & Assoc.
Entrant
Jerome Gould
Art Director
Robert Marona
Illustrator
Morton Salt Company
Client

570
Blau/Bishop & Assoc. Entrant
Al Van Cleven
Art Director
Hinckley & Schmitt
Client

571
Gerstman + Meyers Inc.
Entrant
H.M. Meyers
Art Director
Jerry Dior
Illustrator
General Cigar Company
Client

572
Ken Prestley
Entrant
Marion Bell Illustrator
Montgomery Ward Design Dept.
Agency
W & L Ad Art Studio
Bear Manufacturing/ Montgomery Ward
Client

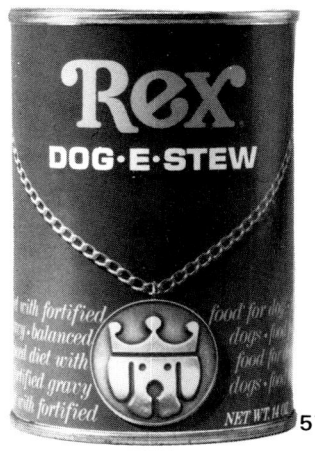

Rex
DOG·E·STEW
NET WT. 14 OZ.
575

Miller
FOUNDED
1855
Miller
ALE
CONTENTS 12 FLUID OZ.
576

2201
6
Lady
Trac II
Razors by Gillette
in shelf display carton
574

RASHanul
577

Percogesic
analgesic/calmative
for enhanced
relief of pain
contains no aspirin
24 tablets
Percogesic
24 tablets
578

573-574
Ray Shaw Entrant
Bruce Ray,
Nick Fader
Designers
Gilette Safety
Razor Division
Client

575
Gould & Assoc.
Art Director
Jerome Gould
Art Director
Laddie Boy,
Div. Nat'l
Pet Foods Co.
Client

576
Walter Landor
Assoc. Entrant
Miller
Brewing Company
Client

577
Gladys Barton
Entrant
Scott-Allison
Pharmaceutical
Client

578
Gerstman + Meyers
Inc. Entrant
R. Gerstman
Art Director
Endo Laboratories
Client

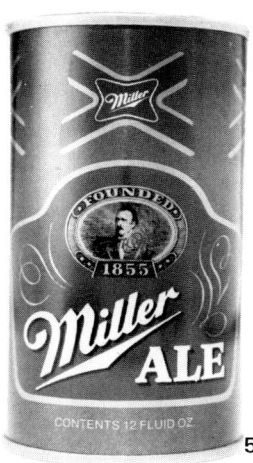

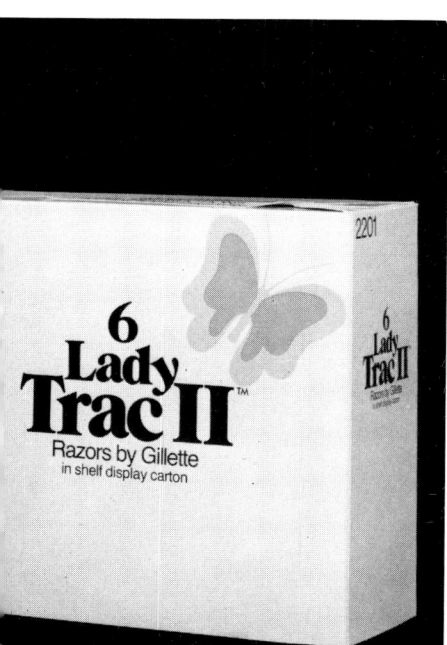

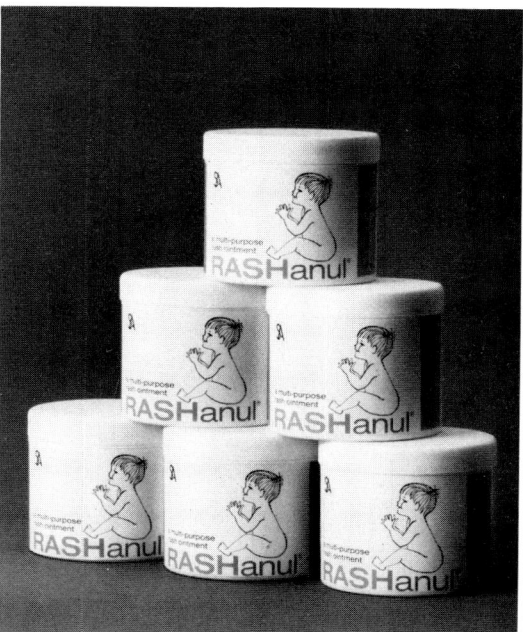

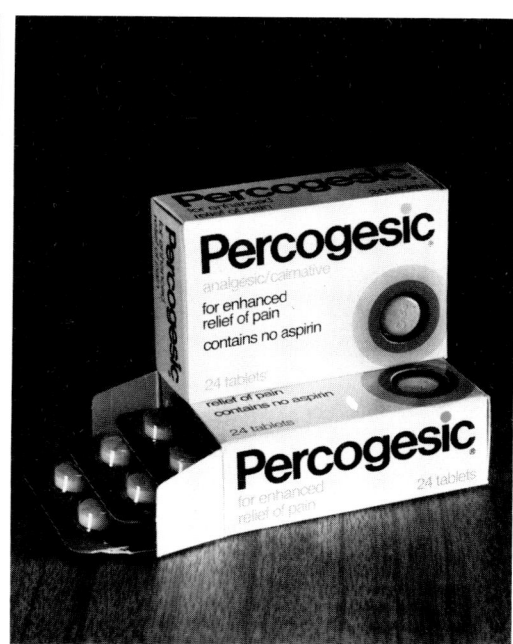

579

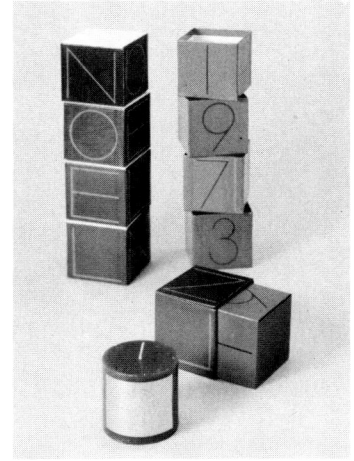

580

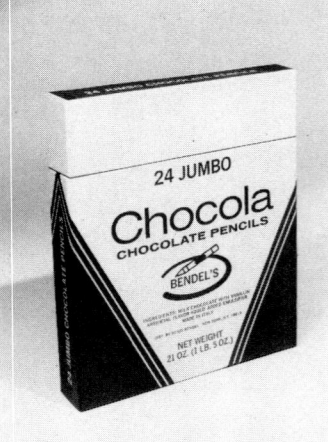

24 JUMBO
Chocola
CHOCOLATE PENCILS
BENDEL'S
NET WEIGHT

581

adam's apple

582

400 gram
Stella

583

RONSON
Cordless
Rechargeable
Electric
Toothbrush
RONSON
Cordless Rechargeable
ELECTRIC TOOTHBRUSH
120/240 VOLT FOR WORLD-WIDE USE

584

8
TRACK
STEREO
PORTABLE
HOME & AUTO
tape cabinet

585

chartpak
knife
center
The new Knife
System for Artists,
Engineers,
Craftsmen.
art knife
frisket knife
3-pack
scalpel

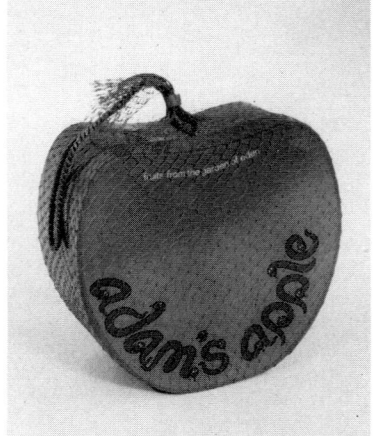

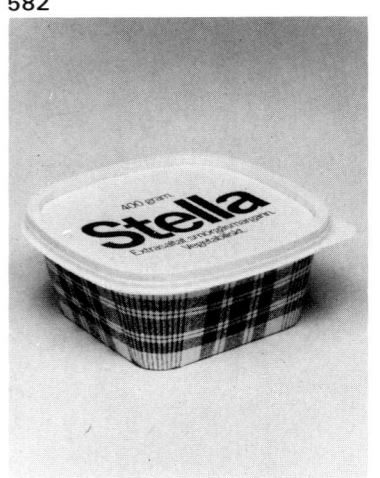

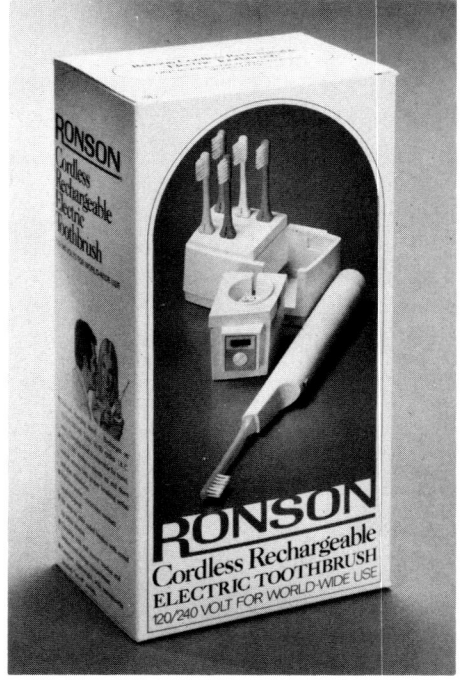

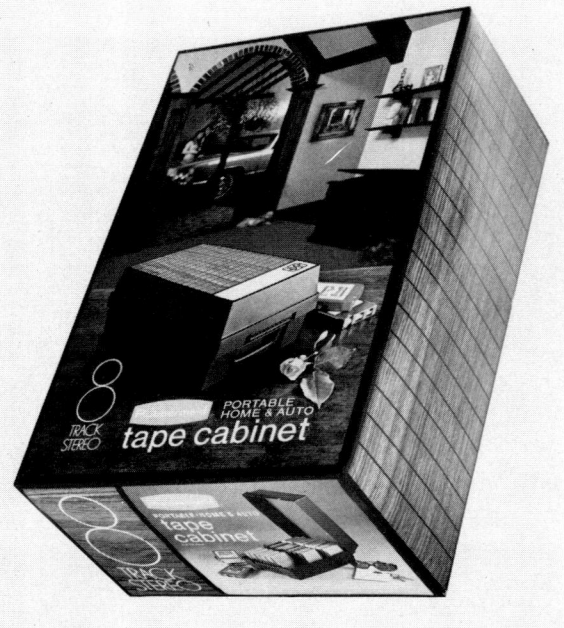

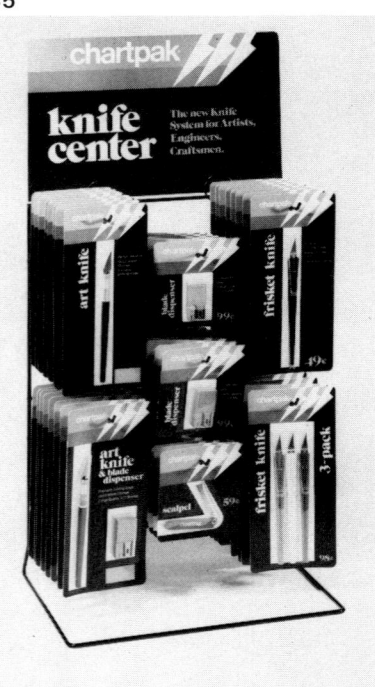

579
Mastropaul Design Inc.
Entrant
Ivan R. Powell
Art Director

580
SCI. Stanley Church Inc.
Entrant
Stanley Church
Art Director
Patti Slade
Artist
Food for Thought
Client

581
SCI. Stanley Church Inc.
Entrant
Stanley Church
Art Director
Ray Barber
Artist
Food For Thought
Client

582
Törnbloms
Entrant
Jan Olson/ Björn Kristiansson
Art Directors
Margirinbolaget
Client

583
Joylene Carpenter
Entrant
Mort Fidler
Art Director
Ronson Corp.
Client

584
Zarney Graphic Artists
Entrant
Fred Boatman
Art Director
EKO Studios
Photographers
Rubbermaid Inc.
Client

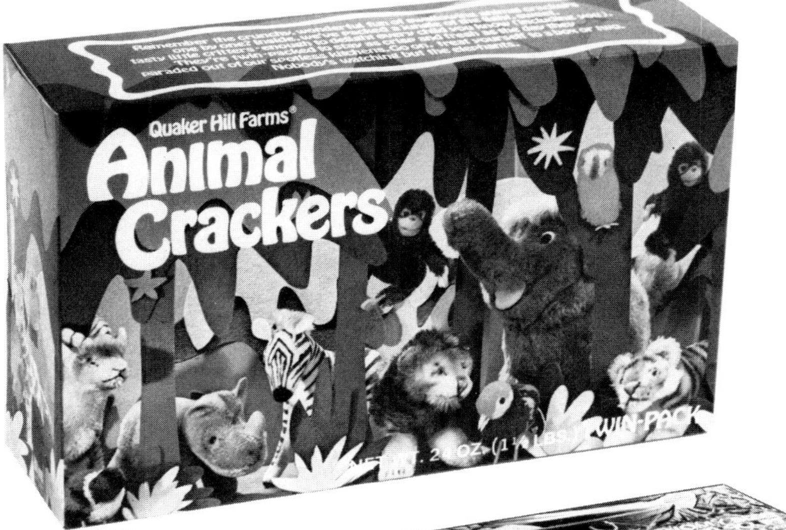
Quaker Hill Farms®
Animal Crackers

587

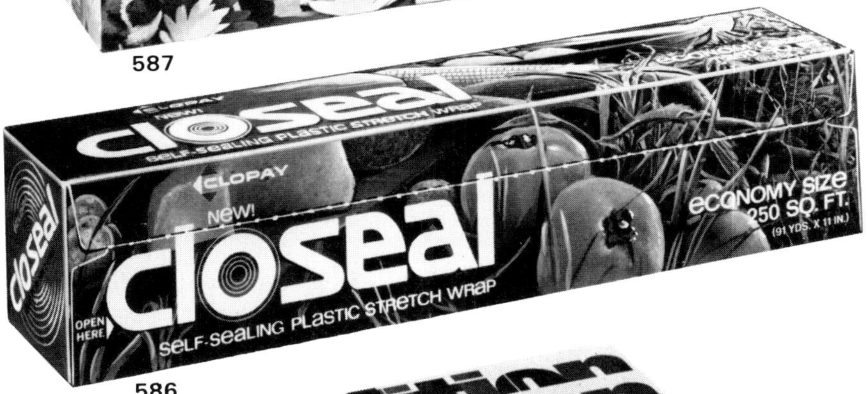
CLOPAY
NEW!
closeal
SELF-SEALING PLASTIC STRETCH WRAP
ECONOMY SIZE
250 SQ. FT.
(91 YDS. X 11 IN.)
OPEN HERE

586

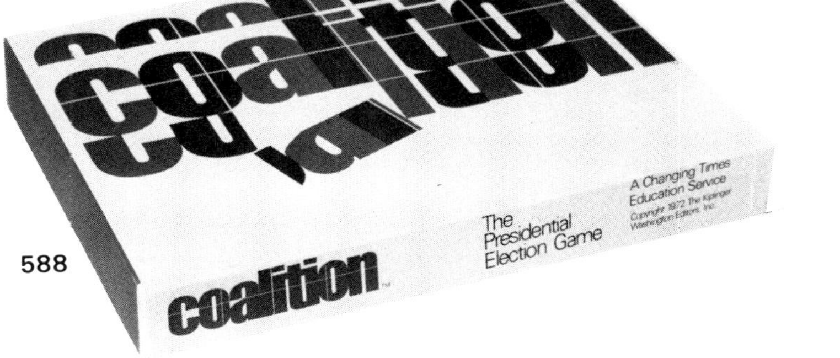
coalition
The Presidential Election Game
A Changing Times Education Service
coalition

588

585
Chartpak,
A Division of
Avery Products
Entrant
Jim Burns
Art Director

586
Clopay Corp.
Entrant
J.T. Wilder
Art Director
Frank Lucas,
David Diehl
Photographers
F. Hulefeld
Studio

587
SCI. Stanley
Church Inc.
Entrant
Stanley Church
Art Director
John McSherry
Photographer
Roy Barber
Type Design
Champion Paper
Package Div.,
Atlas Biscuit
Client

588
Donald A. Dean
Entrant
Changing Times
Education Service
Client

589

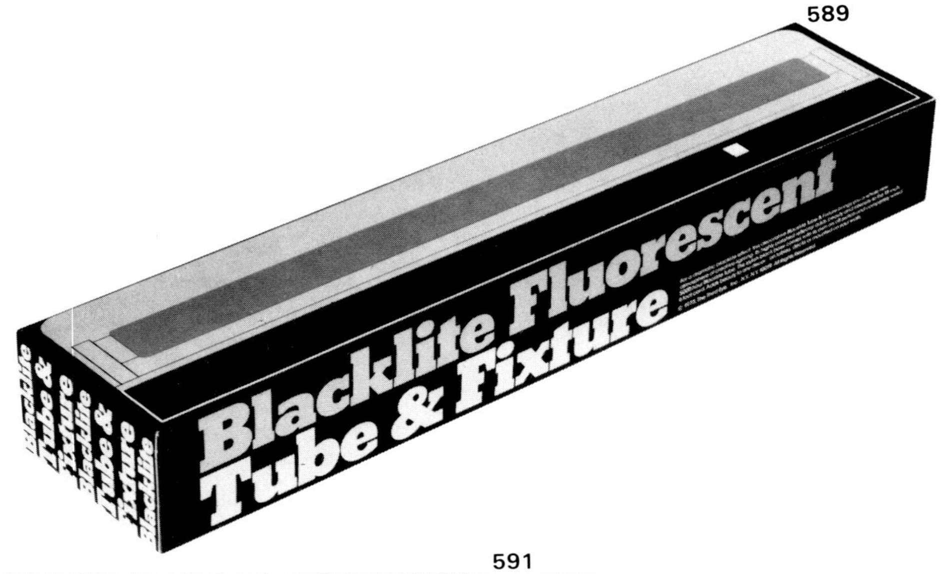
Blacklite Fluorescent
Tube & Fixture

590

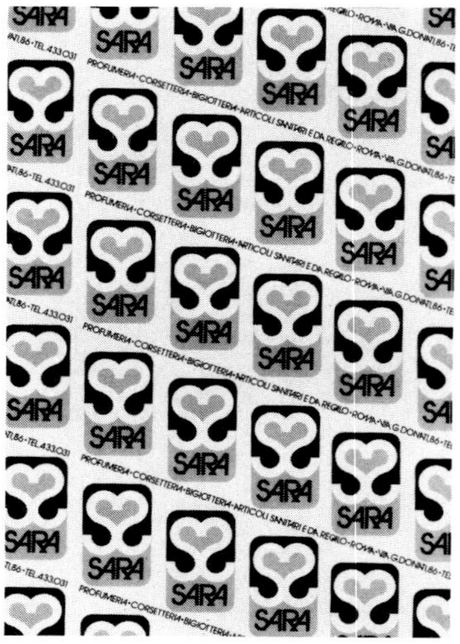
SARA

591

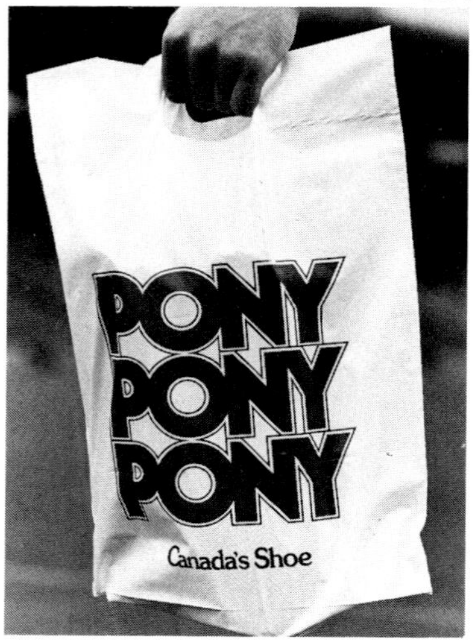
PONY
PONY
PONY
Canada's Shoe

592

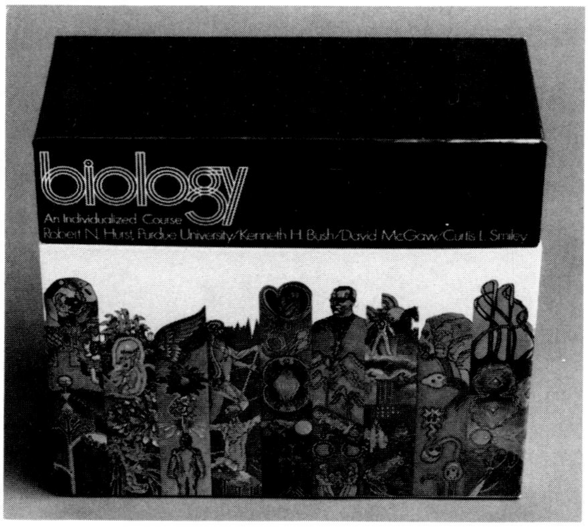
biology
An Individualized Course
Robert N. Hurst, Purdue University/Kenneth H. Bush/David McGaw/Curtis L. Smiley

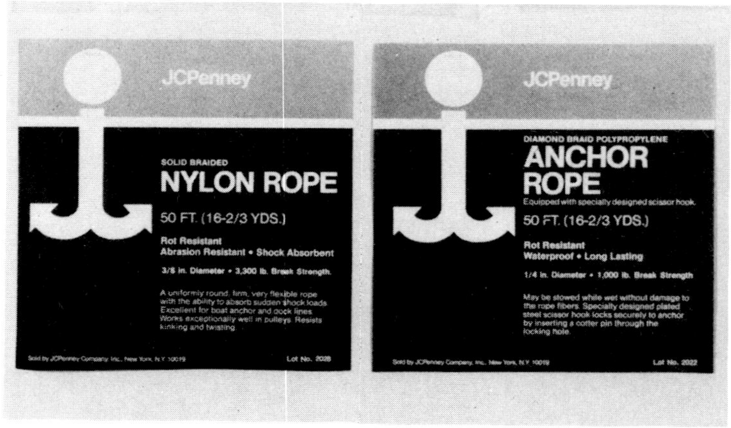
JCPenney
SOLID BRAIDED
NYLON ROPE
50 FT. (16-2/3 YDS.)
Rot Resistant
Abrasion Resistant • Shock Absorbent
JCPenney
DIAMOND BRAID POLYPROPYLENE
ANCHOR ROPE
Equipped with specially designed scissor hook.
50 FT. (16-2/3 YDS.)
Rot Resistant
Waterproof • Long Lasting

593

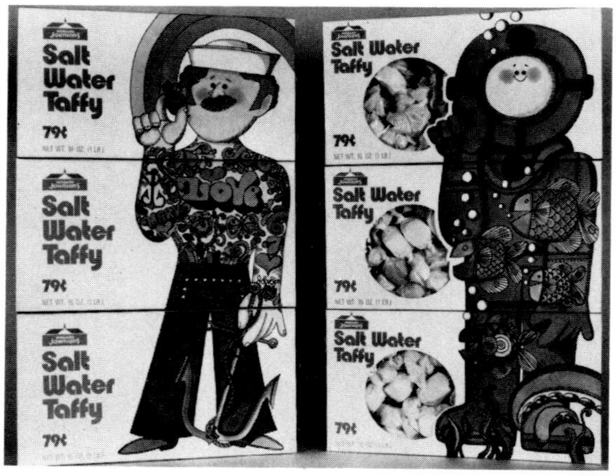
Salt Water Taffy
79¢

594

589
The Third Eye Inc. Entrant
Linda Brewer Art Director
John Brewer Illustrator

590
Rinaldo Cutini Entrant
SARA-Perfumes-Gifts Client

591
Typsettra Limited Entrant
John Lloyd Art Director
Terry O'Malley Copywriter
Vickers & Benson Ltd., Toronto Agency
Pony Sporting Goods Limited Client

592
William Weaver Entrant
Kindley-Lenowitz Studio
Designese Inc. Atlanta, Ga. Client

593
Dan Burch Entrant
Dan Burch Advertising Agency
Wellington Puritan Mills, Inc. Client

595

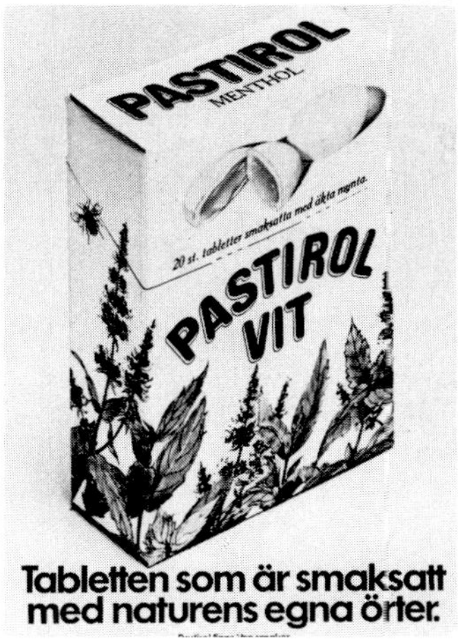
PASTIROL
MENTHOL
PASTIROL
VIT
Tabletten som är smaksatt
med naturens egna örter.

596

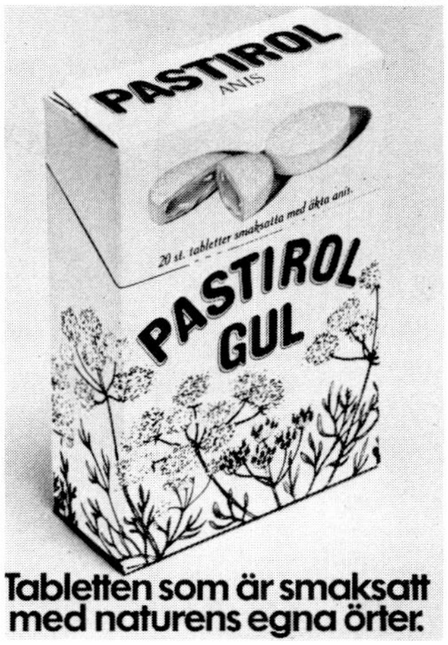
PASTIROL
ANIS
PASTIROL
GUL
Tabletten som är smaksatt
med naturens egna örter.

597

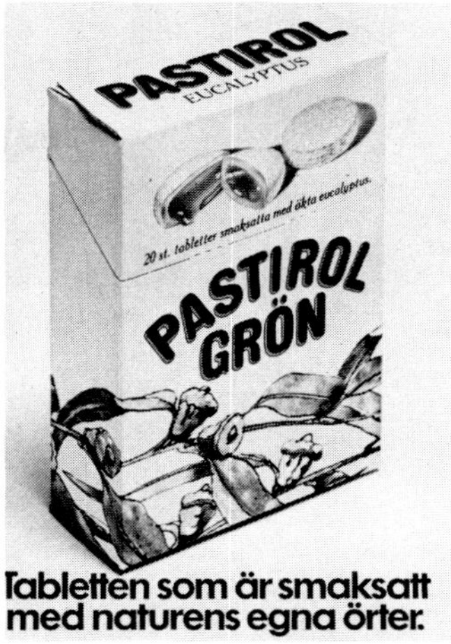
PASTIROL
EUCALYPTUS
PASTIROL
GRÖN
Tabletten som är smaksatt
med naturens egna örter.

598

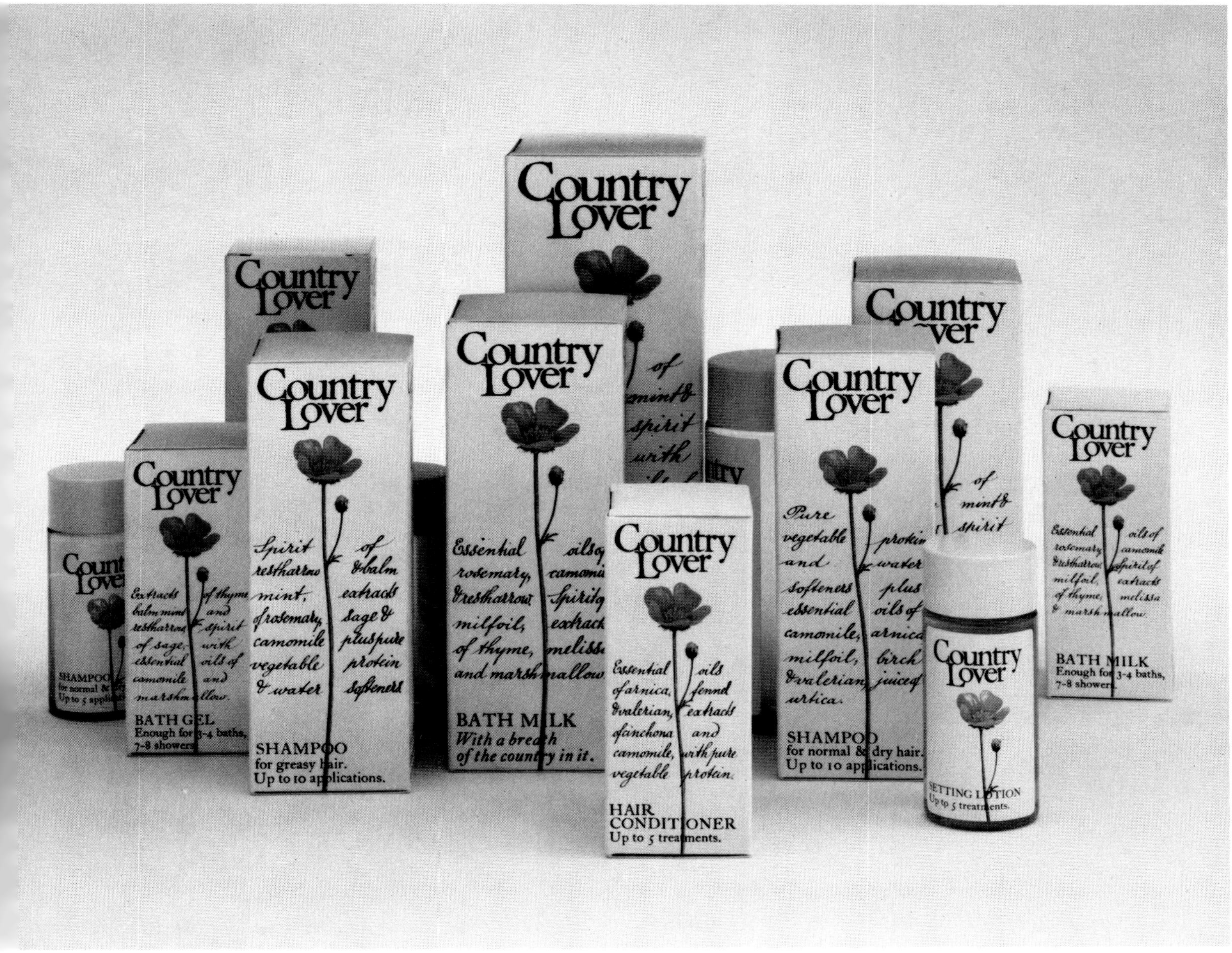
Country Lover
BATH MILK
With a breath of the country in it.
SHAMPOO
for greasy hair.
Up to 10 applications.
HAIR CONDITIONER
Up to 5 treatments.
SHAMPOO
for normal & dry hair.
Up to 10 applications.
SETTING LOTION
Up to 5 treatments.
BATH MILK
Enough for 3-4 baths, 7-8 showers.
BATH GEL

594
Gerstman + Meyers Inc. Entrant
R. Downing, R. Gerstman Art Directors
Jerry Dior Illustrator
Howard Johnson Company Client

595-597
Ericson & Co. AB Entrant
Saljolagsgruppen Client

598
Lloyd, Clark, Rowe Ltd. Entrant
Linda Butler/Kim Clark Art Directors
Norman Barber Illustrator
Country Lover Client

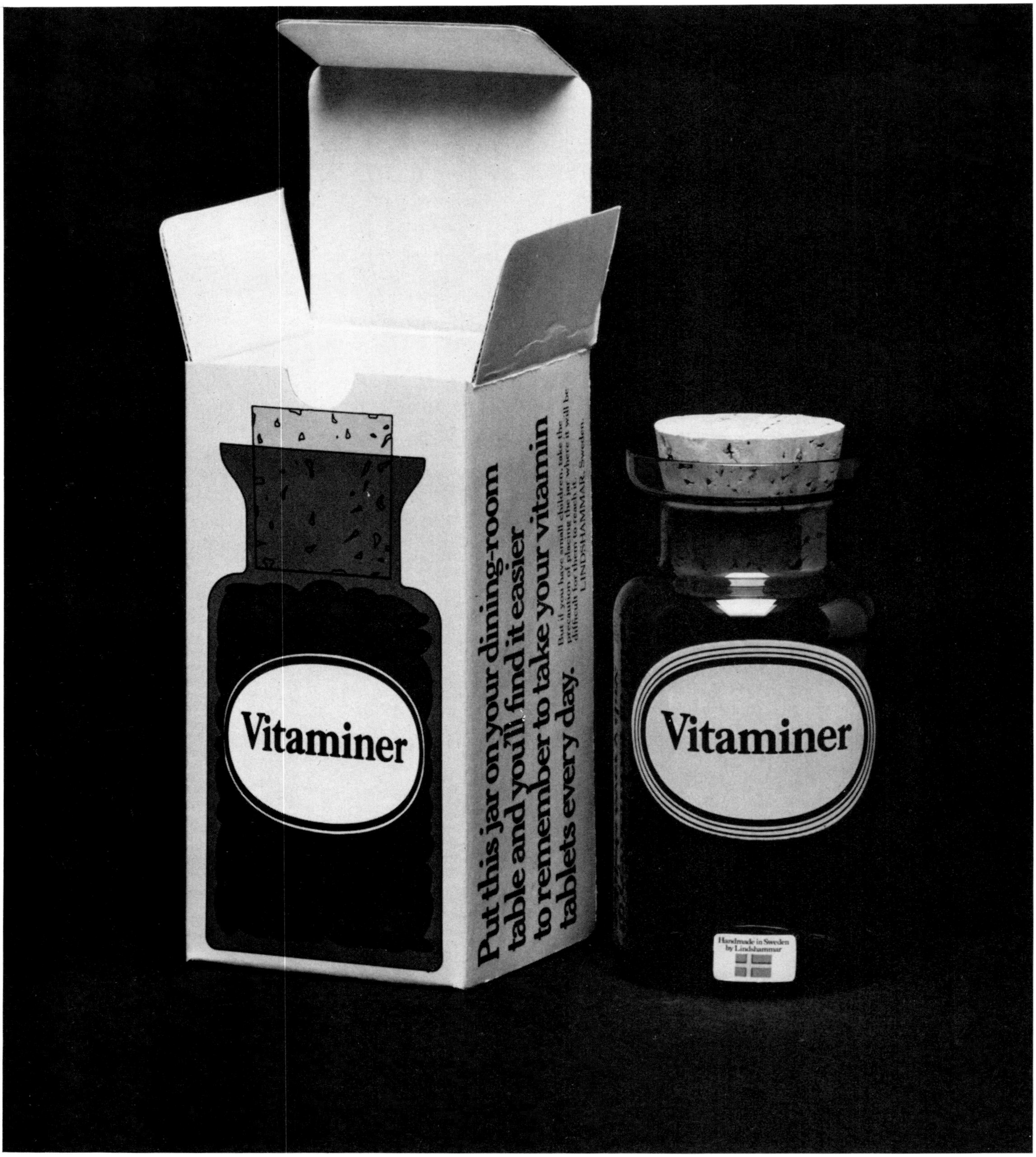
Vitaminer
Put this jar on your dining-room
table and you'll find it easier
to remember to take your vitamin
tablets every day.
But if you have small children, take the
precaution of placing the jar where it will be
difficult for them to reach it.
LINDSHAMMAR, Sweden.
Vitaminer
Handmade in Sweden
by Lindshammar

599
Ericson & Co. AB Entrant
Lindshammar Client

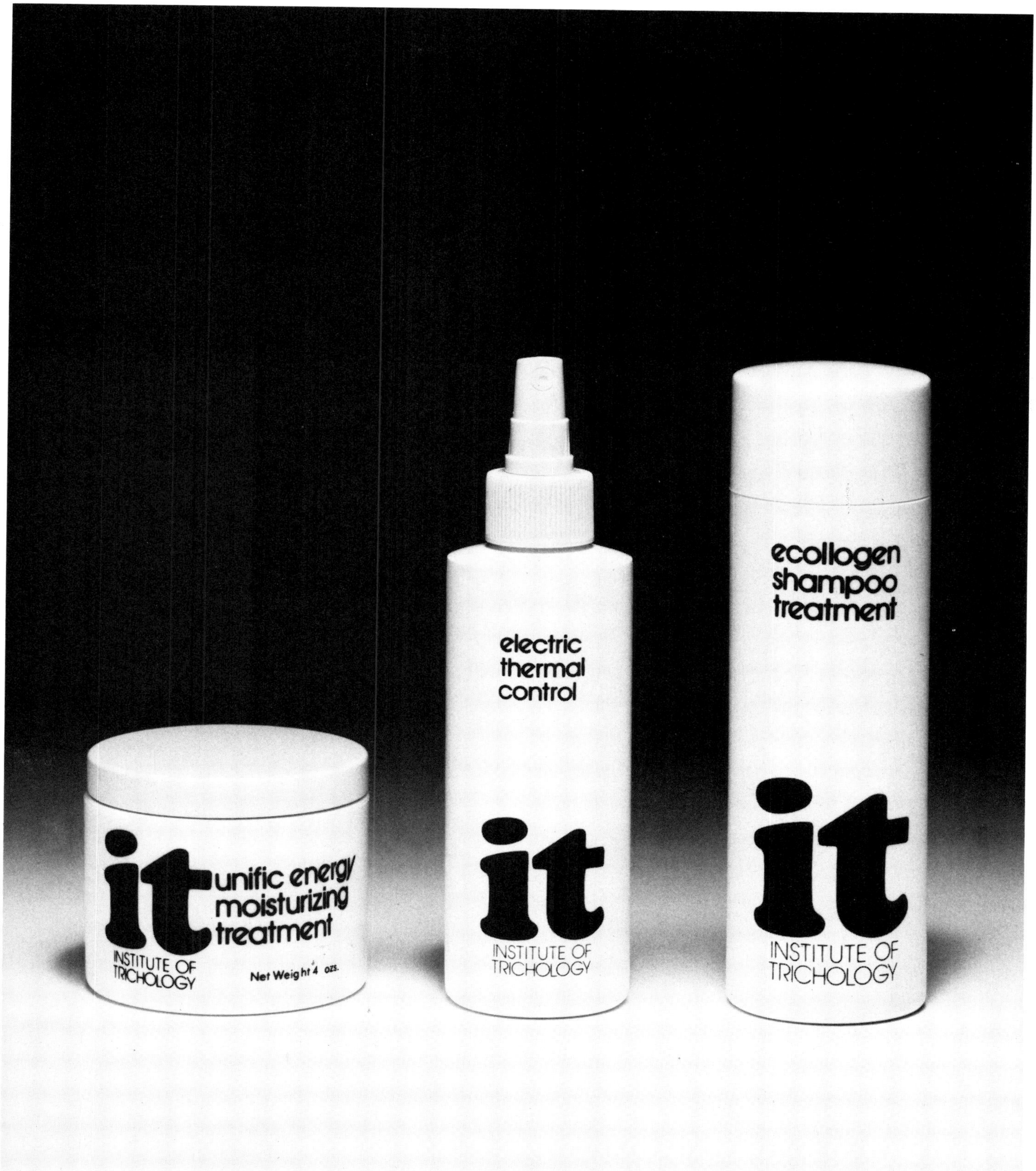
it
unific energy
moisturizing
treatment
INSTITUTE OF
TRICHOLOGY
Net Weight 4 ozs.
electric
thermal
control
it
INSTITUTE OF
TRICHOLOGY
ecollogen
shampoo
treatment
it
INSTITUTE OF
TRICHOLOGY

600
Joe Oliveri Entrant
Eric Vose Illustrator
Diagnostics & Designs Agency
Institute of Trichology Client

601

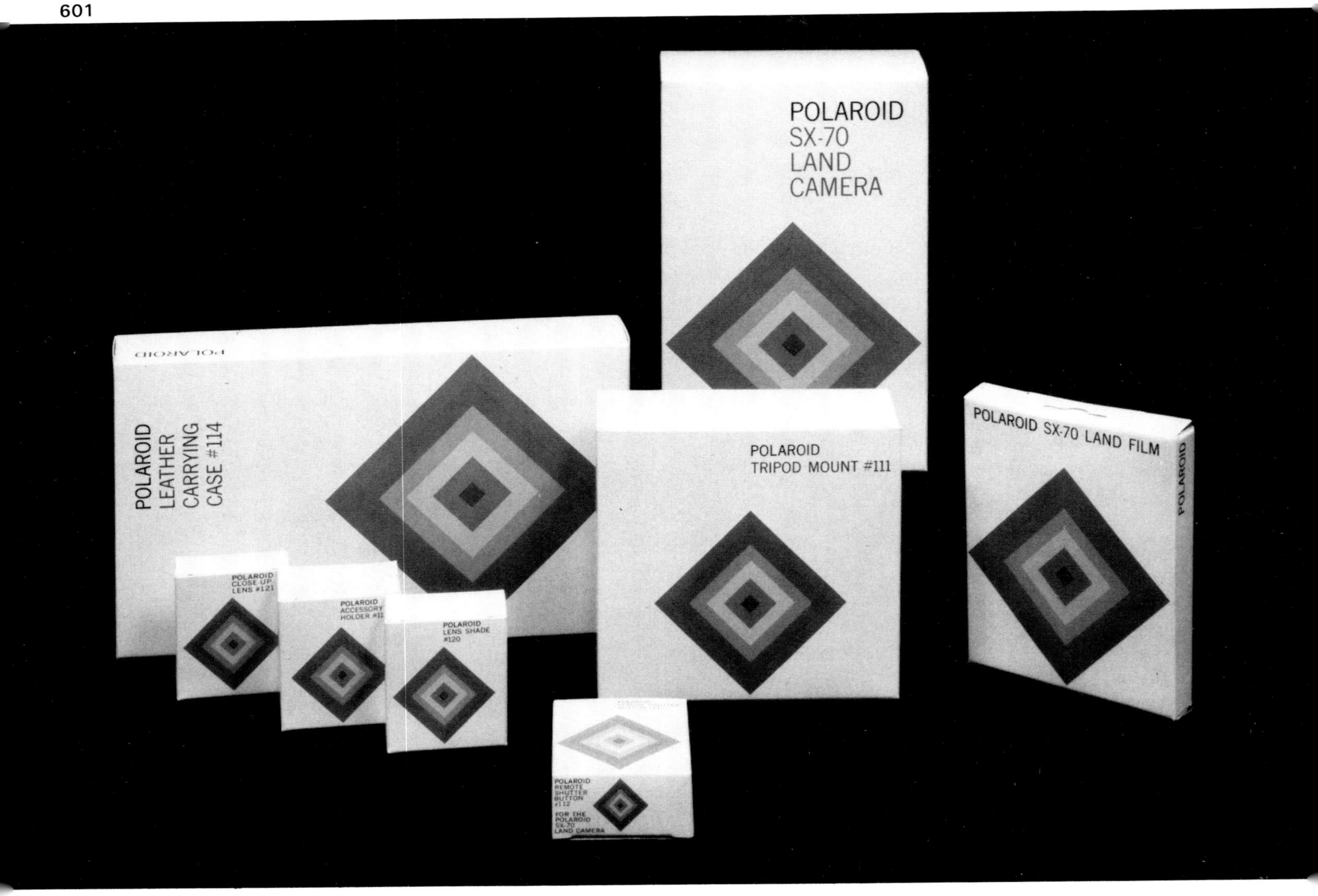
POLAROID
SX-70
LAND
CAMERA
POLAROID
LEATHER
CARRYING
CASE #114
POLAROID
TRIPOD MOUNT #111
POLAROID SX-70 LAND FILM
POLAROID
POLAROID
CLOSE-UP
LENS #121
POLAROID
ACCESSORY
HOLDER
POLAROID
LENS SHADE
#120
POLAROID
REMOTE
SHUTTER
BUTTON
#112
FOR THE
POLAROID
SX-70
LAND CAMERA

601
Polaroid Corporation Entrant
William Field, Paul Giambarba Art Directors

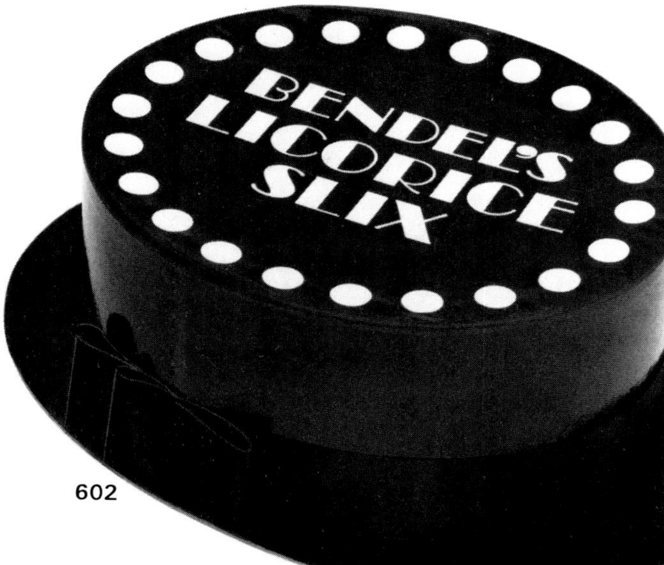
BENDEL'S
LICORICE
SLIX

602

603

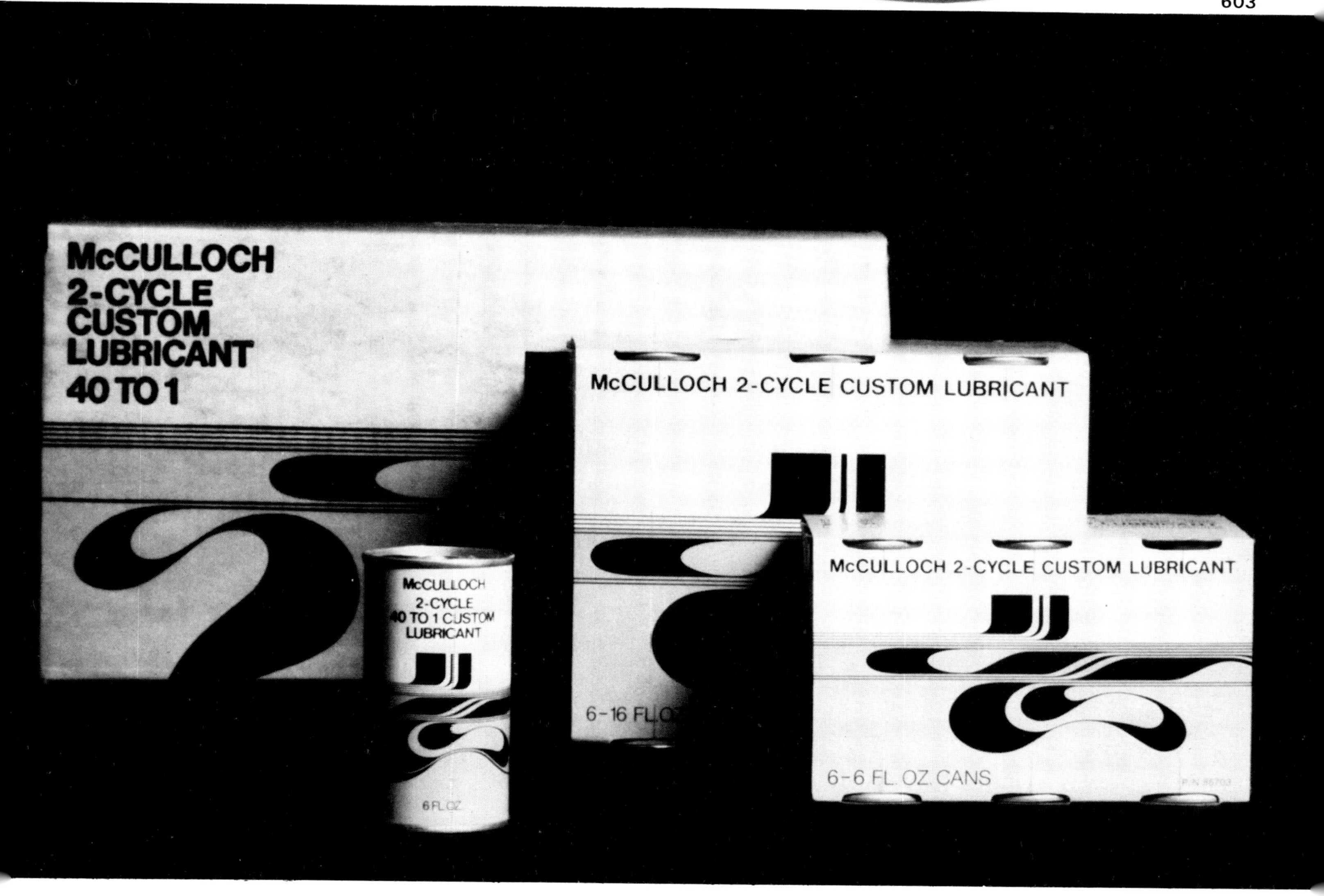
McCULLOCH
2-CYCLE
CUSTOM
LUBRICANT
40 TO 1
McCULLOCH 2-CYCLE CUSTOM LUBRICANT
McCULLOCH 2-CYCLE CUSTOM LUBRICANT
McCULLOCH
2-CYCLE
40 TO 1 CUSTOM
LUBRICANT
6 FL. OZ.
6-16 FL. OZ
6-6 FL. OZ. CANS

602
SCI. Stanley Church, Inc. Entrant
Stanley Church Art Director
Patti Slade Designer
Food for Thought Client

603
Weller & Juett Inc. Entrant
Don Weller Art Director
Don Weller, Jim Van Noy Illustrators
McCulloch Corp. Client

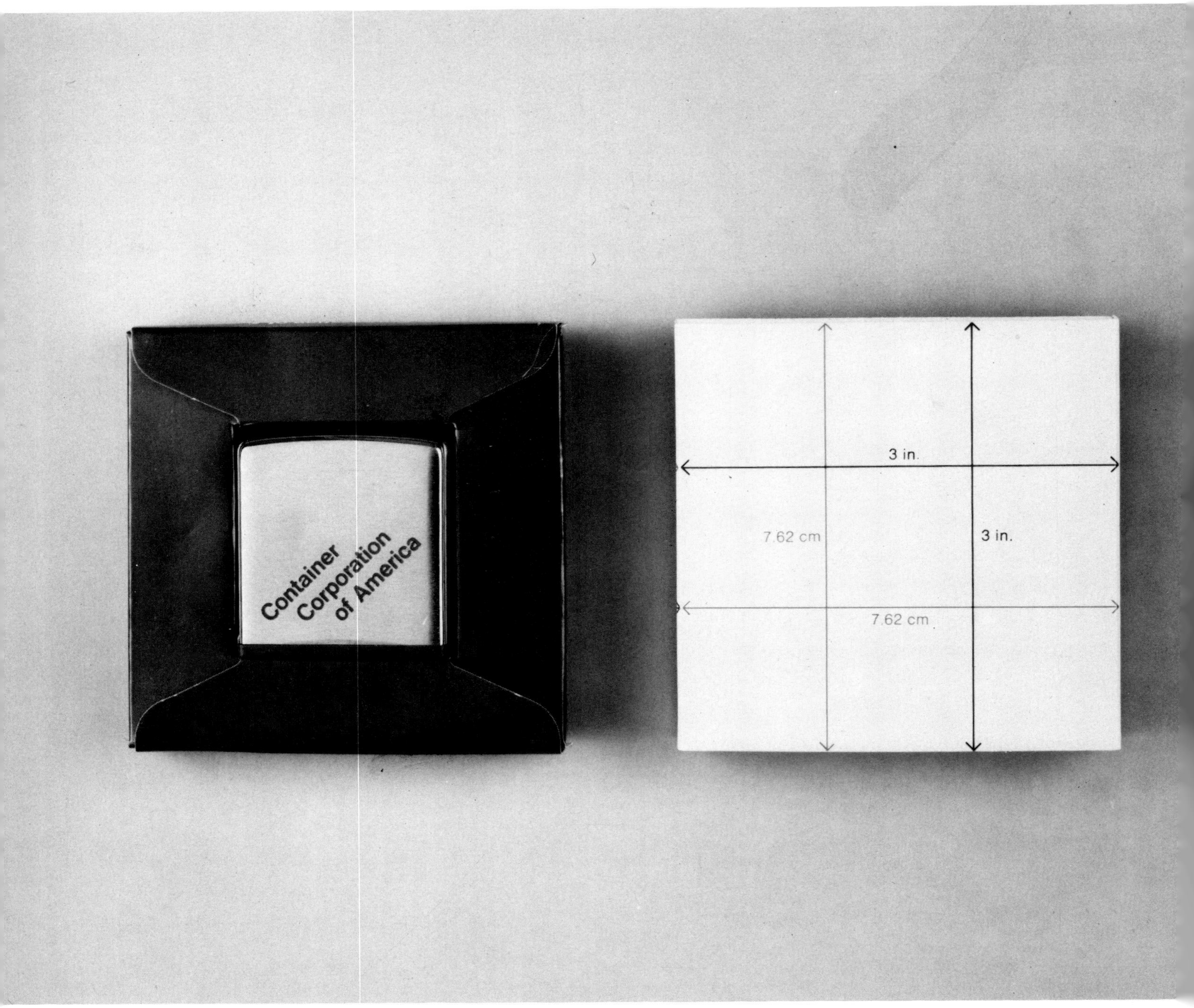
Container
Corporation
of America
3 in.
7.62 cm
3 in.
7.62 cm

604
Container Corp. of America Entrant
R.E. Loth, Bill Bonnell Art Directors

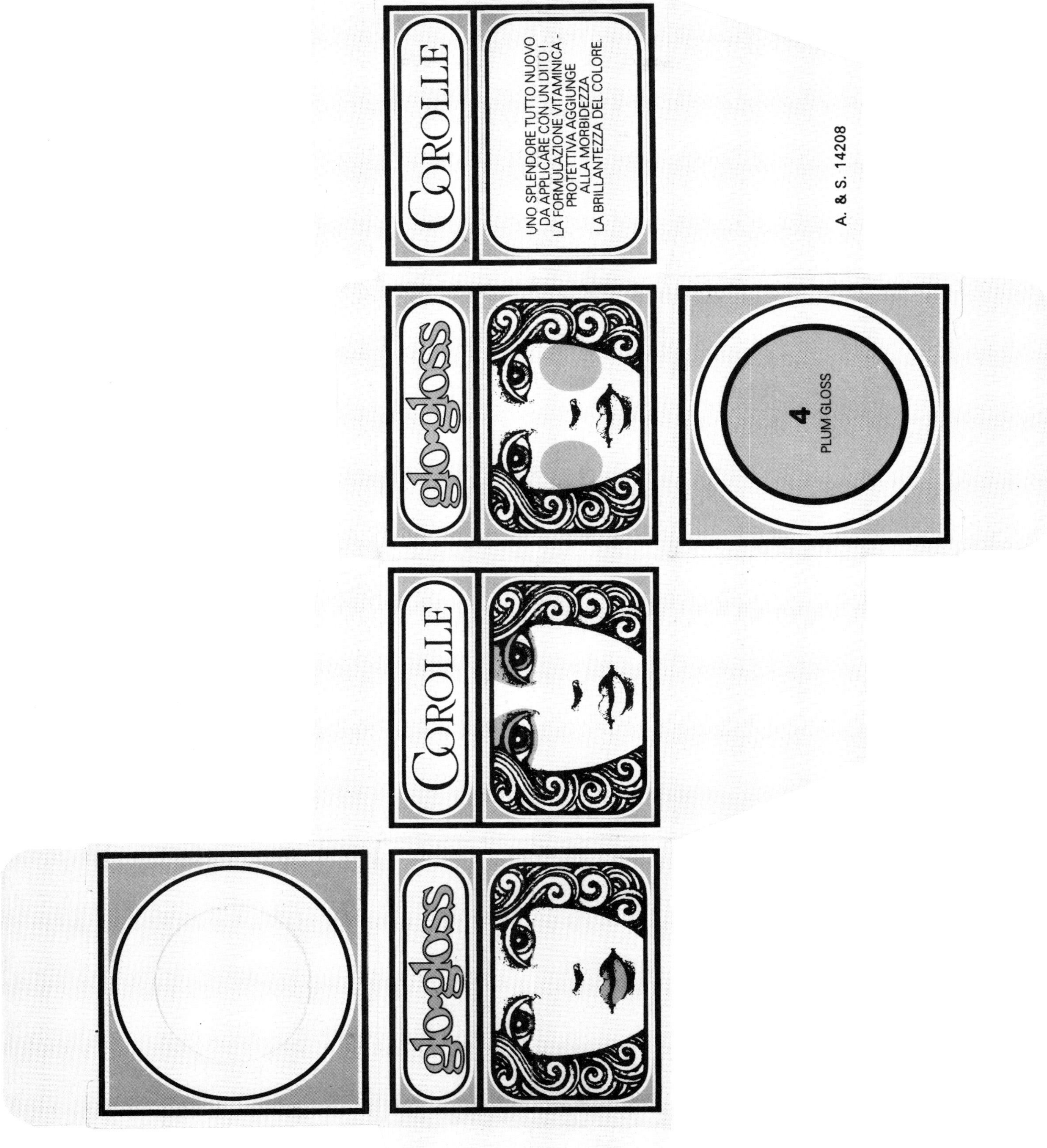
COROLLE
UNO SPLENDORE TUTTO NUOVO
DA APPLICARE CON UN DITO !
LA FORMULAZIONE VITAMINICA -
PROTETTIVA AGGIUNGE
ALLA MORBIDEZZA
LA BRILLANTEZZA DEL COLORE.
A. & S. 14208
glo-gloss
4
PLUM GLOSS
COROLLE
glo-gloss

605
Lubalin, Delpire Cie. Entrant
Annegret Beier Art Director
John Alcorn Illustrator
Delpire-Advico Agency
Corolle Client

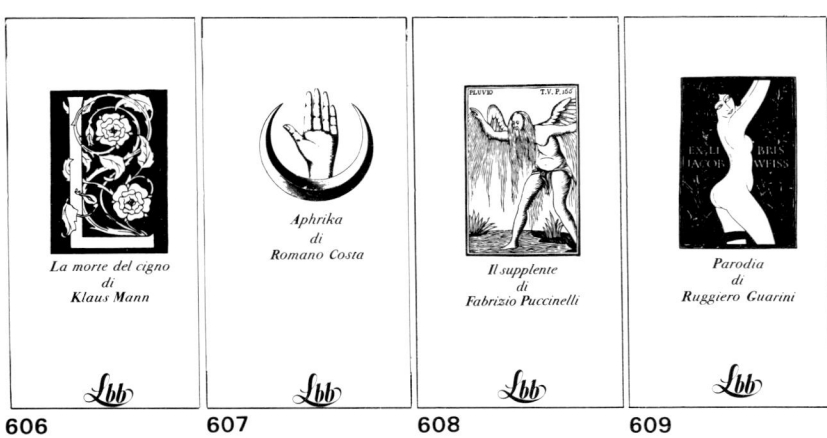

La morte del cigno
di
Klaus Mann
Lbb

606

Aphrika
di
Romano Costa
Lbb

607

Il supplente
di
Fabrizio Puccinelli
Lbb

608

Parodia
di
Ruggiero Guarini
Lbb

609

before you do anything else . . . relax
loosen up
float
disappear
don't think for a while. just feel . . .
you're inside a drop of water and it's drawing out
. . . slowly
you're a m e l t i n g candle
you're a feather floating gently to the ground
an iceberg gradually melting into the sea
a flower slowly withering
very tired and falling asleep
10
11

610

stretch your image of yourself
begin to see all the different people you are
and all the different people you could be
turn yourself into another person for a few minutes
imagine what it would be like to be . . .
16
17

611

I. ARE YOU READY FOR IMPROVISATION?
You are if you are in touch with your senses and your imagination. It isn't hard to be that way — it's just that a lot of people forget about their five senses and imagine they don't have an imagination. Really, all you have to do is . . .
get in touch with your senses
touch your imagination
8
9

612

OPEN
END
(a sourcebook for improvisation)

613

LE
KARABA

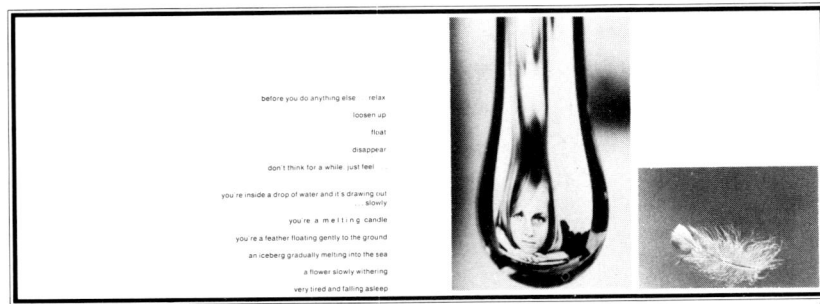

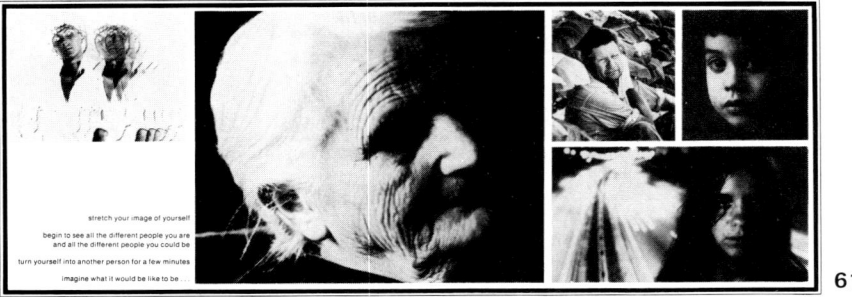

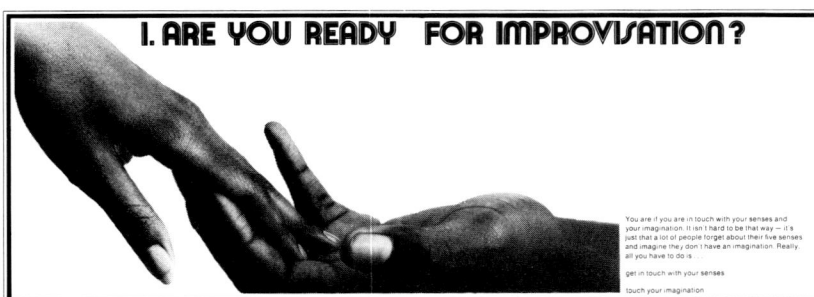

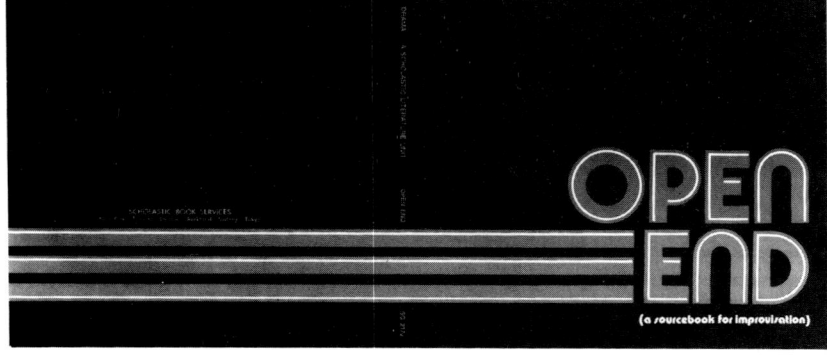

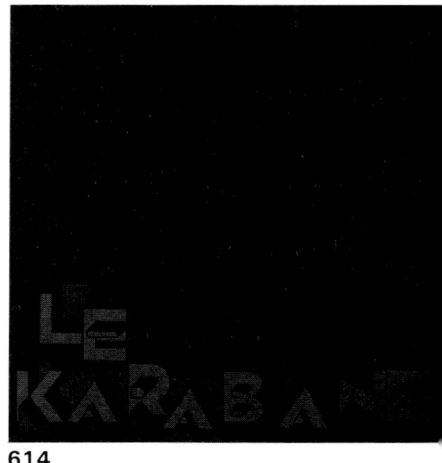

614

606-609
Franco Ricci Entrant

610-613
Pat Wosczyk
Entrant
Bonnie Bishop
Art Director
Scholastic Magazines Inc
Agency

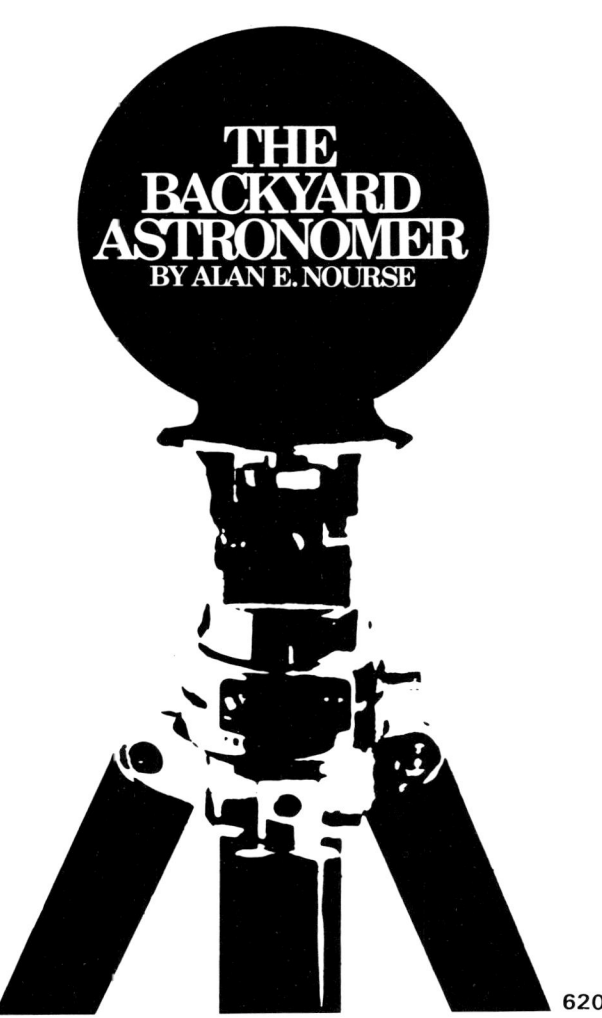

THE
BACKYARD
ASTRONOMER
BY ALAN E. NOURSE

620

MARCUS
GARVEY
DANIEL S. DAVIS

615

The School Newspaper
HOW IT WORKS, HOW TO WRITE FOR IT
BY NANCI A. LYMAN
Illustrated With Photographs

616

617

CHARLES NEIDER
THE AUTHENTIC
DEATH OF
HENDRY JONES
INTRODUCTION BY WIRT WILLIAMS
THIS MAY BE THE GREATEST
WESTERN EVER WRITTEN.

618

PROBLEMS
IN LATIN
AMERICAN
HISTORY
THE MODERN PERIOD
JOSEPH S. TULCHIN

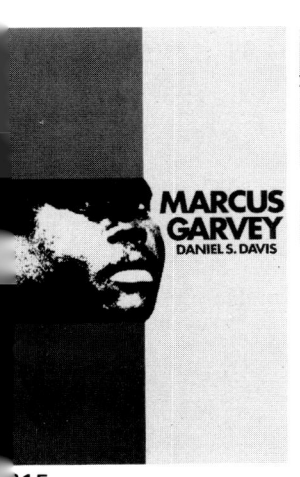

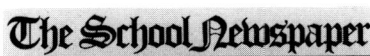

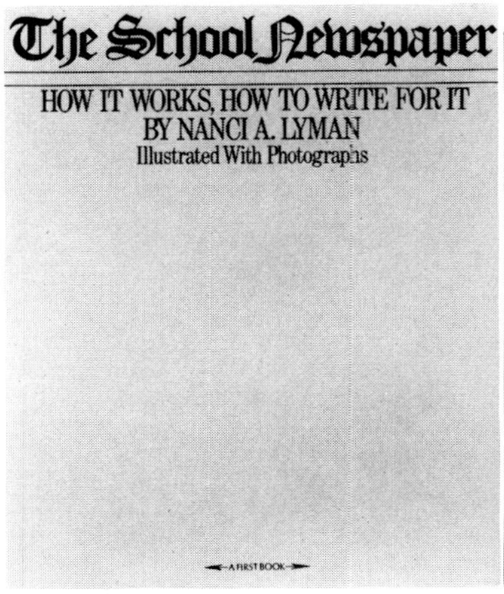

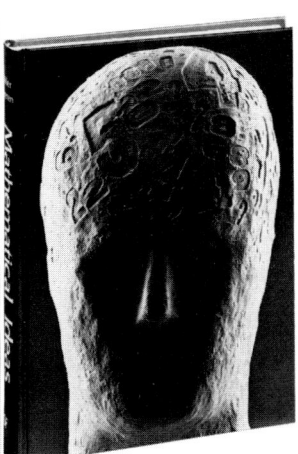

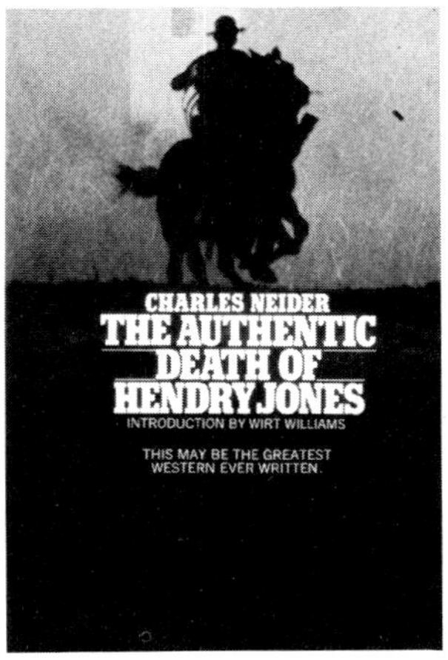

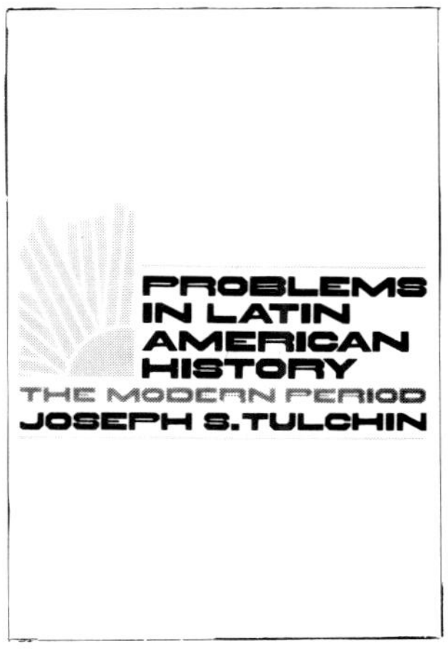

619

614
Lubalin, Delpire & Co. Entrant
Annegret Beier Art Director
Francis Peneaud Letterer
Delpire Advico Agency
Meridien Hotels —Dakar Client

615
Franklin Watts, Inc. Entrant
Judie Mills Art Director

616
Franklin Watts, Inc. Entrant
Judie Mills Art Director
One + One Studio Studio

617
Free Chin Entrant
Hal Kearney Art Director
Scott, Foresman & Co. Client

618
One + One Studio Entrant
Catherine Hopkins Art Director
Harper & Row, Publishers Client

619
Lawrence Daniels & Friends, Inc. Entrant
Larry Daniels Art Director
Harper & Row, Publishers Client

620
Franklin Watts, Inc. Entrant
Judie Mills Art Director
One + One Studio Studio

621

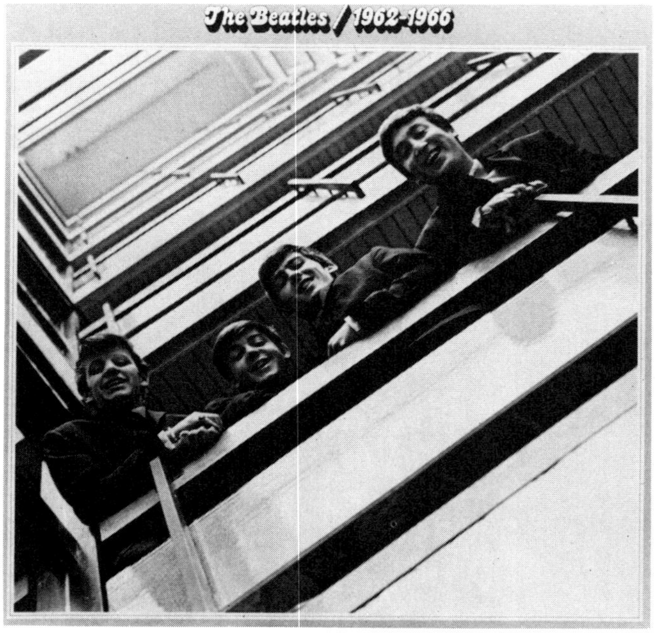
The Beatles / 1962-1966

622

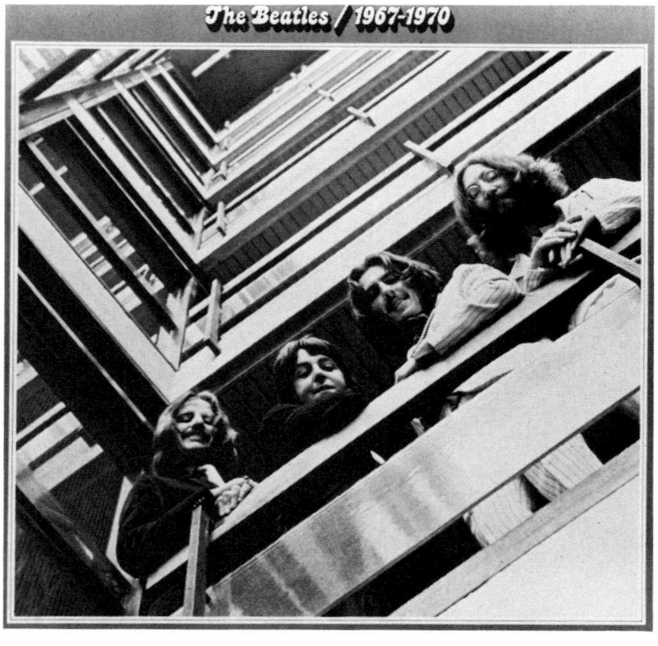
The Beatles / 1967-1970

621-622
Wilkes & Braun, Inc. Entrant
Tom Wilkes Art Director
Apple Records Client

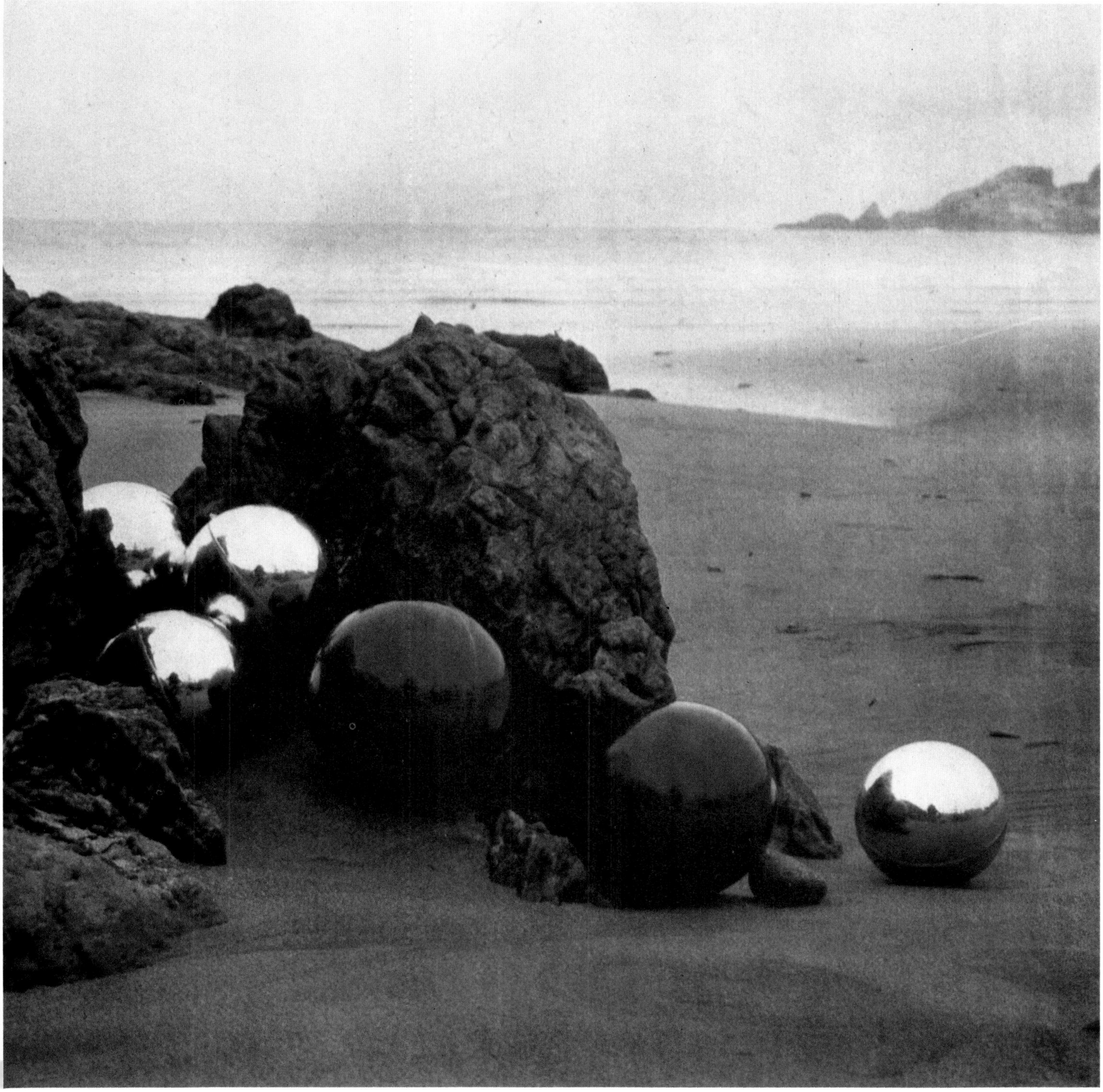

623
Claude Dieterich Entrant
Casal's Studio Studio
IEMPSA Client

624

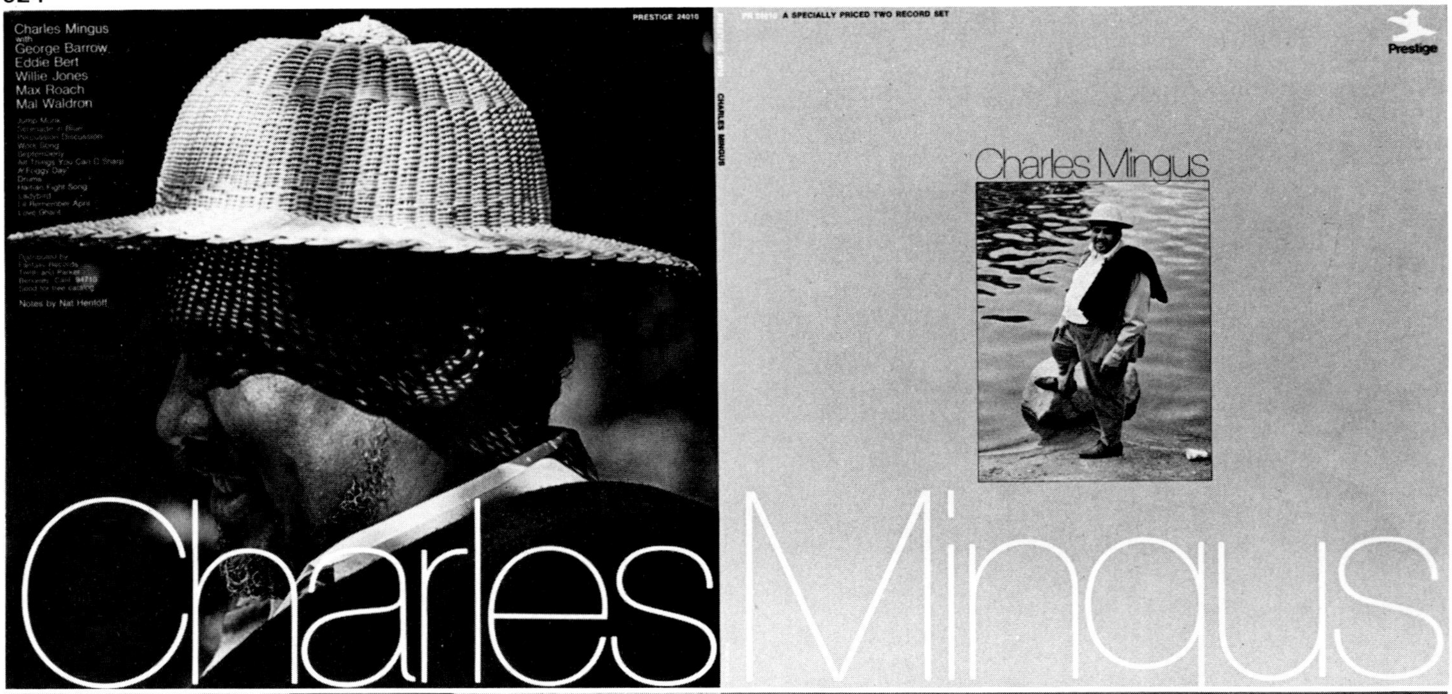
Charles Mingus
with
George Barrow
Eddie Bert
Willie Jones
Max Roach
Mal Waldron
Notes by Nat Hentoff
PRESTIGE 24010
CHARLES MINGUS
A SPECIALLY PRICED TWO RECORD SET
Prestige
Charles Mingus
Charles Mingus

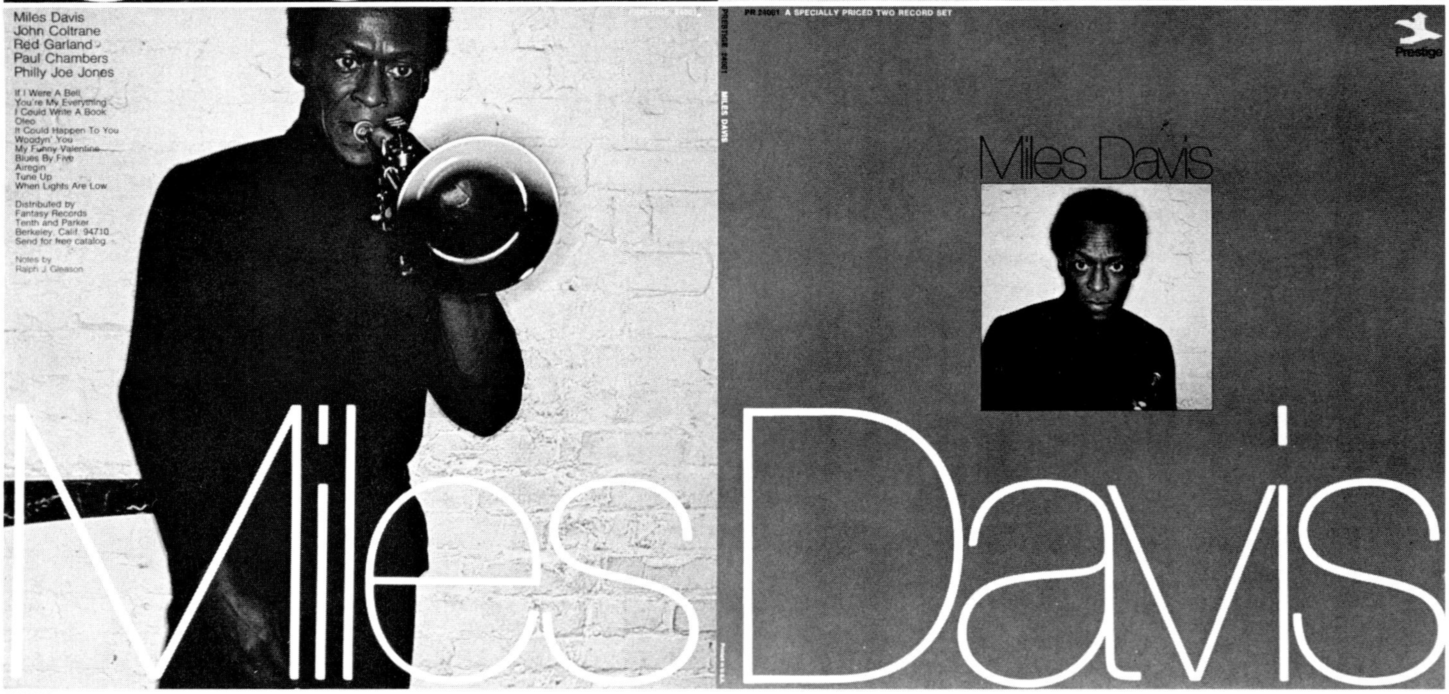
Miles Davis
John Coltrane
Red Garland
Paul Chambers
Philly Joe Jones
If I Were A Bell
You're My Everything
I Could Write A Book
Oleo
It Could Happen To You
Woodyn' You
My Funny Valentine
Blues By Five
Airegin
Tune Up
When Lights Are Low
Distributed by
Fantasy Records
Tenth and Parker
Berkeley, Calif. 94710
Send for free catalog
Notes by
Ralph J. Gleason
PRESTIGE 24001
MILES DAVIS
PR 24001 A SPECIALLY PRICED TWO RECORD SET
Prestige
Miles Davis
Miles Davis

625

626

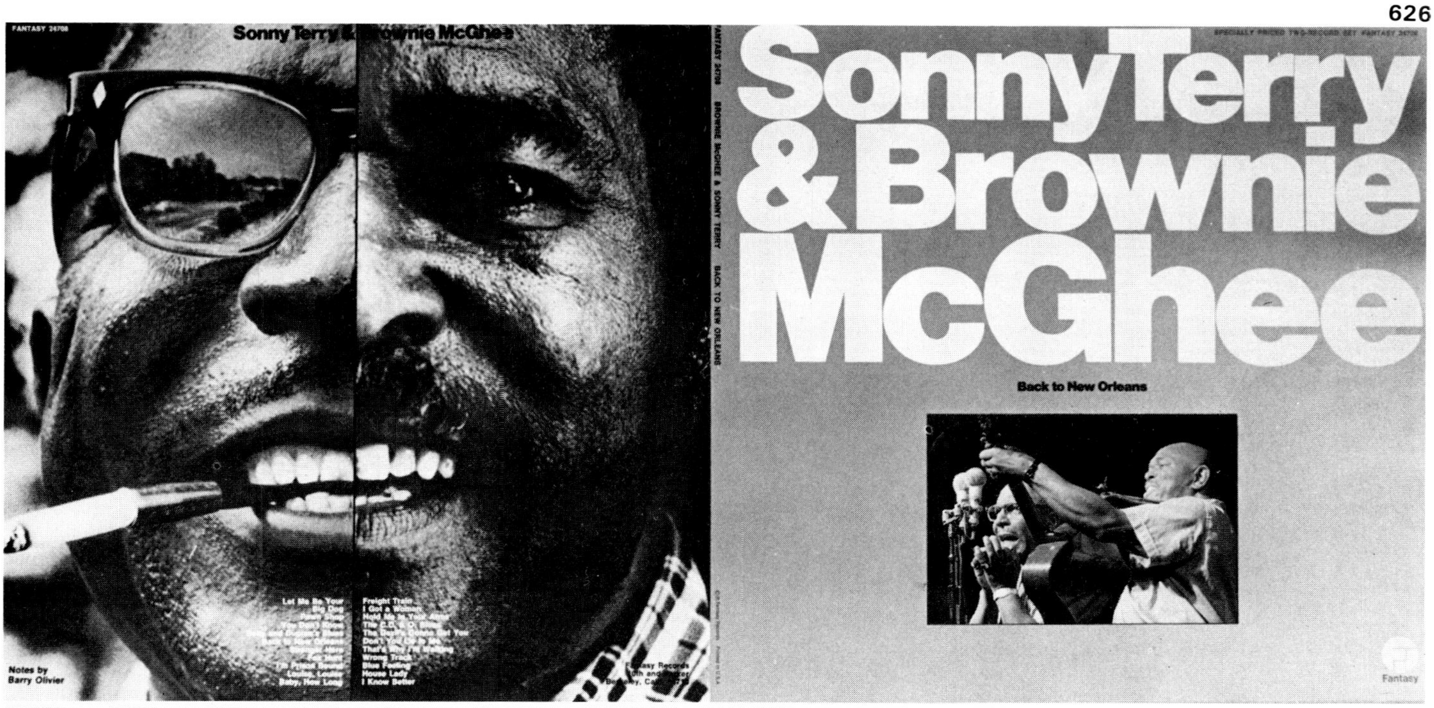
FANTASY 24708
Sonny Terry & Brownie McGhee
Notes by
Barry Olivier
Sonny Terry
& Brownie
McGhee
Back to New Orleans
Fantasy

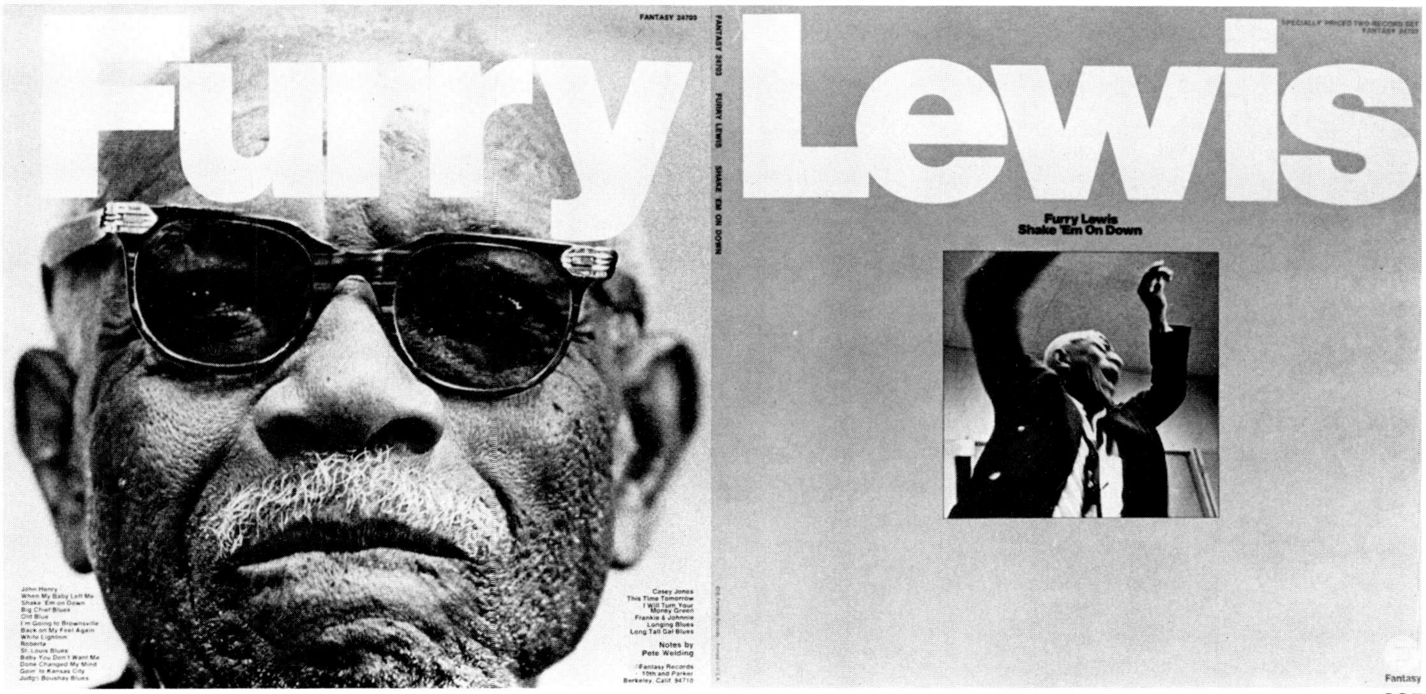
FANTASY 24703
Furry
Lewis
Furry Lewis
Shake 'Em On Down
Notes by
Pete Welding
Fantasy

627

624-627
Tony Lane Entrant
Tony Lane Art Director
Jim Marshall Illustrator
Tony Lane, Lee Friedlander Photographers
Fantasy/Prestige/Milestone Records Clients

628

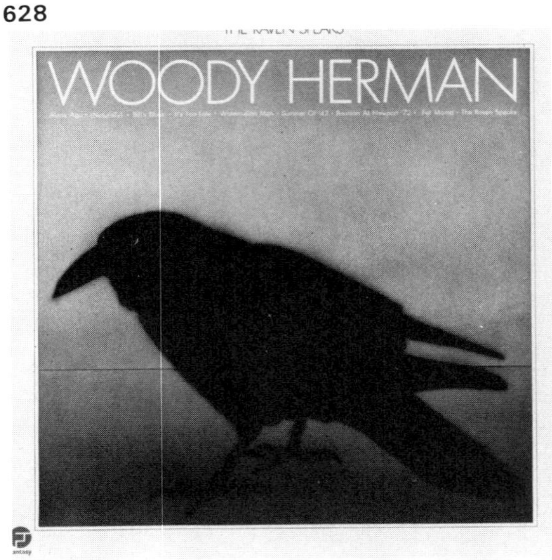
WOODY HERMAN

629

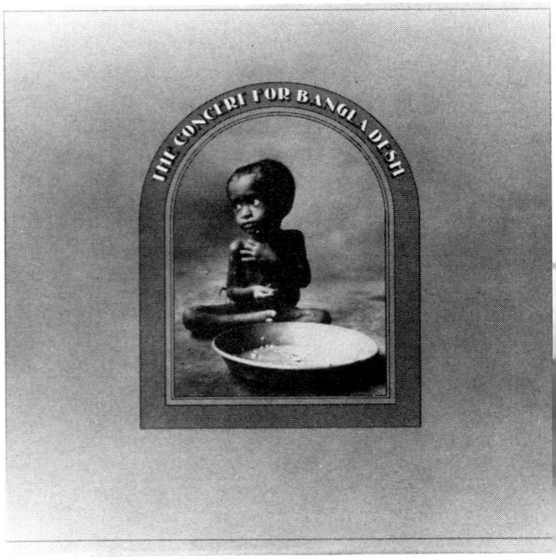
THE CONCERT FOR BANGLA DESH

631

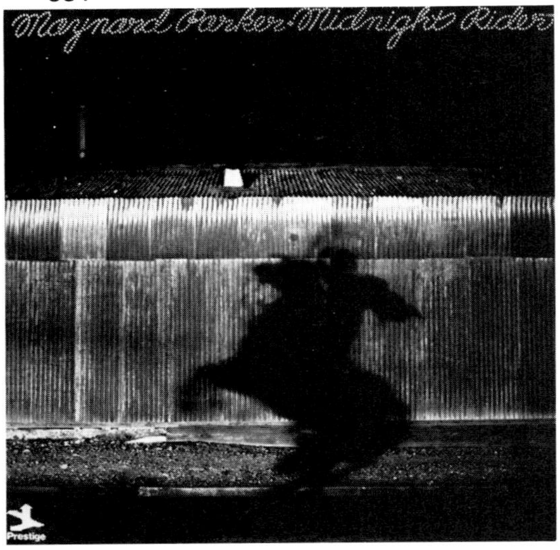
Maynard Parker · Midnight Rider
Prestige

630

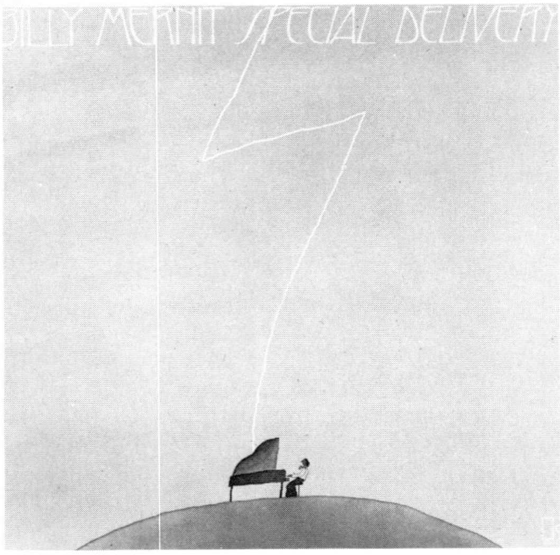
BILLY MERNIT SPECIAL DELIVERY

632

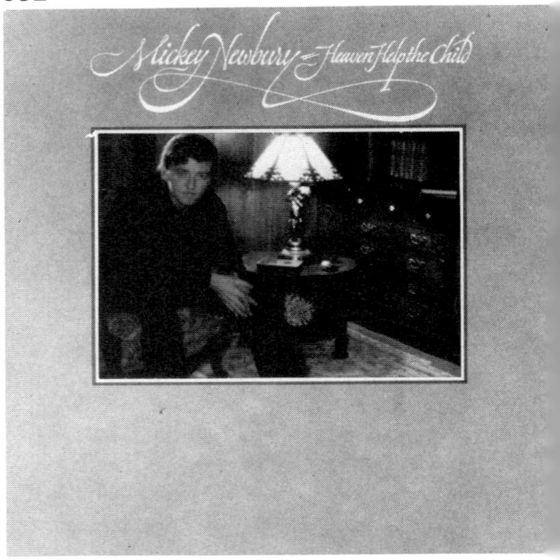
Mickey Newbury — Heaven Help the Child

633

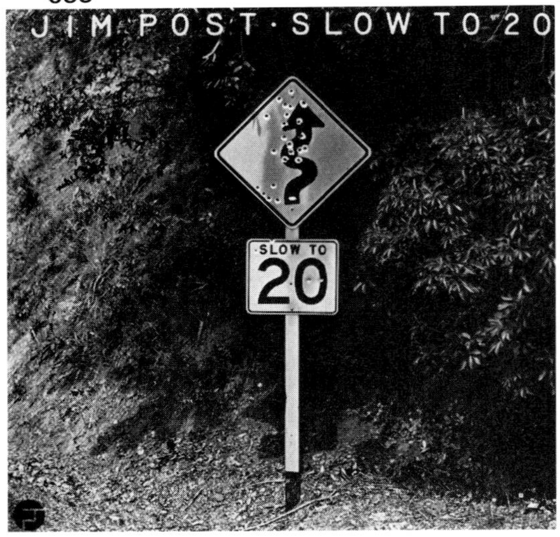
JIM POST · SLOW TO 20
SLOW TO
20

634

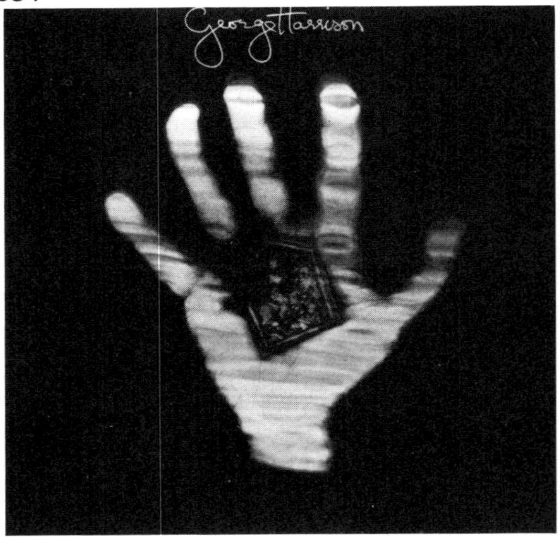
George Harrison

635

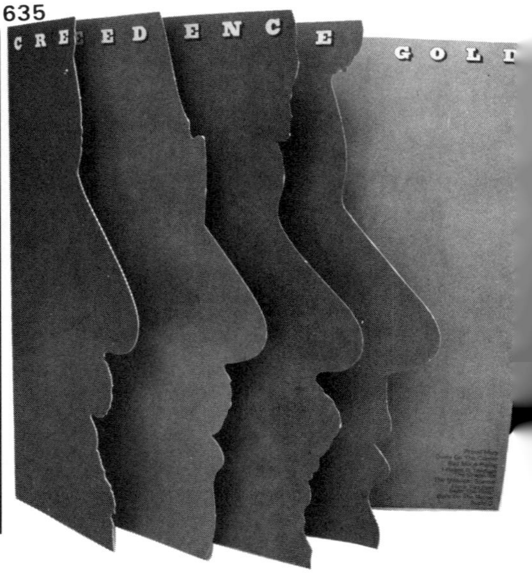
C R E E D E N C E

628
Tony Lane
Entrant
Fantasy/Prestige/ Milestone Records
Clients

629
Wilkes & Braun, Inc.
Entrant
Tom Wilkes
Art Director
Apple Records
Client

630
Elektra Records
Entrant
Robert L. Heimall
Art Director
Guy Billout
Illustrator

631
Tony Lane
Entrant
Fantasy/Prestige/ Milestone Records
Clients

632
Elektra Records
Entrant
Robert L. Heimall
Art Director

633
Tony Lane
Entrant
Fantasy/Prestige/ Milestone Records
Clients

636

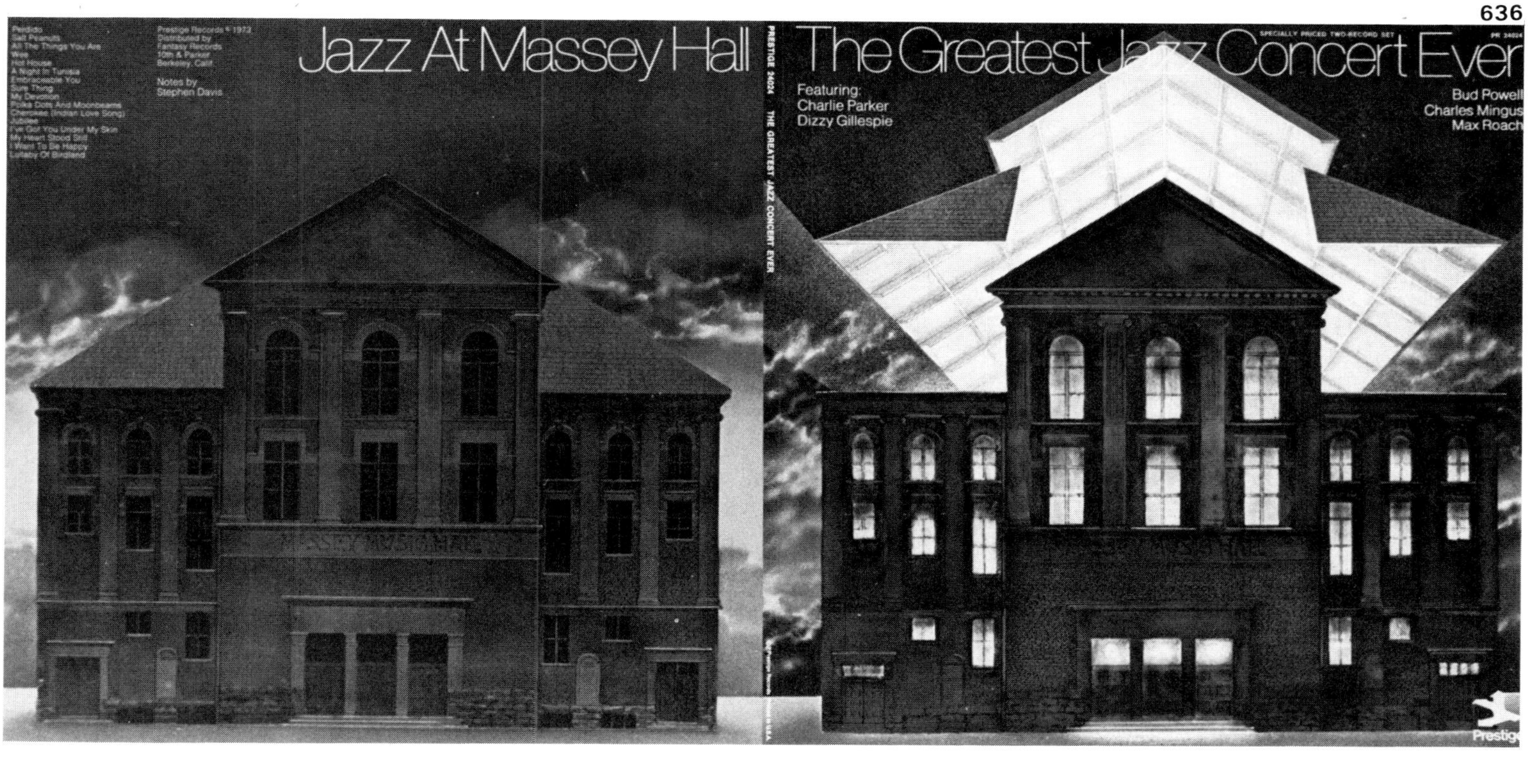

Notes by
Stephen Davis
Jazz At Massey Hall
PRESTIGE 24024 THE GREATEST JAZZ CONCERT EVER
SPECIALLY PRICED TWO-RECORD SET
PR 24024
The Greatest Jazz Concert Ever
Featuring:
Charlie Parker
Dizzy Gillespie
Bud Powell
Charles Mingus
Max Roach
Prestige

634
Wilkes & Braun, Inc. Entrant
Tom Wilkes
Art Director
Kendall Johnson, Ken Marcus
Photographers
Apple Records
Client

635
Tony Lane
Entrant
Fantasy/Prestige/ Milestone Records
Clients

636
Tony Lane
Entrant
Philip Carroll
Illustrator
Fantasy/Prestige/ Milestone Records
Clients

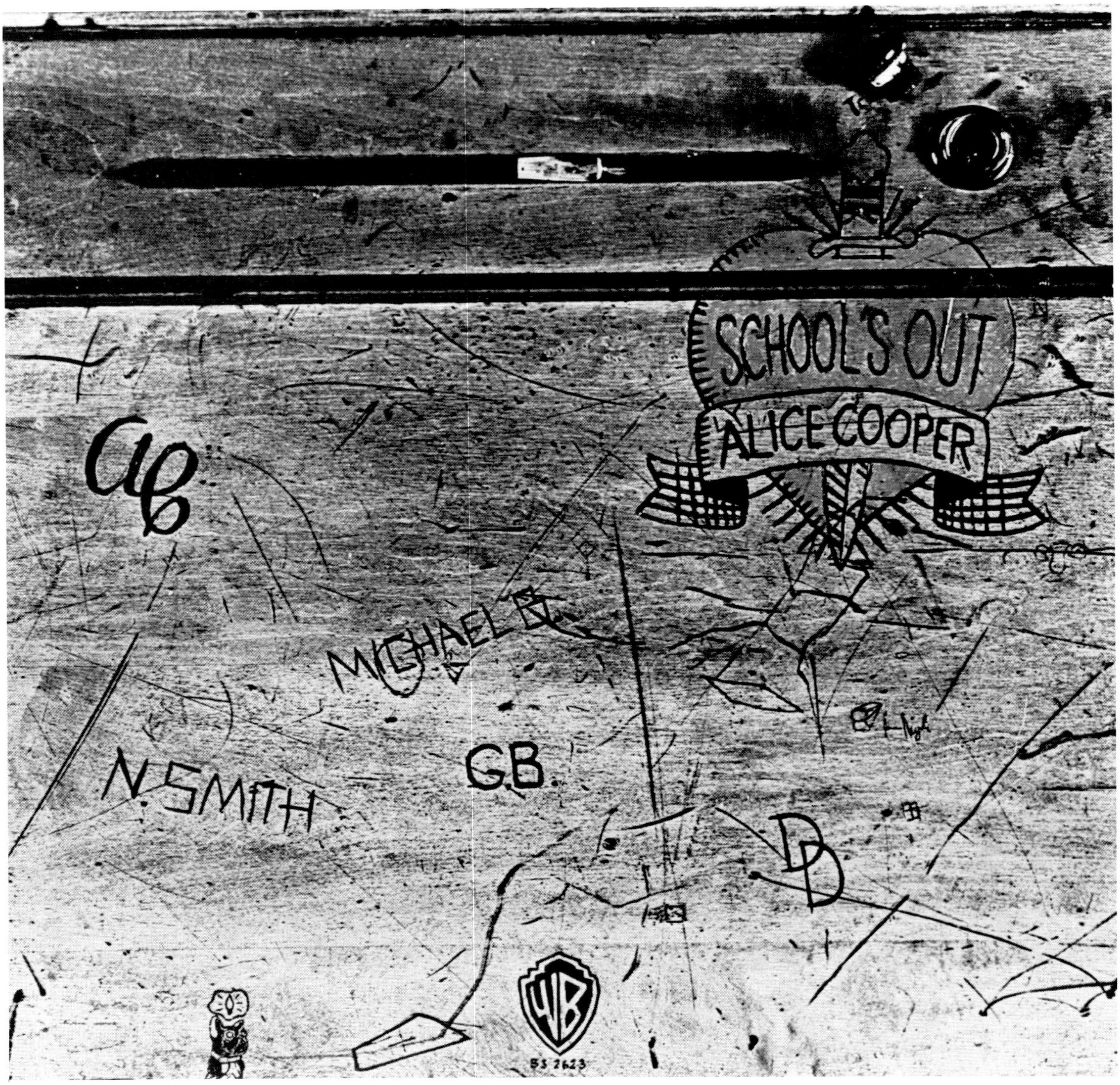
SCHOOL'S OUT
ALICE COOPER
MICHAEL B.
N.SMITH
GB
DD
BS 2623

637
Wilkes & Braun, Inc. Entrant
Craig Braun Art Director
Robert Otter Photographer
Warner Bros. Records Client

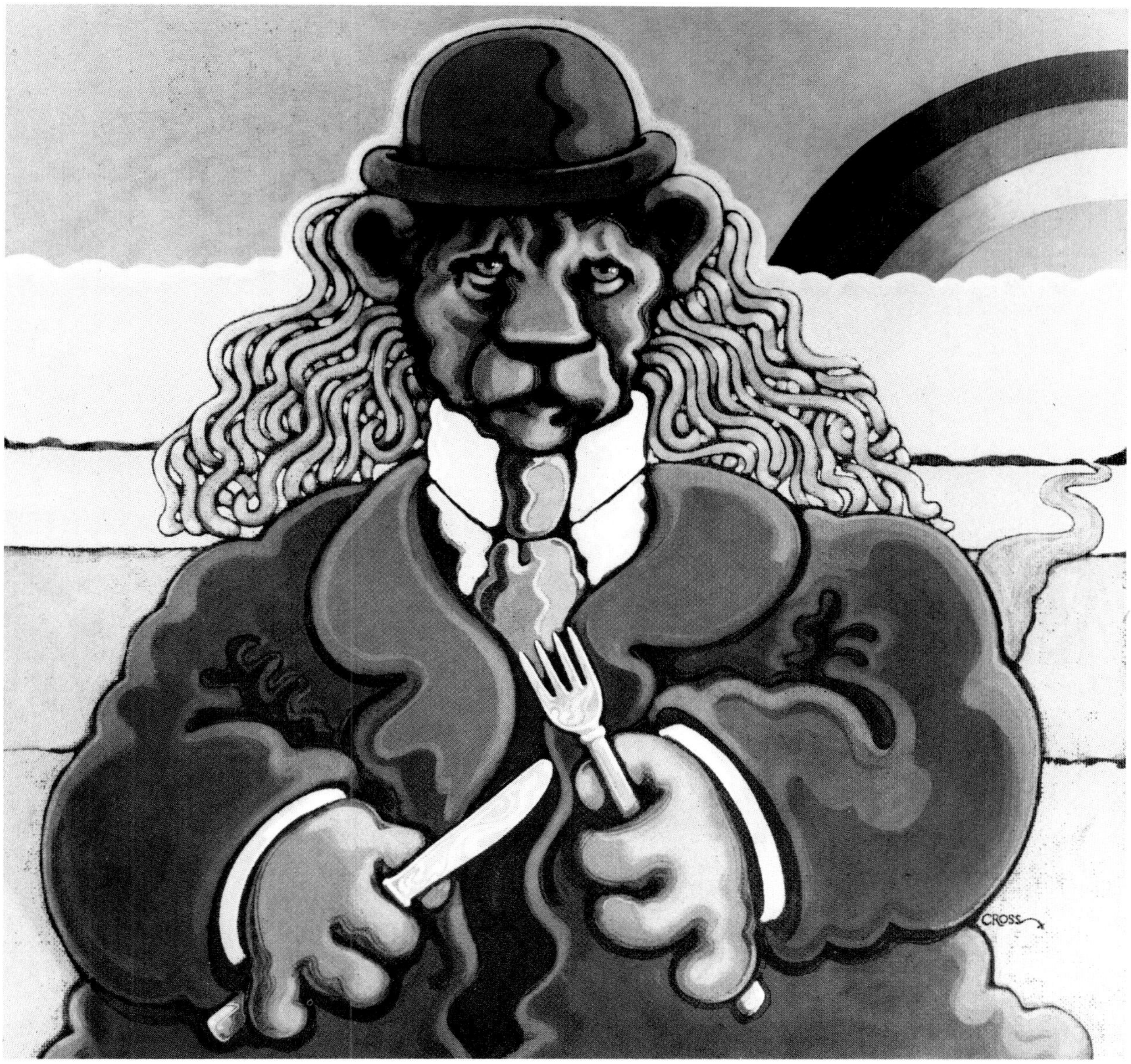
CROSS

638

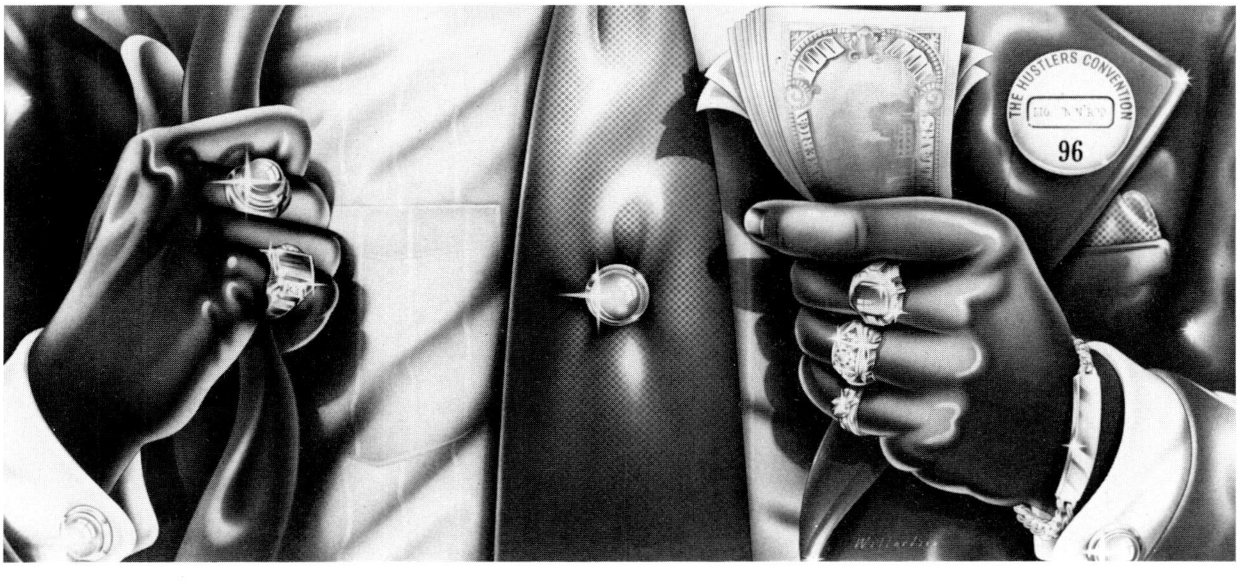
THE HUSTLERS CONVENTION
96

639

638
London Records, Inc. Entrant
Vince Biondi Art Director
Peter Cross Illustrator
Queens Lithographing Corp. Studio

639
Wilkes & Braun, Inc. Entrant
Craig Braun Art Director
Dave Willardson Illustrator
Douglas Records Client

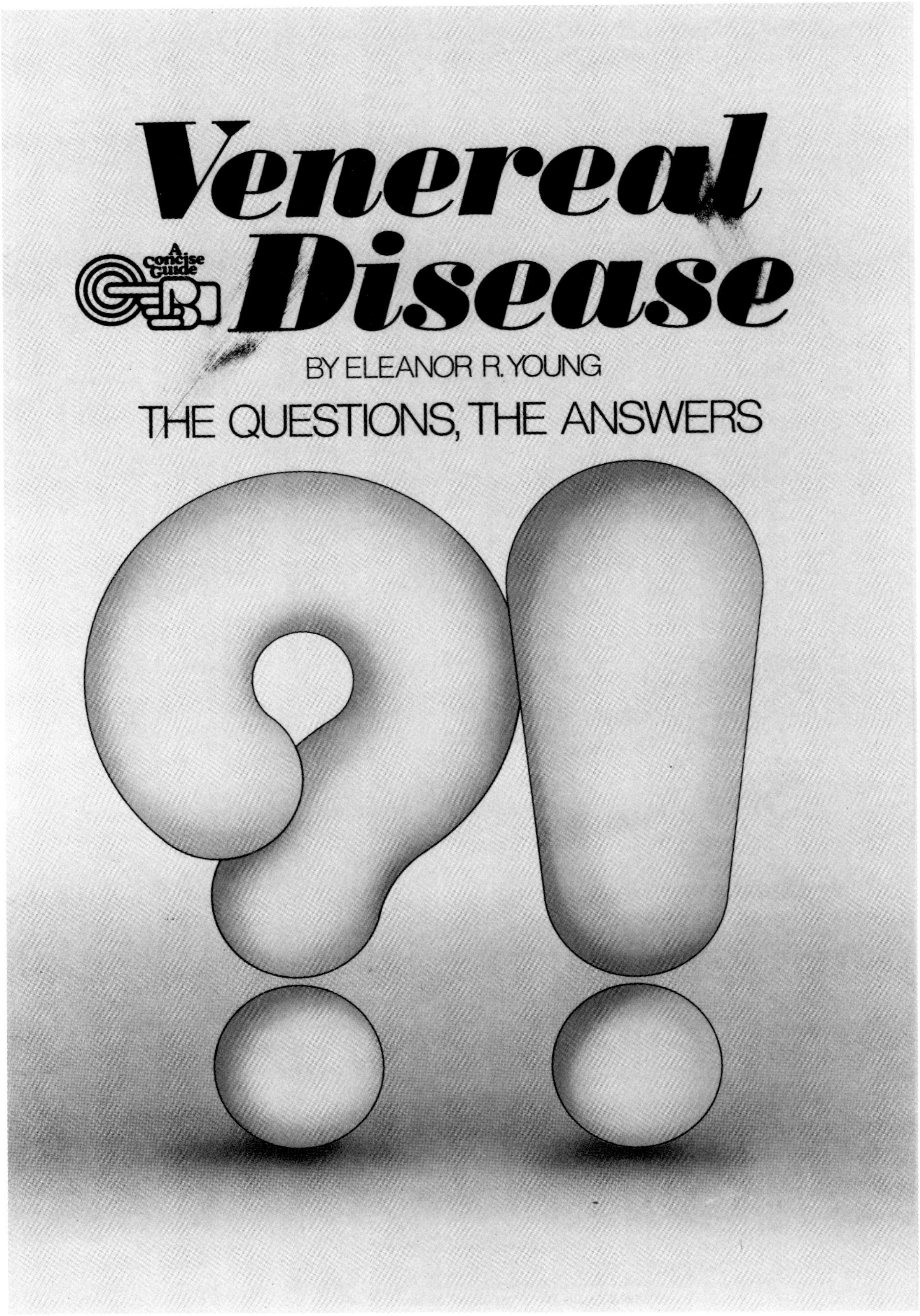
Venereal
A concise Guide
Disease
BY ELEANOR R. YOUNG
THE QUESTIONS, THE ANSWERS

640
Franklin Watts Inc. Entrant
Judie Mills Art Director
Michael Horen Illustrator

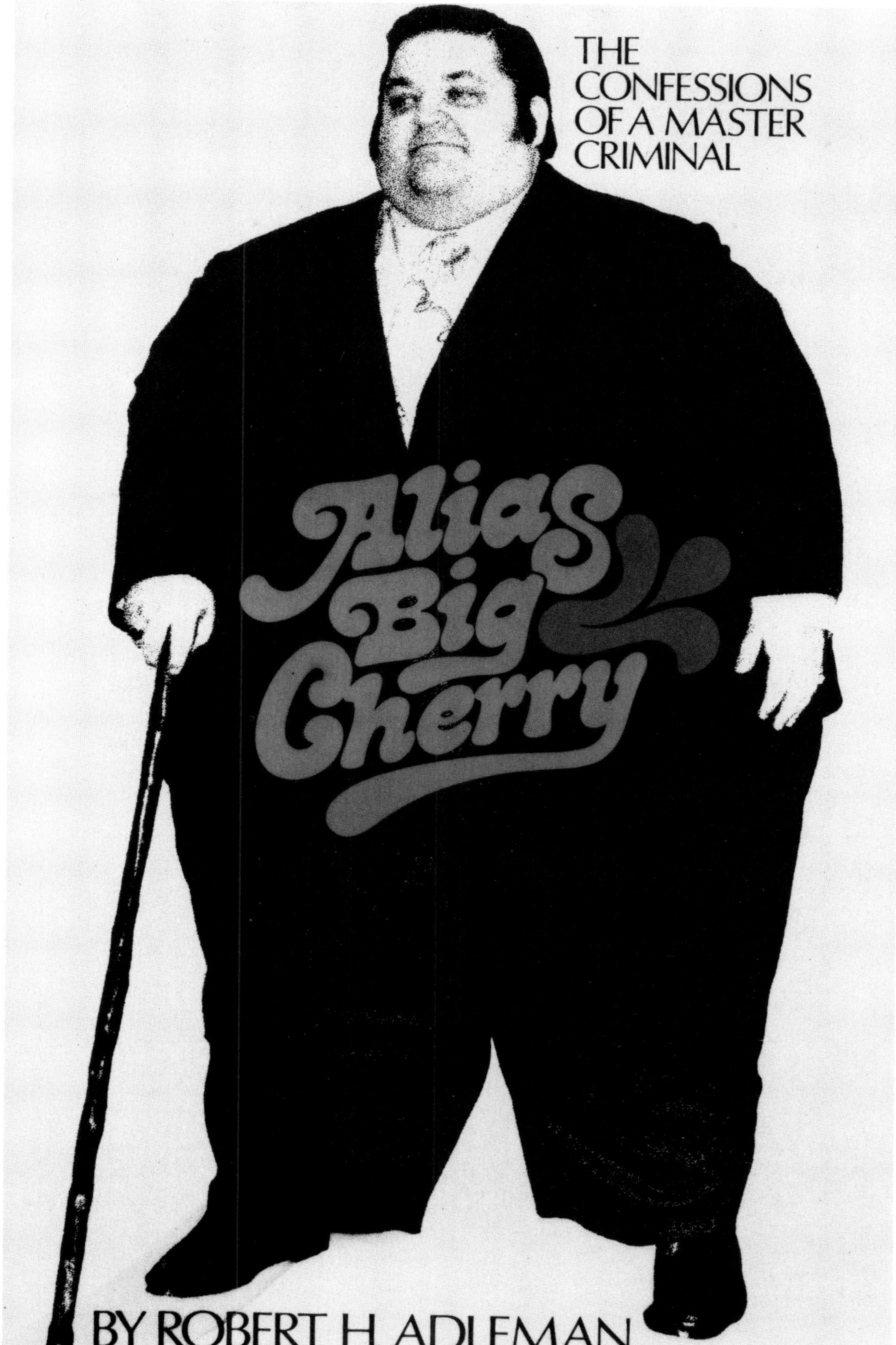
THE
CONFESSIONS
OF A MASTER
CRIMINAL
Alias
Big
Cherry
BY ROBERT H. ADLEMAN

641
Wendell Minor Entrant
Lynn Braswell Art Director
The Dial Press Client

642

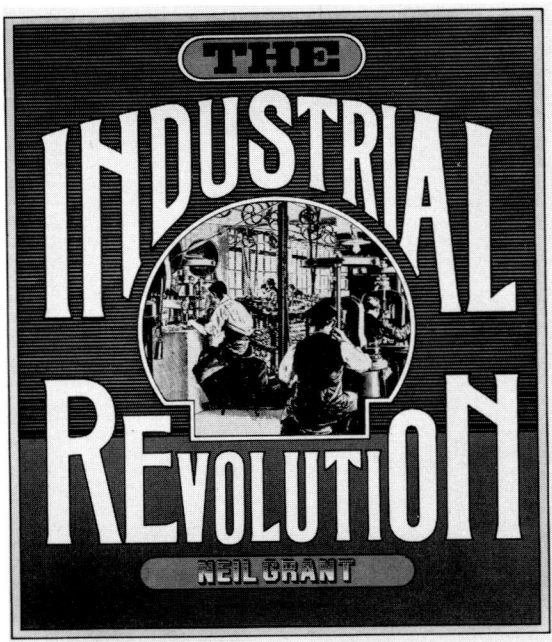

THE
INDUSTRIAL
REVOLUTION
NEIL GRANT

643

FLARE
FRANK BUXTON
AND BILL OWEN
THE BIG BROADCAST 1920-1950
AVON
380-16675-395
THE BIG BROADCAST
1920-1950
A NEW, REVISED, AND GREATLY EXPANDED EDITION OF
RADIO'S GOLDEN AGE
THE COMPLETE REFERENCE WORK
FRANK BUXTON AND BILL OWEN

644

FLARE/AVON/14418/$3.95
$4.45 IN CANADA
Richard W. Langer
GROW IT!
THE BEGINNER'S COMPLETE IN-HARMONY-WITH-NATURE
SMALL FARM GUIDE
FROM VEGETABLE AND GRAIN GROWING TO LIVESTOCK CARE

645

FLARE/AVON/XK118/$3.95
$4.45 IN CANADA
James Trager
THE FOOD BOOK
"It should answer any of the 150,000 questions that might enter the mind of a person interested in food... It's a great reference work, an encyclopedia in one volume... I salute Mr. Trager."
JAMES A. BEARD

646

WAY TO GO, TEDDY
DONALD HONIG

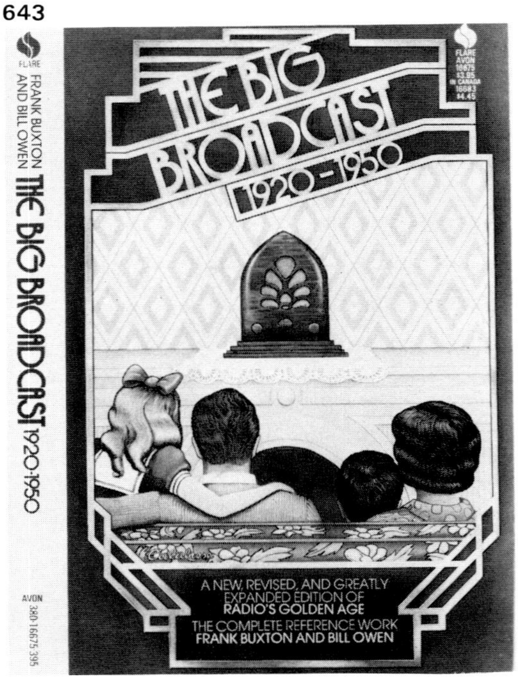

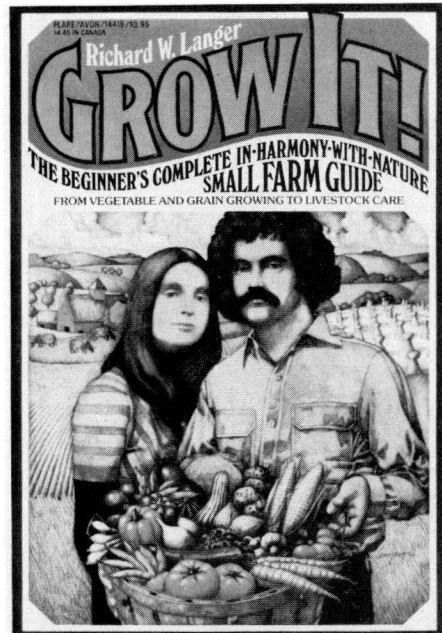

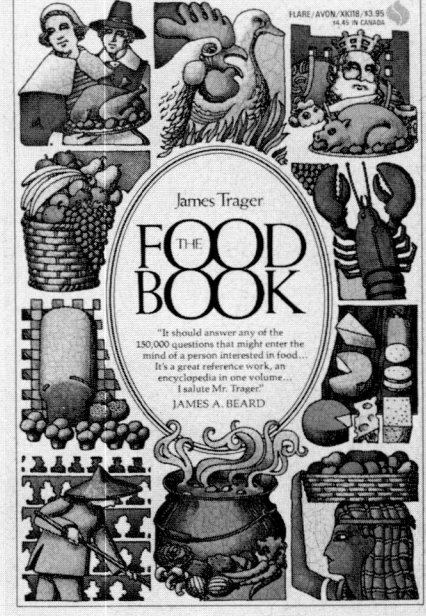

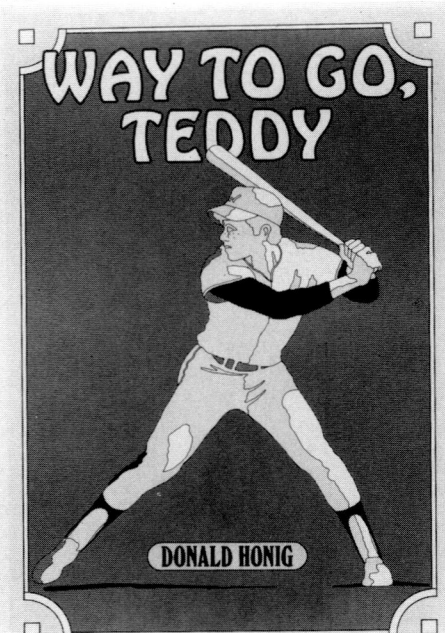

642
Mark Rubin Design
Entrant
Judie Mills
Art Director
Franklin Watts (Juvenile) Client

643
Vincent Calabrese
Entrant
Barbara Bertoli
Art Director
Avon Books
Client

644
Avon Books
Entrant
Barbara Bertoli
Art Director
Jerry Cosgrove
Illustrator

645
Avon Books Inc.
Entrant
Barbara Bertoli
Art Director
Jerry Cosgrove
Illustrator

646
Mark Rubin Design
Entrant
Judie Mills
Art Director
Franklin Watts (Juvenile) Client

647

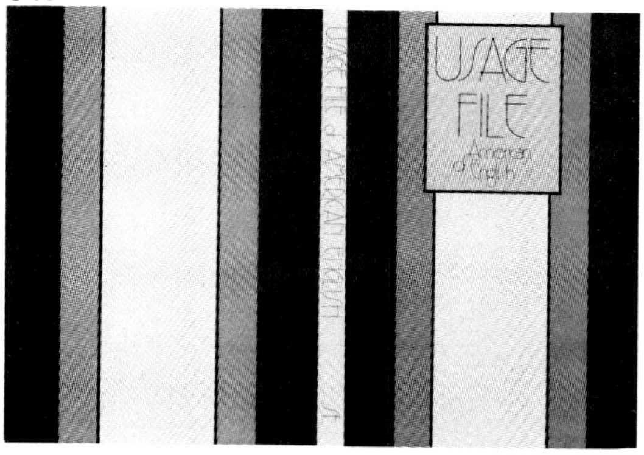
USAGE FILE
American English

648

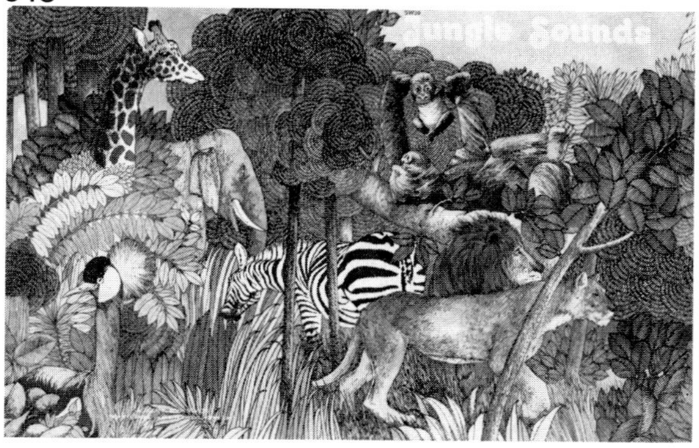
Jungle Sounds

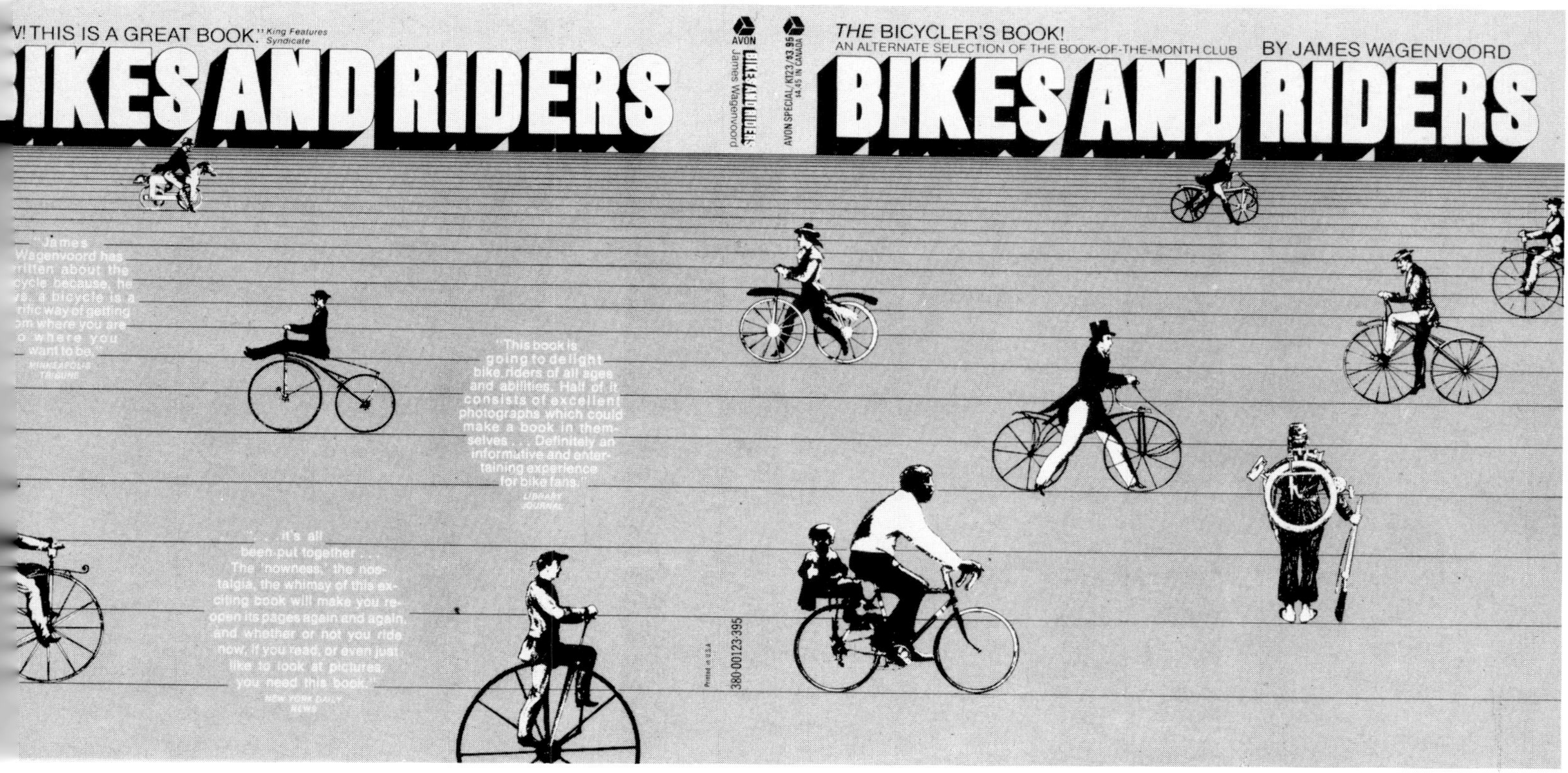
THE BICYCLER'S BOOK!
AN ALTERNATE SELECTION OF THE BOOK-OF-THE-MONTH CLUB
BY JAMES WAGENVOORD
BIKES AND RIDERS
AVON
AVON SPECIAL
"This book is going to delight bike riders of all ages and abilities. Half of it consists of excellent photographs which could make a book in themselves . . . Definitely an informative and entertaining experience for bike fans."
LIBRARY JOURNAL
". . . it's all been put together . . . The 'nowness,' the nostalgia, the whimsy of this exciting book will make you reopen its pages again and again, and whether or not you ride now, if you read, or even just like to look at pictures, you need this book."
NEW YORK DAILY NEWS
380-00123-395
BIKES AND RIDERS

649

647
Bronwyn Moore
Entrant
Hal Kearney
Art Director
Scott, Foresman & Co.
Client

648
Skip Sorvino
Entrant
Phil Slater
Art Director
Ray Cruz
Illustrator
Scholastic Magazine
Client

649
Avon Books Inc.
Entrant
Barbara Bertoli
Art Director

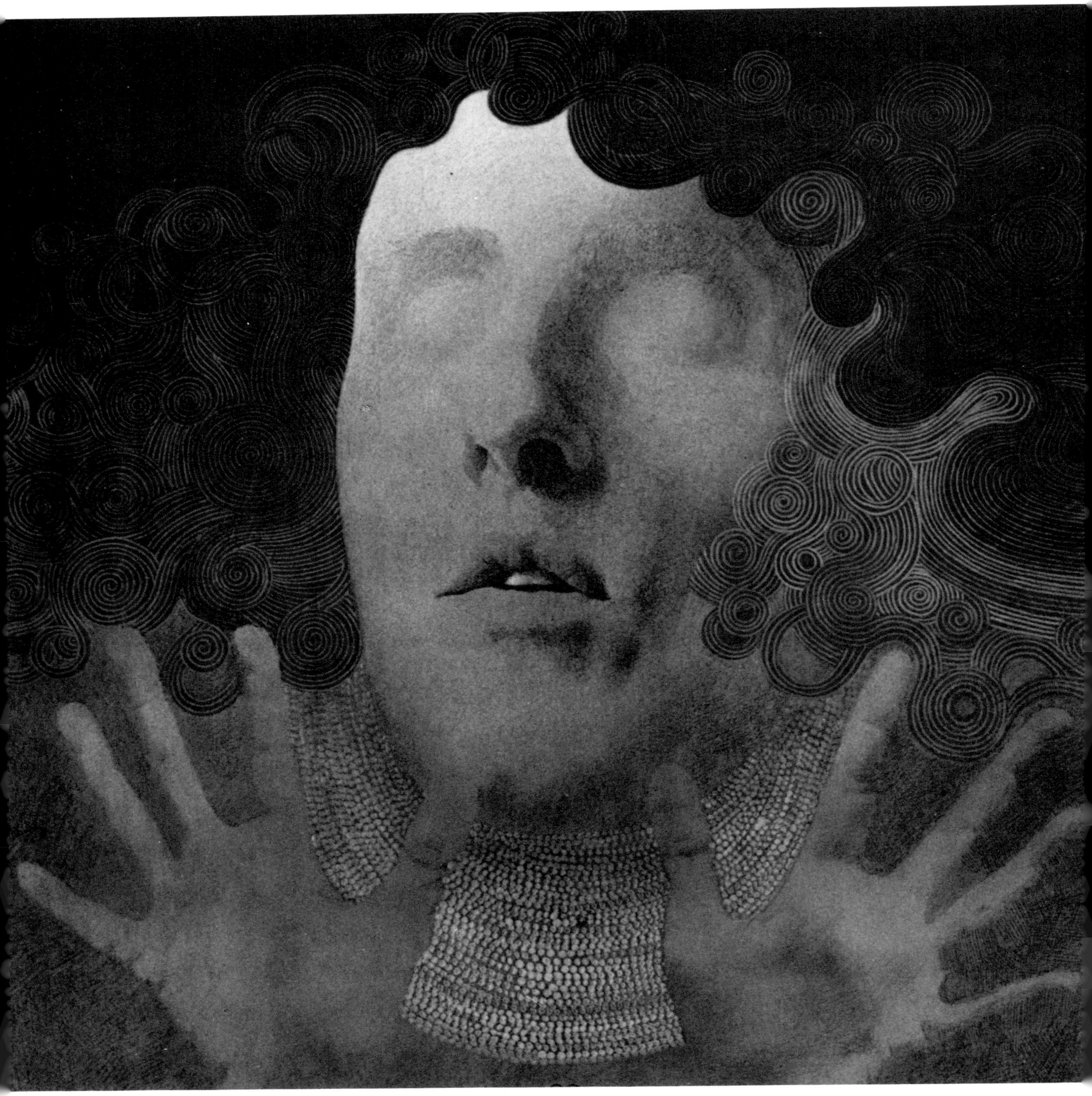

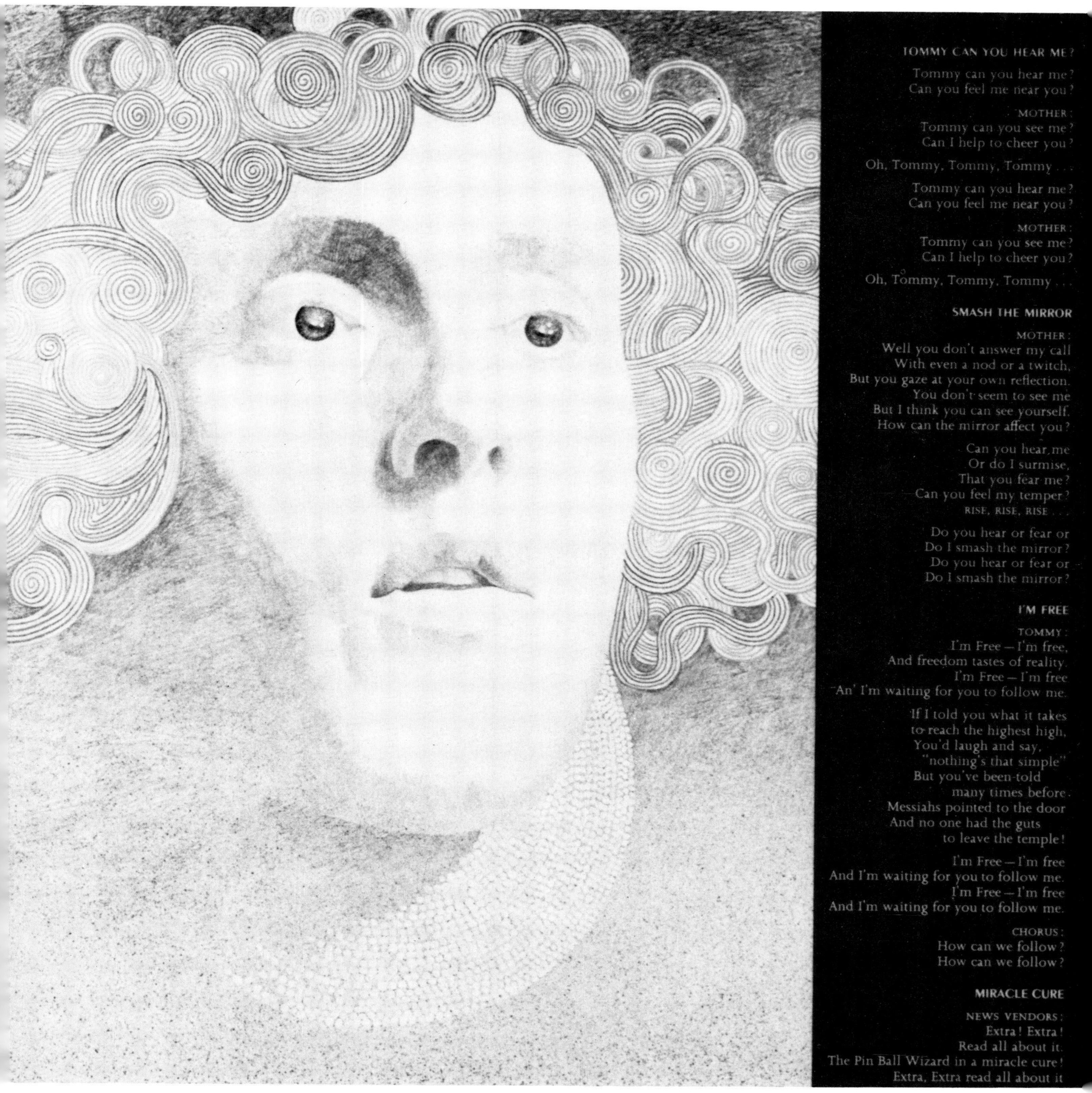
TOMMY CAN YOU HEAR ME?
Tommy can you hear me?
Can you feel me near you?
MOTHER:
Tommy can you see me?
Can I help to cheer you?
Oh, Tommy, Tommy, Tommy . . .
Tommy can you hear me?
Can you feel me near you?
MOTHER:
Tommy can you see me?
Can I help to cheer you?
Oh, Tommy, Tommy, Tommy . . .
SMASH THE MIRROR
MOTHER:
Well you don't answer my call
With even a nod or a twitch,
But you gaze at your own reflection.
You don't seem to see me
But I think you can see yourself.
How can the mirror affect you?
Can you hear me
Or do I surmise,
That you fear me?
Can you feel my temper?
RISE, RISE, RISE . . .
Do you hear or fear or
Do I smash the mirror?
Do you hear or fear or
Do I smash the mirror?
I'M FREE
TOMMY:
I'm Free – I'm free,
And freedom tastes of reality.
I'm Free – I'm free
An' I'm waiting for you to follow me.
If I told you what it takes
to reach the highest high,
You'd laugh and say,
"nothing's that simple"
But you've been told
many times before.
Messiahs pointed to the door
And no one had the guts
to leave the temple!
I'm Free – I'm free
And I'm waiting for you to follow me.
I'm Free – I'm free
And I'm waiting for you to follow me.
CHORUS:
How can we follow?
How can we follow?
MIRACLE CURE
NEWS VENDORS:
Extra! Extra!
Read all about it.
The Pin Ball Wizard in a miracle cure!
Extra, Extra read all about it

650
Wilkes & Braun Inc. Entrant
Craig Braun Art Director
Richard Amsel, Robert Heindel, Wilson McClean, Jim Manos, Alex Gnidziejko, David Byrd, Mark English (shown), Doug Johnson, Robert Grossman, Charles White III, Richard Harvey Illustrators
Ode Records Client

651

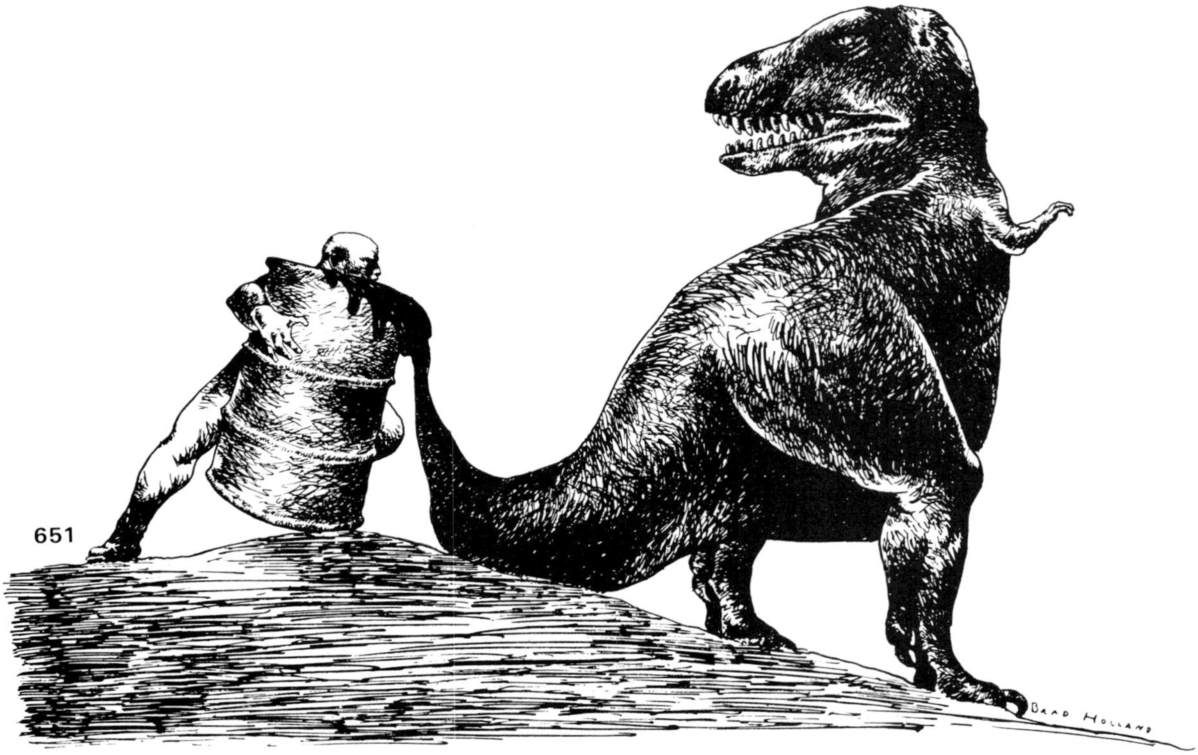
BRAD HOLLAND

652

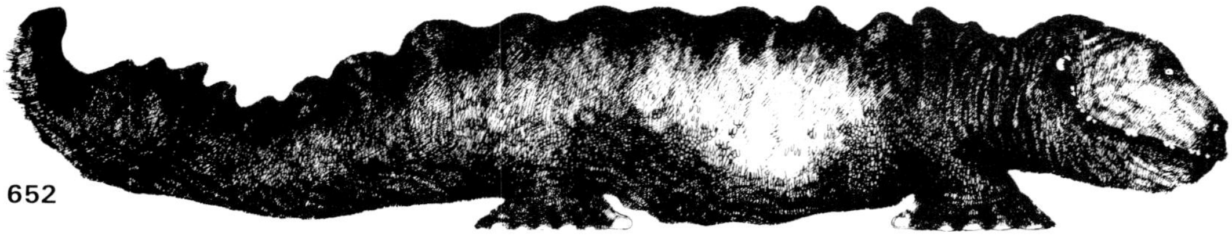

651
Brad Holland Entrant
J.C. Suares Art Director
The New York Times Client

652
Jacqueline Dedell Entrant
Everson Museum of Art Client

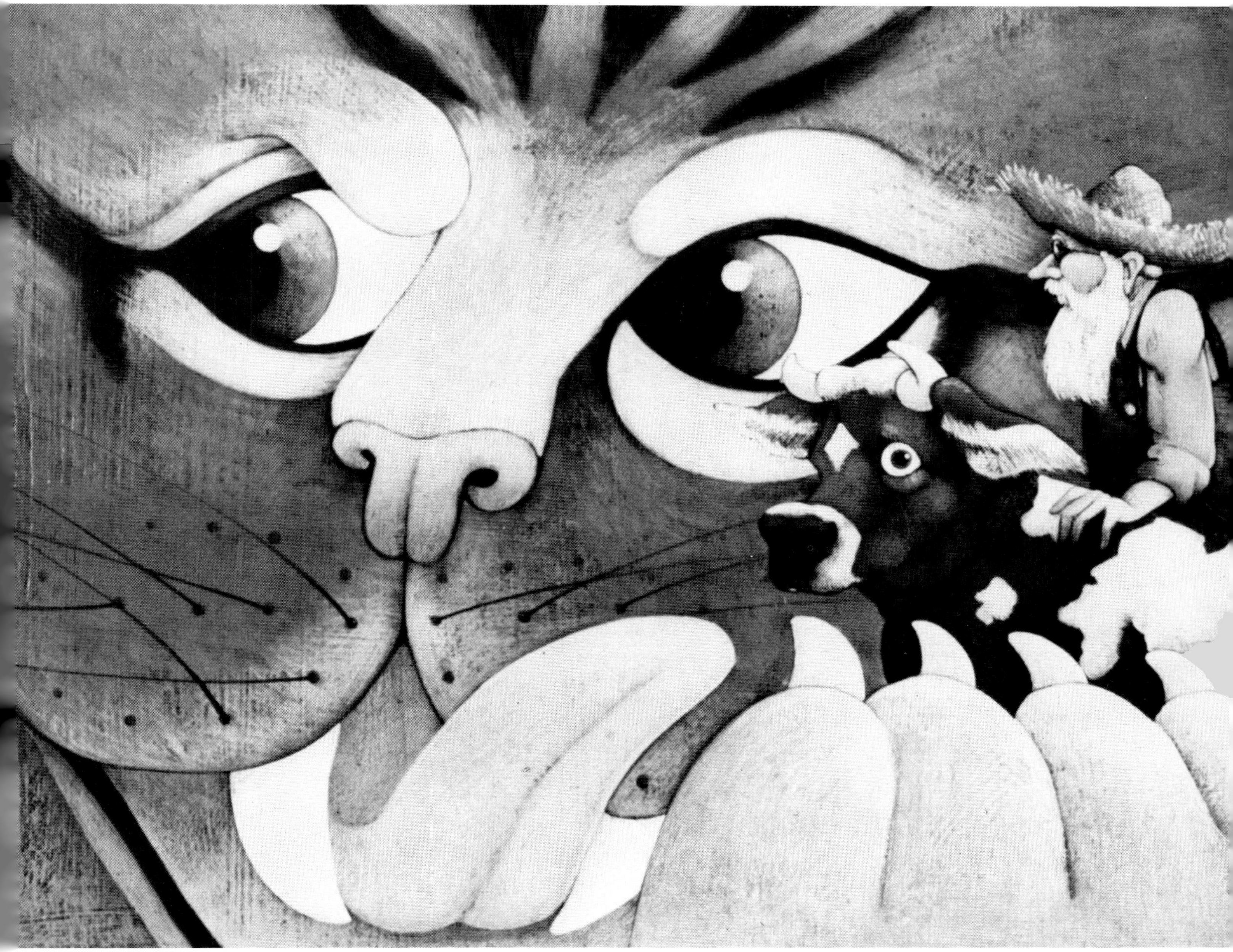

653
Jackie L.W. Geyer Entrant
Zlata Paces Art Director
Marsh MacMillan Publishing House Client

654

STAGGERWING AND ME
the joys of breaking loose in an aging but beautiful biplane
article By TOM MAYER

655

A Little Celebration
The cake isn't very big to celebrate a 25th anniversary. But then, neither was the transistor invented by Bell Laboratories scientists in 1947. From their invention have sprung amazing new communications systems, medical advances,
space exploration—the creation of whole new industries and millions of jobs—and a broad range of new technological developments improving the way we all work, and play, and live. Happy Anniversary

656

子
Het jaar van de rat (Tzu)

657

丑
L'année du boeuf (Ch'ou)

658

寅
Het jaar van de tijger (Yin)

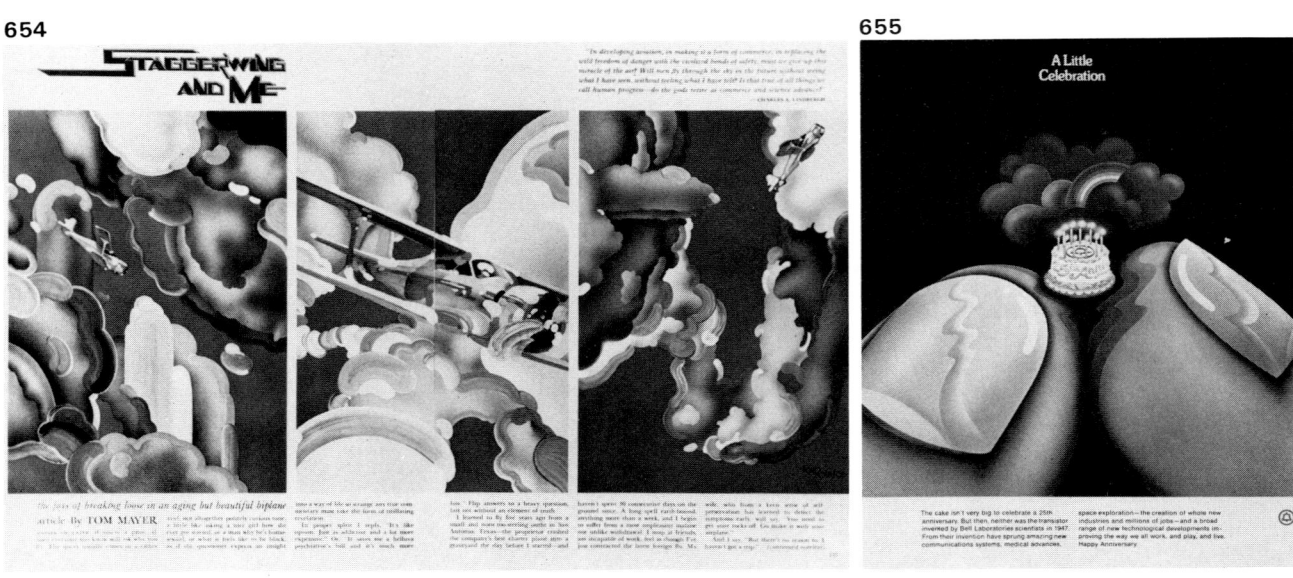

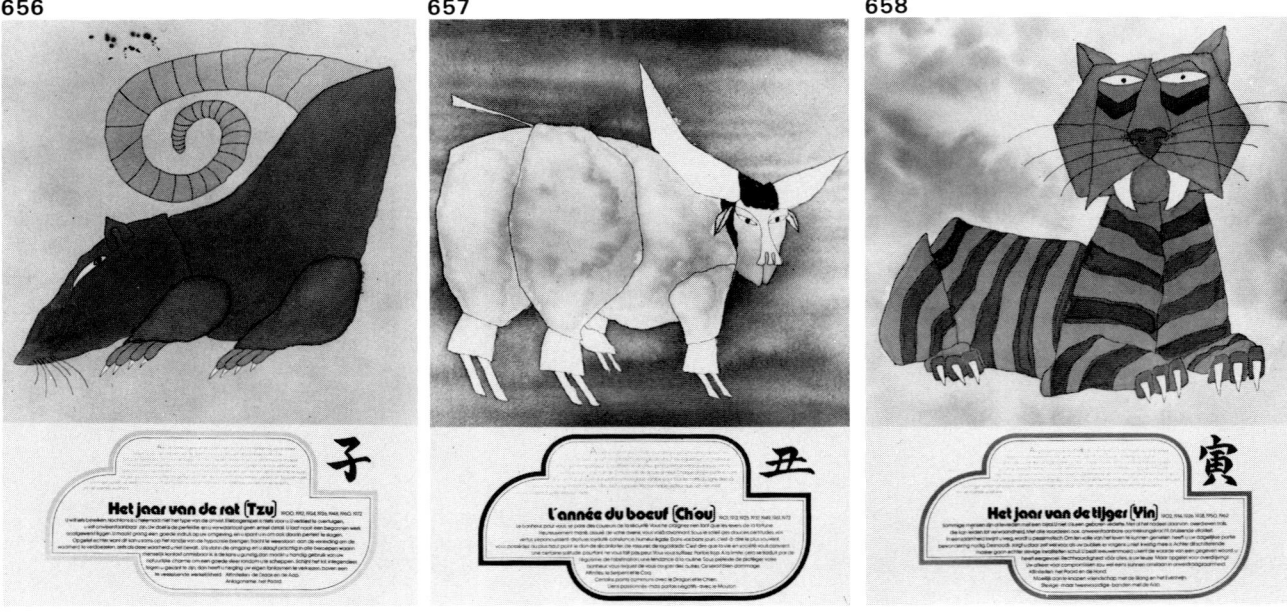

654
Playboy Enterprises, Inc. Entrant
Arthur Paul Art Director
Doug Johnson Illustrator
Roy Moody Designer
Playboy Magazine Client

655
Saul Bass & Associates Entrant
Herb Kessler, Art Goodman Art Directors
Mamoru Shimokochi, Art Goodman Designers
Mamoru Shimokochi Illustrator
American Telephone & Telegraph Client

656-658
Michel Waxmann Entrant
Waxmann Design Studio
Wyeth Laboratories USA (Belgium) Client

660

DART
EXTRAVAGANZA
NUMBER
ONE 72

659

Literary Cavalcade
JANUARY 1973
Buffalo Bill: I believe I . . . am a . . . hero . . . A HERO
Arthur Kopit's INDIANS

661

DOCTOR ON THE SPOT
Whether you're an emergency physician or a physician in an emergency, the problems and practices of the emergency room are your department. Because emergencies aren't planned, they happen, and they often happen around you. So no matter how often —or seldom—you set foot in an ED, here are tips on emergency problems and emergency medicine to help you in your practice— gleaned, of course, from the recent meeting of the American College of Emergency Physicians in San Francisco.

662

663

The American Scene
"Poor, often black, confined in public facilities, they are easily accessible and can be persuaded to participate in virtually any experiment recommended by a physician."
World 12/5/72
21

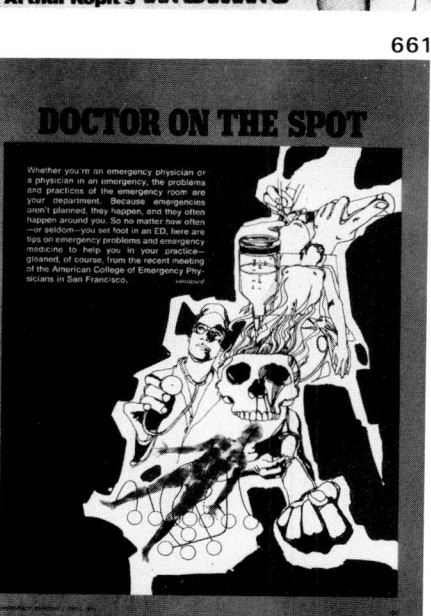

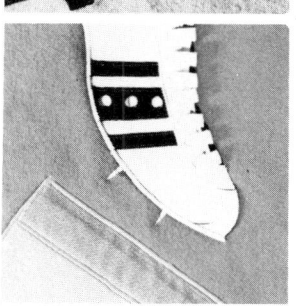

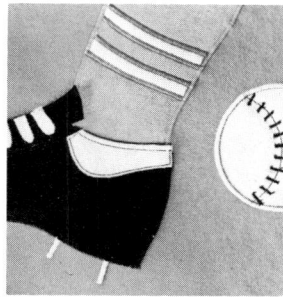

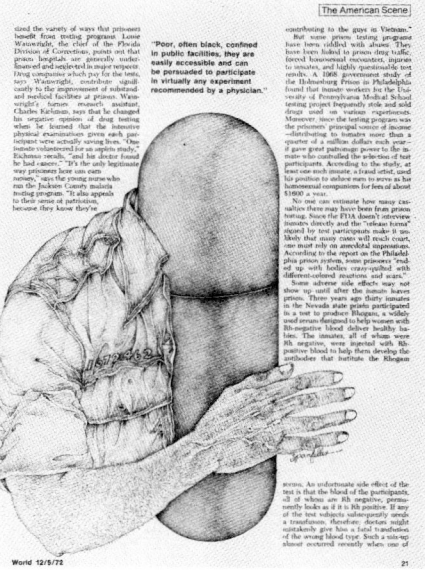

659
Steven Duckett
Entrant
Scholastic Magazine Inc.
Client

660
TY Graphics
Entrant
Tom Yurcich
Art Director
The Cleveland Darter Club Client

661
Emergency Medicine
Entrant
Ira Silberlicht
Art Director
David Passalacqua
Illustrator

662
Peter Good Entrant
Don Easdon Art Director
Creamer, Trowbridge, Case & Basford Agency
Spot-Bilt Client

663
World Magazine
Entrant
Judith Adel, Marcia McElrath
Art Directors

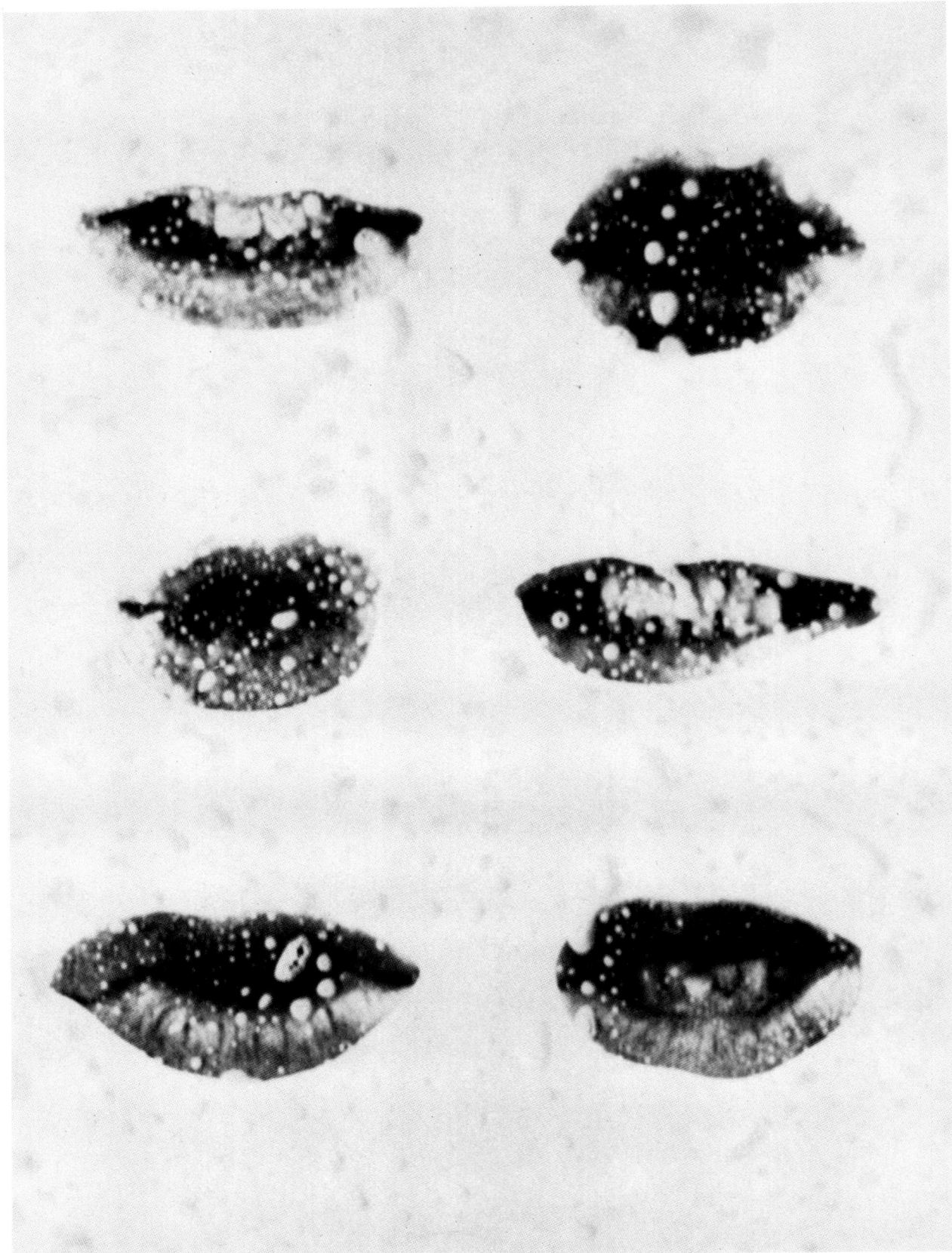

664

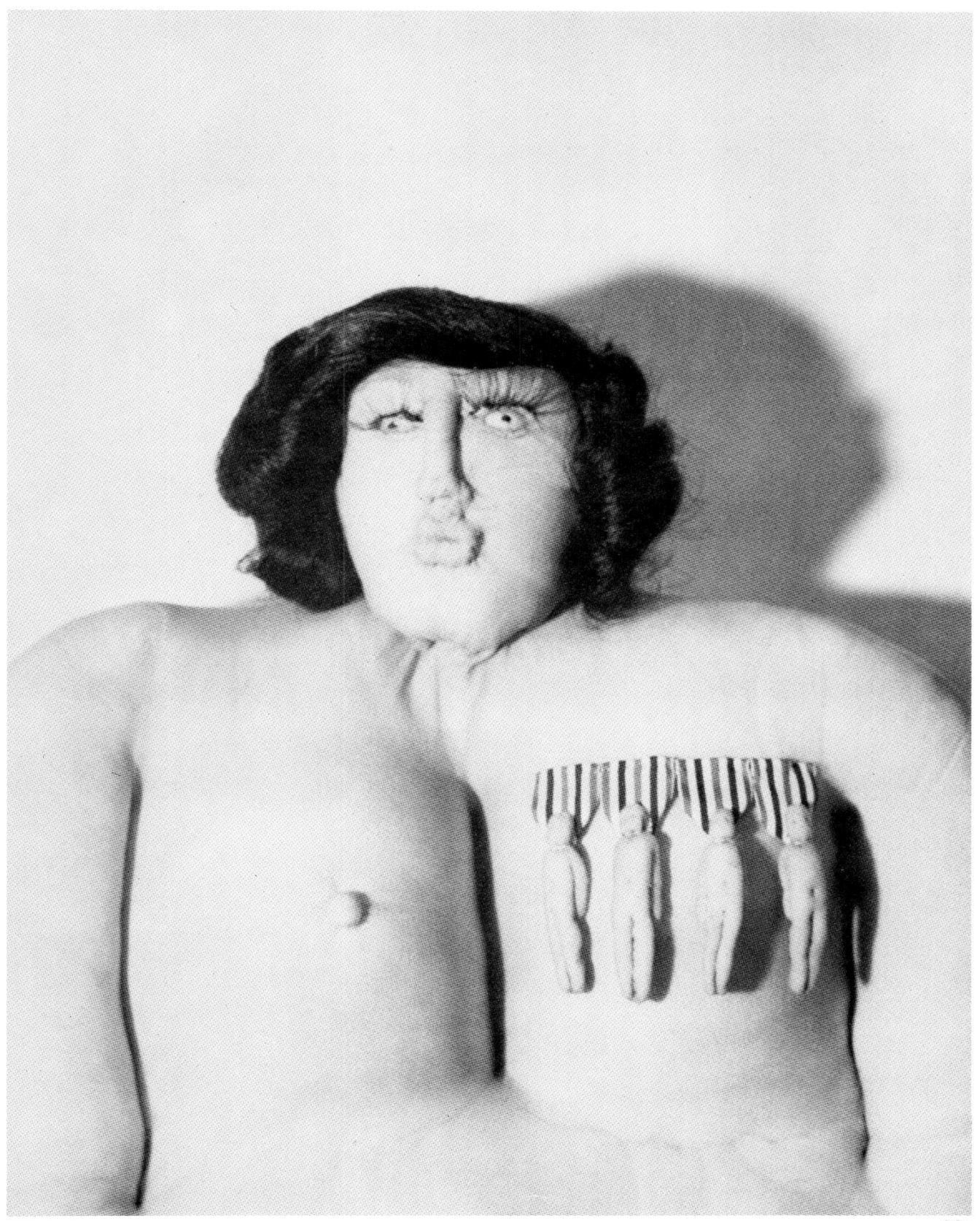

664-665
Nanette Hucknall, Judith Jampel, Arlene Pacchiano Entrants

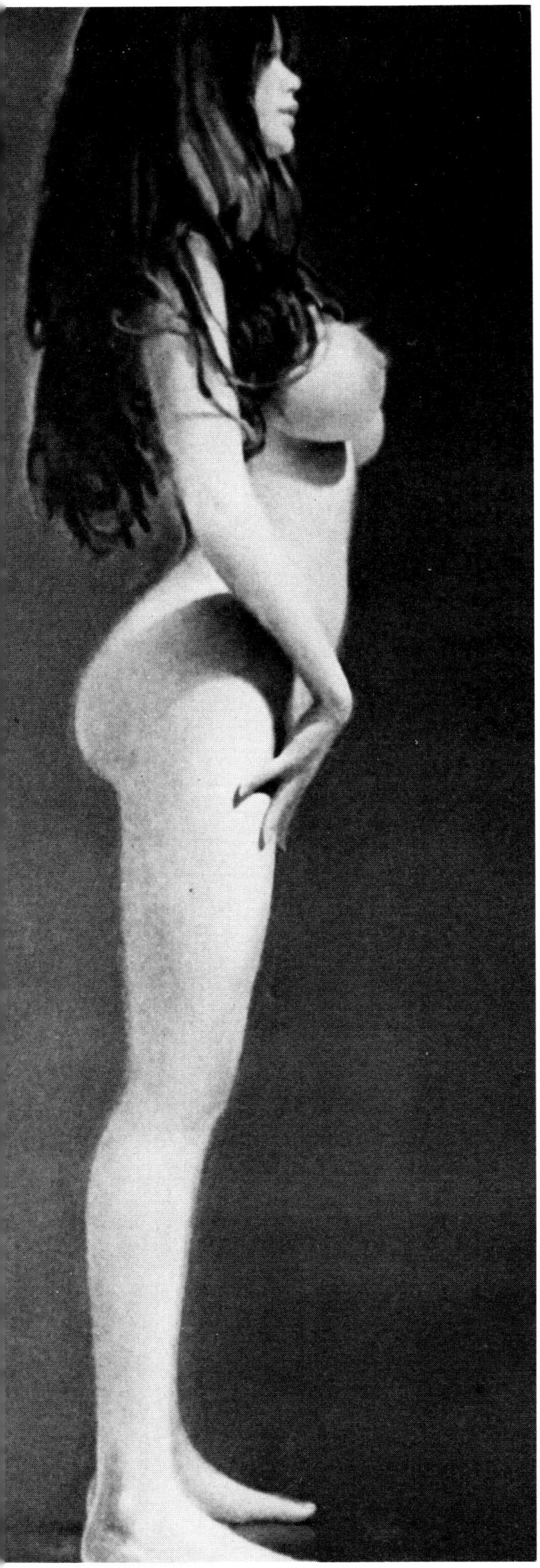

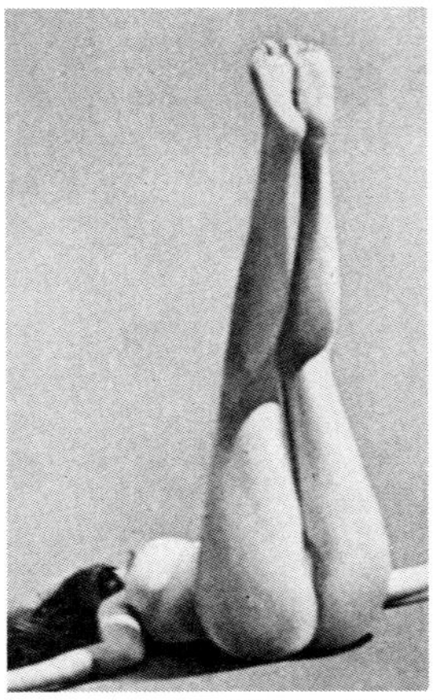

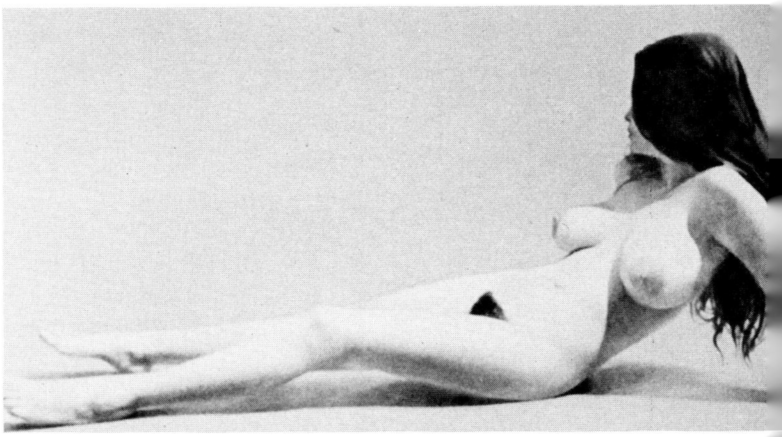

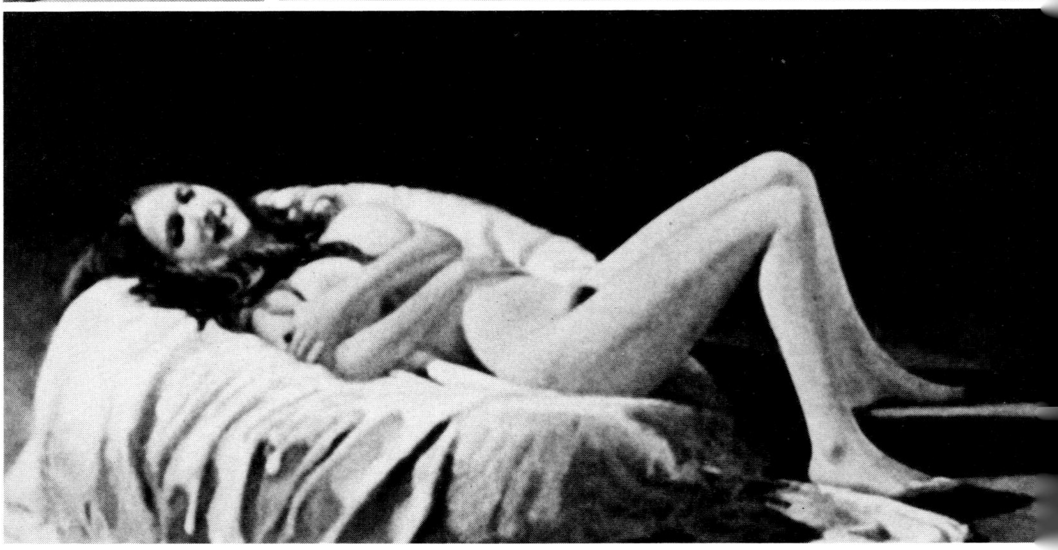

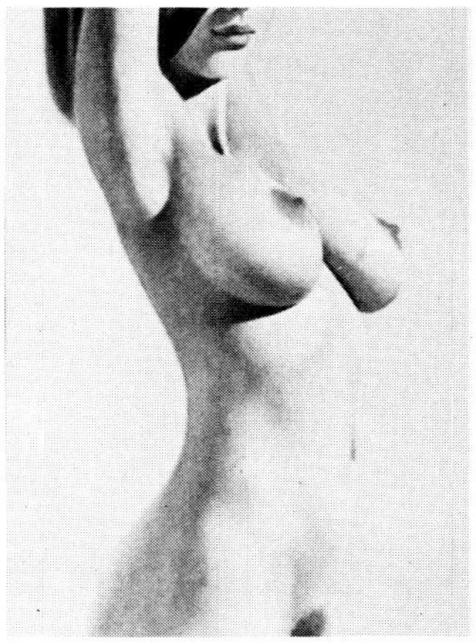

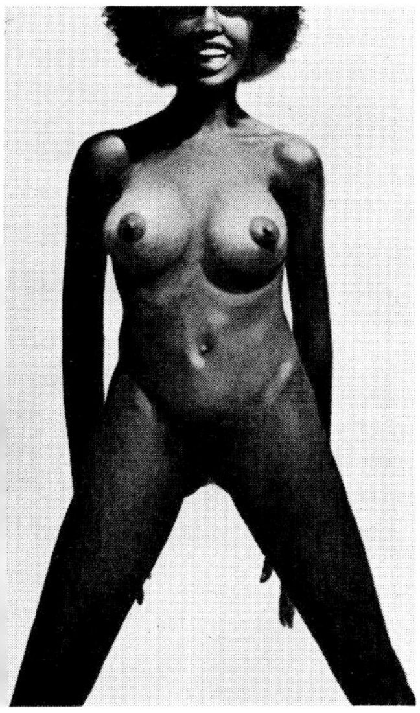

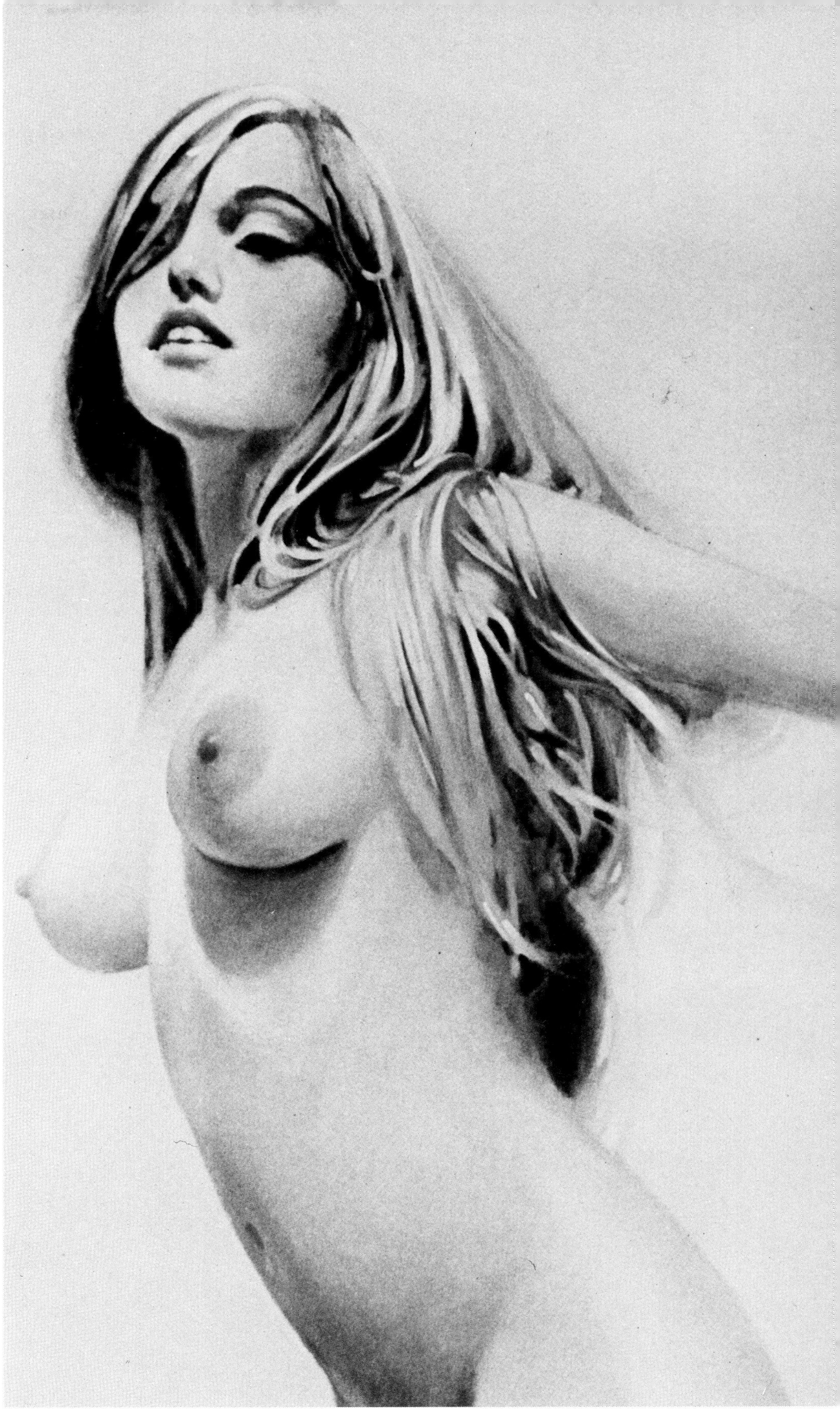

666-673
Playboy Enterprises Inc. Entrant
Arthur Paul Art Director
Martin Hoffman Illustrator
Kerig Pope Designer
Playboy Magazine Client

675

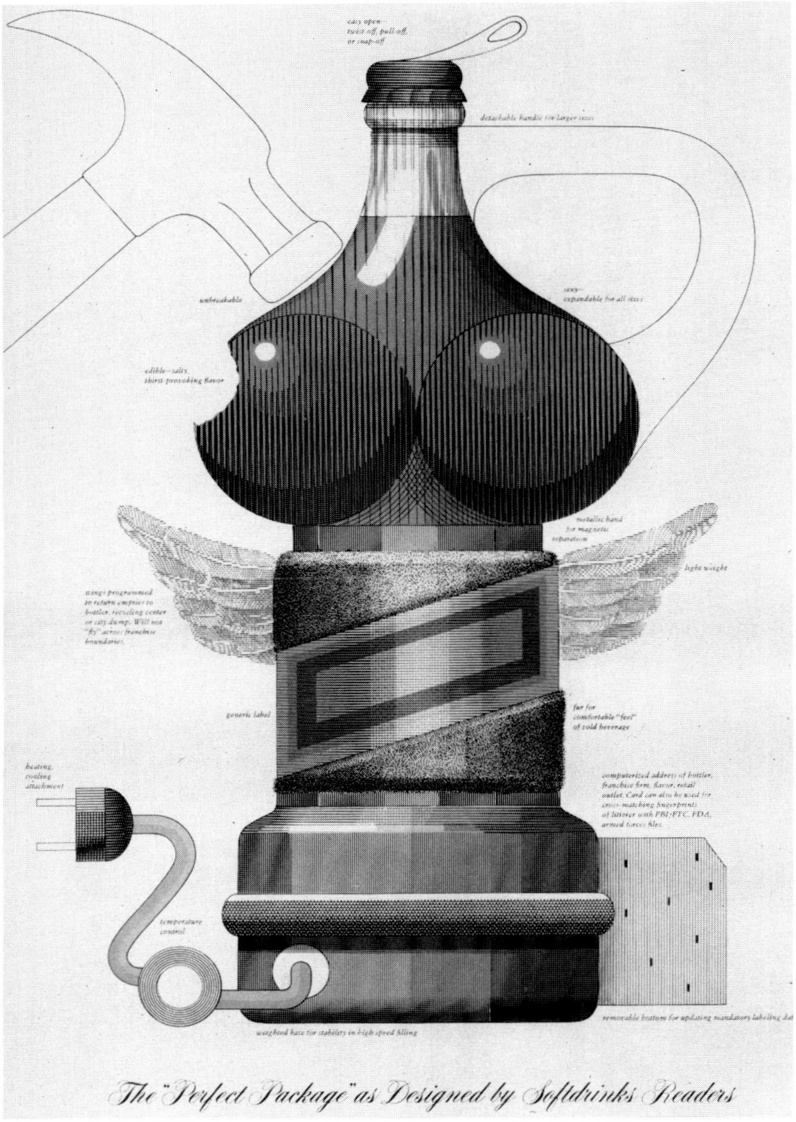
easy open—
twist-off, pull-off,
or snap-off
detachable handle for larger sizes
unbreakable
sexy—
expandable for all sizes
edible—salty,
thirst-provoking flavor
metallic band
for magnetic
separation
light weight
generic label
fur for
comfortable "feel"
of cold beverage
heating,
cooling
attachment
temperature
control
removable bottom for updating mandatory labeling da
weighted base for stability in high speed filling
The "Perfect Package" as Designed by Softdrinks Readers

674

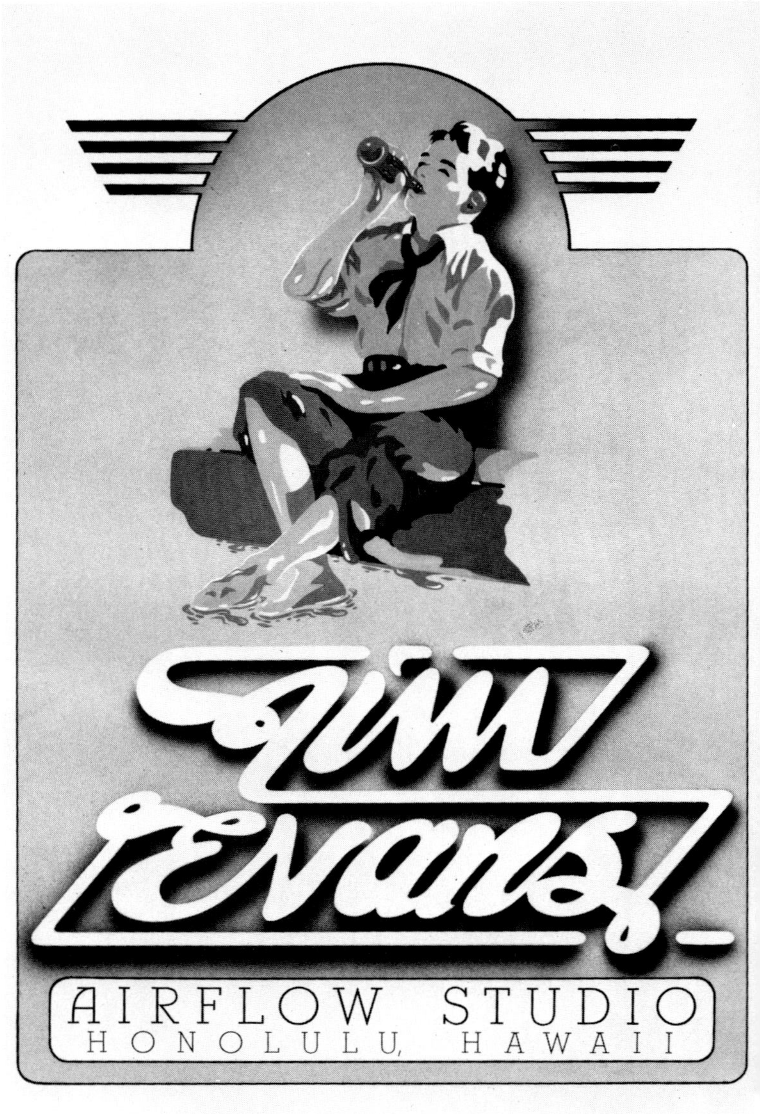
Jim Evans
AIRFLOW STUDIO
HONOLULU, HAWAII

675
Norman Gorbaty Design Inc. Entrant
Norman Gorbaty Art Director
Norman Gorbaty, Brian Ganton Illustrators
Soft Drinks Magazine Client

674
Jim Evans Entrant
Airflow Studio Client

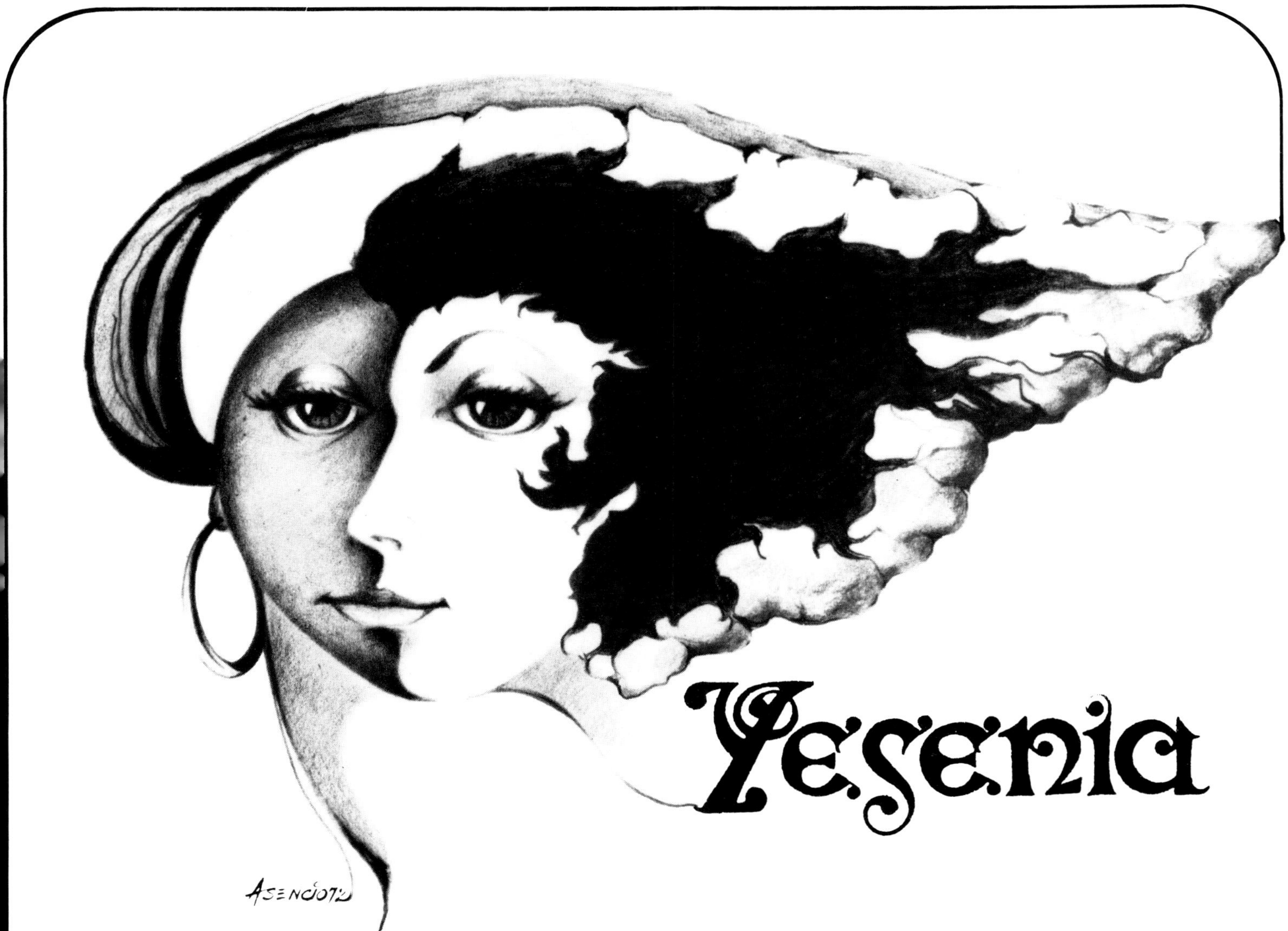
Yesenia
ASENCIO72

676
Marcelino Miyares Entrant
John J. Asencio Art Director
O.M.A.R. Co. Agency
Division Chevrolet Client

677

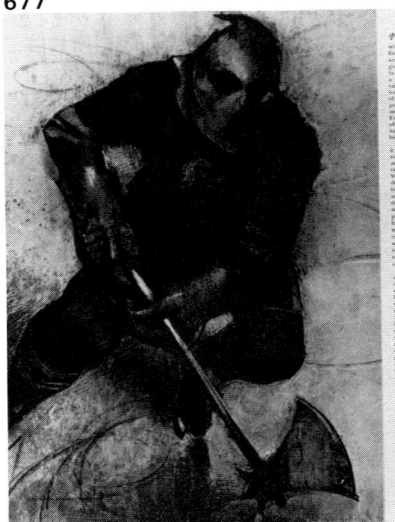

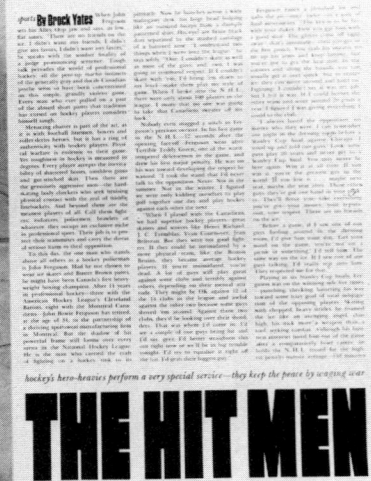

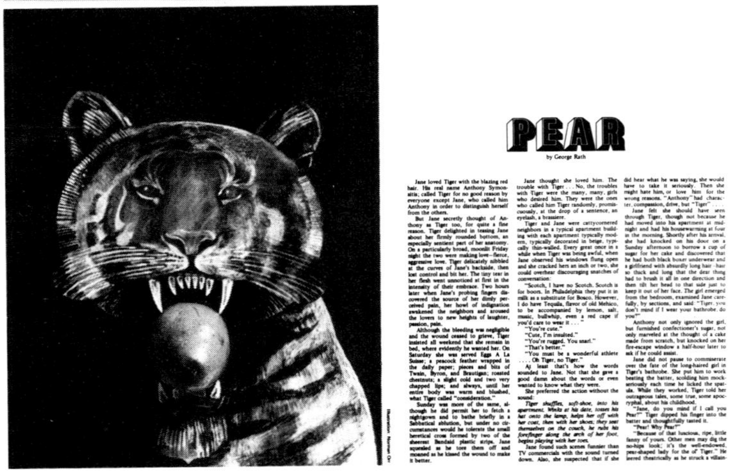

By Brock Yates
hockey's hero-heavies perform a very special service—they keep the peace by waging war
THE HIT MEN

PEAR
by George Rath

678

677
Playboy Enterprises, Inc. Entrant
Arthur Paul Art Director
Harvey Dinnerstein Illustrator
Len Willis Designer
Playboy Magazine Client

678
Steven Jacobs Design, Inc. Entrant
Steve Jacobs Art Director
Norman Orr Illustrator
Bill Arbogast Photographer
California Girl Magazine Client

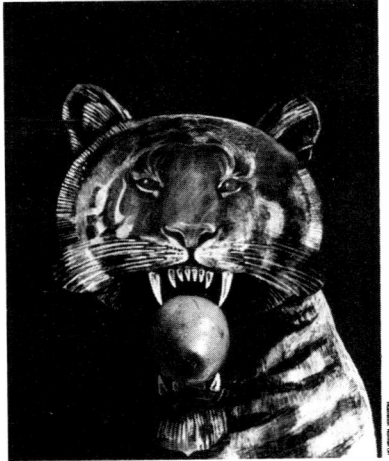

THE BLACK KING OF THE NUMBERS GAME

Blue Boy's got the man's number...
and takes it ... at 600 to 1

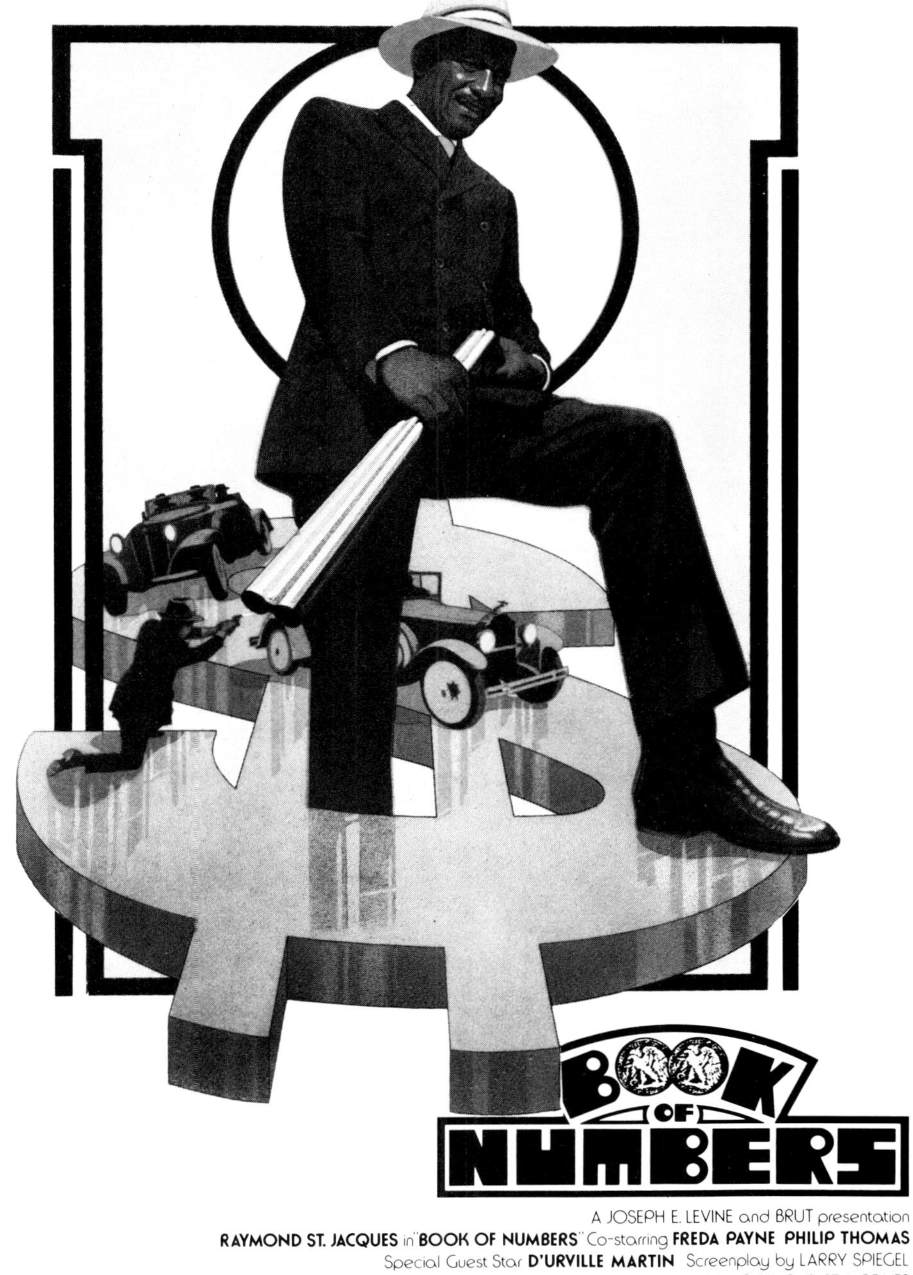
BOOK OF NUMBERS

A JOSEPH E. LEVINE and BRUT presentation
RAYMOND ST. JACQUES in "**BOOK OF NUMBERS**" Co-starring **FREDA PAYNE PHILIP THOMAS**
Special Guest Star **D'URVILLE MARTIN** Screenplay by LARRY SPIEGEL
Based on the novel by ROBERT DEANE PHARR Produced and Directed by RAYMOND ST. JACQUES
An AVCO EMBASSY RELEASE in Color Original Soundtrack Available on BRUT RECORDS

R

679
Communications Quorum, Inc. Entrant
Barry Kaufman, Richard Lomonaco Art Directors
Alex Gnidziejko Illustrator
Avco-Embassy Films Client

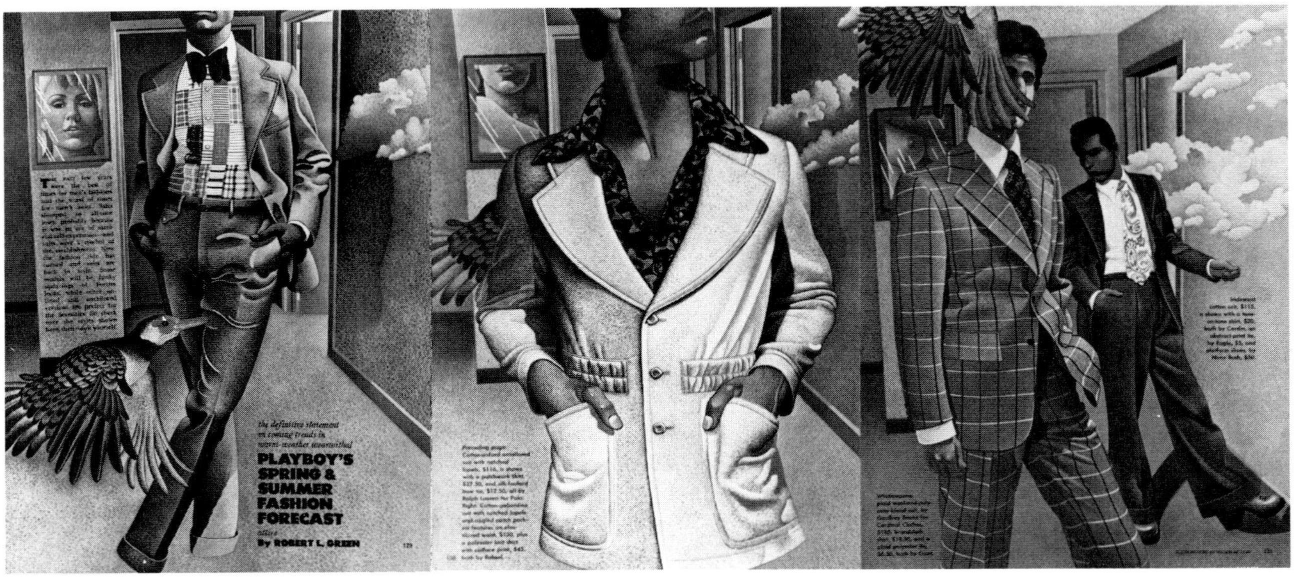
PLAYBOY'S SPRING & SUMMER FASHION FORECAST
By ROBERT L. GREEN

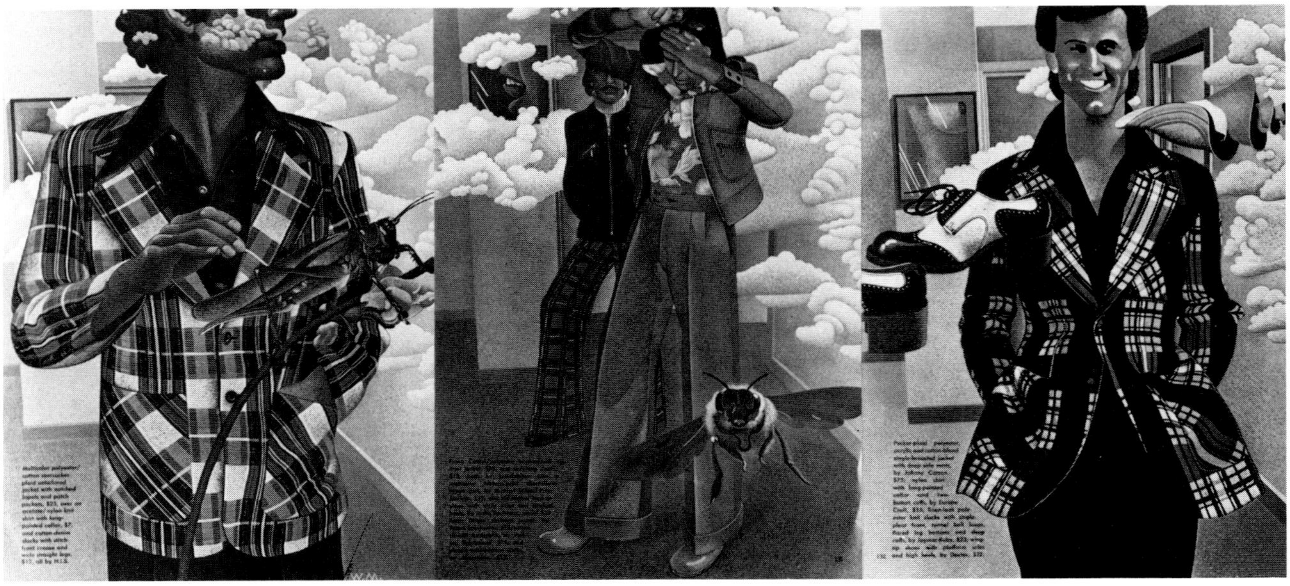

680-683
Playboy Enterprises Inc. Entrant
Arthur Paul Art Director
Wilson McLean Illustrator
Tom Staebler Designer
Playboy Magazine Client

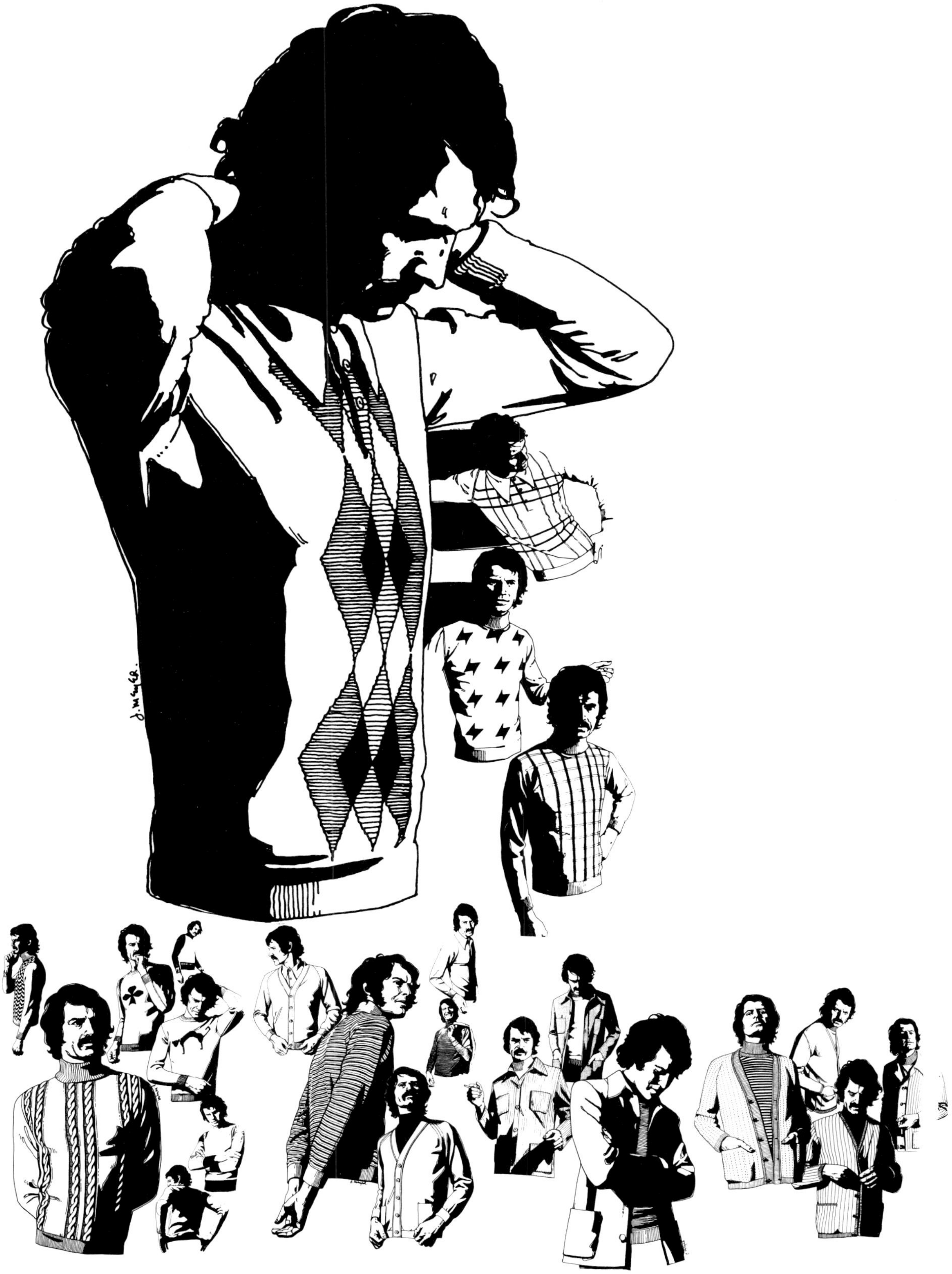

684-688
Lorraine & Crystal Entrants
Simone Osterlly Art Director
John Meyer Illustrator
Brookfield Knitting (Pty.) Ltd. Client

689

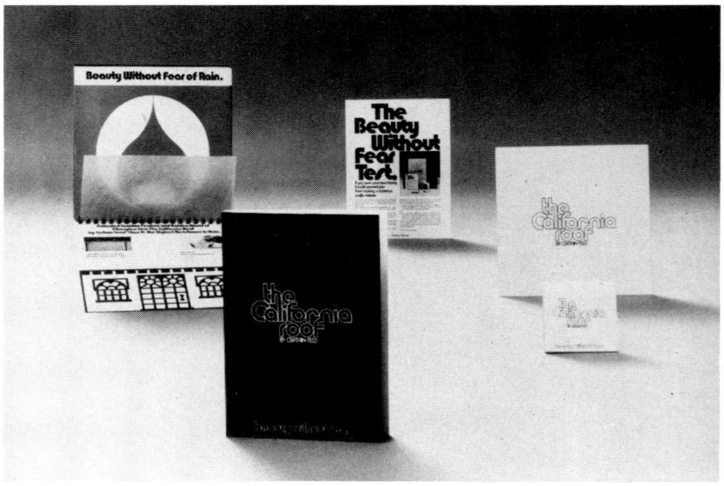
Beauty Without Fear of Rain.
The Beauty Without Fear Test.
the California roof

690

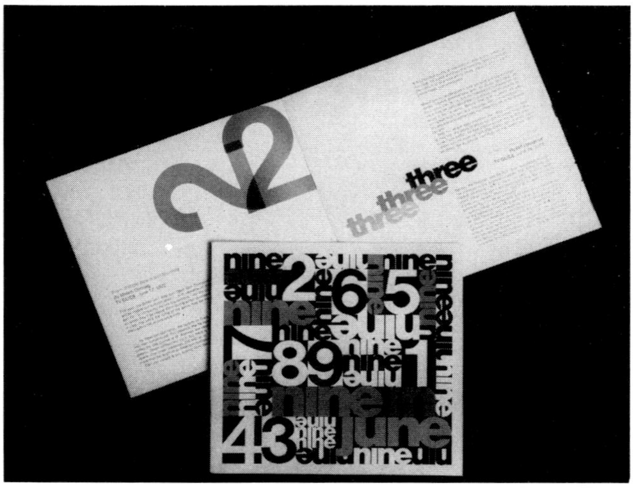
three
three
three

691

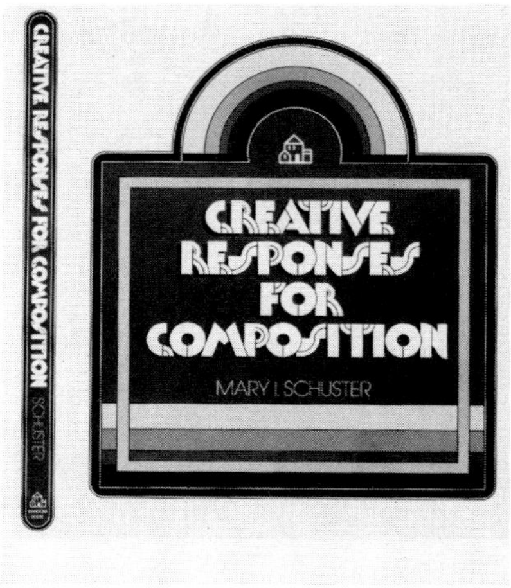
CREATIVE RESPONSES FOR COMPOSITION
MARY I. SCHUSTER
CREATIVE RESPONSES FOR COMPOSITION SCHUSTER

692

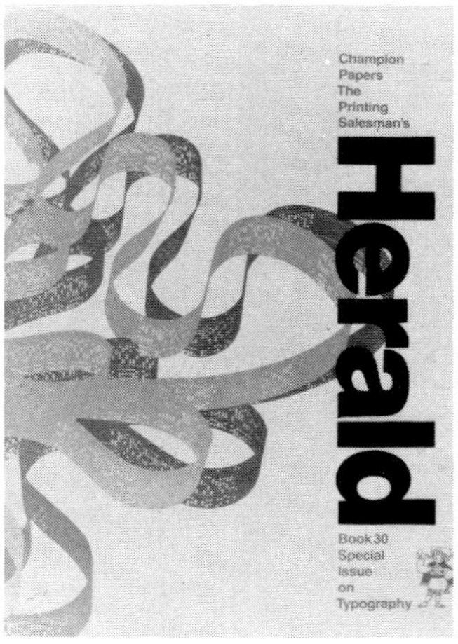
Champion Papers
The Printing Salesman's
Herald
Book 30
Special Issue on Typography

693

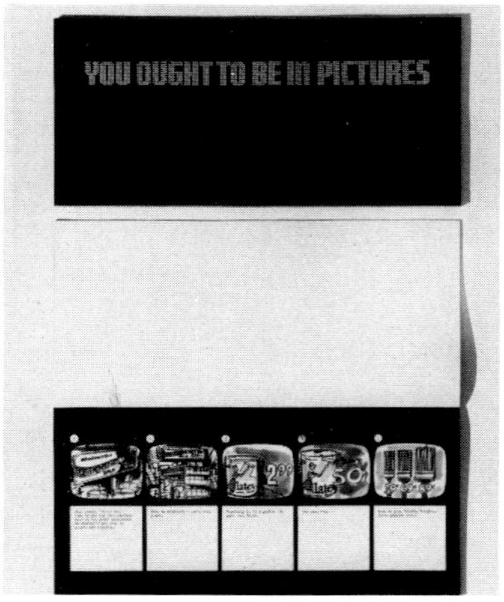
YOU OUGHT TO BE IN PICTURES

694

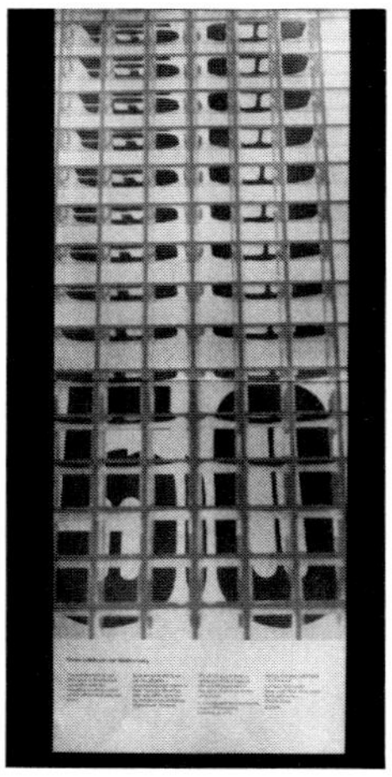

689
Lee Elliot Entrant
S. Schlatner Art Director
The Infinity Group, Inc. Agency
Certain-teed Products Corporation Client

690
TV Guide Entrant
John Brown Art Director
Liz Thompson Illustrator

691
Mark Rubin Design Entrant
Stan Wheatman Art Director
Mark Rubin Letterer
Random House Client

692
Peter Wittman Entrant
Noel Martin Art Director
Peter Wittman Inc. Studio
Champion Papers Client

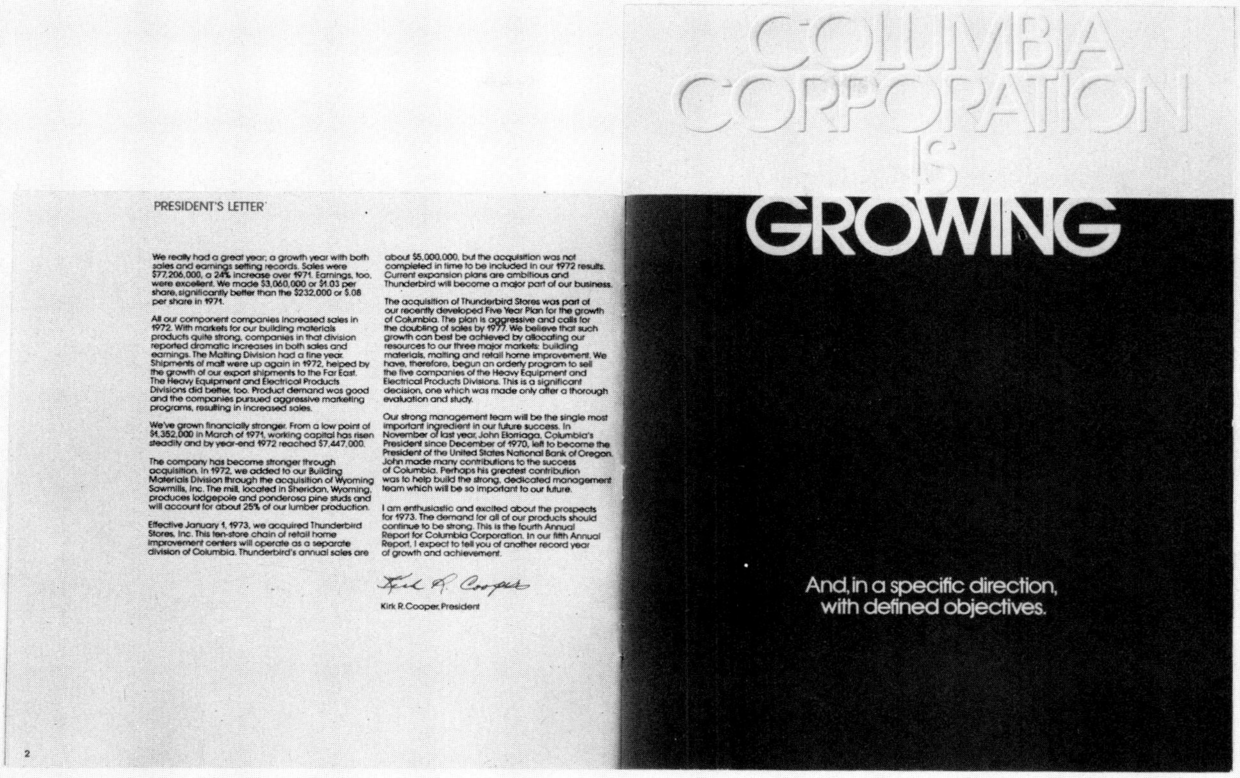

PRESIDENT'S LETTER

We really had a great year; a growth year with both sales and earnings setting records. Sales were $77,206,000, a 24% increase over 1971. Earnings, too, were excellent. We made $3,060,000 or $1.03 per share, significantly better than the $232,000 or $.08 per share in 1971.

All our component companies increased sales in 1972. With markets for our building materials products quite strong, companies in that division reported dramatic increases in both sales and earnings. The Malting Division had a fine year. Shipments of malt were up again in 1972, helped by the growth of our export shipments to the Far East. The Heavy Equipment and Electrical Products Divisions did better, too. Product demand was good and the companies pursued aggressive marketing programs, resulting in increased sales.

We've grown financially stronger. From a low point of $4,352,000 in March of 1971, working capital has risen steadily and by year-end 1972 reached $7,447,000.

The company has become stronger through acquisition. In 1972, we added to our Building Materials Division through the acquisition of Wyoming Sawmills, Inc. The mill, located in Sheridan, Wyoming, produces lodgepole and ponderosa pine studs and will account for about 25% of our lumber production.

Effective January 1, 1973, we acquired Thunderbird Stores, Inc. This ten-store chain of retail home improvement centers will operate as a separate division of Columbia. Thunderbird's annual sales are about $5,000,000, but the acquisition was not completed in time to be included in our 1972 results. Current expansion plans are ambitious and Thunderbird will become a major part of our business.

The acquisition of Thunderbird Stores was part of our recently developed Five Year Plan for the growth of Columbia. The plan is aggressive and calls for the doubling of sales by 1977. We believe that such growth can best be achieved by allocating our resources to our three major markets: building materials, malting and retail home improvement. We have, therefore, begun an orderly program to sell the five companies of the Heavy Equipment and Electrical Products Divisions. This is a significant decision, one which was made only after a thorough evaluation and study.

Our strong management team will be the single most important ingredient in our future success. In November of last year, John Elorriaga, Columbia's President since December of 1970, left to become the President of the United States National Bank of Oregon. John made many contributions to the success of Columbia. Perhaps his greatest contribution was to help build the strong, dedicated management team which will be so important to our future.

I am enthusiastic and excited about the prospects for 1973. The demand for all of our products should continue to be strong. This is the fourth Annual Report for Columbia Corporation. In our fifth Annual Report, I expect to tell you of another record year of growth and achievement.

Kirk R. Cooper, President

COLUMBIA CORPORATION IS GROWING

And, in a specific direction, with defined objectives.

695

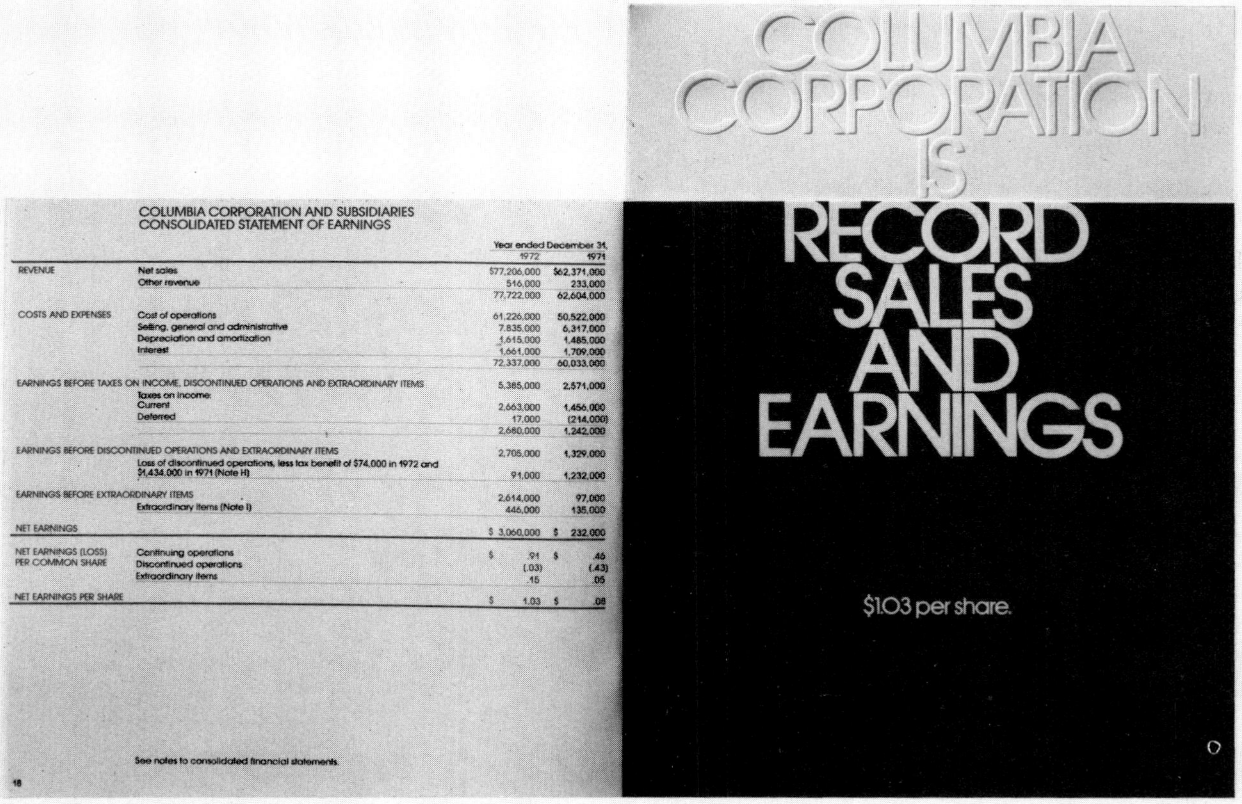

COLUMBIA CORPORATION AND SUBSIDIARIES
CONSOLIDATED STATEMENT OF EARNINGS

		Year ended December 31, 1972	1971
REVENUE	Net sales	$77,206,000	$62,371,000
	Other revenue	516,000	233,000
		77,722,000	62,604,000
COSTS AND EXPENSES	Cost of operations	61,226,000	50,522,000
	Selling, general and administrative	7,835,000	6,317,000
	Depreciation and amortization	1,615,000	1,485,000
	Interest	1,661,000	1,709,000
		72,337,000	60,033,000
EARNINGS BEFORE TAXES ON INCOME, DISCONTINUED OPERATIONS AND EXTRAORDINARY ITEMS		5,385,000	2,571,000
	Taxes on income:		
	Current	2,663,000	1,456,000
	Deferred	17,000	(214,000)
		2,680,000	1,242,000
EARNINGS BEFORE DISCONTINUED OPERATIONS AND EXTRAORDINARY ITEMS		2,705,000	1,329,000
	Loss of discontinued operations, less tax benefit of $74,000 in 1972 and $1,434,000 in 1971 (Note H)	91,000	1,232,000
EARNINGS BEFORE EXTRAORDINARY ITEMS		2,614,000	97,000
	Extraordinary items (Note I)	446,000	135,000
NET EARNINGS		$ 3,060,000	$ 232,000
NET EARNINGS (LOSS) PER COMMON SHARE	Continuing operations	$ .91	$ .46
	Discontinued operations	(.03)	(.43)
	Extraordinary items	.15	.05
NET EARNINGS PER SHARE		$ 1.03	$ .08

See notes to consolidated financial statements.

COLUMBIA CORPORATION IS RECORD SALES AND EARNINGS

$1.03 per share.

696

693
Lou Dorfsman Entrant
Peter Tomlinson Illustrator
Lou Dorfsman, Ted Andresakes Designers
CBS/Broadcast Group Agency
CBS Stations Client

694
Brian O'Neill Entrant
Wolf von dem Bussche Illustrator
Davis-Delaney-Arrow Client

695-696
Robin Rickabaugh Entrant
Heidi and Robin Rickabaugh Art Directors
Gary White Advertising Inc. Agency
Columbia Corporation Client

697

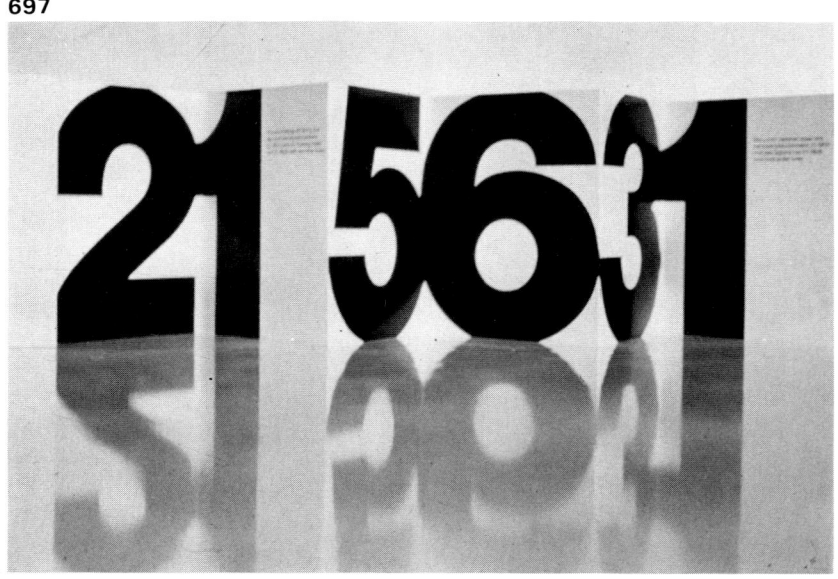

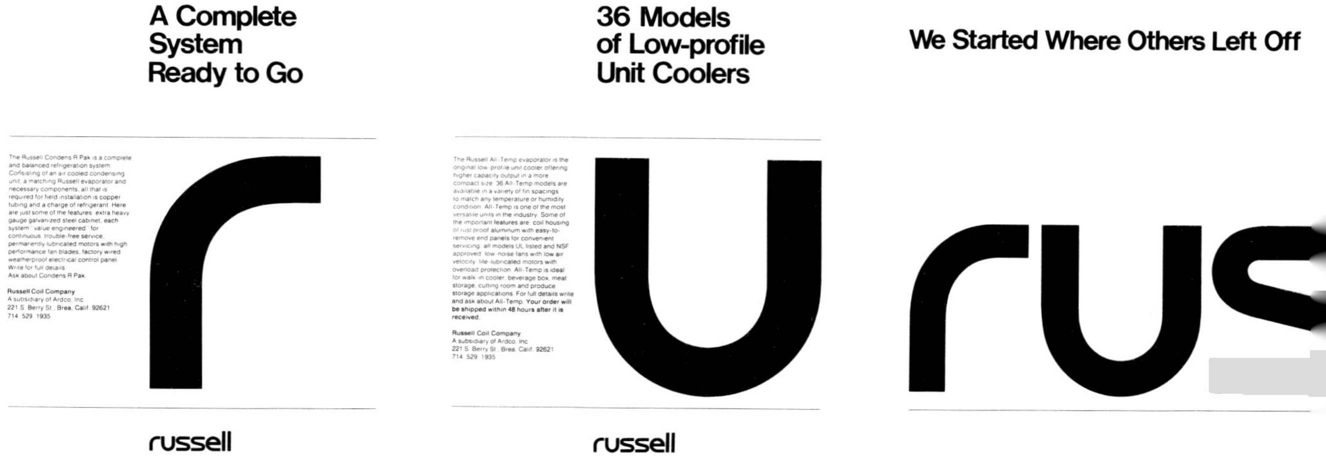

A Complete System Ready to Go
The Russell Condens R Pak is a complete and balanced refrigeration system. Consisting of an air cooled condensing unit, a matching Russell evaporator and necessary components, all that is required for field installation is copper tubing and a charge of refrigerant. Here are just some of the features: extra heavy gauge galvanized steel cabinet, each system "value engineered" for continuous, trouble-free service, permanently lubricated motors with high performance fan blades, factory wired weatherproof electrical control panel. Write for full details. Ask about Condens R Pak.
Russell Coil Company
A subsidiary of Ardco, Inc.
221 S. Berry St., Brea, Calif. 92621
714 529 1935
r
russell
36 Models of Low-profile Unit Coolers
The Russell All-Temp evaporator is the original low-profile unit cooler offering higher capacity output in a more compact size. 36 All-Temp models are available in a variety of fin spacings to match any temperature or humidity condition. All-Temp is one of the most versatile units in the industry. Some of the important features are: coil housing of rust proof aluminum with easy-to-remove end panels for convenient servicing; all models UL listed and NSF approved; low-noise fans with low air velocity; life-lubricated motors with overload protection. All-Temp is ideal for walk-in cooler, beverage box, meat storage, cutting room and produce storage applications. For full details write and ask about All-Temp. Your order will be shipped within 48 hours after it is received.
Russell Coil Company
A subsidiary of Ardco, Inc.
221 S. Berry St., Brea, Calif. 92621
714 529 1935
u
russell
We Started Where Others Left Off
rus

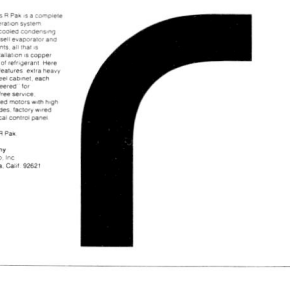

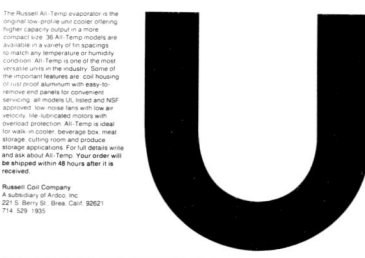

698

697
Arie J. Geurts Design Entrant
Aire J. Geurts Art Director
Unimark International, Johannesburg Client

698-702
Center for Advanced Research in Design Entrant
John Massey Art Director
Rick Eiber Designer
Russell Coil Co. Client

SPORTS DIGEST

703

VIDEOSONICS

704

bayhead YACHT CORP.

705

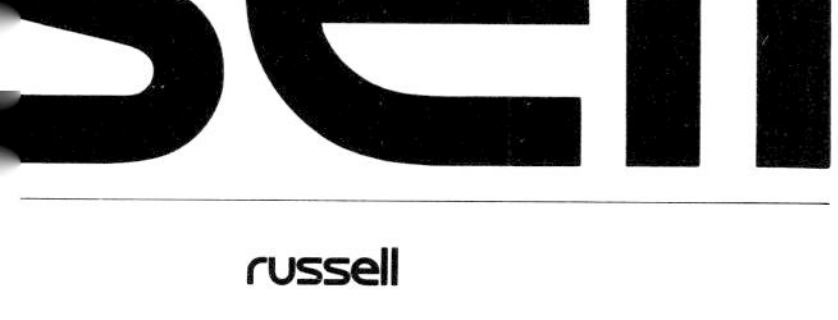
sell
russell

700

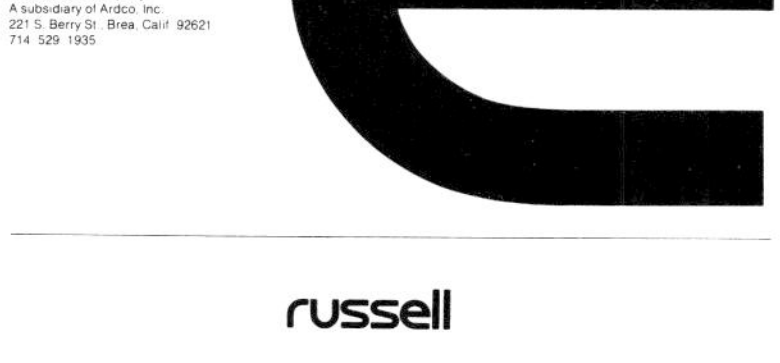
42 Models
of Air Cooled
Condensers
e
russell

701

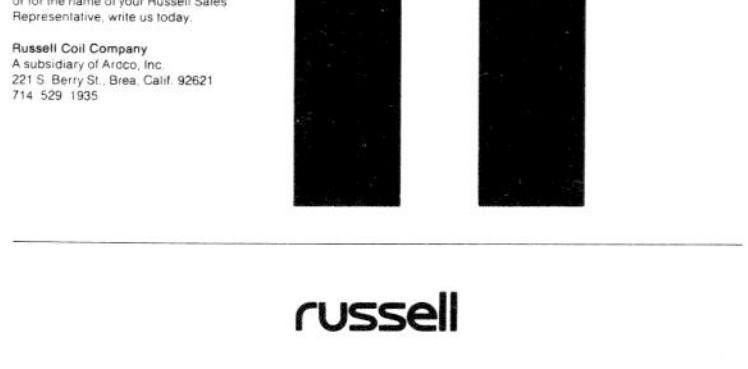
One Step Better
ll
russell

702

703
Robert Miles Runyan & Assoc. Entrant
Robert Miles Runyan Art Director
Scott Reid Designer
Sports Digest Client

704
Joel Shukovsky Entrant
Videosonics Client

705
Lubalin, Smith, Carnase Entrant
Roger Ferriter Art Director
Bayhead Yacht Corporation Client

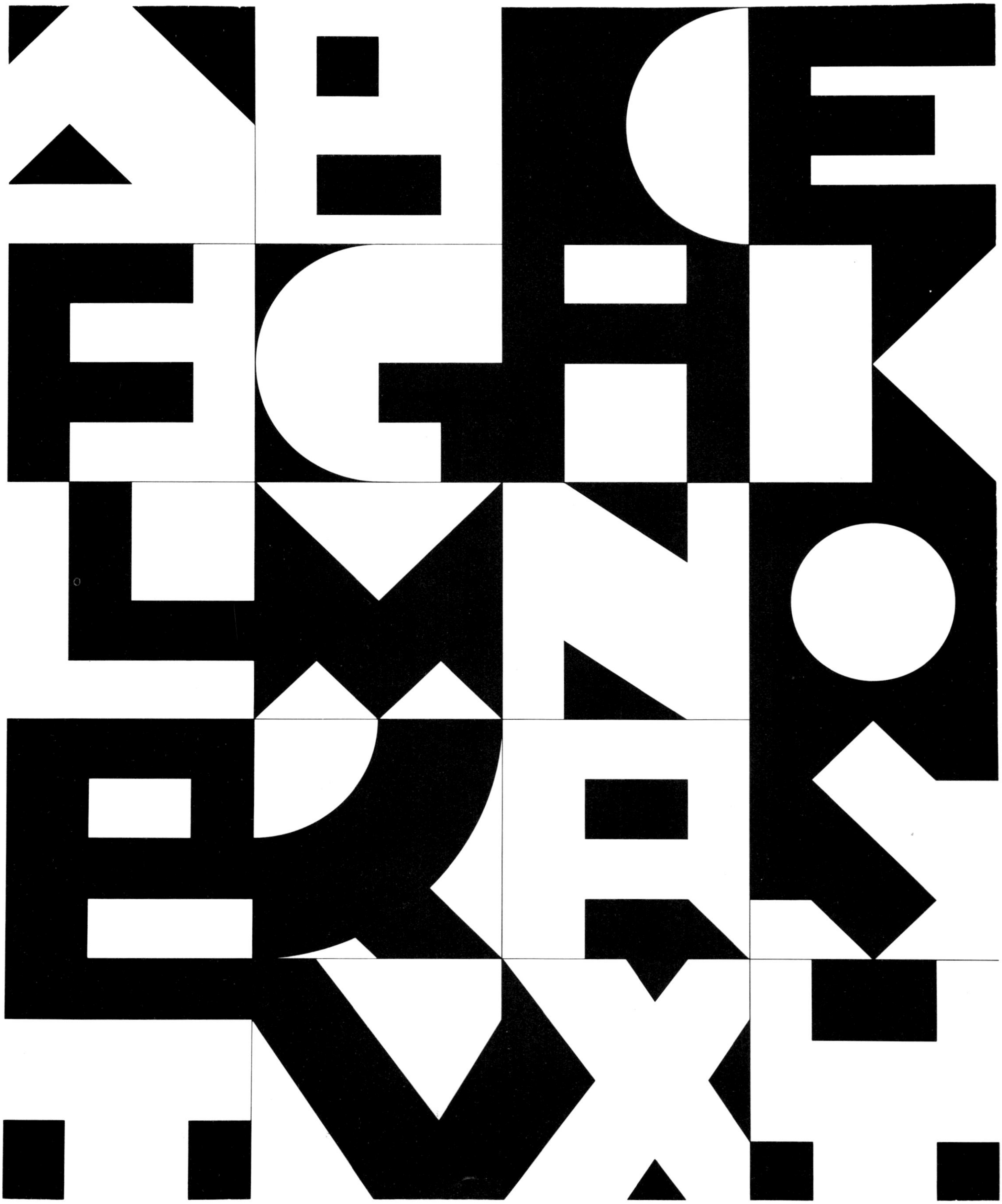

706
Brian O'Neill Entrant
Mike Schacht Art Director
Davis/Delaney/Arrow Agency
Champion Papers Client

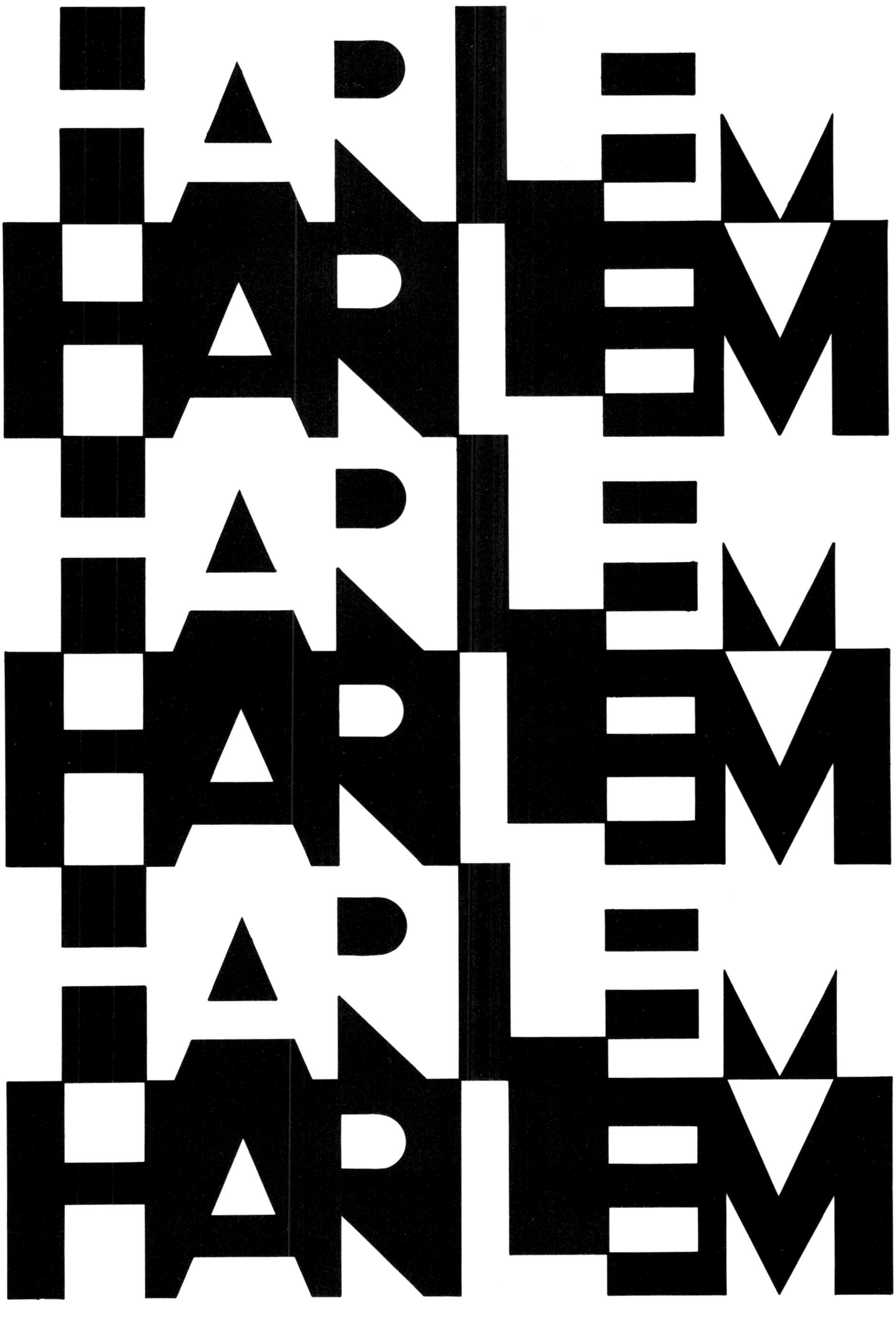
HARLEM
HARLEM
HARLEM

707
Jean-Michel Wargniez Entrant
Havas Conseil Agency

708

709

710

711

708
Thomas A. Rigsby Entrant
Phillips-Brown and TriArts, Inc. Agency
Patterson & Associates Studio
American Security Bank Client

709
Designers Ross, Stewart & Winner Entrant
Frank Ross, Dan Stewart Art Directors
Creative Typographers Client

710
Boatright, Oden & Payton, Inc. Entrant
John Boatright Art Director
Memphis & Shelby County Airport Authority Client

711
David M. Reed Entrant
David M. Reed, Lindy Kunishima Art Direc
Lindy Kunishima Illustrator
Reed/Kaina Adv. Inc. Agency
Hawaii+Foreign Trade Zone #9 Client

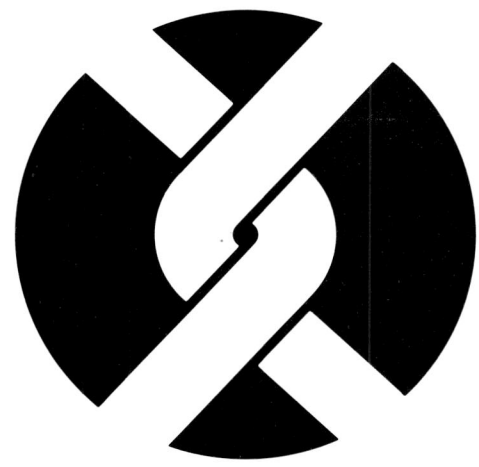

712

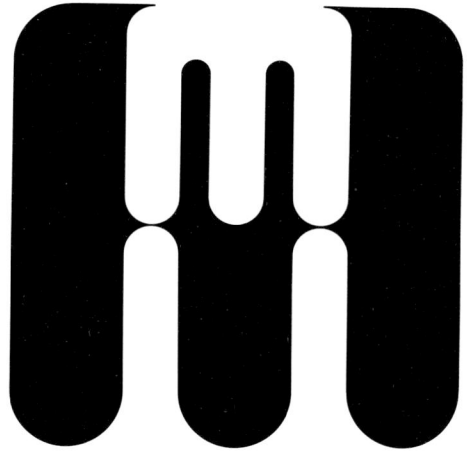

713

714

715

712
Robert Miles Runyan & Associates Entrant
Robert Miles Runyan Art Director
Gary Hinsche Designer
American Protection Industries Client

713
Rinaldo Cutini Entrant
Marcello Masi Client

714
Designers Ross, Stewart & Winner Entrant
Frank Ross, Dan Stewart Art Directors
Old Number Seven Music Co. Client

715
The Dombrosky/Peck Coalition, Inc. Entrant
Joe Herrick Art Director
Washington Investment Planning Co., Inc. Client

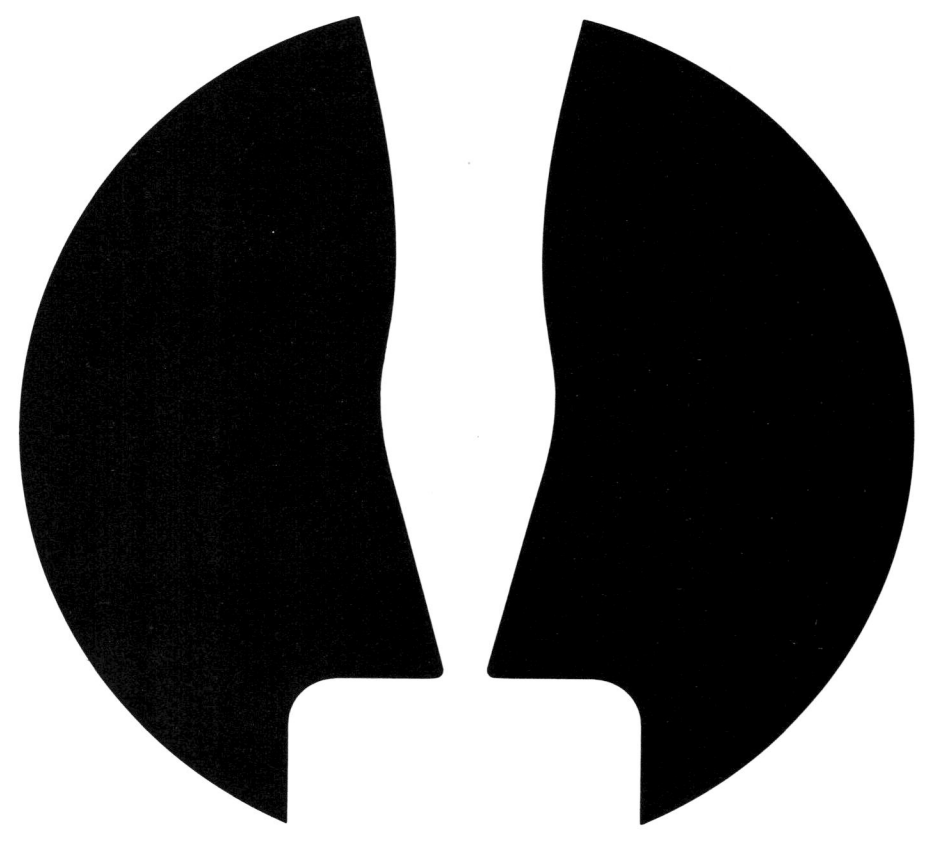

716
Leonard Rochlin Entrant
Leonard Rochlin Design Associates Studio
Martin Partners, Inc. Agency
Northside Psychiatric Hospital Client

717
Weller & Juett Inc. Entrant
Don Weller, Dennis S. Juett Art Directors
Dan Hanrahan Illustrator
Lithographix, Inc. Client

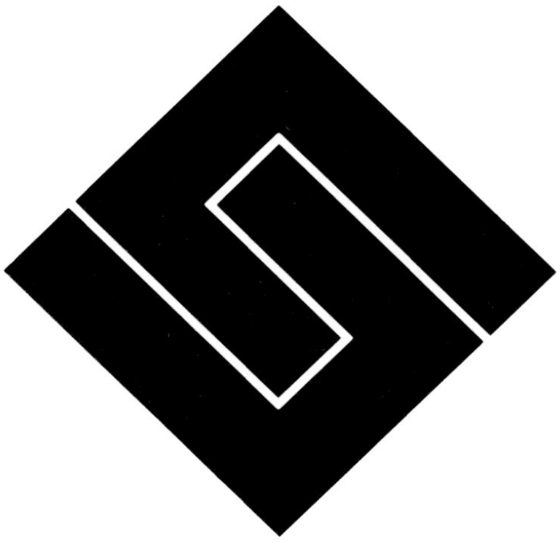

718

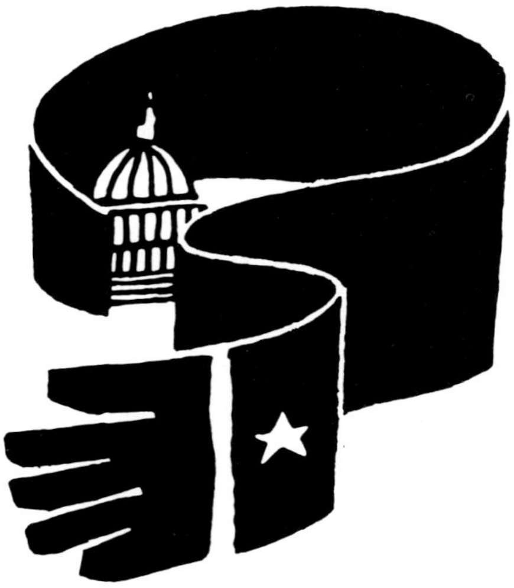

719

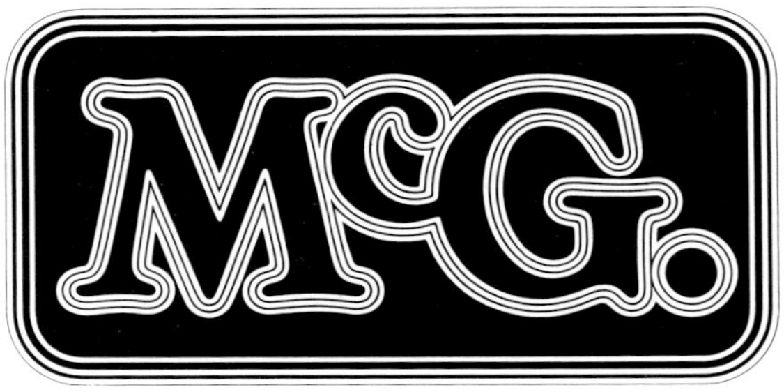
McG.

720

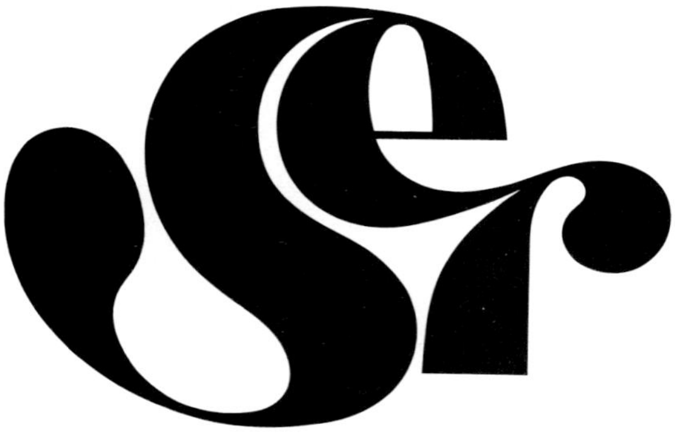
Ser

721

718
Raymond Lee & Associates Limited Entrant
Raymond Lee
Art Director
Durastone Limited (Lockstone) Client

719
Saul Bass & Associates Inc.
Entrant
Art Goodman, Morrie Marsh
Art Directors
Art Goodman
Illustrator
American Documentary Films
Client

720
Lubalin, Smith, Carnase
Entrant
Herb Lubalin
Art Director
Citizens Committee for McGovern/Shriver
Client

721
Claude Dieterich
Entrant
"Ser" Editorial
Client

722

723

724

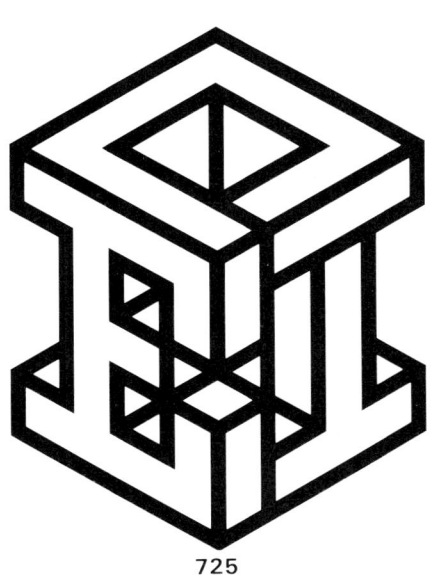

725

722
on Leenhouts,
Reinhard Polstra
Entrants
. Leenhouts
Art Director
Bruna Boekhandel
Client

723
COM 3 (Soyster &
Ohrenschall, Inc.)
Entrant
Gerrit Dreyhage,
Charles Norton,
Tom Wallerich Art Directors
Wild Horse Mesa
Client

724
Powell & Associates
Entrant
Bill Powell
Art Director
Leland Realty &
Land Company Client

725
Lubalin, Smith, Carnase Entrant
Herb Lubalin Art Director
Delpire Cie. Illustrator
Lubalin, Delpire Cie.,
Espace Interieur Clients

726

727

728

729

730

731

732

733

734

726
Ronald Wolin
Entrant
Ronald Wolin,
Norm Friant
Art Directors
Leo Monahan
Illustrator
Grey Advertising
Agency
American Honda
Client

727
Akihiko Seki
Entrant
The Emelin
Theatre
Client

728
George & Me
Entrant
Bruce Fallert,
George Kubricht
Art Directors
Step 2, Inc.
Client

729
Arie J. Geurts
Design
Entrant
Arie J. Geurts
Art Director
Carlton Lighting
Client

730
Peter Good
Entrant
Kupper/
Grant Inc.
Agency
Hartford
National Bank,
Money Center
Client

731
Weller &
Juett Inc.
Entrant
Don Weller,
Dennis Juett
Art Directors
Don Weller
Illustrator
Fred Schmid
Associates
Client

732
Arie J.
Geurts Design
Entrant
Salli Geurts
Art Director
Metamorphosis
Client

733
Courtland
Thomas White
Entrant
Courtland
Thomas White,
Inc. Agency
United
Neighborhood
Houses of
New York
Client

734
Michael
Doret
Entrant
Barry
Smith
Client

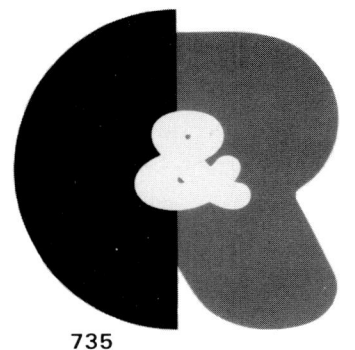
735

736

737

738

739

740

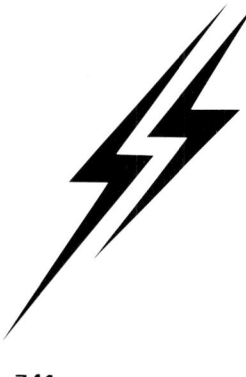
741

742

743

735
W. Chris Gorman Entrant
W. Chris Gorman Associates Studio
American Business Press Client

736
Selame Design Associates Entrant
Joe Selame Art Director
Joe Selame, Richard Edlund Designers
Foreign Autopart Client

737
William F. Finn Entrant
James Wilkins Art Director
William F. Finn & Associates Agency
Stewart Blood Center Client

738
Rinaldo Cutini Entrant
SARA-Perfumes-Gifts Client

739
Fernando Medina Entrant
Lintas España Agency
Sofico Vacaciones Client

740
Kiviat/Rappoport Inc. Entrant
Stephen Kiviat Art Director
Robert Cooney Illustrator

741
Steve Sohmer, Inc. Entrant
Tom Clemente Art Director

742
Fillman Advertising, Inc. Entrant
James M. Gobberdiel Art Director
Jack Davis Illustrator
Jack Davis Graphics Studio
Do Duds Laundry & Dry Cleaning Client

743
Caputo Design Entrant
Ralph Caputo Art Director
Boston Assoc. for Childbirth Education Client

Peter Revson

744
Robert Miles Runyan & Assoc. Entrant
Robert Miles Runyan Art Director
Robert Runyan, Ron Jeffries Designers
Peter Revson Client

745
Spyros Dellaportas Entrant
Mary Charlton Illustrator
Bronson Design Studio Client

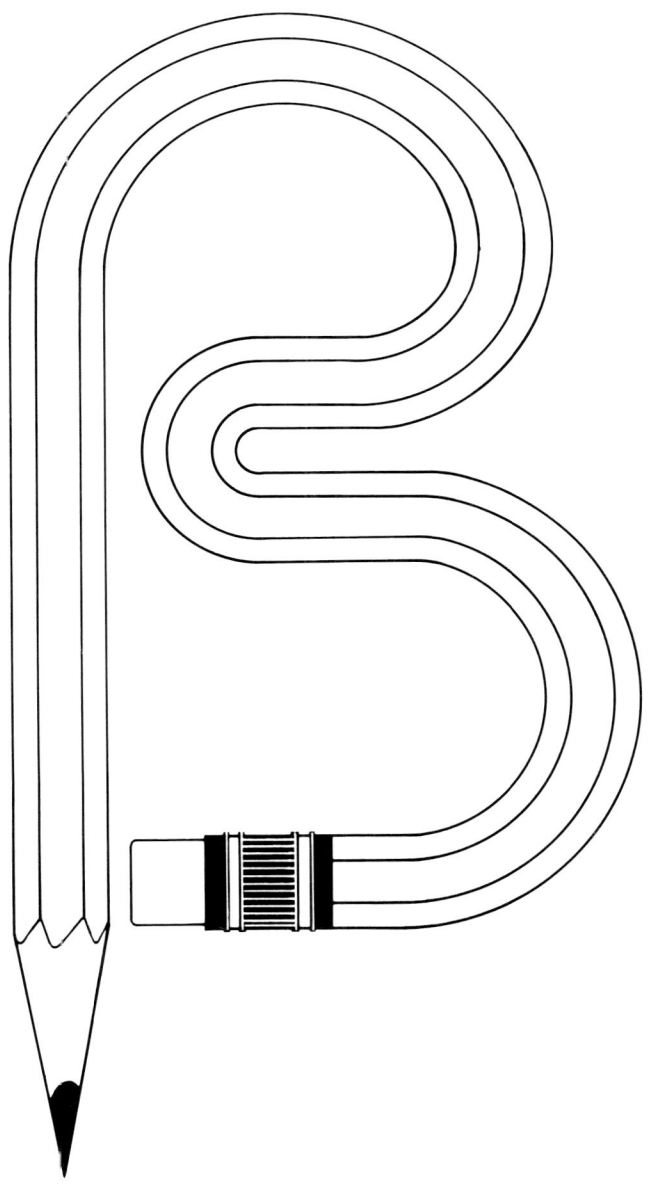

746

COTTON INCORPORATED
COTTON INCORPORATED
J. DUKES WOOTERS, JR.
President
COTTON INCORPORATED

747

athens paper

748

BROWN BAG RECORDS
BROWN BAG RECORDS
BROWN BAG RECORDS

749

AMERICAN ARCHIVES
AMERICAN ARCHIVES

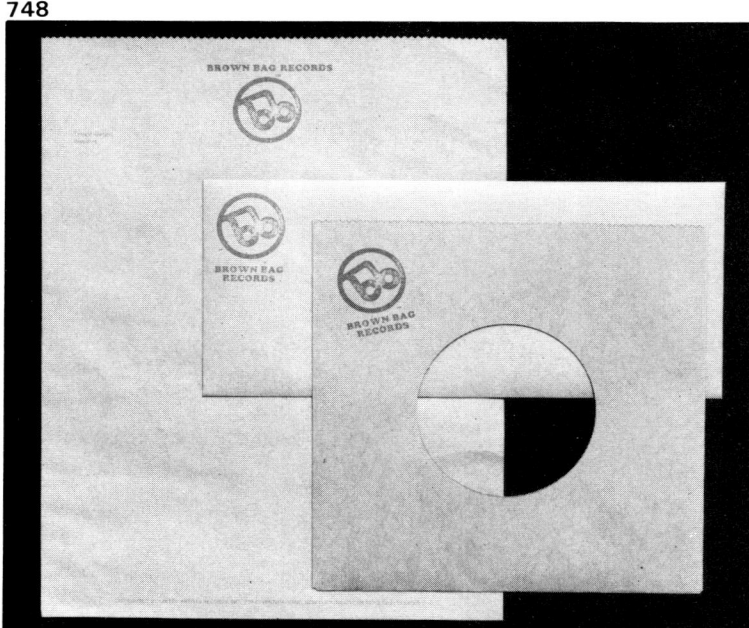

746
Walter Landor Associates Entrant
Cotton Incorporated Client

747
Harmon & Crook Entrant
Ken White Art Director
Dean St. Clair Illustrator
Ray Pike Studios Photographer
Athens Paper Co. Client

748
Wilkes & Braun Inc. Entrant
Tom Wilkes, Craig Braun Art Directors
Tom Wilkes Illustrator
Terry Knight Enterprises, Ltd. Client

749
Sun Associates Entrant
Chris Zarlengo Art Director
International Silver/ American Archives Client

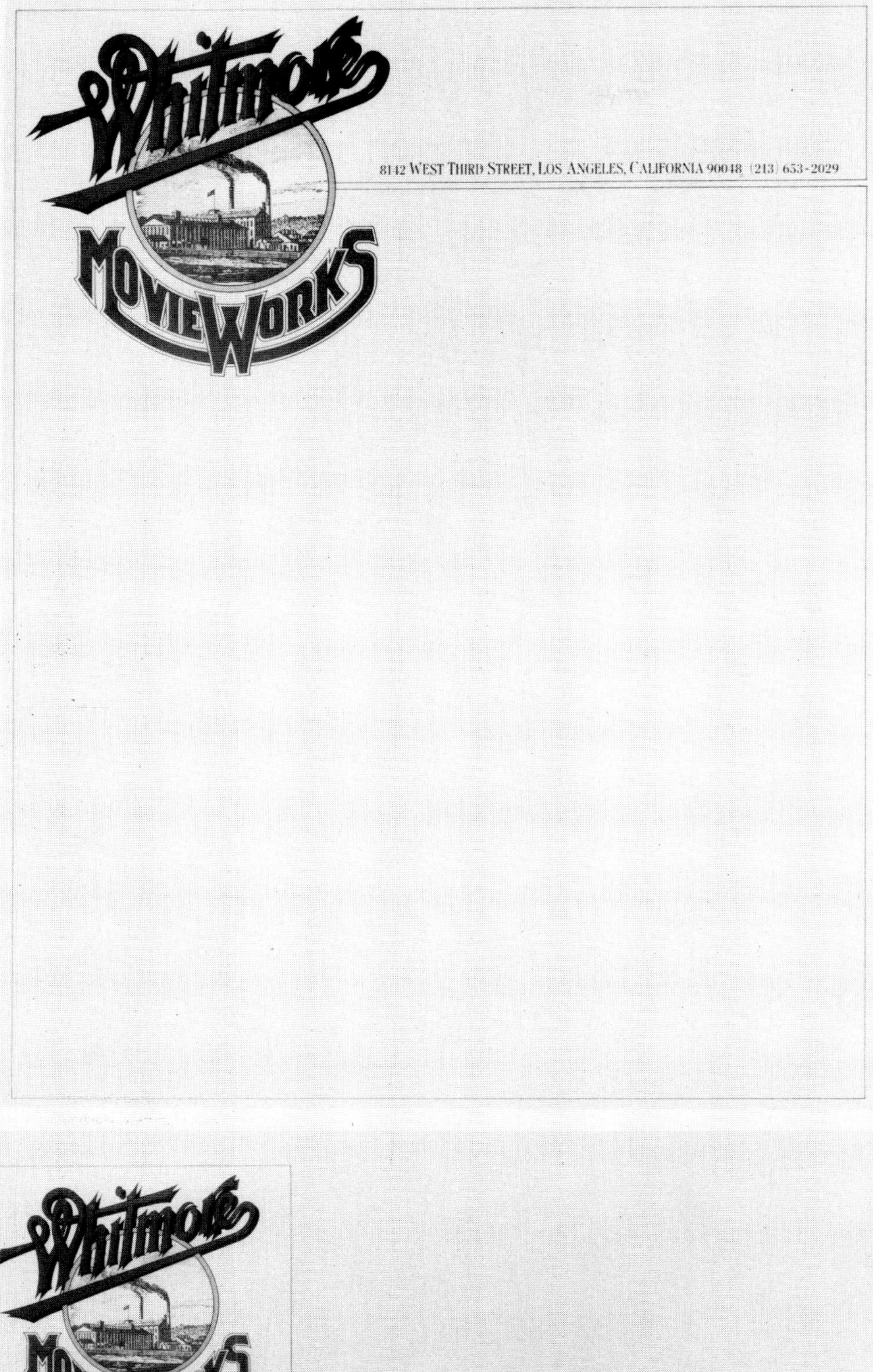
Whitmore
MOVIE WORKS
8142 WEST THIRD STREET, LOS ANGELES, CALIFORNIA 90048 (213) 653-2029

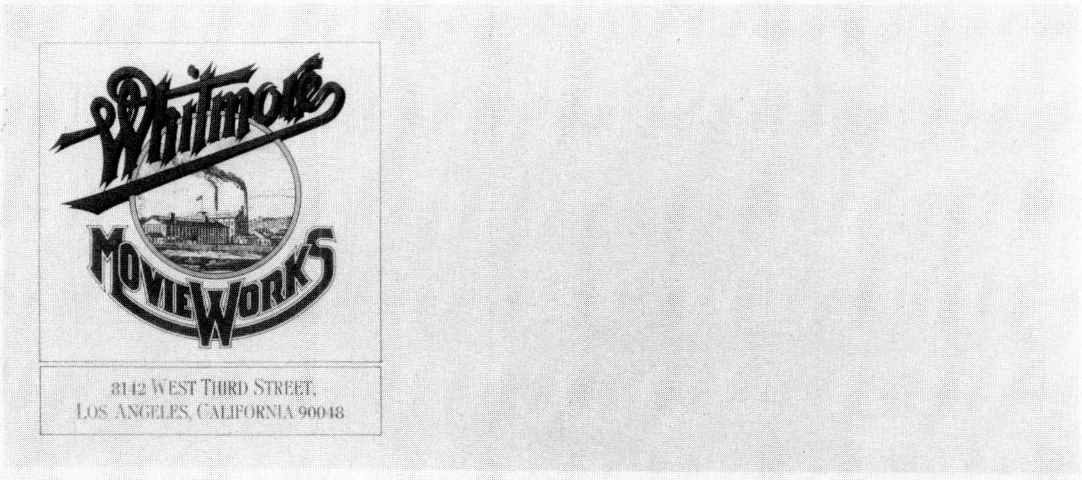
Whitmore
MOVIE WORKS
8142 WEST THIRD STREET,
LOS ANGELES, CALIFORNIA 90048

750
Michael Doret Entrant
Mary Lou Whitmore Art Director
Whitmore Movie Works Client

751

THE INVIRONMENTAL IMPERATIVE...ILLUMINATED CEILING SYSTEMS
TRILOGY

752

Leonard J. Schwartz Enterprises
29 North Main Street
West Hartford, Connecticut 06107
Telephone (203) 521-7024
Real Estate / Development / Construction / Investments

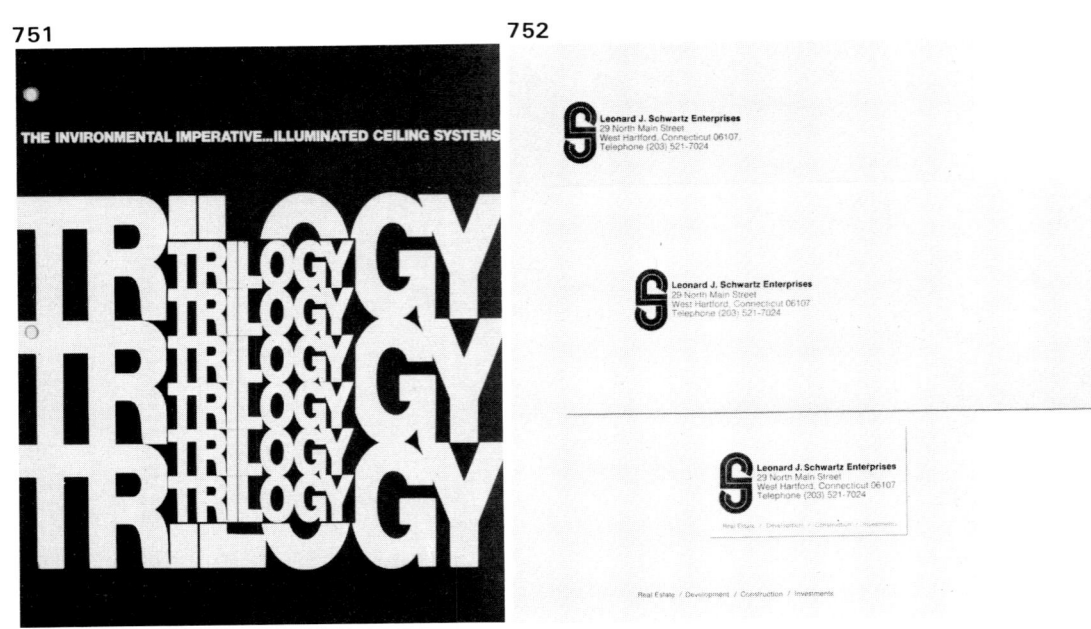

753

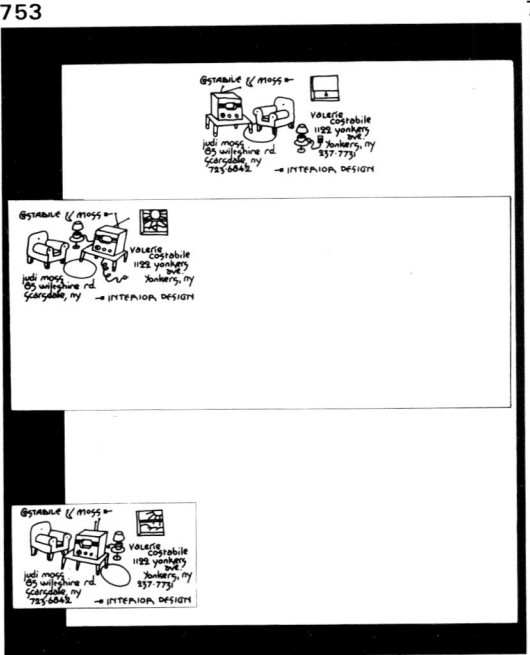

754

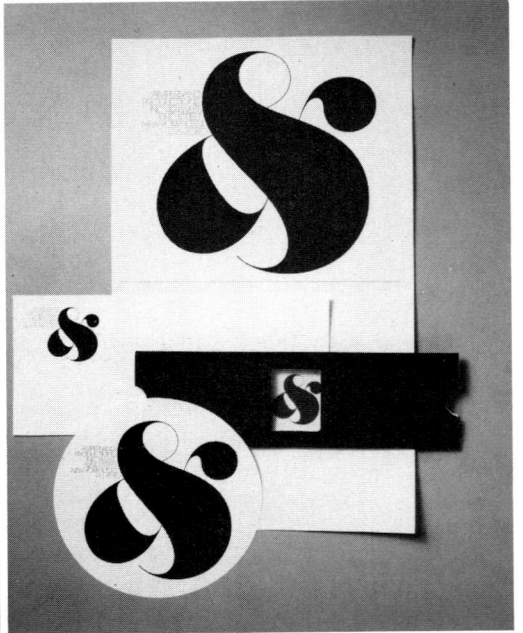

751
Edward Lamport Assoc. Entrant
Edward Lamport Art Director
Neo-Ray Lighting Systems Client

752
Bonnie Lang Entrant
Designers East Agency
Leonard J. Schwartz Enterprises Client

753
Robert Antonik Entrant
Robert Antonik, John Cohoe Art Directors
Morgan Press, Inc. Studio
Costabile and Moss Client

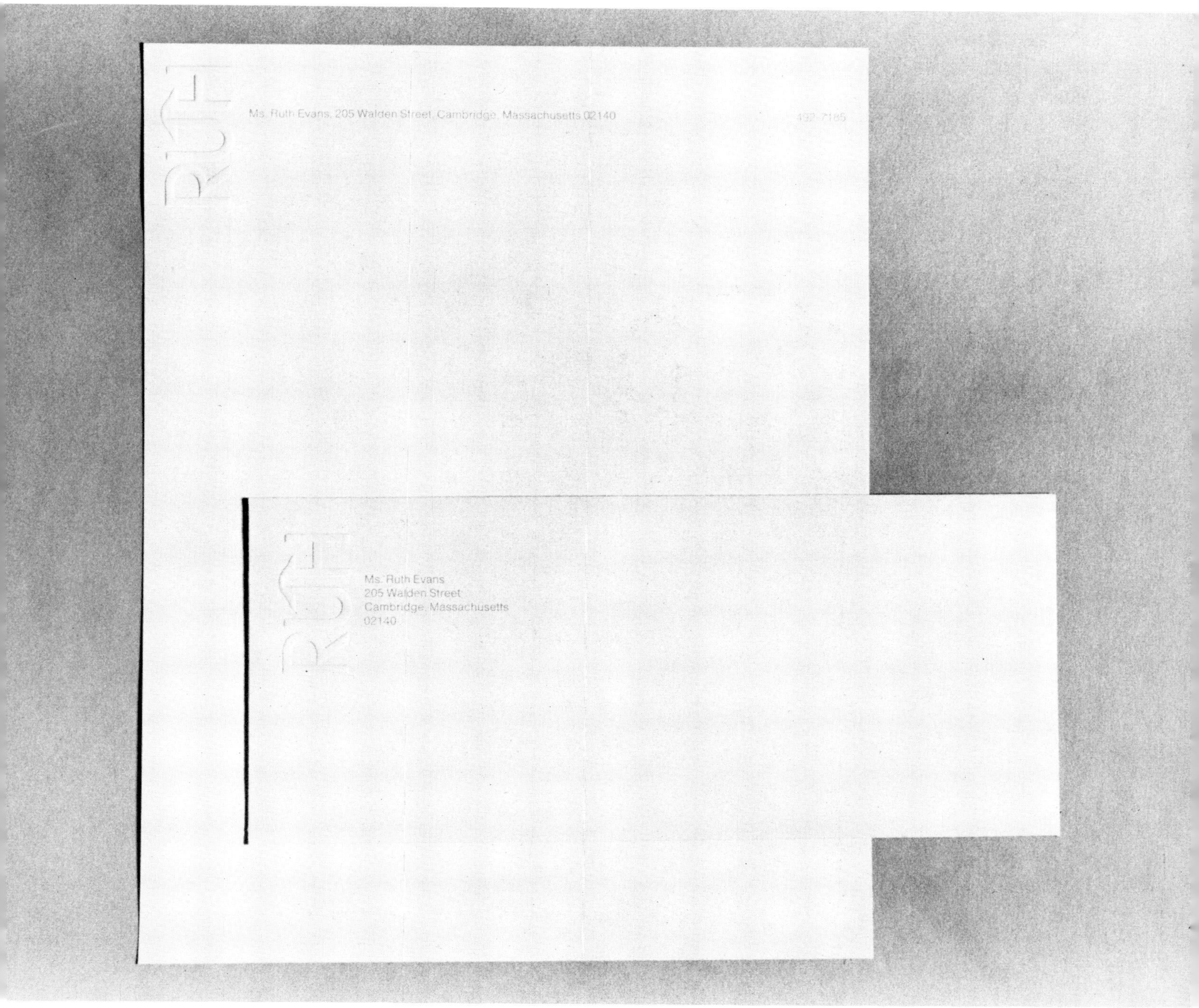
Ms. Ruth Evans, 205 Walden Street, Cambridge, Massachusetts 02140
Ms. Ruth Evans
205 Walden Street
Cambridge, Massachusetts
02140

755

754
Lubalin, Smith, Carnase Entrant
Herb Lubalin Art Director
Ampersand Productions Client

755
Ms. Ruth Evans Entrant

756

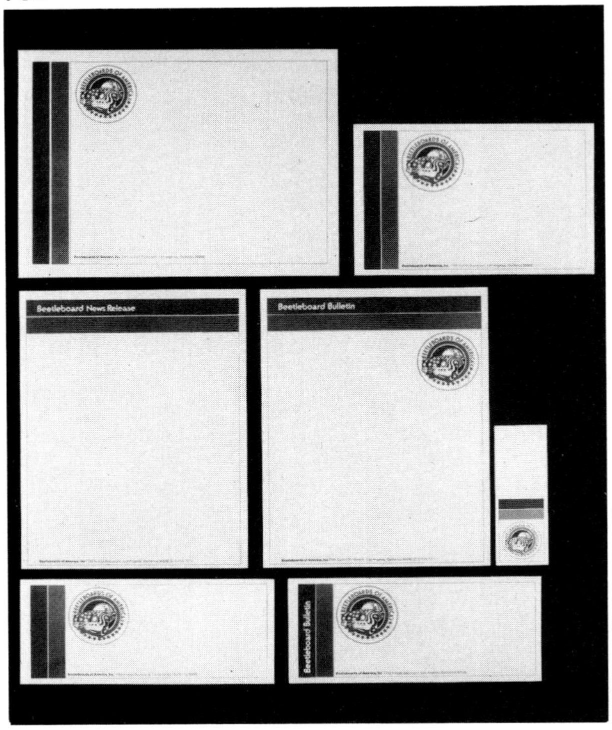
Beetleboard News Release
Beetleboard Bulletin
Beetleboard Bulletin

757

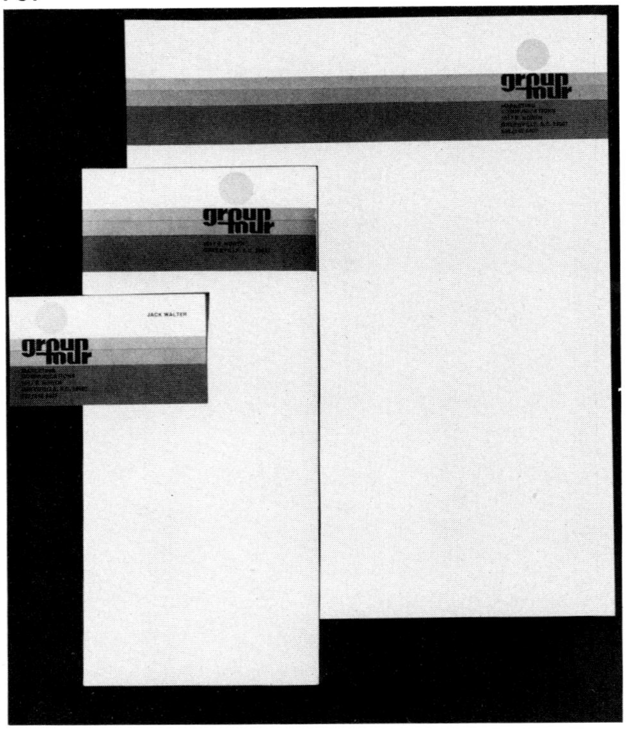
JACK WALTER

758

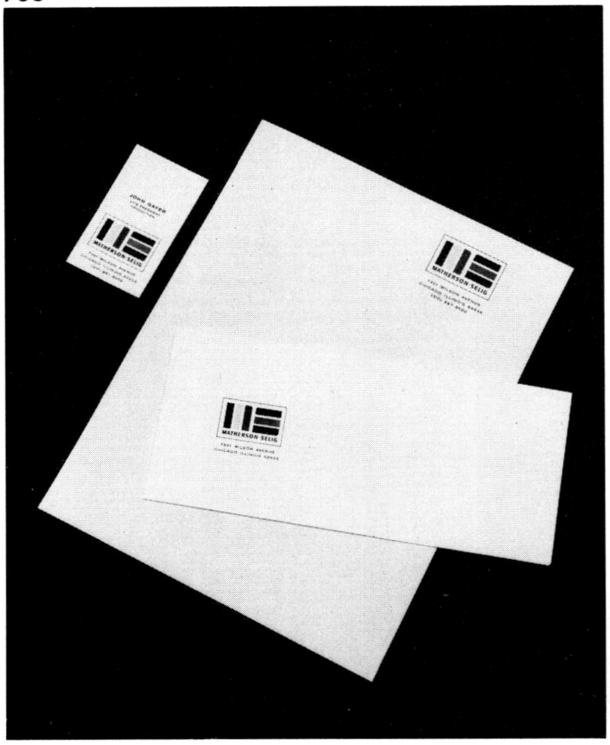
MATHERSON SELIG
MATHERSON SELIG

759

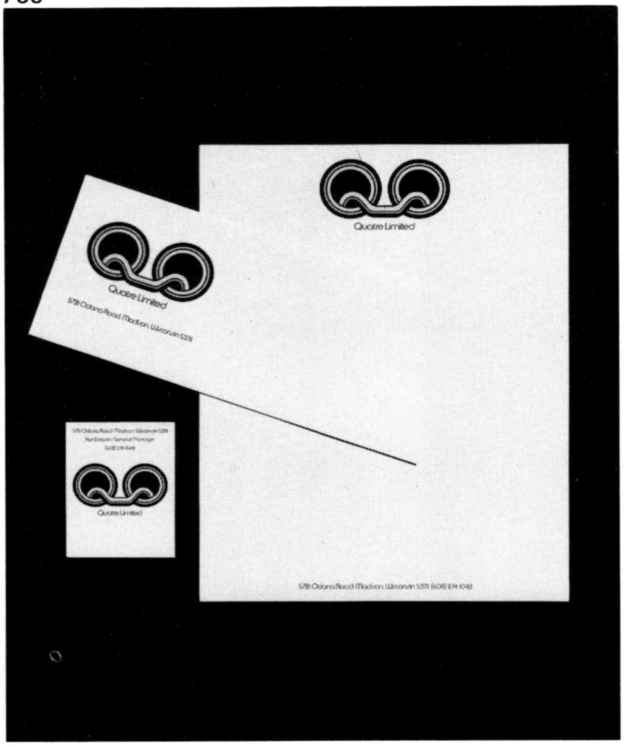
Quatre Limited
Quatre Limited
Quatre Limited

756
Charles E. Bird Incorporated Entrant
Joe Iwanaga Art Director
House of Design Studio
Dick Sokohara Illustrator
Beetleboards of America, Inc. Client

757
Group Four, Inc. Entrant
Grant Treaster, Jr., Richard Sefton Art Directors

758
Ian Scher Entrant
Ian Associates, Inc. Agency
Diversity Printing Corp. Studio
Matherson-Selig Color Card Co. Client

759
Marshall Smith & Assoc. Entrant
Nicholas Warrillow Art Director
Paul Tofte Artist
Strauss Printing Production
Quatre, Ltd. Client

760

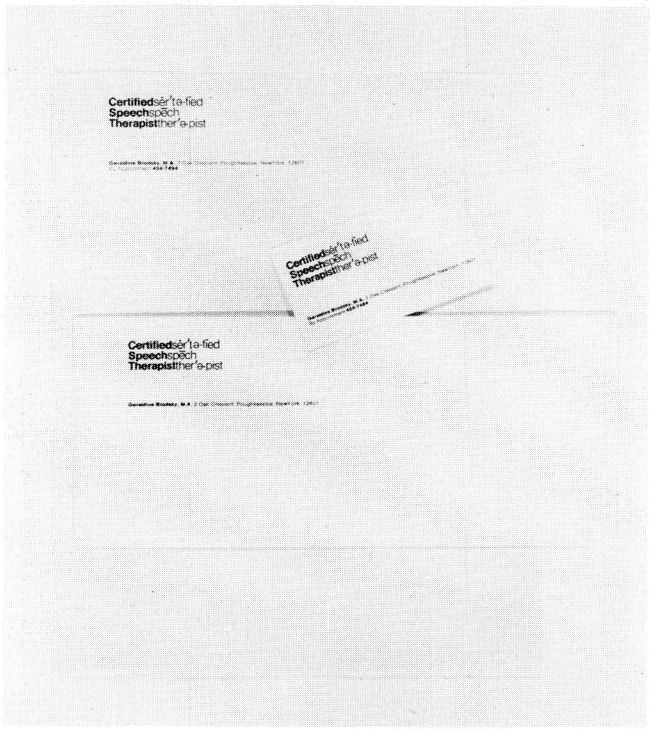
Certifiedsér'ta-fied
Speechspēch
Therapistther'a-pist

761

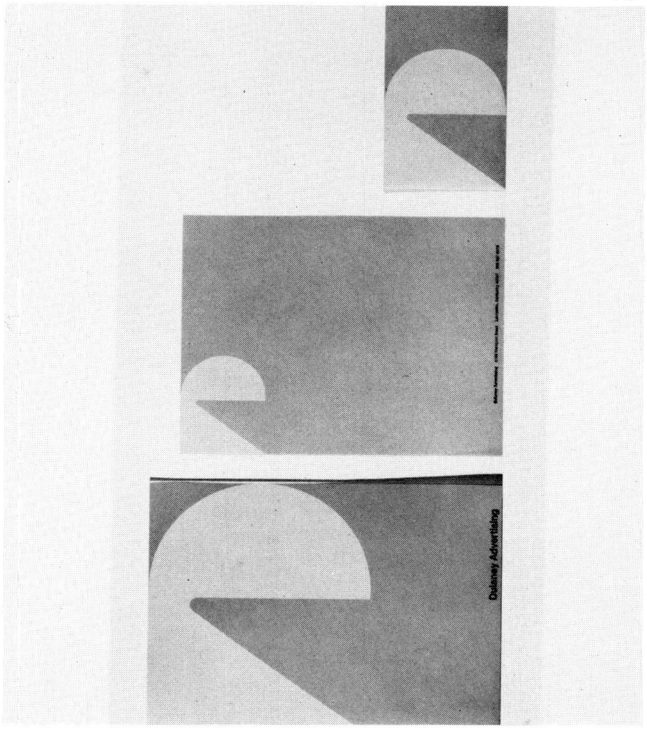
Dulaney Advertising

762

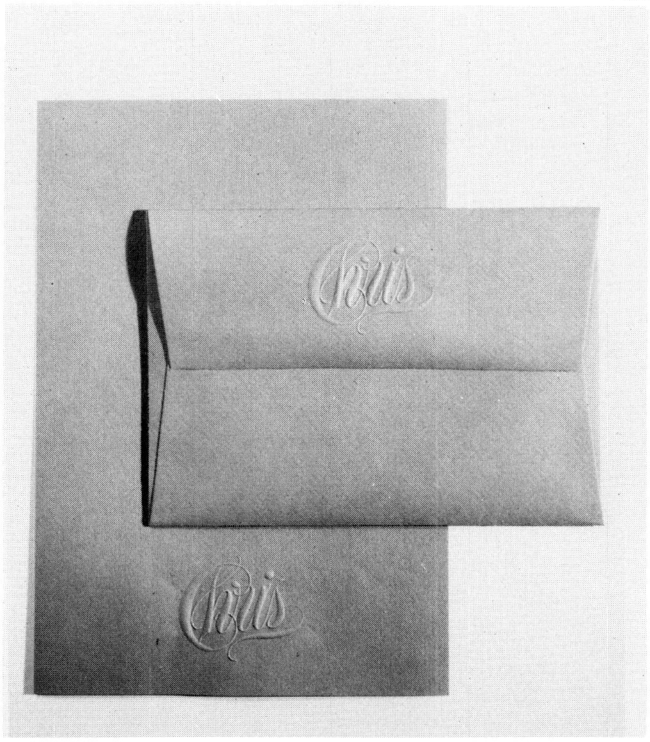
Chris

763

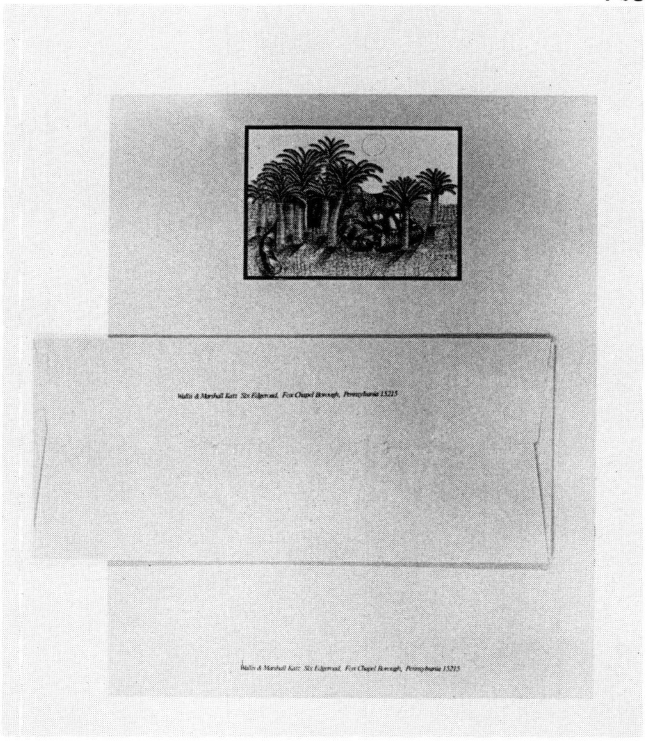

760
John Van Dyke Stram Entrant
Geraldine Brodsky Client

761
Designers Ross Stewart & Winner Entrant
Harriet Winner, Frank Ross, Dan Stewart Art Directors
Dulaney Advertising Client

762
Lubalin, Smith, Carnase Entrant
Tom Carnase Art Director
Chris Crane Cl ent

763
J.M. Essex Design Center Entrant
J. Michael Essex Art Director
Ed Zelinsky Illustrator
WQED Design Center Agency
Wallis and Marshall Katz Clients

764

Exhibit Graphics, Inc.
5-28 47th Road, Long Island City 11101 (212) 361-8069
Designers and Manufacturers of Exhibits, Displays, Showrooms, Interiors

765

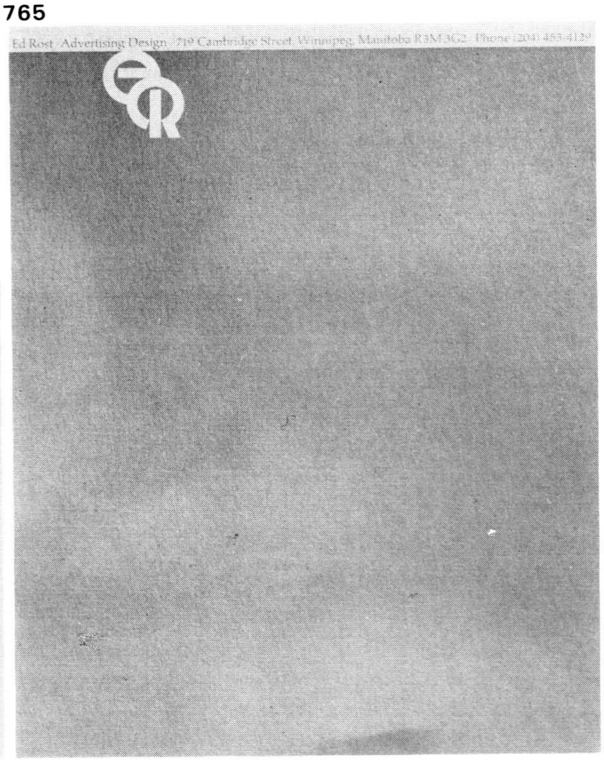
Ed Rost · Advertising Design · 719 Cambridge Street, Winnipeg, Manitoba R3M 3G2 · Phone (204) 453-4129

766

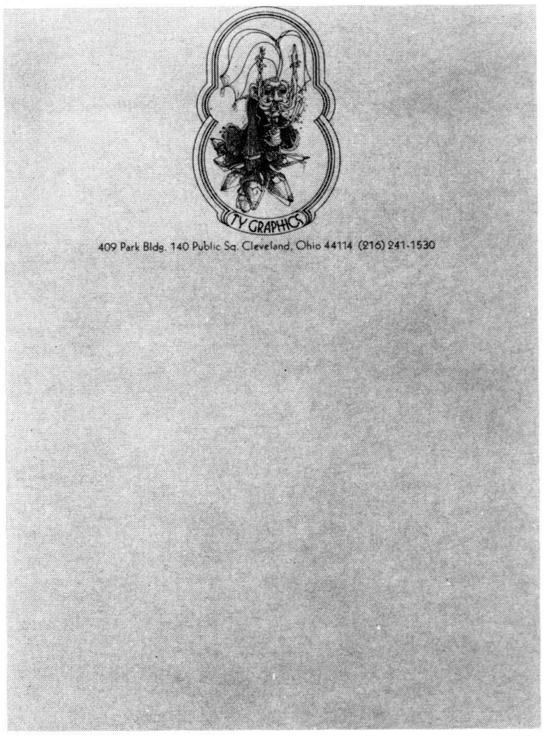
TY GRAPHICS
409 Park Bldg. 140 Public Sq. Cleveland, Ohio 44114 (216) 241-1530

767

Freight House Design, post office box 1163 Darien Conn 06820

764
Bob Salpeter
Entrant
Lopez Salpeter Inc.
Agency
Exhibit Graphics Inc.
Client

765
Ed Rost
Entrant

766
TY Graphics
Entrant
Tom Yurcich
Art Director

767
Bob Salpeter
Entrant
Lopez Salpeter Inc.
Agency
Freight House Design
Client

768

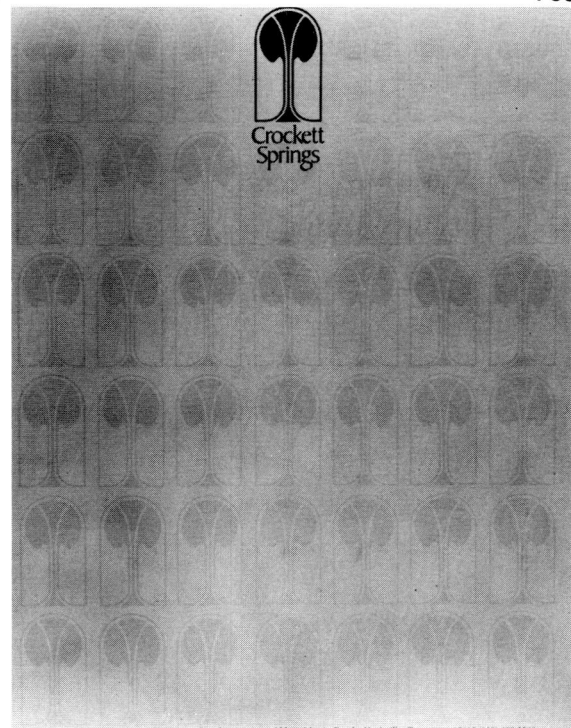

Treftadaeth Cymru
Treftadaeth Ewrop
Blwyddyn yr Adeiladau
Pwyllgor Cymru
Llywydd:
Ei Uchelder Brenhinol Tywysog Cymru
Cadeirydd: T. Mervyn Jones
European
Architectural
Heritage Year
Wales Committee
President:
H.R.H. The Prince of Wales
Chairman: T. Mervyn Jones
1975
Tŷ Croeso, Llandaf, Caerdydd CF5 2YZ
Welcome House, Llandaff, Cardiff CF5 2YZ

769

Crockett
Springs
John Coleman Hayes, Jr. & Associates Developers 2109 Abbott Martin Road Nashville, Tennessee 37215 (615) 292-5542

770

promotion
graphics inc.

771

Tuborg Breweries Ltd., 610 Lincoln St., Waltham, Mass. 02154 (617) 890-3600
TUBORG
BEER

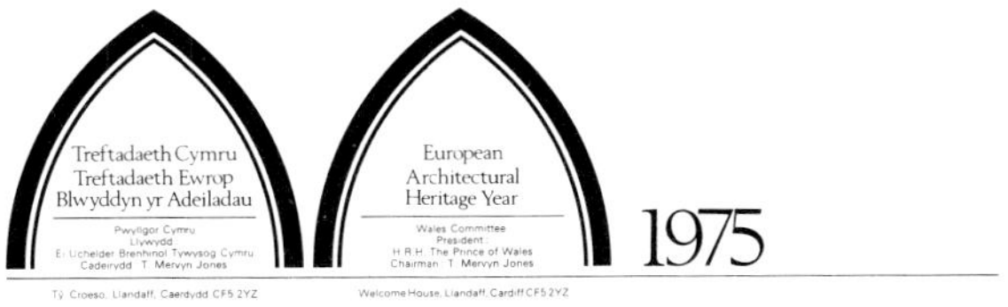

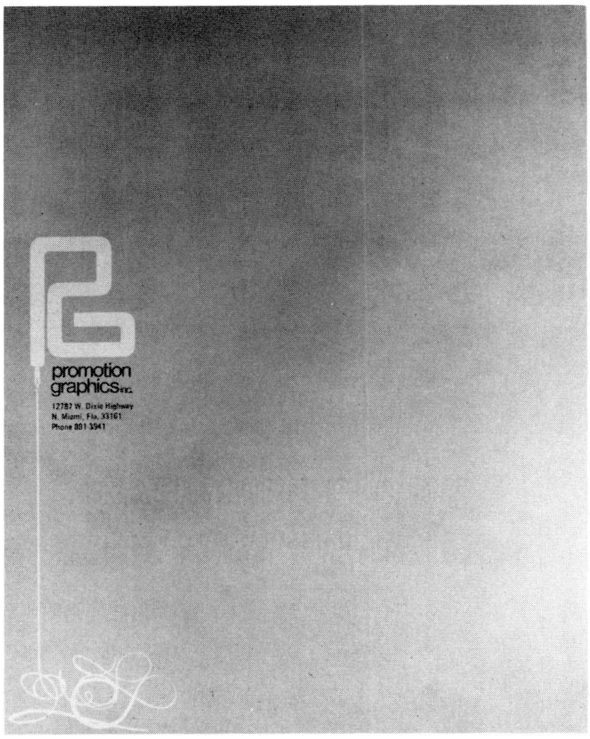

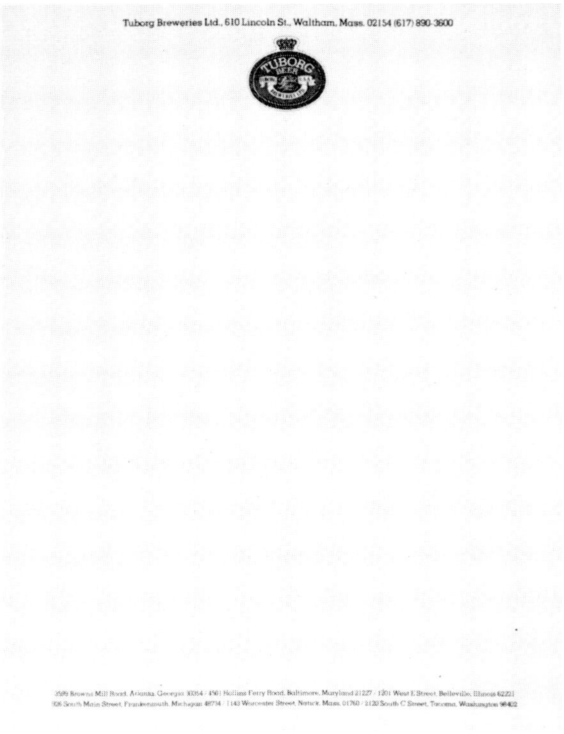

768
Wales Tourist Board
Entrant
Harry Williams
Art Director
European Architectural Heritage Year 1975 Client

769
Dan Girouard Entrant
Brad Whitfield Art Director
Design Graphics, Inc. Studio
John Coleman Hayes Jr. & Associates Client

770
Promotion Graphics
Entrant
Fred Barrett
Art Director

771
Robert Cipriani—Gunn Assoc. Entrant
Oney Shade, Robert Cipriani
Art Directors
Tuborg Breweries Client

772

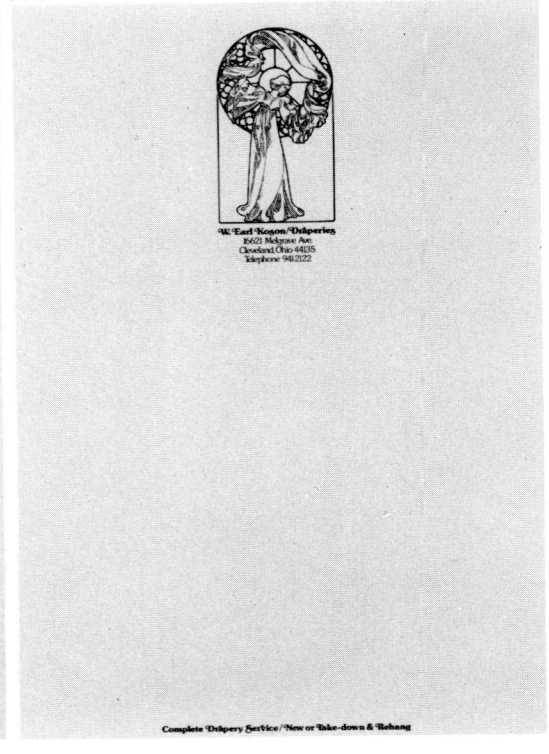

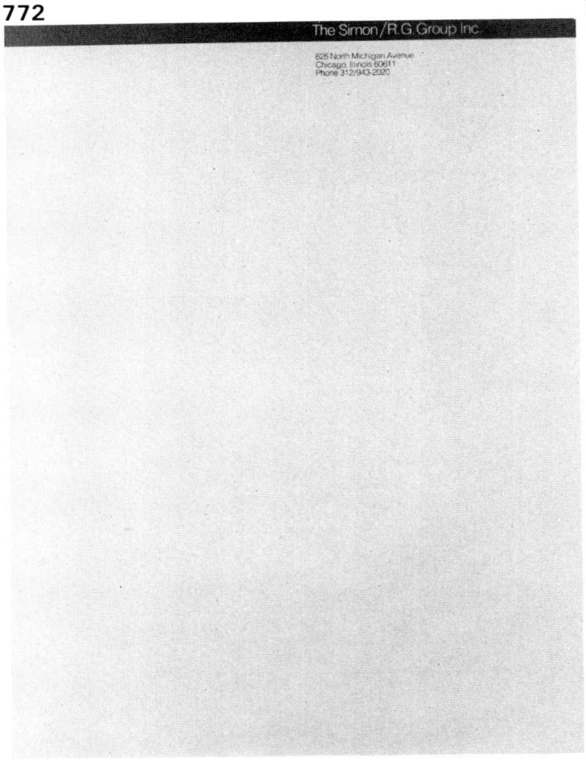

The Simon/R.G. Group Inc.
625 North Michigan Avenue
Chicago, Illinois 60611
Phone 312/943-2020

773

W. Earl Koson/Draperies
16621 Melgrave Ave.
Cleveland, Ohio 44135
Telephone 941-2122
Complete Drapery Service/New or Take-down & Rehang

774

Developers Diversified
Three Commerce Park Square • 23200 Chagrin Boulevard • Cleveland, Ohio 44122 • Tel: (216) 292-4900
Branch Office: 9500 Gandy Boulevard • St. Petersburg, Florida 33702 • Tel: (813) 522-5541

775

Gary Player Golfing Safaris

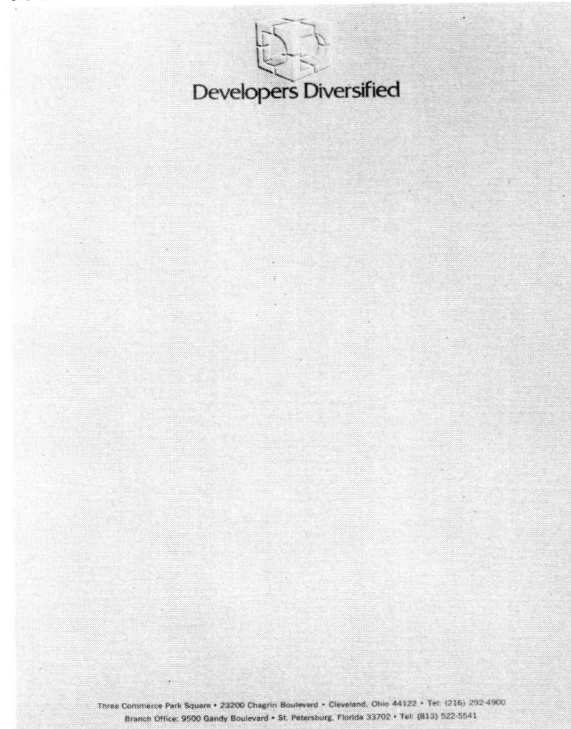

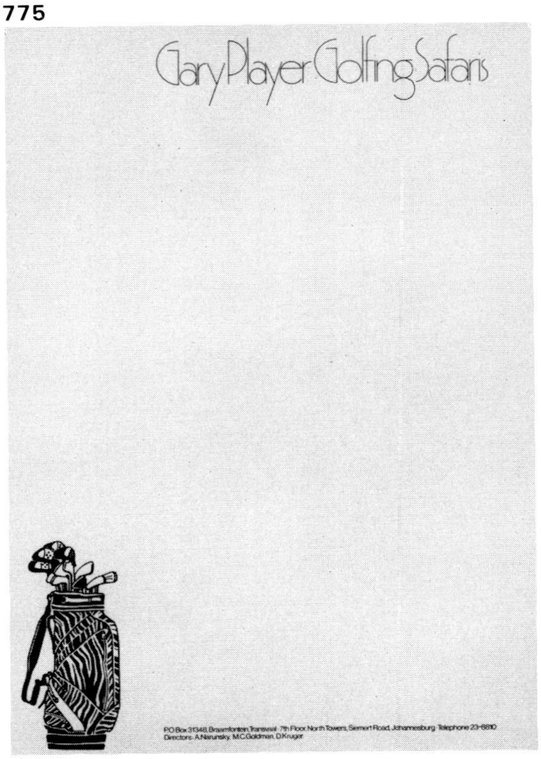

772
Center for Advanced Research in Design Entrant
John Massey Art Director
Rick Eiber Designer
I. Simon/R.G. Group Inc. Client

773
TY Graphics Entrant
Tom Yurcich Art Director
W. Earl Koson/ Draperies Client

774
Joseph J. Toth Entrant
Dix & Eaton Inc. Agency
Kalman Corp. Studio
Developers Diversified Client

775
Lorraine & Crystal Entrant
Jill Henderson Art Director
Gary Player Golfing Safaris Client

776

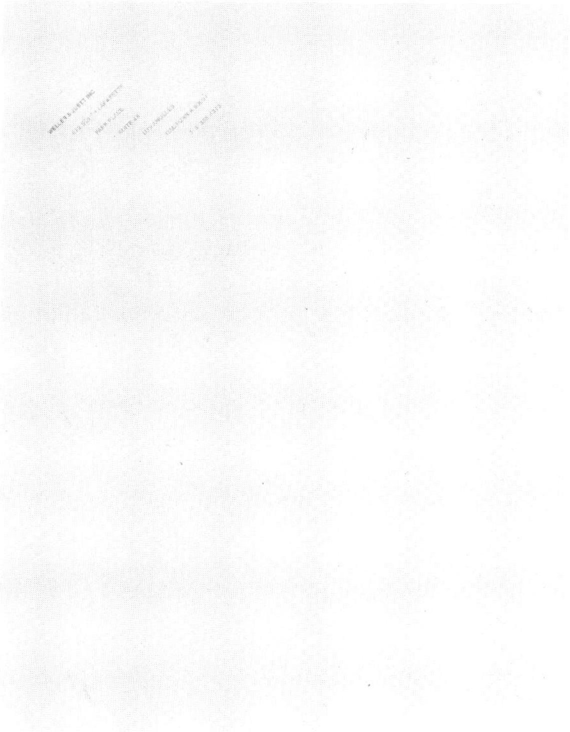

777

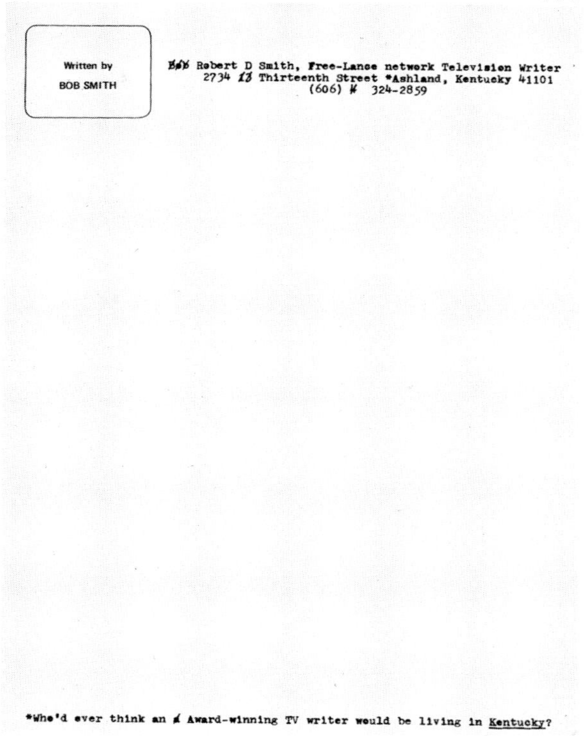

Written by
BOB SMITH

Bob Robert D Smith, Free-Lance network Television Writer
2734 13 Thirteenth Street *Ashland, Kentucky 41101
(606) N 324-2859

*Who'd ever think an ≠ Award-winning TV writer would be living in Kentucky?

778

Greenwood Plaza Terrace, Englewood, Colorado 80110 (303) 770-2262

779

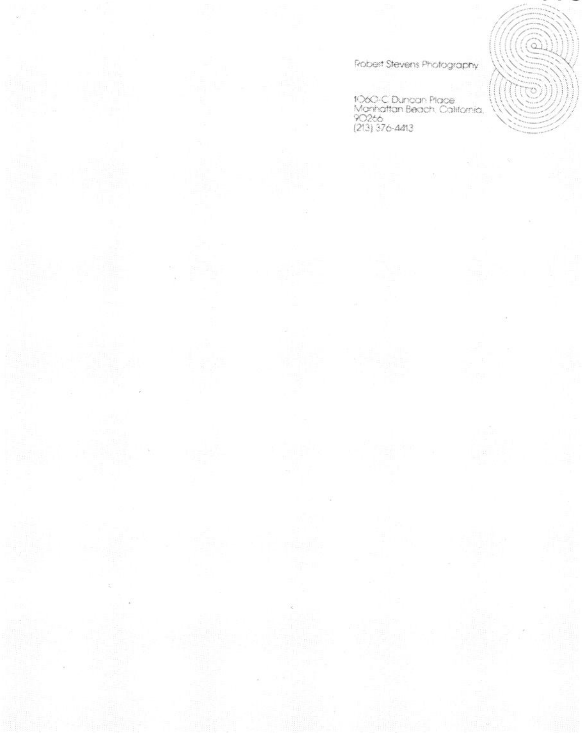

Robert Stevens Photography

1060-C Duncan Place
Manhattan Beach, California
90266
(213) 376-4413

776
Weller & Juett Inc.
Entrant
**Dennis Juett,
Don Weller**
Art Directors

777
David E. Carter
Entrant
Bob Smith
Client

778
Communication Arts, Inc.
Entrant
Richard A. Foy
Art Director
Continental West Realty
Client

779
Robert Miles Runyan & Associates Entrant
Robert Miles Runyan
Art Director
Gary Hinsche
Designer
Robert Stevens Photography Client

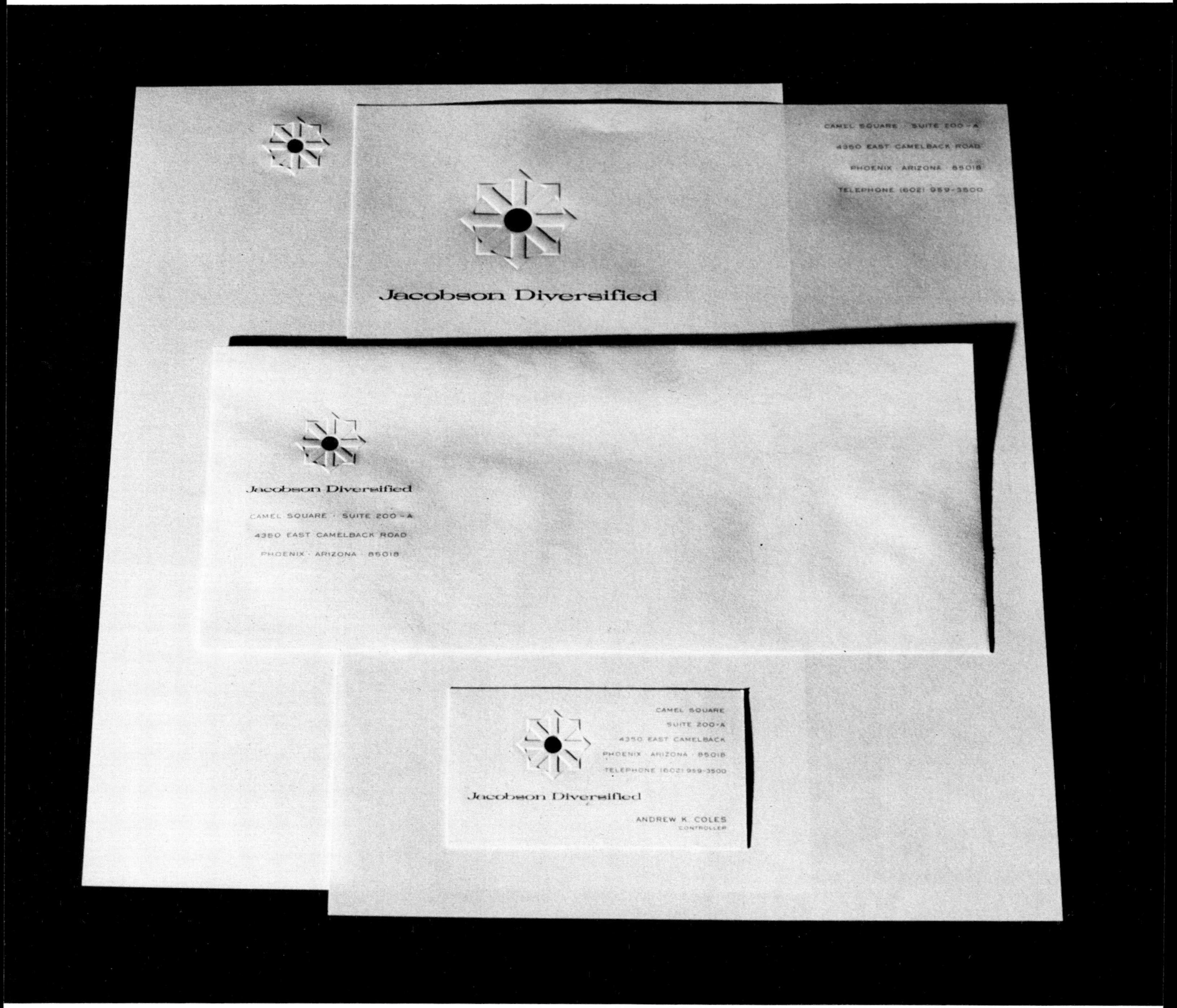
CAMEL SQUARE · SUITE 200-A
4350 EAST CAMELBACK ROAD
PHOENIX · ARIZONA · 85018
TELEPHONE (602) 959-3500
Jacobson Diversified
Jacobson Diversified
CAMEL SQUARE · SUITE 200-A
4350 EAST CAMELBACK ROAD
PHOENIX · ARIZONA · 85018
CAMEL SQUARE
SUITE 200-A
4350 EAST CAMELBACK
PHOENIX · ARIZONA · 85018
TELEPHONE (602) 959-3500
Jacobson Diversified
ANDREW K. COLES
CONTROLLER

780
Marie Martel Entrant
Distinctive Designs Agency
Jacobson Diversified Client

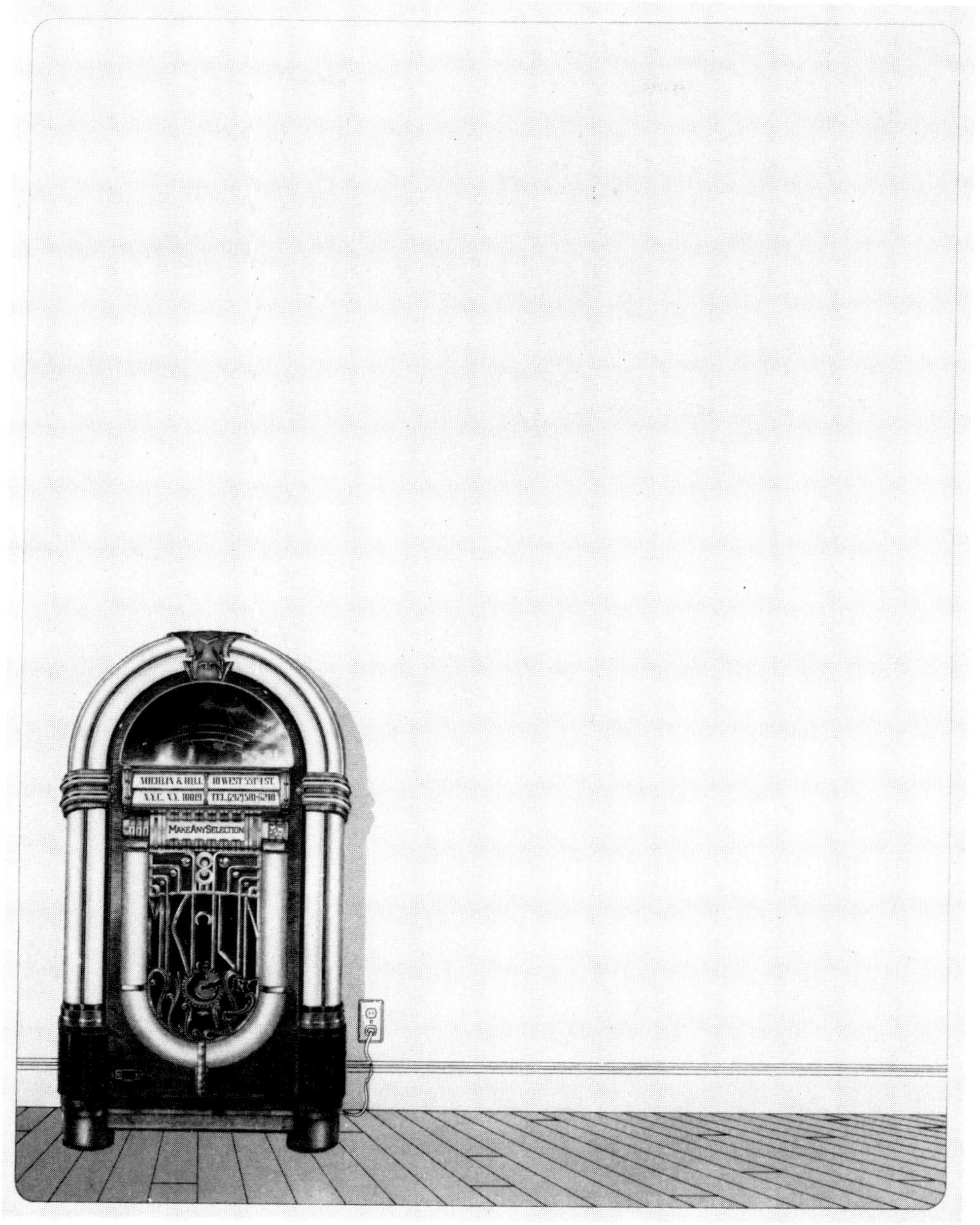
MICHLIN & HILL
40 WEST 55TH ST.
N.Y.C. N.Y. 10019
TEL.(212)581-5210
MAKE ANY SELECTION

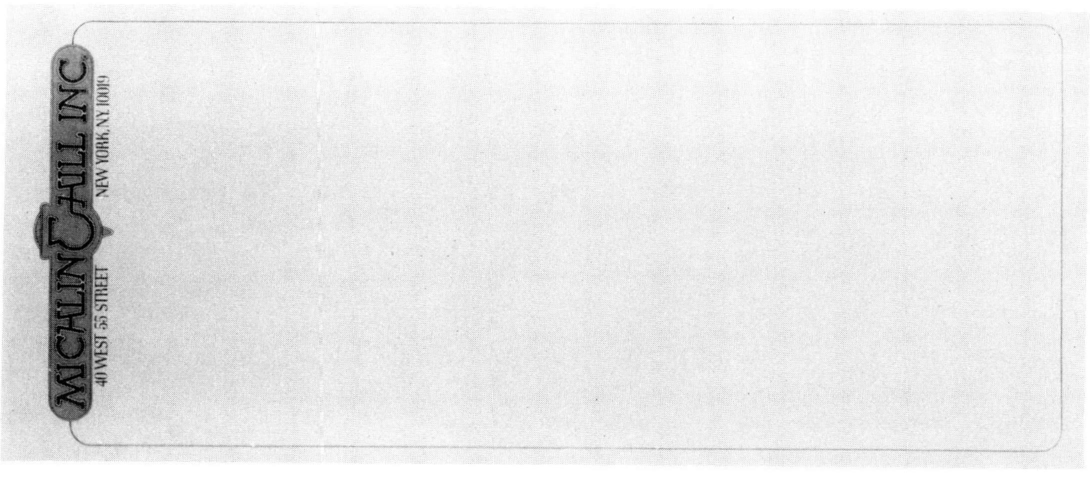
MICHLIN & HILL INC
40 WEST 55 STREET
NEW YORK, NY 10019

781
Michael Doret Entrant
Charles White Illustrator
Fluid Drive Studio Studio
Michlin & Hill Inc. Client

782

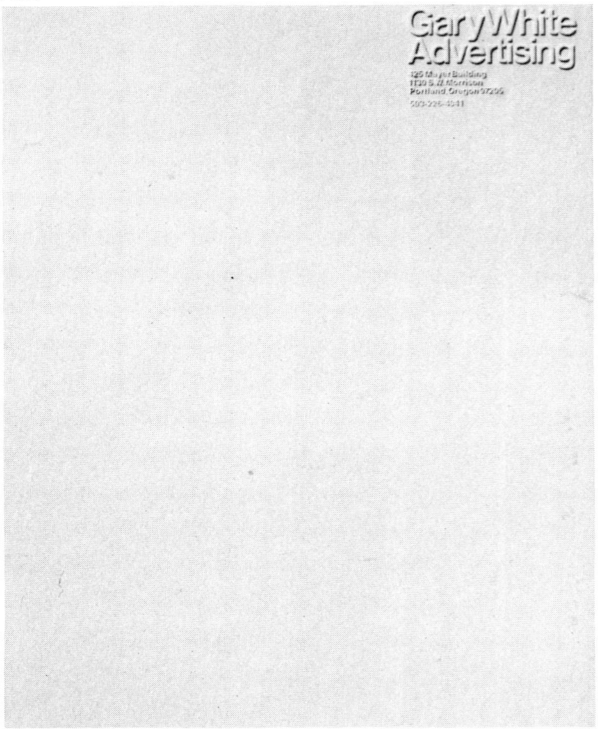
Gary White
Advertising

783

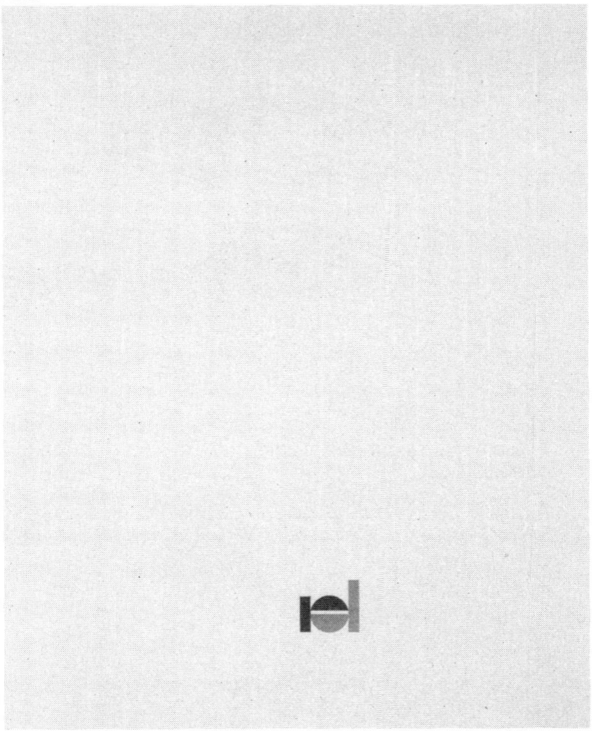

784

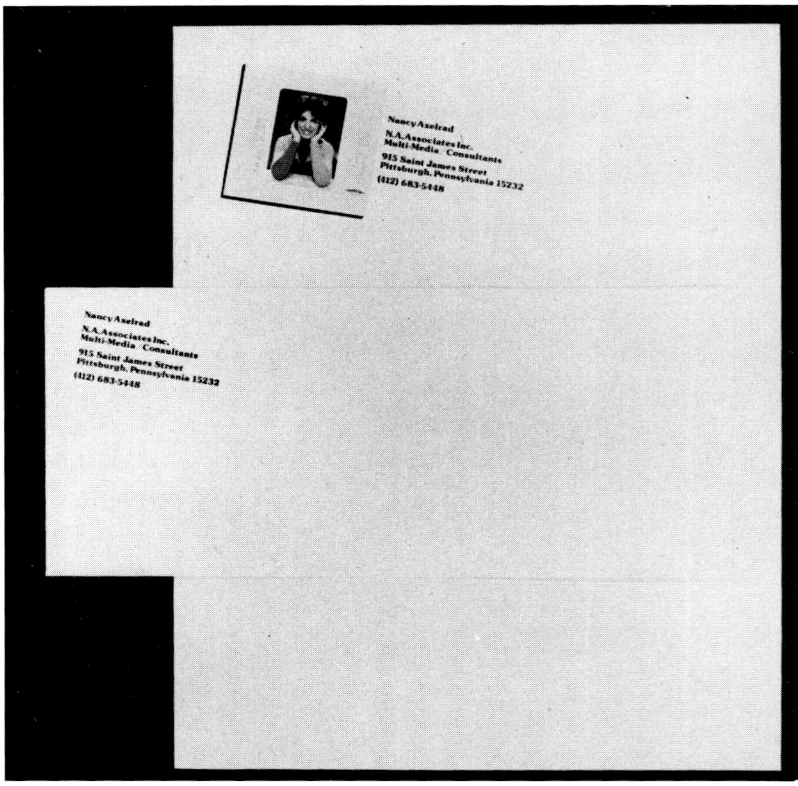
Nancy Axelrad
N.A. Associates Inc.
Multi-Media Consultants
915 Saint James Street
Pittsburgh, Pennsylvania 15232
(412) 683-5448
Nancy Axelrad
N.A. Associates Inc.
Multi-Media Consultants
915 Saint James Street
Pittsburgh, Pennsylvania 15232
(412) 683-5448

785

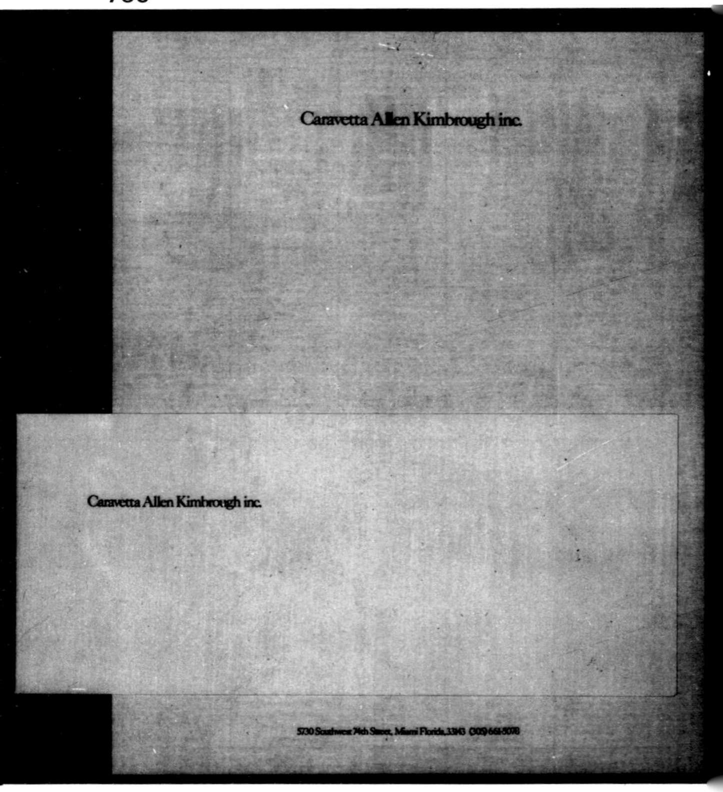
Caravetta Allen Kimbrough inc.
Caravetta Allen Kimbrough inc.
5730 Southwest 74th Street, Miami Florida, 33143 (305) 661-5078

782
Robin Rickabaugh
Entrant
Heidi and Robin Rickabaugh
Art Directors
Gary White Advertising
Client

783
Reynaldo DaCosta
Entrant
Diseño Grafico
Studio

784
J.M. Essex Design Center
Entrant
J. Michael Essex
Art Director
WQED Design Center
Agency
Nancy Axelrad
Client

785
Caravetta Allen Kimbrough inc.
Entrant
Fred Caravetta
Art Director

788

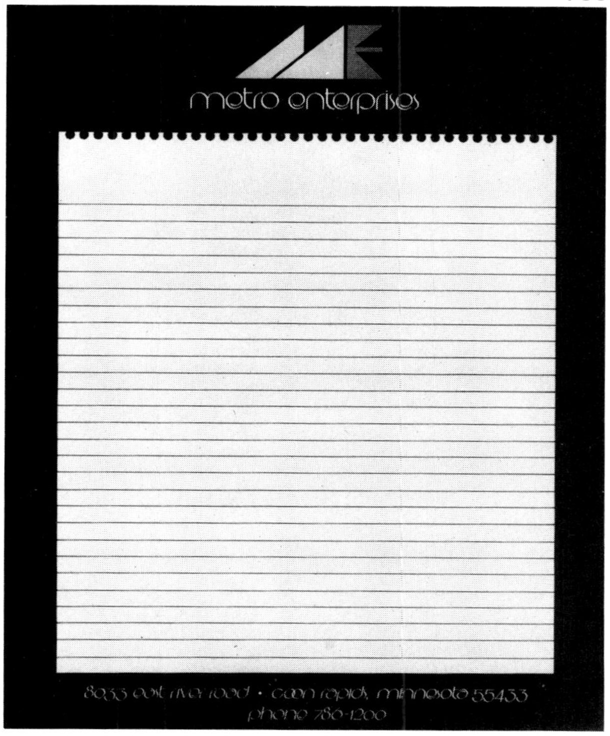

metro enterprises
8033 east river road • coon rapids, minnesota 55433
phone 786-1200

787

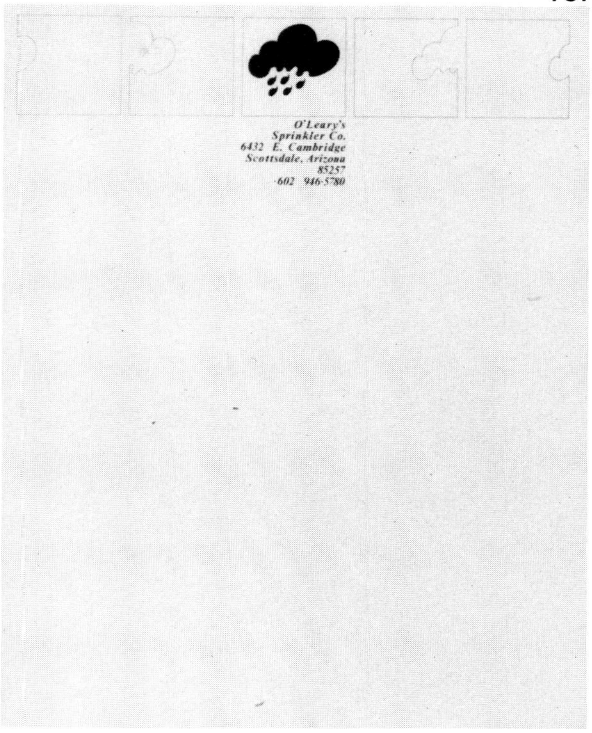

O'Leary's
Sprinkler Co.
6432 E. Cambridge
Scottsdale, Arizona
85257
602 946-5780

786

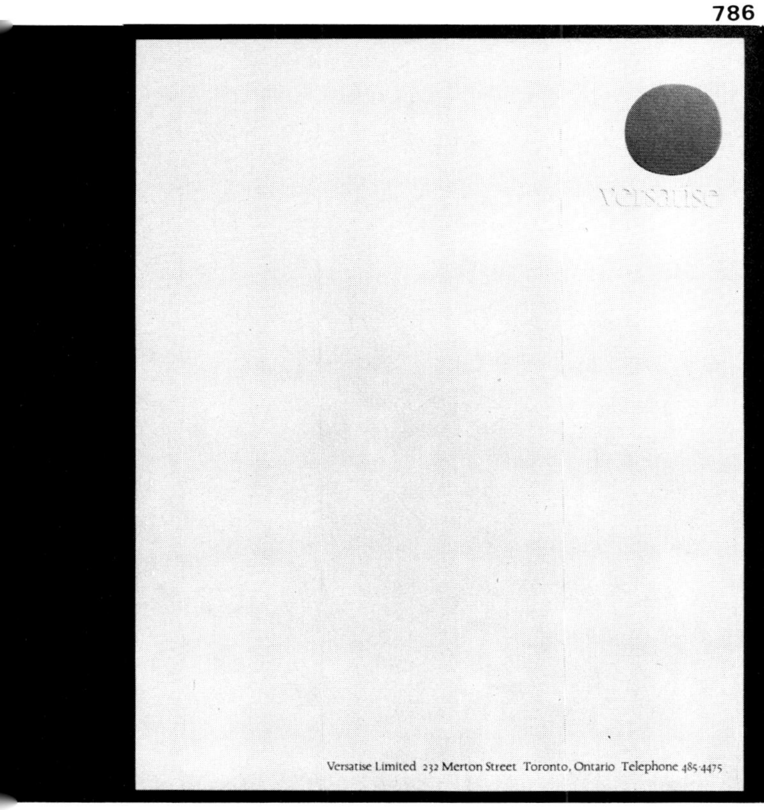

versatise
Versatise Limited 232 Merton Street Toronto, Ontario Telephone 485 4475

789

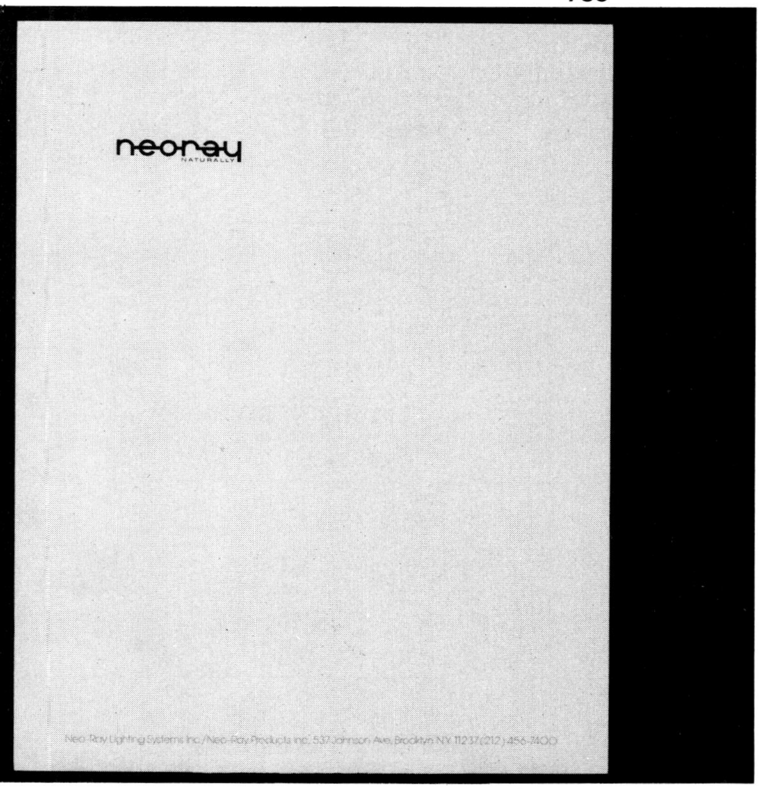

neo-ray
NATURALLY
Neo-Ray Lighting Systems Inc./Neo-Ray Products Inc. 537 Johnson Ave. Brooklyn NY 11237 (212) 456-7400

786
Versatise Limited
Entrant
Jackie Young
Art Director

787
Steven Sessions
Entrant
O'Leary's Sprinkler Co.
Client

788
Clarence W. Foster
Entrant
McGill Graphic Arts
Agency
Metro Enterprises
Client

789
Edward Lamport
Assoc. Entrant
Edward Lamport
Art Director
Neo-Ray
Lighting Systems
Client

790

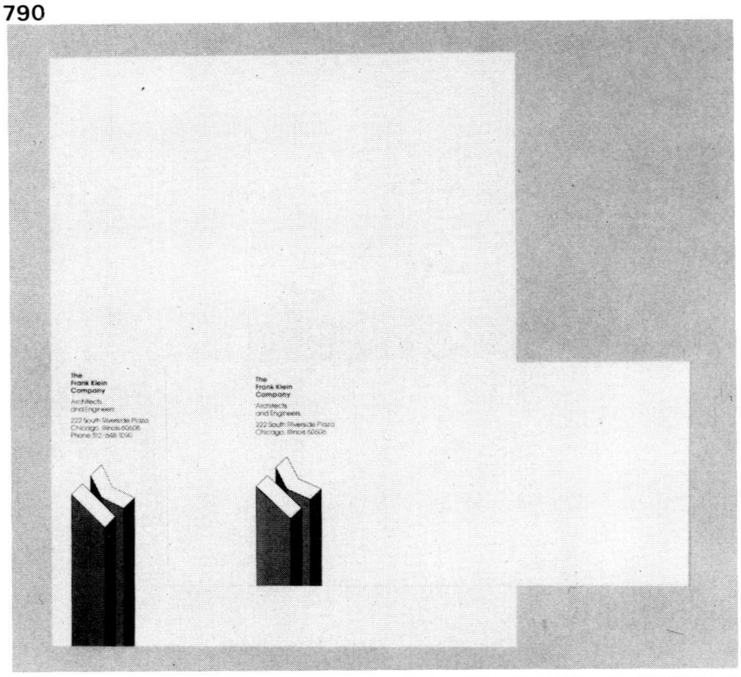
The Frank Klein Company
Architects and Engineers
222 South Riverside Plaza
Chicago, Illinois 60606

791

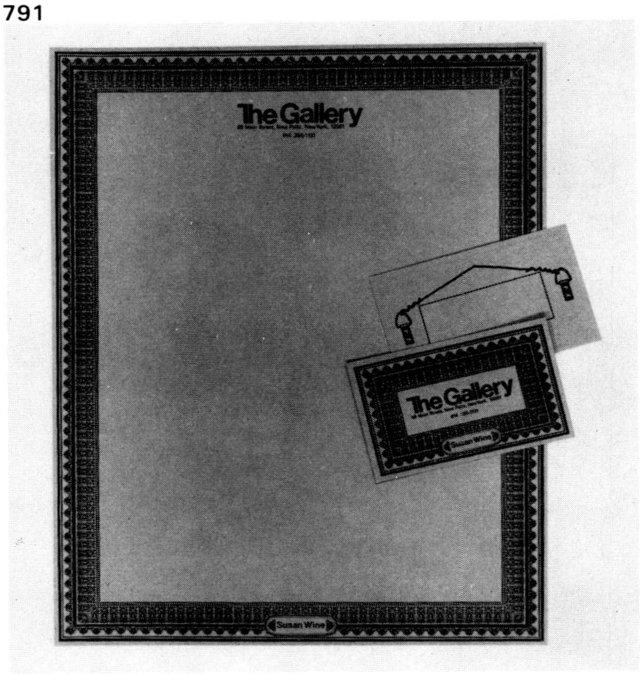
The Gallery
The Gallery
Susan Wine
Susan Wine

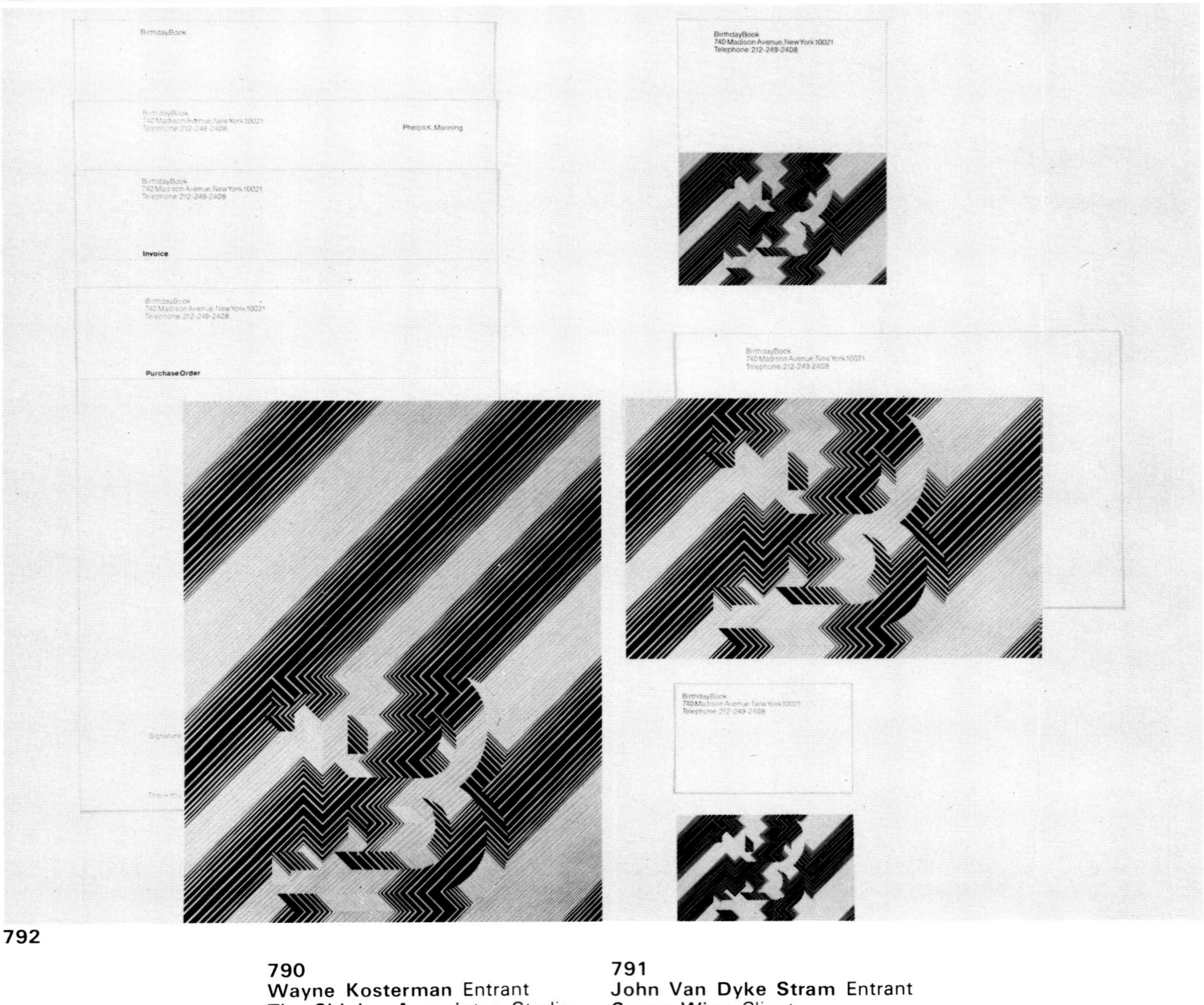
BirthdayBook
BirthdayBook
740 Madison Avenue, New York 10021
Telephone 212-249-2408
Phelps K. Manning
Invoice
Purchase Order

792

790
Wayne Kosterman Entrant
The Shipley Associates Studio
The Frank Klein Company Client

791
John Van Dyke Stram Entrant
Susan Wine Client

TERRY STEVENSON PHOTOGRAPHY
250 FIFTH AVENUE NEW YORK 10001 889-6199
TERRY STEVENSON PHOTOGRAPHY
250 FIFTH AVENUE · NEW YORK 10001
TERRY STEVENSON PHOTOGRAPHY
250 FIFTH AVENUE NEW YORK 10001 889-6199
MAURY OREN/REPRESENTATIVE · PL-3-1971
TERRY STEVENSON PHOTOGRAPHY
250 FIFTH AVENUE · NEW YORK 10001 · 889-6199
Nº 0251
TERRY STEVENSON PHOTOGRAPHY
250 FIFTH AVENUE NEW YORK 10001 889-6199

793

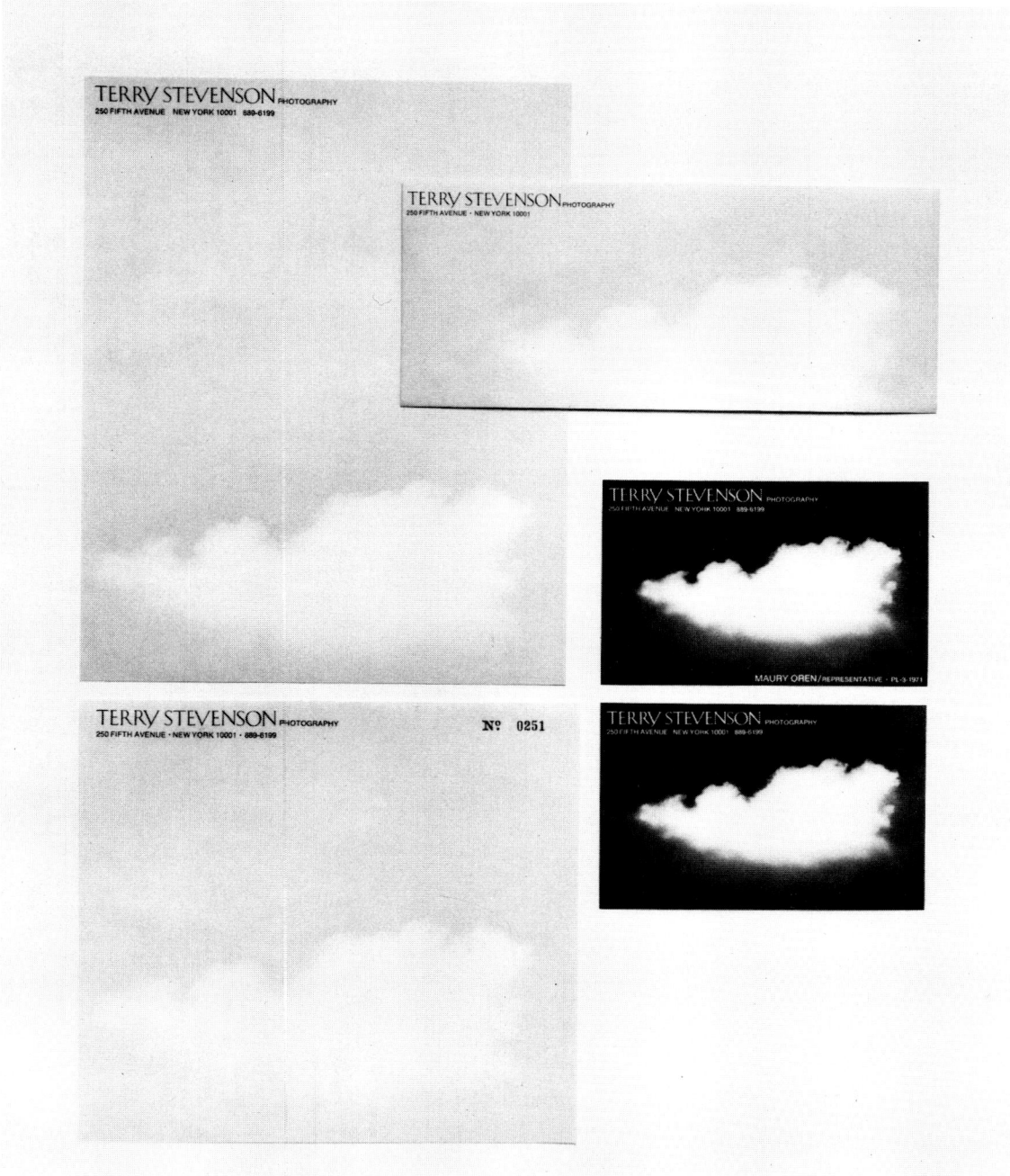

792
William R. Tobias Design Entrant
William Tobias, Upendra Shah Art Directors
Upendra Shah, James Orlandi Illustrators
Birthday Book Client

793
Terry Stevenson Entrant
Guy Dolen, Terry Stevenson Art Directors
Guy Dolen, Inc. Studio

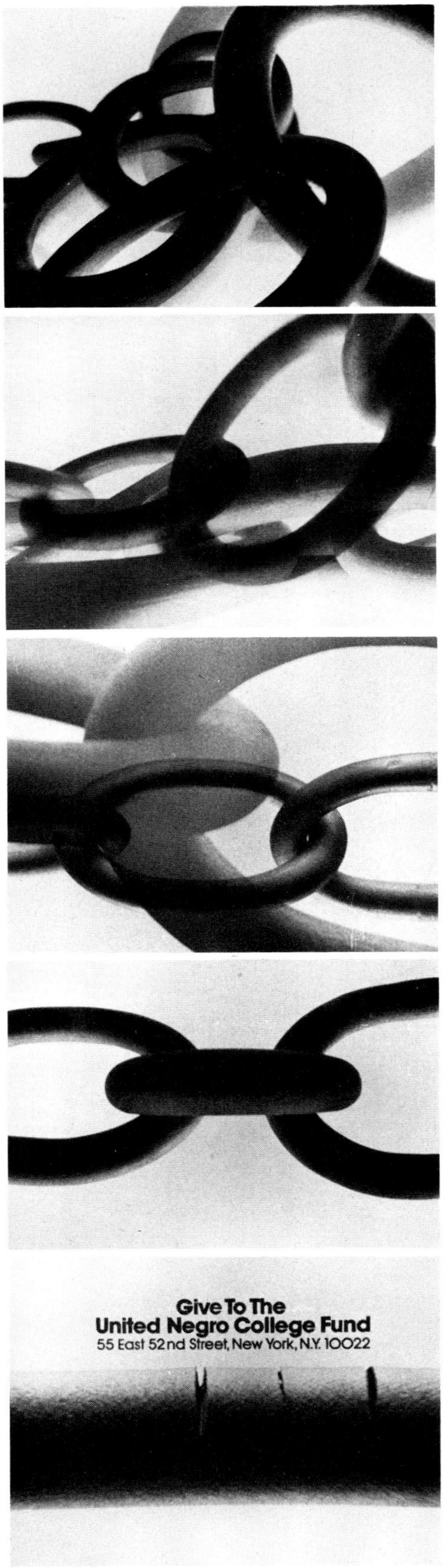
Give To The
United Negro College Fund
55 East 52nd Street, New York, N.Y. 10022

794
Ken Etheridge Entrant
Young & Rubicam Inc. Agency
Lear Levin Studio
The United Negro College Fund Client

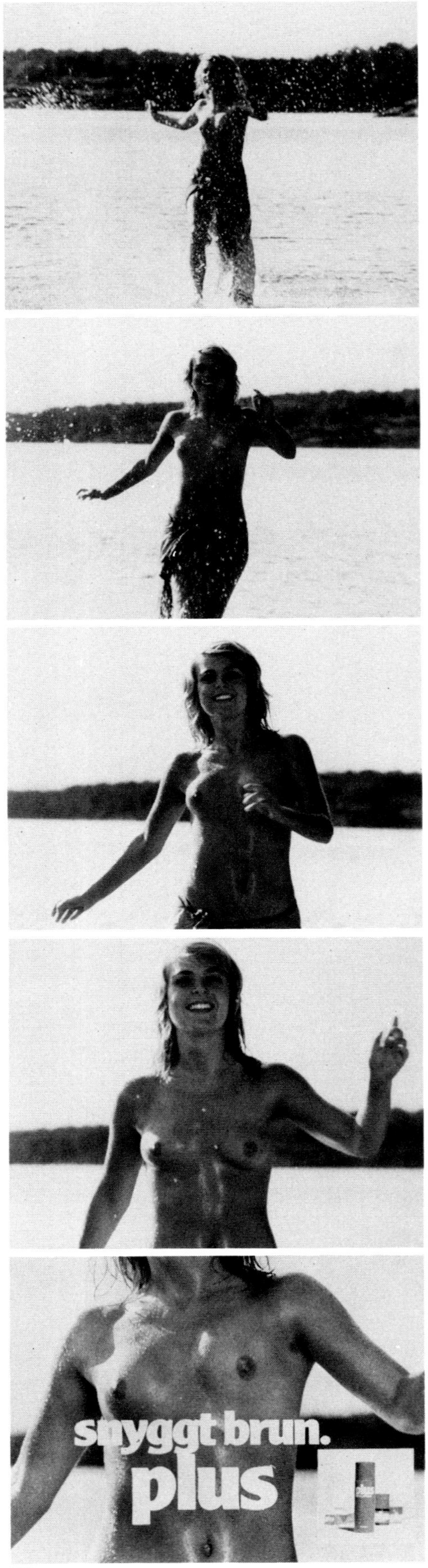
snyggt brun.
plus

795
Marknads Kommunikation AB Entrant
Jorma Kosunen Art Director
Christer & Arne Prod. AB Photographers
Barnängen AB Client

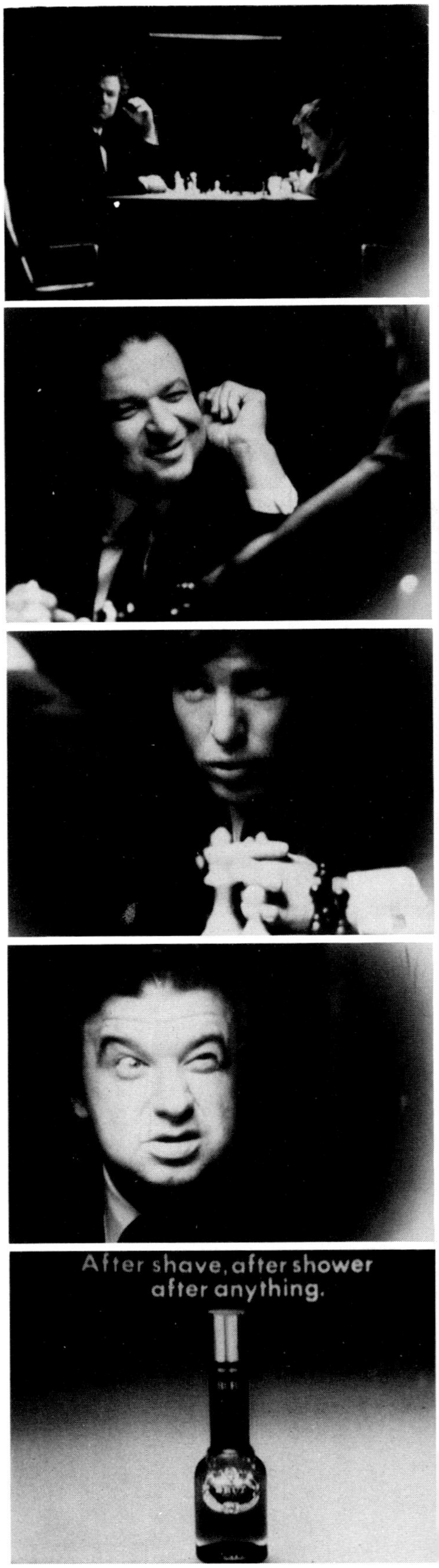
After shave, after shower
after anything.

796
Nadler & Larimer Inc. Entrant
Irwin Goldberg Art Director
Tulchin Productions Studio
Faberge Inc., Brut Lotion Client

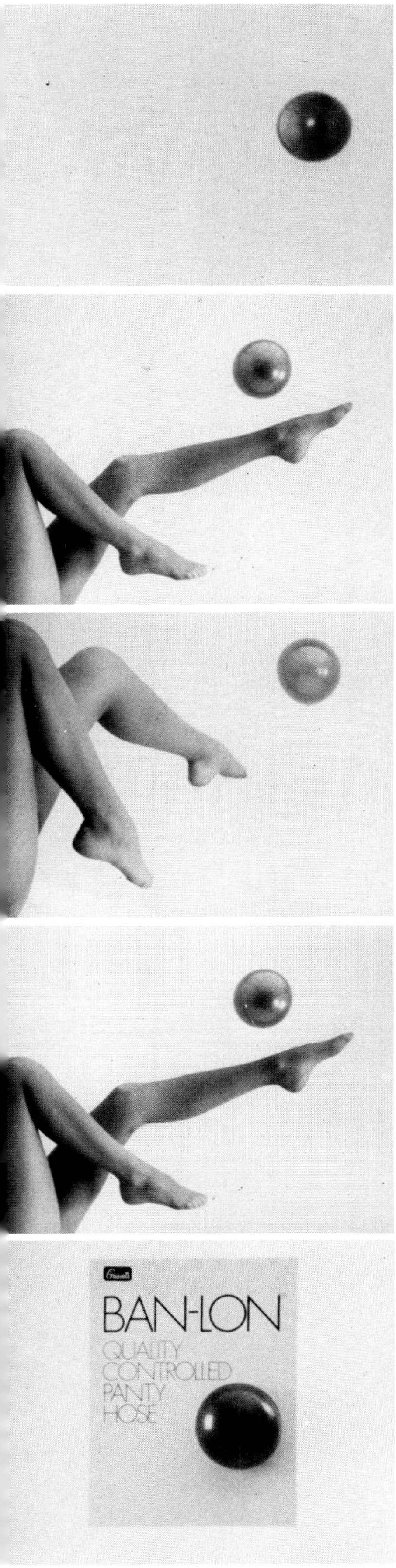
BAN-LON
QUALITY
CONTROLLED
PANTY
HOSE

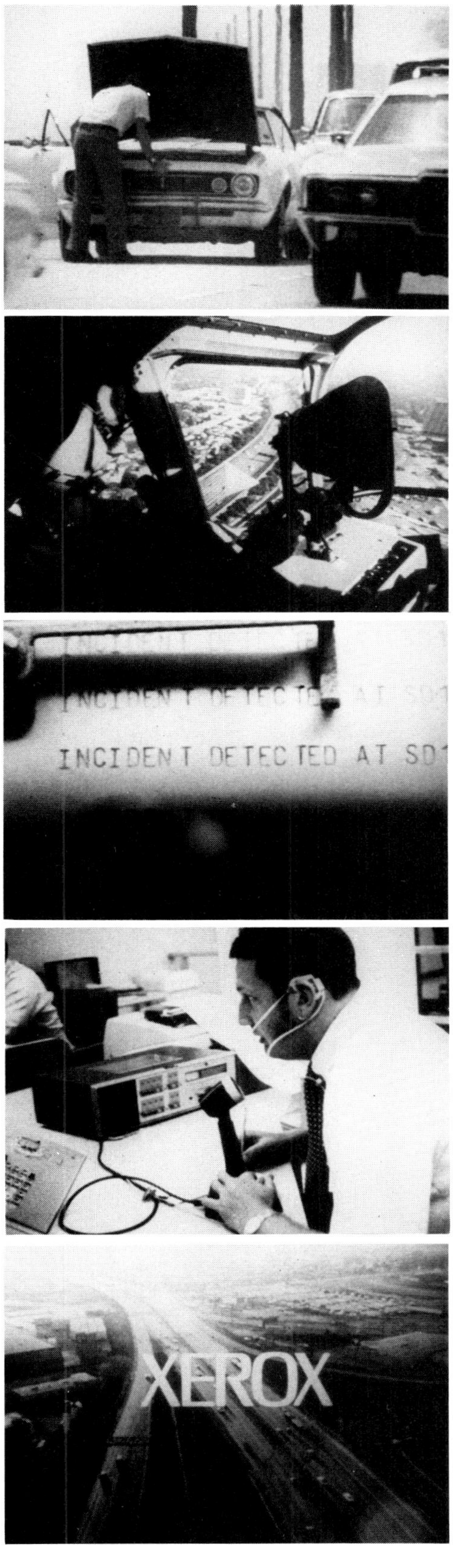
INCIDENT DETECTED AT SD
XEROX

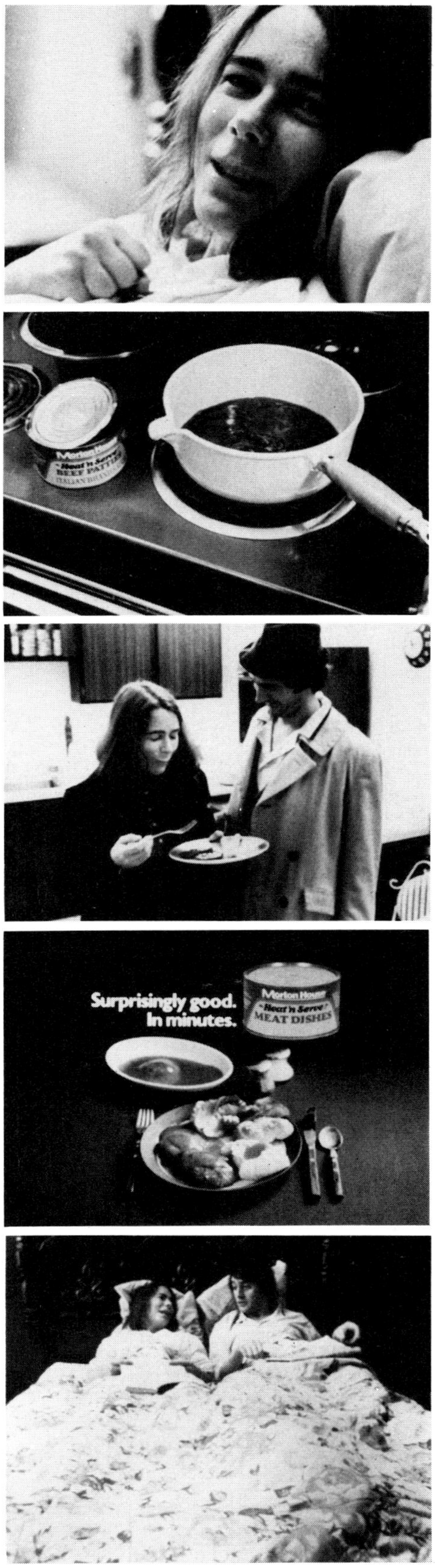
Surprisingly good.
In minutes.
Morton House
MEAT DISHES

797
Don Wise & Co. Entrant
Richard Trask Art Director
Sunlight Pictures Studio
Bancroft Licensing (Ban-Lon) Client

798
Needham, Harper & Steers Entrant
Allen Kay Art Director
Plus Two Studio
Xerox Corporation Client

799
Albert Jay Rosenthal & Co. Entrant
David Francis Art Director
Morton House Client

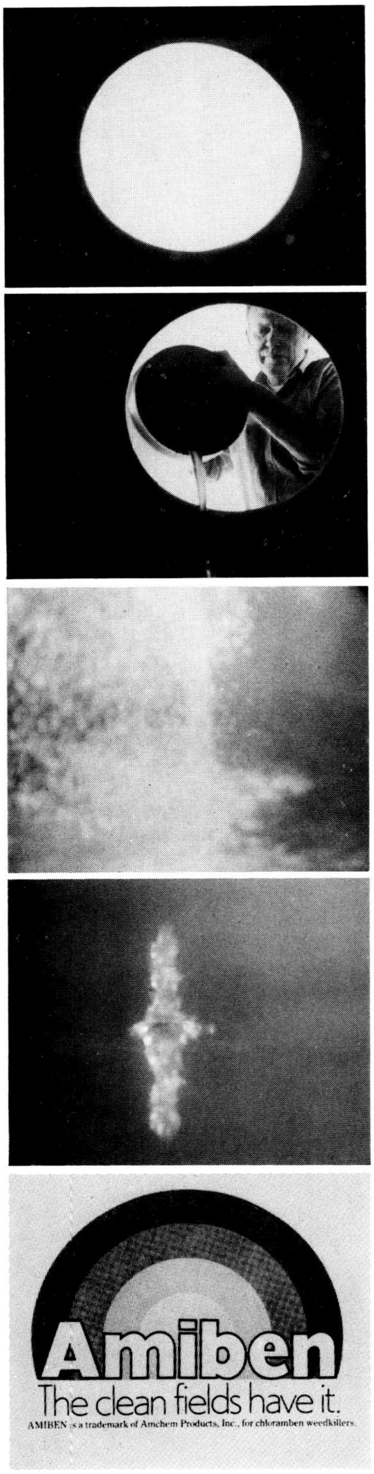
Amiben
The clean fields have it.
AMIBEN is a trademark of Amchem Products, Inc., for chloramben weedkillers.

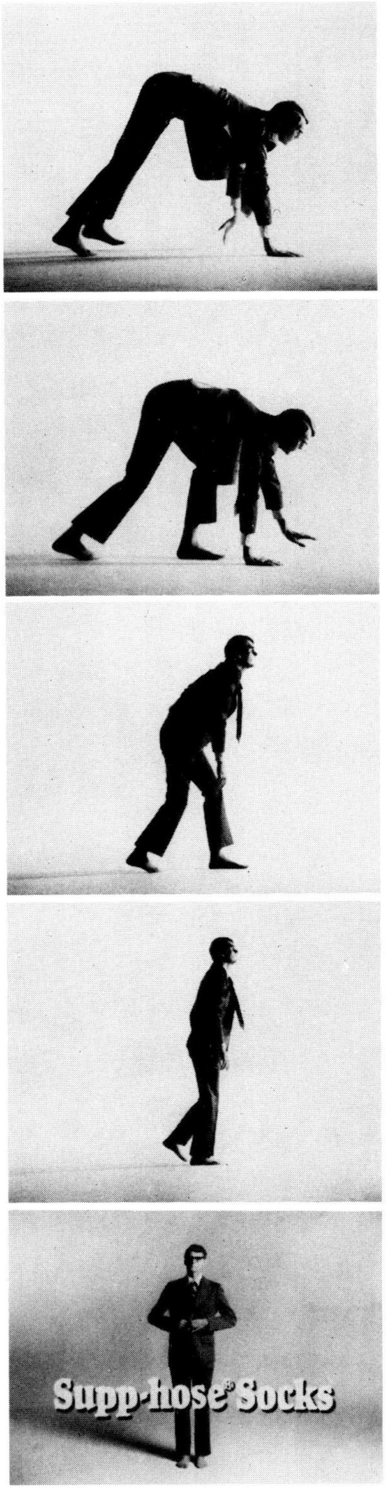
Supp-hose® Socks

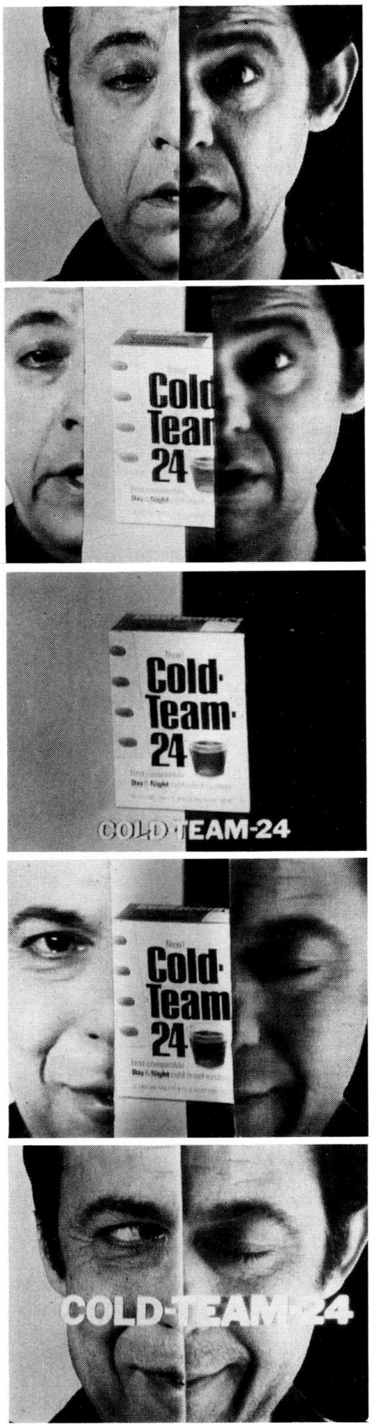
Cold·Team·24
COLD·TEAM-24
COLD-TEAM-24

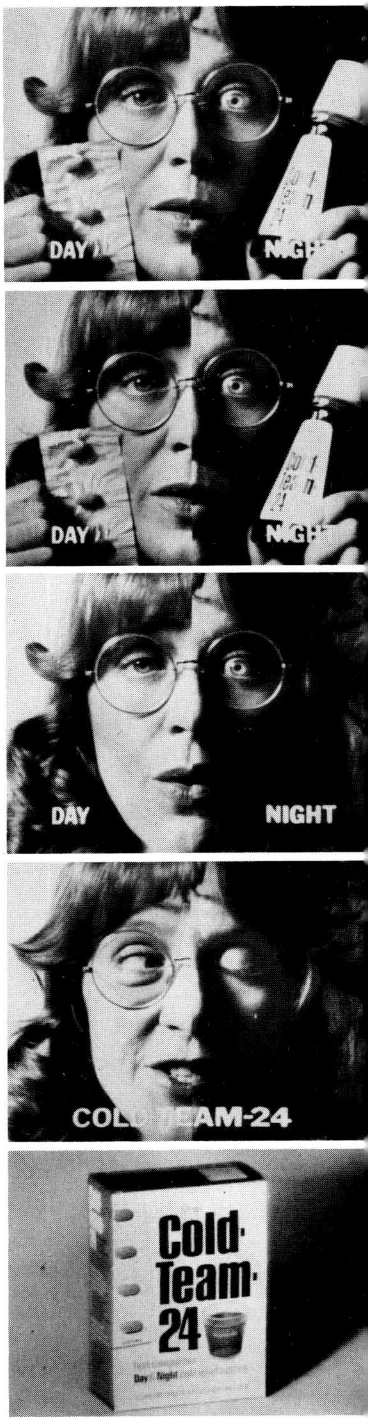
DAY
NIGHT
COLD·TEAM-24
Cold·Team·24

800
Lewis & Gilman Adv. Entrant
Anthony Leone Art Director
Phil Kimmelman Assoc. Animator
Lee Lacy Prod. Studio
Amchem Client

801
Lawrence Dunst Entrant
Frank Camardella Art Director
Irving Penn Photographer
Daniel & Charles Assoc. Ltd. Agency
Independent Artists Studio
Kayser-Roth Client

802-803
Judy White Entrant
Herb Passberger Art Director
PKL Advertising Inc. Agency
Zoe Productions Studio
Chesebrough-Pond's Inc. Client

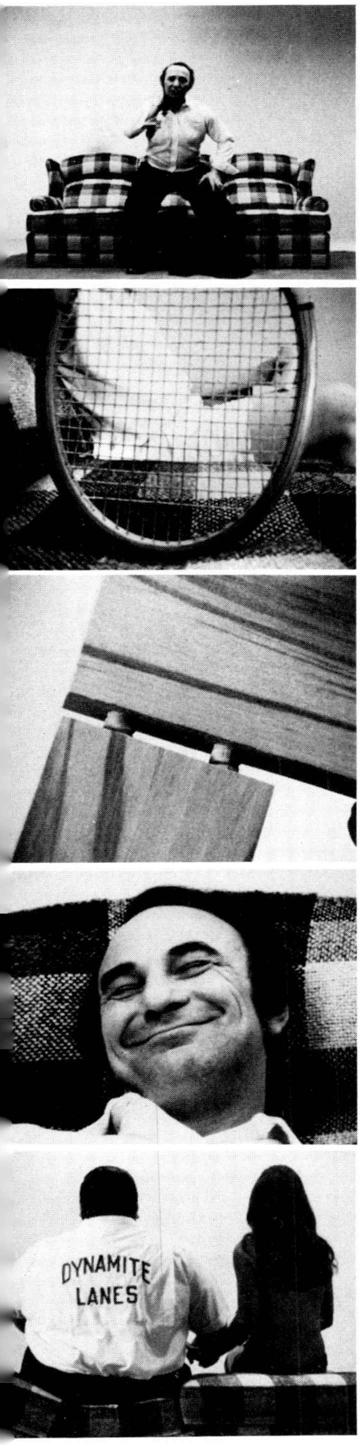
DYNAMITE
LANES

804
Jack O'Grady Photo Productions Entrant
Al Adas Art Director
Rich Kellner Copywriter
Studio Seven (Chicago) Studio
Kroehler Mfg. Company Client

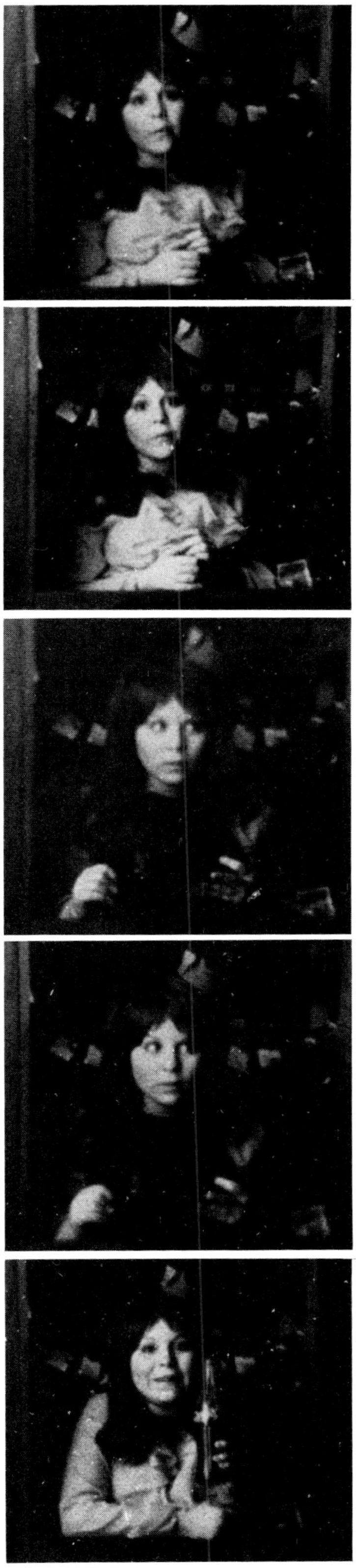

805
Alan Brooks Entrant
Don Toriello Art Director
McCann-Erickson Agency
Alan Brooks Productions Studio
Coca Cola Client

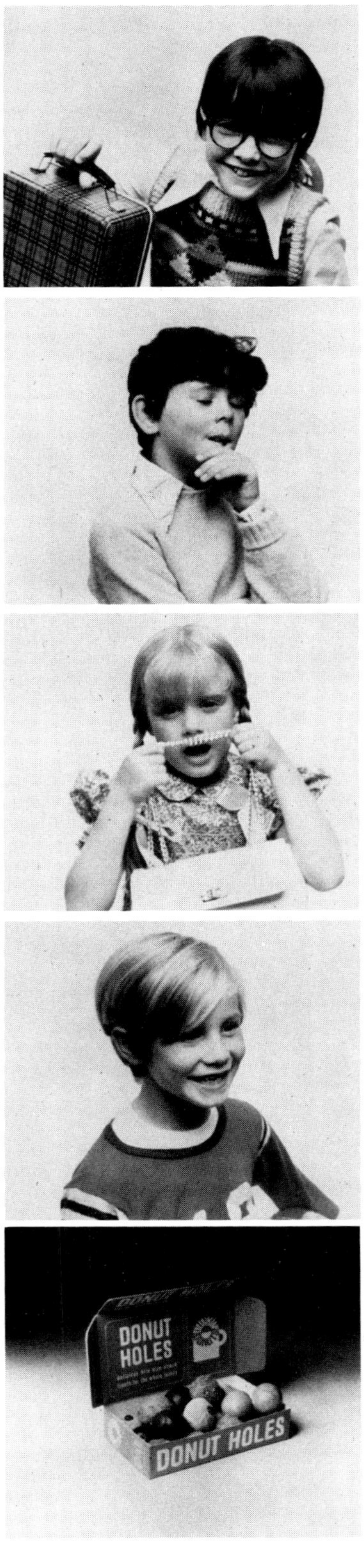
DONUT
HOLES
DONUT HOLES

806
Hill, Holliday, Connors, Cosmopulos, Inc. Entrant
Dick Pantano, Stavros Cosmopulos, J. Hill Art Directors
Horn/Griner Studio
Dunkin' Donuts Client

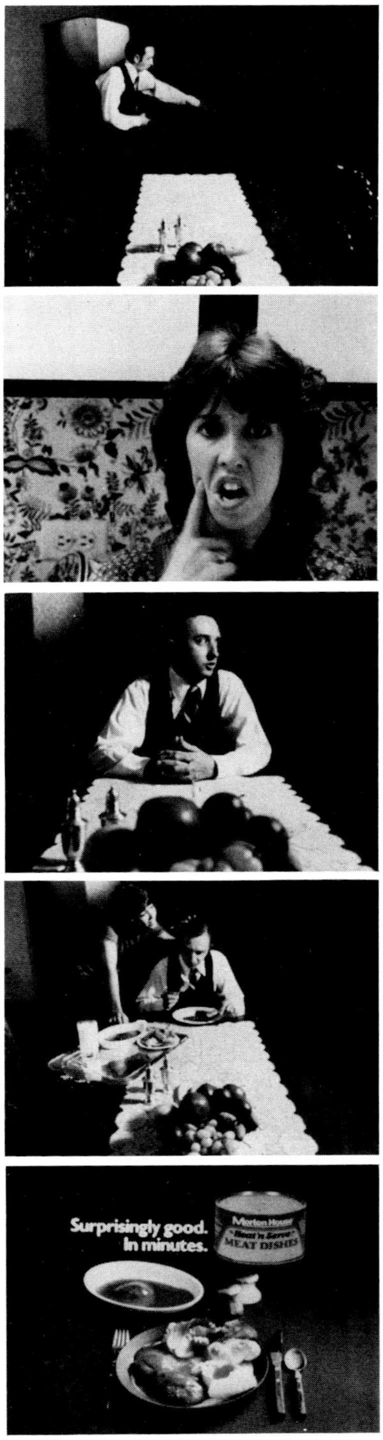
Surprisingly good.
In minutes.
MEAT DISHES

807
Albert Jay Rosenthal & Co. Entrant
David Francis Art Director
Morton House Client

TV2 News

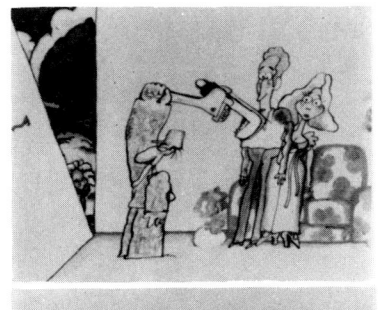

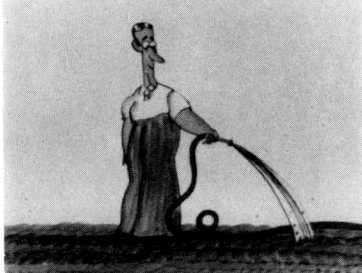

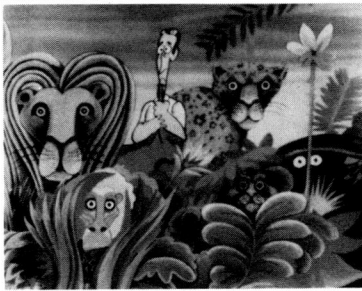

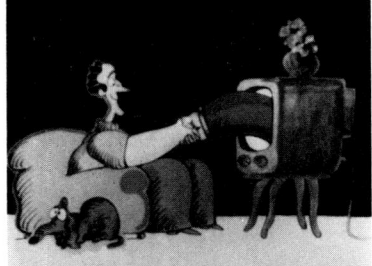

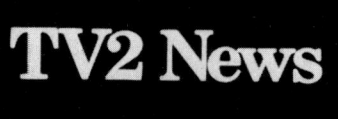

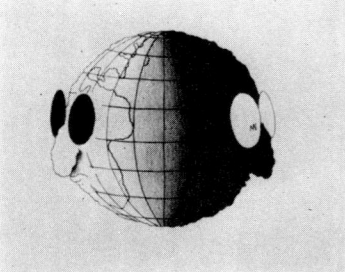

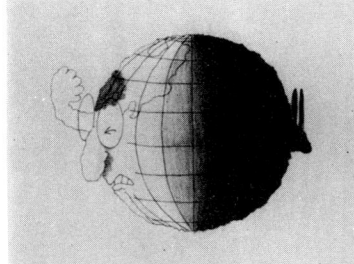

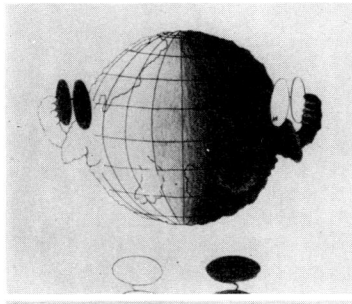

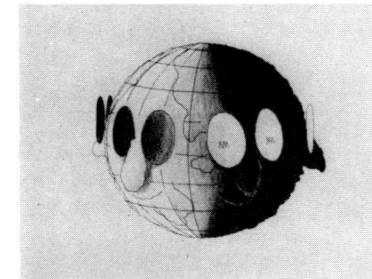

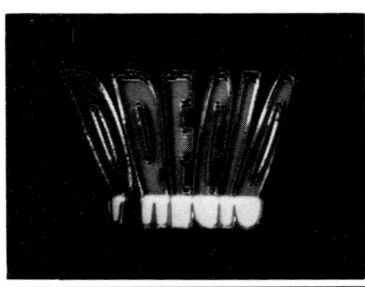

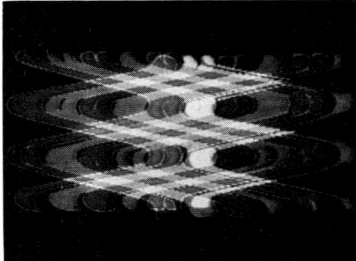

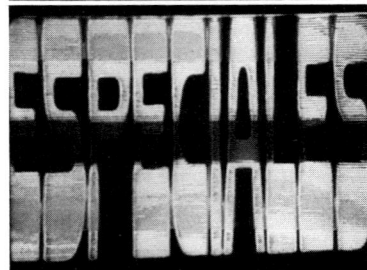

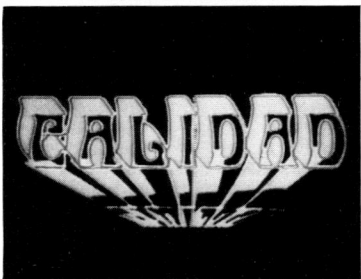

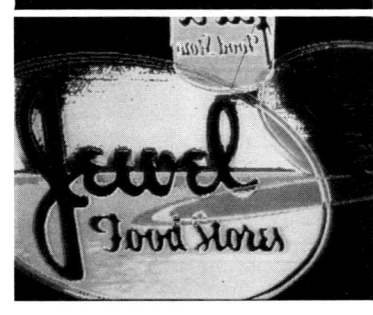

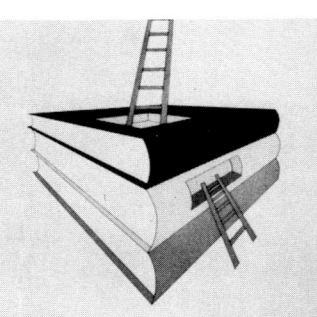

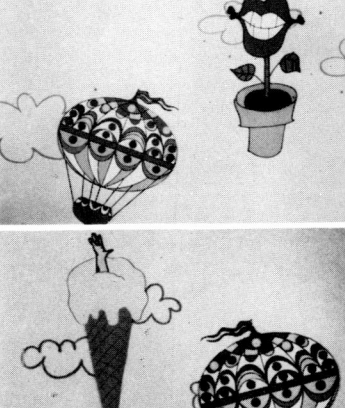

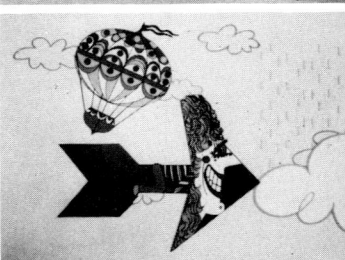

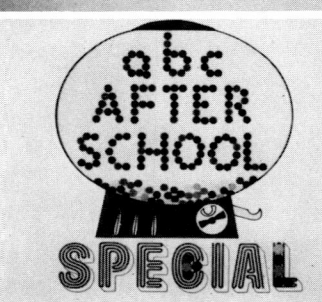

808
Van Brunt & Co. Chicago
Entrant
Lee Gleason
Art Director
Bob Kurtz & Friends
Studio
WBBM-TV
Client

809
Charles Sawyer
Entrant
Rod Capawana
Art Director
Warner Bicking and Fenwick Agency
Zanders Animation Parlour Studio
Corning Optical
Client

CALIDAD
Jewel
Food Stores

810
M. Miyares Entrant
Silvio Gayton
Art Director
Bob Blansky Animator
O.M.A.R. Co. Agency
Dolphin Productions (N.Y.)
Studio
Jewel Food Stores
Client

abc
AFTER
SCHOOL
SPECIAL

811
Elinor Bunin Productions Inc.
Entrant
Elinor Bunin
Art Director
Jack Dazo Animator
American Broadcasting Company TV
Client

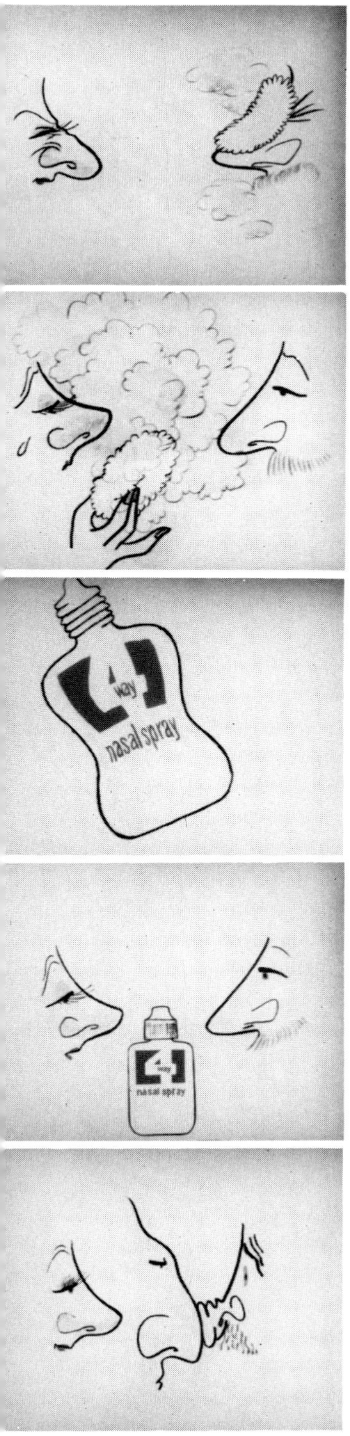

nasal spray

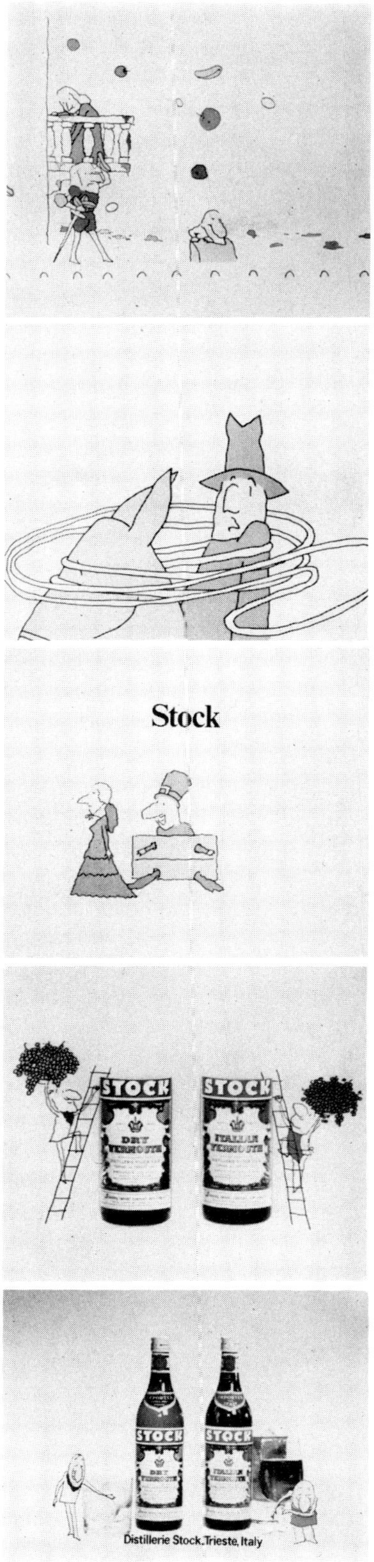

Stock
STOCK
STOCK
Distillerie Stock, Trieste, Italy

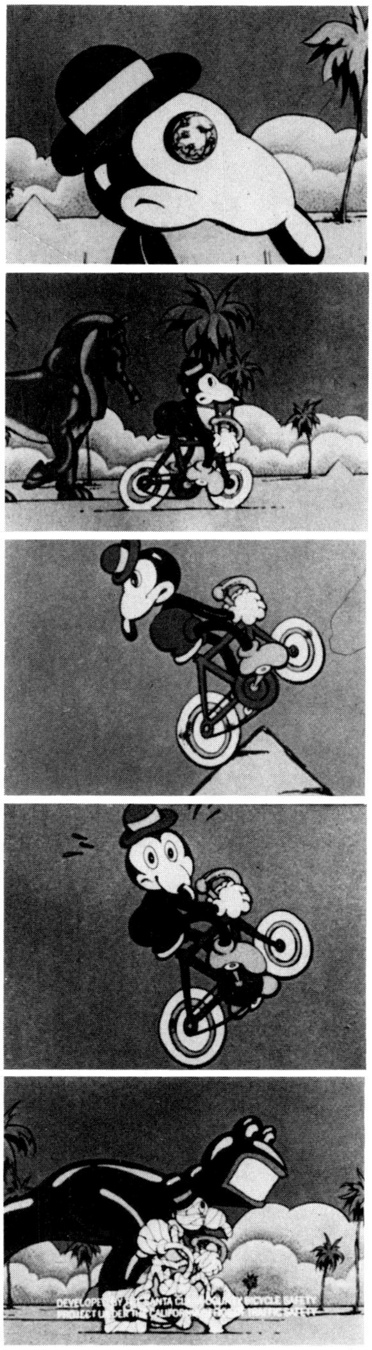

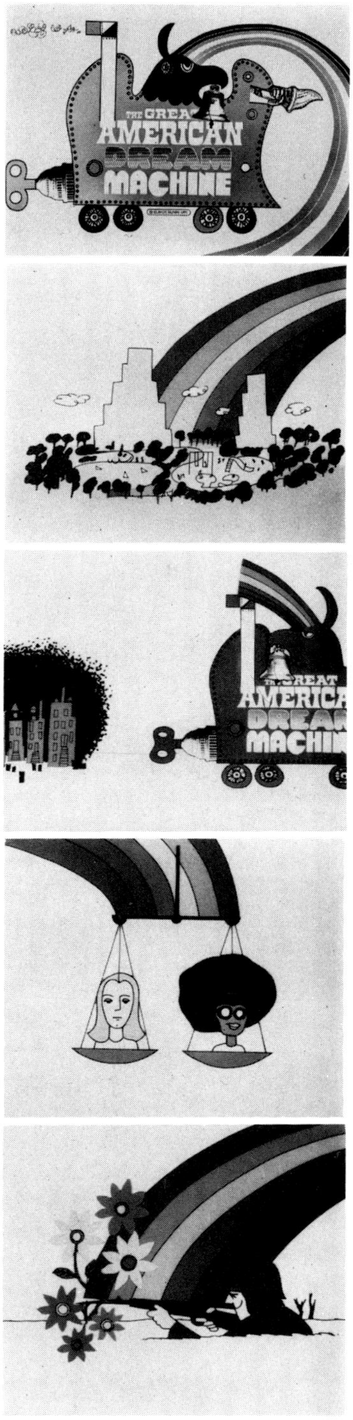

THE GREAT AMERICAN DREAM MACHINE

812
Needham, Harper & Steers
Entrant
John Murray
Art Director
Summerstar
Studio
Bristol-Myers
Client

813
George Fried
Entrant
Robert Blechman
Animator
Shaller Rubin Co. Inc.
Agency
Goodnoff Productions
Studio
Schenley Industries
Client

814
Ed Meyers Entrant
Victor Moscoso
Illustrator
Meyers & Muldoon
Advertising Agency
Animation House
Studio
City of San Jose
Client

815
Elinor Bunin Productions Inc.
Entrant
Elinor Bunin Illustrator
Jack Dazo Animator
National Educational Television Client

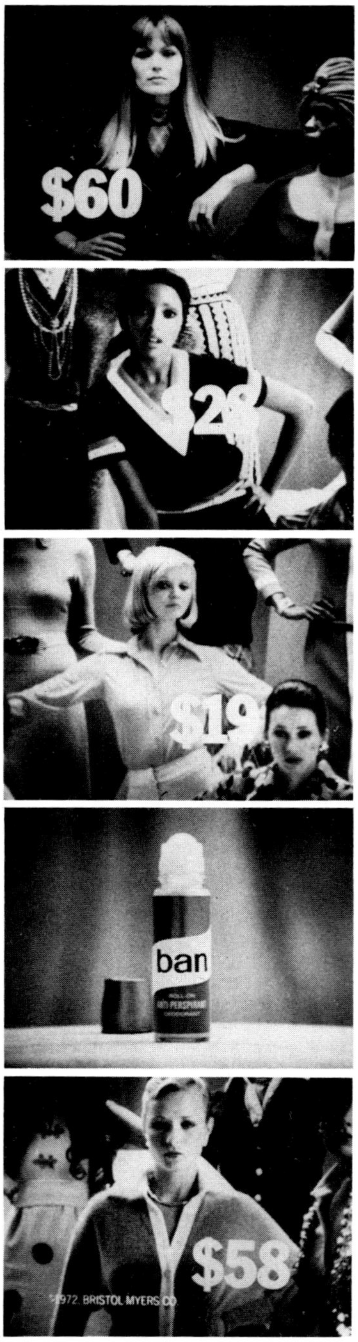
$60
$19
ban
$58
©1972 BRISTOL MYERS CO

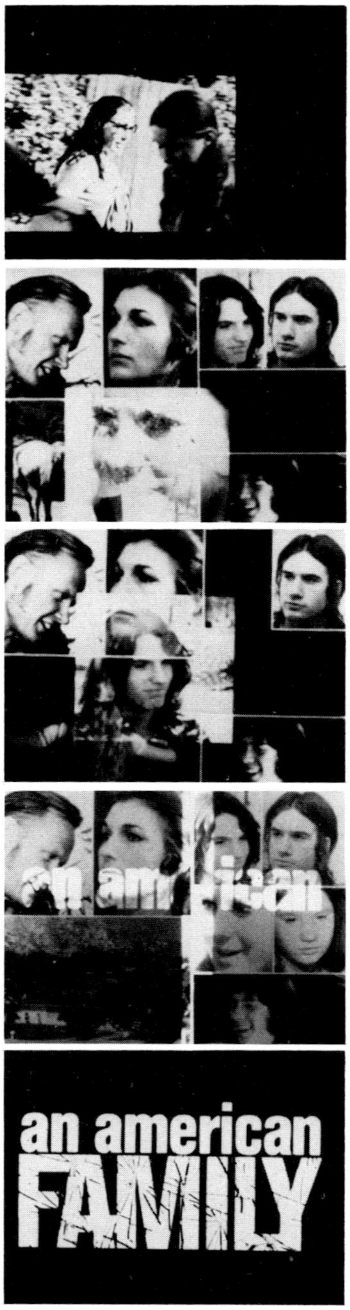
an american
FAMILY

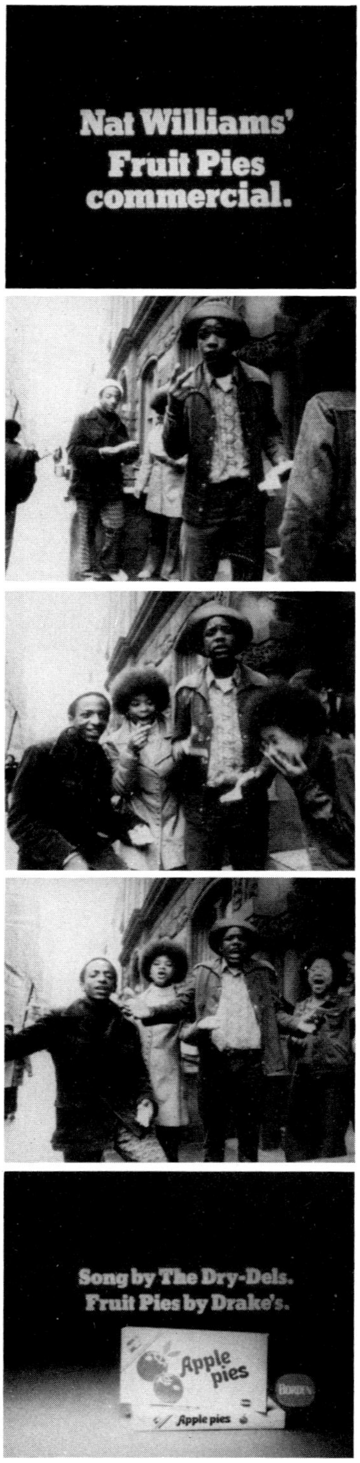
Nat Williams'
Fruit Pies
commercial.
Song by The Dry-Dels.
Fruit Pies by Drake's.
Apple pies

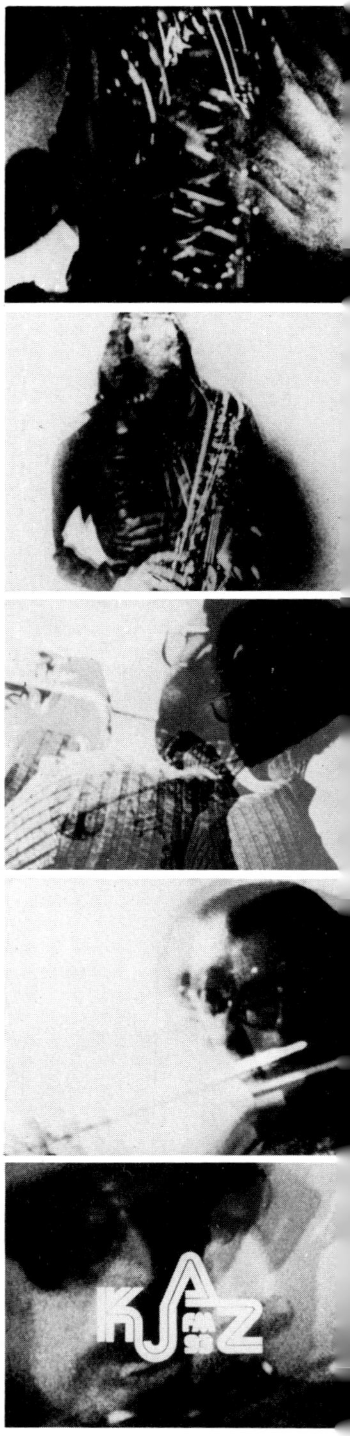

816
Lawrence Dunst
Entrant
Frank Camardella
Art Director
Ken Duskin
Photographer
Daniel & Charles Assoc. Ltd.
Agency
Wakeford/Orloff Inc.
Studio
Bristol-Myers
Client

817
Elinor Bunin Productions Inc.
Entrant
Elinor Bunin
Art Director
Alan Raymond
Photographer
Stonecutters
Editor
Craig Gilbert/ Public Broadcasting Service
Client

818
Needham, Harper & Steers
Entrant
Harry Webber
Art Director
Horn/Griner
Studio
Drakes-Borden
Client

819
Ed Meyers
Entrant
Meyers & Muldoon Advertising
Agency
M Films
Studio
KJAZ Radio
Client

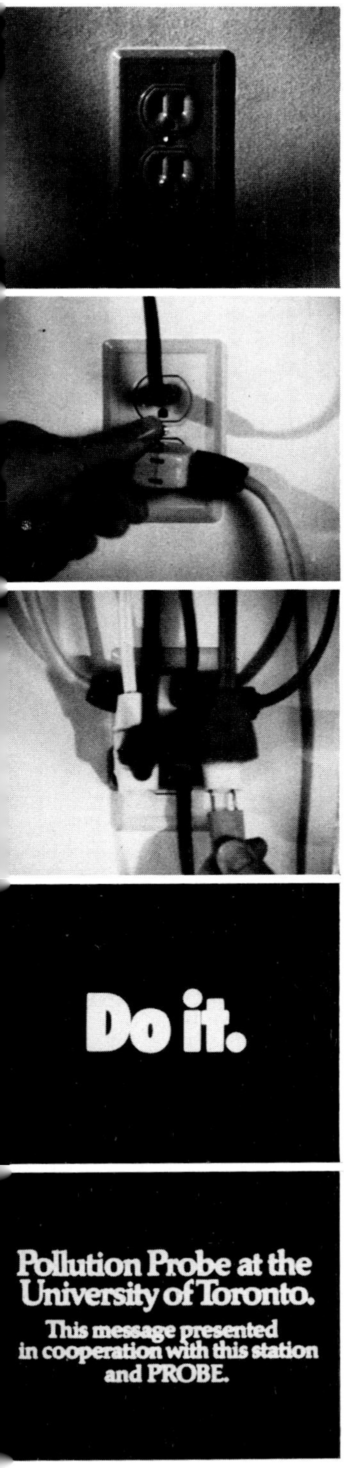
Do it.
Pollution Probe at the University of Toronto.
This message presented in cooperation with this station and PROBE.

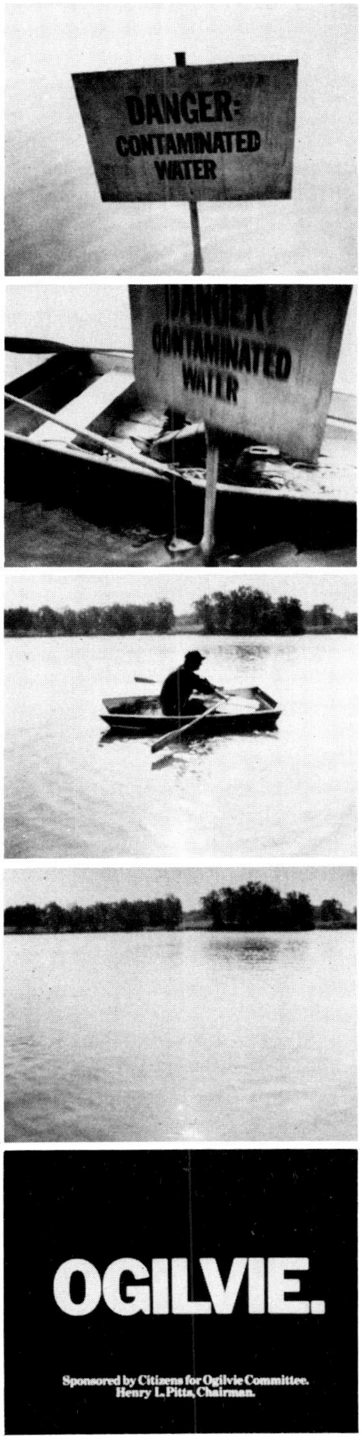
DANGER:
CONTAMINATED
WATER
OGILVIE.
Sponsored by Citizens for Ogilvie Committee.
Henry L. Pitts, Chairman.

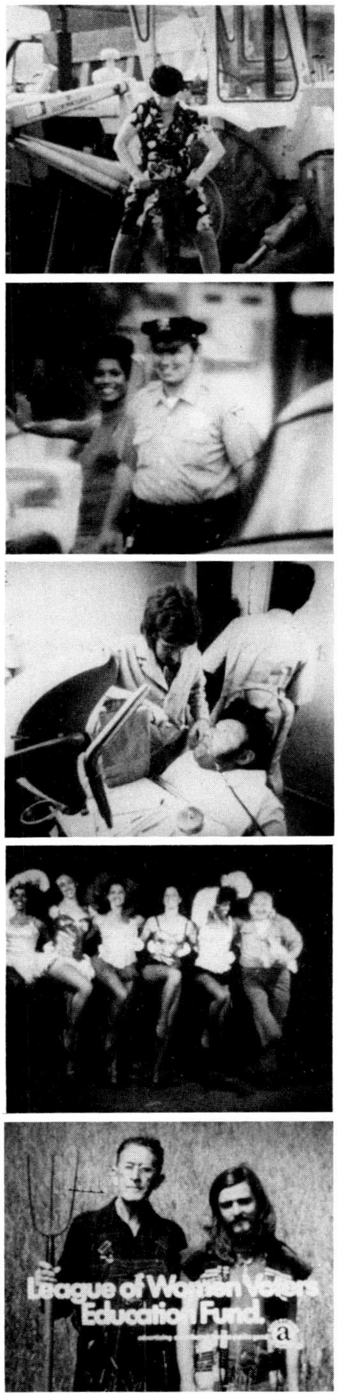
League of Women Voters
Education Fund.

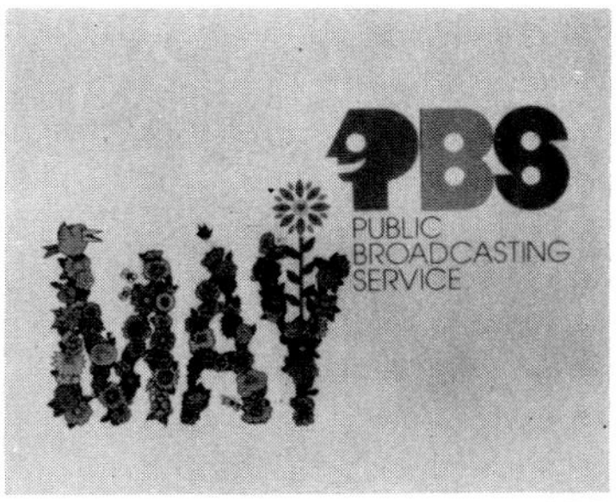
PBS
PUBLIC
BROADCASTING
SERVICE
MAY

823

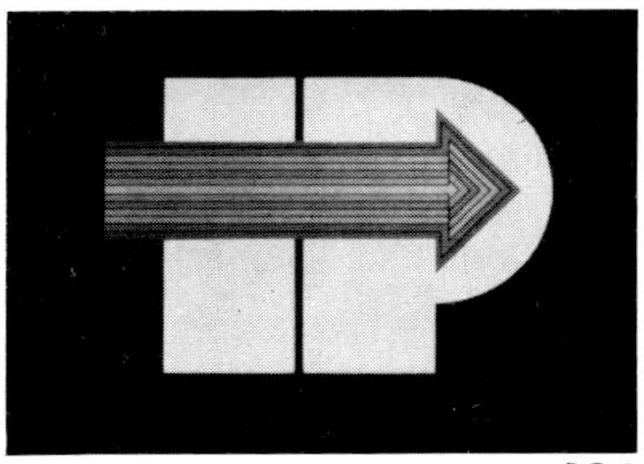

824

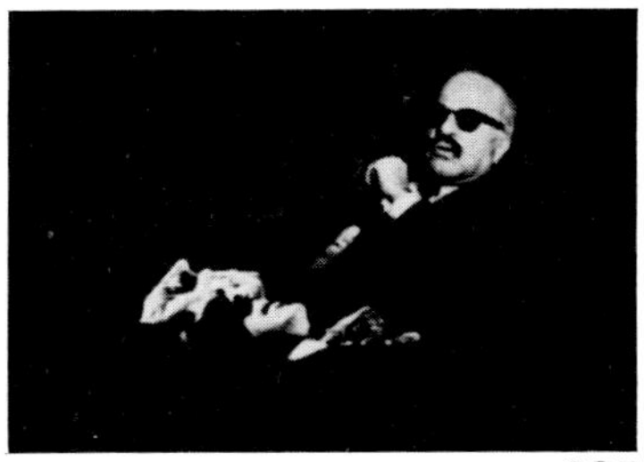

825

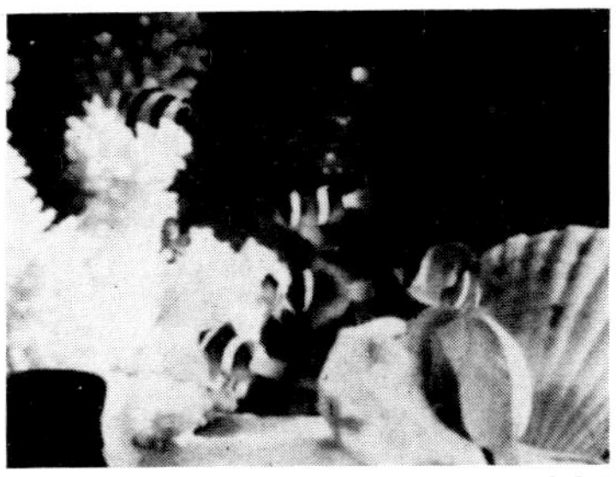

826

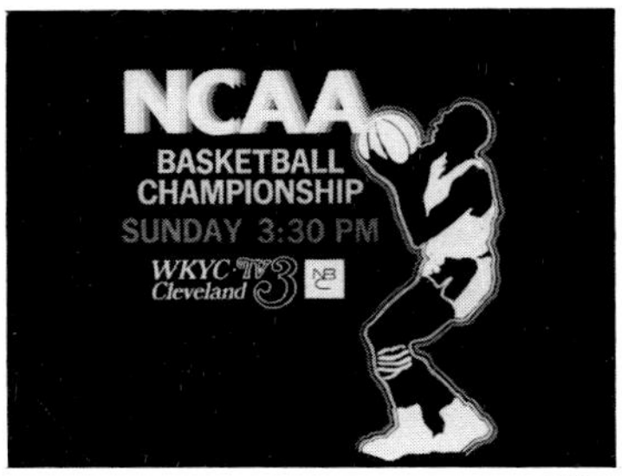
NCAA
BASKETBALL
CHAMPIONSHIP
SUNDAY 3:30 PM
WKYC
Cleveland

827

820
Vickers & Benson Ltd. Entrant
T. O'Malley, T. Hill
Art Directors
Projections
Studio
Pollution Probe, University of Toronto
Client

821
Van Brunt & Co. Chicago Entrant
Dick Lemmon
Art Director
Joe Sedelmaier
Agency
Citizens for Governor Ogilvie
Client

822
Needham, Harper & Steers Entrant
Allen Kay
Art Director
David Langley
Studio
League of Women Voters
Client

823-826
Lubalin, Smith, Carnase Entrant
Herb Lubalin
Art Director
Lawrence K. Grossman Inc.
Agency
Public Broadcasting Service
Client

827
Alphonsio McQueen
Entrant
Harlan Guthrie
Art Director
WKYC-TV, NBC
Client

828

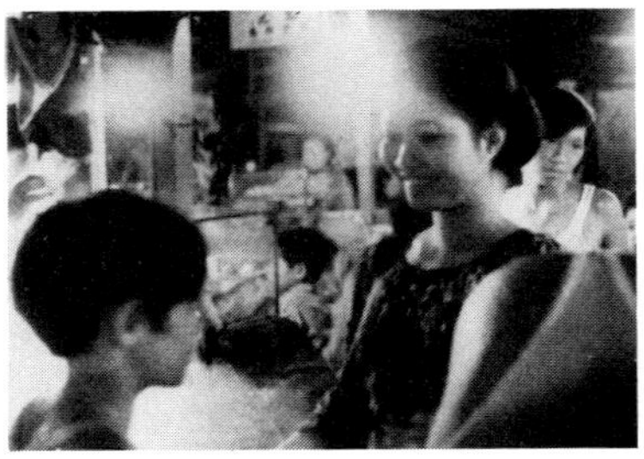

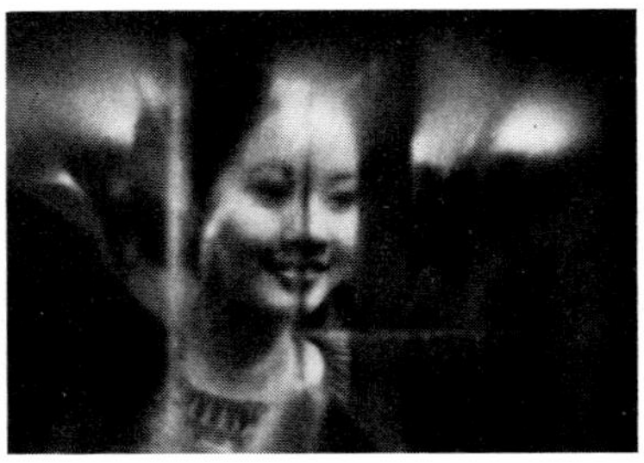

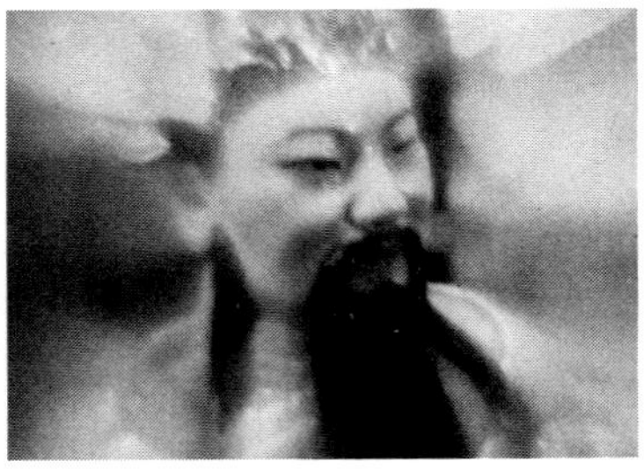

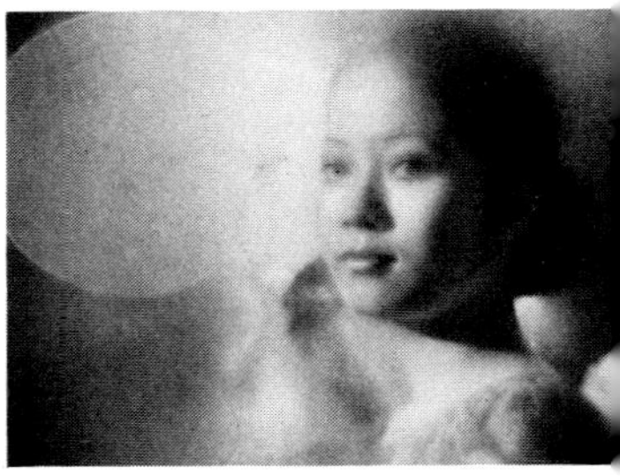

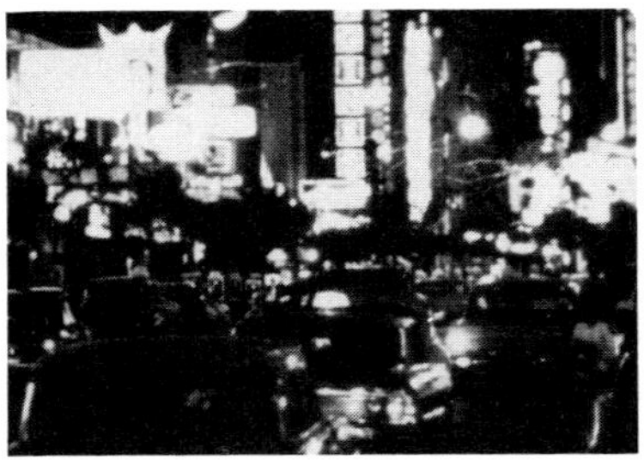

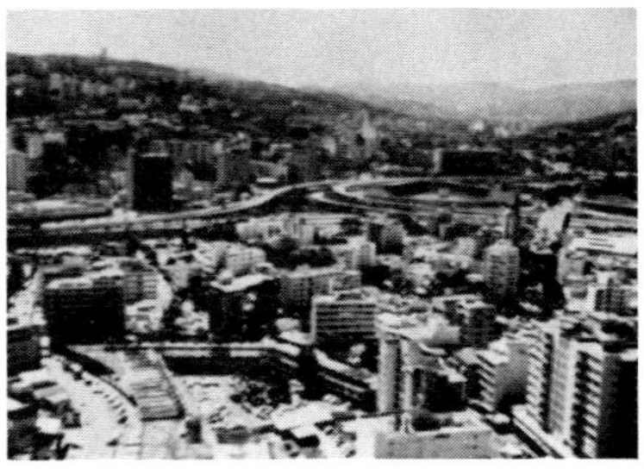

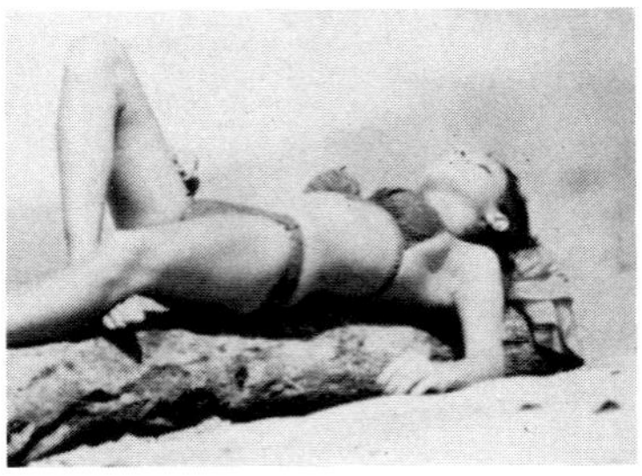

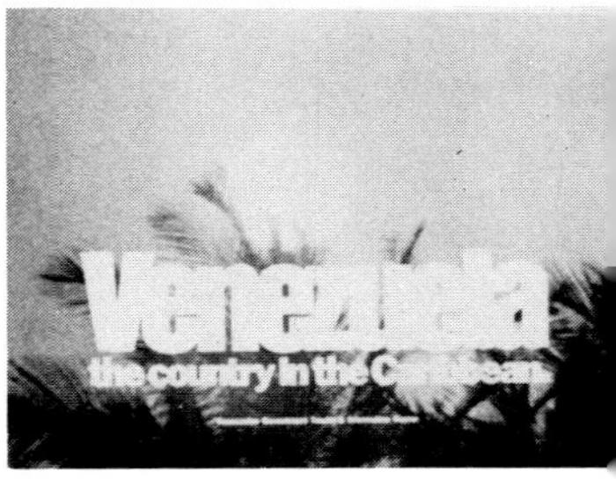
Venezuela
the country in the Caribbean

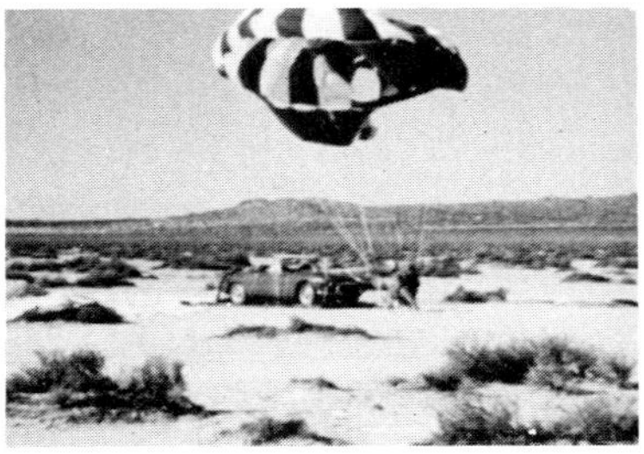

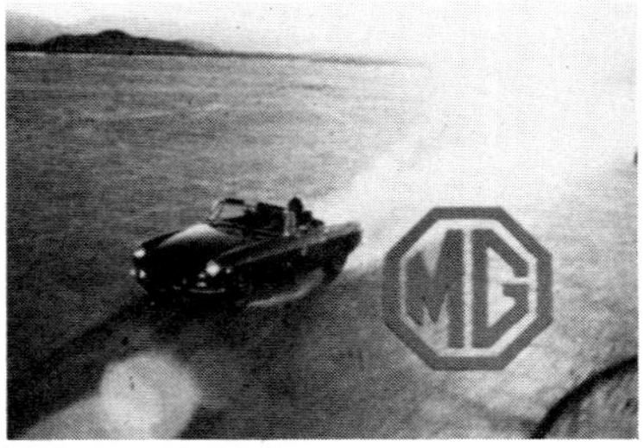
MG

831

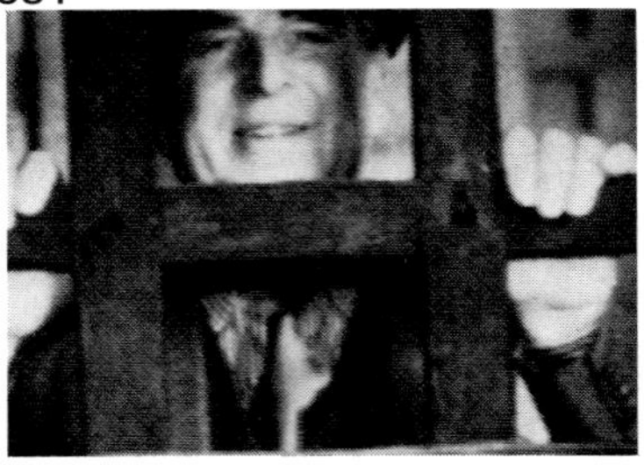

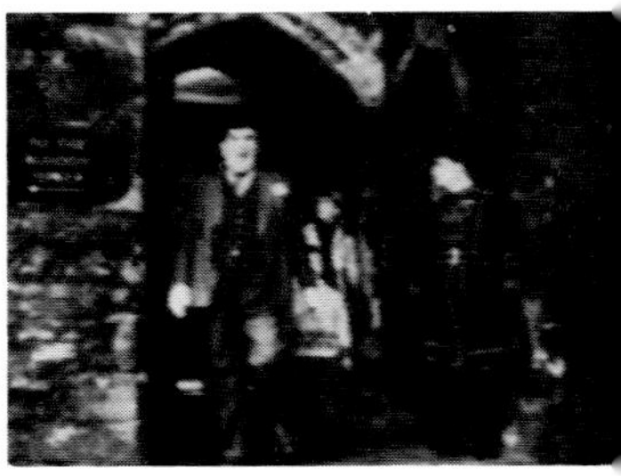

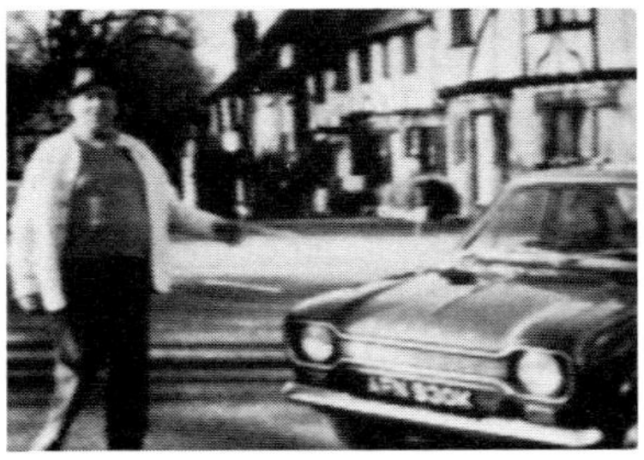

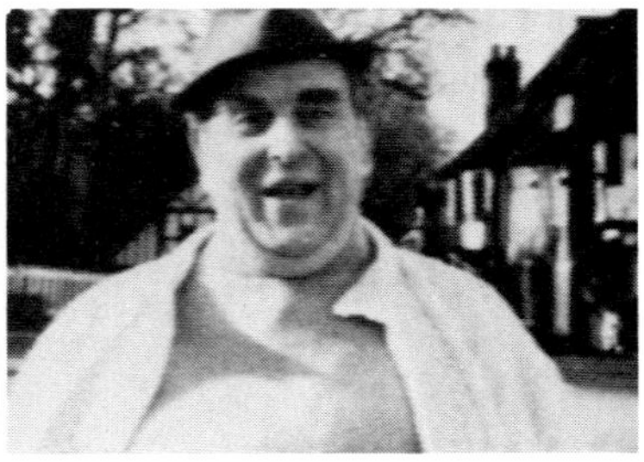

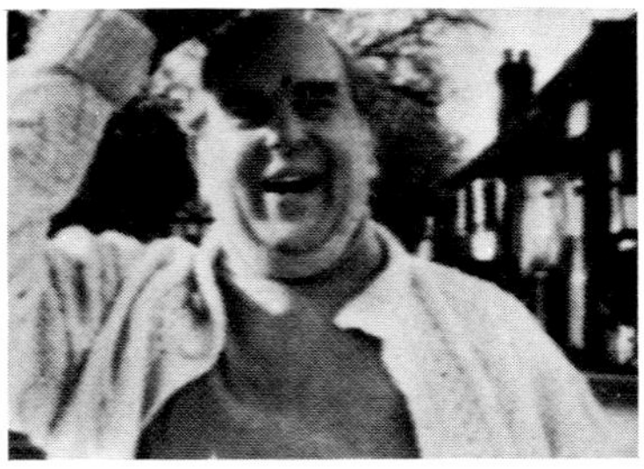

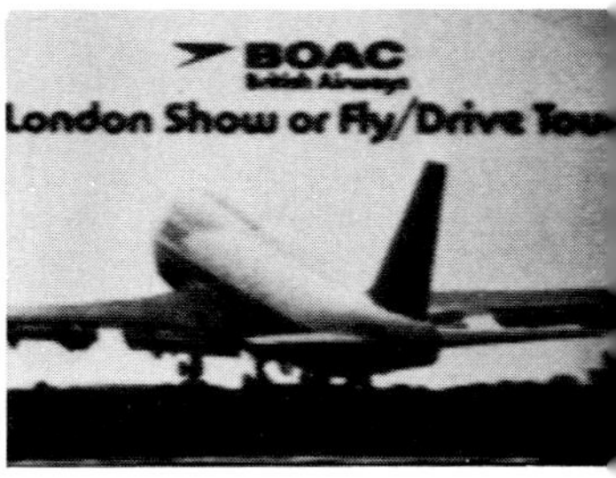
BOAC
London Show or Fly/Drive

836

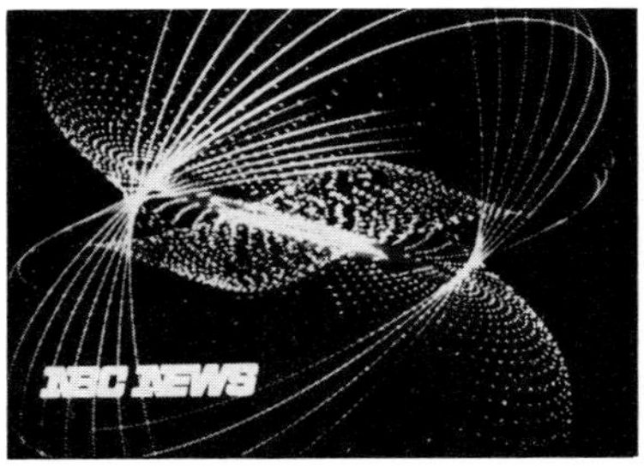
NBC NEWS

837

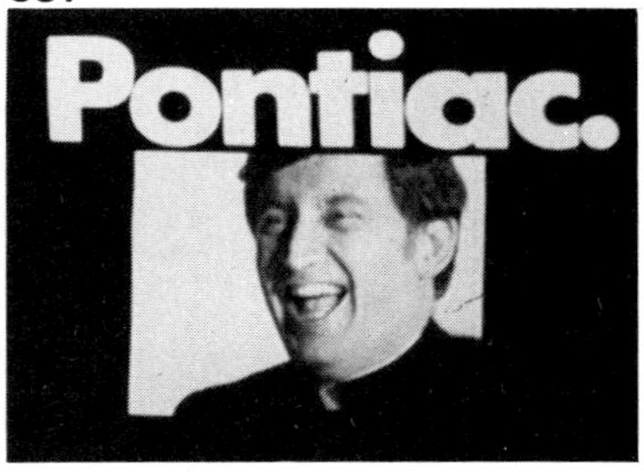
Pontiac.

838

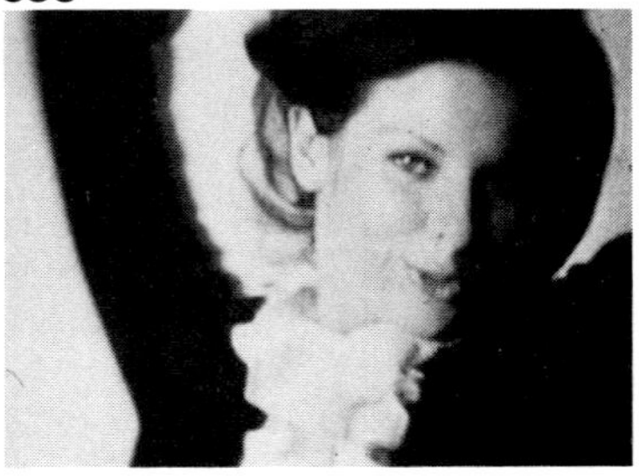

839

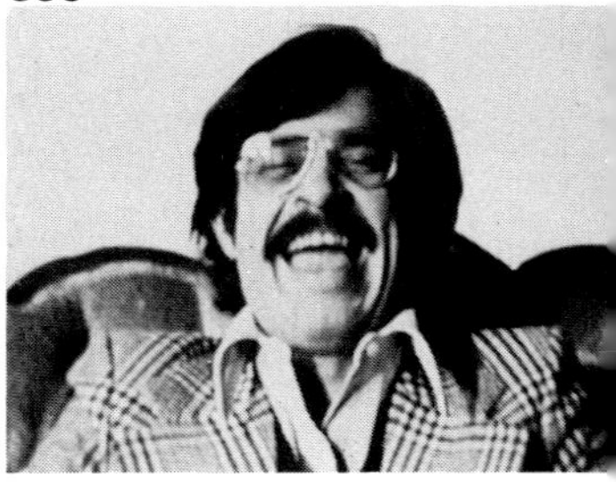

842

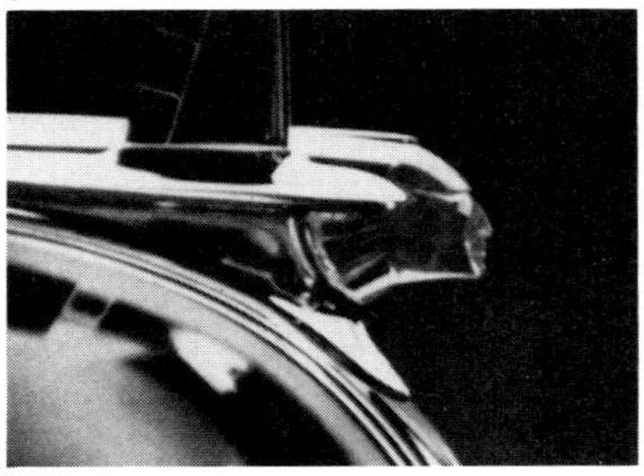

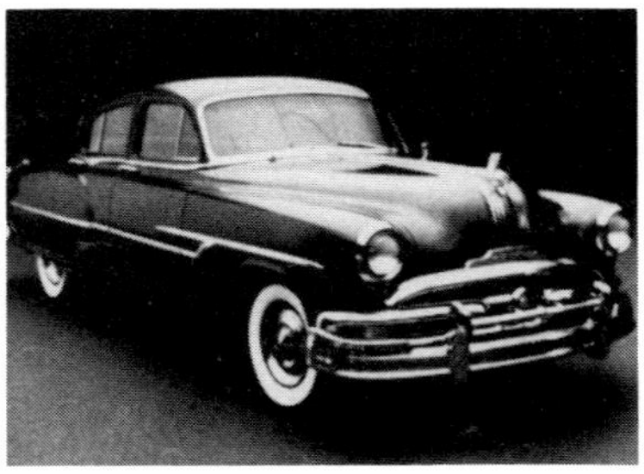

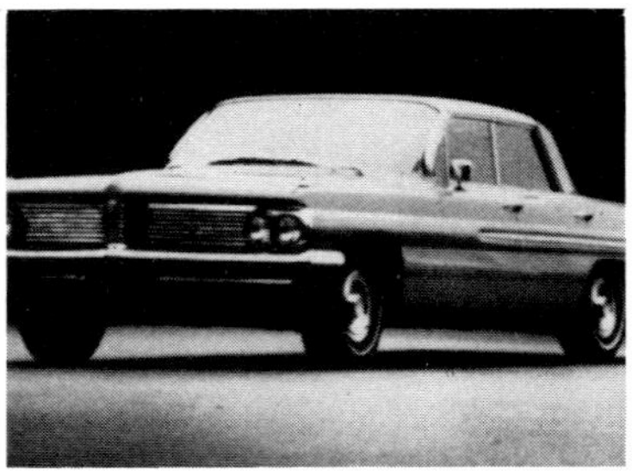

843

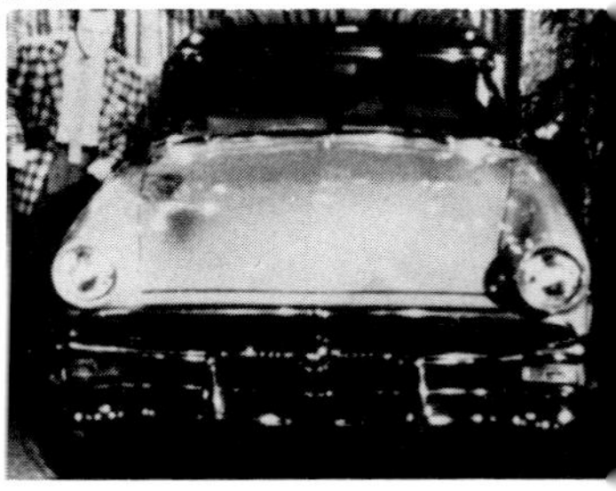

828
Caroline Soong Entrant
John Ashenhurst Art Director
Batey Advertising Pty. Ltd. Agency
Ross Wood Productions Studio
Singapore Airlines Ltd. Client

829
Arthur Roberts & Hill Advertising Entrant
R. Nussbaum, M. Rubin Art Directors
Editors Corner Studio
Venezuelan Government Tourist and Information Center Client

830
Marce Mayhew Entrant
Bozell & Jacobs Agency
Cascade Studio
M.G. Cars Client

831
Eli A. Tulman Entrant
Tinker Dodge & Delano Agency
James Garrett Studio
BOAC Client

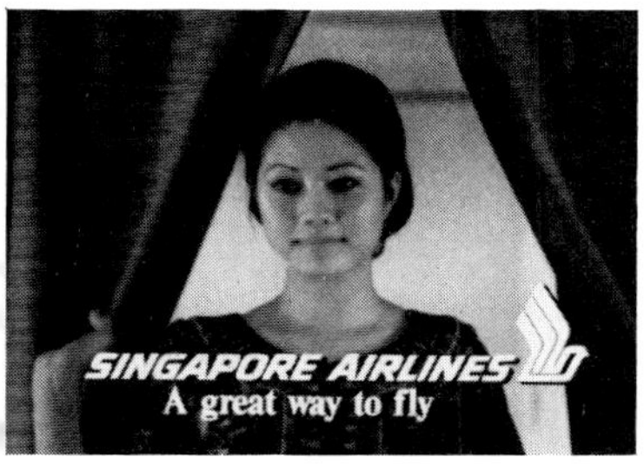
SINGAPORE AIRLINES
A great way to fly

829

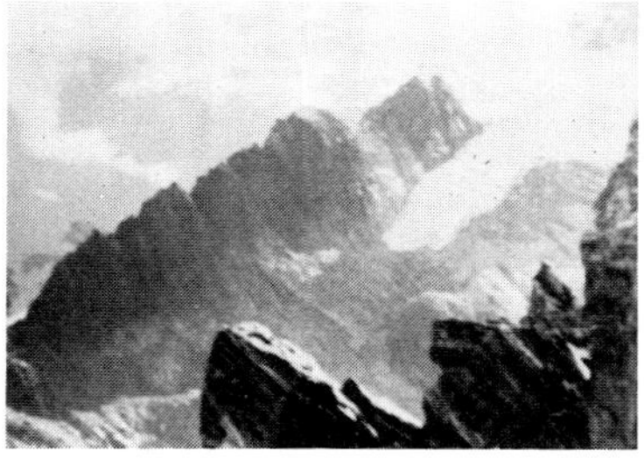

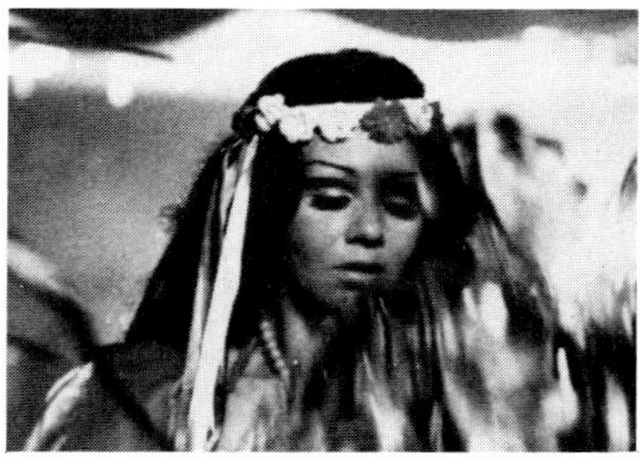

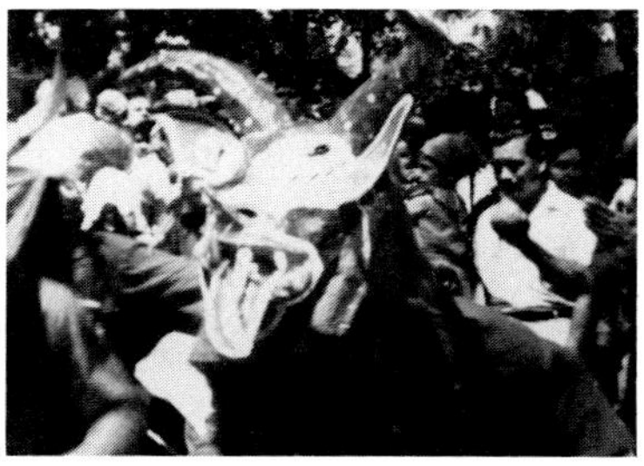

830

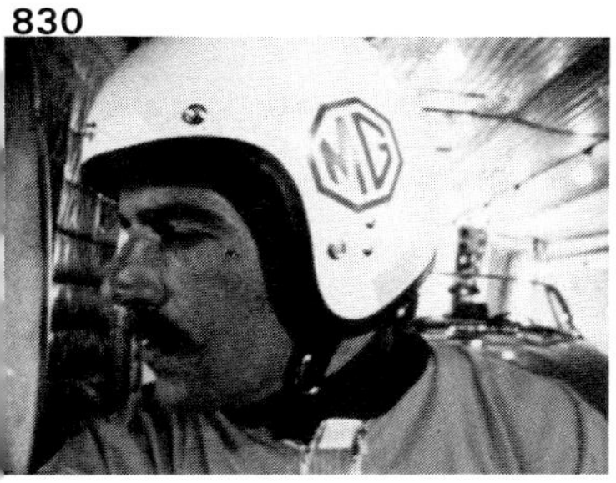

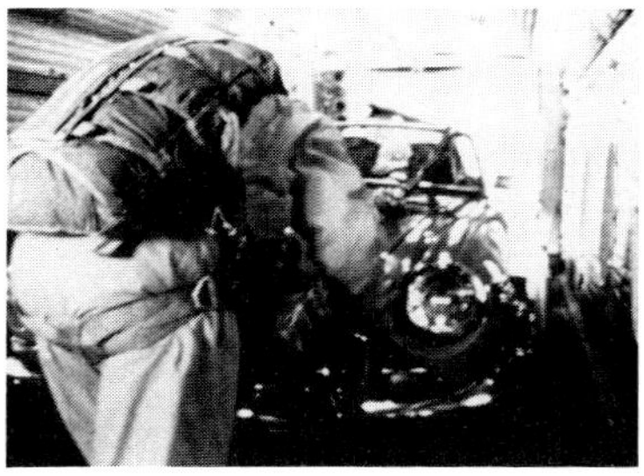

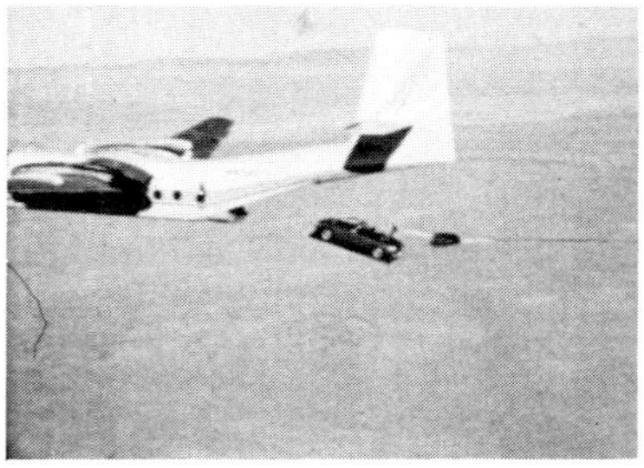

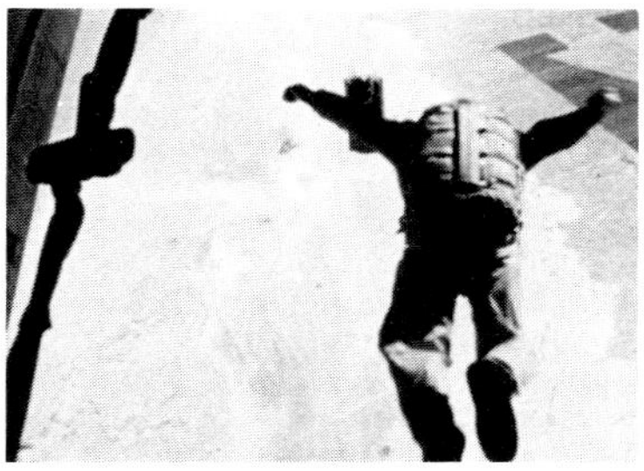

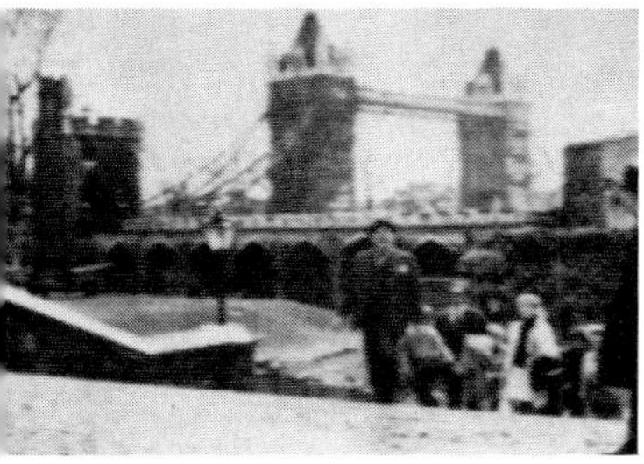

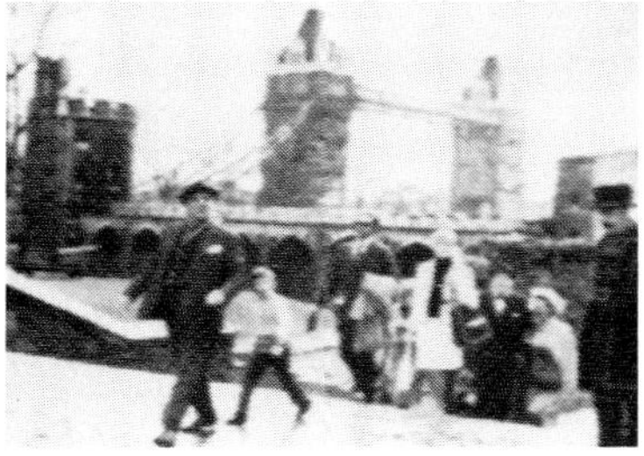

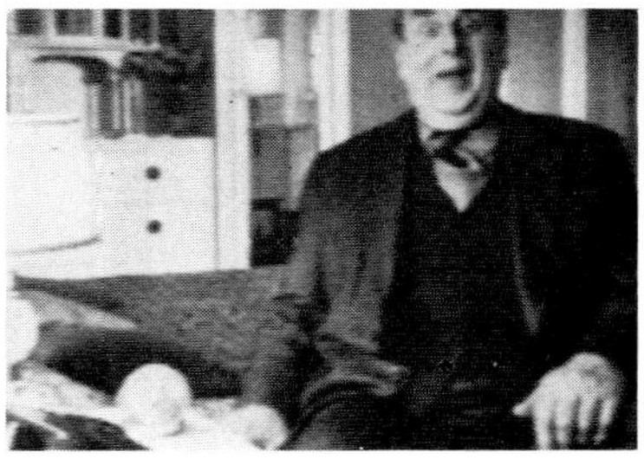

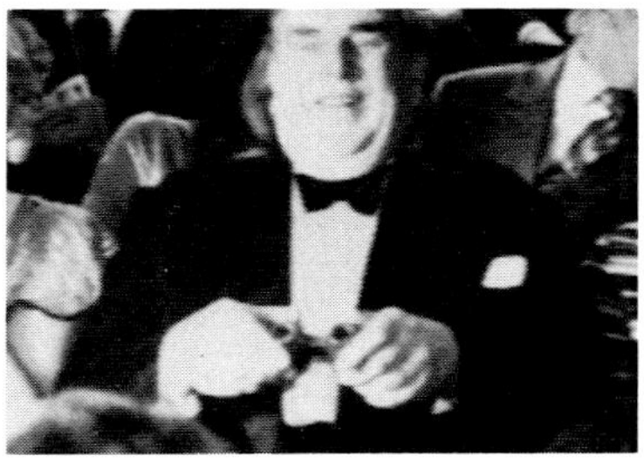

832

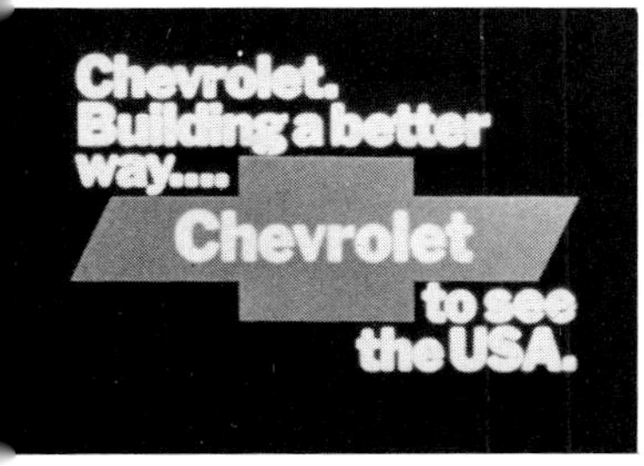
Chevrolet.
Building a better
way....
Chevrolet
to see
the USA.

833

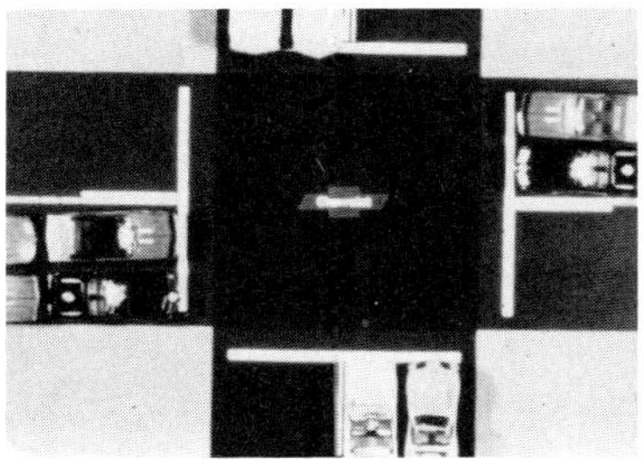

834

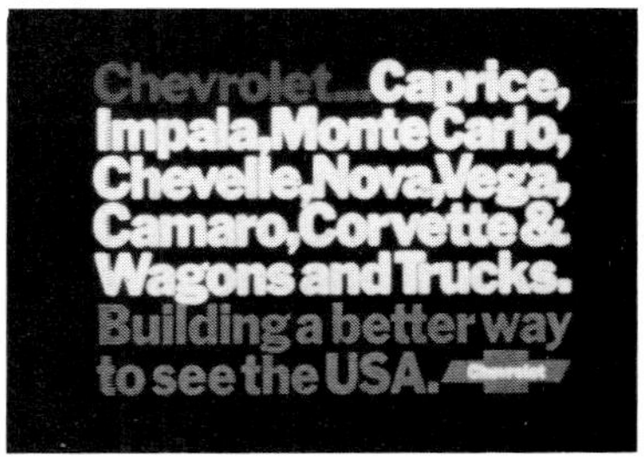
Chevrolet...Caprice,
Impala, Monte Carlo,
Chevelle, Nova, Vega,
Camaro, Corvette &
Wagons and Trucks.
Building a better way
to see the USA.

835

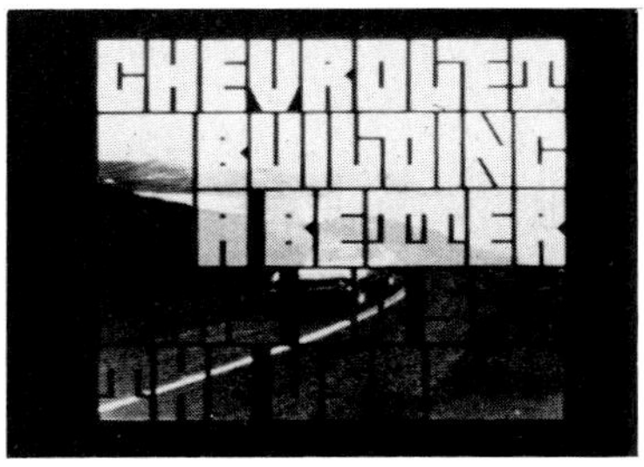
CHEVROLET
BUILDING
A BETTER

840

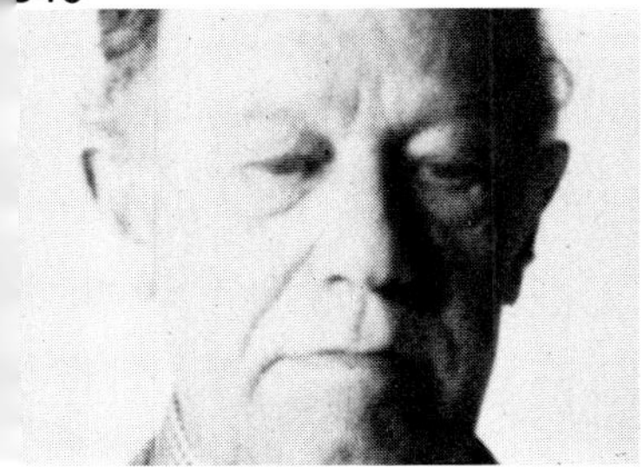

841

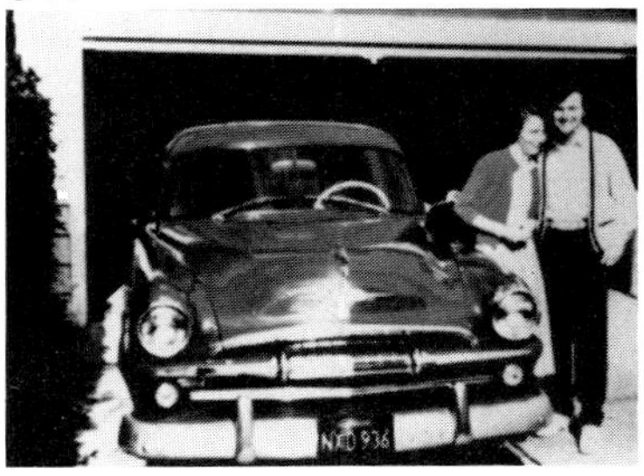

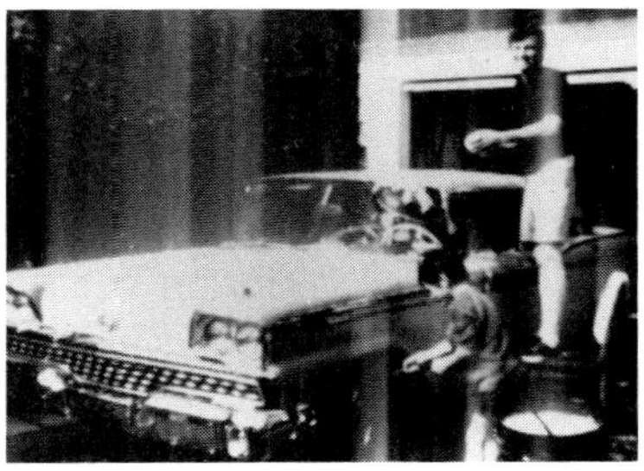

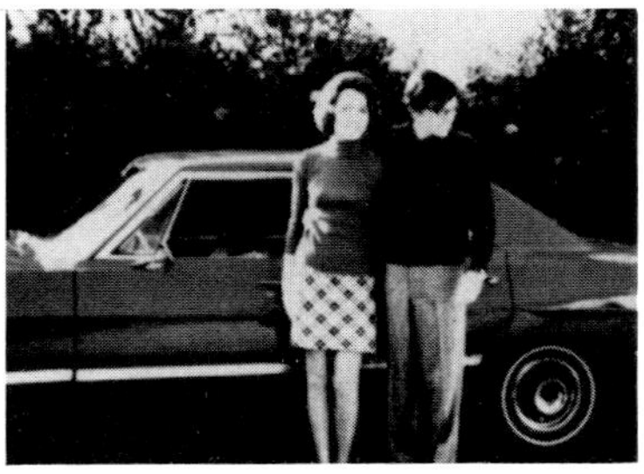

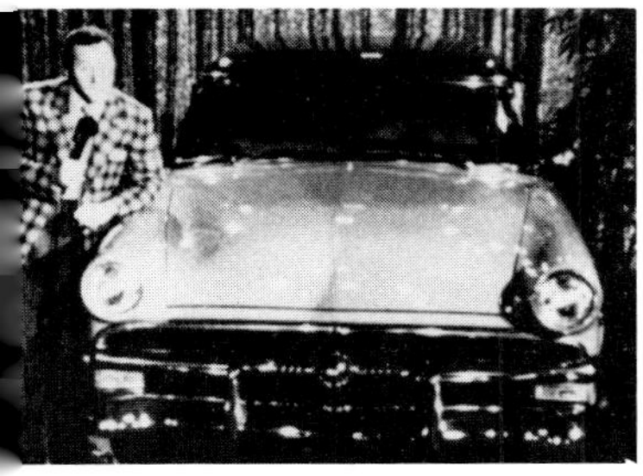

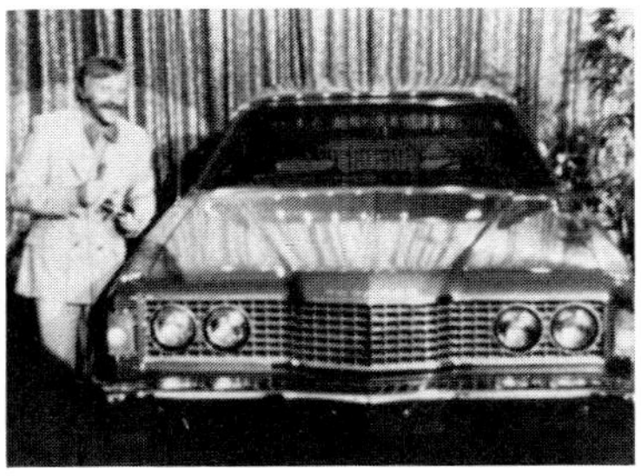

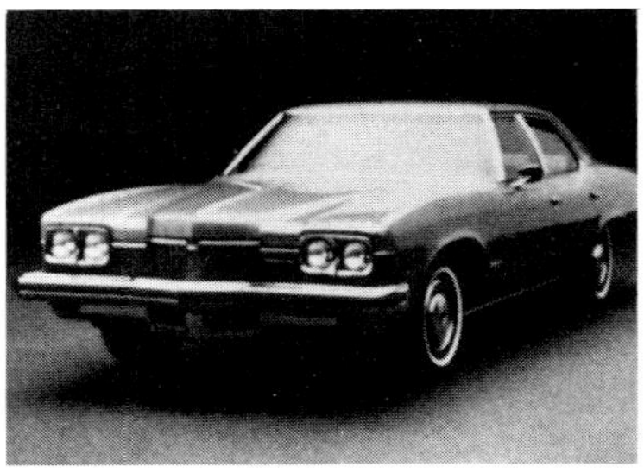

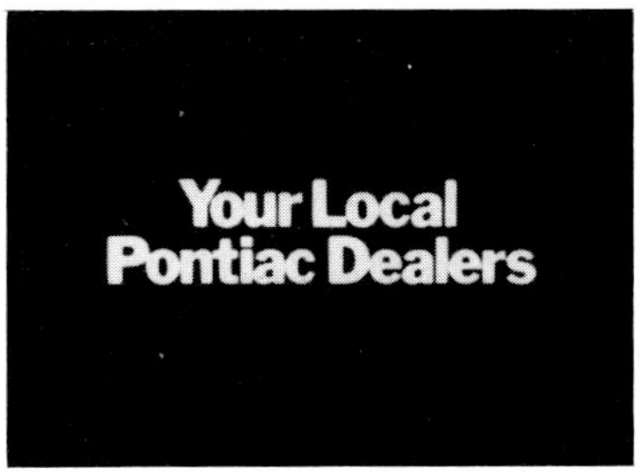
Your Local
Pontiac Dealers

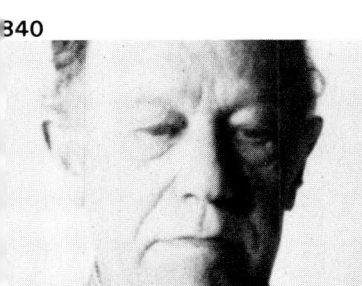

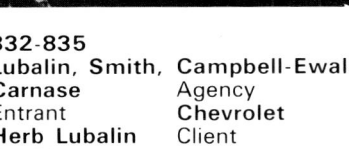

832-835
Lubalin, Smith, Carnase
Entrant
Herb Lubalin
Art Director
Campbell-Ewald
Agency
Chevrolet
Client

836
Bob Greenwell
Entrant
Jerry Kresh
Photographer
NBC
Client

837-840
Hill, Holliday, Connors, Cosmopulos, Inc.
Entrant
Dick Pantano, Stavros Cosmopulos
Art Directors
Videocom Studio
Pontiac Client

841-843
Van Brunt & Co. Chicago
Entrant
John Sapienza
Art Director
Dick Stone
Studio
Chicago Pontiac Dealers
Client

A

ABC News, 338
AC&R Advertising, 206
A.I.M.S., 288
AMF/Head, 106
A.P.D./British Tobacco, 565
Abbey, Hansard Advertising, 508
Acs, Sandor, 483
Adamec, Donald A., 417
Adamec Assoc., 417
Adas, Al, 804
Addison-Wesley Publishing Co., 420
Adel, Judith, 293, 299, 663
Adult Basic Learning Center, 233
Advertising Association, 263
Advisor, 121
Air Industries Corporation, 438
Air Jamaica, 395
Airflow Studio, 674
Aktipis, Helga, 485
Al Majal Magazine, 51, 287
Alaska Airlines, 506
Albert, Jade, 273
Alcorn, John, 605
Alcorn, Richard, 482
Allardyce-Hampshire Ltd., 112
Alliance One, 341
Alten, Cohen, Naish, 175
Alten, Larry, 175
Ambrose, Ken, 9, 106, 202
American Archives, 749
American Broadcasting Company TV, 811
American Business Press, 735
American Can Company, 496
American Dental Association, 245
American Dietaids, 529
American Documentary Films, 363, 719
American Greetings Corporation, 356, 531
American Honda, 726
American Institute of Graphic Arts, 549
American Protection Industries, 712
American Road Builders Assn., 238
American Savers Club, 355
American Seating, 416
American Security Bank, 708
American Stair-Glide Corp., 58
American Symphony Orchestra League, 344
American Telephone & Telegraph, 655
Amft, Robert, 319
Ampersand Productions, 754
Ampersand Studios, 227
Amsel, Richard, 650
Analog Devices, Inc., 490
Andresakes, Ted, 346, 524, 693
Andrews, Bill, 351
Andrus, Fay Ping, 430
Animation House, 814
Ansado, Jean, 536
Anselmo, John, 47, 442
Anselmo, John, Design Assoc., Ltd., 442
Antioch School of Law, 504
Antonik, Robert, 753
Apol, Lysander, 361
Appelbaum & Curtis, 260
Apple Records, 621, 629, 634
Applied Materials Inc., 477
Arbogast, Bill, 391, 407, 678
Arbogast Photography, 391
Arisman, Marshall, 235
Arizona Natural Resources, Inc., 114
Armitage, Frank, 517
Art Group 50, 369
Arthur Roberts & Hill Advertising, 829
Asada, Katsuji, 97, 133
Asencio, John J., 676
Ashenhurst, John, 828
Asociación de Artes y Estudios Experimentales, Lima, Peru, 298
Athens Paper Co., 747
Atlantic Richfield Co., 252
Atlantis Hotel, 119
Atlas Biscuit, 587
Audience Magazine, 285
Austin Nichols (Wild Turkey), 267
Australian Tourist Commission, 129, 339
Auxco, 343
Avco-Embassy Films, 679
Avery Products, Chartpak Division, 585
Avon Books Inc. 643, 644, 645, 649
Awolo American, 527
Ayer, N.W., Philadelphia, 537
Ayer Design, 426
Axelrad, Nancy, 784
Axelrod, Don, 554

B

BOAC, 19, 831
Babitz, Jeff, 288
Backpacker Magazine, 60
Bahrt, Irving, 257, 336
Bailey, Conrad, 396
Baird, Donald, 508
Baker, Kiley, Plastics, 527
Baker, Stan, 49, 321
Baldwin, Fred, 330
Baldwin-Wallace College, 406
Ballard, James L., 512
Ban-Lon, 262, 797
Bank of America, 419
Banks, Robert, 51, 287
Banner Press, 508
Barber, Norman, 598
Barber, Ray, 562, 581, 587
Barboza, Anthony, 25
Barclay, Art, 262
Barnangen AB, 1, 795
Barrett, Fred, 459, 770
Barton, Gladys, 577
Bartone, Laurence, 117
Bass, Saul, & Associates Inc., 372, 655, 719
Batey Advertising Pty. Ltd., 828
Baxter, Rebecca, 5
Bayhead Yacht Corporation, 705
Baystate West Motor Hotel, 394
Bean, Jeremiah, 237
Bear Manufacturing, 572
Beard, Cy, 256
Beard, Pete, 540
Beckenstein, Arthur, 292
Beckerman, Arnold, 215
Beene, Geoffrey, 100
Beetleboards of America, Inc., 756
Beier, Annegret, 605, 614
Beiersdorf AG, Hamburg, 98
Bell, Marion, 572
Bellerose, Mark, 418
Benay, Joel, 547
Bengtsson, Jan, 324
Bergquist, Claes, 375
Berk, Ann, 135, 359
Bernard, Walter, 304, 309
Bernstein, Rein & Boasberg, 58
Bertoli, Barbara, 643, 644, 645, 649
Besalel, Ely, 53
Besalel Ltd., 53
Bichsel Photographic Illust., 65
Bilagare, Vi, 364
Bilecky, John, 509
Billings, Bob, 331, 513
Billout, Guy, 630
Biondi, Vince, 638
Bird, Charles E., Inc., 539, 756
Birthday Book, 382, 792
Bishop, Bonnie, 237, 610
Bivans, Scott, 439
Bixler, Dan A., 272
Blank, Peter J., 60, 482, 488
Blansky, Bob, 809
Blau/Bishop & Assoc., 570
Blechman, Robert, 813
Bliss & Laughlin, 439
Bloch, Thomas, 47, 442
Blomquist, Sven O., Annosbyrå AB, 310
Blumenthal, Martin, 66
Boatman, Fred, 584
Boatright, John, 710
Boatright, Oden & Payton, Inc., 710
Bobbish, John, 554
Bobetski, Ted, 554
Bolanos, Louis, 259
Bonnell, Bill, 205, 396, 436, 560, 604
Book Production Industry, 306, 308
Booren, Rob van, 229
Borden: Comstock, 177
Borg Textiles, 240
Borgstrom, Gun, 273
Bosshard, A., 119
Bostitch, Inc., 193
Boston, City of, 212
Boston Assoc. for Childbirth Education, 743
Boston Globe, 314
Boughton, Chris, 540
Bower, Joseph, 296
Bozell & Jacobs, 830
Bradbury, George, 329
Bradbury-McCormick, 316
Bragg, Bob, 493, 494
Brand-Edmonds-Packett, 239
Braswell, Lynn, 641
Braun, Craig, 637, 639, 650, 748
Braun, Ickes, 337
Braverman, Al, 5, 66
Breslau, Alan, 529, 557
Bresner, Stuart O., 159, 162
Brewer, John, 37, 589
Brewer, Linda, 37, 589
Brian, Robert, Advertising, Inc., 114, 254
Brigham Young University, 23, 433
Bristol-Myers, 32, 96, 812, 816
British Leyland Motors, Inc., 370
Broadway-Hale Stores, Inc., 443
Brodsky, Geraldine, 760
Bronson Design Studio, 745
Brookfield Knitting (Pty.) Ltd., 684
Brooks, Alan, 805
Brooks, Alan, Productions, 805
Brown, David, 264
Brown, John, 555, 690
Brown, Richard, 245, 250, 252, 323
Bruna Boekhandel, 722
Brut Lotion, 796
Buchanan, J. Brett, 384
Buell, Charles, 558
Bunin, Elinor, 311, 815, 817
Bunin, Elinor, Productions Inc., 811, 815, 817
Burch, Dan, 593
Burch, Dan, Advertising, 593
Burger King Corp., 244
Burlockoff, Sam, 287
Burns, Jim, 585
Burry's Div., Quaker Oats, 372
Bush, Marlin, 406
Business Committee for the Arts, 215
Business Week Magazine, 317
Bussche, Wolf von dem, 475, 694
Butler, Linda, 36, 598
Byrd, David, 650

C

CBS/Broadcast Group, 524, 693
CBS News, 524
CBS Stations, 693
CBS Television Network, 107
COM 3 (Soyster & Ohrenschall, Inc.), 723
CRM Books, 517
Cabot, Cabot & Forbes Land Trust, 480
Cahoon, John Photography, 318
Cailor/Resnick, 537
Calabrese, Vincent, 643
Calder, Alexander, 376
Caldwell, Kuhn, 101, 347
California Girl Magazine, 294, 678
Camardella, Frank, 96, 801, 816
Campbell-Ewald, 832
Campbell-Mithun, Inc., 131
Cap Tech Inc., 467
Capawana, Rod, 124, 810
Cappabianca Displays, 316
Caputo, Ralph, 743
Caputo Design, 743
Caravetta, Fred, 234, 244, 785
Caravetta, Allan, Kimbrough, inc., 234, 244, 785
Carheden, Hakan, 131
Carlton Lighting, 729
Carnase, Tom, 762
Carpenter, Joylene, 583
Carrier, Mike, 354
Carroll, Philip, 636
Carter, David E., 558, 777
Carter, Richard, 517
Casal's Studio, 623
Casarola, Angelo, 97
Cascade, 830
Case-Hoyt, 342
Catalano, Sal, 237
Catania, Richard, 99
Ceco Publishing Co., 282, 286
Celedonia, Arthur, 187
Center for Advanced Research in Design, 335, 698, 772
Century Expanded, 358, 529, 557
Certain-teed Products Corporation, 689
Champion International, 371, 376
Champion Papers, 516, 692, 706
Champion Papers, Package Div., 587
Chan, Paul, 419
Changing Times Education Service, 588
Charlton, Mary, 745
Chassagne, Claude, 496
Chesebrough-Pond's Inc., 802

Chevrolet, 282, 832
Chevron Chemical Co., 248
Chin, Free, 617
Chirurg & Cairns Advertising, 118, 255
Christer & Arne Production AB, 1, 795
Church, Stanley, 562, 580, 581, 587, 602
Church & Dwight Co., Inc., 125
Churchill, Patti, 286
Chwast, Seymour, 235
Ciba-Geigy Corporation, 49, 321
Cipriani, Robert, 113, 418, 455, 771
Cipriani, Robert, -Gunn Assoc., 418, 771
Citizens Committee for McGovern/Shriver, 235, 720
Citizens for Governor Ogilvie, 821
Claridge, John, 264
Clark, Kim, 36, 598
Clarke, Gerald, Inc., 187
Clemente, Tom, 519, 741
Cleveland Darter Club, 660
Clopay Corp., 586
Cober, Alan E., 42
Coca Cola, 805
Cochran, Jacqueline, 102
Cochrane, Cary, 509
Cochrane Chase & Co., 190, 249
Cocozza, Thomas, 508
Cohen, Jeff, 134
Cohoe, John, 753
Colangelo, Ted, 329, 483
Colangelo, Ted, Assoc., 329
Cole, Henderson, Drake, Inc., 152, 353, 379, 422
Cole, Jim, 152, 353, 379, 422
Coleman, John, 769
Colgate-Palmolive, 557
Collins Foods International Inc., 469
Columbia Broadcasting System, Inc., 346
Columbia Corporation, 695
Combustion Engineering, Inc., 495
Communication Arts, Inc., 778
Communications Quorum, Inc., 679
Communigraphics, 458
Compton Advertising, 261
Conboy, John, 110
Concombres, 20
Conde Nast Publications, 62, 68, 283
Conley, John, 42, 43, 79, 340
Connecticut Savings Bank, 168
Connor, Woody, 25
Container Corporation of America, 205, 396, 436, 560, 604
Continental West Realty, 778
Cooney, Robert, 740
Cornelia, Bill, 330
Corning Optical, 810
Corolle, 605
Corporate Annual Reports, 4, 486, 491, 492, 495
Corrao, John S., 421
Cosgrove, Bob, 50, 369
Cosgrove, Jerry, 645
Cosmopolitan en Español Magazine, 268
Cosmopulos, Stavros, 122, 168, 212, 385, 394, 455, 806
Costabile and Moss, 753
Cotton Incorporated, 746
Country Lover, 36, 598
Craddock, Barry, 263
Cramp, Bob, 98
Crane, Chris, 762
Crawford, Bob, 239
Creamer, Trowbridge, Case & Basford, 193, 386, 563, 662
Creative Communications S.A., 10, 55
Creative Services, 48, 556
Creative Typographers, 709
Crescent Cardboard Co., 514
Cripps, David, 210
Cross, Dave, 236
Cross, Peter, 638
Crouch, Paul, 484
Cruz, Ray, 53, 648
Crystal, Barry, 104, 527
Cunningham, Robert, 338
Cunningham, Tallman, Pennington, 409
Cutini, Rinaldo, 590, 713, 738
Cynar, S.A. Mendrisio, 155, 397

D

DaCosta, Reynaldo, 783
Daeppen, Otto, 49, 321
Daigneault, Gilles, 20, 281
Daily Newspapers U.S. & Canada, 519
Dallison, Ken, 370
Dance Theater Workshop of N.Y., 382
Daniel & Charles Associates, Ltd., 96, 801, 816
Daniels, Larry, 619
Daniels, Lawrence, & Friends, Inc., 619
Dann, Ed, 337
D'Anna, Russell, 301
Davidson, Marty, 323
Davis, Jack, 742
Davis, Jack, Graphics, 742
Davis, Richard, 80
Davis-Delaney-Arrow, 440, 449, 694, 706
Davol Inc., 386
Dazo, Jack, 811, 815
Deafenbaugh, Chuck, 400
Deakin, Roger, 210
Dean, Donald A., 588
De Beers Consolidated Mines Ltd., 426
de Cesare, John, 525
Dedell, Jacqueline, 233, 652
Deere & Company, 28, 39, 457
Dellaportas, Spyros, 745
Del Monte Corp., 115, 117, 392
Delpire Advico, 605, 614
Delpire et Cie, 725
Demarchelier, Patrick, 62
Demarest, Sharron, 544
Demlin, William W., 306, 308
Design Graphics, Inc., 769
Designers East, 752
Designers Ross Stewart & Winner, 8, 380, 428, 709, 714, 761
Designsense, Inc., 567, 592
Destefano, Tony, 550
Deur, Paul, 378
Deltona Corp., 459
Developers Diversified, 774
Diagnostics & Designs, 600
Dial Press, 641
Diamond, Harry, 42, 43, 79
Diehl, David, 586
Dieterich, Claude, 298, 564, 623, 721
Digital Equipment Corp., 507
Diners Club, Lima, Peru, 564
Dinnerstein, Harvey, 677
Dior, Christian, Perfumes, 101, 347
Dior, Jerry, 571, 594
Diseno Grafico, 783
Distinctive Designs, 780
Diversity Printing Corp., 758
Division Chevrolet, 676
Dix, Seldon, 545
Dix & Eaton Inc., 774
Dixon, John, 485
DiZinno, Hugo, 184
d Morgan, Jonathan, 540
Do Duds Laundry & Dry Cleaning, 742
Dolen, Guy, 793
Dolen, Guy, Inc., 793
Dolphin Productions (N.Y.), 809
Dombrovsky/Peck Coalition Inc., 357, 398, 715
Donaldson, Bryan, 459
Doret, Michael, 734, 750, 781
Dorfsman, Lou, 107, 346, 524, 693
Dorian, Marc, 220
Dorian, Marc, Inc., 220
Dorne, Dick, 519
Dorr-Oliver Inc., 269
Douglas Records, 639
Dow, George, 455
Downing, R., 594
Drakes-Borden, 818
Drayton, Bob, 59
Dreyhage, Gerrit, 723
Drier, Bill, 108
Drown, Jerry, 494
Duckett, Steven, 64, 659
Duerr, Herman, 282
Duevell, William, 338
Dugdale, John, 370
Dulaney Advertising, 761
Dunkin' Donuts, 806
Dunst, Laurence, 96, 801, 816
du Pont Glore Forgan, 358
Durastone Limited (Lockstone), 256, 718
Durotest Corporation, 34, 533
Duskin, Ken, 816
Dynamic Skis, 113

E

EKO Studios, 584

Earthrise Design Inc., 509
Easdon, Don, 662
Eastman Kodak Company, 334
Eck, Frank, 386
Editorial America S.A., 268
Editors Corner, 829
Edlund, Richard, 736
Eiber, Rick, 698, 772
Eiger & Forer, 108
Einess, Jack, 306, 308
Eisenman, Stan, 3, 30
Eisenman and Enock Inc., 3, 30, 303, 473
Electronic Associates, Inc., 187
Elektra Records, 630, 632
Elizabeth Arden Inc., 536
Elliot, Lee, 689
Elliott, Shaw, Inc., 18
Ellmore, James, 19
Emelin Theatre, 727
Emergency Medicine, 278, 661
Endo Laboratories, 578
Endress, John Paul, 67, 267
English, Mark, 305, 650
Enock, David, 3, 30
Epstein, H., 338
Ericson & Co., AB, 121, 364, 375, 595, 599
Espace Intérieur, 725
Esquire Magazine, 74, 280
Essex, J. Michael, 307, 763, 784
Essex, J.M., Design Center, 307, 509, 763, 784
Essman, Robert N., 317
Etheridge, Ken, 25, 794
Euro Advertising Ltd., 263, 264
European Architecural Heritage Year 1975, 768
Evans, Jim, 674
Evans, Ruth, 755
Everson Museum of Art, 652
Exhibit Graphics, Inc., 764
Exxon Corporation, 42, 43, 79, 340

F

FMC Chemicals, 251
Faberge, Inc., 67, 103, 796
Fader, Nick, 31, 573
Faia, Donald, 535
Fallert, Bruce, 728
Fantasy Records, 7, 624, 628, 631, 633, 635, 636
Farner, Dr. Rudolf, AG BSR, 155, 397
Faughender, Carlton, 356, 531
Fazio, Joe, 568
Federal Reserve Bank of San Francisco, 498
Fedynak, Raymond, 9, 202
Fegley, Richard, 85
Feiffer, Jules, 235
Ferriter, Roger, 705
Fessler, Al, 117, 248, 392
Fidler, Mort, 583
Field, William, 462, 601
Fillman Advertising, Inc., 742
Finger, Herb, 456
Finlay Kaiser Inc., 467, 469
Finn, William F., 737
Finn, William F., & Associates, 737
First National City Bank of N.Y., Investment Management Group, 453
Fisher-Harrison Printing Co., 354
Flagler Federal Savings & Loan Association, 234
Florafax, 393
Florian, Hal, 547
Florida Bar, 227
Florio, Val C., 352
Fluid Drive Studio, 781
Fluidmaster, Inc., 190
Flurer, Ursula, 38
Flying Tiger Corporation, 40, 487
Folkan, 228
Food For Thought, 580, 581, 602
Food Graphics Inc., 554
Foote, David, 48, 556
Foray Art Studios, 167
Ford, Byrne & Associates, 343, 345
Ford, Byrne & Brennan, 532
Ford, J.W., Company, 50, 369
Foreign Autopart, 736
Forsman, Birgitta, 443, 464
Fortune, Bill, 190, 249
Foss, Robert L., 227

Foster, Clarence W., 788
Foster, Gib, 552
Foster, Steve, 511
Foster Wheeler Corp., 9, 202
Foy, Richard A., 778
Francis, David, 799, 807
Francis & Shaw Inc., 518
François, André, 43
Franklin Book Programs, Inc., 10, 55
Frazier, Alan, 252
Freese, Tom, 474
Freight House Design, 767
French, Doug, 461
French Government Tourist Office, 130
Friant, Norm, 726
Friary, Terry, 128
Fridén, Par, 310
Fried, George, 813
Friedlander, Lee, 624
Friedman, Michael, 399
Frost, Hugh, 238
Frybarger, Richard, 457
Frykholm, Stephen, 54, 561
Fuller, Joel, 400
Fuller, Joel Vann, 400, 403
Fuqua Industries, Inc., 493
Fury, Len, 4, 491

G

GKO&S Werbeagentur GmbH & Co. KG, 98
Galati, Jim, 21
Ganton, Brian, 63, 284, 496, 675
Garcia, Tony, 159
Gardner, Charles, 109
Garrett, James, 831
Gary Player Golfing Safaris, 775
Gatsby Mens Wear, 175
Gayton, Silvio, 809
Geigy Pharmaceuticals, 525, 568
Gelberg, Bob, 259
General American Trans. Corp., 271, 552
General Cigar Company, 571
General DataComm, 483
General Foods Corp., 547
George & Me, 728
Gerstman, R., 578, 594
Gerstman + Meyers Inc., 571, 578, 594
Gervasi, Doug, 301
Gescheidt, Alfred, 64
Geurts, Arie J., 32, 697, 729
Geurts, Arie J., Design, 697, 729, 732
Geurts, Salli, 732
Geyer, Jackie, 184, 521, 653
Giaccaloni, Mike, 106
Giambarba, Paul, 601
Giardini/Russell, Inc., 429, 480, 490
Gibbs Assoc., the Design Group, 400, 403
Gifted Resource Center, 534
Gilbert, Craig, 817
Gill, Don, 511
Gillette Company, 24, 461
Gillette Safety Razor Division, 31, 573
Giovanopoulos, Paul, 235
Gips, Philip, 383
Girouard, Dan, 769
Glamour Magazine, 62, 68, 283
Gleason, Lee, 808
Gleckler, Gayle, 177
Glinn, Burt, 3, 30, 473
Glynn, John, 455
Gnidziejko, Alex, 650, 679
Gobberdiel, James M., 742
Gold, Bill, 367
Gold, Charles, 488
Goldberg, Irwin, 67, 103, 267, 796
Goldsholl, Morton, 474
Goldsholl Associates, 474
Goldsmith, Vern, 114, 254
Gomez, Ignacio, 180
Good, Peter, 662, 730
Goode, Rex, 318
Goodman, Arthur, 372, 655, 719
Goodnoff Productions, 813
Gorbaty, Norman, 496, 675
Gorbaty, Norman, Design, Inc., 63, 284, 496, 675
Gorham, John, 540
Gorman, W. Chris, 341, 735
Gorman, W. Chris, Associates, 341, 735
Gorman, Jeff, 126
Gould, Jerome, 565, 569, 575
Gould & Assoc., 565, 569, 575
Grace, W. R., & Co., 486
Granges Essem Plast. Upplands Vasby, 310
Grant, Foster, AR, 471
Grant, Howard, 426
Grant, William, 555
Graphic Communications, 23, 433
Graphic Communications Center, 419, 456
Graphics 4 Inc., 421
Graphicsgroup, Inc., 175, 355, 368, 511
Graphics Institute, Inc., 342
Grasso, Lou, 167
Greater Miami Retailers Assoc., 236
Green, Norman, 235
Green, Sidney, Associates, 504
Greenwell, Bob, 836
Gregory, Mike, 540
Grember, John, 330
Grey Advertising, 726
Grossman, Alvin, 75
Grossman, Lawrence K., Inc., 823
Grossman, R., 271
Grossman, Robert, 235, 650
Group Four, Inc., 757
Guerard, Jim, 438
Guidziejko, Alex, 292
Gulotta, Paul, 125
Gunn, Ian, 9, 202
Gunn Associates, 113, 418, 455
Guthrie, Harlan, 827
Gylling (Sony), 324

H

Haas, Ernst, 240
Haling, George, 495
Hall, Tarra, 127
Halt, James G., 522
Hamill, George, 167
Hammermill Paper Company, 522
Hamway, Ed, 80
Hanopole, Irwin, 35
Hanrahan, Dan, 717
Hanser, Larsson & Röstlund AB, 154
Hardwood House, 335
Harmon & Crook, 747
Harper & Row, Publishers, 618, 619
Harper's Bazaar, 273
Harris, Brownie, 400
Harris, Burt, 393
Harrison, Peter, Associates, Inc., 475
Hart Products Company, 8
Hartford National Bank Money Center, 730
Hartman, George, 62, 68, 283
Harvard Engraving, 59
Harvey, Richard, 650
Hass, Derrick, 263, 264
Havas Conseil, 707
Hawaii—Foreign Trade Zone #9, 711
Hayes, John Coleman, Jr. & Associates, 769
Head Ski and Sportswear, 500
Hege, Laszlo, 278
Heimall, Robert L., 630, 632
Heimann, Heinz, 10, 55
Heindel, Robert, 650
Hemsley, Nigel, 210, 270
Henderson, Dick, 152, 353, 422
Henderson, Jill, 775
Hera Annonsbyrå AB, 41, 216
Herring, Jerry, 553
Herrick, Joe, 399, 715
Hess, Richard, 125, 492
Hettinga, Frans, 229
Heublein Inc., 159, 489
Heublein-Smirnoff, 162
Highland National Bank of Newburgh, 111
Hij Herenmode, 361
Hill, Holliday, Connors, Cosmopulos, Inc., 122, 168, 212, 385, 394, 806, 837
Hill Jay, 122, 806
Hill, T., 820
Hillebrand, Burt, 260
Hinckley & Schmitt, 570
Hinrichs, Kit, 34, 471, 533
Hinrichs Design Assoc., 34, 471, 533
Hinsche, Gary, 443, 712, 779
Hirsch, Bernard, 18
Hirschfeld, Al, 135
Hoffman, Martin, 666
Hoflich, Richard, 353
Holiday Magic Cosmetics, 535
Holland, Brad, 651
Homelite, 250
Honeywell Photographic, 131
Hopkins, Catherine, 618
Horen, Michael, 640
Horn/Griner, 806, 818
Horowitz, Ryszard, 101, 426
Horton, Rick, 521
Hospital Audiences Inc., 340
House of Design, 539, 756
House of Ronnie, 22
Howard Johnson Company, 594
Howlett, Margaret, 82, 295
Hucknall, Nanette, 333, 664
Hudson Shatz Painting Company, 342
Huey, Lock, 383
Hulefeld, F., 586
Hume, Smith, Mickelberry, 108
Hurll, Holmes, 418
Hutnick, Richard, 171

I

IBM, 423, 437
IEMPSA, 623
INA Corp., 345
Ian Associates, Inc., 758
Ichida, Grant, 356
Ilford Inc., 124
Independent Artists, 801
Infinity Group Inc., 689
Inner Circle Magazine, 286
Institute of Trichology, 600
Intercept, 383
Interlink Advertising Ltd., 210
Intermedia, Inc., 50, 369
International City Corporation, 353
International Flavors & Fragrances Inc., 440, 449
International Silver, 749
In-Town Living Council, 357
Irving, Jay, 206
Irwin, Elliott, 129, 339
Isaacs, Robert, 407
Isaacs, Shelley, 245
Israel, Ed, 452
Itel Corporation, 180, 456
Iwanaga, Joe, 539, 756

J

J. B. Packaging, 264
Jacobs, Kenn, 334
Jacobs, Robert, 22
Jacobs, Steve, 294, 391, 398, 407, 678
Jacobs, Steven, Design, Inc., 294, 391, 398, 407, 678
Jacobson Diversified, 780
Jamaica Tourist Board, 427
Jampel, Judith, 664
Jansu, Rudy, 205
Japan Air Lines, 97, 133
Jayserka, Nirmal, 10, 55
Jennard, Jerry, 553
Jensen, John, 58
Jewel Food Stores, 809
Jiebel, Craig, 50, 369
Johnson, Barry, 514
Johnson, Barry, Studio, 514
Johnson, Doug, 650, 654
Johnson, Kendall, 634
Jones, Jack, 135
Jordan, Ken, 568
Juett, Dennis, 57, 717, 731, 776
Juhl Advertising Agency, 272
Jung, Ed, 534

K

KJAZ Radio, 319
Kahan, Louis, 371
Kahn, Steve, 438
Kaiser, Michael, 467, 469
Kal, Merrick & Salan, Inc., 238
Kalman Corp., 774
Kamerer, John R., 110
Kantor, Norman, 215
Kaprielian, Walter, 395, 547
Katz, Jacobs, Douglas, Inc., 21, 22
Katz, Marshall, 763
Katz, Rick, 22
Katz, Wallis, 763
Kaufman, Allan, 177
Kaufman, Barry, 679
Kay, Allen, 102, 130, 266, 798, 822
Kay, Rusty, 40, 487
Kayser-Roth, 801
Kearney, Hal, 77, 319, 617, 647
Keenan, Larry, Jr., 456
Keep the Archipelago Clean Committee, 216

Keig, Susan Jackson, 512
Kellner, Rich, 804
Kelly, John, 458
Kelly, Nason, Inc., 125
Kelly, Tony, 205
Kelvin Group Part., 553
Kemsley, William, 60, 482, 488
Kent, Nancy V., 69, 80, 300
Kent State University Theater, 384
Kentucky Electric Steel Co., 558
Kessler, Herb, 655
Ketchum, MacLeod & Grove, Inc., 97, 133, 184, 395, 547
Kidder, Fred C., 464
Kimmelman, Phil, Assoc., 800
Kindley-Lenowitz Design Associates, 567, 592
King, Lee, & Partners, 215, 271, 552
Kirkland, Douglas, 69, 300
Kirsch, Art, 476
Kiviat, Stephen, 740
Kiviat/Rappoport Inc., 740
Kleckner, Valerie, 27, 29, 520
Klein, Frank, Company, 790
Klim, Matt, 489
Klim, Matt, & Assoc. Inc., 489
Kloppenburg, Switzer & Teich, 132
Knapp, Richard, 317
Knight, Terry, Enterprises Ltd., 748
Knowles, Thomas J., 61
Knox, Harry, & Assoc., 48, 556
Kolbe, Kurt, 517
Koltun Brothers, 57
Koner, Marvin, 4, 491
Koppers, 521
Koson, W. Earl/Draperies, 773
Kosterman, Wayne, 790
Kosunen, Jorma, 1, 324, 795
Kraftco Corporation, 479, 497
Kramer, Daniel, 304
Kraus, Gerald, 187
Kresh, Jerry, 836
Krieger, Harold, 99, 102, 127
Kristiansson, Björn, 582
Krivisky, Steve, 66
Kroehler Mfg. Company, 804
Kubricht, Geoge, 728
Kunishima, Lindy, 711
Kupper/Grant Inc., 730
Kurfees Paint Company, 380
Kurtz, Bob, & Friends, 808
Kurz, Ch., 119
Kwan, Anita, 540

L

Lacy, Lee, Prod., 800
Lafitte, Frank, 6, 26, 85
Lamp Magazine, 42, 43
Lamport, Edward, 751, 789
Lamport, Edward, Assoc., 751, 789
Landings on Skidaway Island, 409
Lando/Bishopric Advertising, 259
Landor, Walter, Assoc., 576, 746
Lane, Tony, 7, 624, 628, 631, 633, 635, 636
Lang, Bonnie, 752
Langley, David, 822
Langmuir, Paul, 563
LaPerle, Thom, 419, 456
Law, A. Norman, 360
Lawrence, Bernard, 500
Lawton, Nancy, 478
Lea, Mary Ann, 77
League of Women Voters, 822
Leasco Corp., 562
Lee, Raymond, 256, 265, 718
Lee, Raymond, & Assoc., Ltd., 256, 265, 718
Leeds Polytechnic, 540
Leenhouts, Tom, 722
Lefmann, Walter, 196, 545
Lefton, Al Paul, 128
Legeckis, Marta, 227
Leland Realty & Land Company, 724
Lemery, Gene, 113, 418
Lemmon, Dick, 821
Lenac, Ralph, 190, 249
Lenox, 118
Leone, Anthony, 800
Lerner, Frank, 65
Leslie Advertising Agency, 445
Letraset USA Inc., 352
Levin, Dan, 112
Levin, Lear, 794

Levine, David, 235
Lewis & Gilman Adv., 800
Lieberman, Archie, 28, 457
Lieberman, Valrie, 500, 504
Lienhart, Jim, 28, 39, 457
Lindshammar, 599
Lintas España, 739
Lithographix, Inc., 717
Little, Arthur D., Inc., 360
Litwin, Richard, 342
Lloyd, Clark, Rowe Ltd., 36, 598
Lloyd, John, 591
Lob, Eric, 271, 552
Loeb Program Board, 373
Logan Carey & Rehag, 463, 466
Lomonaco, Richard, 679
London Records, 638
Long, Steve, 461
Lopez, Salpeter Inc., 243, 549, 764, 767
Lorraine & Crystal, 104, 527, 684, 775
Lorraine, Jacques, 104
Loth, R.E., 436, 604
Loth, Robert, 205, 436
Love, Michael, 21
Low, Markus J., 49, 321
Lowe, Jacques, 10, 55
Lowe's Industries, Inc., 494
Lowes, Thomas, Associates, 522
Lubalin, Delpire Cie., 605, 614, 725
Lubalin, Herb, 235, 427, 499, 720, 725, 754, 823, 832
Lubalin, Smith, Carnase 5, 66, 235, 427, 499, 705, 720, 725, 754, 762, 823, 832
Lucas, Frank, 586
Luft, Jim, 520
Lynch, Warren, 8

M

M Films, 819
MG Cars, 830
Mabey, Trousdell, 271, 537, 552
Mácha, Svatopluk, 131
Macmillan Publishing Company, 653
Madeira School, 421
Magleby, McRay, 23, 430
Mago Inforna, 525
Maine, State of, 385
Maisel, Jay, 10, 55, 486
Malast, Margret, 38
Malcolm, Stan, Adv. Art., 462
Maloney, Bill, 235
Maltz, Doris, 323
Mancini, J., 437
Manos, Jim, 650
Manpower, 126
Marco, Phil, 46, 496
Marcus, Ken, 634
Margino, Al, 167
Margirinbolaget, 582
Marini, Climes & Guip, Inc., 184, 521
Marini, Larry, 521
Marknads Kommunikation AB, 1, 324, 795
Marona, Robert, 569
Marsh, Morrie, 719
Marshall, Jim, 624
Martel, Marie, 780
Martin, Noel, 692
Martin, Robert, 251
Martin Partners, Inc., 716
Masi, Marcello, 713
Massey, John, 335, 698, 772
Mastropaul Design Inc., 579
Matchabelli, Prince, 99
Matherson-Selig Color Card Co., 758
Matsumoto, Tosh, 133, 347
Mayhew, Marce, 830
McCall's Magazine, 75
McCallum, Frank, 215
McCann-Erickson, Inc., 117, 248, 392, 805
McCann-Erickson (Nederland) BV, 115, 229
McCarthy, Lynn, 392
McCarthy, Tom, 440, 449
McCarty, Michael, 458
McCathern, George, 358, 529, 557
McCormack Hemsley Palmer Ltd., 270
McClean, Wilson, 650
McCrary, Jim, 377
McCulloch Corp., 603
McDonald & Little Advertising, 511
McElrath, Marcia, 293, 663
McGill Graphic Arts, 788
McInnes, John, 519
McKeown, Wesley B., 2

McLean, Wilson, 680
McMullan, James, 235
McQueen, Alphonsio, 827
McSherry, John, 587
Mechanicus, Philip, 229
Medcom, Inc., 257, 292, 305, 336
Medina, Fernando, 739
Medisan AB, 154
Meinzinger, George, 469
Melander, Lars, 41, 216, 228
Melange, 553
Memphis & Shelby County Airport Authority, 710
Mendoza, Mauricio, 268
Menell, Don, 60, 488
Merck, Sharp Dohme, 508
Meridien Hotels, Dakar, 614
Metamorphosis, 732
Metro Enterprises, 788
Metropolitan Pittsburgh Public Broadcasting, 307
Meyer, John, 684
Meyer, Oscar, & Co., 454
Meyers, Ed, 814, 819
Meyers, H.M., 571
Meyers & Muldoon Advertising, 814, 819
Miami Herald, the, 236
Michael, J., 509
Michelin Tires, 128
Michlin & Hill Inc., 781
Midland Bank, 270
Mierop, Craig, 118
Miho, James, 371, 376, 516
Miho, Tomoko, 335
Miho Inc., 371, 376, 516
Milestone Records, 7, 624, 628, 631, 633, 635, 636
Miller, Earl, 58
Miller, Herman, Inc., 54, 561
Miller, Kevin, 334
Miller, Mark, 255
Miller, Martin A., 342
Miller Brewing Company, 576
Mills, Judie, 615, 616, 620, 640, 642, 646
Minor, Wendell, 641
Miyares, Marcelino, 676, 809
Mochizuki, Art, 40, 438, 443, 487
Modern Bride, 279
Monahan, Leo, 726
Monks, Arthur, Assoc., 429
Montgomery, David, 98
Montgomery Ward, 572
Moody, Roy, 654
Moore, Bronwyn, 647
Moore, James, 273
Morecraft/Oliwa, 29
Morello, Joe, 245, 250
Morgan Press, Inc., 753
Mori, Kenn, 279
Morris, Stephen, 226
Morrison, Jim, 238
Morton House, 799, 807
Morton Salt Company, 569
Moscoso, Victor, 814
Moulin, Thomas, 498
Muller, Jordan Herrick Inc., 9, 106, 127, 202, 251
Murder Ink, 510
Murray, John, 812
Murray, Southam, 484
Murrie White & Associates, 28, 39, 457
Museum of Science, 455

N

NBC, 836
NR Promotions, 167
NYC Off-Track Betting Corp., 139, 374, 460
NYU Publications Bureau, 373
Nader-Lief, Inc., 126, 439
Nadler & Larimer, Inc., 67, 103, 267, 796
Nathan, Richard, 257, 336
National Educational Television, 815
National General Corporation, 464
National Pet Foods Co., Laddie Boy Div., 573
Needham, Harper & Steers, 102, 105, 130, 134, 250, 252, 266, 798, 812, 818, 822
Negrin, Robert, 374
Nemeth, Bruce, 288
Nemser, Robert, 495
Neo-Ray Lighting Systems, 751, 789

Nestle, 554
New England Mutual Life Insurance, 122
Newman, Rickie, 120
New York Magazine, 304, 309
New York Times, 651
Nibco, Inc., 272
Niles, David, 418
Noble, Richard, 287
Northside Psychiatric Hospital, 716
Norton, Charles, 723
Nussbaum, R., 829
Nyquist, Ray, 271, 552

O

O.M.A.R. Co., 676, 809
O'Day, Bill, 139, 374, 460
Ode Records, 46, 650
Odell Hardware Co., 354
Odette, Jack, 453, 504
Odette Associates Inc., 453, 500, 504
Odyssey House, 243
O'Grady, Jack, Photo Productions, 804
O'Grady, Jack, Studios Inc., 330
Ojne, Ben, 98, 247
Old Number Seven Music Co., 714
O'Leary's Sprinkler Co., 787
Olivo, Gary N., 305
Olivo, John, 261
Oliveri, Joe, 600
Olson, Jan, 582
O'Malley, T., 591, 820
One + One Studio, 616, 618, 620
O'Neill, Brian, 370, 440, 449, 694, 706
Ong, James, 479, 497
Ong & Associates, Inc., 479, 497
Orlandi, James, 792
Orr, Norman, 678
Osterlly, Simone, 684
Otter, Robert, 637

P

PKL Advertising Inc., 99, 510, 802
Pacchiano, Arlene, 664
Paces, Zlata, 653
Paganucci, R.V., 423, 437
Palsa, Joseph R., 56
Palsa, Joseph R., & Assoc., 56
Pantano, Dick, 168, 212, 394, 806, 837
Panuska, Robert, 244
Paper Prism, 354
Parker, Phil, 105
Paschke, Ed, 289
Passalacqua, David, 661
Passberger, Herb, 510, 802
Patterson, Rhodes, 205
Patterson & Associates, 708
Paul, Arthur, 6, 26, 85, 289, 290, 302, 654, 666, 677, 680
Peachtree Corners, 379
Pearl, Norton, 398
Pedersen, B. Martin, 326, 381
Pedersen Design, Inc., 326, 381
Peneaud, Francis, 614
Penn, Irving, 96, 100, 801
Pennington, Ewen, 409
Pepper, Bob, 453
PepsiCo, 3, 30, 303, 473
Perez, Hector, 373
Perez, Jose A., 373
Perspectives Inc., 20, 281
Peterson, Bob, 5
Petrower, Joel, 296, 297, 316
Phair, Joseph H., 97, 133
Philips, Robert, 252
Phillips, Bernard, 270
Phillips-Brown and TriArts, Inc., 708
Photography Inc., 8
Pictorial Powers Conway, 135
Piedmont Industries, 171
Pierce, Don, 113
Pike, Ray, Studios, 747
Pima College, 458
Pinnacle Books Inc., 550
Playboy Magazine, 6, 26, 85, 289, 290, 302, 485, 654, 666, 677, 680
Playboy Enterprises, Inc., 6, 26, 85, 289, 290, 302, 485 654, 666, 677, 680
Plus Two, 798
Polaroid Corporation, 462, 601
Pollock, A.L., 484
Polstra, Reinhard, 722
Pontiac, 837

Pontiac Dealers Chicago, 841
Pony Sporting Goods Limited, 591
Pope, Kerig, 6, 26, 85, 290, 302, 666
Powell, Bill, 515, 724
Powell, Ivan R., 579
Powell & Associates, 515, 724
Pratt-Read, 220
Prestige Records, 7, 624, 628, 631, 633, 635, 636
Prestley, Ken, 572
Progressive Architecture, 296, 297, 316
Projections, 820
Promotion Graphics, 459, 770
Public Broadcasting Service, 817, 823
Puhlmann, Rico, 68, 283
Push Pin Studios, 547

Q

Quatre, Ltd., 759
Queens Litographing Corp., 638

R

RAM Golf Corp., 132
Raleigh Lithograph, 359
Ramberg, Christina, 290
Rampley, Ronald, 463, 466
Random House, 691
Ray, Bruce, 31, 573
Raymond, Alan, 817
Raymond, David, 507
Redbook Magazine, 27, 29, 520
Reder, Ed, Advertising, 260
Reed, David, 218, 711
Reed/Kaina Adv., Inc., 218, 711
Reid, Scott, 703
Reinhold Publishing Co., 296, 297, 316
Renfro, Ed, 235
Revson, Peter, 744
Reynolds, R. J., Military Division, 109
Ricci, Franco, 147, 606
Ricci Studio Relazione, 147
Richardson Seigle Rolfs & McCoy Inc., 331, 506, 513
Richmond, Will, 406
Rickabaugh, Heidi, 695, 782
Rickabaugh, Robin, 695, 782
Ries, Henry, 128
Rigsby, Thomas A., 708
Ris Paper Company, 383
Ritter, Richard, 426
Rivera, Pablo, 479
Roach, Jerry, 393
Robinson, Roy, Photography, 331
Rochlin, Leonard, 716
Rochlin, Leonard, Design Associates, 716
Rodriguez, Emilio, Jr., 268
Rodriguez, William, 359
Rogalski, Herbert, 314
Rogers, Chuck, 493
Romano, Dave, 108
Rondesics, Inc., 152, 422
Ronson Corp., 583
Rosato, Fred, 555
Rosenberg, Arnold, 103
Rosenfeld, Jerry, 114, 254
Rosenthal, Albert Jay, & Co., 109, 393, 799, 807
Ross, Dick, 220
Ross, Frank, 8, 380, 428, 709, 714
Rost, Ed, 765
Rostock, Edward, 127
Rothman, Frank, 301
Rotmil, Charles, 18
Roulston & Co., 56
Rubbermaid Inc., 584
Rubin, Mark, 691, 829
Rubin, Mark, Design, 642, 646, 691
Rule, Robin, 279
Rumford Press, 352
Rumrill-Hoyt, 334
Runyan, Robert Miles, 40, 438, 443, 464, 487, 703, 712, 744, 779
Runyan, Robert Miles, & Associates, 40, 438, 443, 464, 487, 703, 712, 744, 779
Rusk, Karen B., 498
Russell, Ethan, 46
Russell, Robert H., 429, 480, 490
Russell Coil Co., 698
Russell/Nicholson, 445
Ryder, Sharon Lee, 297

S

SCI, Stanley Church Inc., 562, 580, 581, 587, 602
SCIC, 147
SCM Corporation, 475
SWECO, Inc., 249
Sagebrush Studio, 177
St. Clair, Dean, 747
St. Vincent, Rick, 269
St. Vincent/Chew/Milone, Inc., 269
Sakahara, Dick, 539
Saljolagsgruppen, 595
Salpeter, Bob, 243, 549, 764, 767
Samardge, Nick, 440, 449
Samsonite Luggage, 110
Sandbank, Henry, 525
Sanders, Bernard B., 344
Sanders, Bill, 236
Sanders & Noe Inc., 344
San Jose, City of, 814
Sapienza, John, 841
Sapinaro, Mario, 171
Sara-Perfumes-Gifts, 590, 738
Sarapochiello, Jerry, 27
Savage & Parsons Ltd., 210
Satra Motors, Ltd., 112
Savage, Naomi, 77
Sav-On Drugs, Inc., 47, 442
Sawyer, Charles, 124, 810
Schacht, Mike, 706
Schaewen, Deidi von, 427
Schenk, Fred, 61
Schenk, Fred, Studio, 61
Schenley Industries, 813
Scher, Ian, 758
Schlatner, S., 689
Schlumberger Ltd., 499
Schmid, Fred Associates, 731
Schmitt, Ted, 129, 339
Scholastic Books, Inc., 237
Scholastic Magazines, Inc., 64, 301, 610, 648, 659
Scholastic Publications, 82, 295
Schottland, Miriam, 293
Schuett, S.T., 445
Schumaker, Bob, 351, 416
Schumaker Deur Designers, 351, 378, 416
Schumann, Ray, Photography Inc., 428
Schwartz, Leonard J., Enterprises, 752
Schwerzmann, J., 155
Scott, Foresman & Co., 77, 319, 617, 647
Scott-Allison Pharmaceutical, 577
Scovill Manufacturing Co., 492
Seager, David M., 344
Searle, G.D., & Co., 257, 305
Searle, R., 271
Sedelmaier, Joe, 821
Sefton, Richard, 757
Segal, Leslie, 486, 492
Seghers, Carroll, II, 489
Segmented Sampling Inc., 246
Seida, Takashi, 281
Seiki, Akihiko, 727
Seiko Watches, 206
Selame, Joe, 736
Selame Design Associates, 736
Selco Mining Corporation Ltd., 265
"Ser" Editorial, 721
Servomation Corporation, 488
Sessions, Steven, 787
Shade, Oney, 771
Shah, Upendra, 792
Shakertown at Pleasant Hill, Ky., 512
Shaller Rubin Co. Inc., 813
Shapers, Don, 463
Shapiro, Ellen, 235
Shaw, Ray, 31, 573
Sheridan, Richard, 139
Shimokochi, Mamoru, 655
Shipley Associates, 790
Shukovsky, Joel, 704
Signorino, Slug, 272
Sigwart, Forrest L., 180
Silano, Ed, 22
Silberlicht, Ira 278, 661
Sillen, Larry, 549
Silver, Marvin, 40, 443, 487
Silverman, Burt, 235
Simon, I./R.G. Group Inc., 772
Simpson Lee Paper Company, 407
Singapore Airlines Ltd., 828
Singer & Cole, 329
Sinn, Paul, 420, 476, 478

Sire, 229
Sisson, Karyl, 438, 443
Six Flags over Georgia, 511
Skelton, Claude, 400
Slade, Patti, 580, 602
Slater, Phil, 648
Slick, Paul, 517
Smallman, Robert E., 282
Smidt, Sam, Assoc., 420, 476, 477, 478
Smiley, Ruth, 60
Smith, Barry, 734
Smith, Bob, 777
Smith, Bucklin & Assoc., Inc., 344
Smith, Gordon, 395, 520
Smith, Marshall, & Associates, 454, 759
Smith, Tyler, 193, 386
Smokler, Jerold, 80, 273
Smosarski, Chris, 540
Smyth Greyhound, 331, 513
Sofico Vacaciones, 739
Soft Drinks Magazine, 63, 284, 675
Sohmer, Steve, 530
Sohmer, Steve, Inc., 530, 741
Sokohara, Dick, 756
Somerset Importers, 105
Sonnenfeld, Leni, 333
Sony Corporation of America, 518
Soong, Caroline, 828
Sorel, Edward, 235
Sorvino, Skip, 648
Souffle, Jim, 250
Sourcebook Magazine, 318
South Florida Dairy Farmers, 108
Southern Bank & Trust, 445
Southern Short Course in
  News Photography, 403
Southland Corporation, 38
Spahr, Mike, 109
Special, Bob, 494
Sperry-Remington, 532
Speyer, Lars, 477
Spiegel-Verlag, Hamburg, 247
Spinoza, Rudy, 251
Sport Magazine, 5, 66
Sports Digest, 703
Spot-Bilt, 662
Springer, Gary, 28, 39
Staebler, Tom, 680
Stack, Richard, 480
Steigman, Stephen, 266
Stein Printing Co., 493, 494
Stendig, Inc., 260
Stephenson, Lynton, 104
Step 2, Inc., 728
Sterling Drug Inc., 4, 491
Sterling Regal, 171
Sternglas, Arno, 358
Stettner, Bill, 162, 254
Stevens, J. P., & Co., Inc., 167
Stevens, Payson, 517
Stevens, Robert, 438
Stevens, Robert, Photography, 779
Stevenson, Terry, 793
Stewart, Dan, 8, 380, 428, 709, 714, 761
Stewart Blood Center, 737
Stock Photos Unlimited of New York, 24
Stone, Dick, 841
Stone, Don, 190
Stonecutters, 817
Stram, John Van Dyke, 760, 791
Strathmore Paper Company, 563
Strauss Printing, 759
Stubis, Tal, 367
Studio Seven (Chicago), 804
Studio White, 361
Stuermer, Pam, 531
Sturzenegger, Mark, 54, 561
Suares, J.C., 651
Sullivan, Jerry, 379
Summerstar, 812
Sun Associates, 749
Sunlight Pictures, 797
Supermarketing, 288
Swanberg, John, 193
Swanstrom, Al, 109
Sweda International, 18
Sweet, Ozzie, 418
Sweet's Div., McGraw-Hill
  Information Systems Co., 337
Syntex Corporation, 476

T

TV Guide, 555, 690
TY Graphics, 660, 766, 773

Tap Manpower, 239
Taplin, Myron, 386
Tappich, J., 155, 397
Tarragon Graphics, 384
Taylor Agency, 535
Teason, Bill, 367
Tedesco, Michael, 518
Teich, Lester, 126
Teich, Rex, 132
Tender, Mickey, 537
Tempees, 21
Thal, Ron, 535
Third Eye, Inc., 37, 589
Thomas, Fred, 331
Thompson, J. Walter, 361
Thompson, Ken, 355
Thompson, Liz, 690
Thompson, J. Walter, 110
Thorpe, Jim, 528
Tichenor, E.S., Co., 428
Time, Inc., 196, 545
Tinker Dodge & Delano, 19, 129, 159,
  162, 177, 339, 831
Tinta-Tryck, 41
Tobias, William R., 382, 792
Tobias, William R., Design, 792
Tofte, Paul, 454, 759
Tomc, Tom, 302
Tomlinson, Pter, 693
Toriello, Don, 805
Törnbloms, 375, 582
Toth, Joseph J., 774
Town and Country Magazine, 69, 80, 300
Trainello, Gennaro, 171, 240
Trask, Richard, 262, 797
Travenol Laboratories, 336
Treaster, Grant, Jr., 757
Trevino, Gil, 518
Tri-Arts Press, 519
Tuborg Breweries, 771
Tulchin Productions, 796
Tulman, Eli A., 19, 831
Tuohy, Arthur, 97, 133
Turner, Pete, 326
Turner, Ronald, 477
Twins Pharmaceuticals (Pty.) Ltd., 104
Two One Two, Ltd., 120
Typographic Workshop, 540
Typesettra Limited, 591

U

Underhill, Les, 114
Unimark International Johannesburg, 32, 697
Union Carbide, 329
United Air Lines, 330
United Brands Co., 25
United Delco Division of G.M. Corp., 286
United Jewish Appeal of New York, 333
United Negro College Fund, 794
United Neighborhood Houses
  of New York, 733
United States Army, 537
United States Information Agency, 51, 287
United States Postal Service, 48, 556
United States Steel, 261
Universal Pictures, 367
University of Toronto Pollution Probe, 820

V

Vaeth, Peter, 152, 422
Van Brunt & Co. Chicago, 808, 821, 841
Van Cleven, Al, 570
Van Dine Horton, 521
Van Gelder Papier—Holland, 523
Van Leeuwen Advertising, 452
Van Noy, Jim, 603
Vareltzis, Ron, 568
Vendikos, Tasso, 124
Venezuelan Government Tourist
  and Information Center, 829
Veno, Joe, 427
Versatise Limited, 786
Vicari, Jim, 118, 255
Vickers & Benson Ltd., 591, 820
Videocom, 837
Videosonics, 704
Virginia Commonwealth University, 400
Visual Arts Gallery, 381
Visual Design, 356, 531
Visual Graphics Corp., 259
Vogel, Alan, 440, 449

Volkman, Roy, 550
Volkswagen of America, Inc., 326
Vos, Peter, 115
Vose, Eric, 600

W

W & L Ad Art, 572
WBBM-TV, 808
WKA Corporate Graphics, Inc.,
  60, 482, 488
WKYC-TV, NBC, 827
WNBC-TV, 135, 359
WQED/Design Center,
  307, 509, 763, 784
WRVR, 53
Wakeford/Orloff Inc., 816
Walden, Jim, 464
Wales Tourist Board, 768
Walker Engraving, 117, 248
Walker, Allan D., 47, 442
Walker, J. Charles, 384
Walker, Kenneth, 546
Wallerich, Tom, 723
Wanek, John, 372
Wargniez, Jean-Michel, 707
Warner Bicking & Fenwick, 124, 810
Warner Bros. Records, Inc., 52, 637
Warren, S.D., Co., 418
Warren, Vic, 331, 506, 513
Warrillow, Nicholas, 454, 759
Warwick, Mike, 540
Washington Investment Planning
  Co., Inc., 715
Washington Post Company, 482
Waterman Advertising, 171, 240
Watson, George, 286
Watts, Franklin, Inc., 615, 616, 620, 640
Watts, Franklin (Juvenile), 642, 646
Waxmann Design, 656
Waxmann, Michel, 656
Weaver, William, 567, 592
Webber, Harry, 818
Weigand, Richard, 74, 280
Weisz Decal Inc., 513
Weisz, Thomas J., Ltd., 111
Weller, Don, 52, 57, 363, 603,
  717, 731, 776
Weller & Juett, Inc.,
  52, 57, 363, 603, 717, 731, 776
Wellington Puritan Mills, Inc., 593
Wenman, David, 206
Werner, Martin, 97, 133
Westbrook, Sam, 227
Westinghouse Electric Corp., 184
Westrom, Gunnel, 154
Wetzel Brothers, Inc., 454
Wheatman, Stan, 691
White, Charles, 650, 781
White, Courtland Thomas, 246, 733
White, Courtland Thomas, Inc., 246, 733
White, Gary, Advertising Inc., 695, 782
White, Judy, 802
White, Ken, 747
White, Nigel, 112
White, Peter, 261
Whitfield, Brad, 769
Whitmore, Mary Lou, 750
Whitmore Movie Works, 750
Whorf, Chris, 52
Wieczkowski, Richard F., 99
Wight, Robin, 263
Wilcox, Shorty, 378
Wild Horse Mesa, 723
Wilder, J.T., 586
Wilkes, Gene, 368, 379
Wilkes, Tom, 46, 377, 621, 629, 634, 748
Wilkes & Braun Inc., 46, 377, 621,
  629, 634, 637, 639, 650, 748
Wilkins, James, 737
Willardson, Dave, 639
Williams, Ernest R., 120
Williams, Harry, 768
Williams, Jim, 50, 369
Williamson, Edwin, 239
Willis, Len, 677
Wilson, Bill, 357, 399
Wilson, Janis, 498
Wilson, Rex, 500
Wilson, Roland B., 122
Wilson, Sue, 477
Wine, Susan, 791
Winner, Harriet, 8, 380, 761
Winslow, Laura, 111

Wirz, Adolf, AG Werbeberatung, 119
Wise, Don, Co., 262, 797
Witter, Dean, & Co., Inc., 463, 466
Wittman, Peter, 371, 376, 516, 692
Wittman, Peter, Inc., 692
Wolf, Bernard, 427
Wolf, Henry, 74, 75, 100, 280, 285
Wolf, Henry, Productions Inc., 74, 75, 100, 280, 285, 309
Wolin, Ronald, 726
Wolverine World Wide, Inc., 351, 378
Wood, Ray, 565
Wood, Ross, Productions, 828
Wood, Tom, 353
World Magazine, 293, 299, 663
World of One, 120
Wortel & Delaere Studio, 523

Wosczyk, Pat, 610
Wright, J., 34, 533
Wright-Manning Co., 474
Wyland, G., 397
Wyeth Laboratories, 292
Wyeth Laboratories USA (Belgium), 656

X

Xerox, 134, 266, 798

Y

Y & R Properties Limited, 484
YMHA, 323
Yim, T.C., Rep., 218
Young, Jackie, 786

Young & Rubicam Inc., 25, 794
Yurcich, Tom, 660, 766, 773

Z

Zanders Animation Parlour, 810
Zarkades, Nicholas, 24, 461
Zarlengo, Chris, 749
Zarney Graphic Artists, 584
Zelcer, Alfred, 289
Zelinsky, Ed, 307, 763
Ziemienski, Dennis, 294
Ziff-Davis Publishing Co., 279
Zoe Productions, 802
Zoecon, 478
Zucker, Herb, 22
Zwisler, Patricia, 480, 490

CREATIVITY 2
A Photographic Review of Creativity '72
1973, 304 pp., 24 pp. in full color, over 900 illus.
ISBN 0-910158-04-5, $17.50 U.S. & Canada.

CREATIVITY 1
A Photographic Review of Creativity '71
1972, 288 pp., 16 pp. in full color, 876 illus.
ISBN 0-910158-02-9, $17.50 U.S. & Canada.

The CREATIVITY Annuals
Standing Order: ISBN 0-910158-10-X.